Hellenistic Literature and Culture

Also available from Bloomsbury

Hellenistic Tragedy: Texts, Translations and a Critical Survey,
by Agnieszka Kotlinska-Toma
New Perspectives on the Hellenistic Peloponnese, edited by Manolis Pagkalos
and Andrea Scarpato
The Politics of Form in Greek Literature, edited by Phiroze Vasunia

Hellenistic Literature and Culture

Studies in Honor of Susan A. Stephens

Edited by
Benjamin Acosta-Hughes,
Jacqueline Arthur-Montagne,
and
Phiroze Vasunia

BLOOMSBURY ACADEMIC
LONDON • NEW YORK • OXFORD • NEW DELHI • SYDNEY

BLOOMSBURY ACADEMIC
Bloomsbury Publishing Plc, 50 Bedford Square, London, WC1B 3DP, UK
Bloomsbury Publishing Inc, 1359 Broadway, 12th Floor, New York, NY 10018, USA
Bloomsbury Publishing Ireland, 29 Earlsfort Terrace, Dublin 2, D02 AY28, Ireland

BLOOMSBURY, BLOOMSBURY ACADEMIC and the Diana logo are trademarks of
Bloomsbury Publishing Plc

First published in Great Britain 2024
Paperback edition published 2025

A catalogue record for this book is available from the British Library.

Library of Congress Cataloging-in-Publication Data
Names: Stephens, Susan A., honouree. | Acosta-Hughes, Benjamin, 1960– editor. |
Vasunia, Phiroze, 1966– editor. | Arthur-Montagne, Jacqueline, editor.
Title: Hellenistic literature and culture : studies in honor of Susan A. Stephens / edited by
Benjamin Acosta-Hughes, Jacqueline Arthur-Montagne and Phiroze Vasunia.
Description: London ; New York : Bloomsbury Publishing, 2023. |
Includes bibliographical references and index.
Identifiers: LCCN 2023017705 (print) | LCCN 2023017706 (ebook) |
ISBN 9781350286016 (hardback) | ISBN 9781350288119 (paperback) |
ISBN 9781350286023 (pdf) | ISBN 9781350286030 (ebook)
Subjects: LCSH: Greek literature, Hellenistic—History and criticism. |
LCGFT: Festschriften.
Classification: LCC PA3081 .H44 2023 (print) | LCC PA3081 (ebook) |
DDC 880.9/001—dc23/eng/20230701
LC record available at https://lccn.loc.gov/2023017705
LC ebook record available at https://lccn.loc.gov/2023017706

ISBN: HB: 978-1-3502-8601-6
        PB: 978-1-3502-8811-9
        ePDF: 978-1-3502-8602-3
        eBook: 978-1-3502-8603-0

Typeset by RefineCatch Limited, Bungay, Suffolk

To find out more about our authors and books visit www.bloomsbury.com
and sign up for our newsletters.

Contents

List of Plates   vii

List of Contributors   viii

Preface   xv

Foreword *Richard Saller*   xvi

Abbreviations   xviii

Part One Archaic and Classical Greek Literature

1   Semonides, Fragment 1 as an Iambic Catalogue in Stanzas
     Christopher Athanasious Faraone   3

2   The Humble and the Grand: Realism in Euripides' *Electra*
     Marco Fantuzzi and Mathias Hanses   16

Part Two Coming to Egypt

3   Through a Glass Darkly: Alexander's Campaign in Egypt
     Daniel L. Selden   45

Part Three Callimachus

4   Neglected Splendors: Alcman's Louvre *Partheneion* and
     Callimachus' Tale of Phrygius and Pieria *Giulio Massimilla*   111

5   Callimachus' Duplicitous *Iambos Don Lavigne*   123

6   From a Small Beginning: Of Sibling and Poetic Order in
     Callimachus *Benjamin Acosta-Hughes*   146

7   "Them He Cannot Take": Callimachus' Epigram for Heraclitus
     Phiroze Vasunia   161

8   Advisory Tops: Callimachus Ep. 54 Gow and Page (1 Pf.)
     Markus Asper   176

9   On a New Papyrus Fragment of Callimachus' *Hecale* (*P.Ant.*
     III 179 add.) *Giovan Battista D'Alessio*   181

10   No Lyre for Heracles *Peter Parsons*   191

11   Strabo's Callimachus *Richard Hunter*   201

Part Four Hellenistic and Roman Culture

12   Seeing Double: Apollonius' Two Phaethons *Ivana Petrovic*   215

13   "Apollonius Speaks Greek, Petiharenpi Speaks Egyptian":
     Cross-Cultural Self-Fashioning in the Serapeum Archive
     Edward Kelting   227

14   Young Snakes, Old Models: Hellenistic Poetics and Literary
     Heritage in Nicander, *Theriaca* 343–58 *Alexander Sens*   239

15   The Death of the Author: Hesiod's Double Burial in Epigrams of
     Mnasalkes (*AP* 7.54 = 18 GP) and Alkaios (*AP* 7.55 = 12 GP)
     and in the Biographical Tradition *Peter Bing*   249

16   Doomscrolling at Segesta: An Allusion to Lycophron in Virgil,
     Aeneid 5. 552–4 *Alessandro Barchiesi*   268

17   Father Ammon and the King *Jay Reed*   284

18   Crinagoras of Mytilene and Octavia *Roland Mayer*   299

19   Poets, Plants, and Riddles *Kathryn Gutzwiller*   308

Part Five Ancient Prose Fiction

20   The *Sparagmos* of Parthenope between Ancient Novel and
     Myth *Jacqueline Arthur-Montagne*   319

21   Alexandria in the Ancient Greek Novels *Stephen A. Nimis*   328

Aftermath

22   Practicing Orthodoxy: Body Language in Sophronius'
     Thaumata Maud Gleason   341

23   Reading Stephens *Lee Palmer Wandel*   355

A Bibliography of Susan A. Stephens   361
Index   366

Plates

1   Alexander's Egypt

2   Barque Chapel, Luxor Temple. Alexander attired as Pharaoh, facing the god Amun

3   Veneration of the Apis bull. Year 21 of Psamtik I (*c.* 644 BCE)

4a The Narmer Palette, verso

4b The Narmer Palette, detail of the lower register, verso

5   Alexander's route from Pēlousion to Memphis

6   Unidentified Pharaoh wearing the *nemes* cloth. Recovered from the sunken harbor of Alexandria, formerly the royal quarters

7   Amun-Rē' presents Queen Mutemwiya with the divine breath of life (♀ *ʿnḫ*). Mortuary Temple of Ḥatšepsut, al-Dayr al-Baḥrī

8   Site of Alexandria / ⲣⲁⲕⲟⲧⲉ

9   Flooding of the Nile. Repetition of the First Occasion

10 The pyramids at Giza rising out of the flood water of the yearly inundation

11 Ptolemaic Alexandria seen from Lake Maryūṭ

12 Cameo of Ptolemy II and Arsinoe II

13a Image from the Papyrus, P. Lille 78b

13b Image from the Papyrus, P. Lille 78b

14 Detail of the Nile Mosaic at Palestrina

15 Detail of the Nile Mosaic at Palestrina

16 The Contest between the Muses and the Sirens (long side). 250–275 CE. Rome

Contributors

Benjamin Acosta-Hughes, Professor of Greek and Latin
Ohio State University, USA

Benjamin Acosta-Hughes is the author of *Polyeideia: The "Iambi" of Callimachus and the Archaic Iambic Tradition* (2002) and of *Arion's Lyre: Archaic Lyric into Helllenistic Poetry* (2010), co-author of *Callimachus in Context: From Plato to the Augustan Poets* (2012), and co-editor of Brill's *Companion to Callimachus* (2011) and of *Euphorion: Oeuvre poétique et autres fragments* (2012).

Jacqueline Arthur-Montagne, Assistant Professor of Classics
University of Virginia, USA

Jacqueline Arthur-Montagne completed her doctorate under Susan Stephens' supervision at Stanford University and has drawn many of her research interests from Susan's work on the Greek novels and papyrology. She is the co-editor of *Documentality: New Approaches to Written Documents in Imperial Life and Literature* (2022) and has authored several articles on ancient prose fiction and Greek literary criticism.

Markus Asper, Professor of Classics
Humboldt University Berlin, Germany

Markus Asper has published on Hellenistic poetry and on the ancient Greek sciences and their literatures. Among his more recent publications are *Thinking in Cases* (2020, editor) and essays on ancient mathematical commentaries, textual authority and epistemic story-telling.

Alessandro Barchiesi, Professor of Classics
New York University, USA

Alessandro Barchiesi, a Latinist with research interests in Hellenistic and Alexandrian texts, has cooperated with Susan Stephens at Stanford and co-edited with her *Rituals in Ink* (2004). His most recent work is the editing of a multi-author commentary on Ovid's *Metamorphoses* (2023).

Giovan Battista D'Alessio, Professor of Classical Philology
University of Naples Federico II, Italy

Giovan Battista D'Alessio was formerly Professor of Greek Language and Literature at King's College London. He has published extensively, with a particular focus on Greek lyric, Hellenistic poetry, and literary papyri.

Peter Bing, Samuel Candler Dobbs Professor of the Classics Emeritus, Emory University, Atlanta, GA, USA and Professor of Classics, University of Toronto, Canada.
University of Toronto, Canada

Peter Bing shares many interests with Susan Stephens, particularly in Hellenistic poetry, the cultural politics of the Ptolemies, including their kingship ideology. In addition to numerous essays on Greek literature, he is the author of *The Well-Read Muse. Present and Past in Callimachus and the Hellenistic Poets* (1988) and *The Scroll and The Marble: Studies in Reading and Reception in Hellenistic Poetry* (2009). He co-edited *Brill's Companion to Hellenistic Epigram* (with J. S. Bruss 2007) and co-authored *Games of Venus: An Anthology of Greek and Roman Erotic Verse from Sappho to Ovid* (with R. Cohen 1991) as well as *Aristaenetus: Erotic Letters. Introduced, Translated and Annotated* (with R. Höschele 2014).

Marco Fantuzzi, Professor of Classics Emeritus
University of Roehampton, UK

Marco Fantuzzi is Professor of Classics Emeritus at the University of Roehampton, London, Visiting Fellow at the Institute of Classical Studies, London, and Research Associate at Trinity College, Dublin.

He has taught at the universities of Trento, Florence, Macerata, Roehampton, and at Columbia University in New York. He has published widely on Hellenistic literature. His publications include *Bionis Smyrnaei Adonidis Epitaphium* (1985); *Ricerche su Apollonio Rodio* (1988); (with R. L. Hunter) *Tradition and Innovation in Hellenistic Poetry* (2004); *Achilles in Love* (2012); *The Rhesus Attributed to Euripides* (2020). He co-edited (with R. Pretagostini) *Struttura e storia dell'esametro greco* (*Gruppo editoriale internazionale*, 1995–6), (with T. Papanghelis) *Brill's Companion to Greek and Latin Pastoral* (2006), and (with C. Tsagalis) *A Companion to the Epic Cycle and Its Fortune in the Ancient World* (2015).

Christopher Athanasious Faraone, Edward Olson Distinguished Professor of Classics
University of Chicago, IL, USA

Christopher Athanasious Faraone's work is primarily concerned with ancient Greek religion and poetry. Recent publications include *The Transformation of Ancient Greek Amulets in Roman Times* (2018), *Hexametrical Genres from the Homer to Theocritus* (Oxford 2021), and articles on ancient Greek magic, poetry, and religion. He is co-editor with S. Torallas Tovar, of *The Greco-Egyptian Magical Formularies*, vol. 1 (2022).

Maud Gleason, formerly Lecturer in Classics
Stanford University, CA, USA

Maud Gleason often enjoyed co-teaching with Susan Stephens at Stanford University. Maud's own scholarly interests focus on exploring the bodily meanings and cultural attitudes hiding in neglected Greek texts from the Roman Empire. She is the author of *Making Men* (1985) and articles on Julian the Apostate, the Desert Fathers, Herodes Atticus and his Roman wife Regilla, Galen, Cassius Dio, Josephus, and Aretaeus. She is currently revising her Jerome lectures on the cultural meanings of a dehumanizing (and quasi-imaginary) disease in the Roman Empire.

Kathryn Gutzwiller, John Miller Burnam Professor of Classics Emerita
University of Cincinnati, OH, USA

Kathryn Gutzwiller has written extensively on Hellenistic poetry, with a focus in recent years on epigrams and visual depictions of texts. Her books include *Theocritus' Pastoral Analogies: The Formation of a Genre* (1991), *Poetic Garlands: Hellenistic Epigrams in Context* (1998, Goodwin Award winner), and *A Guide to Hellenistic Literature* (2007). She has also edited *The New Posidippus: A Hellenistic Poetry Book* (2005), and among her articles she has published "New Menander Mosaics from Antioch," in collaboration with Ömer Çelik, *American Journal of Archaeology* (2012).

Mathias Hanses, Melvin and Rosalind Jacobs Endowed Fellow in the Humanities and Associate Professor of Classics and Ancient Mediterranean Studies, African Studies, and African American Studies
Penn State University, PA, USA

Mathias Hanses works on Greek and Roman drama; Africana receptions of Ancient Greece and Rome; and race, status, and difference in the Roman world. His first book is called *The Life of Comedy after the Death of Plautus and Terence* (2020). He is currently working on a second project, under contract, titled *Black Cicero: W. E. B. Du Bois, the Ancient Romans, and the Future of Classical Scholarship*.

Richard Hunter, Regius Professor of Greek Emeritus
University of Cambridge, UK

Richard Hunter is a Fellow of Trinity College, Cambridge. His most recent books are *The Measure of Homer* (2018), (with R. Laemmle) *Euripides, Cyclops* (2020), *The Layers of the Text: Collected Papers on Classical Literature 2008–2021* (2021), and *Greek Epitaphic Poetry: A Selection* (2022).

Edward Kelting, Assistant Professor of Literature and Classical Studies
University of California, San Diego, CA, USA

Edward Kelting works on Roman Egypt, Latin literature, and the cultural history of the Imperial Period. His monograph-in-progress, based on a dissertation he wrote under the supervision of Susan Stephens, is titled *Egyptian Things: Translating Egypt to Early Imperial Rome*. Other recent publications have focused on Juvenal's *Satires*, Apuleius' *Metamorphoses*, and Philostratus' *Life of Apollonius*.

Don Lavigne, Associate Professor of Classics
Texas Tech University, TX, USA

Don Lavigne is editor of *Helios*. His work centers upon the oral-poetic landscape of early Greece and its impact on the Hellenistic and later Roman poets, with a particular focus on gender, performance, and genre. He is currently finishing a book that explores archaic Greek inscribed epigram in the context of early Greek song culture.

Giulio Massimilla, Professor of Greek Literature
University of Naples Federico II, Italy

Giulio Massimilla is the author of a two-volume critical edition, with introduction and commentary, of Callimachus' *Aetia* (1996, 2010). He has written on archaic Greek lyric, Attic drama, ancient Greek literary criticism, Hellenistic poetry, imperial and Late Antique Greek epic, ancient Greek novels, Greek literary papyri, and the reception of classical antiquity in contemporary literature.

Roland Mayer, Emeritus Professor of Classics
King's College London, UK

Roland Mayer's main field of research and publication has been the Latin literature of the early empire. Susan and he have known one another since they were both graduate students in California, and so she is his oldest and firmest friend.

Stephen A. Nimis, formerly Professor of Comparative Literature
American University in Cairo, Egypt

Stephen A. Nimis was also formerly Professor of Classics, Miami University of Ohio, Oxford OH, USA. His research was on major narrative forms: epic, drama, and the novel. Over the years he benefited enormously from the counsel, support, and remarkable scholarship of Susan Stephens, for which he is deeply grateful.

Peter Parsons, formerly Regius Professor of Greek Emeritus
University of Oxford, UK

Peter Parsons was Lecturer in Papyrology from 1960 to 1989 and Regius Professor of Greek at the University of Oxford from 1989 until his retirement in 2003. His research centred on Hellenistic poetry and on unedited papyri, literary and documentary. For many years he was chairman of the Oxyrhynchus Papyri Project of the British Academy. Peter Parsons died in 2022.

Ivana Petrovic, Hugh H. Obear Professor and Chair of Classics
University of Virginia, Charlottesville, VA, USA

Ivana Petrovic is editor of *Greece and Rome*. Ivana wrote a monograph on the cult of Artemis in Hellenistic poetry (2007) and co-edited several volumes.

Together with Andrej Petrovic, Ivana is currently working on a large-scale diachronic study of belief in Greek religion; the first volume *Inner Purity and Pollution in Greek Religion. Vol. I: Early Greek Religion* was published in 2016.

Jay Reed, Professor of Classics and Comparative Literature
Brown University, Providence, RI, USA

Jay Reed has published commentaries on Bion of Smyrna (in the series Cambridge Classical Texts and Commentaries, 1997) and Ovid, *Metamorphoses* X–XII (in the Fondazione Lorenzo Valla series, Scrittori greci e latini, 2013, forthcoming in revised and augmented form from Cambridge, 2023) and *Virgil's Gaze*, a monograph on the poetics of Roman identity in Virgil's *Aeneid* (2007), as well as explanatory notes for the R. Humphries translation of the *Metamorphoses* (2018) and many papers, mainly on Hellenistic and Roman literature and culture and their reception.

Richard Saller, Kleinheinz Family Professor of European Studies
Stanford University, CA, USA

Richard Saller is the author of *Personal Patronage under the Early Empire* (1982) and *Patriarchy, Property and Death in the Roman Family* (1994), co-author of *The Roman Empire: Economy, Society and Culture* (2nd ed., 2014), and co-editor of the *Cambridge Economic History of the Greco-Roman World* (2007).

Daniel L. Selden, Research Professor of Literature
University of California, Santa Cruz, USA

Daniel L. Selden holds a doctoral degree in Comparative Literature from Yale and taught at Columbia University, Stanford, and the New School for Social Research before accepting a permanent appointment on the faculty at Santa Cruz. A former Getty Scholar and Beaufort Fellow at St. John's College, Cambridge, he has also held visiting appointments at Emory, the Oriental Institute at the University of Chicago, and the Università degli Studi di Padova. In 2019 he delivered the Charles Beebe Martin Memorial Lectures at Oberlin College under the title *Holy Wandering: The Worlding of the Alexander Romance*.

Alexander Sens, Markos and Eleni Tsakopoulos Kounalakis Professor of Hellenic Studies and Dean of the Graduate School of Arts and Sciences
Georgetown University, Washington, DC, USA

Alexander Sens has written extensively on the poetry of the late classical and early Hellenistic periods. His most recent book is *Hellenistic Epigrams: A Selection* (2020).

Phiroze Vasunia, Professor of Greek
University College London, UK

Phiroze Vasunia's publications include *The Gift of the Nile* (2001), *Zarathushtra and the Religion of Ancient Iran* (2007), and *The Classics and Colonial India* (2013). He is the editor of numerous volumes, including *Classics and National Cultures* (2010), which he jointly edited with Susan Stephens.

Lee Palmer Wandel, WARF Michael Baxandall and Linda and Stanley Sher Professor of History
University of Wisconsin-Madison, WI, USA

Lee Palmer Wandel is the author of *Always Among Us: Images of the Poor in Zwingli's Zurich* (1990, 2001, 2003), *Voracious Idols and Violent Hands: Iconoclasm in Reformation Zurich, Strasbourg, and Basel* (1995, 1999), *The Eucharist in the Reformation: Incarnation and Liturgy* (2006), *The Reformation: Towards a New History* (2011), and *Reading Catechisms, Teaching Religion* (2016). She is currently working on a book tentatively titled *The Matter of the Liturgy*.

Preface

"Susan doesn't want a fuss and will recoil at the thought of a *Festschrift*," is what quite a few friends said to us in the early stages of this book. Perhaps so. We were simply unable to resist. Susan Stephens has influenced the study of ancient Greek literature and been a mentor to so many students and colleagues over the years that we had to thank her—and what better way to honor her than to present her with a volume on her favorite subjects! This book is a small token of our appreciation; it is offered with admiration and gratitude, and in friendship.

We would like to thank the Department of Classics at Stanford University, Susan's home for so many years, for making the publication of this book possible. Our thanks, in particular, to Professors Grant Parker, Walter Scheidel and Richard Saller for their help with the publication. Grant has been particularly resourceful in the later stages of publication. We would also like to thank Alice Wright and Lily Mac Mahon at Bloomsbury for shepherding the book through the press. Roza El-Eini was a fast and efficient copyeditor. Marina Pavlidou Elamin offered expert help with the index. Our thanks to the many contributors who made this volume a reality and who put up with delays during the editing process. And, most of all, we would like to thank Susan for her many brilliant and learned contributions to Greek Studies. Long may she flourish!

Foreword

Richard Saller
Stanford University

The contributions in this volume attest to the important influence Susan Stephens' books and articles have had on the fields of Hellenistic literature and the intercultural dynamics in Ptolemaic Egypt. Her scholarly record is enviable.

What should not be lost in the praise of her research is that along with her scholarship she has been a mainstay of the Department of Classics, of the School of Humanities and Sciences, and of Stanford University. Research universities need that rare breed of professors who are respected for their research and teaching, and are also willing generously to devote themselves to the functioning of the institution. Susan has been exemplary on all counts. An alumna of both the undergraduate and doctoral programs of Stanford, Susan then dedicated her career to the improvement of a great university, serving three times as department chair and twice as a dean.

My first contact with Susan came in a departmental review in May 2001 during one of her terms as chair. The review committee's report noted that the chair had "a lucid and realistic" assessment of the department, reflecting one of Susan's most valuable character traits for the institution—her penchant to tell it how it is, unadorned by happy talk. As department chair, she was able to outline a new vision for Classics, and was actively engaged in the hiring of faculty to energize the department. Later, during the years that we worked together in the Dean's Office of the School of Humanities & Sciences, I came to have a deep appreciation of her knowledge of the many programs housed in the School and her directness mixed with an ironic sense of humor.

Susan could be impatient with ineptness and bureaucracy, which made it all the more remarkable that she was willing to serve on and to chair a very long list of (sometimes tedious) university committees over the years. In her early years as a faculty member, she worked to support Feminist Studies and to promote the much-needed more equal treatment of women. In later decades, she served on every university committee appointed to oversee undergraduate and graduate programs. Her knowledge and experience made her an obvious choice to join in the university's essential (but thankless) process of reaccreditation by the Western Association of Schools and Colleges; she successfully managed the task with her typical efficiency.

In short, Stanford University and the Department of Classics would not be what they are today without Susan's devotion, energy, and acuity, and so I am delighted to have this volume as a tribute to her many contributions.

Abbreviations

Names of Greek and Latin authors and texts are largely abbreviated in the style of the *Oxford Classical Dictionary* (4th ed., 2012) or given more explicitly.

Part One

Archaic and Classical Greek Literature

Semonides, Fragment 1 as an Iambic Catalogue in Stanzas

Christopher Athanasious Faraone
University of Chicago

Close analysis of the structure of Semonides 1 shows that the twenty-four iambic trimeters preserved uniquely by Stobaeus[1] have lost a single verse and comprise a complete catalogue poem that had originally been composed carefully in five-verse stanzas. Commentators often complain that it is a bad poem[2] and I will not defend it, except to point out that this assessment has much to do with our modern inability to appreciate how the genre of catalogue poetry, although at times mind-numbing to us, might have been of interest and even entertaining for an ancient audience. Indeed, Semonides 1 is not at all unlike other more famous archaic catalogues composed in elegiac couplets, such as Tyrtaeus 12, Solon 27 ("Ages of Man") and the mid-section of his "Hymn to the Muses" (Solon 13:33–62). Scholars have, moreover, often noted the "elegiac" tone and content of Semonides 1 and some have even suggested that Semonides Fragment 1 was deeply influenced by Solon 13.[3] But there is more to be said: Fragment 1 not only reflects the same content and structure of the elegiac catalogues of Solon and other poets,[4] it is also organized as an iambic version of the five-couplet stanza found in a number of elegiac poems of archaic period.[5] We shall see, however, that Semonides' use of stanzas in this poem seems to be a kind of experiment, because the few other long archaic poems that have survived in iambic trimeters, for example, Semonides 6 or Solon 24, show no sign of stanzaic composition.

It is, in fact, a great pleasure to offer this study to my former teacher, because tracing the experimentation of Greek poets with established meters, genres, and canons has, of course, been central to her own work on Callimachus, Theocritus, and Apollonius, which continues to illuminate a Hellenistic poetics characterized by creative experimentation with archaic and classical models.[6] Her teaching has, in fact, long encouraged me to see such experimentation—especially in meters and genres—at work in archaic and early classical period as well and for this I am grateful.[7]

Semonides Fragment 1 begins like many elegiac poems, by addressing a young man and invoking the collectivity to which this youth belongs in a single sentence that runs for five trimeters:[8]

> ὦ παῖ, τέλος μὲν Ζεὺς ἔχει βαρύκτυπος
> πάντων ὅσ' ἐστὶ καὶ τίθησ' ὅκη θέλει,
> νοῦς δ' οὐκ ἐπ' ἀνθρώποισιν, ἀλλ' ἐπήμεροι
> ἃ δὴ βοτὰ ζώομεν, οὐδὲν εἰδότες
> ὅκως ἕκαστον ἐκτελευτήσει θεός.

Boy, loud-thundering Zeus controls the outcome of everything there is and disposes it as he wishes. There is no intelligence among men, but we live like grazing animals, subject to what the day brings, with no knowledge of how the god will bring each thing to pass.

Stanza 1

This first section of the poem is organized by a *men*-and-*de* construction—τέλος μὲν Ζεὺς ἔχει (1) and νοῦς δ' οὐκ ἐπ' ἀνθρώποισιν (3)—that divides the stanza into two unequal parts with the first two verses focused on the reality of human life (Zeus controls everything) and the second three on our human inability to comprehend this. Semonides, moreover, has composed the final verse in ring-composition, which returns us to the thought that the *telos* of all human life is in divine hands (1: <u>τέλος</u> μὲν Ζεὺς ἔχει and 5: ἕκαστον ἐκ<u>τελευτήσει</u> θεός).[9]

And when Semonides speaks of the lack of human knowledge he includes himself, by first referring to "mortals" (3: ἀνθρώποισιν) and then by using the inclusive "we live" (4: ζώομεν), an inclusion that recalls, in fact, the first two couplets of Solon's catalogue of human (mis)perceptions, a section of thirty elegiac couplets that is preserved in the midst of his "Hymn to the Muses," but has traditionally been recognized as a separate poem[10] or a kind of "set-piece" easily placed a the longer poem (13.33–42):[11]

> θνητοὶ δ' ὧδε νοέομεν ὁμῶς ἀγαθός τε κακός τε,
>   †ἐν δηνην† αὐτὸς δόξαν ἕκαστος ἔχει,
> πρίν τι παθεῖν· τότε δ' αὖτις ὀδύρεται· ἄχρι δὲ τούτου
>   χάσκοντες κούφαις ἐλπίσι τερπόμεθα.
> χὤστις μὲν νούσοισιν ὑπ' ἀργαλέῃσι πιεσθῇ,
>   ὡς ὑγιὴς ἔσται, τοῦτο κατεφράσατο·

ἄλλος δειλὸς ἐὼν ἀγαθὸς δοκεῖ ἔμμεναι ἀνήρ,
    καὶ καλὸς μορφὴν οὐ χαρίεσσαν ἔχων·
εἰ δέ τις ἀχρήμων, πενίης δέ μιν ἔργα βιᾶται,
    κτήσεσθαι πάντως χρήματα πολλὰ δοκεῖ.

And thus we mortals, whatever our estate, think that the expectation which each one has is progressing well(?), until he suffers some mishap, and then afterwards he wails. But until then we take eager delight in empty hopes. Whoever is oppressed by grievous sickness thinks that he will be healthy; another man of low estate considers that it's high and that he's handsome though his form is without beauty. If someone is lacking means and is constrained by the effects of poverty, he thinks that he will assuredly acquire much money.

Here Solon, after evoking a kind of universal sentiment ("we mortals think . . ." and "we take eager delight . . ."), provides us with a long catalogue, that begins with three examples, each of which takes up a full couplet beginning with a pronoun that is linked syntactically as part of a regular series: χὤστις μὲν (37), ἄλλος (39), and εἰ δέ τις (41).[12] The poet, moreover, enhances the unity of this section of the poem by replicating a key term and idea: he places the word δόξα[13] in the first couplet to signal the beginning of this catalogue of (mis)perceptions and wishful thinking, a theme that he reiterates in the last two couplets by using the cognate verb δοκεῖ to illustrate two specific cases, first in line 39 and then again in line 42, where it stands as the very last word of this five-couplet stanza. Solon 13 then continues for another twenty lines that fall into two elegiac stanzas. They begin with another general statement, "Everyone has a different pursuit" (43: σπεύδει δ' ἄλλοθεν ἄλλος), and then give us a list of examples, all but the first limited to a couplet (or a pair of them) that also begins with a reiterative pronoun: the merchant (43: ὁ μὲν); the plowman (47: ἄλλος); the craftsman (49: ἄλλος); the poet (51: ἄλλος); the seer (53: ἄλλον); and the healer (57: ἄλλοι).[14]

Solon's "catalogue of vocations" is, of course, more complicated then this simple list suggests, but it suffices to give us a sense of how elegiac catalogues were structured couplet by couplet, precisely what we see in the mid-section of Semonides 1, where the poet moves from his initial discussion (see above) of divine *telos* to a catalogue divided in three stanzas that itemizes our foolish human expectations (6–10) and the forces in the world that frustrate these hopes (11–15), a list that then continues, like Solon's two-stanza catalog of vocations, into the next stanza (16–20):[15]

ἐλπὶς δὲ πάντας κἀπιπειθείη τρέφει
ἄπρηκτον ὁρμαίνοντας· οἱ μὲν ἡμέρην

μένουσιν ἐλθεῖν, οἱ δ᾿ ἐτέων περιτροπάς·
νέωτα δ᾿ οὐδεὶς ὅστις οὐ δοκεῖ βροτῶν
πλούτῳ τε κἀγαθοῖσιν ἵξεσθαι φίλος.

φθάνει δὲ τὸν μὲν γῆρας ἄζηλον λαβὸν   11
πρὶν τέρμ᾿ ἵκηται, τοὺς δὲ δύστηνοι βροτῶν
φθείρουσι νοῦσοι, τοὺς δ᾿ Ἄρει δεδμημένους
<   >
πέμπει μελαίνης Ἀΐδης ὑπὸ χθονός·

οἱ δ᾿ ἐν θαλάσσῃ λαίλαπι κλονεόμενοι   16
καὶ κύμασιν πολλοῖσι πορφυρῆς ἁλὸς
θνήσκουσιν, εὖτ᾿ ἂν μὴ δυνήσωνται ζόειν·
οἱ δ᾿ ἀγχόνην ἅψαντο δυστήνῳ μόρῳ
καὐτάγρετοι λείπουσιν ἡλίου φάος.

Yet hope and confidence nourish all in our eagerness for the impossible. Some
wait for the morrow to come, others for the revolving seasons, and there is no
one who does not expect that he will arrive at the next year as the friend of
wealth and prosperity.

Stanza 2

But unenviable old age comes first and seizes one man before he reaches his goal,
while miserable illnesses that beset mortals destroy others <. . .> and others, laid
low by Ares, Hades sends beneath the dark earth.

Stanza 3

Others die at sea tossed about by a gale and the turbulent sea's many waves,
whenever they are unable to gain livelihood (on land), and others fasten a noose
in a wretched death, leaving the sun's light by their own choice.

Stanza 4

In the first section of the catalogue (Stanza 2) the poet begins with another
universal statement (6: πάντας) that recalls how Solon starts his own catalogue
of vocations (13.43: σπεύδει δ᾿ ἄλλοθεν ἄλλος). There follows a list, again as in
Solon, which in this case moves quickly from two plural examples (7: οἱ μέν . . .
8: οἱ δ᾿) to a third final example in the singular (9: οὐδεὶς ὅστις). The stanza,
moreover, focuses on units of time in all three of its internal verses: a day (7-8:
ἡμέρην μένουσιν ἐλθεῖν), the turning of the years (8: ἐτέων περιτροπάς), and
then the new year (9: νέωτα). Semonides, however, makes no mention of time in
the other four stanzas. This stanza also ends with a verb of expectation (δοκεῖ)
that recalls the very first word of the stanza ἐλπὶς.[16] We saw above this same kind

of ring-composition at the end of the first stanza of the catalogue in Solon 13, where the verb δοκεῖ appears twice (lines 39 and 42) and likewise recalls the references to δόξαν and ἐλπίσι at the start of the stanza (34 and 36).[17]

In the second section of this iambic catalogue (11–15 = Stanza 3), however, Semonides moves to a different theme, one that describes how old age, sickness and death frustrate human expectations at every turn. Here form follows content, for the poet inverts the shape of the catalogue in the previous stanza, first by making mortals the grammatical objects, rather than the subjects, of verbs, and then by giving us a single example (11: τὸν μὲν) followed by two in the plural (12: τοὺς δὲ and 13: τοὺς δ᾽):[18]

Stanza 2 (mortal agents)	Stanza 3 (mortal objects)
7: οἱ μέν	11: τὸν μὲν
8: οἱ δ᾽	12: τοὺς δὲ
9: οὐδεὶς ὅστις	13: τοὺς δ᾽

The formal effect, then, is one of ring-composition and chiasmus across stanzas: Stanza 3 pessimistically inverts and thereby unravels the form of Stanza 2 and in the process also contradicts its content, namely the foolish hopes of mankind. In the third part of this catalogue (= Stanza 4), Semonides continues to describe the disasters that frustrate human expectations, again framing the stanza with ring-composition at the start of the first, middle and last verse, which each begin with a third-person verb whose subject (old age, diseases and Hades) is a bane to mankind: φθάνει δὲ τὸν μὲν γῆρας (11), φθείρουσι νοῦσοι (13) and πέμπει μελαίνης Ἀΐδης (15).[19] He emphasizes, moreover, the common themes of the third and fourth stanzas by closing each with images of the dead going off to the underworld—πέμπει μελαίνης Ἀΐδης ὑπὸ χθονός (15) and λείπουσιν ἠλίου φάος (20)—and he unifies the catalogue even more by repeating with similar sounds a present-tense, third-person plural verb at the start of the third verse of each of the three internal stanzas (8: μένουσιν, 13: φθείρουσι v- and 18: θνήσκουσιν), emphasizing the verb in all three cases by a sense break at or just before the midline caesura.

The final stanza neatly summarizes the catalogue and wraps up the fragment, which many rightly believe to be a complete poem (21–5):[20]

οὕτω κακῶν ἄπ᾽ οὐδέν, ἀλλὰ μυρίαι
βροτοῖσι κῆρες κἀνεπίφραστοι δύαι
καὶ πήματ᾽ ἐστίν. εἰ δ᾽ ἐμοὶ πιθοίατο,
οὐκ ἂν κακῶν ἐρῷμεν, οὐδ᾽ ἐπ᾽ ἄλγεσιν
κακοῖς ἔχοντες θυμὸν αἰκιζοίμεθα.

Thus nothing is without misery, but countless death-demons and unforeseen sorrows and disasters exist for mortals. But if they were to take my advice, we would not long for misfortunes nor would we torment ourselves by having our hearts set on bitter pains.

The summary adverb οὕτω, here at the start of this fifth and final stanza, signals the close of the catalogue and the poem, as does the brief resumé of the catalogue of human disasters in the third and fourth stanzas: death-demons (22: κῆρες), ruins (22: δύαι), and pains (23: πήματ'). This stanza is framed and emphasized by the threefold repetition of κακῶν (21), κακῶν (24) and κακοῖς (25), a word that does not appear in the rest of the poem. Semonides, moreover, increases the sense of closure in the final two verses, when he recalls the end of the first stanza by reverting to the universalizing first person (24–5: οὐκ ἂν κακῶν ἐρῷμεν ... οὐδ' αἰκιζοίμεθα) that he used in line 4 (ζώομεν, οὐδὲν εἰδότες)[21] and by interjecting himself as a source of advice at the start of the final sentence of the poem (24: εἰ δ' ἐμοὶ πιθοίατο), where he reminds us of the parainetic frame of the poem, in which the presumably older speaker offers advice to a nameless youth. In addition to the responding and chiastic counterpoint within the three-stanza catalogue itself, we find that all five of the stanzas of Semonides 1 share some important structural parallels, most notably, all but the fifth and final stanza end with echoing disyllabic nouns: θεός, φίλος, χθονός, and φάος. Commentators have noted a similar and more elaborate effect in the initial stanza of Mimnermus 2.1–10, where in an amazing display of ring-composition the poet sees to it that the key thematic words at the ends of lines 1–3 (ὥρη, ἠελίου, ἥβης) are systematically answered and thereby undone in reversed order by the same words, which appear in the second half of the poem at the ends of lines 7–9 (ἥβης, ἠέλιος, ὥρης).[22]

Finally, what are we to make of the fact that Stobaeus transmits the middle stanza of this catalogue with only four iambic verses? As it turns out, elegiac catalogues, often organized in a regular couplet-by- couplet construction, are sometimes plagued by lacunae that are hard to detect, especially when a full line or a full member of the list disappears. Solon 27 (the "Ages of Man" poem), for instance, survives as a nine-couplet fragment, but its overall architecture suggests that Solon originally composed the poem as a regularly paced and continuous list that divides up human life ten couplets. We know this, because Solon assigned a full couplet to each hebdomad (= unit of seven years) and began each with a number, all except the seventh and eighth hebdomad, as we can see the second half of the poem (9–18):

πέμπτῃ δ᾽ ὥριον ἄνδρα γάμου μεμνημένον εἶναι
  καὶ παίδων ζητεῖν εἰσοπίσω γενεήν.
τῇ δ᾽ ἕκτῃ περὶ πάντα καταρτύεται νόος ἀνδρός,
  οὐδ᾽ ἔρδειν ἔθ᾽ ὁμῶς ἔργ᾽ ἀπάλαμνα θέλει.
ἑπτὰδὲ νοῦν καὶ γλῶσσαν ἐν ἑβδομάσιν μέγ᾽ ἄριστος
  ὀκτώ τ᾽· ἀμφοτέρων τέσσαρα καὶ δέκ᾽ ἔτη.
τῇ δ᾽ ἐνάτῃ ἔτι μὲν δύναται, μαλακώτερα δ᾽ αὐτοῦ
  πρὸς μεγάλην ἀρετὴν γλῶσσά τε καὶ σοφίη.
τὴν δεκάτην δ᾽ εἴ τις τελέσας κατὰ μέτρον ἵκοιτο,
  οὐκ ἂν ἄωρος ἐὼν μοῖραν ἔχοι θανάτου.

In the fifth it is time for a man to be mindful of marriage and to
  look for a line of sons to come after him.
In the sixth a man's mind is being trained for everything and he
  is no longer as willing to commit acts of foolishness.
In the seventh, he is far the best in thought and speech, *and in
  the eighth*, a total of fourteen years
In the ninth he still has ability, but his speech and wisdom give
  weaker proof of a high level of excellence.
If one were to complete stage after stage and reach *the tenth*, he
  would not have death's allotment prematurely.

The unexpected compression of the seventh and eighth hebdomad and the pentameter lamely composed as an arithmetic lesson (ἀμφοτέρων τέσσαρα καὶ δέκ᾽ ἔτη) make it clear that: (i) at some point in its transmission from antiquity an entire couplet dropped out of our text, a couplet that once described fully the features of the eighth hebdomad;[23] and (ii) at some later point in time a diligent but untalented scribe, realizing that the eighth hebdomad was missing, rewrote lines 13–15 (the seventh hebdomad) by ejecting the original pentameter and replacing it with his own truncated version of the missing eighth hebdomad.[24]

Given all the other signs of rigorous stanzaic structure in Semonides 1, it is likewise probable that a single iambic trimeter has vanished from the third stanza, especially in a fragment solely preserved by Stobaeus, who in recent years has emerged as an unreliable source, who often truncates and rewrites poetic fragments or combines two different fragments into one.[25] Unlike the case of the "Ages of Man" catalogue (Solon 27), where there are cardinal numbers to orient us at the start of each couplet, it is more difficult to say where a verse has dropped out of the third stanza of Semonides 1, but the parallelism revealed above between Stanzas 2–4 can help us narrow it down. The chiastic response of οἱ μέν (7), οἱ δ᾽ (8) and οὐδεὶς ὅστις (9) with τὸν μέν (11), τοὺς δέ (12) and τοὺς δ

(13) and the parallel placement of the plural third-person verbs at the start of the third verse of each of the catalogue stanzas suggest strongly that the first three verses of Stanza 3 were composed as a continuous unit, while the ending of line 15 (χθονός) nicely fits the rhyming pattern of the last words in three of the three other stanzas. All of this leads to the conclusion that the fourth trimeter in the third stanza has disappeared. where it presumably provided a fuller description of those who die in warfare.

Let me close by offering a descriptive outline of the stanzaic structure of Semonides 1:

First Stanza (the gods hold the *telos* of human life, of which humans are ignorant): A single sentence organized by μέν and δέ and ring composition: τέλος μὲν Ζεὺς ἔχει (1) and ἐκτελευτήσει θεός (5).

Second Stanza (a coherent catalogue of foolish human expectations): A single sentence organized by ring composition: ἐλπὶς (6) and δοκεῖ (9).

Third Stanza (a coherent catalogue of forces that foil human expectations): Probably a single sentence organized by ring composition: φθάνει δὲ τὸν μὲν γῆρας (11) and πέμπει μελαίνης Ἀΐδης (15).

Fourth Stanza (a coherent extension of the previous catalogue of forces that foil human expectations): A single sentence with no ring-composition, but there is responsion of ideas between the end of this stanza and the end of the previous: πέμπει μελαίνης Ἀΐδης ὑπὸ χθονός (15) and λείπουσιν ἡλίου φάος (20).

Fifth Stanza: A summation of the whole poem (21: οὕτω) organized by ring-composition: κακῶν ἄπ᾽ οὐδέν (21) οὐδ᾽ ἐπ᾽ ἄλγεσιν κακοῖς ἔχοντες θυμὸν αἰκιζοίμεθα (24–5).

Most commentators believe that this fragment was probably a single poem and by taking into account a lost trimeter in Stanza 3, we can see this unity more clearly: Semonides composed this poem as a series of five interlocking stanzas, four of which comprise a single sentence and all of which are five iambic trimeters in length.

Finally, we should return to the question raised at the start: did Semonides take a popular elegiac form (the stanzaic catalogue in five-couplet stanzas) and compose a poem in iambic trimeters that in a similar manner are divided into five-verse stanzas and display both ring-composition and responsion? Some have pointed out (see note 3) that in this fragment Semonides seems to imitate Solon 13, and we have certainly seen above that in the first two couplets of Fragment 1 he seems to echo the language of the first stanza of Solon's catalogue. And there is more: the three stanzas that make up the central catalogue of Semonides 1 also imitate the shape of Solon's three-stanza catalogue, for example, the fact that in both catalogues the third stanzas seem to continue the syntax of the second and both are very different from the first. I would suggest, therefore, that Semonides, in addition to echoing the content of Solon 13 has also borrowed its stanzaic form by composing his poem in a series of tightly knit five-couplet stanzas. There is, moreover, the possibility that this stanzaic poem in iambs may have been a one-off experiment, because our two other long iambic poems Semonides' Fragment 6 and Solon 24 are clearly *not* composed in regular stanzas. It seems best, therefore, to argue that Semonides 1 was some kind of experiment in rendering the content and form of the stanzaic catalogues of elegy into an iambic poem, an experiment that was not, as far as we can tell from extant iambic poetry, repeated again. But we can nonetheless appreciate it as an experiment in condensation and to some degree in miniaturization. The argument for influence depends, finally, on dating Solon's birth to the decade before Semonides', but there are arguments for making Semonides' birthdate earlier[26] Given the difficulty of arriving at precise dates for seventh-century poets, it seems best to talk of similarities between the Semonidean and the Solonian catalogues and that one was imitating the other or that both were working with the stock features of archaic catalogues that ran across different poetic genres.

Notes

1 Because recent papyrological publications have shown that Stobaeus or his copyists were capable of mistakenly combining two separate poems or excerpts into a single citation, we need to be suspicious of the integrity of fragments like this one that survive only in his *Florilegium*; see Sider (2001), 272–80. Earlier Campbell (1984ʳ, 54–6, had stressed Stobaeus' tendency to edit out erotic poetry and personal references, even to the point of rewriting a poem to remove some of them. Many thanks to Joel Lidel and David Sider who read and commented on earlier versions of this paper; the errors that remain are, of course, all mine.

2 See, e.g., Fränkel (1973), 202 ("feeble and erratic"); and Babut (1971), 17, who decries the mediocrity of the poem and its lack of originality, citing much earlier

bibliography to support his view. For an excellent defense of its qualities, however, see Carson (1984).

3   Steffen (1973).

4   For a survey, see Faraone (2005).

5   Weil (1862); Rossi (1953/4); and Faraone (2008).

6   See, especially, Stephens (2003), 12; Acosta-Hughes and Stephens (2012), 55–7, 82; or Stephens (2017), 3.

7   See, e.g., Faraone (2004).

8   For this text and English translation, see Gerber (1999), 298–301, who in turn generally uses the text of West (1992). For the initial greeting ὦ παῖ at the start of an elegiac poem and often, as here, as the first word of the poem (most common in the *Theognidea*); see Gerber (1984), 125.

9   Gerber (1984), 128, "ring-composition which rounds off the first section of the poem," citing Römisch (1933), 49.

10 Scholars have long debated whether Fragment 13 is a single and unified poem and (if it is) how we are to identify its rhetorical or logical units. They generally see line 33 as the beginning of a new section that introduces the second half of the poem; see Gerber (1970), 124, and Anhalt (1993), 33–4, for a summary of earlier discussions. Buchner (1939), 170–90, and Maddalena (1943), 1–2, likewise think that 33–62 are a single unit, but offer no subdivision of the thirty lines. For the stanzaic structure here, see Faraone (2005) and (2008), 35–40.

11 For the text of Solon, I use the text of West (1992) and the translation Gerber (1999), who generally uses West's text.

12 Gerber (1999), *ad loc.*, and other editors suggest plausibly that lines 39–40 refer to *two* different cases (hence the comma at the end of 39): the low-born man, who thinks he is noble, and the ugly one, who believes he is handsome. But if this is so, it violates the one-person-per-couplet pattern that we see in the rest of this poem, in Solon's "Ages of Man" (discussed below) and in most of the other elegiac catalogues. Mülke (2002), 292, however, is surely right to think that Solon has the stock Greek phrase καλός κ'ἀγαθός in mind here and has produced, albeit in a chiastic manner, its poetic opposite: "And another man of low estate thinks himself noble and handsome, though he has a displeasing shape."

13 The verbal range of the Greek word δόξα are difficult to capture in translation. Campbell (1967), 234, concisely summarizes this double meaning as follows (my emphases): "Mortals, both good and evil, are (unlike Zeus, whose view is comprehensive) deluded by false *beliefs* and false *hopes*."

14 Faraone (2008), 36–9.

15 This is the text and translation of Gerber (1999) with minor changes in the latter. Neither he nor any other editor intuits, as I do, a missing trimeter in the middle stanza (11–15), a common problem in stichic catalogues that I address below.

16 Gerber (1984: 129): "In δοκεῖ we have essentially a continuation of the previous ἐλπὶς." He lists as comparanda Solon 13.33–6, Bacch. 20B. 8–12 and Euripides *Hec.* 370–1.

17 Gerber (1984), 130.

18 Gianotti (1977), 138, and Gerber (1984), 131, note a "balanced abbcc structure," but for some reason they ignore οὐδεὶς ὅστις (line 9).

19 Another feature of the third stanza is the status of the entities which or who attack the woebegone mortals: "old age" (11: γῆρας) seizes them, "illnesses" (12: νοῦσοι) destroy them, Ares (12: Ἄρει) lays them low, and Hades (15: Ἀΐδης) sends them beneath the earth. In a modern text and translation we distinguish, of course, the first two agents (abstract ideas and therefore common nouns) from the two deities ("Ares" and "Hades") who follow, despite the fact that the names of both were also used as common nouns for "war" and "the underworld" and that in later times both γῆρας and νοῦσοι could be personified as human banes.

20 Gerber (1984), 134–5, who cites several other commentators, sees Fragment 1 as a complete poem, at the end of which Semonides advises us to focus on the present and not be deluded by vane hopes for the future. Some, however, have felt the ending to be too negative or pessimistic, e.g. Fränkel (1973), 202, who suggests the lines preserved by Stobeaus were "followed by an injunction to enjoy life and the present moment, that is to say, an invitation to festive drinking." Steffen (1973) even argues that Fragments 2–4 originally were part of the lost ending of Fragment 1.

21 Gerber (1984), 128, rightly calls it "a kind of ring-composition." West (1992), *ad loc.* follows Ahrens in emending ζώομεν to ζόουσιν.

22 See Faraone (2008), 20–2, for discussion and full bibliography.

23 Faraone (2008), 65–9.

24 We can also see this process in the textual transmission of a five-couplet epigram of Leonidas of Tarentum: the last three couplets (all end-stopped) begin with the same verb in the same form and as a result the middle couplet has completely disappeared in the Palatine recension, a fact that would have been lost on us entirely were the full text not preserved in the alternate Planudean recension. See the comments of Gow and Page (1965) on Leonidas no. 11 *ad loc.*

25 See note 3 above.

26 See, e.g., Carey (2009), 162, who dates Semonides to the first half of the seventh century and speaks of Solon 13 as the "the closest parallel."

Bibliography

Acosta-Hughes, B. and S. A. Stephens (2012), *Callimachus in Context. From Plato to the Augustan Poets*, Cambridge: Cambridge University Press.

Anhalt, E. K. (1993), *Solon the Singer: Politics and Poetics*, Lanham, MD: Rowman and Littlefield.

Babut, D. (1971), "Sémonide et Mimnerme," *Revue des Études Grecques*, 84: 17–43.

Bartol, K. (1992), "Where was Iambic Poetry Performed? Some Evidence from the Fourth Century B.C.," *Classical Quarterly*, 42: 65–71.

Boedeker, D. and D. Sider, eds. (2001), *The New Simonides*, Oxford: Oxford University Press.

Buchner, K. (1939), "Solons Musengedicht," *Hermes*, 87: 163–90.

Budelmann, F., ed. (2009), *Cambridge Companion to Greek Lyric*, Cambridge: Cambridge University Press.

Campbell, D. (1967), *Greek Lyric Poetry: A Selection of Early Greek Lyric, Elegiac and Iambic Poetry*, Bristol: Bristol Classical Press.

Campbell, D. (1984), "Stobaeus and Early Greek Lyric Poetry," in D. E. Gerber (ed.), *Greek Poetry and Philosophy: Studies in Honor of Leonard Woodbury*, 51–60, Chico, CA: Scholars Press.

Carey, C. (2009), "Iambos," in F. Budelmann (ed.), *Cambridge Companion to Greek Lyric*, 149–67, Cambridge: Cambridge University Press.

Carson, A. (1984), "How Bad a Poem is Semonides Fragment 1?" in D. E. Gerber (ed.), *Greek Poetry and Philosophy: Studies in Honor of Leonard Woodbury*, 59–72, Chico, CA: Scholars Press.

Dale, A. M. (2002), "Stichos and Stanza," *Classical Quarterly*, 56: 46–50.

Faraone, C. A. (2004), "Hipponax Frag. 128W: Epic Parody or Expulsive Incantation?" *Classical Antiquity*, 23: 209–45.

Faraone, C. A. (2005), "Catalogues, Priamels and Stanzaic Structure in Early Greek Elegy," *Transactions of the American Philological Association*, 135: 249–65.

Faraone, C. A. (2008), *The Stanzaic Architecture of Ancient Greek Elegy*, Oxford: Oxford University Press.

Fränkel, H. (1973), *Early Greek Poetry and Philosophy*, New York: Harcourt Brace Jovanovic.

Gerber, D. E. (1970), *Euterpe: An Anthology of Early Greek Lyric, Elegiac, and Iambic Poetry*, Amsterdam: Hakkert.

Gerber, D. E. (1984), "Semonides Fr. 1 West: A Commentary," in D. E. Gerber (ed.), *Greek Poetry and Philosophy: Studies in Honor of Leonard Woodbury*, 125–35, Chico, CA: Scholars Press.

Gerber, D. E. (1999), *Greek Elegiac Poetry from the Seventh to the Fifth Centuries B.C.*, Loeb Classical Library, 258, Cambridge, MA: Harvard University Press.

Gerber, D. E., ed. (1984), *Greek Poetry and Philosophy: Studies in Honor of Leonard Woodbury*, Chico, CA: Scholars Press.

Gianotti, G. F. (1977), *Il canto dei Greci*, Torino: Loescher.

Gow, A. S. F. and D. Page (1965), *The Greek Anthology: Hellenistic Epigrams*, Cambridge: Cambridge University Press.

Lloyd-Jones, H. (1995), *Female of the Species: Semonides on Women*, Park Ridge, NJ: Noyes Press.

Maddalena, A. (1943), "Per l'interpretazione dell'elegia di Solone alle Muse," *Rivista di filologia e di istruzione classica*, 21: 1–12.

Mülke, C. (1943), *Solons politische Elegien und Iamben*, Munich: K. G. Sauer.

Römisch, E. (1933), *Studien zu älteren griechischen Elegie*, Frankfurt: Klostermann.

Rossi, F. (1953/1954), "Studi su Tirteo," *Atti dell'Istituto Veneto*, 112: 369–437.

Sider, D. (2001), "'As is the Generation of Leaves' in Homer, Simonides, Horace and Stobaeus," in D. Boedeker and D. Sider (eds.), *The New Simonides*, 272–88, Oxford: Oxford University Press.

Steffen, V. (1973), "De Semonide iambographo vitae humanae aestimatore," *Scripta minora selecta*, vol. 1, 7–87, Wroclaw: Wydawnictwo Polskiej Akademii Nauk.

Stephens, S. (2003), *Seeing Double: Intercultural Poetics in Ptolemaic Alexandria*, Berkeley, CA: University of California Press.

Stephens, S. (2017), "Alexandria: The New Center," *Electryone*, 5: 1–16.

Weil, H. (1862), "Über Spuren strophischer Composition bei den alten griechischen Elegikern," *Rheinisches Museum*, 17: 1–13.

West, M. L., ed. (1992), *Iambi et Elegi Graeci ante Alexandrum Cantati*, 2 vols, 2nd ed., Oxford: Oxford University Press.

2

The Humble and the Grand

Realism in Euripides' *Electra**

Marco Fantuzzi

Professor of Classics Emeritus, University of Roehampton, London

Mathias Hanses

Penn State University

Introduction

An Attic hydria datable to the second half of the sixth century BCE pictures five women, elegantly dressed and wearing jewelry, collecting water at a fountain house. For decades, between around 525 and 490 BCE, this iconography remained popular in Athens. It was represented on seventy-one black-figured and four red-figured vases.[1] Based on these images and other archaeological evidence, it has been concluded that, in archaic Athens, the wives and daughters of citizen families, possibly including aristocratic families (as suggested by the jewelry), frequented fountains, and thus probably enjoyed greater freedom and easier access to public spaces than their peers did in subsequent years. By the later fifth century, however, literary sources come to describe the task of fetching water as tedious, unpleasant, and normally left to the enslaved. Most famously, the female semi-chorus of *Lysistrata* (411 BCE), forced by wartime conditions to complete unusual duties, enter the scene carrying pitchers on their heads and complaining about the disgraceful conditions under which they have had to draw water (*Lys.* 327–32). In this period, we no longer encounter vase representations of (elite) women at the fountain-house, so this iconographic motif seems to have stopped being of interest to members of the upper classes (the only ones who could afford elaborate vases) after the archaic age.[2]

It is worth observing, therefore, that when Euripides' Electra appears on the stage in the play that bears her name, she enters from a rustic cottage carrying a pitcher on her head and stating that she is going to draw water from a spring. Since the pitcher belongs in the everyday life of the non-elite, it realistically represents the princess's newly humble station in the countryside. We use "realistically" here to refer to "materialistic realism." The term is defined as "an attempt to reflect one's experience of the natural and human world without any intercession of some notion of an ideal and perfect form" that is stimulated by an interest in the variety of human experience, in mutability and individuality.[3] In Aeschylus' *Choephoroi*, it had been the enslaved women of the chorus who carried libation vessels. Electra herself bore the offerings she was about to dedicate on her father's tomb. In Sophocles' *Electra*, which may or may not have preceded Euripides' play of the same name, she enters holding an urn with her father's ashes. All of these objects have religious and ritualistic connotations. The pitcher, then, that Electra carries in Euripides marks a striking difference from the Aeschylean and Sophoclean plays—a secular adaptation to a materialistic, domestic dimension. If vessels are, as it seems,[4] powerful vehicles of meaning in Aeschylus' and Sophocles' tragedies, then the contrast created by the Euripidean Electra's novel appearance and actions must have struck the spectators immediately and intensely.

Notably, examples of lifelike depictions of humble settings and characters and everyday occupations became more common from the third century onward,[5] when—in the words of Susan Stephens—"Artists in the Hellenistic period of both plastic and textual arts were self-conscious in their turning away from the idealizing heroic, as the role of war and its heroizing values were becoming less relevant to the lives of those who ran ancient cities and the taste for images closer to themselves grew more attractive."[6] In Stephens' analysis, the cup of Theocritus' *Id.* 1 with its depictions of common professions, erotic anxiety, and old age, or Hecataeus' statue of Philitas in Posidippus, define a new aesthetic that challenges the heroic paradigm of earlier poetry.[7]

In this chapter, we will be arguing that Euripides' *Electra* serves as a prototype, and a trendsetter, for this development as Stephens defined it. The play provides an early example of realistic portrayals of humble settings or characters, and it both makes explicit but also calls into question the role that noble birth and the heroic dimension play in exemplifying virtue.[8] *Electra*'s approach to realism in fact takes various forms, focusing on credibility in the presentation of characters and environment. This relates especially to the creation of an atmosphere of domesticity through the use of everyday objects and costumes that reflect a setting in the countryside.[9] Furthermore, Euripides sets expectations of clarity, logic, and reason, displaying throughout an "insistence on what is convincing at the level of everyday experience."[10] For instance, the characters approach psychological accuracy even and especially in the portrayal of obsessiveness and unheroic traits.

Relying on these features, Euripides' *Electra* effectively deglamorizes the traditional mythological atmosphere of Greek tragedy by populating the stage with characters who, at least in the first half of the play, often behave as if they were contemporary Athenians or humble characters from the *Odyssey*, such as Eumaeus and his swineherds,[11] rather than distanced and unattainable Iliadic heroes of the epic past.[12] In the second half, *Electra* moves from the lowly realm of everyday life to the grand and grandiose, most notably events surrounding the Trojan War and depictions of intra-familial murder. However, even here the play points to the true toll of bloodshed if realistically portrayed. Throughout, the play does not abandon such conventional, non-illusory, and hence not strictly speaking "realistic" features of tragedy as music, song, and dance. Yet, we argue that Euripides puts these varied elements to use in the service of even more fully foregrounding *Electra*'s realistic elements.

The above dynamics will be explored in two interconnected sections. The first focuses on *Electra*'s prologue, and especially on the titular character's opening monody. Here, Electra employs a New Musical aria (i.e., a mode of performance that appears to have been typical of royal women in tragedy) to demonstrate her high birth. The young woman thereby creates a jarring contrast to—and calls all-the-more emphatic attention to—her visual appearance, which portrays poverty in a realistic fashion. The result is a deliberate act of multi-medial rhetoric designed to convince spectators that she has been gravely wronged. In the second section, the focus lies on Euripides' demythologization of objects and personalities throughout the rest of the play. Characters here question traditional ways of defining nobility through royal lineage (including Electra's own approach to the topic) and call attention to the gruesomeness of war and murder, thus redefining some of the most grandiose events of Greek myth as ultimately inspiring terror.

Section 1: Old Clothes and New Music in the Prologue of Euripides' *Electra*

Modern readers of Euripides' *Electra* have claimed with some consistency that mourning did not, in fact, "become" the titular heroine. In the play's prologue, Agamemnon's daughter enters dressed in rags. Her hair is cropped and filthy, and she is carrying a water jug on her head. This costume reflects Electra's new social status: she has been married to a lowly farmer to remove any future children from the line of royal succession. Soon, she proceeds to sing a monody centered on the sorrow she has experienced following her father's murder, her mother Clytemnestra's new marriage to Aegisthus, and her brother Orestes' exile. It is clear, however, that Electra has cut her own hair and that she is carrying the jug of her own volition (the farmer offers to relieve her of the burden at 64–76). She could possibly even access nicer clothes if she so desired (the chorus suggest she borrow from them the beautiful garments appropriate to the ongoing Festival of Hera at 190–2). Accordingly, Electra's focus on her own burdens has struck many as ostentatious and overly emotional.[13] Then again, there have also been those who defend Electra against her detractors, most famously Froma Zeitlin, who argued that the character employs her clothes deliberately as an "outward token of her inner isolation."[14] Michael Lloyd agrees that rather than condemn Electra based on modern prejudices against self-pity, we should account for her need to make a convincing case—to the theatergoers and to the gods—that she has been wronged.[15] Accordingly, Melissa Mueller has identified Euripides' Electra as "the first postmodern heroine—the first to consciously manipulate her audience's reaction with props (and verbally to "flag" that this is what she is doing)."[16]

In what follows, we expand upon this observation and posit that Electra's opening aria constitutes no piece of self-centered hysteria, but rather a carefully crafted piece of rhetoric. The young woman's song provides clear demonstrations of her inherent royalty and thereby calls even more attention to her costume, which puts her humble circumstances on vividly realistic display. Through her rags, shaved head, and water pitcher, Electra highlights the departure from what she perceives to be her true nature, and from what she would have looked like in earlier versions of the same story. In particular, the visuals of her entrance would have clashed with memories of Aeschylus' *Oresteia*, which—it has been argued—may have been reperformed a few years before the original staging of Euripides' *Electra* (between about 420 and 413 BCE).[17] In Aeschylus, Electra still lived in her dead father's palace, availed herself of enslaved attendants, and the object she carried at the start was no humble pitcher, but a libation vessel. By contrast, the Euripidean Electra has fallen deeper than her Aeschylean (and, for that matter, her Sophoclean) counterpart, in that she has been deprived of all royal accouterments. Considering the visual nature of tragic performances, this shift would have been noticeable even if it had gone unaddressed. Yet, Euripides' Electra goes out of her way throughout the scene to highlight her lowly appearance through words and apparently also through gestures, and to point out that it is neither out of necessity nor out of sheer emotionality that she is carrying a humble vessel on her head. Rather, she clarifies in her very first lines (delivered still in the iambic trimeters of spoken verse) that her appearance reflects her intention to make a deliberate rhetorical point (54–9):

> ὦ νὺξ μέλαινα, χρυσέων ἄστρων τροφέ,
> ἐν ᾗ τόδ' ἄγγος τῷδ' ἐφεδρεῦον κάρᾳ
> φέρουσα πηγὰς ποταμίας μετέρχομαι—
> οὐ δή τι χρείας ἐς τοσόνδ' ἀφιγμένη,
> ἀλλ' ὡς ὕβριν δείξωμεν Αἰγίσθου θεοῖς—
> γόους τ' ἀφίημ' αἰθέρ' ἐς μέγαν πατρί.

Oh dark Night, nurse of the golden stars, in which I bear this pitcher sitting here on my head as I go for water from the stream—not that I've come to such a degree of need, but to display Aegisthus' hubris to the gods—and send laments for my father into the broad heaven.

Electra is meticulous, here, in calling attention to her close-cut hair and water jug, and in asserting her own agency in the choice of her attire. Her insistent use of deictics, likely accompanied by pointing, focuses the audience's gaze on the details of her visual appearance. In turn, her use of first-person verbs underlines that she is in full control of her own actions. In a purpose clause, she explains that she embraces her humble costume and her prop to demonstrate Aegisthus' culpability. Accordingly, the jug will serve as a visual reminder of Aegisthus' guilt for as long as it remains on the stage. As Michael Lloyd emphasizes, to point out an offender's *hubris* in such manners constitutes no act of self-indulgence, but a ritual necessity for the gods to spring into action.[18] We should therefore not see Electra's use of rags and pitcher as deceptive. Rather, she is throwing into relief an important aspect of her real-life experience.[19]

Notably, as Electra likewise emphasizes in the passage, this rhetorical act consists not of one, but of two components. In addition to her humble and "realistic" appearance, the success of her act of persuasion is also predicated on the dirge she is about to sing (γόους τ' ἀφίημ', 59). After all, Electra's costume and prop are useful only because they contrast so strongly with her regal upbringing. Electra's inherent royalty may no longer be visible, but in the monody that she announces in line 59, this "true" nature will, as it were, prove audible. Here, the testimony to Electra's royal personality lies not simply in the words she sings, but also in the very fact that they are sung.

Indeed, we ought to note that *Electra*'s opening monody may constitute an early instance of the later fifth century's impressive "New Music."[20] This innovative performance style combined revolutionary approaches to the construction of instruments with challenging choreography and great musical extravagance. Its origins lay in the emergence of a new class of professional double-pipe players, which paralleled the rise of professional actors. The New Music was influential in both dithyrambic and nomic performances, and on the tragic stage its trendsetters included Agathon, as well as Euripides and his musical collaborator Cephisophon.[21] While the New Music attracted the scorn of Plato and Aristotle, it appears to have been widely popular with less conservative swaths of the Athenian audience.[22]

External evidence for *Electra*'s likely adherence to the new style includes a papyrus fragment (PVindob. G 2315) preserving part of the original musical notation for Euripides' *Orestes* (408 BCE). A prominent feature of the papyrus is the lengthening or doubling of sung syllables in line with New Musical precepts to fit more than one *aulos* tone. Aristophanes mocks such privileging of music over language in his caricature of Euripidean songs in *Frogs* (εἰειειειειλίσσετε at 1314 and εἰειειλίσσουσο at 1349). Significantly, the comic playwright alludes to lines from *Electra* for this parody, as Kerr Borthwick has noted (Ar. *Ran.* 1317–18 = Eur. *El.* 435–7).[23] This suggests that our play, too, would have been New Musical.

As Electra thus begins to sing, she continues to call attention not just to the nature of her plight, but also to the very fact that her media of choice are music and dance. Three lines to this effect open the first strophe and repeat at the beginning of the first antistrophe. Here, Electra addresses herself (112–14 = 127–9):

σύντειν᾽ (ὥρα) ποδὸς ὁρμάν· ὤ,
ἔμβα ἔμβα κατακλαίουσα
ἰώ μοί μοι.

Press on—this is the hour—your urgent step; O, go forward, forward, sorrowing.
O me, O me!

A differently worded version of this self-exhortation to sing and dance occurs in the first mesode, which separates the first strophe from the first antistrophe (125–6):

ἴθι τὸν αὐτὸν ἔγειρε γόον,
ἄναγε πολύδακρυν ἀδονάν.

Come, rouse the same lament, raise up the pleasure of abundant tears.

Electra here emphasizes that she is singing and dancing while she is actually singing and dancing. The pun on the two meanings of πούς (both the metrical unit of her song and her actual foot) contained in line 112 and repeated in line

127 neatly summarizes the duality.[24] Such moments of metapoetry are familiar from tragic choruses.[25] In this instance, the wordplay draws the listeners' attention to what kind of person typically delivers monodies in Greek tragedy. Edith Hall has highlighted that the majority of monodists are of royal descent, non-Athenian, and female.[26] We can think, for example, of Io in *Prometheus Bound* or Iphigenia in Euripides' *Iphigenia at Aulis*.[27] Where exceptions occur, they are often used in the service of characterization. In Euripides' *Orestes*, for example, an enslaved Phrygian man delivers a solo in contexts so effeminizing as to reaffirm, rather than weaken, the association of monody and femininity. In *Ion*, the titular hero sings a song, but the play is so concerned with the royal boy's transition to full manhood—after which he ceases to sing—that this too cannot count as an example to the contrary. Finally, Aeschylus' Xerxes is royal and foreign, and though biologically male, he too is portrayed as effeminate.

There was at least a tendency, then, for monodies to be sung by a woman from a royal family, or by someone sharing in several of her characteristics, especially in Euripides. Accordingly, listeners could have associated any character beginning a monody with at least a certain degree of royalty and of femininity, and they might have considered the very fact that Electra delivers an aria an expression of her lofty descent. It is in keeping with this observation that Electra repeatedly underscores her regal origins in the words she sings. For example, she explicitly calls herself a "royal daughter" (κούρᾳ τᾷ βασιλείᾳ) in line 186. Earlier, in lines 115–21, which follow immediately on Electra's initial self-exhortation to sing and dance, she similarly points out her royal parentage:

ἐγενόμαν Ἀγαμέμνονος
καί μ᾽ ἔτικτε Κλυταιμήστρα
στυγνὰ Τυνδάρεω κόρα,
κικλήσκουσι δέ μ᾽ ἀθλίαν
Ἠλέκτραν πολιῆται.
φεῦ φεῦ σχετλίων πόνων
καὶ στυγερᾶς ζόας.

I am the daughter of Agamemnon, and Clytemnestra bore me, Tyndareus' hateful child. The people of my city call me wretched Electra. Alas, alas for my harsh toils and my hateful life.

Electra underscores that her father was the noble king Agamemnon (115), and that her mother—while not herself admirable—is the daughter of the honorable Tyndareus (117). Befitting the suggestion that the singer's royal descent is underlined by the medium of song, the verses in question are notable for their sound. For example, both words in verse 115, ἐγενόμαν and Ἀγαμέμνονος, intersperse a gamma followed by a succession of nasals with alphas, epsilons, and omicrons. As a result, they sound exceedingly similar. The taus, kappas, mus, and lambdas in καί μ' ἔτικτε Κλυταιμήστρα (117) create a comparable effect. Other musical features include the anadiplosis φεῦ φεῦ of line 120, which recalls similar doublings in lines 113 = 128 (ἔμβα ἔμβα) and 114 = 129 (ἰώ μοί μοι) and anticipates line 137 (ὧ Ζεῦ Ζεῦ), as well as such exceedingly alliterative lines as 159–62 (ἰώ μοι <ἰώ> μοι / πικρᾶς μὲν πελέκεως τομᾶς / σᾶς, πάτερ, πικρᾶς , . . . βουλᾶς "O me, me for the bitter cut of the axe / upon you, father, and the bitter plan"). Here, the tendency towards "doubling" is particularly pronounced, and as was mentioned above, such repetition of identical words and sounds is a feature of the New Music. At the same time, then, as Electra brings up her royal parents, her performance's New Musical features would have further highlighted the connection between the young woman's lofty heritage and her song. The resultant clash with her humble costuming would have increased in intensity with each new line sung as part of the monody.

This portrayal of Electra as a royal singer whose sufferings are externalized through a costume that realistically reifies her newly humble status continues in the second strophe. Here, Electra draws even more emphatic attention to her visual appearance, apparently through pointing and gestures, perhaps because the initial shock of seeing her shorn head may have started to wear off (140–9):

θὲς τόδε τεῦχος ἐμᾶς ἀπὸ κρατὸς ἑ-
λοῦσ', ἵνα πατρὶ γόους νυχίους
ἐπορθροβοάσω·
†ἰαχὰν ἀοιδὰν μέλος
Ἀίδα, πάτερ, σοι†
κατὰ γᾶς ἐνέπω γόους
οἷς ἀεὶ τὸ κατ' ἦμαρ
λείβομαι, κατὰ μὲν φίλαν
ὄνυχι τεμνομένα δέραν
χέρα τε κρᾶτ' ἔπι κούριμον
τιθεμένα θανάτῳ σῷ.

Take this vessel from my head and set it down so I may raise high (?) for my father these nocturnal cries of lamentation, crying out a song of Hades for you (?), father. Down through the earth I utter the laments with which continually day by day I pine, slashing with nails this throat of mine beating hand against shorn head in sorrow at your death.

At this point in the monody, Electra lowers the pitcher off her head. She then calls attention, once again, to the fact that she is singing and dancing. Finally, she proceeds to tear at her neck and shaven scalp. Putting down the jug would therefore not have shifted the audience's attention away from the visual reminders of Electra's plight. On the contrary, it appears that Electra removes the prop because all aspects of her performance are intensifying.[28] Notably, the second strophe differs from earlier parts of the monody in that it consists of only one continuous sentence with parallel first-person singular verbs at or near the end of their *cola* or periods (ἐπορθροβοάσω; ἐνέπω; λείβομαι), which is typical of the New Music.[29] Perhaps, then, the second strophe's single, continuous, musical line would have been reflected in a greater fluidity in her dance moves,[30] which in turn could have helped Electra underline her inborn grace. This visual would have further heightened the jarring contrast between a musical performance reflecting royal femininity, and the shocking sight of Electra's cropped head, which the singer actively lacerates at the end of the strophe.

It seems likely that such gestures drawing the audience's eyes to the actor's realistic costuming would not just have occurred here, but also elsewhere in the monody. After all, David Wiles suggests for tragic choruses that the phenomenon of strophic responsion that has strophes match the metrics of their antistrophes was reflected in the dance moves as well.[31] The choreuts would, according to this theory, have performed similar mimetic movements during similar parts of their song. The same principle might apply to a monody like Electra's,[32] which too is arranged into strophes and antistrophes. The actor could accordingly have engaged in similar gesturing throughout the song. Obvious further candidates for such highlighting of Electra's realistic costuming through tearing and pointing include the second mesode. Here, Electra compares herself to a swan (150–6):

ἒ ἔ, δρύπτε κάρα·
οἷα δέ τις κύκνος ἀχέτας
ποταμίοις παρὰ χεύμασιν
πατέρα φίλτατον καλεῖ,
ὀλόμενον δολίοις βρόχων
ἕρκεσιν, ὣς σὲ τὸν ἄθλιον,
πάτερ, ἐγὼ κατακλαίομαι ...

Ah ah, tear my head—and as some moaning swan by river's streams calls to its dearest father, who has perished in the guileful corded net, so do I, father, mourn for you and your wretched fate, ...

In antiquity, swans were considered remarkable for their filial piety, and for the beauty of the songs they sing at the moment of death. The bird therefore provides a fitting image for a daughter who demonstrates her ability to perform an aria for her father even in the face of great sorrows. Contrasting with the dignity of the simile is the humility of Electra's realistic costume, to which she again calls attention by physically tearing the skin on her head, thereby producing an upsetting presentation of the damage that her present plight is doing to the sensibilities she expresses through music.

Concluding, thus, our reading of the prologue and looking ahead briefly to the play's parodos, it is worth noting that further gestures at her head would at this later point have accompanied Electra's exchange with the arriving chorus. This song connects seamlessly to the end of her monody, and Electra's contribution reflects the same concerns as her aria. It also neatly summarizes the point of her performance thus far and points ahead to topics that will surface later in the play (183–8):

σκέψαι μου πιναρὰν κόμαν·
καὶ τρύχη τάδ' ἐμῶν πέπλων,
εἰ πρέποντ' Ἀγαμέμνονος
κούρᾳ τᾷ βασιλείᾳ
τᾷ Τροίᾳ θ', ἃ 'μοῦ πατέρος
μέμναταί ποθ' ἁλοῦσα.

Look at my filthy hair, this threadbare clothing of mine, and see if they are seemly for Agamemnon's royal daughter, and for Troy which does not forget she once was conquered by my father.

Electra here persists in gesturing at her head, and as in her solo, she stresses that her realistically ragged appearance contrasts with her inherent royalty, which she has been expressing through song. As was the case throughout the prologue, Electra thus employs music suggestive of a woman's regal attributes to create a clash with the lowly costuming that points to her new place among the non-elite. In fact, the performance that Electra delivers jointly with the chorus was remembered as one of Greek tragedy's most gripping,[33] and the choreuts soon abandon their initial skepticism of the singer. Electra seems, therefore, to have made her case convincingly, at least for the time being. Still, it is likewise true that as the play progresses, Euripides' characters begin to call into question the very definition of nobility that is central to Electra's claim to pity. She may have demonstrated her descent from kings and reminded the spectators of her father's role in the Trojan War. Yet, in the next section, we turn to the question of how the play presents a newly realistic take on these aspects of her story as well, and not just on the acts of everyday domesticity to which she calls attention in her opening monody.

Section 2: The Humble and the Grand

Considering that Euripides' *Electra* was first performed well after the premiere of Aeschylus' *Choephoroi* (and perhaps also after Sophocles' *Electra*) it should be safe to say that the young woman's presentation in rags constitutes an innovation, and a departure from her portrayal in prior tragedies. However, as we just saw, Euripides' Electra does retain much of her royal pride. Bellicose feelings and a strong need for revenge simmer below the surface of her song. It is in line with this observation that, as we noted above, she presents the act of drawing water not as something she is compelled to do by real indigence, but rather as a role she has chosen to assume in order to provoke the gods' indignation and pity for the humiliating life imposed on her by Aegisthus (54–9).

Electra must therefore have seemed doubly displaced in the eyes of her divine audience (and the Athenian audience).[34] Not only was she living in a farmer's cottage instead of a royal palace (an inappropriate environment), but she was also about to draw water from a rustic stream (an inappropriate occupation). Electra reminds the audience of this radical misplacement in terms of social geography in the first words she speaks to her farmer-husband, making explicit that the activity in which she is engaging is below her station (the peasant emphasizes the same at 64–6: τί γὰρ τάδ᾽, ὦ δύστην᾽, ἐμὴν μοχθεῖς χάριν / πόνους ἔχουσα, πρόσθεν εὖ τεθραμμένη, / καὶ ταῦτ᾽ ἐμοῦ λέγοντος οὐκ ἀφίστασαι; "Why, unhappy woman, do you labor at these tasks for my sake, taking on drudgery, when you were finely raised before, and do not refrain from them though I tell you to?"). Later on, when the women of the chorus invite Electra to participate in the procession to the temple of Hera, she again describes her everyday life as a humiliation that keeps her from sharing in the lofty life of the other high-born Argive brides, thus showing, as we have seen, the clearest awareness that she remains in control of her appearance and its effects. The women of the chorus understand (and initially disapprove of) Electra's strategy (193–5). Yet, Electra manages not only to draw the chorus over to her side, but also to incite Orestes to take action against Aegisthus and Clytemnestra. Here is how she addresses her brother when she is still unaware of his identity, considering him merely a foreign guest-friend (303–10):

ἄγγελλ᾽ Ὀρέστηι τἀμὰ κἀκείνου κακά,
πρῶτον μὲν οἵοις ἐν πέπλοις αὐλίζομαι,
πίνῳ θ᾽ ὅσῳ βέβριθ᾽, ὑπὸ στέγαισί τε
οἵαισι ναίω βασιλικῶν ἐκ δωμάτων,
αὐτὴ μὲν ἐκμοχθοῦσα κερκίσιν πέπλους
[ἢ γυμνὸν ἔξω σῶμα καὶ στερήσομαι]
αὐτὴ δὲ πηγὰς ποταμίους φορουμένη.
ἀνέορτος ἱερῶν καὶ χορῶν τητωμένη …

Report to Orestes these troubles that are mine and his as well. First, the kind of clothes I must lie in, the dirt I am loaded with, the kind of shelter I live in, exiled from those royal halls, working the shuttle to make clothes with my own labor [or else I shall have my body unclothed and be deprived], and carrying fresh water from the stream myself, missing festive rites, excluded from choruses …

At the end of this part of the tragedy where, in an innovative departure from the traditional myth, Electra lists the ordinary details of her daily life, we find a recapitulative list of the items that characterize her humbleness. The practice and the "theory" of her tragic state seem, here, to be intimately connected to one another and loaded with a metatheatrical dimension. Through the proud princess' explicit admission that she is not in so lowly a condition as she pretends to be, but that she is rather strategically up-playing her plight, we see Euripides detailing the main tokens through which he has constructed her humility. In doing so, he primes the audience for the specific reactions he is hoping to provoke. At the same time, the persistence of the vengeful pride that still characterizes Electra even in the midst of her humiliation points the way toward her return to the traditional role of avenger.

Significantly, what we may call the theory and practice of tragic humbleness are combined not only in Electra's words. In dialogue with his sister and reacting to the admirable behavior of the peasant, Orestes utters a long deliberation on the subject of virtue. As he sees it, virtue is a quality that, contrary to prior opinion, is not reserved only for those of privileged background or wealth but evident also among the lower classes. It shows itself through actions (367–82):

οὐκ ἔστ᾽ ἀκριβὲς οὐδὲν εἰς εὐανδρίαν·
ἔχουσι γὰρ ταραγμὸν αἱ φύσεις βροτῶν.
ἤδη γὰρ εἶδον ἄνδρα γενναίου πατρὸς
τὸ μηδὲν ὄντα, χρηστὰ δ᾽ ἐκ κακῶν τέκνα,
λιμόν τ᾽ ἐν ἀνδρὸς πλουσίου φρονήματι,
γνώμην δὲ μεγάλην ἐν πένητι σώματι.

[πῶς οὖν τις αὐτὰ διαλαβὼν ὀρθῶς κρινεῖ;
πλούτῳ; πονηρῷ τἄρα χρήσεται κριτῇ.
ἢ τοῖς ἔχουσι μηδέν; ἀλλ' ἔχει νόσον
πενία, διδάσκει δ' ἄνδρα τῇ χρείᾳ κακόν.
ἀλλ' εἰς ὅπλ' ἐλθών; τίς δὲ πρὸς λόγχην βλέπων
μάρτυς γένοιτ' ἂν ὅστις ἐστὶν ἀγαθός;
κράτιστον εἰκῇ ταῦτ' ἐᾶν ἀφειμένα.]
οὗτος γὰρ ἀνὴρ οὔτ' ἐν Ἀργείοις μέγας
οὔτ' αὖ δοκήσει δωμάτων ὠγκωμένος,
ἐν τοῖς δὲ πολλοῖς ὤν, ἄριστος ηὑρέθη.

Well, nothing is precise when it comes to virtue! For there is confusion in the natures of men. Before now I have seen a worthless man sprung from a noble father, and estimable children from low born parents; emptiness I have seen in a rich man's thinking, and a great mind in a poor man's body. How then shall a man distinguish and rate them correctly? By wealth? A faulty guide he will then be using! Or by lack of possessions? Yet poverty is unhealthy, and trains a man in badness, because of his need. Turning, then, to arms? Yet who when facing an enemy's spears can testify which man is the virtuous one? It is best to let these things go and leave them in disorder. For this man, who is not eminent among the Argives, nor yet puffed up by family reputation, but belongs amongst the many, has been found excellent.

This speech (given in an abridged version here) is extraordinarily long, somewhat loose in its arrangement, and parts of it have been suspected of interpolation.[35] But, whether all of these lines are by Euripides does not impinge on our analysis. Orestes' main focus lies on the difficulty of identifying virtue, and on his rejection of the widespread assumption that identifies virtue with nobility of birth, or εὐγένεια (much like his sister had done at the start of the play). Indeed, the whole drama, well beyond the long scene on Electra's resistance to the traditional tokens of Orestes' identification (508-46), revolves around the (un)certainty of recognition, and the audience is asked to revisit the subject again and again. It is only the evaluation of a person's qualities on a case-by-case basis, and an assessment of their positive impact on society, that should be the parameter to assess what virtue is. Now, the occasion for Orestes' speech is provided by the generosity of the peasant, who wants to host the foreigner and his companion (Pylades) in his cottage even though he is poor (362), thus showing his social usefulness despite his lack of resources. Immediately after Orestes has finished, Electra makes an acrid comment, objecting to the farmer's invitation (ὦ τλῆμον, εἰδὼς δωμάτων χρείαν σέθεν / τί τούσδ᾽ ἐδέξω μείζονας σαυτοῦ ξένους; "You thoughtless man! You know the poverty of your home; so why have you received these guests who are greater men than you?" 404–5). Placed briefly after Orestes' *rhesis*, these words would have made Electra seem like a more questionable character.

Orestes' speech thus provides a larger ideological backdrop, so to speak, against which to evaluate the peasant's humbleness, as well as Electra's. It reinscribes democratic Athenian values for an audience that would likely be sympathetic to this stance.[36] The lines furthermore revive a polemic against aristocratic views—subscribed to by Theognis and others—according to which ethical ἀρετή and social relevance cannot be separated from εὐγένεια.[37] It is appealing to suppose that in placing Orestes' words at the end of the first part of the tragedy, Euripides meant to provide a defense of his juxtaposition of a pseudo-humble Electra and an actually impoverished peasant in the supposedly lofty genre of tragedy, and to invite further reflection on the topic.

We ought to remember in this context that dressing royal characters in rags seems to have been a hallmark of Euripides, which Aristophanes had begun to mock already in his parody of *Telephus* in *Acharnians* (425 BCE).[38] There the character Dicaeopolis dresses in rags and a Mysian cap in order to appear "as wretched as possible" (οἷον ἀθλιώτατον, 384), thus attempting to convince the patriotic Acharnians of his peace plan. During the preparations, Dicaeopolis asks Euripides for the rags to wear (414–17) in order to imitate Telephus, king of the Mysians, who in his Euripidean nameplay (438 BCE) had disguised himself as a beggar in order to be able to enter the royal palace at Argos.[39] Closer in time to *Electra*, the theme of royals strategically disguised in humble costumes recurs in Euripides' *Helen* (412 BCE), where Menelaus appears on stage in rags and considers explicitly how his get-up will strengthen the story of his shipwreck (1079–80).[40] We would surmise that *Electra*'s exploration of the same topic, and apparent defense of the playwright's choices, constitutes a moment of Euripidean paracomedy in line with recent suggestions by Craig Jendza (2020). More specifically, Euripides replies to the paratragedy of *Acharnians* and thereby paves the way for a further contribution to the topic in Aristophanes' *Frogs*.

Frogs, of course, comes many years after *Electra*. In the relevant passage, Aeschylus has just expressed the idea that tragedy must instruct society to perform great deeds, such as winning wars (cf. 1026–7, 1030–1). He comes back to the same point a few lines after stating, significantly, that demigods use more sublime forms of clothing and expression than mortals (1058–62):

'ἀλλ', ὦ κακόδαιμον, ἀνάγκη
μεγάλων γνωμῶν καὶ διανοιῶν ἴσα καὶ τὰ ῥήματα τίκτειν.
κἄλλως εἰκὸς τοὺς ἡμιθέους τοῖς ῥήμασι μείζοσι χρῆσθαι·
καὶ γὰρ τοῖς ἱματίοις ἡμῶν χρῶνται πολὺ σεμνοτέροισιν.
'ἀμοῦ χρηστῶς καταδείξαντος διελυμήνω σύ.

Look, you wretch [= Euripides], great thoughts and ideas force us to produce expressions that are equal to them. And anyway, it suits the demigods to use sublime expressions, just as they wear much more impressive clothing than we do; that is where I set a good example that you completely corrupted.

Euripides then tries to understand how he was responsible for that corruption (τί δράσας; "How so?" 1062b), and Aeschylus promptly explains (1063–4a):

πρῶτον μὲν τοὺς βασιλεύοντας ῥάκι' ἀμπισχών, ἵν' ἐλεινοὶ
τοῖς ἀνθρώποις φαίνοιντ' εἶναι.

First, you made your royals wear rags, so that they would strike people as being piteous.

In the context of his poetological discourse, Aristophanes' rendition of Aeschylus points to the audience's pity as the desired effect of Euripides' application of a humble everyday appearance to royal characters. Electra likewise explains her ostentatiously humble clothing and behavior as intended to provoke indignation and compassion. Aristophanes' Aeschylus may have had Euripides' Electra in mind, then, perhaps among other Euripidean characters, when he critiqued the tragedian's portrayal of royal characters. Whatever the case may be, the point is that both Electra the Euripidean character and Aeschylus the tragic poetologist of Aristophanic comedy attempt to explain the adoption of humble clothing and provide the same explanation. Even if the parallel is a coincidence, it still lends weight to the idea that Euripides' Electra spoke in a quasi-parabatic authorial voice, defending not only her own embrace of her humble clothing, but also Euripides' more frequent reliance on this particular strategy.

Moving now into later parts of *Electra*, we might like to remember that Bernard Knox once observed that: "The effect of the domestic atmosphere of the first half of the play is to strip every last shred of heroic stature from Electra and Orestes, so that we see their subsequent actions not as heroic fulfillment of a god's command, but rather as crimes committed by men 'as they are.'"[41] Upon this reading, Euripides' emphasis on the humble everyday life of Electra and the peasant (notably appreciated by Orestes) prepares the audience for the second half of the tragedy, where the killing of Clytemnestra and Aegisthus is portrayed as one instance of matricide and another simply of cruel butchery,[42] rather than as acts of divinely-sanctioned and righteous revenge for Agamemnon's death. In this context, the first stasimon (432–86) depicts the deaths of Aegisthus and Agamemnon in darkly realistic tones as acts of brutal violence—this despite the initial cheer and glamorous atmosphere surrounding the tale of Greek ships sailing to Troy and their ultimate victory.[43]

In the first strophe/antistrophe the chorus focus on the Greek fleet that carried Achilles and Agamemnon to Troy accompanied by the merry dances of the Nereids.[44] The mention of the antagonists in the events connected to the "anger of Achilles" immediately points to the last year of the war, and thus indirectly evokes the intertext of the Iliadic ecphrasis of Achilles' second shield.[45] Euripides stresses the relation between this shield and the earlier one he is about to describe by reminding us that the first panoply was also created by Hephaestus (line 444), thus highlighting similarities to the second one of the *Iliad* (18.462–7).[46] In a notable distinction, however, the first shield mentioned at *Il.* 17.194–7 and 18.82–5 had been a wedding gift from the gods to Achilles' father Peleus.[47] Here is part of the description in the Euripidean version (lines 452–78):

Ἰλιόθεν δ᾽ ἔκλυόν τινος ἐν λιμέσιν
Ναυπλίοις βεβῶτος
τᾶς σᾶς, ὦ Θέτιδος παῖ,
κλεινᾶς ἀσπίδος ἐν κύκλῳ
τοιάδε σήματα †δείματα
Φρύγια† τετύχθαι·
περιδρόμῳ μὲν ἴτυος ἕδραι
Περσέα λαιμοτόμαν ὑπὲρ ἁλὸς
ποτανοῖσι πεδίλοις κορυφὰν Γοργόνος ἴσχειν,
Διὸς ἀγγέλῳ σὺν Ἑρμᾷ,
τῷ Μαίας ἀγροτῆρι κούρῳ
ἐν δὲ μέσῳ κατέλαμπε σάκει φαέθων
κύκλος ἁλίοιο
ἵπποις ἂμ πτεροέσσαις
ἄστρων τ᾽ αἰθέριοι χοροί,
Πλειάδες Ὑάδες, †Ἕκτορος
ὄμμασι† τροπαῖοι·
ἐπὶ δὲ χρυσοτύπῳ κράνει
Σφίγγες ὄνυξιν ἀοίδιμον ἄγραν
φέρουσαι· περιπλεύρῳ δὲ κύτει πύρπνοος ἔσπευ–
δε δρόμῳ λέαινα χαλαῖς
Πειρηναῖον ὁρῶσα πῶλον.

ἄορι δ' ἐν φονίῳ τετραβάμονες ἵπποι ἔπαλλον,
κελαινὰ δ' ἀμφὶ νῶθ' ἵετο κόνις.

From a man arrived from Troy in Nauplia's harbour I heard, O son of Thetis, that on the circle of your famous shield these emblems were fashioned, terrors for the Phrygians. On the rim's encircling field was Perseus above the brine on flying sandals, holding, throat severed, the Gorgon's head, in company with Zeus' herald Hermes, that rustic son of Maia. And on the buckler's centre shone, radiant, the circle of the sun on his winged horses, and ethereal choruses of stars—Pleiades, Hyades—to turn back Hector's eyes. And on the helm of beaten gold were Sphinxes bearing in their talons their sung prey; and on the hollow corselet, breathing fire, sped at a run the lioness on clawed feet, as she saw the Peirenean colt. And on the slaughtering sword leapt four-stepping horses and dust was billowing dark about their backs.

In Euripides' narrative, already the mention of the Nereids and the setting at Cheiron's cave depart from the Iliadic description of the second panoply and thus set the stage for *Electra*'s challenging stance. The motif of the Nereids bringing the arms to Achilles on the back of dolphins is quite common in late-fifth-century iconography, especially at Athens,[48] but in the *Iliad* Thetis alone had carried (16.616–17) and delivered (19.10–11) the second shield to Achilles. Yet, the aspect of Euripides' challenge to Homer that concerns us most are the various glimpses the chorus women provide of such realistically sinister aspects of the war as fright, blood, or death. At the same time that they celebrate the war of Troy as a glorious event worthy of epic, they show through these other, unavoidably bloody elements the day-to-day of warfare, which is frequently delivered in the female voice in Euripidean tragedy.[49] The chorus' concentration on images of fright in the iconography of the shield also has a metaliterary value, since it is especially here that Euripides issues his challenge to Homer.[50] Although the second shield resembles the first in that it is δεινός . . . σμερδαλέος ("terrible and awful to behold," 20.259–60), and although the glare from Achilles' arms frightened enemies already in Homer's description (22.134–7), the Iliadic second shield of Achilles had mainly displayed varied (almost encyclopaedic) aspects of human everyday or festive life, individual or social, or the natural world.[51] Apart from the extended picture of a city besieged by a hostile army that may recall the larger story of which the ecphrasis is a small part,[52] all the other scenes were non-martial and thus foreign to the warlike perspective of the *Iliad*. This has led a few scholars to believe that the Iliadic ecphrasis was a pure digression, and that it served solely for the delectation of the readers,[53] creating for their relaxation a peaceful view of the world alternative to the tension of the war and largely disconnected from it.[54]

In direct contrast to Homer, Euripides' first arming of Achilles is brimming with precisely such images of fright as one might expect to find on a shield, and which do survive on actual shields from antiquity.[55] The images in question served to scare the enemy and suggest a magical equivalence in aggressive strength between the creatures and warriors depicted and the bearer of the shield himself. It is in this manner that such objects indeed became "δείματα for the Phrygians" (456–7).[56] The gorgon's head featured on Achilles' Euripidean shield was in fact particularly common in this context, especially in the Archaic age,[57] and the sphinx, Perseus, and chimaera are also attested frequently as shield decorations.[58] Pheidias' statue of Athena Parthenos, for one, carried a shield with a gorgon-head, a breastplate with the same motif, and a helmet with a sphinx on either side.[59] Of course, figures such as a gorgon, sphinx, chimaera, or Perseus do not belong in real life, inasmuch as they are mythical entities; however, since they were often represented on ancient shields, they do belong in the real everyday life of archaic warriors.

There is a dual opposition, then, to Homeric precedent, contained in the Euripidean stasimon. On the one hand, Euripides' real-life military equipment stands in stark contrast to the extra-martial encyclopaedia that Homer ascribes to Achilles' second shield. On the other hand, Euripides' chorus replaces the heroic grandeur that characterizes the Greeks' "invincible armada" at the beginning of the ode with a series of realistic glimpses at the terrors that characterize an actual war. In other words, the realism of the arms and of their images of fright and death is in tune with the prevailing, fearful mood of the rest of the play, and with the dark atmosphere of the double execution of Aegisthus and Clytemnestra that is still to come. It also works well with the realistic atmosphere that Euripides adopts for the first part of *Electra* more so than, perhaps, anywhere else in the plays known to us. It is just that we have now switched from the realism of humble, everyday life to an examination of the realistic dimensions of a supposedly "grand" event such as the war of Troy.[60]

Conclusions

The final parts of the play bring to their logical conclusion the varied elements of Euripidean realism that define *Electra*. The spectators had been asked on numerous occasions to see familiar characters from fresh "realistic" perspectives

A princess sings in manners demonstrating her royal birth, but she has been placed in humble rags reflecting real life that foreground her suffering. Her brother, in turn, finds that the lowly peasant displays greater nobility than some so-called "noble" men. Indeed, if realistically portrayed, even the glorious Trojan War inspires a sense of grandeur but also of terror. As the tragedy concludes, Euripides appears to want the theatergoers to derive similar observations from the murder of Clytemnestra and Aegisthus. Even early on, the farmer had summarized the couple's actions in the following zeugma (8–10):

> ἐν δὲ δώμασιν
> θνῄσκει γυναικὸς πρὸς Κλυταιμήστρας δόλῳ
> καὶ τοῦ Θυέστου παιδὸς Αἰγίσθου χερί.

> but in his home [Agamemnon] was killed by his wife, Clytemnestra, with her guile and the violence of Thyestes' son, Aegisthus.

According to the peasant, Euripides' Clytemnestra is a murderer, but unlike in Aeschylus and Sophocles, she did not herself wield the "man-killing axe." This may make her seem less deserving of punishment than in other versions. Furthermore, the farmer goes on to describe Clytemnestra's subsequent treatment of Electra as an honest attempt at saving her daughter from the clutches of Aegisthus (27–30):

> ὠμόφρων ὅμως
> μήτηρ νιν ἐξέσωσεν Αἰγίσθου χερός.
> ἐς μὲν γὰρ ἄνδρα σκῆψιν εἶχ' ὀλωλότα,
> παίδων δ' ἔδεισε μὴ φθονηθείη φόνῳ.

> but her mother, cruel though she was, rescued her from Aegisthus' violence. For her husband's death, you see, she had a pretext, but the children's slaying she feared might rouse resentment.

Indeed, Electra takes deliberate advantage of Clytemnestra's (grand)motherly feelings when she pretends to have given birth in order to lure her victim to her humble abode (656–8).[61] In their ensuing *agon* (988–1138), each of the two women gets to make a strong case for her own position. If the matricide was a debatable deed already in the *Oresteia*, it would therefore have appeared an even more problematic act in Euripides. Furthermore, Clytemnestra does not take recourse to the sacrifice of Iphigenia in justifying her actions but rather blames Agamemnon's adultery (1030–4), which she avenged employing Aegisthus as an instrument (1046–8). This adds a further "realistic" touch, as she is portrayed as a betrayed wife whose experience is more easily relatable than that of a queen enraged by an infanticide. And in fact, the realism of Clytemnestra's portrayal extends not only to her psychology but also to the bloodshed to which she and Aegisthus succumb. Aegisthus unwittingly offers Orestes a friendly and pious welcome right before he is struck down, and his death is described with gruesome anatomic precision (839–43). In turn, Clytemnestra begs her children in her final moments to spare themselves the pollution that they will incur by killing their mother (1165). It makes sense, then, that the ensuing violence is condemned as disproportionate not only by the chorus, but also by the god Castor. As he and his brother are swung in on the *mechane* after the murder of their sister Clytemnestra, he proclaims (1242–4):

> ἀφίγμεθ᾽ Ἄργος, ὡς ἐσείδομεν
> σφαγὰς ἀδελφῆς τῆσδε, μητέρος δὲ σῆς.
> δίκαια μέν νυν ἥδ᾽ ἔχει, σὺ δὲ οὐχὶ δρᾷς.

we have come to Argos, as we observed the slaughter of the sister here, your mother. Her punishment is just, but not your deed.

At the very end of the play, Euripides thus abandons realism and reverts to a traditional moment of divine intervention. Nevertheless, it is precisely the playwright's realism reaching its logical end point that triggers Castor's comments as *deus ex machina*. In Euripides' *Electra*, more lifelike depictions of famous moments in Greek myth always point out that human pain goes deeper than the spectators might have suspected. Electra suffers profoundly when she is reduced to a humble setting, but her response still suggests that the lowly peasant might be a better person than the royal characters who interact with him. Moreover, both Electra and Clytemnestra have understandable reasons for their actions that make sense if we ascribe to them a realistic psychology. Whether at Troy or at Argos, the deeds these "noble" characters commit, if realistically considered, instill profound horror. They thus open a substantial new field to be explored in Euripides' experimentations with tragedy.

Notes

* The Greek of Euripides' *Electra* as cited in this paper is based on Diggle (1981) in consultation with Basta Donzelli (1995); Roisman and Luschnig (2011); and Cropp (2013). Translations of *Electra* are from Cropp (2013) with occasional modifications;

translations of Aristophanes, *Frogs* are from Henderson (2002). This paper greatly benefited from generous feedback by Martin Cropp. The authors also wish to thank Claire Catenaccio, Helene Foley, and Erin M. Hanses for their comments on the first section when it was in earlier stages of composition.

1　Trümper (2012).

2　Rotroff and Lamberton (2006), 7–8.

3　Pollitt (1986), 141.

4　Cf. most recently Mueller (2016), 114–16; Billings (2018).

5　Cf. Gellie (1981), 3; Michelini (1987), 182–3.

6　Stephens (2018), 45.

7　Ibid., 61.

8　Cf. Michelini (1987), 183.

9　Goff (1999–2000), 94–7.

10　Cropp (2013), 1; see also Gellie (1981).

11　Michelini (1987), 185–6.

12　Arnott (1981), 181.

13　Cf., e.g., Grube (1961); O'Brien (1964); Knox (1979); Raeburn (2000). To some, Electra's seemingly exaggerated emotionality is connected to the farmer's claim that he has not slept with his wife (42–53), which they view as having a destabilizing effect on the young woman. See Zeitlin (1970), 666; King (1983), 111–15; Hall (2010), 134; Roisman and Luschnig (2011), on 44; Cropp (2013), on 44.

14　Zeitlin (1970), 648.

15　Lloyd (1986).

16　Mueller (2016), 47.

17　Arguments to date the *Electra* around 420 BCE rely largely on metrical evidence. Possible references to later events suggest the play may have been staged around 413 BCE; see Roisman and Luschnig (2011), 28–32 and Cropp (2013), 31–3. Newiger (1961), esp. 427–30, finds reminiscences of a recent revival of the *Oresteia* in Ar. *Nub.* He argues that Euripides' *Electra* should be placed near the date of this reperformance. See also Webster (1971), 34; Hammond (1984), 379 n. 19; Konstan (1985), 176 n. 2; Wilson (2000), 22; Biles (2006–7); Revermann (2006), 19–20, 66–87; Mueller (2016), 203–4 n. 6. For connections between Aeschylus' *Oresteia* and Euripides' *Electra*, both here and in what is commonly called Euripides' "parody" of Aeschylus' recognition scene (*El.* 518–44), see most recently Roisman and Luschnig (2011) ad loc.; Torrance (2011) and (2013), 13–33; and Mueller (2016), 42–69, 88–105, 111–33.

18　Lloyd (1986), 3. See also Fraenkel (1950) on Aesch. *Ag.* 1317 (adducing also Aesch. *Cho.* 983, Lysias 3.15, and Antiphon 1.29). Lloyd (1986) adds Aesch. *Cho.* 246 and Eur. *Tro.* 998.

19　The costume thus serves the opposite purpose of what a disguise would accomplish. For such ironies, compare Muecke (1982).

20 On New Music, see West (1992), 356–90; Csapo and Slater (1995), 331–48; Csapo
    (1999–2000); Hall (2002), 8–9, 18–24; Csapo (2004). Kranz ([1933] 1988) first
    identified *Electra* as belonging to the new style, but still used a different terminology.
    See further Csapo (2009); and Cropp (2013), 166–8. For a call to include the presence
    of New Music in the interpretation of Greek tragedies, see Wilson (1999–2000), 428.
21 For Cephisophon and his relationship to Euripides, see *Vit. Eur.*; Kassel-Austin, *PCG*
    3.2,596; and the translation of the relevant schol. Ar. *Ran.* at Kovacs (1994), 61.
22 For Plato's and Aristotle's argument that the New Music "effeminized" its listeners,
    see Barker (1984), 124–82. For the influence of Pericles' associate Damon of Oa on
    this line of thinking, see Wallace (2004).
23 Borthwick (1994); Csapo (2004), 223.
24 See Torrance (2013), ch. 1.
25 Cf. esp. Henrichs (1994–5, 1996).
26 See Hall (1999), (2002) 8–9, (2006), 288–320. Hall credits Maas (1929), 20, with some
    of the groundwork. We have not been able to consult Beverley (1997).
27 Of course, some soloists, like Sophocles' Ajax and Philoctetes, are highborn, but not
    female. Yet, in Aeschylus and, particularly, the later Euripides, exceptions are few.
28 In 1971, Wilfried Barner suggested that it was only at the beginning of this second
    strophe—as Electra lowers the jug off her head—that she would have started singing
    (289). Considering her consistent use of lyric meters from the beginning of the first
    strophe, and her sustained references to the musicality of her performance, this
    seems impossible. It appears more likely that the *intensity* of her song and
    choreography would have changed when she put down the jug.
29 Csapo (2004), 225.
30 On Greek tragic dance, see Lawler (1964) and Naerebout (1997), esp. 149–289.
31 Wiles (1997), 87–113.
32 For mimetic dancing in monodies, cf. Barner (1971), 287–90; Csapo (1999–2000),
    419–29; as well as [Arist.] *Pr.* 19 with Hall (2002), 13.
33 See Plut. *Lys.* 15, *Nic.* 29, and *Pel.* 29 with Hall (2002), 36, (2006), 312, and (2010),
    233. Note also Herod. 3.14, where the Persian king Cambyses humiliates Egyptian
    noblemen precisely by reducing their daughters to the class-inappropriate activity of
    carrying water jugs on their heads. Like Electra, the girls lament, and the nobles'
    response is one of genuine pity.
34 See Lloyd (1986), 3–4; Zeitlin (1970), 648–9.
35 See Cropp (2013), 161, for the quotation and a review of the various interventions in
    the text and defenses of the authenticity of the paradosis. Cf. also Goldhill (1986),
    more recently followed by Egli (2003), 226–7.
36 Basta Donzelli (1978), 242–3.
37 Cf. in particular *TrGF* 61b with Collard and Cropp (2004), 76–8; Karamanou (2017),
    199–207.

38 Jendza (2020), 93, 83–91.
39 On *Telephus* and *Acharnians*, see also Platter (2007), 143–76.
40 Jendza (2020), 91–102.
41 Knox (1979), 254, cf. also 252–3.
42 Cf. O'Brien (1964), 30–1.
43 Compare King (1980). Contrast Gellie (1981), 7.
44 The analysis that follows presupposes materials from Fantuzzi (2021), 348–57.
45 *Pace* Lowenstam (1993), 209, who maintains that Euripides does not distinguish between the first and second armor of Achilles and simply ignores the second armor described in *Iliad* 18.
46 See in detail Torrance (2013), 79.
47 Cropp (2013), 169–70.
48 Cf. Barringer (1995).
49 Cf. King (1980), 198.
50 As Heffernan (1993), 23, puts it correctly: "after Homer, all ecphrasis becomes doubly paragonal: a contest staged not just between the word and the image, but also between one poet and another."
51 Cf. also Aelius Theon, *Rhetores Graeci* ii.119 Spengel.
52 Becker (1995), 114.
53 Ibid., 150.
54 However, the shield's cosmological breadth could be pertinent to the Iliadic narrative in more than one way. Cf., e.g., Taplin (1980) and Dubel (1995) on the shield as a representation of the complex extra-martial world which Achilles renounces in choosing *kleos* and death.
55 See also Hes. [*Sc.*] 144-319 and Cropp (2013), on 452–77.
56 Cf. Philipp (2004), 32–7.
57 Cf. Chase (1902), 106–7; Philipp (2004), 34–5, 103, 222–32.
58 Cf. *LIMC* IV.2, 285f., 299–301; Philipp (2004), 192–4, 319–20; Csapo (2009), 100 n. 8. As apotropaic figures, the sphinx, gorgon, Pegasus, and lion (cf. 474) are very frequently represented in funereal iconography and thus point to the slaughter of Agamemnon. They also foreshadow the imminent execution of Clytemnestra and Aegisthus; cf. Csapo (2009), 101.
59 Cf. Csapo (2009), 102–3.
60 Compare King (1980), 212.
61 Cf. also Arnott (1981), 184–5.

Bibliography

Arnott, W. G. (1981), "Double the Vision: A Reading of Euripides' *Electra*." *Greece and Rome*, 28: 179–92.

Barker, A. (1984), *Greek Musical Writings, Volume I: The Musician and His Art*, Cambridge: Cambridge University Press.

Barner, W. (1971), "Die Monodie," in W. Jens (ed.), *Die Bauformen der griechischen Tragödie*, 277–320, Munich: Wilhelm Fink.

Barringer, J. M. (1995), *Divine Escorts: Nereids in Archaic and Classical Greek Art*, Ann Arbor, MI: University of Michigan Press.

Basta Donzelli, G. (1978), *Studio sull'Elettra di Euripide*, Catania: Università di Catania, Facoltà di lettere e filosofia.

Basta Donzelli, G. (1995), *Euripides: Electra*, Stuttgart: Teubner.

Becker, A. S. (1995), *The Shield of Achilles and the Poetics of Ekphrasis*, Lanham, ME: Rowman & Littlefield.

Beverley, E. J. (1997), "The Dramatic Function of Actors' Monody in Later Euripides," DPhil. thesis, University of Oxford.

Biles, Z. P. (2006–7), "Aeschylus' Afterlife: Reperformance by Decree in 5th C. Athens?" *Illinois Classical Studies*, 31/2: 206–42.

Billings, J. (2018), "Orestes' Urn in Word and Action," in M. Telò and M. Mueller (eds.), *The Materialities of Greek Tragedy: Objects and Affect in Aeschylus, Sophocles, and Euripides*, 49–62, London: Bloomsbury Academic.

Borthwick, E. K. (1994), "New Interpretations of Aristophanes' *Frogs* 1294–1328," *Phoenix*, 48: 21–41.

Chaniotis, A., ed. (2021), *Unveiling Emotions III: Arousal, Display, and Performance of Emotions in the Greek World*, Stuttgart: Franz Steiner Verlag.

Chase, G. H. (1902), "The Shield Device of the Greeks," *Harvard Studies in Classical Philology*, 13: 61–127.

Collard, C. and M. J. Cropp (2004), *Euripides: Selected Fragmentary Plays*, vol. 2, Liverpool: Aris & Phillips.

Cropp, M. J. (2013), *Euripides Electra*, 2nd ed., Oxford: Oxbow Books.

Csapo, E. (1999–2000), "Later Euripidean Music," *Illinois Classical Studies*, 24–5: 399–426.

Csapo, E. (2004), "The Politics of the New Music," in P. Murray and P. Wilson (eds.), *Music and the Muses: The Culture of 'Mousikē' in the Classical Athenian City*, 207–48, Oxford: Oxford University Press.

Csapo, E. (2009), "New Music's Gallery of Images: The 'Dithyrambic' First Stasimon of Euripides' *Electra*," in J. R. C. Cousland and J. R. Hume (eds.), *The Play of Texts and Fragments: Essays in Honour of Martin Cropp*, 93–110, Leiden: Brill.

Csapo, E. and W. Slater (1995), *The Context of Ancient Drama*, Ann Arbor, MI: University of Michigan Press.

Diggle, J. (1981), *Euripidis fabulae*, vol. 2, Oxford: Clarendon Press.

Dubel, S. (1995), "L'arme et la lyre: Remarques sur le sense du bouclier d'Achille dans l'*Iliade*," *Ktema*, 20: 245–57.

Egli, F. (2003), *Euripides im Kontext zeitgenössischer intellektueller Strömungen*, Munich: K.G. Saur.

Fantuzzi, M. (2021), "Describing Images/Connoting Feelings: Choral Ekphrasis in Euripides," in A. Chaniotis (ed.), *Unveiling Emotions III: Arousal, Display, and Performance of Emotions in the Greek World*, 345–72, Stuttgart: Franz Steiner Verlag.

Fraenkel, E. (1950), *Aeschylus:* Agamemnon, Oxford: Clarendon Press.

Gellie, G. H. (1981), "Tragedy and Euripides' *Electra*," *Bulletin of the Institute of Classical Studies*, 28: 1–12.

Goff, B. (1999–2000), "Try to Make it Real Compared to What? Euripides' *Electra* and the Play of Genres," *Illinois Classical Stuudies*, 24–5: 93–105.

Goldhill, S. (1986), "Rhetoric and Relevance: Interpolation at Euripides *Electra* 367–400," *Greek, Roman and Byzantine Studies*, 27: 157–71.

Goldhill, S. and R. Osborne, eds. (1999), *Performance Culture and Athenian Democracy*, Cambridge: Cambridge University Press.

Grube, G. M. A. (1961), *The Drama of Euripides*, New York: Barnes and Noble.

Hall, E. (1999), "Actors' Song in Tragedy," in S. Goldhill and R. Osborne (eds.), *Performance Culture and Athenian Democracy*, 96–122, Cambridge: Cambridge University Press.

Hall, E. (2002), "The Singing Actors of Antiquity," in P. Easterling and E. Hall (eds.), *Greek and Roman Actors: Aspects of an Ancient Profession*, 3–38, Cambridge: Cambridge University Press.

Hall, E. (2006), *The Theatrical Cast of Athens: Interactions between Ancient Greek Drama and Society*, Oxford: Oxford University Press.

Hall, E. (2010), *Greek Tragedy: Suffering under the Sun*, Oxford: Oxford University Press.

Hammond, N. G. L. (1984), "Spectacle and Parody in Euripides' *Electra*," *Greek, Roman and Byzantine Studies*, 25: 373–87.

Henderson, J. (2002), *Aristophanes iv:* Frogs, Assemblywomen, Wealth, Cambridge, MA and London: Harvard University Press.

Henrichs, A. (1994–5), "'Why Should I Dance?': Choral Self-Referentiality in Greek Tragedy," *Arion*, 3: 56–111.

Henrichs, A. (1996), "Dancing in Athens, Dancing on Delos: Some Patterns of Choral Projection in Euripides," *Philologus*, 140: 48–62.

Herington, C. J. (1985), *Poetry into Drama: Early Tragedy and the Greek Poetic Tradition*, Berkeley, CA: University of California Press.

Jendza, C. (2020), *Paracomedy: Appropriations of Comedy in Greek Tragedy*, New York: Oxford University Press.

Jens, W., ed. (1971), *Die Bauformen der griechischen Tragödie*, Munich: Wilhelm Fink.

Karamanou, I. (2017), *Euripides, "Alexandros": Introduction, Text and Commentary*, Berlin: De Gruyter.

King, H. (1983), "Bound to Bleed: Artemis and Greek Women," in A. Cameron and A. Kuhrt (eds.), *Images of Women in Antiquity*, 109–27, Detroit, MI: Wayne State University Press.

King, K. C. (1980), "The Force of Tradition: The Achilles Ode in Euripides' *Electra*," *Transactions of the American Philological Association*, 110: 195–212.

Knox, B. M. W. (1979), *Word and Action: Essays on the Ancient Theater*, Baltimore, MD: Johns Hopkins University Press.

Konstan, D. (1985), "Philia in Euripides' *Electra*," *Philologus*, 129: 176–85.

Kovacs, D. (1994), *Euripidea*, Leiden: Brill.

Kranz, W. (1933), *Stasimon*, Berlin: Weidmann.

Lawler, L. B. (1964), *The Dance of the Ancient Greek Theatre*, Iowa City, IA: University of Iowa Press.

Lloyd, M. (1986), "Realism and Character in Euripides' *Electra*," *Phoenix*, 40: 1–19.

Lowenstam, S. (1993), "The Arming of Achilleus on Early Greek Vases," *Classical Antiquity*, 12: 199–218.

Maas, P. (1929), *Griechische Metrik*, Leipzig: Teubner.

Michelini, A. N. (1987), *Euripides and the Tragic Tradition*, Madison, WI: University of Wisconsin Press.

Muecke, F. (1982), "'I Know You—by Your Rags': Costume and Disguise in Fifth-Century Drama," *Antichthon*, 16: 17–34.

Mueller, M. (2016), *Objects as Actors: Props and the Poetics of Performance in Greek Tragedy*, Chicago, IL, and London: University of Chicago Press.

Murray, P. and P. Wilson, eds. (2004), *Music and the Muses: The Culture of "Mousikē" in the Classical Athenian City*, Oxford: Oxford University Press.

Naerebout, F. G. (1997), *Attractive Performances. Ancient Greek Dance: Three Preliminary Studies*, Amsterdam: Gieben.

Newiger, H.-J. (1961), "Elektra in Aristophanes' *Wolken*," *Hermes*, 89: 422–30.

O'Brien, M. J. (1964), "Orestes and the Gorgon: Euripides' *Electra*," *American Journal of Philology*, 85: 13–39.

Philipp, H. (2004), *Archaische Silhouettenbleche und Schildzeichen in Olympia*, Berlin and New York: De Gruyter.

Platter, C. (2007), *Aristophanes and the Carnival of Genres*, Baltimore, MD: Johns Hopkins University Press.

Pollitt, J. J. (1986), *Art in the Hellenistic Age*, Cambridge: Cambridge University Press.

Raeburn, D. (2000), "The Significance of Stage Properties in Euripides' *Electra*," *Greece & Rome*, 47: 149–68.

Revermann, M. (2006), *Comic Business: Theatricality, Dramatic Technique, and Performance Contexts in Aristophanic Comedy*, Oxford: Oxford University Press.

Roisman, H. M. and C. A. E. Luschnig (2011), *Euripides'* Electra*: A Commentary*, Norman, OK: University of Oklahoma Press.

Rotroff, S. I. and R. D. Lamberton (2006), *Women in the Athenian Agora*, Athens: American School of Classical Studies at Athens.

Stephens, S. (2018), *The Poets of Alexandria*, London: I.B. Tauris.

Taplin, O. (1980), "The Shield of Achilles within the *Iliad*," *Greece & Rome*, 27: 1–21.

Torrance, I. (2011), "In the Footprints of Aeschylus: Recognition, Allusion, and Metapoetics in Euripides," *American Journal of Philology*, 132: 177–204.

Torrance, I. (2013), *Metapoetry in Euripides*, Oxford and New York: Oxford University Press.

Trümper, M. (2012), "Gender and Space, 'Public' and 'Private,'" in S. L. James and S. Dillon (eds.), *A Companion to Women in the Ancient World*, 288–303, Chichester: Wiley-Blackwell.

Wallace, R. W. (2004), "Damon of Oa. A Music Theorist Ostracized?", in P. Murray and P. Wilson (eds.), *Music and the Muses: The Culture of "Mousikē" in the Classical Athenian City*, 249–68, Oxford: Oxford University Press.

Webster, T. B. L. (1971), *Greek Tragedy*, Oxford: Clarendon Press.

West, M. L. (1992), *Ancient Greek Music*, Oxford: Oxford University Press.

Wiles, D. (1997), *Tragedy in Athens: Performance Space and Theatrical Meaning*, Cambridge: Cambridge University Press.

Wilson, P. (1999–2000), "Euripides' Tragic Muse," *Illinois Classical Studies*, 24–5: 42–9.

Wilson, P. (2000), *The Athenian Institution of the Khoregia: The Chorus, the City and the Stage*, Cambridge: Cambridge University Press.

Zeitlin, F. I. (1970), "The Argive Festival of Hera and Euripides' *Electra*," *Transactions of the American Philological Association*, 101: 645–69.

Part Two

Coming to Egypt

3

Through a Glass Darkly

Alexander's Campaign in Egypt

Daniel L. Selden
University of California, Santa Cruz

> *One can only think of language as a network, a net over the entirety of things, over the totality of the real. It inscribes on the plane of the real this other plane, which we here call the plane of the symbolic.*
>
> Jacques Lacan, *Le Séminaire, I*
> *Les écrits techniques de Freud* (1953–4)[1]

Itinerary

From a detached, though hardly disengaged perspective, Greek and Roman historians writing under Roman rule[2] relate that after the brutal siege of Tyre (333 BCE), which wrested from Darius III (OPers. 𐎭𐎠𐎼𐎹𐎺𐎢𐏁 *Dārayavauš*)[3] his last remaining seaport, Alexander III of Macedonia marched his troops down through the Iranian satrapy of Eber-Nāri ("Beyond the River")[4] to Ġazzah, the key *entrepôt* of southern Palestine, where, in an equally legendary siege, his forces once again proved to be invincible.[5] With his communication and supply lines back to Macedonia now wholly unobstructed, Alexander marched across the northern Sinai (*biꜣ*) along the so-called "Ways of Horus" (*Wꜣ.wt Ḥr*), the ancient trade and military route that linked Egypt to the Levant,[6] crossing over at Pēlousion (Eg. *Pr-ꜣImn*; *Snw*; Aram. סין *Sīn*)[7] into the unresisting satrapy of Mudrāya (𐎸𐎢𐎭𐎼𐎠𐎹).[8] Here, in the course of imposing Macedonian dominion over Egypt, his "longing" (*póthos*) propelled him to linger at what for Greek and Roman historians, at least, looked to be three unrelated sites:[9] Memphis, the capital of Egypt under Persian rule; Rhakōtis, a coastal village on the Western fringes of the Nile Delta; and Sīwah, a desert oasis some 3,000 kilometers southwest of Rhakōtis, which the Hellenic world knew only metonymically as the "Oracle of Zeus-Ammon."[10]

Historians, ancient as well as modern, differ regarding the order in which Alexander visited these places, and this difference is instructive. According to Arrian (*c.* 86–146 BCE), Alexander sailed from the satrapal seat at Memphis down the Canopic branch of the Nile to Rhakōtis whence, after laying the foundations for Alexandria, he marched west, accompanied by a select group of light-armed soldiers, along the Mediterranean littoral to Amunia—modern Marsā Maṭrūḥ—and from there south across the Sahara to the oasis of Sīwah (Plate 1).[11] Q. Curtius Rufus (first century CE), however, reports that from Memphis, Alexander marched directly west across the desert to the Oracle of Ammon and only after that north to Rhakōtis, on his way out of Egypt back to Eber-Nāri. Plutarch (*c.* 46–*c.* 119 CE) confirms Arrian (Rhakōtis → Ammon), but Diodorus Siculus (*c.* 90–*c.* 30 BCE) and M. Junianus Justinus (second–third century CE) support Curtius (Ammon → Rhakōtis). Plutarch, Diodorus, and Justin, however, make no mention of Memphis whatsoever. Clearly there were discrepancies among the early sources upon which the later Alexander historians depended.[12] Greek and Roman writers evidently saw no particular connection between these far-flung places—hence their appeal to Alexander's fancy (*póthos*)—and absent any discernible underlying logic, it ultimately made no difference in what order he visited these sites, or whether or not Memphis comprised part of the itinerary. What *póthos* names here, then, is a logic of illogic, which becomes recuperable within mainstream Greco-Roman historical discourse to the extent that writers could represent (*mimeisthai*) Alexander's character (*ēthos*), in all its vagaries, as what Aristotle called a *homalōs anōmalon*, that is, a constantly inconstant disposition,[13] concomitantly thereby lending his expedition spatial as well as temporal coherence.[14]

If we change our frame of reference, however, and ask how the activities that Greek and Roman historians ascribe to Alexander during his six-month stay in Egypt looked not to Macedonians, Greeks, or Romans, but to the newly subject populace of Egypt and above all to the Egyptian priesthood,[15] the logic linking these three stopping points comes more clearly into focus. Extant monuments at Karnak, Luxor, the Baḥrīya Oasis, and Elephantinē indicate that from the time he took control of Egypt, Alexander—like the Iranian pharaohs who preceded him—had Egyptian artists represent him as King of the Two Lands (⚏ *tꜣ wy*) (Plate 2).[16] In this connection, the three principal sites that he visited during his tour of the country allowed him, according to a logic that is peculiarly Egyptian, to legitimate himself as Pharaoh, a task incumbent upon every new Egyptian king, but particularly so when there was a dynastic break or an anomaly in the succession.[17] No one of these stopping points has full meaning in and of itself, but in conjunction, the triad rehearses a traditional and readily recognizable symbolic pattern, deeply rooted in the Egyptian ideology of kingship from the Predynastic Era on. As such, each of these stopping points functions, within the imperial Roman narratives, as a site or geographic node productive of a multiplicity of different and even contradictory meanings.[18] Without any claim to the historicity of the sequence, then, the exposition here will take up each station in turn, in the order that best allows their signification to unfold: Memphis—Sīwah—Rhakōtis.[19] Collectively, the extant Greek and Roman narratives of Alexander's Egyptian enterprise form a network of related texts which, taken together, convey more than any one of the accounts discloses on its own.[20] This accordingly necessitates a synchronic reading across the narratives as a set. Here, however, the constraints on space permit me only to discuss the first of these sites in any depth—viz., Memphis and the activities that the historians ascribe to Alexander there. Towards the end of the essay, I will discuss Sīwah and Rhakōtis more briefly in order to give some sense of the symbolic triad as a whole. This focus has the advantage of providing what Freud termed a *Mustervorbild*,[21] that is, a preliminary account, offered in advance of a more exhaustive presentation for purposes that are mainly propaedeutic and which therefore require an exposition of critical approaches that are either necessary or useful for such an undertaking.

Legitimation

In the Egyptian ideology of kingship, Memphis ⚏ (< *Mn-nfr* "Enduring is the Perfection"), occupied a privileged position. Situated just below the apex of the Delta, where Lower Egypt and Upper Egypt meet, the city had, since the mythopoetic union of the Two Lands (⚏ *zmꜣ tꜣ.wy*) sometime in the third millennium BCE, served as the capital and premier religious center of the country, a preeminence that it later shared with Thebes (⚏ *Wꜣs.t*), without eclipsing its own luster. Many kings built their principal residences ⚏

ḥnw) elsewhere—in the New Kingdom, for example, Amenḥotep III (1391–1353 BCE) constructed his palace of "The Dazzling Aten" (𓉐𓇳 *Pn-ṯḥn-ʾItn*) at Malqata on the west bank of the Nile at Thebes,[22] while Ramesses II (*c.* 1303–1213 BCE) chose to move his court to the newly erected "House of Ramesses" (𓉐𓇳 *Pr Rꜥ-msi-s[w]*), situated in the eastern Delta, roughly 100 kilometers upstream from Memphis on the Pēlusiac branch of the Nile. Nonetheless, as the papyri from Achaemenid Elephantinē attest,[23] Memphis remained a thriving political, commercial, military, and artistic center down through the Persian occupation, from which the state apparatus continued to issue royal edicts, appoint government officials, and crown Egypt's kings.[24] In fact, from the Middle Kingdom on, documents frequently refer to the city as either 𓌇𓏤𓊖 *mḫꜣ.t tꜣ.wy* "Balance of the Two Lands" or as 𓋹𓏤𓏏 *ꜥnḫ tꜣ. wj* "Life of the Two Lands,"[25] metaphorically the hinge or suture between Lower and Upper Egypt.[26]

According to Arrian, when Alexander reached Memphis, "he sacrificed to a multiplicity of gods, but especially to Apis" (θύει ἐκεῖ τοῖς τε <u>ἄλλοις θεοῖς</u> καὶ τῷ Ἄπιδι),[27] and staged a gymnastic and poetic competition (καὶ ἀγῶνα ἐποίησε γυμνικόν τε καὶ μουσικόν), for which "the artists most distinguished in these talents come to him from Greece" [3.1.4]. As Arrian recounts this spectacle, he records an exhibition, unprecedented not only for Egypt, but for the Levantine-Mediterranean world as a whole. Other rulers had paid cult to alien gods, and Alexander himself, along his march from Tyre into Egypt, is said to have sacrificed to YHWH with the High Priest at the Temple in Jerusalem.[28] Never before, however, do historical annals record so visible a public celebration drawn so conspicuously from two proximate yet wholly different cultures—so divergent, in fact, that according to an oft cited passage in Herodotus, each culture followed norms that were inverse to the customs of the other.[29] Offerings to Egyptian deities, coupled with Hellenic games—an institution alien to Egypt[30]—suggests, as Susan Stephens has argued, that already for Alexander and his successors the "Two Lands" conjoined at Memphis were now conceptually no longer just Lower and Upper Egypt, but also, resituating within a wider geopolitical framework the logic of unity in difference affirmed throughout classical Egyptian literature and art, the joining of Greece with Egypt.[31]

Why, among Alexander's reverence for "a multiplicity of gods" (ἄλλοις θεοῖς), does Arrian single out his sacrifice to Apis (� *Ḥpw*)—the divine bull who, as the earthly embodiment of the god Ptaḥ, resided in a sanctuary that formed part of Memphis' main temple complex (𓉗𓏏𓂓𓊪𓏏𓎛 *Ḥw.t kꜣ Ptḥ* "Temple of the Kꜣ of Ptaḥ")?[32] Greeks and Macedonians in Alexander's entourage, as well perhaps as Egyptians literate in Greek, were likely to have been familiar with Herodotus' account (*logos*) of how the Achaemenid king Kambysēs II (OPers. 𐎣𐎲𐎢𐎪𐎡𐎹 *Kabūjiya*; Eg. ⟨◯𓎡𓃀𓍒⟩ *Kmbd̠*) [r. 530–522 BCE], after conquering Egypt in 525, gratuitously killed the Apis bull, flogged his attendant priests, and executed his Egyptian devotees.[33] However compelling Herodotus' portrait of the 'mad Kambysēs" (*hupomagróteros*)—a story that continues to circulate popularly today[34]—his narrative constitutes a multilayered fiction that weaves together motifs drawn from disparate East Mediterranean literary and historical traditions—principally Akkadian, Egyptian, Iranian, and Greek.[35] Accordingly, Kambysēs II's reputation has less to do with the veracity of Herodotus' account— as Hayden White reminds us: "All stories are fictions"[36]—than with the narrative's illocutionary force,[37] in this case a series of vituperative and verdictive speech acts which, although by definition neither true nor false,[38] occasioned long-term perlocutionary effects, blackening among other things Kambysēs' reputation. "An utterance [*énonciation*]," Shoshana Felman stresses, "is always, irreducibly, *in excess* over its statement [*énoncé*], . . . [and] it is precisely this excess of utterance over the statement it makes that [J. L.] Austin christens 'illocutionary force,' or 'force of utterance,' attempting, as he stresses, to contrast *force* and *meaning*."[39] Building, then, on the performative excess in Herodotus' vilification of Kambysēs, while bracketing its constative value, Alexander's sacrifice to the living Apis afforded him the means to distance himself symbolically from the antecedent Persian occupation,[40] as well as demonstrate with an illustratory gesture his personal investment in the Apis cult and, more broadly, Egyptian religion in general.[41]

Of all the tenets that challenged Hellenized denizens and visitors to Egypt, animal worship proved perennially the most difficult for them to entertain.[42] In paying homage to the Apis bull, then, Alexander not only sent a clear message to his comrades that he gave credence to an irreducibly Egyptian deity, nationally recognized and popular throughout the whole of the Two Lands, but for whom there was no Macedonian or Greek equivalent in the way that YHWH the aniconic god of the *Yĕhûdîm* or the Canaanite Ba'al could be readily assimilated to Zeus (Plate 3).[43] At the same time, moreover, in worshiping an animal, Alexander effectively collapsed the Great Chain of Being (*scala naturae*) that Aristotle had erected,[44] which distinguished gods and men categorically from animals and plants, a doctrine that in the West, at least, became a cornerstone of Late Antique, Medieval, and Early Modern thought.[45]

On the other hand—and perhaps more importunately—Apis had in Egypt close affinities with kingship.[46] The Narmer Palette, a predynastic ritual implement dated to the early thirty-first century BCE, already portrays the king as a bull destroying a fortified city, goring his opponents [Plates 4a–b].[47] Similarly, the Palermo Stone (*c.* twenty-fifth century BCE), which preserves the royal annals of the early Egyptian state, shows that the connection between king and the Apis cult dates back at least as far as the First Dynasty.[48] From the New Kingdom on, moreover, down through the Roman Period, the epithet 𓄿 *k3 nḫt* ("Victorious Bull") appears ubiquitously in royal titles. In all of these contexts, the bull symbolizes the virility and power of the Pharaoh. Hence the Sed-Festival—a celebration of the king's vitality on the occasion of his thirtieth regnal year[49]—included the "running of the Apis" (𓉐𓌢𓂻𓊡𓎼𓄿𓏏 *pḥrr Ḥpw*), a rite in which the king raced with (or against) the Apis bull, so as to demonstrate his continued vitality and vigor.[50]

Alexander's offering to Apis has to be understood, then, as an initial step towards legitimating his succession to the Egyptian throne. From histories, inscriptions, and artistic renderings, moreover, we know that Alexander not only participated in the religious life of Memphis. He also financed the restoration and embellishment of Egyptian temples that had fallen into disrepair, a duty incumbent upon all Egyptian kings at their assumption of the throne. Most importantly, Alexander restored the Barque Chapel at Luxor Temple, a sanctuary closely tied to the ideology of kingship, partly through the yearly Opet Festival, (𓎛𓃀𓄤𓏏𓊮𓉐 *ḥb nfr n 'Ip.t*), a fertility ritual enacted at the onset of the inundation, in which the ruling king united with the god Amun in the inner sanctum of the temple, a rite envisioned as a sacred marriage (*hieros gamos*). As John Darnell explains: "[T]he Opet Festival celebrated the renewal of the *k3*-force of Amun, and the transmission of the spirit of kingship in the eternal present. As a ritual of annual renewal, the Opet Festival could reconfirm the royal coronation."[51] In keeping with the temple decorations that Alexander funded elsewhere in Egypt, the reliefs adorning the Barque Chapel at Luxor already portray him attired as the king of Egypt (see Plate 2), wearing the Double Crown (*sḫm.ti*) which combines the white crown of Upper Egypt with the red crown of Lower Egypt. In this case, however, the stakes were somewhat higher: the inscriptions and reliefs that adorn the chapel, situated immediately before the forecourt of the naos, effectively inscribe Alexander in the Opet Festival, which by implication both confirms his coronation and renews his vigor. Whether the priests of Memphis also officially crowned Alexander King of Egypt has been a subject of much dispute, though recent publications by scholars conversant with the languages and culture of Late Period Egypt, have tended to affirm this.[52] The recent discovery Alexander's full pharaonic titulary (𓇳𓏤𓋹𓏏 *nḥb.t*) on a pedestal from the Temple of Amun in the Baḥrīyah Oasis has, in part, helped to substantiate this argument.[53] At the very least, the titulary—a protocol traditionally bestowed upon a king at his enthronement—makes clear that even if not ritually crowned, the Egyptian priesthood accepted Alexander as the divinely appointed king of the Two Lands. "As with every pharaoh," writes Francisco Bosch-Puche, "he [viz., Alexander] was recognized as the legitimate king and interpolated in the traditional theocracy, as is clearly shown by the fact that he is thus identified in the royal titulary bestowed upon him."[54]

Beginning with the Middle Kingdom, pharaonic titularies consisted of a series of five titles, each followed by a different eponym, which together made up the king's "Great Name" (𓏞𓏤𓏤 *rn wr*). Although often formulaic and commonly defective, royal titularies also served as attestations to the king's divine descent or his affiliation with one or more of Egypt's national gods. Thus, Tuthmosis III records his birth name as (𓅝𓄤𓏏) (*Dḥwti msi[.w] nfr ḫpr*) "Thoth is born, perfect in form") which effectively identifies the king as Thoth (*Dḥwti*) incarnate. At the same time, royal titularies also articulated the duties or priorities that the king had chosen for his reign, in particular his ability to "smite" (𓌨𓏭 *ḥwi*) the Nine Bows,[55] the ancestral enemies of Egypt—Asiatics, Nubians, Libyans, and later Greeks—so as to establish order (𓏇𓐙 *Mꜣꜥ. t*) in the Two Lands and ward off chaos and transgression (𓊃𓆑𓏏 *izf.t*).[56] Given these parameters, in which rule, representation, and violence all stand intertwined,[57] the priests at Memphis devised for Alexander a Great Name that incorporates him into the pharaonic tradition even as it registers his difference:[58]

Ḥr-Rꜥ: ḥqꜣ ḥqꜣ.w nw tꜣ r ḏr=f

Nb.ty: mꜣi wr pḥty iti ḏw.w tꜣ.w ḫꜣs.wt

Ḥr-nbw: kꜣ n ḥwi Bꜣq.t ḥqꜣ wꜣḏ-wr šnw n itn

Ni-sw.t bi.ti: stp n Rꜥ mri 'Imn

Zꜣ Rꜥ: Zꜣ 'Imn 'Ilksnd[rs]

mri 'Imn-Rꜥ [nb] iri sḥr.w mi Rꜥ [ḏ.t]

Horus-Rēʿ: Ruler of the rulers of the earth in its entirety

Two Mistresses: Lion of great strength who seizes the mountains, lands, and deserts

Horus of Gold: Bull who protects Egypt, ruler of the sea and all that the sun encircles

King of Upper and Lower Egypt: Chosen of Rēʿ, Beloved of Amun

Son of Rē': Son of Amun, Alexan[der]
Beloved of Amun-Rē', [Lord] who Conducts Politics, like Rē' [forever]

In form, the titulary is completely orthodox,[59] from the *serekh*-panel ( *srḥ* "palace façade") that encloses his Horus name through the Two Mistresses and Golden Horus names to the cartouches that provide magical protection by surrounding both his Throne Name (*praenomen*) and his Birth Name (*nomen*).[60] Taken as a whole, however, most of the names that make up Alexander's titulary stand out as unconventional or at least unprecedented in the formularies of previous kings. Typically, rulers from the Middle Kingdom on bore Horus or other titulary names that underscored the traditional duties of the pharaoh: to govern, to protect, and to make the Two Lands flourish:

Sšmw t3.wy
Sesostris II: "He who guides the Two Lands"

k3 nḫt mri R^c ptpt ḫ3s.t nb(.t) ḫr ṯb.wt=f
Ramesses II: "Strong Bull beloved of Rē' who has trampled every foreign land under his sandals"

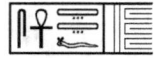

s^cnḫ t3.wy.fy
Menṯuḥotep III: "He who regenerates the Two Lands"

At Luxor, Alexander's Horus name reads: (*mk Km.t* "Defender of Egypt"),[61] but other extant versions of his titulary make only fleeting reference to the welfare of Egypt, for example: *k3 n ḥwi B3q.t* "Bull who protects Egypt," a phrase embedded in the more complex syntagm of the Golden Horus name.[62] Instead, the titulary stresses Alexander's role as "a ruler who rules other rulers": *ḥq3 ḥq3.w*—that is, the sovereign not simply of Egypt (*B3q.t* "Shining One"), but of the world in its entirety (*t3 r ḏr=f*).[63] The formulation *ḥq3 ḥq3.w* derives more or less directly from the Assyrian royal protocol *Šar šarrāni*, which Tukulti-Nunarta I (r. 1244–1208 BCE) introduced, as well as its calque used to denominate kings in Old Persian (*xšāyaθiya xšāyaθiyānām* "King of Kings"), even though surviving titularies from the Assyrian and Persian occupations of Egypt do not employ these designations.[64] Royal inscriptions as well as bas-reliefs from the Ramesside and Third Intermediate Periods often depict the king repelling or annihilating non-Egyptian peoples: Ramesses II (r. 1279–1213), for example, bore the title "Strong Bull who Shatters the Asiatics" (𓆎𓈖𓏏𓄊 *k3 nḫt s3 st. tyw*), while Shoshenq I (r. 943–922 BCE) styled himself "He Who Smites the Nine Bows, Victorious in every Land" (𓉐𓈖𓏏 *ḥwi pd.wt-9 wr nḫt.w m t3.w nb.w*). Neither, however, laid claim to the type of world domination that Alexander's royal titulary projects. Considering that when he took control of Mudrāya, he had yet to subdued the Achaemenid State (*xšaça-*)[65] in its entirety, his titulary must either have been optimistically proleptic or, more likely, composed in retrospect, sometime after the battle of Gaugamēla and the death of Darius III (331 BCE).[66] As such, in formulating the Great Name for Alexander, the Egyptian priests aimed simultaneously to validate his usurpation of the Egyptian throne and, as an outsider, to mark his difference, in effect the same titulary strategy that the priesthood had used for earlier foreign kings— Hyksos, Kushite, Libyan, Persian, and so forth.[67]

According to our extant sources, then, Alexander while in Memphis employed three different, yet closely related strategies to legitimate himself as Pharaoh: (1) he repaired and augmented temples throughout Egypt, most importantly the Barque Chapel at Luxor; (2) he sacrificed to the Apis bull in an effort to differentiate himself from the Ariyan Pharaohs who preceded him, as well as to indicate his acceptance of even those Egyptian cults that Macedonians and Greeks found most alien and unappealing; and (3) he assumed the fivefold titulary traditional for the king of Egypt, which marked his accession to the throne.[68] In performing these three long-established rites, Alexander—whether present or absent for their enactment—interpolated himself symbolically into Egyptian monarchical traditions that, in one form or another, went back as far as the fourth millennium BCE. In so doing, he effectively reaffirmed the historical continuity of his office, drawing for the present on the prestige of the past, and arranging matters, as Q. Curtius puts it, in such a way as to make no changes in the native customs of the Egyptians (*ut nihil ex patrio Aegyptiorum more mutaret*).[69]

Figuration

The accounts that Greek and Roman historians provide of Alexander's occupation of Egypt survive in narratives shot through with shards of the pharaonic coronation rites (☥‿𓆣 *ḫ^{c}w nsw* "Apparition of the King"),[70] components which the Greek and Roman historians themselves, while presumably transmitting what they found in their sources, in all likelihood did not understand.[71] One of the key questions that imposes itself here, then, concerns the manner in which Greco-Roman historians configured the relationship between the Hellenic and the non-Hellenic material at their disposal. Historians writing under the Roman Empire relied primarily on narrative as their preferred mode of representation, which means that every historical account constituted what W. K. Wimsatt called a "verbal icon,"[72] that is, a linguistic artefact that *prima facie* must be analyzed as such. Hayden White has made the argument for what he calls the "figural realism" of historical discourse, or the "mimesis effect" that historical narrations aim to produce, repeatedly and from a variety of perspectives over the past sixty years:

> The historian's characteristic instrument of encodation, communication and exchange is ordinary educated speech. This implies that the only instruments that he has for endowing his data with meaning ... are the techniques of figurative language. All historical narratives presuppose figurative characterizations of the events they purport to represent and explain. And this means that historical narratives, considered purely as verbal artifacts, can be characterized by the mode of figurative discourse in which they are cast.[73]

The orders of figuration that White assumes here are what Kenneth Burke identified as the four "master tropes"—metaphor, metonymy, synecdoche, and irony.[74] The style, emplotment, and ideological proclivity of any particular historical narrative derive from the tension between the *cognitive content* of the message and the *principal mode of figuration*—that is, the dominant trope of the narration[75]—which both prefigures the historical field and "shapes" the message of the historical text.[76] This tropology, White shows, "constitutes a virtual 'logic' of narration that, once perceived, allows us to understand why these discourses are organized the way they are both on their surfaces and in their depths."[77]

In his *Anabasis Alexandri*, Arrian employs different constitutive figures or tropes to organize different parts of his narration.[78] In representing Alexander's march from Pēlusion to Memphis, Arrian first selects those "facts" among his sources that he wishes to retain—narratemes already in discursive form[79]—and then proceeds to replot them according to the trope of metonymy. Roman Jakobson, in a celebrated essay,[80] showed that the twofold character of language— that is, the *selection* of discrete lexical items (phonemes, morphemes, tagmemes, etc.) and their *combination* into syntagmatic units of a higher order[81]—corresponds, at a more complex level of discursive integration, to the pair of tropes that Greek rhetoricians called *metaphor* and *metonymy*.[82] As a figure of speech (σχῆμα λέξεος / *figura dictionis*), Jakobson observed, metaphor operates on the principle of *similarity*, substituting one word or phrase for another on the basis of a perceived likeness across disparate semantic domains.[83] Metonymy, by contrast, works on the principal of *contiguity*, substituting the term for one entity for that of another perceived to lie either spatially or logically proximal to it—part for whole, cause for effect, container for contained, and so forth. Unlike metaphor, however, the two terms at play in the metonymy belong to the same conceptual domain.[84] Extended to larger units of discourse, moreover, beyond the level of the word or phrase, metaphor and metonymy also function as figures of thought (σχῆμα διανοίας / *figura sententiae*):[85] Thus, Jakobson observes, "The development of discourse may take place along two different semantic lines: one topic may lead to another either through their similarity or through their contiguity."[86]

Fleshing out Jakobson's observation here, White, with a bit more specificity, adds that metonymy in particular governs "the arrangement of phenomena into temporal series of spatial sets,"[87] an observation that reconceptualizes metonymy as a trope that has both a temporal and a spatial dimension. Arrian's account of Alexander's march from Pēlusion to Memphis illustrates this spatio-temporal complexity rather well, tracking Alexander as he moves through time as well as space:

ὁ δὲ εἰς μὲν Πηλούσιον φυλακὴν εἰσήγαγε, τοὺς δὲ ἐπὶ τῶν νεῶν ἀναπλεῖν κατὰ τὸν ποταμὸν κελεύσας ἔστε ἐπὶ Μέμφιν πόλιν, αὐτὸς ἐφ᾽ Ἡλιουπόλεως ἤει, ἐν δεξιᾷ ἔχων τὸν ποταμὸν τὸν Νεῖλον, καὶ ὅσα καθ᾽ ὁδὸν χωρία ἐνδιδόντων τῶν ἐνοικούντων κατασχὼν διὰ τῆς ἐρήμου ἀφίκετο ἐς Ἡλιούπολιν. ἐκεῖθεν δὲ διαβὰς τὸν πόρον ἧκεν ἐς Μέμφιν καὶ θύει ἐκεῖ τοῖς τε ἄλλοις θεοῖς καὶ τῷ Ἄπιδι καὶ ἀγῶνα ἐποίησε γυμνικόν τε καὶ μουσικόν, ἧκον δὲ αὐτῷ οἱ ἀμφὶ ταῦτα τεχνῖται ἐκ τῆς Ἑλλάδος οἱ δοκιμώτατοι.

Alexander installed a garrison at Pēlousion while he, having ordered his naval officers to sail up the river as far as the city of Memphis, proceeded to Hēliopolis, keeping the river Nile always to his right, and taking possession of all the districts that he came upon, as their inhabitants surrendered, he arrived through the desert at Hēliopolis. From there, fording the river, he reached Memphis where he sacrificed to a plurality of gods, including Apis, and put on both athletic and poetic competitions, for which the most notable performers came to him from Greece.[88]

Metonymy here clearly prefigures Arrian's historical account of Alexander's passage from Pēlusion to Memphis, both at the level of syntax and at the level of sense (Plate 5).[89] In its grammatical structure—a concatenation linking clauses of different types, both finite and adverbial—the coordination of one phrase with another is not always immediately apparent, forcing the reader to construct the sentence out of its component parts.[90] The prepositional phrase διὰ τῆς ἐρήμου ("through the desert"), for example, can be construed either with the preceding clause (χωρία ... κατασχὼν διὰ τῆς ἐρήμου) or with the clause that follows it (διὰ τῆς ἐρήμου ἀφίκετο ἐς Μέμφιν). Conceptually, moreover, the passage maps Alexander and his army's movements through a series of contiguous spaces. First, at the end of their long march across the Northern Sinai, a corps of Macedonian guards (*phulakē*) enter and occupy the immediately adjoining fortress of Pēlousion (𓉐𓏤𓇋𓏠𓈖𓅆𓉐 *Pr-'Imn* "House / Temple of Amun"). Meanwhile, Alexander sends his navy upriver to Memphis, while he himself advances adjacent to his fleet from one geographically proximate district or estate to another, χωρίον by χωρίον, hugging the east bank of the Nile as far as Hēliopolis (𓉺𓊖 *'Iwn.w* "The Pillars").[91] Although Arrian finds nothing to say about Alexander's stay at Hēliopolis, the temple estate (𓉗𓉐 *ḥw.t*) there had for millennia figured as one of the premiere intellectual and religious centers of all Egypt.[92] According to the Heliopolitan cosmogony, the temple compound stood at the site where on "the first occasion" (𓊃𓊪𓏤𓉔𓏤 *zp tpy*), in "the time before there were two things," the self-fashioning god Atum (𓏏𓂋𓅆 *'Itmw*) emerged from the dark, primeval, and chaotic waters (𓏌𓏌𓏌 *nwn*), seated upon the Mound of Creation (𓐪𓄿𓄿𓂦 *q33*), whence he brought the cosmos into being stage by stage.[93] There is perhaps a chiastic symmetry at play here insofar as the man destined to rule the world in its entirety (*ḥq3 t3 r ḏr=f*) stops to pay his respects at the site where the world initially came into being. Finally, from Hēliopolis, Alexander crosses over form the east to the west bank of the Nile, whence he proceeds upriver to Memphis, a move that Arrian describes in language that effectively foregrounds the metonymic figuration that underpins the composition of the episode as a whole: ἐκεῖθεν δὲ διαβὰς τὸν πόρον ἧκεν ἐς Μέμφιν.

Immediately following what we might best describe as a metalinguistic foregrounding of his narrative tropology,[94] Arrian writes into his account a second tropological turn, imposed upon the first, expressed through the paratactic juxtaposition of two exogenic cultural events—the first Egyptian (divine offerings [𓊵𓏏𓊪𓏤𓏤𓏤 *ḥtp.w-nṯr*] to the bull-god Apis),[95] the other Greek (athletic competitions [ἀγῶνες *agōnes*])[96]—a collocation considered earlier in the context of its broader East Mediterranean geopolitical setting.[97] Not only are these practices mutually unintelligible across cultural constituencies. At a syntactic level, the narrative presents the two spectacles as contiguous, connected in Arrian's prose only by the bare conjunctive καί, with no suggestion of any relationship between them or any indication of their order, time, or place. René Dirven calls this type of figuration "linear metonymy," a version of the trope which "keeps the separate existence of the two elements in the metonymy intact, but . . . does not allow the elements to replace each other."[98] While syntax remains inherently metonymic, here the syntagm also bears semantic weight. "Grammar," as R. W. Langacker has shown, "is not autonomous vis-à-vis semantics, but rather incorporates it. An expression's meaning is just the semantic pole of the symbolic assembly comprising it. Semantic composition is thus an aspect of grammatical composition."[99] This follows from Edward Sapir's well-known neo-Kantian tenet that grammatical categories reflect "not so much our intuitive analysis of reality as our ability to compose that reality into a variety of formal patterns,"[100] a precept whose implications Benjamin Whorf summed up succinctly: "Language is not simply a reporting device for experience but a defining framework for it."[101] What linear metonymy makes possible, if not inevitable, then, is that Alexander's offerings to Apis stand adjacent to, yet also independent of, the Greek games that he also staged in the Achaemenid satrapal seat at Memphis. As such, it is not only the conjunction of these two events that Arrian conveys along the axis of linguistic combination, but also their detachment, a decoupling or polarization which, through a further turn of the metonymic screw, refigures each of these actions as a *synecdoche* for its respective culture: animal cults typified, to the Greek mind at least, what was most peculiar about the Egyptian world, just as the *agōn* from Homer and Hesiod on represented one of the defining features of Panhellenic Greece.[102] As such, Arrian places Egyptian and Greek practices on equal footing, without judgment or hierarchization, and without one impinging on or mixing with the other—they remain separate as it were, but equal.[103]

In this account, then, the first in which Alexander engages directly with Egyptian politico-religious institutions, Arrian portrays Egyptian and Hellenic cultures as parallel formations which neither meet nor impact one another, anticipating in this regard Ptolemaic institutions such as the dual legal system in which traditional Egyptian law and its judicial apparatus operated alongside a corpus of traditional Greek law and court proceedings amalgamated from various Hellenic city-states.[104] As a way to configure the relationship between Egyptian and Greek practices, this double tracking has a long institutional and scholarly history that survives up through the present day. The same division resurfaces, for example, in J. P. Mahaffy's lectures on *The Progress of Hellenism in Alexander's Empire*, published in 1905, which invoke Arrian's metonymically motivated separatism as a framework for understanding the new Greek papyri and archeological finds from Ptolemaic and Roman Egypt, partly published in the Napoleonic *Description de l'Égypte* (1809–29 CE), with ongoing excavations made under the auspices of Queen Victoria's Consul-General of Egypt, Evelyn Baring, First Earl of Cromer. So Mahaffy informs his audience:

> You will be impatient to know how the old culture of Egypt harmonised with [the] splendour of Alexandria. The fact is that the first and second Ptolemies thought very little about Egypt, except as a source of revenue, and as a nation to be kept quiet while it fed the glory of the Graeco-Macedonian rule. For military purposes the Egyptians were accounted nearly useless, and as regards literature and science, no attempt was made to examine and utilise the lore of the priests. We may depend upon it that these priests were not willing to impart it to the upstart Greeks, and the hieroglyphic writing and strange language were almost impenetrable barriers to the few Greeks who attempted to learn them. So the wisdom and the art of Memphis, Thebes, and Hēliopolis, and all the other splendid old Egyptian cities *remained a thing apart* and foreign to the Alexandrians; the Egyptians were regarded as a foreign and subject population, only fit to labor and pay taxes and no systematic attempt was made to Hellenize them ... [Thus,] we may be certain that everything that they were proud of in the royal quarter of Alexandria was as purely Greek as they knew how to build it. *No statues of Egyptian gods and hieroglyphic ornaments could find a place in these buildings.* I went to Egypt to satisfy myself on this point, and it was surprising how scarce such combinations proved to be.[105]

Franck Goddio's underwater finds in the Ptolemaic Palace Quarter, now submerged beneath the harbor of modern Alexandria,[106] not only expose Mahaffy's patently racist delusions (Plate 6). They serve as a reminder that the same fantasmatic projection of an "impenetrable barrier" separating Egyptians from Greeks—a trope borrowed from Germaine de Staël's *De l'Allemagne* (1814)[107]—continues to inform contemporary treatments of Teminid Egypt today, which persistently rely on the same metonymic figuration to which Arrian had recourse in his *Anabasis*. This divide, which effectively attempts to seal off Greek culture from "contamination" with Egypt, shows up clearly in reviews of Susan Stephen's groundbreaking study, *Seeing Double: Intercultural Poetics in Ptolemaic Alexandria* (2003). Here are two assessments of the book chosen more or less at random:

As the Satrap Stele shows, festive occasions were contexts in which Egyptian petitions could be made. Ptolemy obliged his petitioners, but the favors were local and specific. By background, language, and culture he was not the "last of the pharaohs" nor was he in the least concerned "to see double." Egyptians might praise and accommodate him, but he did not see himself or his kingship as a multicultural hybrid.

Robin Lane Fox
"King Ptolemy: Centre and Periphery" (2015)

[T]he poetic output of the Hellenistic period seems to have a quite different agenda, which has less to do with a willing exploration of the interface of Greek and Egyptian culture than with the exploration of a Greek cultural identity in Greek terms.

Simon Goldhill
Review of *Seeing Double: Intercultural Poetics in Ptolemaic Alexandria*,
by S. Stephens (2005)

Between Arrian's recourse to metonymy in configuring the historical field of the *Anabasis* and the use to which Lane Fox and Goldhill put the same trope, there is a crucial difference. In Arrian, the synecdoches that he employs to stand for Egyptian and for Greco-Macedonian culture respectively serve an equipollent function that sets both cultures on equal terms. Mahaffy and his contemporary successors, however, inflect this division hierarchically in a manner complicit with the colonialist and neo-colonialist agendas of the modern world-system.[108]

Narration

Alexander's journey from Pēlousion to Memphis and the various celebrations in which he participated while staying there form a finite, self-contained narrative sequence which exhibits both continuity of action (πρᾶξις) and consistency of subject matter (χρῆμα). Though not demarcated as such in modern editions of the *Anabasis*, Arrian indicates the discursive boundaries of this sequence through the corelative spatial indices that frame this portion of his text: εἰς Πηλούσιον . . . ἐκ Μέμφιος (3.1.3–3.1.4). Roland Barthes, in his programmatic study of *la langue du récit*,[109] designates this type of discursive sequence a *unité fonctionnelle*. "The *functional character* of certain segments of the story (*histoire*)," Barthes points out, "establishes them as [meaningful discursive] units."[110] From a linguistic point of view, moreover, a function—in Barthes' sense of the term—constitutes a unit of content (*unité de contenu*), not of expression or of form.[111] Functional units concern "what an utterance means" (*"ce que veut dire" un énoncé*), not the grammatical or rhetorical components of verbal expression (*énonciation*).[112] More generally, A.-J. Greimas notes: "Syntactical unities (above the level of the phrase) are in fact unities of content."[113] For Barthes, therefore, the structural analysis of any narrative takes as its point of departure an inventory of the various *unités fonctionnelles* that constitute the text, some conveyed in a few words, others at greater length:

> In order to determine the basic narrative units, it is necessary never to lose sight of the functional character of the segment under consideration, and to realize in advance that those segments will not necessarily coincide with the forms traditionally attributed to the various parts of narrative discourse (actions, scenes, paragraphs, dialogues, inner monologues, etc.).[114]

As a functional discursive unit, then, Arrian's account of Alexander's progress from Pēlousion to Memphis not only depicts Alexander's latest additions to his serial annexation of the satrapies of Achaemenid Iran (OPers. *dahyāva*). Concomitantly, Arrian portrays Alexander's military occupation of the Two Lands as coincident with his appropriation of the charisma and symbolic capital that kings of Egypt traditionally possessed.[115] To put this in other terms: Alexander, in Arrian's account, takes over both the repressive apparatus of the state (i.e., military [⟨hieroglyphs⟩ *mšʿ*] and presumably the police [⟨hieroglyphs⟩ *šnʿ.w*]),[116] as well as the ideological institutions of Late Period Egyptian culture, the two main functives of royal power.[117]

Alexander's stay at Memphis initiated the process of his legitimation as Pharaoh and hence the solidification of his jurisdiction over Egypt, its religious rites, and its titular denominations, all of which were necessary but evidently not sufficient to confirm him as king of the Two Lands (⟨hieroglyphs⟩). Accordingly, Greco-Roman historians discuss two other sites that Alexander visited—Sīwah and Rhakōtis—but apparently, as with the ceremonies at Memphis, they did not recognize either their connection to royal legitimation or their interdependence, such that from one historical account to another, the localities appear in different order, or remain absent from the account altogether. Louis Hjelmslev in his *Omkring sprogteoriens grundlæggelse* [*Prolegomena to a Theory of Language*] ([1943] 1993), taking his point of departure from Saussure's demonstration that language is a system of pure *values*,[118] stresses the importance of dependency for the understanding of any utterance or text, be it a morpheme or an extended narration:

Analysis consists in registering the dependencies between certain terms (Dan. *termer*[i.e., a delimited portion of the discourse[119]]; sing. *term*), which we may call, in accordance with established usage, the parts of the text, and which have existence precisely by virtue of these dependencies and only by virtue of them. The fact that we can call these terms "parts" and this whole procedure a division or analysis, is due to the fact that there also exist dependencies between these terms and the totality (i.e., the text) into which one says they "enter," dependencies which it is likewise the task of the analysis to register ... Each of the parts can be defined only by the relations that exist (1) between it and other coordinated parts, (2) between the whole and the parts of the next degree, and (3) between the set of relations and dependencies and their parts. After we have recognized this, the "objects" of naïve realism are, from our point of view, nothing but intersections of bundles of such dependencies.[120]

For Hjelmslev, then, the critical analysis of linguistic artifacts does not aim solely at the division of the "object" (in this case, a text or set of texts) into its constituent parts, but rather seeks an analysis that will reveal the mutual dependencies among its various components. If we take Memphis, Sīwah, and Rhakōtis as the three principal *termer* that figure in the Egyptian *logoi* of the Greco-Roman historians of Alexander, each forms, at a higher level of discursive integration, a *unité fonctionnelle*, themselves comprised of several secondary narrative units. However, we cannot, as Hjelmslev suggests, understand them in isolation—by concentrating, say, on the oracle at Sīwah or the foundation of Alexandria alone[121]—but only through the dependencies that they bear to one another within the Greco-Roman historical accounts. Each of the terminal points where Alexander stopped on his circuit through Lower Egypt (　𓏏𓄿𓅓𓎛𓅱 *T3-mḥw*) serves to further his legitimation as king of Egypt, though each in a distinctly different way. As noted at the outset, all that space allows me here is to discuss the two remaining *termer* in brief in order to elicit the most basic connections.

Sīwah: Q. Curtius recounts that Alexander traveled through the farthest reaches of the Western Desert (*per vastas solitudines*) to the remote oasis of Sīwah (𓇋𓄿𓈖𓈖𓈖𓈖 *Sḫt i3m.w* "Field of Trees"; Berber ⵉⵙⵉⵡⴰⵏ "Isiwan") in order to consult what the Greco-Roman world knew as the oracle of Zeus-Ammon, a shrine situated at the confluence of Berber, Egyptian, and Greek political and economic interests.[122] When Alexander approached what Egyptians called simply the Temple of Amun (𓉐𓏏𓇋𓏠𓈖𓅆 *Pr-'Imn*), the eldest of the priests came forward and addressed Alexander as "son" (*filium* / παῖς), explaining that this was the designation that Alexander's father, Amun, had bestowed upon him. In effect, then, the priesthood at Sīwah substantiated the paternity written into Alexander's Birth Name as attested in the titulary from Baḥrīyah: ⟨𓅱𓇋𓏤𓂝𓍽⟩ *Z3 'Imn 'Irksnd[rs]* "Son of Amun, Alexander," thereby actualizing the epithet and so further substantiating Alexander's claim to the Egyptian throne.[123] However risible or hubristic to Macedonians and Greeks the notion of Alexander's divine paternity might seem—Plutarch credits Alexander's deific aspirations to a grammatical mistake in the transmission of the oracle from Egyptian into Greek[124]—the response of the Chief Prophet (𓊹𓎛𓏺 *ḥm-nṯr tpy*) effectively writes Alexander into the Egyptian cycle of divine succession which from the New Kingdom on had become a central tenet of the Egyptian ideology of kingship.[125] According to this myth, first attested in the mortuary temple of Ḥatšepsut (r. 1507–1458 BCE) at al-Dayr al-Baḥrī (𓆓𓋴𓂋𓉐 *Ḏsr ḏsr.w* "Holy of Holies"). Amun-Rēʿ appears in divine form before Mutemwiya, the wife of the reigning king, Tuthmosis II (Plate 7). The two engage sexually, and from this union the queen—a mortal woman—bears a divine heir to the Egyptian throne, a son (or, in this case, daughter) whose shaping Amun-Rēʿ oversees and to whom the female-king will return after death. What the myth of the divine birth (𓄟𓋴𓏏𓊹 *msw.t nṯr*) attempts, to address, then, is the rift that had opened up between the realm of the gods (𓊹𓊹𓊹 *nṯr.w*) and the realm of human beings (𓂋𓀀𓏥 *rmṯ*), who were at one time united,[126] through the ritual production of a king who is both fully human and fully divine, thereby sublating the opposition altogether.[127] Depending on one's frame of cultural reference, then, Alexander's descent from Amun appears either as an extravagant folly or as a cosmic necessity that guarantees the continuity and divinity of the pharaonic succession. Unlike the parity between Egyptian and Greek celebratory rites which Arrian portrays at Memphis, here Alexander's ostensibly divine decent from Amun (Grk. *Zeus*) polarizes the two traditions which now stand at odds with one another.

    RHAKŌTIS: the third and final *term* in Alexander's tour of Egypt was the village of Rhakōtis (𓊪𓉐𓂝𓈎𓂧𓊖 *R-ʿ-qd* "Worksite," "Under Construction"),[128] situated on a thin slip of land between the Mediterranean Sea and Lake Maryūṭ (Plate 8), just west of the Canopic branch of the Nile, where "marsh-dwellers" (𓇋𓂧𓎛𓇌𓅱 *idḥy.w*) had lived since the time of the Old Kingdom (*c.* 2700–2200 BCE).[129] Marching east from the village of Ἀμμωνία—the doubled μ marks this as a Greek spelling (Arab. مطروح مرسى *Marsā Maṭrūḥ*) along the Mediterranean littoral, Alexander, struck by the village of Rhakōtis, situated between two bodies of water, ordered that a city be constructed at that site. Two facets of Alexander's building program here relate directly to the circuit of legitimation that runs from Memphis through Sīwah to Rhakōtis. First, from the pre-Dynastic period on, kingship and monumental building—temples, palaces, tombs, populous cities[130]—stood in a relationship of mutual support in which the king commissioned large-scale building projects such that architecture functioned as a metonym for royal power.[131] Hence the *serekh*-panel (i.e., a palace façade) in which rulers from the early Dynastic period on engraved their names.[132] In fact, among the first things that a newly crowned pharaoh might do to mark a change of dynasty or reign was to construct a new royal city to serve as his capital. Thus, Amenemḥat I (*c.* 1994–1962 BCE), on his accession to the throne moved the government from Thebes to *'Iṯi tꜣ.wy* ($\boxed{\underline{\underline{\bar{x}}}}$ "He who seizes the Two Lands"), the city that he founded in the Faiyum Oasis. Similarly, Smendes I ($\boxed{\text{𓇋𓇓𓅱𓏏𓊵𓏏𓀭}}$ *Ni-sw Bꜣ-n-Ḏd.t mri-'Imn:* *c.* 1076–1052 BCE), the first ruler of the Twenty-First dynasty, established his royal residence at Tanis ($\boxed{\text{𓊨𓈖𓏏}}$ *Ḏꜥn.t*) in the northeastern region of the Delta. Given such historical precedents, then—and there are many others—Alexander's orders to construct a new metropole on the site of Rhakōtis figures as part of his efforts to meet the expectations of a legitimately consecrated Pharaoh.[133]

Second, the water surrounding the tuft of land on which Rhakōtis stood constitutes a geoglyph of the Mound of Creation ($\boxed{\text{𓈎}}$ *qꜣꜣ*) that rose out of the primeval waters on the First Occasion, cosmogonic precepts to which Alexander would have also been exposed at Hēliopolis.[134] Not only did the annual inundation of the Nile produce at its peak patches of green ground that resembled islands floating in the stream (Plate 9); many Egyptian architectural forms—pyramids, obelisks, temples, royal residences—served to reify the moment of the First Occasion in stone, with buildings situated so that at the peak of the flood they appeared as if they were emerging out of the river waters (Plate 10). In this regard, Erik Hornung explains that for Egyptian culture "creation was perceived not as a single, isolated event, but as a process that entailed constant repetition. The world could become repeatedly as new and perfect as it had been at the time of its origin."[135] Not unlike Pi-Ramesses, then, a metropolis strewn across an archipelago of islands nestled within the twists and turns of the Pelusiac branch of the Nile, Alexander chose to plant his own Residence ($\boxed{\text{𓉔𓈖𓂋𓏤}}$ *ḥnꜥ-v*) at *R-ꜥ-qd* where the natural setting recalled the mound that had emerged out of the chill waters as the sun arose over the hillside on the first day of the First Occasion (cf.: $\boxed{\text{𓎛}}$ *ḥꜥ* "Primeval Mound"; $\boxed{\text{𓎛𓇋}}$ *ḥꜥi* "to rise, appear," as well as "to be crowned," or "to assume the throne"). According to a logic that is peculiarly Egyptian, then, the construction of a city, palace, temple, or tomb fashioned in a form mimetic of the Primeval Mound recollected and reenacted allegorically the investiture of the king, complementary ways of returning to and repeating what had taken place *in illo tempore*.[136] For Alexander, then, the foundation of *R-ʿ-qd / Alexándreia* not only evoked the origin of the world that he would go on to subdue. According to the Alexander Romance—which represents not the letter but the spirit of Alexander's expedition—he proceeds to renew that world through the establishment of political, social, and cosmic order (⟨𓐙𓂝𓏏⟩ *mꜣʿ.t*) and the eradication of chaos, falsehood, injustice, and crime (⟨𓄋𓏏⟩ *izf.t*) (Plate 11).[137]

Signification

To analyze all of Alexander's dealings at Sīwah and Rhakōtis as the Greek and Roman historians present them, as well as their dependencies upon each other and their respective links to the matter of Memphis, involves complexities whose exposition we must postpone to another occasion. Nonetheless, even in so abbreviated a discussion, a number of commonalities emerge. While each of the *termer* in the Greco-Roman narratives constitutes a site directly associated with the Egyptian ideology of kingship and therefore furthers the function of legitimizing Alexander's role as Pharaoh, each also transpires along a seam where the Greek and Egyptian worlds meet, in effect suturing two radically different cultures in a way that displaces earlier, more restricted trading centers such as Naukratis or Thōnis.[138] To take an obvious example, the Alexander of the Roman imperial histories does not seek out Amun-Rēʿ in his principal residence at Karnak, easily accessible from Memphis up the Nile,[139] but marches instead three hundred miles across the Western Desert to Sīwah, a site already known to the Greek and Roman world as the oracle of Zeus-Ammon, where Greek colonists from Cyrene would have encountered Egyptians from the Nile valley. Tropologically, moreover, in the same way that metonymy constitutes the dominant mode of figuration that organizes on all levels Arrian's account of Alexander's passage from Pēlousion to Memphis, so the two remaining *termer* of Alexander's Egyptian venture are, as verbal artefacts, likewise figurally encoded—each, however, by way of a different trope: Memphis: *metonymy*; Sīwah: *syllēpsis* [i.e., Stephens' "seeing double"];[140] and Rhakōtis: *allegory*.[141] Whereas metonymy sets Hellenic over and against Egyptian culture side-by-side without one overlapping with the other, *syllēpsis* [σύλληψις "taking together, conjunction"],[142] as it configures the historical narratives concerning Alexander's fortunes at the oracle of Sīwah, superimposes one signification upon another such that words, phrases, whole passages of text read one way within the symbolic system of the Greeks and another when framed within the semantic structure of Late Egyptian. Arrian, for example, writes regarding Sīwah: "Alexander marveled (ἐθαύμασε) at the place and consulted (ἐχρήσατο) the god's oracle."[143] Here, the collocation ἐθαύμασε ∧ ἐχρήσατο constitutes a hendiadys which conjures up 𓇋𓃀𓄿𓏏 *bi3y.t*, the Egyptian term for "oracle," derived from the noun's most basic meaning "wonder." Accordingly, the passage references conjointly Greek procedures for oracular consultation, as well as the very different divinatory protocols in Egypt.[144] Finally, in the narratives regarding Rhakōtis, the Roman imperial historians situate the construction of Alexandria within a complex network of allegorical signs drawn from multiple cultures which do not so much describe the place referentially as convey its meaning in advance of the construction. As Paul de Man explained:

> [It is] necessary, if there is to be allegory, that the allegorical sign refer to another sign that precedes it. The meaning constituted by the allegorical sign can only consist in the *repetition* (in the Kierkegaardian sense of the term) of a previous sign with which it can never coincide, since it is of the essence of this previous sign to be pure anteriority.[145]

Removed, then, in relation to its own origin, allegory establishes its meaning within this temporal difference, which in Egypt, from the Predynastic Era on, generates the rhetoric of the Fist Occasion (*zp tpy*) and its material reproductions that, as we have seen, overdetermines the site of Ἀλεξάνδρεια / ⲣⲁⲕⲟⲧⲉ.[146]

As we come to the end of our Egyptian tour, we return—following Louis Hjelmslev and the further elaboration of his work by Fredric Jameson and Hayden White[147]—to what we can most accurately describe as the *content of the form*, that is, the function that non- or pre-semantic grammatical, syntactic, tropological, generic, and structural features of the discourse, all of which properly belong to the plane of expression, but nonetheless play an significant role in the constitution of the plane of content, thereby blurring what the texts themselves reveal to be an arbitrary, if nonetheless conveniently heuristic, distinction.[148] Instead of the binary opposition between signifier and signified that dominated semiology from the Stoics through Saussure, Hjelmslev proposed a four-term set of positions:

	FORM	CONTENT
CONTENT	form of content	content of content
FORM	form of form	<u>content of form</u>

In this connection, Roman Jakobson speaks of "the semantic load of grammatical appliances,"[149] such as we find, for example, in the syntax of Mallarmé, whose scrupulously calculated syntactic disarticulations, Barbara Johnson notes, creates "an excess, not a deficiency, of meaning."[150] Rather than a break with the poetic past, moreover, the "semantic load" of Mallarmé's convoluted syntax perpetuates a literary device—in Shklovskiĭ's sense of приём—long central to the tradition of Indo-European verse.[151] As Annette Teffeteller observes, with reference to Eliot rather than to Mallarmé:

> T. S. Eliot's view of the poet's task as "to force, to dislocate if necessary, language into his meaning" reflects an Indo-European tradition that continues in the hymns of the Vedic and Greek poets. It is a tradition that valorizes complexity of thought, systematic ambiguity, multivalency, multiple levels of literal and metaphorical meaning held in equipoise ... And all of this complexity of meaning is encoded in the intricate interplay between the syntactic, the metrical, and the stylistic structures of the poetic grammar.[152]

Rhetoric, considered as a system of figures and tropes,[153] expressly introduces semantic dislocations of this type, which give rise in turn to a plurality of meanings, some compatible with one another, others not[154]—yet, so can grammar and syntax which constitute their linguistic foundation and support.

This was the case, as we saw, with Arrian's account of Alexander's entry into Egypt and his ensuing march upstream to Memphis, a cohesive sequence of narration, emplotted metonymically, which Arrian divides between two sentences. In the first of these, Arrian has so arranged the syntax that, like the proem to the Virgil's *Aeneid*, it unfolds between the names of two well-known and strategically important cities: Pēlousion (*Pr-'Imn*) → Hēliopolis (*'Iwn.w*), positioned at either end of the sentence so as in effect to bracket the statement as a whole:

> ὁ δὲ εἰς μὲν <u>Πηλούσιον</u> φυλακὴν εἰσήγαγε, τοὺς δὲ ἐπὶ τῶν νεῶν ἀναπλεῖν κατὰ τὸν ποταμὸν κελεύσας ἔστε ἐπὶ Μέμφιν πόλιν, αὐτὸς ἐφ᾽ Ἡλιουπόλεως ἤει, ἐν δεξιᾷ ἔχων τὸν ποταμὸν τὸν Νεῖλον, καὶ ὅσα καθ᾽ ὁδὸν χωρία ἐνδιδόντων τῶν ἐνοικούντων κατασχὼν διὰ τῆς ἐρήμου ἀφίκετο ἐς <u>Ἡλιούπολιν</u>.

> At Pēlousion, [Alexander] installed a garrison while he, having ordered his naval officers to sail up the river as far as the city of Memphis, proceeded to Hēliopolis,

keeping the river Nile always to his right, taking possession of all the districts that he came upon, as their inhabitants surrendered, he arrived through the desert at Hēliopolis.

Between these two geographic nodes, linked here by way of the Nile (𓇋𓏏𓂋𓈗 *itrw* "the River"), the syntactic sweep of the sentence, in which Alexander takes possession (κατασχών) of one Lower Egyptian district (χωρίον) after another, or perhaps more likely each of the Egyptian nomes (𓈅𓏏 *sp3.t*)[155] along the way—all of them remain anonymous, as if the details of local Egyptian administration or the villages where the inhabitants of Lower Egypt lived, made no difference to Alexander whatsoever. On the one hand, we might construe this as *Arrian*'s assessment of Alexander's interest in local Egyptian affairs, yet on the other the anonymity could also mark a signifying gap. After all, even though *Aegyptus* had been a Roman praefecture since 30 BCE, what would Lower Egyptian toponyms such as 𓏶𓏶𓏶𓊖 *'Im3w* or 𓇌𓂋𓅱𓊖 *T3rw*, for which no Greek or Latin denomination survives, have signified to a Roman imperial readership of the first or second century CE, even if the names occurred in other sources? For most, such toponyms could only represent exotica, phantasmatic places, like one of Italo Calvino's *Città invisibili* or the fabled wonders beyond *Thule*.

To the extent that Diodorus, Arrian, Q. Curtius, Plutarch, and Justin all narrate Alexander's expedition as what White terms a "temporal series of spatial sets," his passage from Pēlousion to Memphis, at least as Arrian relates it, constitutes a *mise-en-abyme* of the *Anabasis Alexandri* as a whole.[156] Starting from the coast of the "Sea in the Middle" (Eg. 𓇅𓂋 *W3d-wr*),[157] Alexander and his troops make the upward march (*anábasis*) to Memphis, annexing one featureless territory after another to the Macedonian Empire, a journey into the heart of an alien land where, at Hēliopolis and Memphis, in particular, Alexander begins to take on the role and the trappings of an Egyptian king: he honors the cult of Apis, assumes the fivefold royal titulary, and had himself represented in Egyptian temples in the garb and regalia of a pharaoh. The scenario here prefigures the crisis at the border between Parthia (OPers. 𐎱𐎼𐎰𐎺 *Parθava-*) and Hyrcania (OPers. 𐎺𐎼𐎣𐎠𐎴 *Varkāna-*),[158] which appears later in the historical accounts where, as part of his efforts to solidify control over the vast Achaemenian domain, Alexander begins to clothe himself in Medio-Persian style and institutes the oriental ritual of *proskúnēsis*.[159] According to Q. Curtius, the events unfolded as follows:

Alexander demanded that the victors over so many nations in paying their respects to him should prostrate themselves on the ground and gradually sought to accustom them to servile duties. Accordingly, he circled his head with a purple diadem such as Darius had worn and assumed Persian dress. In fact, he used to say that he was wearing the spoils of the Persians, but with them he had assumed their customs and an insolence of spirit accompanied the magnificence of his attire. These practices, corrupted by luxury and foreign customs, were openly detested by the veteran soldiers of Philip, and in the whole camp the feeling and discussion was the same [6.6.3–9].[160]

Ultimately, then, Arrian's account of Alexander's trip to Memphis, however seductive its denotative lure,[161] constitutes a figure for the trajectory of Alexander's expedition as a whole, tracing his increasing penetration from the Mediterranean littoral to Bābilim, Pārsa and beyond, into the northeastern most reaches of the Achaemenid state. Crossing the Āmū Daryā (Grk. *Ôxos*) into Sogdiana (OPers. 𐎿𐎢𐎦𐎢𐎭 *Suguda-*), Alexander married Rôxánē (OPer. *Rauxšnā-*), the daughter of the Bactrian noble Oxyártēs (OPers. *Huxšaθra-*), thereby joining in the flesh the Hellenic with the Ariyan,[162] beyond the level of court protocol or dress. Accordingly, Arrian's *Anabasis* constitutes a *récit spéculaire* insofar as it contains an internal duplication in which the text represents itself, a historiographical device already familiar from Herodotus.[163] In the terms of Lucien Dällenbach, we are dealing here with an *énoncé synecdochique* in which a portion of Arrian's text stands in for his narration as a whole, be it at the level of the *énoncé*, the *énonciation*, or the *code du récit*, if not all three.[164]

One of the remarkable features of Alexander's *iter ad Aegyptum*, at least as Diodorus, Arrian, Q. Curtius, and Plutarch portray it, is that everything in these accounts signifies, and multiple times over–down to the smallest linguistic, thematic, or structural detail, textual gaps included, and it does so in multiple registers and across multiple cultural frames of reference—not only Greek, Macedonian, and Egyptian, but also Iranian, Semitic, Nubian, and Berber. As such, the Greco-Roman accounts of Alexander in Egypt, and Arrian in particular, present us with what Barthes described as a "galaxy of signifiers, not a structure of signifieds,"[165] drawn from multiple, culturally specific signifying systems, a plurality which precludes both the possibility of closure and the type of discursive totalization or finitude that Aristotle valorizes as whole, entire, and complete in all its parts (ὅλον).[166] The many networks of signification that traverse these texts inevitably interact with one another—even beyond the cognizance or "intentions" of the writer—though none of them proves able to supersede the others.[167] To complicate matters further, the Roman imperial historians of Alexander had to deal not only with several, often irreconcilable frames of cultural reference. They also had to reckon with signifying systems in place at multiple points in time. To put the question most broadly: what did Alexander's annexation of Egypt mean to the Afro-Eurasian world in 332–331 BCE, and what did his expedition signify for Roman readers—including the ethnically diverse denizens of Roman Egypt[168]—in the first and second centuries CE when Rome campaigned persistently (54 BCE–217 CE) against the Parthian Empire (Parth. *Parθaw*)?

"Every signification," Jacques Lacan reminds us, "only ever refers back (*renvoyer*) to another signification."[169] Lacan alludes here to the process of "infinite semiosis," which Charles Sanders Peirce introduced in his early work on semiotics (1865–7).[170] As opposed to the dyadic model of the sign (*signifiant / signifié*) on which Saussure based his *Cours de linguistique générale* (1916), Peirce refined the procedure of signification with his insistence on the presence of a third element, what he called the *interpretant*,[171] which intervenes in any relationship which a sign or, as Peirce calls it, *representamen*, bears to the object that it represents. Paul de Man again usefully explains the implication of Peirce's interpretant, both for the process of signification as a whole and, more particularly, for what de Man designates here as rhetorical reading:

> [For Peirce,] the sign is to be interpreted if we are to understand the idea it is to convey, and this is so because the sign is not the thing but a meaning derived from the thing by a process ... that is not simply generative, i.e., dependent on a univocal origin. The interpretation of a sign is not, for Peirce, a meaning but another sign; it is a reading, not a decodage, and this reading has, in its turn to be interpreted into another sign, and so on *ad infinitum*. Peirce calls the process by means of which "one sign gives birth to another" pure rhetoric, as distinguished from pure grammar which postulates the possibility of unproblematic, dyadic meaning, and pure logic, which postulates the possibility of the universal truth of meanings. Only if the sign engendered meaning in the same way that the object engenders the sign, that is, by representation, would there be no need to distinguish between grammar and rhetoric.[172]

If signs are in and of themselves merely interpretants of other signs this commits Peirce, as Albert Atkin notes, "to the claim that an infinity of further signs must both *proceed* from and *precede* any given sign."[173] This is precisely the point upon which Lacan seizes: "In grasping the function of the sign, one is always referred from one sign to another. Why? Because the system of signs, as they are concretely instituted, *hic et nunc*, forms in and of itself a whole (*forme par lui-même un tout*). That is to say, that it institutes an order from which there is no exit (*un ordre qui est sans issue*)."[174] Language, then, taken as a system of arbitrarily constituted signs, provides us no access to "the real," which Lacan famously defined as "that which cannot come into representation" (*ce qui résiste absolument à la symbolisation*),[175] a formulation that he largely owes to Kant.[176]

Peirce certainly envisioned that a single sign would give rise to different *interpretants* in the minds of different individuals, both for persons who inhabit the same language (e.g., Greek), as well as interlocutors who dwell in two or three distinct language systems (Greek / Egyptian / Aramaic / Berber / Beja, etc.), as would be the case, for example, with the *representamen* ΑΠΙΣ | ḤPW [Copt. ⲍⲁⲡⲉ]. As Rossella Fabbrichesi, in an essay on the fallibilism of inquiry in the philosophy of Peirce,[177] observes:

> [T]he *signification* process—that is, the process of knowledge—is an unending process of translation in which meaning resides in the in-between, in the referring, in the vague area of transit. Vague because never precisely achieved. Meaning and eventually also the meaning of reality, is not a thing, a *res*, but, as Peirce puts it, is an indefinitely future event ... This means that any truth we gain, any theory we are leading to, is fallible, uncertain, and inexact, dragged as it is in the infinite chain of semiosis ... Peirce elsewhere calls this process "mellonization," from the Greek μέλλον, which means, "being about to." Reality has then to be intended as a "habit of expectation.[178]

For Peirce, then, "mellonization" and "infinite semiosis" constitute two sides of the same cognitive predicament. Cumulatively, the semiotic process by which one interpretant replaces or translates another unfolds in a temporality of μέλλησις, that is, of suspended expectation as to what is perpetually "about to be." Accordingly, Arrian's account of Alexander's trip to Memphis constitutes nothing so much as a palimpsest of such *mellēseis*, a site for the uptake of one interpretant after another, reaching back to a time well before Callisthenes and looking forward to the innumerable successive reiterations of Alexander's life up through W. W. Tarn, Paul Cartledge, Robin Lane Fox, and Oliver Stone who, in what Hjelmslev would call their "naïve realism," nourish the hope that, with the rigor of the "scientific" historiography that Leopold von Ranke developed,[179] "the way it actually was" (*wie es eigentlich gewesen*) will emerge objectively at some point in the future,[180] on the far side of semiological constraints (*Zwange*),[181] and the "vertiginous possibilities of referential aberration" that the rhetoric of tropes inevitably induces.[182]

Hayden White locates this crux partly in the recurrent methodological confusion in historical accounts between *concepts* and *things*, on the one hand, and the insufficiently theorized distinction between a *fact* and an *event*, on the other:

[T]he term "history" is the signifier of a concept rather than a *reference* to a thing or domain of being having material presence. This concept may have as its signified either "the past" or something like "temporal process" but these, too, are concepts rather than things. Neither has a material presence. Both are known only by way of "traces" or material entities which indicate not so much what the things that produced them were, as, rather, the fact that "some thing" passed by a certain place or did something in that place. What it was that had passed by or what it had done in that place will remain a mystery, the solution to which may be inferred or intuited, but the nature of which must remain conjectural— indeed, must remain a possibility only and therefore a "fiction."[183]

In the case of Alexander, what few material traces remain of his tour through Egypt survive only in Egyptian artefacts: (1) his five-fold royal titulary inscribed on a stone block in the Baḥrīya oasis; (2) the bas-reliefs and statues that represent Alexander in Pharaonic dress, according to the Egyptian canon of proportions, in temples, both major and minor, scattered about Egypt (Luxor, Karnak, Elephantinē (*ꜣbw*), Hermopolis (*Ḥnmw*), Hibis, and the colossal wreck of "Alexander's Temple" that lies in ruins in Baḥrīya; and (3) the hieroglyphic texts, mostly formulaic, that accompany the statues and reliefs. These material indices, considered in the context of their native culture, are, as we have seen, sufficient to configure the *concept* of legitimation as a possible *event*, a conjecture bolstered by later and derivative historical narrations, but which, given the disjointed nature of the material remains and our ignorance of the time or circumstances their production, cannot be established as a *fact*. In this connection, White observes:

> [A]though modern professional historians limit themselves to assertions about the past that can be derived from the study of documents, monuments, and other traces of the past's reality, the kind of study of such evidence licensed by the historical profession is so *ad hoc*, merely commonsensical, and fragmentary that not even the criterion of coherence can be met without a great deal of patching up that is of a figurative (and therefore fiction-making) kind.[184]

Perhaps White has in mind here Feste's retort to Olivia in *Twelfth Night*: "Anything that's mended is but patched" [I.5.43]. Reading Diodorus, Plutarch, Arrian, and Q. Curtius Egyptologically, however—that is, against the grain—yields a good deal more ideological coherence, particularly when viewed from within to the conventions of Egyptian historiography,[185] than do the Greek and Latin narratives of Alexander in Egypt, which remain irreducibly desultory, contradictory, and lacunose.

Joan Didion, at the opening of *The White Album* (1979), a collection of essays that documents the fracturing of social, political, psychic, and cultural life, principally in California, from the late 1960s through the mid-1970s, offers the following remarks regarding the narrative imagination:

> We tell ourselves stories in order to live. The princess is caged in the consulate. The man with the candy will lead the children into the sea. The naked woman on the ledge outside the window on the sixteenth floor is a victim of accidie, or the naked woman is an exhibitionist, and it would be "interesting" to know which. We tell ourselves that it makes some difference whether the naked woman is about to commit a mortal sin or is about to register a political protest, or is about to be, the Aristophanic view, snatched back into the human condition by the fireman in priest's clothing just visible in the window behind her, the one smiling at the telephoto lens. We look for the sermon in the suicide, for the social or moral lesson in the murder of five. We interpret what we see, select the most workable of the multiple choices. We live entirely, especially if we are writers, by the imposition of a narrative line upon disparate images, by the "ideas" with which we have learned to freeze the shifting phantasmagoria which is our actual experience.[186]

For over two millennia now, we have been telling ourselves stories about the life and deeds Alexander "the Great," and it would be "interesting" to know why. In the West, we cling to the conviction that somehow it still matters whether the priests at Sīwah proclaimed Alexander the son of Amun, or whether Alexander and Hephaestion were lovers, or if Alexander actually burned all extant copies of the Avesta in Iran. Professional historians treat these matters as if these were at least *potential* facts that might one day be established *in futuro*, and so create conjectural— and hence irreducibly fictitious—narratives about them, stringing the "events" together as a series of historical *tableaux* that function according to what Derrida has called the "*movement of supplementarity*," insofar as they simultaneously complete (*supplémenter*) and replace (*suppléer*) the irrecuperable particulars of an existence perhaps better described as one of accidence, serial discontinuity, and geopolitical confusion. We can analyze the stories about Alexander's life that we continue to tell, what they signify and how, but instead of attempting to establish their veracity, perhaps the more conscientious task today lies in the attempt to understand what these stories as stories have achieved historically, culturally, and politically in the shaping of the Afro-Eurasian world within and across cultures, in what ways they have allowed us to live, why we still persist in telling them, and whether, in the twilight of modernity, we should continue to care about establishing what Alexander III of Macedon did or did not do at all.

Wenn die Philosophie ihr Grau in Grau malt, dann ist eine Gestalt des Lebens alt geworden, und mit Grau in Grau läßt sie sich nicht verjüngen, sondern nur erkennen; die Eule der Minerva beginnt erst mit der einbrechenden Dämmerung ihren Flug.

G. W. F. Hegel, *Grundlinien der Philosophie des Rechts* (1820)

Notes

1 Lacan: "Le langage n'est concevable que comme un réseau, un filet sur l'ensemble des choses, sur la totalité du réel. Il inscrit sur le plan du réel cet autre plan que nous appelons ici le plan du symbolique" (1975), 288.

2 Recent overviews of Alexander in the Roman imagination include Spencer (2011); Peltonen (2019). In this context, see also Taietti (2016).

3 On the name and its significance, see Schmitt (1990). See further, Briant (2003).

4 On the relatively complex subject of the satrapies of the Achaemenid Empire, see Petit (1990); Jacobs (1994, 2011). N. S. Gill posted a chart of the satrapies on the ThoughtCo. website on February 26, 2020, at: https://www.thoughtco.com/satrapies-of-the-achaemenid-persians-120229 (accessed May 7, 2023).

5 For informed discussion of most aspects of Alexander's activities in Egypt, see the essays collected in Grieb, Nawotka, and Wojciechowska (2014).

6 See Gardiner (1920); Hoffmeier and Moshier (2013); Hussein and Alim (2015).

7 See Stanley, Bernasconi, and Jorstad (2008). Cf. Ezekiel 30:15: סין מעוז מצרים.

8 For an overview of Alexander's expedition, see Badian (1985).

9 E.g., Ἐπὶ τούτοις δὲ πόθος λαμβάνει αὐτὸν ἐλθεῖν παρ' Ἄμμωνα ἐς Λιβύην (*Anabasis* 3.3).

10 Among the references in Greek literature to the Oracle of Zeus Ammon antedating Alexander are: Herodotus, *Inquiry* 1.46; Pindar, *Pythian* 4.29; Aristophanes, *Birds* 619; Euripides, *Alcestis* 115; Aristotle, *Athenian Constitution* 61; etc. In Plato's *Politikós*, Theodoros of Cyrene describes Ammon as "our deity" (257b).

11 Pausanias, in describing the acropolis at Sparta remarks:

Farther on from here is a sanctuary of Ammon. From the first the Lacedaemonians are known to have used the oracle in Libya more than any other Greeks. It is said also that when Lysander was besieging Aphytis in Pallene Ammon appeared by night and declared that it would be better for him and for Lacedaemon if they ceased from warring against Aphytis. And so Lysander raised the siege and induced the Lacedaemonians to worship the god still more. The people of Aphytis honor Ammon no less than the Ammonian Libyans.

3.18.3

12 See Pearson (1960).

13 Aristotle, *Poetics* 1454a27–8: τέταρτον δὲ τὸ ὁμαλόν. κἂν γὰρ ἀνώμαλός τις ᾖ ὁ τὴν μίμησιν παρέχων καὶ τοιοῦτον ἦθος ὑποτεθῇ, ὅμως ὁμαλῶς ἀνώμαλον δεῖ εἶναι. For an overview of the question of "personal identity," together with the main bibliography, see Heller, Sosna, and Wellbery (1987); Olson (2021).

14 Here the fundamental discussion remains Kant 1781/1787: A19–49/ B33–73. The most significant post-Kantian interventions dealing with the spatio-temporal continuity of the subject are, with regard to the present context, Freud (1919, 1920, 1923); Bergson (1968); Lacan (1945); Lefebvre (2000).

15 Helpful in this context, are Bresciani (1958a–b, 2012); Assmann (1999); Lurson (2016); Bredow (2017); Budka (2019); Sabbahy (2021). For ties between the Greek and Egyptian worlds in the fourth century BCE, see Pasek (2022).

16 For a succinct overview of Alexander's (self-)representation in Egypt, see Schäfer (2007).

17 For a useful overview of Alexander's strategies of pharaonic legitimation, see Pfeiffer (2014). On Egyptian royal legitimation more generally, see Otto (1969); Blöbaum (2006); Roth (2006); Levin and Müller (2017); Maderna-Sieben (2018).

18 See Freud ([1915] 1946), "Anhang C: Wort und Ding."

19 For a concise overview of Egyptian history in this period, see van de Mieroop (2021), 290–323.

20 See Selden (2020). Basic texts on autopoiesis include Maturana and Varela (1972); Luhmann (1984, 2002); Meadows (2008).

21 E.g., Freud (1916), 312. The textbook example here is the dream specimen that Freud calls "Der Traum von Irmas Injektion" (1900), 66–84, in fact a piece of self-analysis.

22 See Cabrol (2000).

23 Porten and Yardeni (1986–99); Porten (2011).

24 Wilkinson (2010), 369–70; Thompson (2012), 1–52; Colburn (2020), 27–94.

25 In the Old Kingdom, the city was known as *Ỉnb.w-ḥḏ* ("White [or: Gleaming] Walls"); documents from the First Intermediate Period refer to *Ḏd-s.wt* ("Everlasting of Places"); and Manetho calls Memphis *Ḥw.t-kꜣ-Ptḥ* ("Mansion of the *Ka* of Ptaḥ"). *Mn-nfr* first appears in the New Kingdom.

26 For the administration of the Egyptian state, see Moreno García (2013, 2020).

27 For *allos* as "alien," see LSJ s.v. II.

28 Josephus, *Jewish Antiquities* 11.8.4–6.

29 Herodotus 2.35.2. See further Froidefond (1971); Vasunia (2001); Moyer (2011).

30 While Egyptians from the First Dynasty on regularly staged ad hoc competitions in a variety of sports (running, wrestling, archery, boxing, stick fighting, swimming), all derivative of military combat and symbolically significant, they had no collective contests on the order of the Panhellenic games and well into the Roman period had difficulty rendering Greek agonistic texts into Egyptian (see Decker 1973). For a

summary account of Egyptian sports, see Kyle (2007), 28–37. For more detail, see Touny and Wenig (1969); Decker (1975, 1987, 2006, 2012); Decker and Herb (1994).

31 Stephens (2003), particularly pp. 238ff. For pictorial examples of this doubleness—the terms hybridity or syncretism are not so useful here—see Venit (2015). On duality as "a mental structuring device [that] the Egyptians lived by, expressing, implicitly or explicitly, a vision of the world and its functioning," see Servajean (2008).

32 On Egyptian animal cults in general and bull cults in particular, see Otto (1938); Vercoutter (1975); Goe (1986); Kessler (1989); Dodson (2005); Fitzenreiter (2013); Colonna (2021). For a concise overview of the Apis cult in the Late Period, see Kater-Sibbes and Vermaseren (1975); Colburn (2020), 74–81; Thompson (2021), 177–96; Marković (2021).

33 Herodotus 3.27–9. For an overview of the Persian occupation of Egypt drawn from the extant hieroglyphic, Demotic, and Greek documents, see Posener (1936); Klasens (1945–8); Bresciani (1958a–b, 2012); Bianchi (1982); Ray (1988); J. H. Johnson (1994); Ruzicka (2012); Wasmuth (2017). On the historiographical problems raised by Herodotos' account, see von Hoffmann and Vorbichler (1980); Gammie (1986); Depuydt (1995).

34 See, for example, *Herodotus: The Madness of Cambyses* (2015).

35 For the historiographical and literary generic details, see Cruz-Uribe (2003); Dillery (2005); Griffin (2006); Konstantakos (2016). Elsewhere I have argued that the Kambysēs episode is programmatic for Hērodotus' *Inquiry* as a whole: Selden (1999).

36 White (1999), 9. White goes on to point out: "stories are not lived; there is no such thing as a real story."

37 The fundamental studies include: Austin (1975); Searle (1970, 1985); Searle and Vanderveken (1985). For Derrida's critique of Searle, see Derrida (1988) and Moati (2009). For speech acts in literature, see Miller (2001) and Felman (2002).

38 See Austin (1975), 1–11.

39 See Felman (2002), 50–4. Cf. Lacan (1966), 892, where he refers to: *la loi par quoi l'énonciation ne se réduira jamais à l'énoncé d'aucun discours.*

40 For a solid overview of the Achaemenid occupation of Egypt, see Colburn (2015, 2020). The standard history, still useful but dated, is Kientiz (1953). On anti-Persian sentiment in post-Achaemenid Egypt, see Devauchelle (1995).

41 On Alexander's "normative inversion" of the literature on Kambysēs' treatment of the Apis bull, see Pfeiffer (2014), 94–6.

42 See Smelik and Hemelrijk (1984); Teeter (2002).

43 Among recent treatments, see Miller (1993), 225–488; Assmann (2003); Leopold and Jensen (2004).

44 Cf. Aristotle, *De generatione animalium* 732a25–733b16.

45 Lovejoy (1933).

46 For the connection between Apis and the king, see Kessler (1989); Aufrère (2020); Marković (2021).

47 Much has and continues to be written on the Narmer Palette. In this context, particularly useful are Ciałowicz (1991); Davis (1992).

48 See Toby (2000), 117. See also Jiménez Serrano (2004). On the depiction of Apis on the Palermo Stone, see Gómez Vázquez (2012).

49 Uphill (1965); Hornung and Staehelin (1974, 2006); Roth (2006).

50 See Jurman (2010).

51 Darnell (2010); Fukaya (2020).

52 See particularly Pfeiffer (2014).

53 Bittel and Hermann (1934), 37. On the "Northern Oasis," see A. Fakhry (1974); Bliss (2006).

54 Bosch-Puche (2013), 131.

55 See Uphill (1965–6); Valbelle (1990); Stadnikow (1995).

56 See Assmann (2001); Karenga (2004); Menu (2005); Ferguson (2016).

57 See Davis (1992); Bestock (2019).

58 For a complete inventory of the Egyptian names and titles attested for Alexander, see Bosch-Puche (2008, 2013, and 2014a–b). See also Bosch-Puche and Moje (2015).

59 *LÄ*, 3: 540–57. For discussion of the Great Name and its various components, see Gauthier (1907–17); von Beckerath (1999); Leprohon (2013). The following website not only lists all known Pharaonic titularies together with their historical variants, but contains a great deal of useful bibliography as well as a reference library: https://pharaoh.se.

60 Cf. Barta (1970); Spieser (2000, 2010); Lightbody (2020).

61 Sethe (1904), II 8, no. 5:2. Both von Beckerath (1999) and Leprohon (2013) predate the publications of Bosch-Puche. See also: https://pharaoh.se/pharaoh/Alexander-the-Great.

62 The misspellings (𓈖𓏏𓊖, 𓐍𓏤𓆳) are copied from the altar.

63 The oecumenical vision of world sovereignty here finds its closest analogue in the Alexander Romance, a multiform Afro-Eurasian network of related texts which, at least in part, originated in Egypt. For an overview, see Stoneman (2007–), 1:xvi–civ; Selden (2010, 2012).

64 See von Beckerath (1999), 220–31.

65 What we today call the "Persian Empire" had, in fact, no proper name. The royal administration simply referred to it as the "State" (*xšaça-*) or the "Regime" (*Herrschaft*). See Schmitt (2014), 285. For further discussion, see Kellens (2002).

66 On "anticipatory" elements in the royal titulary, see Leprohon (2010).

67 See Budka (2019); Cooper (2018); Mourad (2015); Ryholt (1997); Rössler-Köhler (1991); Loprieno (1988).

68 Cf. Wasmuth (2017), 221–70.

69 Q. Curtius Rufus, *Historiae* 4.7.5. Cf. *contra* Plutarch, *Alexander* 28.1: καθόλου δὲ πρὸς μὲν τοὺς βαρβάρους σοβαρὸς ἦν.

70 On pharaonic coronations, see Frankfort (1948), esp. 101–47; Gardiner (1953); Fairman (1958); Barta (1980); Munro (1984); Fehlig (1986); Morris (2010).

71 For the sources available to the Alexander historians writing under the Roman Empire, see Pearson (1960) along with Auberger (2001) and Badian (2012), 48–57. On the fidelity of the Alexander Historians to their sources, see Bosworth (1988, 2003). To the extent that Egypt was a province of the Roman Empire when most of the extant Alexander historians worked, it would certainly have been possible to have learned something of Egyptian political ideology.

72 Wimsatt (1954).

73 White (1978), 94. On the tropological construction of historical discourse in general, see White (1973), 281–486, (1978), 81–134, and (1999), 1–26.

74 Burke (1941). Cf. Bloom (1975), esp. 83–105, and (2004), esp. 1–12.

75 On the discursive dominant, see Jakobson (1981b).

76 White (2010), 165.

77 Ibid., 173.

78 For a different set of tropological abductions in Arrian's *Anabasis*, see Selden (2018a).

79 So White on the fiction of factual representation: "factual statements . . . are linguistic entities and belong to the order of discourse" (1999: 28).

80 Jakobson ([1956] 1971).

81 Cf. Saussure (1997), 171–84; Jakobson ([1956] 1971), 72–6.

82 On μεταφορά—Isocrates, *Evagoras* 9.6; Aristotle, *Poetics* 1457b6 and *Rhetoric* 1410b36. On μετωνυμία—[Plutarch], *De Homero* 2, 286; Quintilian 8.6.23. Cf. du Marsais (1730), s.vv.; Fontanier ([1830] 1977), s.vv.; Lausberg (1973), s.vv.

83 For a basic introduction to semantic domains, see Langacker (1987), 147–82; Croft (2003); Mendoza Ibáñez (2003).

84 Cf. White (1973), 51:

> In Metonymy, phenomena are implicitly apprehended as bearing relationships to one another in the modality of part-part relationships, on the basis of which one can effect a reduction of one of the parts to the status of an aspect or function of the other. To apprehend any given set of phenomena as existing in the modality of part-part relationships (not, as in Metaphor, object-object relationships) is to set thought the task of distinguishing between those parts which are representative of the whole and those which are simply aspects of it . . . By Metonymy, then, one can simultaneously distinguish between two phenomena and reduce one to the status of a manifestation of the other.

85 For the distinction, see *Rhetorica ad Herennium*, IV.xiii.18; Quintilian, *Institutio oratoria* IX.1.16. Recent work on metonymy in cognitive linguistics includes Lakoff and Johnson (1980); Lakoff (1987); Gibbs (1994); Fass (1997); Panther and Radden (1999); Dirven and Pörings (2003); Barcelona (2003); al-Sharafi (2004); Panther, Thornburg, and Barcelona (2009). All of these discussions devolve from Jakobson ([1956] 1971), and Lacan (1966), esp. "L'instance de la lettre dans l'inconscient, ou la raison depuis Freud" (493–530).

86 Jakobson ([1956] 1971), 90. Matzner (2016) makes interesting remarks on particular passages of poetry; however, there are (a) too many bibliographical gaps in his discussion of metonymy (Fontanier, Nietzsche, Lacan, Derrida, Sarah Kofman, White, Barbara Johnson, Spivak, Hillis Miller, Harold Bloom, Shoshana Felman, etc.) to actually mount any rigorous "rethinking" of metonymy, and (b) his discussion contains fundamental confusions regarding what it means to read a text rhetorically.

87 White (2010), 173.

88 Arrian, *Anabasis Alexandri* 3.1.3–4.

89 Cf. Jakobson (1981a).

90 On tagmemes, see Bloomfield (1933), 166–8; Cook (1969); Pike (1982).

91 For an overview of Hēliopolis, see Kákosy (1977). Recent discussions of the site include: Quirke (2011); Raue (2016–17); Nuzzolo and Krejčí (2017); Naether (2019); Bruwier and Doyen (2019); Ashmawy, Dietze, and Raue (2020).

92 Myśliwiec (1978–9); Bickel (1994); Allen (1995); Calmettes (2019).

93 For an extended discussion of the Edfu version of this cosmogony, which centers on Horus, see Reymond (1969); Finnestad (1985).

94 On the linguistics of metalanguage, see Jakobson (1960, 1985); Barthes ([1959] 2002); Jaworski, Coupland, and Galasinski (2004).

95 Arrian's text reads θύει "sacrifice," a term culturally inappropriate which provides a good example of Arrian's projection of Greek practices and norms onto Egyptian culture. Egyptian gods received "offerings" of bread, bear, and other food stuffs, but ritual slaughter, when it occurred at all, was peripheral to the rite itself. On the role of sacrifice in Egypt, see Quaebegeur (1993); Dodson (2009); Frankfurter (2011).

96 See Nietzsche (1872a).

97 Above p. 48.

98 Dirven (2003), 100–1.

99 Langacker (2009), 47. See also Jakobson (1981a).

100 Sapir (1921), 125.

101 Cf. Whorf (2012), 252, 257.

102 The indispensable gloss is Nietzsche (1872b). For a representative contemporary treatment, see Barker (2009).

103 On the United States doctrine of "separate but equal," see *Plessy v. Ferguson*, 163 U.S. 537 (1896); *Brown v. Board of Education of Topeka*, 347 U.S. 483 (1954).

104 See Seidl (1968); Theodorides (1974); Manning (2003); Lippert (2012, 2016); Keenan, Manning, and Yiftach-Firanko (2014); Yiftach (2015).

105 Mahaffy (1905), 73–5, italics added.

106 Goddio (1998); Goddio, et al. (2004, 2008); Bischoff and Gerigk (2016). More material is available online: https://www.franckgoddio.org.

107 De Staël (1814), part 2, chapter 1 *ad finem*: "La littérature, les arts, la philosophie, la religion des deux peuples [viz. les Français et les Allemands], attestent cette différence; et *l'éternelle barrière du Rhin* sépare deux régions intellectuelles qui, non moins que les deux contrées, sont étrangères l'une à l'autre" (italics added).

108 On neocolonialism, see Fanon (1961); Sartre (1964); Nkrumah (1965); Amin (1971); Constantino (1978); Coslett (2020). On the modern world-system, see Wallerstein (2011), vol. 4; Arrighi and Silver (1999); Grosfoguel and Cervantes-Rodríguez (2002); Babones and Chase-Dunn (2012).

109 Barthes ([1966] 2002).

110 Barthes ([1971] 1966), 835–6. For the narratological sense of "function," see Propp (1998), emphasis added. In a later publication ([1970] 2002), Barthes proposes the term *lexie* ("lexia") to designate a unit not of narrative, but of reading; see ([1970] 2002), 129–30.

111 Hjelmslev ([1943] 1993), 44–55 = Hjelmslev (1968–71), 65–79. In most respects, the French translation is superior to the English of Hjelmslev (1969).

112 Barthes ([1966] 2002): 837.

113 Greimas (1966), 5.

114 Ibid.

115 On charisma, see Weber (1922), 753–817, and (1968). On symbolic capital, see Bourdieu (1972, 2001). For rituals enhancing pharaonic charisma, see Kemp (1976); Koska (2019).

116 See Agut-Labordère (2017).

117 Althusser (2011). Althusser employs these terms to describe a completely different historical and economic situation, but the distinction that he makes here between repressive and ideological fits other historical contexts as well, where they inevitably appear in very different forms. Good introductions to Egyptian culture of the Late Period include: Goff (1979); Myśliwiec (2000); Jay (2006); Manassa (2007); Vandorpe (2019); Klotz (2019).

118 See Saussure (1997), 150–69.

119 See OED, s.v. term.

120 Hjelmslev ([1943] 1993), 26–7 = Hjelmslev (1968–71), 43–4.

121 For a recent example, see Anson (2021).

122 See Fakhry (1973).

123 See Caneva (2012).

124 Plutarch, *Alexander* 27.8–11.

125 See Assmann (1982); Brunner (1986); Rikala (2003).

126 See Hornung (1997).

127 On the principal of *sublation / Aufhebung*, see Hegel (1986), § 96, Zusatz; Erdmann
   (1843), § 33.

128 On the name, see Cheveau (1999).

129 See Véron et al. (2006); Stanley et al. (2007).

130 Wilkinson (1999), 192–7; cf. Selden (1998), 393–5.

131 See Selden (1998), 394–405. More recent discussions include: Bács and Beinlich
   (2017); Budka (2019); Sabbahy (2021); Troche (2021), chapter 3.

132 See above, pp. 51–2.

133 So Justin 11.11: Reuersus ab Hammone Alexandream condidit et coloniam
   Macedonum caput esse Aegypti iubet.

134 See above p. 56.

135 Hornung (1999), 35. Cf. Eliade (1947).

136 Cf. Selden (2018b).

137 On the concept of *Ma 'at*, see n. 54. In the words of Kandake as represented in one
   of the Armenian Alexander Romances: "Alexander, [you have] maintained [your]
   power by doing kindness to your friends … For not by war alone have you subdued
   the world and its people, but by great wisdom" (Wolohojian 1969: 81 and 139). See
   also Badian (2012), 1–19; Selden (2011).

138 See Stephens (2003), esp. 1–73 and 238–57. Standard overviews of the subject are
   Helck (1995); Vittmann (2003). On Naukratis, in particular, see Möller (2000);
   James (2003); Bresson (2005); Villany and Schlotzhauer (2006). On Hērakleion,
   Robinson and Goddio (2015); for the Egyptian names and their orthography,
   see Gauthier (1925–31), vol. 4, 32; von Bomhard (2012), 77–8, 88–9. Eg. *hōne* >
   Sahid. ⲍⲱⲛⲉ "estuary, or marshland."

139 For the centrality of Karnak and the cult of Amun, see Blyth (2006); Gabolde
   (2018); Becker, Blöbaum, and Lohwasser (2020).

140 See Selden (1994).

141 See Selden (2018b).

142 Du Marsais (1730), 143, provides the classic definition of σύλληψις: a trope "in
   which the same word is taken in two different senses within the same clause"; cf.
   Fontanier ([1830] 1977), 105; Riffaterre (1980).

143 Arrian, *Anabasis* 3.4.5.

144 For Greek oracular divination, see Parke (1967); Eidinow (2007); Stoneman (2011).
   On Egyptian oracular procedures, see Schenke (1960); von Lieven (1999, 2016);
   Dunand (2022).

145 De Man (1983), 207; cf. Deleuze (1968).

146 See Finnestad (1985); Allen (1995); Selden (2020).

147 Hjelmslev ([1943] 1993), 44–55 = Hjelmslev (1968–71), 65–706. For an overview of Jameson's recourse to "the content of the form," see Eagleton (2009). Of Jameson's numerous works that deal with the issue, I would single out Jameson (1971, 1981, 1992, 1999), and (2007), xiii–xix. White (1973, 1990) are obvious points of departure.

148 Hjelmslev ([1943] 1993), 44–55 = (1968–71), 65–79. Cf. Eco (1971); White (1990).

149 See Jakobson (1981a).

150 Johnson (1980), 68.

151 See Shklovskiï (1929).

152 Teffeteller (n.d.).

153 So, famously, Nietzsche (1872b):

> Was ist also Wahrheit? Ein bewegliches Heer von Metaphern, Metonymien, Anthropomorphismen kurz eine Summe von menschlichen Relationen, die poetisch und rhetorisch gesteigert, übertragen, geschmückt wurden, und die nach langem Gebrauche einem Volke fest, canonisch und verbindlich dünken: die Wahrheiten sind Illusionen, von denen man vergessen hat, dass sie welche sind, Metaphern, die abgenutzt und sinnlich kraftlos geworden sind, Münzen, die ihr Bild verloren haben und nun als Metall, nicht mehr als Münzen in Betracht kommen.
>
> Cf. de Man (1979a): 103–18.

154 So Quintilian, *Institutio oratoria* 9.1.4: "est igitur tropos sermo a naturali et principali significatione translatus ad aliam ornandae orationis gratia, vel, ut plerique grammatici finiunt, *dictio ab eo loco, in quo propria est, translata in eum, in quo propria non est*; figura, sicut nomine ipso patet, conformatio quaedam orationis remota a communi et primum se offerente ratione." See, however, Nietzsche's seminar, "Darstellung der antiken Rhetorik" ([1872–3] 1989: 20–4), which claims that all language is rhetorical by nature, thereby sublating the opposition between "literal" and "figurative":

> Es ist aber nicht schwer zu beweisen, daß was man, als Mittel unbewußter Kunst in der Sprache u. deren Werden thätig waren, ja daß die Rhetorik eine Fortbildung der in der Sprache gelegenen Kunstmittel ist am hellen Lichte des Verstandes. Es giebt keine unrhetorische „Natürlichkeit" der Sprache, an die man appelliren könnte: die Sprache selbst ist das Resultat von lauter rhetorischen Künsten ... Alle Wörter aber sind an sich u. von Anfang <an>, in Bezug auf ihre Bedeutung Tropen ... Eigentlich ist alles Figuration, was man gewöhnliche Rede nennt.
>
> KGA II, 4: 425-6

155 It is not clear what χωρίον means in this context. The domains at issue here may well correspond to an official Egyptian administrative district ($\overline{\underline{\text{⊟}}}$ ı *sp3.t*), which Greek writers from Herodotus [2.4] on called νομός.

156　See Gide (1948), 41.

157　Cf. Grant (1969); Norwich (2007); Abulafia (2011); Broodbank (2013).

158　See Plutarch, *Life of Alexander* 45.1: ἐντεῦθεν εἰς τήν Παρθικὴν ἀναζεύξας καὶ σχολάζων πρῶτον ἐνεδύσατο τήν βαρβαρικὴν στολήν.

159　See Bowden (2013); Matarese (2013); Mullen (2018).

160　Q. Curtius, *Historiae* 6.6.3–9.

161　Cf. Jakobson (1960); White (1999).

162　On the ethnonym "Ariyan," see Schmitt (2014), s.v.

163　Selden (1999).

164　Dällenbach (1977), 62.

165　Barthes (1970), 122.

166　Cf. Aristotle, *Poetics* 1450b: ὅλον δέ ἐστιν τὸ ἔχον ἀρχὴν καὶ μέσον καὶ τελευτήν. For the semantics of ὅλον, see LSJ s.v. Indispensable here is Derrida (1972b), 247–324 ("La mythologie blanche"); de Man (1979a), 3–19 ("Semiology and Rhetoric").

167　Cf. Barthes ([1970] 2002), 122–3.

168　See Riggs (2012); Bagnall (2021).

169　Lacan (1975), 272 (condensed):

> Nous trouvons là manifesté ce principe fondamental de la sémantique, qui est que tout sémantème renvoie à l'ensemble du système sémantique, à la polyvalence de ses emplois. Aussi bien, pour tout ce qui est proprement du langage, en tant qu'il est humain, c'est-à-dire utilisable dans la parole, il n'y a jamais univocité du symbole. Tout sémantème est toujours à plusieurs sens.

170　See Savan (1988); Lizka (1996); Short (2007); Atkin (2015), 124–63, and (2022), §2.2.

171　See Peirce's 1867 paper, "On a New List of Categories," in Peirce (1992–8), vol. 1, 101.

172　De Man (1979a), 8–9. For an account of "infinite semiosis" as it fits into Peirce's philosophical development, see Atkin (2022).

173　Atkin (2015), 135.

174　Lacan (1975) 288.

175　Ibid., 80.

176　As one among many such formulations in the first *Kritik*, see Kant (1781), 190:

> Denn wir haben es doch nur mit unseren Vorstellungen zu tun; wie Dinge an sich selbst (ohne Rücksicht auf Vorstellungen, dadurch sie uns affizieren,) sein mögen, ist gänzlich außer unserer Erkenntnissphäre. Ob nun gleich die Erscheinungen nicht Dinge an sich selbst, und gleichwohl doch das Einzige sind, was uns zur Erkenntnis gegeben werden kann, so soll ich anzeigen, was dem Mannigfaltigen an den Erscheinungen selbst für eine Verbindung in der Zeit zukomme, indessen daß die Vorstellung desselben in der Apprehension

jederzeit sukzessiv ist. So ist z.E. die Apprehension des Mannigfaltigen in der Erscheinung eines Hauses, das vor mir steht, sukzessiv. Nun ist die Frage: ob das Mannigfaltige dieses Hauses selbst auch in sich sukzessiv sei, welches freilich niemand zugeben wird. Nun ist aber, sobald ich meine Begriffe von einem Gegenstande bis zur transzendentalen Bedeutung steigere, das Haus gar kein Ding an sich selbst, sondern nur eine Erscheinung, d.i. Vorstellung, deren transzendentaler Gegenstand unbekannt ist; was verstehen ich also unter der Frage: wie das Mannigfaltige in der Erscheinung selbst (die doch nichts an sich selbst ist) verbunden sein möge? Hier wird das, was in der sukzessiven Apprehension liegt, als Vorstellung, die Erscheinung aber, die mir gegeben ist, ohnerachtet sie nichts weiter als ein Inbegriff dieser Vorstellungen ist, als der Gegenstand derselben betrachtet, mit welchem mein Begriff, den ich aus den Vorstellungen der Apprehension ziehe, zusammenstimmen soll. Man sieht bald, daß, weil Übereinstimmung der Erkenntnis mit dem Objekt Wahrheit ist, hier nur nach den formalen Bedingungen der empirischen Wahrheit gefragt werden kann, und Erscheinung, im Gegenverhältnis mit den Vorstellungen der Apprehension, nur dadurch als das davon unterschiedene Objekt derselben könne vorgestellt werden, wenn sie unter einer Regel steht, welche sie von jeder anderen Apprehension unterscheidet, und eine Art der Verbindung des Mannigfaltigen notwendig macht. Dasjenige an der Erscheinung, was die Bedingung dieser notwendigen Regel der Apprehension enthält, ist das Objekt.

177 See Cooke (2007).

178 Fabbrichesi (2018b), 180. Cf. ibid. (2018a), 1–2:

Since 2010 the philosophical arena has seen the rise of a new battle—maybe, the most ancient battle that philosophy has fought. It is the problem of the status of reality. More precisely, the aim of this battle has been to defend the Existence of Reality against those who have argued that "reality" is only a mode of speech and interpretation. As is known, many important philosophers, both Italian and foreign, have taken part in this battle, and obviously agreements, negotiations, or even unbridgeable differences have emerged. It is also known that it is Maurizio Ferraris who started the debate (first and foremost against himself, namely, against the interpreter of Nietzsche deeply rooted in the hermeneutic and Vattimian faith), with various volumes and articles, and then with the pugnacious *Manifesto of New Realism*. My intention [here] . . . is to enter this debate in order to raise a different sort of question, not whether reality exists or doesn't exist—a strongly commonsensical and therefore not deeply philosophical position— but what we do, what we want to obtain, when we use terms such as "real," "objective," "given." In pragmatist fashion, I would like to ask the same question that Peirce asked 150 years ago: what effects does our belief in reality produce? As Peirce wrote, when we deem something "real," we mean that that something can cause a certain belief capable of producing relevant practical effects. Real things lead me to do certain actions and not others. Thus, the problem of realism must be addressed accordingly: what are the conceivably practical habits and behaviors that the belief in the existence of reality produces? The problem is then to distinguish true beliefs (that is, those beliefs that remove doubt and allow me to act with confidence) from false beliefs (that is, purely fictional beliefs with no effective grasp on the world).

179　See Ranke (2010); White (1973), 163–90; Braw (2017); Ankersmit (2012); Boldt (2015); Krieger (1977); Iggers (1983); Iggers and Powel (1990); Maurer (2006).

180　Ranke (1824), 1:vi: "Man hat der Historie das Amt, die Vergangenheit zu richten, die Mitwelt zum Nutzen zukünftiger Jahre zu belehren, beigemessen. So hoher Ämter unterwindet sich gegenwärtiger Versuch nicht; er will bloß zeigen, *wie es eigentlich gewesen*," italics added.

181　Cf. Nietzsche (1906), § 522: "Wir hören auf zu denken, wenn wir es nicht in dem sprachlichen Zwange thun wollen, wir langen gerade noch bei dem Zweifel an, hier eine Grenze als Grenze zu sehen."

182　De Man (1979a), 10: "Rhetoric radically suspends logic and opens up vertiginous possibilities of referential aberration."

183　White (2014), x.

184　Ibid., xi.

185　For Egyptian modes of rethinking and rewriting the past, see Hornung (1966); Manassa (2003, 2013); Gozzoli (2006); Lutz (2014).

186　Didion (1979), 11.

I have known Susan Stephens now for almost half a century. Over the years, she has played many different roles in my life and in my intellectual formation—teacher, mentor, colleague, friend. As an undergraduate at Yale in the mid-1970s, she first introduced me to Hellenistic poetry, though her stay on Yale's faculty in Classics was destined to be brief. We reconnected in the late 1980s when I moved West to join the Literature Department at the University of California, Santa Cruz, in part through our mutual friend John J. Winkler. Susan was instrumental in bringing me to Stanford and, although I ultimately returned to UCSC, we talked and met frequently, sometimes daily, over the course of the 1990s and early 2000s, sharing ideas about Hellenistic literature, particularly in its connection to Egyptian culture. Susan is an exacting and capacious scholar situated on the cutting edge of the profession, whose unflagging support for her students is, in my experience, virtually unparalleled. Were it not for Susan, I would not have gone on to do the kind of work in intercultural poetics that has sustained my career.

Bibliography

Abel, C. (1884), *Über den Gegensinn der Urworte*, Leipzig: Wilhelm Friedrich.

Abulafia, D. (2011), "Mediterranean History as Global History," *History and Theory*, 50: 220–8.

Agut, D. and J. Carlos Moreno-Garcia (2016), *L'Égypte des pharaons: De Narmer à Dioclétien*, Paris : Belin.

Agut-Labordère, D. (2017), "Administrating Egypt under the First Persian Period: The Empire as Visible in the Demotic Sources," in B. Jacobs (ed.), *Die Verwaltung im Achämenidenreich: imperiale Muster und Strukturen*, 677–97, Wiesbaden: Harrassowitz.

Ahi, V. and T. F. H. Allen (1996), *Hierarchy Theory*, New York: Columbia University Press.

al-Sharafi, A. G. M. (2004), *Textual Metonymy: A Semiotic Approach*, New York: Palgrave Macmillan.

Allen, J. P. (1995), *Genesis in Egypt: The Philosophy of Ancient Egyptian Creation Accounts*, 2nd ed., San Antonio, TX: Van Siclen Books.

Almond, I. (2004), *Sufism and Deconstruction: A Comparative Study of Derrida and Ibn 'Arabi*, New York: Routledge.

Alter, R. (2011), *The Art of Biblical Poetry*, 2nd ed., New York: Basic Books.

Althusser, L. (2011), "Idéologie et appareils idéologiques d'État (Notes pour une recherche)," in *Sur la réproduction*, 263–306, Paris: Presse universitaires de France.

Amin, S. (1971), *Neo-Colonialism*, New York: Monthly Review Press.

Anderson, A. R. (1932), *Alexander's Gate, Gog and Magog, and the Inclosed Nations*, Cambridge, MA: The Medieval Academy of America.

Andrej, M. (2020). "The Myth of the War of the Seven Against Thebes and Pausanias Educational Topography," *Hypothekai* 4: 171–206.

Ankersmit, F. R. (2012), *Meaning, Truth, and Reference in Historical Representation*, Ithaca, NY: Cornell University Press.

Anson, E. M. (2021), "Alexander's Foundation of Alexandria," *International Journal of Military History and Historiography*, 42 (2): 1–23.

Arrighi, G. and B. J. Silver (1999), *Chaos and Governance in the Modern World-System*, Minneapolis, MN: University of Minnesota Press.

Ashmawy, A., K. Dietze and D. Raue, eds. (2020), *Heliopolis: Kultzentrum unter Kairo*, Heidelberg: Propylaeum.

Assmann, J. (1982), "Die Zeugung des Sohnes: Bild, Spiel, Erzählung und das Problem des ägyptischen Mythos," in J. Assmann, W. Burkert and F. Stolz (eds.), *Funktionen und Leistungen des Mythos: Drei altorientalische Beispiele*, 13–61, Fribourg: Vandenhoeck & Ruprecht.

Assmann, J. (1999), *Ägypten: Eine Sinngeschichte*, 5th ed., Berlin: S. Fischer Verlag.

Assmann, J. (2001), *Ma'at: Gerechtigkeit und Unsterblichkeit im alten Ägypten*, 2nd ed., Munich: Beck.

Assmann, J. (2003), *Die Mosaische Unterscheidung: oder der Preis des Monotheismus*, 2nd ed., Munich: Carl Hanser.

Atkin, A. (2015), *Peirce*, London: Routledge.

Atkin, A. (2022), "Peirce's Theory of Signs," in E. N. Zalta and U. Nodelman (eds.), *The Stanford Encyclopedia of Philosophy* (Fall 2022 Edition), Stanford, CA: Metaphysics Research Lab, Stanford University. Available online: https://plato.stanford.edu/archives/fall2022/entries/peirce-semiotics/ (accessed May 5, 2023).

Auberger, J. (2001), *Historiens d'Alexandre*, Paris: Les Belles Lettres.

Aufrère, S. H., ed. (2020), *Les taureaux de l'Égypte ancienne*, Nîmes: Association égyptologique du Gard.

Austin, J. L. (1975), *How to Do Things with Words*, 2nd ed., ed. J. O. Urmson and Marina Sbisà, Cambridge, MA: Harvard University Press.

Babones, S. J. and C. Chase-Dunn (2012), *Routledge Handbook of World-Systems Analysis*, London: Routledge.

Bács, T. A., ed. (2002), *A Tribute to Excellence: Studies Offered in Honor of Ernő Gaál, Ulrich Luft, László Török*, Budapest: Eötvös Loránd Tudományegyetem.

Bács, T. A. and H. Beinlich, eds. (2017), *Constructing Authority: Prestige, Reputation and the Perception of Power in Egyptian Kingship*, Wiesbaden: Harrassowitz.

Badian, E. (1985), "Alexander in Iran," in I. Gershevitch (ed.), *The Cambridge History of Iran, Volume 2: The Median and Achaemenian Periods*, 420–501, Cambridge: Cambridge University Press.

Badian, E. (2012), *Collected Papers on Alexander the Great*, Abingdon: Routledge.

Badir, S. (2018), *Hjelmslev*, Paris: Les Belles Lettres.

Bagnall, R., ed. (2021), *Roman Egypt: A History*, Cambridge: Cambridge University Press.

Bakhtin, M. (1963), *Problemy poètiki Dostoevskogo*, 2nd ed., Moscow: Sovetskij Pisatel'.

Bakhtin, M. (2017), *Slovo v Romane*, Sankt-Peterburg: Pal'mira.

Bal, M. (2017), *Narratology: Introduction to the Theory of Narrative*, Toronto: University of Toronto Press.

Barcelona, A., ed. (2003), *Metaphor and Metonymy at the Crossroads: A Cognitive Perspective*, Berlin: Mouton de Gruyter.

Bareš, L., F. Coppens, and K. Smolarikova, eds. (2010), *Egypt in Transition: Social and Religious Development of Egypt in the First Millennium* BCE, Prague: Czech Institute of Egyptology.

Barker, E. T. E. (2009), *Entering the Agon: Dissent and Authority in Homer, Historiography, and Tragedy*, Oxford: Oxford University Press.

Barta, W. (1970), "Der Königsring als Symbol zyklischer Wiederkehr," *Zeitschrift für Ägyptische Sprache und Altertumskunde*, 98: 5–16.

Barta, W. (1980), "Thronbesteigung und Krönungsfeier als unterschiedliche Zeugnisse königlicher Herrschaftsübernahmem," *Studien zur altägyptischen Kultur*, 8: 33–53.

Barthes, R. ([1957] 2002), *Mythologies, Œuvres completes*, vol. 1, 671–821, Paris: Seuil.

Barthes, R. ([1959] 2002), "Littérature et métalanguage," *Œuvres complètes*, vol. 2, 364–5, Paris: Seuil.

Barthes, R. ([1965] 2002), *Eléments de sémiologie, Œuvres complètes*, vol. 2, 631–702, Paris: Seuil.

Barthes, R. ([1966] 2002), "Introduction à l'analyse structurale des récits," *Œuvres complètes*, vol. 2, 828–65, Paris: Seuil.

Barthes, R. ([1967] 2002), *Système de la mode, Œuvres complètes*, vol. 3, 895–1251, Paris: Seuil.

Barthes, R. ([1970] 2002), *S/Z, Œuvres complètes*, vol. 3, 119–346, Paris: Seuil.

Barthes, R. ([1971] 2002), "Réflexions sur un manuel," *Œuvres complètes*, 3: 945–51, Paris: Seuil.

Barthes, R. (2002), *Œuvres complètes*, 5 vols, ed. E. Marty, 2nd ed., Paris: Seuil.

Bartholomae, C. (1904), *Altiranisches Wörterbuch*, Straßburg: K. J. Trübner.

Becker, M., A. I. Blöbaum, and A. Lohwasser, eds. (2020), *Inszenierung von Herrschaft und Macht im ägyptischen Tempel: Religion und Politik im Theben des frühen 1. Jahrtausends v. Chr.*, Münster: Zaphon.

Beekes, R. (2010), *Etymological Dictionary of Greek*, 2 vols, Leiden: Brill.

Bergson, H. (1968), *Durée et simultanéité*, 7th ed., Paris: Presses universitaires de France.

Bestock, L. (2019), *Violence and Power in Ancient Egypt: Image and Ideology before the New Kingdom*, London: Routledge.

Bianchi, R. S. (1982), "Perser in Ägypten," *LÄ*, IV: 943–51.

Bickel, S. (1994), *La cosmogonie égyptienne avant le Nouvel Empire*, Göttingen: Vandenhoeck & Ruprecht.

Bischoff, J. and C. Gerigk, eds. (2016), *Diving to the Pharaohs: Franck Goddio's Discoveries in Egypt*, Göttingen: Steidl.

Bittel, K. and A. Hermann (1934), "Grabungsbericht Hermopolis 1933," *Mitteilungen des Deutschen Instituts für Ägyptische Altertumskunde in Kairo*, 5: 11–44.

Bliss, F. (2006), *Die ägyptischen Oasen / Oasenleben, Vol. II: Die ägyptischen Oasen Bahriya und Farafra in Vergangenheit und Gegenwart*, Bonn: Politischer Arbeitskreis Schulen.

Blöbaum, A. I. (2006), *"Denn ich bin ein König, der die Maat liebt": Herrscherlegitimation im spätzeitlichen Ägypten: Eine vergleichende Untersuchung der Phraseologie in den offiziellen Königsinschriften vom Beginn der 25. Dynastie bis zum Ende der makedonischen Herrschaft*, Aachen: Shaker.

Bloom, H. (1975), *A Map of Misreading*, New York: Oxford University Press.

Bloom, H. (2004), *The Art of Reading Poetry*, New York: HarperCollins.

Bloomfield, L. (1933), *Language*, New York: Holt, Rinehart, and Winston.

Blyth, S. (2006), *Karnak: Evolution of a Temple*, London: Routledge.

Boardman, J., N. G. L. Hammond, D. M. Lewis, and M. Ostwald, eds. (1988), *The Cambridge Ancient History, Second Edition, Vol. IV. Persia, Greece and the Western Mediterranean c. 525 to 479 B.C.*, Cambridge: Cambridge University Press.

Boldt, A. D. (2015), *The Life and Work of the German Historian Leopold von Ranke (1795–1886): An Assessment of His Achievements*, Lewiston: Edwin Mellen Press.

Bonnet, C., A. Declercq, and I. Slobodzianek, eds. (2012), *Les représentations des dieux des autres*, Caltanissetta: Salvatore Sciascia.

Bosch-Puche, F. (2008), "L'autel' du temple d'Alexandre le Grand à Bahariya retrouvé," *Bulletin de l'Institut Français d'Archéologie Orientale du Caire*, 208: 29–44.

Bosch-Puche, F. (2013), "The Egyptian Royal Titulary of Alexander the Great, I: Horus, Two Ladies, Golden Horus, and Throne Names," *Journal of Egyptian Archaeology*, 99: 31–154.

Bosch-Puche, F. (2014a), "Alexander the Great's Egyptian Names in the Barque Shrine at Luxor Temple," in V. Grieb, K. Nawotka, and A. Wojciechowska (eds.), *Alexander the Great and Egypt: History, Art, Tradition*, 55–88, Wiesbaden: Harrassowitz.

Bosch-Puche, F. (2014b), "The Egyptian Royal Titulary of Alexander the Great, II: Personal Name, Empty Cartouches, Final Remarks, and Appendix," *Journal of Egyptian Archaeology*, 100: 89–109.

Bosch-Puche, F. and J. Moje (2015), "Alexander the Great's Name in Contemporary Demotic Sources," *Journal of Egyptian Archaeology*, 101: 340–8.

Bosworth, A. B. (1988), *From Arrian to Alexander: Studies in Historical Interpretation*, Oxford: Clarendon Press.

Bosworth, A. B. (2003), "Plus ça change . . . Ancient Historians and their Sources," *Classical Antiquity*, 22: 167–98.

Bourdieu, P. (1972), *Esquisse d'une théorie de la pratique*, Geneva: Droz.

Bourdieu, P. (2001), *Langage et pouvoir symbolique*, Paris: Fayard.

Bowden, H. (2013), "On Kissing and Making Up: Court Protocol and Historiography in Alexander the Great's 'Experiment with Proskynesis,'" *Bulletin of Classical Studies*, 56: 55–77.

Brady, F., J. Palmer, and M. Price, eds. (1973), *Literary Theory and Structure: Essays in Honor of William K. Wimsatt*, New Haven, CT: Yale University Press.

Braw, J. D. (2007), "Vision as Revision: Ranke and the Beginning of Modern History," *History and Theory*, 46: 45–60.

Bredow, I. von, (2017), *Kontaktzone Vorderer Orient und Ägypten: Orte, Situationen und Bedingungen für primäre griechisch-orientalische Kontakte vom 10. bis zum 6. Jahrhundert v. Chr.*, Stuttgart: Franz Steiner.

Bresciani, E. (1958a), "La satrapia d'Egitto," *Studi Classici e Orientali*, 7: 132–88.

Bresciani, E. (1958b), "The Persian Occupation of Egypt," in I. Gershevitch (ed.), *The Cambridge History of Iran, Volume 2: The Median and Achaemenian Periods*, 502–28, Cambridge: Cambridge University Press.

Bresciani, E. (2012), "EGYPT i. Persians in Egypt in the Achaemenid period," *Encyclopaedia Iranica*, VIII/3, 247–9. Available online: http://www.iranicaonline.org/articles/Egypt-I (accessed May 9, 2023).

Bresson, A. (2005), " Naucratis: De l'emporion à la cite," *Topoi*, 12/13: 133–55.

Briant, P. (2003), *Darius dans l'ombre d'Alexandre*, Paris: Fayard.

Bröckelmann, D. and A. Klug, eds. (2006), *In Pharaos Staat: Festschrift für Rolf Gundlach zum 75. Geburtstag*, Wiesbaden: Harrassowitz.

Broodbank, C. (2013), *The Making of the Middle Sea: A History of the Mediterranean from the Beginning to the Emergence of the Classical World*, Oxford: Oxford University Press.

Brose, M., P. Dills, F. Naether, L. Popko, and D. Raue, eds. (2019), *En détail—Philologe und Archäologie im Diskurs: Festschrift für Hans-Werner Fischer-Elfert*, vol. 2, Berlin: De Gruyter.

Brunner, H. (1986), *Die Geburt des Gottkönigs: Studien zur Überlieferung eines altägyptischen Mythos.* 2nd ed., Wiesbaden: Harrassowitz.

Brunner-Traut, E. (1961), "Pharao und Jesus als Söhne Gottes," *Antaios*, 2: 266–84.

Bruwier, M.-C. and F. Doyen, eds. (2019), *Héliopolis d'Égypte: la ville du soleil*, Bruxelles: Safran.

Bruwier, M.-C. and F. Doyen, eds. (2019), *Héliopolis—La ville du soleil*, Bruxelles: Fondation Boghossian.

Budka, J., ed. (2019), *Egyptian Royal Ideology and Kingship under Periods of Foreign Rulers: Case Studies from the First Millennium BC*, Wiesbaden: Harrassowitz.

Burkard, G (1995), "Literarische Tradition und historische Realität: die persische Eroberung Ägyptens am Beispiel Elephantine II: Indizien gegen eine Zerstörung der Tempel," *Zeitschrift für ägyptische Sprache und Altertumskunde*, 122: 31–7.

Burke, K. (1941), "Four Master Tropes," *Kenyon Review*, 3: 421–38.

Bury, J. B. (1890), *The Nemean Odes of Pindar*, London: Macmillan.

Cabrol, A. (2000), *Amenhotep III, le magnifique*, Monaco: du Rocher.

Calmettes, M.-A. (2019), "La religion d'Iounou: cosmogonie et monothéisme originel," in M.-C. Bruwier and F. Doyen (eds.), *Héliopolis—La ville du soleil*, 11–22, Bruxelles: Fondation Boghossian.

Caneva, S. G. (2012), "D'Hérodote à Alexandre: L'appropriation gréco-macédonienne d'Ammon de Siwa, entre pratique oraculaire et légitimation du pouvoir," in C. Bonnet, A. Declercq, and I. Slobodzianek (eds.), *Les représentations des dieux des autres*, 193–219, Caltanissetta: Salvatore Sciascia.

Carrithers, M., S. Collins, and S. Lukes, eds. (1985), *The Category of the Person: Anthropology, Philosophy, History*, Cambridge: Cambridge University Press.

Chantraine, P. (1979), *La Formation des noms en grec ancien*, reprint, Paris: Klincksieck.

Cheveau, M. (1999), "Alexandrie et Rhakôtis: Le point de vue des Égyptiens," in J. Leclant and R. Vian des Rives (eds.), *Alexandrie: Une mégapole cosmopolite*, 1–10, Paris: Académie des Inscriptions et Belles Lettres.

Ciałowicz, K. (1991), *Les palettes égyptiennes aux motifs zoomorphes et sans décoration: Études de l'art prédynastique.* Kraków: Uniwersytet Jagielloński.

Colburn, H. P. (2015), "Memories of the Second Persian Period in Egypt," in J. Silverman and C. Waerzeggers (eds.), *Political Memory in and after the Persian Period in Egypt*, 165–202, Atlanta, GA: SBL Press.

Colburn, H. P. (2020), *Archaeology of Empire in Achaemenid Egypt*, Edinburgh: Edinburgh University Press.

Collins, B. J., ed. (2002), *A History of the Animal World in the Ancient Near East*, Leiden: Brill.

Colonna, A. (2021), *Religious Practice and Cultural Construction of Animal Worship in Egypt from the Early Dynastic to the New Kingdom: Ritual Forms, Material Display, Historical Development*, Oxford: Archaeopress.

Cook, W. A. (1969), *Introduction to Tagmemic Analysis*, New York: Holt, Rinehart, and Winston.

Cooke, E. F. (2007), *Peirce's Pragmatic Theory of Inquiry: Fallibilism and Indeterminacy*, New York: Continuum.

Cooper, J. (2018), "Kushites Expressing 'Egyptian' Kingship: Nubian Dynasties in Hieroglyphic Texts and a Phantom Kushite King," *Ägypten und Levante*, 28: 143–67.

Coslett, D. E., ed. (2020), *Neocolonialism and Built Heritage: Echoes of Empire in Africa, Asia, and Europe*, London: Routledge.

Croft, W. (2003), "The Role of Domains in the Interpretation of Metaphors and Metonymies," in R. Dirven and R. Pörings (eds.), *Metaphor and Metonymy in Comparison and Contrast*, 161–205, Berlin: Mouton de Gruyter.

Cruz-Uribe, E. (2003), "The Invasion of Egypt by Cambyses," *Transeuphratène*, 25: 9–60.

Cupane, C. and B. Krönung, eds., (2016), *Fictional Storytelling in the Medieval Eastern Mediterranean and Beyond*. Leiden: Brill.

Dällenbach, L. (1977), *Le récit spéculaire: Essai sur la mise en abyme*, Paris: Seuil.

Darnell, J. C. (2010), "Opet Festival," in J. Dieleman and W. Wendrich (eds.), *UCLA Encyclopedia of Egyptology*, Los Angeles. Available online: https://escholarship.org/uc/item/4739r3fr (accessed May 9, 2023).

Davis, W. (1992), *Masking the Blow: The Scene of Representation in Late Prehistoric Egyptian Art*, Berkeley, CA: University of California Press.

de Man, P. (1979a), *Allegories of Reading: Figural Language in Rousseau, Nietzsche, Rilke, and Proust*, New Haven, CT: Yale University Press.

de Man, P. (1979b), "Autobiography as De-facement," *MLN*, 94: 919–30.

de Man, P. (1983), *Blindness and Insight: Essays in the Rhetoric of Contemporary Criticism*, 2nd ed., Minneapolis, MN: University of Minnesota Press.

de Man, P. (1986), "The Return to Philology," in *The Resistance to Theory*, 21–6, Minneapolis, MN: University of Minnesota Press.

de Man, P. (1990), "Roland Barthes and the Limits of Structuralism," *Yale French Studies*, 77: 177–90.

de Man, P. (1996), *Aesthetic Ideology*, ed. A. Warminski, Minneapolis, MN: University of Minnesota Press.

de Man, P. (1996), "The Epistemology of Metaphor," in A. Warminski (ed.), *Aesthetic Ideology*, 34–50, Minneapolis, MN: University of Minnesota Press.

de Staël, G. (1814), *De l'Allemagne*, Paris: F. A. Brockhaus.

Decker, W. (1973), "Bemerkungen zum Agon für Antinoos in Antinoupolis (Antinoeia)," *Kölner Beiträge zur Sportwissenschaft*, 2: 38–56.

Decker, W. (1975), *Quellentexte zu Sport und Körperkultur im alten Ägypten* (Sankt Augustin: Hans Richarz).

Decker, W. (1987/92), *Sport und Spiel im Alten Ägypten* (Munich: C. H. Beck) = *Sports and Games in Ancient Egypt*, trans. A. Guttmann (New Haven: Yale University Press, 1992).

Decker, W. (2006), *Pharao und Sport* (Mainz: P. von Zabern).

Decker, W. (2012), *Sport am Nil: Texte aus drei Jahrtausenden ägyptischer Geschichte*, Hildesheim: Arete.

Decker, W. and M. Herb (1994), *Bildatlas zum Sport im Alten Ägypten: Corpus der bildlichen Quellen zu Leibesübungen*, 2 vols, Leiden: Brill.

Deleuze, G. (1968), *Différence et répétition*, Paris: Presses universitaires de France.

Denniston, J. D. (1954), *The Greek Particles*, 2nd ed., Oxford: Clarendon Press.

Depuydt, L. (1995), "Murder in Memphis: The Story of Cambyses's Mortal Wounding of the Apis Bull (*ca.* 523 B.C.E.)," *Journal of Near Eastern Studies*, 54: 119–26.

Derrida, J. (1967), *De la grammatologie*, Paris: Minuit.

Derrida, J. (1972a), *La dissémination*, Paris: Seuil.

Derrida, J. (1972b), *Marges de la philosophie*, Paris: Minui.

Derrida, J. (1988), *Limited Inc*, Evanston, IL: Northwestern University Press.

Derrida, J. (1996), *Le Monolinguisme de l'autre—ou la prothèse de l'origine*, Paris: Galilee.

Derrida, J. (1997), *De l'hospitalité: Anne Dufourmantelle invite Jacques Derrida à répondre*, Paris: Calmann-Levy.

Derrida, J. (1999), *Donner la mort*, Paris: Galilée.

Devauchelle, D. (1995), "Le sentiment anti-perse chez les anciens Égyptiens," *Transeuphratès*, 9: 67–80.

di Branco, M. (2011), *Alessandro Magno: Eroe arabo nel medioevo*, Rome: Salerno.

Didion, J. (1979), *The White Album*, New York: Simon and Schuster.

Dillery, J. (2005), "Cambyses and the Egyptian Chaosbeschreibung Tradition," *Classical Quarterly*, 55 (2): 387–406.

Dirven, R. (2003), "Metonymy and Metaphor: Different Mental Strategies of Conceptualization," in R. Dirven and R. Pörings (eds.), *Metaphor and Metonymy in Comparison and Contrast*, 75–111, Berlin: Mouton de Gruyter.

Dirven, R. and R. Pörings, eds. (2003), *Metaphor and Metonymy in Comparison and Contrast*, Berlin: Mouton de Gruyter.

Dodson, A. (2005), "Bull Cults," in S. Ikram (ed.), *Divine Creatures: Animal Mummies in Ancient Egypt*, 72–105, Cairo: American University in Cairo Press.

Dodson, A. (2009), "Rituals Related to Animal Cults," in J. Dieleman and W. Wendrich (eds.), *UCLA Encyclopedia of Egyptology*, 1 (1), Los Angeles. Available online: https://escholarship.org/uc/item/6vk541n0.

Dominick, W. and J. Hall (2010), *A Companion to Roman Rhetoric*, Chichester: Blackwell Publishing.

Doufikar-Aerts, F. (2010), *Alexander Magnus Arabicus: A Survey of the Alexander Tradition through Seven Centuries: From Pseudo-Callisthenes to Ṣūrī*, Leiden: Peeters.

Droysen, J. G. (1875), *Grundriss der Historik*, Leipzig: Veit.

du Marsais, C. C. (1730), *Des tropes, ou, Des diferens sens dans lesquels on peut prendre un même mot dans une même langue*, Paris: J.-B. Brocas.

Dunand, F. (2022), *Selon l'ordre du dieu: pratiques oraculaires en Égypte ptolémaïque et romaine*, Paris: de Brocard.

Eagleton, T. (2009), "Jameson and Form," *New Left Review*, 59: 123–37.

Eco, U. (1971), *Le forme del contenuto*, Milan: Bompiani.

Eidinow, E. (2007), *Oracles, Curses, and Risk among the Ancient Greeks*, Oxford: Oxford University Press.

Eixenbaum, B. ([1918] 1986), "Как сделана 'Шинель' Гоголя," in О прозе. О поэзии: сборник статей, 45–64, Ленинград: Художественная литература.

el-Sharkawy, A. (1997), *Der Amun-Tempel von Karnak: die Funktion der grossen Säulenhalle*, Berlin: Köste.

Eliade, M. (1947), *Le mythe de l'éternel retour: Archétypes et répétition,* Paris: Gallimard.

Eliade, M. (1957), *Das Heilige und das Profane: Vom Wesen des Religiösen*, Hamburg: Rowohlt.

Erdmann, J. E. (1843), *Grundriss der Logik und Metaphysik*, 2nd ed., Halle: Lippert.

Encyclopedia Iranica (2012), "DARIUS v. Darius III," VI/1, 51–4. Available online: http://www.iranicaonline.org/articles/darius-v (accessed May 9, 2023).

Erikson, E. H. (1954), "The Dream Specimen of Psychoanalysis," *Journal of the American Psychoanalytic Association*, 2: 5–56.

Fabbrichesi, R. (2018a), "Semiotics and the Something: A Pragmatist Perspective on the Debate on Realism," *European Journal of Pragmatism and American Philosophy*, X-1. OpenEdition Journals. Doi.org/10.4000/ejpap.1151.

Fabbrichesi, R. (2018b), "The Continuity of the Infinite Semiosis and the Fallibilism of Inquiry in C.S. Peirce," in E. B. Ghizzi, L. F. N. de Souza Dantas, M. S. Madeira, M. E. Quilici Gonzalez, M. Broenz, and M. Aiubb (eds.), *Sementes de Pragmatismo na Contemporaneidade*, 179–88, Sao Paulo: FiloCzar.

Fairman, W. H. (1958), "The Kingship Rituals of Egypt," in S. Hooke (ed.), *Myth, Ritual, and Kingship: Essays on the Theory and Practice of Kingship in the Ancient Near East and in Israel*, 74–14, Oxford: Oxford University Press.

Fakhry, A. (1974), *The Oases of Egypt*, 2 vols, Cairo: American University in Cairo Press.

Fanon, F. (1961), *Les damnés de la terre*, Paris: Maspero.

Farrington, A. (2013), "The *Pythia* of Sicyon," *Nicephoros*, 26: 109–37.

Fass, D. (1997), *Processing Metonymy and Metaphor*, Greenwich, CT: Ablex Publishing.

Fehlig, A. (1986), "Königskrone und Horusauge," *Göttinger Miszellen*, 90: 11–25.

Felman, S. (2002), *The Scandal of the Speaking Body: Don Juan with J. L. Austin, or Seduction in Two Languages*, Stanford, CA: Stanford University Press.

Ferguson, R. J. (2016), "The Ancient Egyptian Concept of Maat: Reflections on Social Justice and Natural Order," *Centre for East-West Cultural & Economic Studies*, No. 15, Robina, Gold Coast: Bond University. http://epublications.bond.edu.au/cewces_papers/13 (accessed May 9, 2023).

Finnestad, R. B. (1985), *Image of the World and Symbol of the Creator: On the Cosmological and Iconological Values of the Temple of Edfu*, Wiesbaden: Harrassowitz.

Fitzenreiter, M., ed. (2013), *Tierkulte im pharaonischen Ägypten und im Kulturvergleich*, Munich: Wilhelm Fink.

Fontanier, P. ([1830] 1977), *Les figures du discours*, Paris: Flammarion.

Förster, F. and H. Riemer, eds. (2013), *Desert Road Archaeology in Ancient Egypt and Beyond*, Köln: Heinrich-Barth-Institut.

Frankfort, H. (1948), *Kingship and the Gods: A Study of Ancient Near Eastern Religion as the Integration of Society and Nature*, Chicago, IL: University of Chicago Press.

Frankfurter, D. (2011), "Egyptian Religion and the Problem of the Category 'Sacrifice,'" in J. W. Kunst and Z. Várhelyi (eds.), *Ancient Mediterranean Sacrifice*, 75–93, Oxford: Oxford University Press.

Fraser, P. M. (1972), *Ptolemaic Alexandria*, 3 vols, Oxford: Clarendon Press.

Fraser, P. M. (1996), *Cities of Alexander the Great*, Oxford: Clarendon Press.

Freud, S. (1900), *Die Traumdeutung*, 1st ed., Leipzig and Vienna: Franz Deuticke.

Freud, S. (1910), "Über den Gegensinn der Urworte," *Jahrbuch für psychoanalytische und psychopathologische Forschungen*, 2: 179–84.

Freud, S. ([1915] 1946), "Das Unbewußte," in A. Freud (ed.), *Gesammelte Werke*, vol. 10, 264–303, London: Imago Publishing.

Freud, S. (1916), *Vorlesungen zur Einführung in die Psychoanalyse*, Leipzig and Vienna: Hugo Heller.

Freud, S. (1919), "Das Unheimliche," *Imago*, 5: 297–324.

Freud, S. (1920), *Jenseits des Lustprinzips*, Vienna: Internationaler Psychoanalytischer Verlag.

Freud, S. (1923), *Das Ich und das Es*, Vienna: Internationaler Psychoanalytischer Verlag.

Froidefond, C. (1971), *Le mirage égyptien dans la littérature grecque d'Homére à Aristote*, Gap: Ophrys.

Fukaya, M. (2020), *The Festivals of Opet, the Valley, and the New Year: Their Socio-Religious Functions*, Oxford: Archaeopress.

Gabolde, L., ed. (2018), *Karnak, Amon-Rê: la genèse d'un temple, la naissance d'un dieu*, Cairo: Institut français d'archéologie orientale.

Gammie, J. G. (1986), "Herodotus on Kings and Tyrants: Objective Historiography or Conventional Portraiture?," *Journal of Near Eastern Studies*, 45: 171–95.

Gardiner, A. (1920), "The Ancient Military Road between Egypt and Palestine," *Journal of Egyptian Archaeology*, 6: 9–116.

Gardiner, A. (1953), "The Coronation of King Ḥaremḥab," *Journal of Egyptian Archaeology*, 39: 13–31.

Gauthier, H. (1907–17), *Le livre des rois d'Egypte*, 5 vols, Paris: Imprimerie de l'Institut français d'archéologie orientale.

Gauthier, H. (1925–31), *Dictionnaire des noms géographiques contenus dans les textes hiéroglyphiques*, 7 vols, Cairo: Imprimerie de l'Institut Français d'Archéologie Orientale.

Gershevitch, I. ed. (1985), *The Cambridge History of Iran, Vol. II: The Median and Achaemenian Periods*, Cambridge: Cambridge University Press.

Gibbs, R. (1994), *The Poetics of Mind: Figurative Thought, Language and Understanding*, Cambridge: Cambridge University Press.

Gide, A. (1948), *Journal 1888–1939*, Paris: Gallimard [Pléiade].

Gilman, S. L., C. Blair, and D. J. Parent, eds. ([1872–3] 1989), *Friedrich Nietzsche on Rhetoric and Language*, Oxford: Oxford University Press, 1989.

Goddio, F. and A. Bernard (1998), *Alexandria: The Submerged Quarters*, London: Periplus.

Goddio, F. and A. Bernard (2004), *Sunken Egypt: Alexandria*, London: Periplus.

Goddio, F., D. Fabre, and C. Gerigk (2008), *Egypt's Sunken Treasures*, 2nd ed., Munich: Prestel.

Goe, H. (1986), "Tierkult," in *LÄ*, VI: 571–87.

Goff, B. (1979), *Symbols of Ancient Egypt in the Late Period*, Berlin: De Gruyter.

Gómez Vázquez, J. A. (2012), "A propósito de ciertas atribuciones al toro Apis en los anales de Palermo/Cairo," *Boletín de la Asociación Española de Egiptología*, 21: 27–38.

Gozzoli, R. (2006), *The Writing of History in Ancient Egypt During the First Millennium BC (ca.1070–180 BC): Trends and Perspectives*, London: Golden House.

Grant, M. (1969), *The Ancient Mediterranean*, London: Weidenfeld & Nicolson.

Greimas, A.-J. (1966), *Sémantique structurale: recherche de méthode*, Paris: Larousse.

Grieb, V., K. Nawotka, and A. Wojciechowska, eds. (2014), *Alexander the Great in Egypt: History, Art, Tradition*, Wiesbaden: Harrassowitz.

Griffin, J. (2006), "Herodotus and Tragedy," in C. Dewald and J. Marincola, *The Cambridge Companion to Herodotus*, 46–59, Cambridge: Cambridge University Press.

Griffin, K. (2018), *All the rḥyt-people Adore: The Role of the rḥyt-people in Egyptian Religion*, GHP Egyptology 29, London: Golden House Publications.

Grosfoguel, R. and A. M. Cervantes-Rodríguez, eds. (2002), *The Modern/Colonial/Capitalist World-System in the Twentieth Century: Global Processes, Antisystemic Movements, and the Geopolitics of Knowledge*, Westport, CT: Praeger.

Heckel, W. and L. A. Trittle, eds. (2011), *Alexander the Great: A New History*, London: J. Wiley & Sons.

Hegel, G. W. F. (1986), *Enzyklopädie der philosophischen Wissenschaften im Grundrisse 1830*, ed. E. Moldenhauer and K. M. Michel, 3 vols, Frankfurt a.M., Suhrkamp.

Helck, W. (1995), *Die Beziehungen Ägyptens und Vorderasiens zur Ägäis bis ins 7 Jahrhundert v. Chr.*, 2nd ed., Darmstadt: Wissenschaftliche Buchgesellschaft.

Heller, T. C., M. Sosna, and D. E. Wellbery, eds. (1987), *Reconstructing Individualism: Autonomy, Individuality, and the Self in Western Thought*, Stanford, CA: Stanford University Press.

Herodotus: The Madness of Cambyses, trans. T. Holland, New York: Penguin, 2015.

Hjelmslev, L. ([1943] 1993), *Omkring sprogteoriens grundlæggelse*, Copenhagen: C. A. Reitzel.

Hjelmslev, L. (1968–71), *Prolégomènes à une théorie du langage, suivi de la structure fondamentale du langage*, trans. U. Canger, Paris: Minuit.

Hjelmslev, L. (1969), *Prolegomena to a Theory of Language*, trans. F. J. Whitfield, Madison, WI: University of Wisconsin Press. The English translation is far inferior to the French one.

Hofmann, I. von and A. Vorbichler (1980), "Das Kambysesbild bei Herodot," *Archiv für Orientforschung*, 27: 86–105.

Hoffmeier, J. K. (2015), *Akhenaten and the Origins of Monotheism*, Oxford: Oxford University Press.

Hoffmeier, J. K. and S. O. Moshier (2013), "A Highway out of Egypt: The Main Road from Egypt to Canaan," in F. Förster and H. Riemer (eds.), *Desert Road Archaeology in Ancient Egypt and Beyond*, 485–510, Köln: Heinrich-Barth-Institut.

Hooke, S., ed. (1958), *Myth, Ritual, and Kingship: Essays on the Theory and Practice of Kingship in the Ancient Near East and in Israel*, Oxford: Oxford University Press.

Hornung, E. (1966), *Geschichte als Fest: Zwei Vorträge zum Geschichtsbild der früher Menschheit*, Darmstadt: Wissenschaftliche Buchgesellschaft.

Hornung, E. (1971), *Der Eine und die Vielen*, Darmstadt: Wissenschaftliche Buchgesellschaft.

Hornung, E. (1997), *Der ägyptische Mythos von der Himmelskuh: Eine Ätiologie des Unvollkommenen*, 3rd ed., Göttingen: Vandenhoeck & Ruprecht.

Hornung, E. (1999), *Geist der Pharaonenzeit*, 2nd ed., Zurich: Artemis & Winkler.

Hornung, E. (2005), *Echnaton: Die Religion des Lichts*, Ostfildern: Schwabenverlag.

Hornung, E. and E. Staehelin (1974), *Studien zum Sedfest*, Geneva: Éditions de Belles-Lettres.

Hornung, E. and E. Staehelin (2006), *Neue Studien zum Sedfest*, Basel: Schwabe.

Hussein, H. and E. Alim (2015), "The Way(s) of Horus in the Saite Period: Tell El-Kedwa and Its Key Location Guarding Egypt's Northeastern Frontier," *Journal of Ancient Egyptian Interconnections*, 7: 39–51.

Iggers, G. G. (1983), *The German Conception of History: The National Tradition of Historical Thought from Herder to the Present*, 2nd ed. (Middletown: Wesleyan University Press).

Iggers, G. and J. M. Powel, eds. (1990), *Leopold von Ranke and the Shaping of the Historical Discipline*, Syracuse, NY: Syracuse University Press.

Ikram, S., ed. (2005), *Divine Creatures: Animal Mummies in Ancient Egypt*, Cairo: American University in Cairo Press.

Jacobs, B. (1994), *Die Satrapienverwaltung im Perserreich zur Zeit Darius III*, Wiesbaden: L. Reichert.

Jacobs, B. (2011), "Achaemenid Satrapies", *Encyclopædia Iranica*, online edition, 2011. Available online: https://www.iranicaonline.org/articles/achaemenid-satrapies; accessed (May 11, 2003).

Jacobs, B. ed. (2017), *Die Verwaltung im Achämenidenreich: imperiale Muster und Strukturen*, Wiesbaden: Harrassowitz.

Jakobson, R. ([1956] 1971), "Two Aspects of Language and Two Types of Aphasic Disturbances," in M. Halle and R. Jakobson, *Fundamentals of Language*, 2nd rev. ed., 68–96, Berlin: Mouton de Gruyter.

Jakobson, R. *Selected Writings*, 9 vols, ed. Stephen Rudy, et al., The Hague: Mouton.

Jakobson, R. (1960), "Linguistics and Poetics," in *Selected Writings*, vol. 3, 18–51, The Hague: Mouton.

Jakobson, R. (1981a), "Poetry of Grammar and Grammar of Poetry," in *Selected Writings*, vol. 3, 87–97, The Hague: Mouton.

Jakobson, R. (1981b), "The Dominant," in *Selected Writings*, vol. 3, 752–6, The Hague: Mouton.

Jakobson, R. (1985), "Metalanguage as a Linguistic Problem," in *Selected Writings*, vol. 7, 113–21, The Hague: Mouton.

James, P. (2003), "Naukratis Revisited," *Hyperboreus: Studia Classica* 9: 235–64.

Jameson, F. (1971), *Marxism and Form: Twentieth-Century Dialectical Theories of Literature*, Princeton, NJ: Princeton University Press.

Jameson, F. (1972), *The Prison-House of Language: A Critical Account of Structuralism and Russian Formalism*, Princeton, NJ: Princeton University Press.

Jameson, F. (1981), *The Political Unconscious: Narrative as a Socially Symbolic Act*, Ithaca, NY: Cornell University Press.

Jameson, F. (1992), *Postmodernism or, The Cultural Logic of Late Capitalism*, Durham, NC: Duke University Press.

Jameson, F. (1999), *Brecht and Method*, London: Verso.

Jameson, F. (2007), *The Modernist Papers*, London: Verso.

Jansen-Winkeln, K. (2002), "Die Quellen zur Eroberung Ägyptens durch Kambyses," in T. A. Bács (ed.), *A Tribute to Excellence: Studies Offered in Honor of Ernő Gaál, Ulrich Luft, László Török*, 309–19, Budapest: Eötvös Loránd Tudományegyetem.

Jaworski, A., N. Coupland, and D. Galasinski, eds. (2004), *Metalanguage: Social and Ideological Perspectives*, Berlin: Mouton de Gruyter.

Jay, J. E. (2006), "Religious Literature of Late Period and Greco-Roman Egypt," *Religion Compass*, 1: 93–106.

Jiménez Serrano, A. (2004), *La Piedra de Palermo: traducción y contextualización histórica*, Madrid: Asociación Española de Egiptología.

Johnson, B. (1980), "Poetry and Syntax: What the Gypsy Knew," in *The Critical Difference: Essays in the Contemporary Rhetoric of Reading*, 67–75, Baltimore, MD: Johns Hopkins University Press.

Johnson, B. (1981), "Translator's Introduction," to J. Derrida, *Dissemination*, vii–xxxiii, Chicago, IL: University of Chicago Press.

Johnson, J. H. (1994), "The Persians and the Continuity of Egyptian Culture," in H. Sancisi-Weerdenburg, A. Kuhrt, and M. Cool Root (eds.), *Achaemenid History, Vol. VIII. Continuity and Change*, 149–59, Leiden: Brill.

Jurman, C. (2010), "Running with Apis: The Memphite Apis Cult as a Point of Reference for Social and Religious Practice in Late Period Elite Culture," in L. Bareš,

F. Coppens, and K. Smolarikova (eds.), *Egypt in Transition: Social and Religious Development of Egypt in the First Millennium* BCE, 224–67, Prague: Czech Institute of Egyptology.

Junge, F. ed. (1984), *Studien zu Sprache and Religion Ägyptens: zu Ehren von Wolfhar- Westendorf, überreicht von seinen Freunden und Schülern*, vol. 2, Göttingen: F. Junge.

Kafka, F. (2020), *Franz Kafka-Ausgabe: Historisch-Kritische Edition sämtlicher Handschriften, Drucke und Typoskripte*, ed. R. Reuß and P. Stängele, 10 vols, Göttingen: Wallstein Verlag.

Kákosy, L. (1977), "Heliopolis," *LÄ*, 2: 1111–13.

Kant, I. (1781/7), *Critik der reinen Vernunft*, Riga: Johann Friedrich Hartknoch.

Karenga, M. (2004), *Maat, The Moral Ideal in Ancient Egypt: A Study in Classical African Ethics*, New York: Routledge.

Kater–Sibbes, G. J. F. and M. J. Vermaseren (1975), *Apis*, 3 vols, Leiden: Brill.

Keenan, J. G., J. G. Manning, and U. Yiftach-Firanko (2014), *Law and Legal Practice in Egypt from Alexander to the Arab Conquest: A Selection of Papyrological Sources in Translation, with Introductions and Commentary*, Cambridge: Cambridge University Press.

Kemp, B. J. (1976), "The Window of Appearance at El-Amarna, and the Basic Structure of this City," *Journal of Egyptian Archaeology*, 62: 8–99.

Kemp, B. J. (2012), *The City of Akhenaten and Nefertiti: Amarna and Its People*, London: Thames & Hudson.

Kemp, B. J. (2018), *Ancient Egypt: Anatomy of a Civilization*, 3rd ed., London: Routledge.

Kessler, D. (1989), *Die heiligen Tiere und der König*, Wiesbaden: Harrassowitz.

Kientiz, F. K. (1953), *Die politisch Geschichte Ägyptens vom 7. bis zum 4. Jahrhundert vor der Zeitwende*, Berlin: Akademie-Verlag.

Klasens, A. (1945–8), "Cambyses en Egypte," *Ex Oriente Lux*, 10: 339–49.

Klotz, D. (2006), *Adoration of the Ram: Five Hymns to Amun-Re from Hibis Temple*, New Haven: Yale Egyptological Seminar.

Konstantakos, I. M. (2016), "Cambyses and the Sacred Bull (Hdt. 3.27–29 and 3.64): History and Legend," in V. Liotsakis and S. Farrington (eds.), *The Art of History: Literary Perspectives on Greek and Roman Historiography* Trends in Classics Suppl, vol. 41, 37–72, Berlin: De Gruyter.

Koska, M. M. (2019), "The Symbolism and Function of the Window of Appearance in the Armarna Period," *Folia Praehistorica Posnaniensa*, 24: 77–97.

Krieger, L. (1977), *Ranke: The Meaning of History*, Chicago, IL: University of Chicago Press.

Kügler, J. (1997), *Pharao und Christus? Religionsgeschichtliche Untersuchung zur Frage einer Verbindung zwischen altägyptischer Königsideologie und neutestamentlicher Christologie im Lukasevangelium.* Bodenheim: PHILO.

Kunst, J. W. and Z. Várhelyi, eds. (2011), *Ancient Mediterranean Sacrifice*, Oxford: Oxford University Press.

Kyle, D. G. (2007), *Sport and Spectacle in the Ancient World*, Malden, MA: Blackwell.

Lacan, J. (1945), "Le temps logique et l'assertion de certitude anticipée: un nouveau sophisme," *Cahiers d'Art*: 32–42.

Lacan, J. (1966), *Écrits*, Paris: Seuil.

Lacan, J. (1975), *Le Séminaire, Livre I: Les écrits techniques de Freud*, Paris: Seuil.

Ladynin, I. (2020), "Udjahorresnet and the Royal Name of Cambyses: The 'Derivative Sacrality' of Achaemenids in Egypt," *Journal of Ancient Egyptian Interconnections*, 26: 88–9.

Lakoff, G. (1987), *Women, Fire, and Dangerous Things: What Categories Reveal about the Mind*, Chicago, IL: University of Chicago Press.

Lakoff, G. and M. Johnson (1980), *Metaphors We Live By*, Chicago, IL: University of Chicago Press.

Langacker, R. W. (1987), *Foundations of Cognitive Grammar*, Stanford, CA: Stanford University Press.

Langacker, R. W. (2009), "Metonymic Grammar," in K.-U. Panther, L. L. Thornburg, and A. Barcelona (eds.), *Metonymy and Metaphor in Grammar*, 45–74, Amsterdam: John Benjamins Publishing.

Lausberg, H. (1973), *Handbuch der literarischen Rhetorik. Eine Grundlegung der Literaturwissenschaft*, 2nd ed., Munich: Max Hueber.

Leclant, J. (1968), "Les rites de purification dans le cérémonial pharaonique du couronnement," in *Proceedings of the XIth international Congress of the International Association for the History of Religions*, 3 vols, vol. 2, 48–51, Leiden: Brill.

Leclant, J. and R. Vian des Rives, eds. (1999), *Alexandrie: Une mégapole cosmopolite*, Paris: Académie des Inscriptions et Belles Lettres.

Lefebvre, L. (2000), *La production de la space*, 4th ed., Paris: Anthropos.

Leopold, A. M. and J. S. Jensen, eds. (2004), *Syncretism in Religion: A Reader*, London: Routledge.

Leprohon, R. J. (2010), "Patterns of Royal Name-Giving," in E. Frood and W. Wendrich (eds.), *UCLA Encyclopedia of Egyptology*, Los Angeles. Available online: https://escholarship.org/uc/item/51b2647c (accessed May 9, 2023).

Leprohon, R. J. (2013), *The Great Name: Ancient Egyptian Royal Titulary*, Atlanta, GA: Society of Biblical Literature.

Lévi-Strauss, C. (1958), *Anthropologie structurale*, Paris: Plon.

Levin, C. and R. Müller, eds. (2017), *Herrschaftslegitimation in vorderorientalischen Reichen der Eisenzeit*, Tübingen: Mohr Siebeck.

Lightbody, D. I. (2020), *On the Origins of the Cartouche and Encircling Symbolism in Old Kingdom Pyramids*, Oxford: Archaeopress.

Liotsakis, V. and S. Farrington, eds. (2016), *The Art of History: Literary Perspectives on Greek and Roman Historiography*, Trends in Classics Suppl., vol. 41, Berlin: De Gruyter.

Lippert, S. (2012), "Law: Definitions and Codification," in E. Frood and W. Wendriche (eds.), *UCLA Encyclopedia of Egyptology*, 1 (1), Los Angeles. Available online: https://escholarship.org/uc/item/0mr4h4fv (accessed May, 9 2023).

Lippert, S. (2016), "Egyptian Law, Saite to Roman Periods," *Oxford Handbook Topics in Classical*, available online at: https://academic.oup.com/edited-volume/43505; accessed 8 August 2023.

Littlemore, J. (2018), *Metonymy: Hidden Shortcuts in Language, Thought and Communication*, Cambridge: Cambridge University Press.

Lizka, J. (1996), *A General Introduction to the Semiotic of Charles Sanders Peirce*, Bloomington, IN: Indiana University Press.

Lloyd, A. B. ed. (2010), *A Companion to Ancient Egypt*, Oxford: Wiley Blackwell.

Loprieno, A. (1988), *Topos und Mimesis: zum Ausländer in der ägyptischen Literatur*, Wiesbaden: Harrassowitz.

Lovejoy, A. O. (1933), *The Great Chain of Being: A Study of the History of an Idea*, Cambridge, MA: Harvard University Press.

Luhmann, N. (1984), *Soziale Systeme: Grundriss einer allgemeinen Theorie*, Frankfurt a.M.: Suhrkamp.

Lurson, B. (2016), *A Perfect King: Aspects of Ancient Egyptian Royal Ideology of the New Kingdom*, Paris: Geuthner.

Lutz, L. (2014), "History-Writing in Ancient Egypt," in W. Grajetzki and W. Wendrich (eds.), *UCLA Encyclopedia of Egyptology*, 1 (1), Los Angeles. Available online: https://escholarship.org/uc/item/73v96940 (accessed May, 9 2023).

Lyotard, J.-F. (1979), *La Condition postmoderne: Rapport sur le savoir*, Paris: Minuit.

Maderna-Sieben, C. (2018), *Königseulogien der frühen Ramessidenzeit: politische Propaganda im Dienst der Legitimierung einer neuen Dynastie*, Heidelberg: Propylaeum.

Mahaffy, J. P. (1905), *The Progress of Hellenism in Alexander's Empire*, Chicago, IL: Chicago University Press.

Manassa, C. (2003), *The Great Karnak Inscription of Merneptah: Grand Strategy in the 13th Century BC*, New Haven, CT: Yale Egyptological Seminar.

Manassa, C. (2007), *The Late Egyptian Underworld: Sarcophagi and Related Texts from the Nectanebid Period*, Wiesbaden: Harrassowitz.

Manassa, C. (2013), *Imagining the Past: Historical Fiction in the New Kingdom*, Oxford: Oxford University Press.

Manning, J. G. (2003), "Egypt: Demotic Law," in R. Westbroo (ed.), *A History of Ancient Near Eastern Law*, vol. 2, 819–62, Leiden: Brill.

Maravelia, A. and N. Guilhou, eds. (2018), *Environment and Religion in Ancient and Coptic Egypt: Sensing the Cosmos through the Eyes of the Divine*, Oxford: Archaeopress.

Marincola, J., ed. (2008), *A Companion to Greek and Roman Historiography*, 2 vols, Chichester: Wiley-Blackwell.

Marković, N. (2021), "Apis is Ptah, Apis is Ra, Apis is Horus, Son of Isis: The Solar Aspects of the Divine Apis Bull and the Royal Ideology of the Late Period (664–332 BCE)," in M. Nuzzolo and J. Krejčí (eds.), *The Rise and Development of the Solar Cult and Architecture in Ancient Egypt*, 235–51, Wiesbaden: Harrassowitz.

Matarese, C. (2013), "Proskynesis and the Gesture of the Kiss at Alexander's Court: The Creation of a new Élite," *Palamedes*, 8: 75–86.

Maturana, H. and F. Varela (1972), *De máquinas y seres vivos: una teoría sobre la organización biológica*, Santiago: Universitaria.

Matzner, S. (2016), *Rethinking Metonymy: Literary Theory and Poetic Practice from Pindar to Jakobson*, Oxford: Oxford University Press.

Maurer, I. (2006), "The Rhetoric of Literary Realism in Leopold von Ranke's Historiography," *Clio*, 35: 309–28.

Meadows, D. H. (2008), *Thinking in Systems: A Primer*, White River Junction, VT: Chelsea Green Publishing.

Mendoza Ibáñez, F. J. R. (2003), "The Role of Mapping and Domains in Understanding Metonymy," in A. Barcelona (ed.), *Metaphor and Metonymy at the Crossroads: A Cognitive Perspective*, 109–32, Berlin: Mouton de Gruyter.

Menu, B. (2005), *Maât: L'ordre juste du monde*, Paris: Éditions Michalon.

Miller, F. (1993), *The Roman Near East: 31 BC–AD 337*, Cambridge, MA: Harvard University Press.

Miller, J. H. (2001), *Speech Acts in Literature*, Stanford, CA: Stanford University Press.

Moati, R. (2009), *Derrida/Searle: Déconstruction et langage ordinaire*, Paris: Presses universitaires de France.

Möller, A. (2000), *Naukratis: Trade in Archaic Greece*, Oxford: Oxford University Press.

Moore, K. R., ed. (2018), *Brill's Companion to the Reception of Alexander the Great*, Leiden: Brill.

Moreno García, J. C. (2020), *The State in Ancient Egypt: Power, Challenges and Dynamics*, London: Bloomsbury.

Moreno García, J. C., ed. (2013), *Ancient Egyptian Administration*, Leiden: Brill.

Morris, E. F. (2010), "The Pharaoh and Pharaonic Office," in A. B. Lloyd (ed.), *A Companion to Ancient Egypt*, 201–17, Oxford: Wiley Blackwell.

Moyer, I. (2011), *Egypt and the Limits of Hellenism*, Cambridge: Cambridge University Press.

Mourad, A.-T. (2015), *Rise of the Hyksos: Egypt and the Levant from the Middle Kingdom to the Early Second Intermediate Period*, Oxford: Archaeopress.

Mullen, J. (2018), "Beyond Persianization: The Adoption of Near Eastern Traditions by Alexander the Great," in K. R. Moore (ed.), *Brill's Companion to the Reception of Alexander the Great*, 233–53, Leiden: Brill.

Mulligan, K. and F. Correia (2021), "Facts," in E. N. Zalta (ed.), *The Stanford Encyclopedia of Philosophy* (Winter 2021 Edition), Stanford, CA: Metaphysics Research Lab, Stanford University. Available online: https://plato.stanford.edu/archives/win2021/entries/facts/ (accessed May 9, 2023).

Munro, Peter (1984), "Die Nacht vor der Thronbesteigung: zum ältesten Teil des Mundöffnungsritual," in F. Junge (ed.), *Studien zu Sprache and Religion Ägyptens: zu Ehren von Wolfhart Westendorf, überreicht von seinen Freunden and Schülern*, vol. 2, 907–28, Göttingen: F. Junge.

Myśliwiec, K. (1978–9), *Studien zum Gott Atum*, 2 vols, Hildesheim: Gerstenberg.

Myśliwiec, K. (2000), *The Twilight of Ancient Egypt: 1st Millennium B.C.*, trans. D. Lorton, Ithaca, NY: Cornell University Press.

Naether, S. (2019), "Heliopolis in Egyptian Literary Texts: Sacred Architecture and Cult Activities," in M. Brose, P. Dills, F. Naether, L. Popko, and D. Raue (eds.), *En détail— Philologie und Archäologie im Diskurs: Festschrift für Hans-Werner Fischer-Elfert*, vol. 2, 773–97, Berlin: De Gruyter.

Nagy, G. (1979), *The Best of the Achaeans: Concepts of the Hero in Archaic Greek Poetry*, Baltimore, MD: Johns Hopkins University Press.

Nagy, G. (1990a), *Greek Mythology and Poetics*, Ithaca, NY: Cornell University Press.

Nagy, G. (1990b), *Pindar's Homer: The Lyric Possession of An Epic Past*, Baltimore, MD: Johns Hopkins University Press.

Nagy, G. (2007), "Lyric and Greek Myth," in R. D. Woodward (ed.), *The Cambridge Companion to Greek Mythology*, 19–51, Cambridge: Cambridge University Press.

Nagy, G. (2015), *Masterpieces of Metonymy: From Ancient Greek Times to Now*, Washington, DC: Center for Hellenic Studies.

Nawotka, K. (2017), *The Alexander Romance by Ps.-Callisthenes*, Leiden: Brill.

Nawotka, K. and A. Wojciechowska, eds. (2016), *Alexander the Great in the East: History, Art, Tradition*, Wiesbaden: Harrassowitz.

Nietzsche, F. (1872a), "Homer's Wettkampf," in *Fünf Vorreden zu fünf ungeschriebenen Büchern*, dedicated to Cosima Wagner, posthumously published, Nietzsche Source, *Digital Critical Edition*. Available online: http://www.nietzschesource.org/?#eKGWB/ CV-CV5 (accessed May 9, 2023).

Nietzsche, F. (1872b), "Über Wahrheit und Lüge im außermoralischen Sinne," posthumously published, Nietzsche Source, *Digital Critical Edition*. Available online: http://www.nietzschesource.org/#eKGWB/WL (accessed May 9, 2023).

Nietzsche, F. ([1872–3] 1989), "Darstellung der antiken Rhetorik," in S. L. Gilman, C. Blair, and D. J. Parent (eds.), *Friedrich Nietzsche on Rhetoric and Language*, 2–206, Oxford: Oxford University Press.

Nietzsche, F. (1906), *Der Wille zur Macht, 1884/88: Versuch einer Umwerthung aller Werthe*, 2nd ed., Leipzig: Naumann.

Nkrumah, K. (1965), *Neo-Colonialism: The Last Stage of Imperialism*, London: Thomas Nelson & Sons.

Norwich, J. J. (2007), *The Middle Sea: A History of the Mediterranean*, New York: Vintage.

Nuzzolo, M. and J. Krejčí (2017), "Heliopolis and the Solar Cult in the Third Millennium B.C.," *Ägypten und Levante*, 27: 357–79.

Nuzzolo, M. and J. Krejčí, eds. (2021), *The Rise and Development of the Solar Cult and Architecture in Ancient Egypt*, Wiesbaden: Harrassowitz.

Olson, E. T. (2021), "Personal Identity," in E. N. Zalta (ed.), *The Stanford Encyclopedia of Philosophy* (Spring 2021 Edition), Stanford, CA: Metaphysics Research Lab, Stanford University. Available online: https://plato.stanford.edu/archives/spr2021/entries/ identity-personal/ (accessed May 9, 2023).

Otto, E. (1938), *Beiträge zur Geschichte der Stierkulte in Aegypten*, Leipzig: J. C. Hinrichs.

Otto, E. (1969), "Legitimation des Herrschens im pharaonischen Ägypten," *Saeculum*, 20: 385–411.

Panther, K.-W. and G. Radden, eds. (1999), *Metonymy in Language and Thought*, Amsterdam: John Benjamins Publishing.

Panther, K.-W., L. L. Thornburg, and A. Barcelona, eds. (2009), *Metaphor and Metonymy in Grammar*, Amsterdam: John Benjamins Publishing.

Parke, H. W. (1967), *Geek Oracles*, London: Hutchinson & Co.

Pasek, S. (2022), *Athen und Ägypten: die Beziehungen zwischen dem Nilland und Attika im 5. und 4. Jh. v. Chr.*, Berlin: Dr. Köster.

Pearson, L. (1960), *The Lost Histories of Alexander the Great*, New York: American Philological Association.

Pédech, P. (2011), *Historiens Compagnons d'Alexandre: Callisthène—Onésicrite—Néarch —Ptolémée—Aristobule*, 2nd ed., Paris: Les Belles Lettres.

Peirce, C. S. (1958), *The Collected Papers of Charles Sanders Peirce*, vols 7–8, ed. A. W. Burks, Cambridge, MA: Harvard University Press.

Peirce, C. S. (1992–8), *The Essential Peirce: Selected Philosophical Writings*, 2 vols, ed. N. Houser and C. Kloesel, Bloomington, IN: Indiana University Press.

Peltonen, J. (2019), *Alexander the Great in the Roman Empire, 150 BC to AD 600*, London: Routledge.

Petit, T. (1990), *Satrapes et satrapies dans l'empire achéménide de Cyrus le Grand à Xerxès Ier*, Paris: Les Belles Lettres.

Pfeiffer, S. (2014), "Alexander der Große in Ägypten: Überlegungen zur Frage seiner pharaonischen Legitimation," in A. Wojciechowska, V. Grieb, and Krzysztof Nawotka (eds.), *Alexander the Great in Egypt: History, Art, Tradition*, 89–106, Wiesbaden: Harrassowitz.

Pfeiffer, S., ed. (2007), *Ägypten unter fremden Herrschern zwischen persischer Satrapie und römischer Provinz*, Frankfurt a. M.: Verlag Antike.

Pike, K. (1982), *Linguistic Concepts: An Introduction to Tagmemics*, Lincoln, NE: University of Nebraska Press.

Porten, B. (2011), *The Elephantine Papyri in English: Three Millennia of Cross-Cultural Continuity and Change*, 2nd ed., Atlanta, GA: Society of Biblical Literature.

Porten, B. and A. Yardeni (1986–99), *Textbook of Aramaic Documents from Ancient Egypt*, 4 vols, Winona Lake, IN: Eisenbrauns.

Posener, G. (1936), *La première domination perse en Égypte. Recueil d'inscriptions hiéroglyphiques*, Cairo: Institut français d'archéologie orientale du Caire.

Propp, V. (1998), *Morfologiya skazki*, 3rd ed., Moscow: Labirint.

Proust, M. (1924), *À la recherche du temps perdu: Sodome et Gomorrhe*, Part I, Paris: Gallimard.

Quaebegeur, J., ed. (1993), *Ritual and Sacrifice in the Ancient Near East*, Leuven: Peeters.

Quirke, S. G. J. (2011), "On/Heliopolis/'Ain Shams: Where Light First Became Enlightenment," in *Alexandria and Other Centres of Thought in Ancient Egypt*, 10–11

December 2009, Bibliotheca Alexandrina, Proceedings, 7–19, Alexandria: Alexandria Center for Hellenistic Studies.

Ranke, L. von (1824), *Geschichten der romanischen und germanischen Völker von 1494 bis 1514*, 2 vols, Leipzig: Reimer.

Ranke, L. von (2010), *The Theory and Practice of History*, ed. G. G. Iggers, trans. W. A. Iggers, New York: Routledge.

Raue, D. (2016–17), "Religion et politique au cœur de l'ancienne Égypte: Le temple d'Héliopolis," *Annuaire, École Pratique des Hautes Études: Ve section—sciences religieuses*, 125: 93–108.

Ray, J. D. (1988), "Egypt 525–404 B.C.," in J. Boardman, N. G. L. Hammond, D. M. Lewis, and M. Ostwald (eds.), *The Cambridge Ancient History, Second Edition, Vol. IV: Persia, Greece and the Western Mediterranean c. 525 to 479 B.C.*, 254–86, Cambridge: Cambridge University Press.

Reymond, E. A. E. (1969), *The Mythical Origin of the Egyptian Temple*, New York: Barnes & Noble.

Riffaterre, M. (1980), "Syllepsis," *Critical Inquiry*, 6: 625–38.

Riggs, C., ed. (2012), *The Oxford Handbook of Roman Egypt*, Oxford: Oxford University Press.

Rikala, Mia (2003), "A Rebirth for the Pharaoh: Reflections on the Classification of the New Kingdom Divine Birth Cycle as a Ritual," *Scripta Instituti Donneriani Aboensis*, 18: 176–88.

Robinson, D. and F. Goddio, eds. (2015), *Thonis-Heracleion in Context*, Oxford: Oxford Centre for Maritime Archaeology.

Rössler-Köhler, U. (1991), *Individuelle Haltungen zum ägyptischen Königtum der Spätzeit: private Quellen und ihre Königswertung im Spannungsfeld zwischen Erwartung und Erfahrung*, Wiesbaden: Harrassowitz.

Roth, S. (2006), "Der Herrscher im Fest: zur rituellen Herrschaftslegitimation des ägyptischen Königs und ihrer Aussendarstellung im Rahmen von Festen," in D. Bröckelmann and A. Klug (eds.), *In Pharaos Staat: Festschrift für Rolf Gundlach zum 75. Geburtstag*, 205–49, Wiesbaden: Harrassowitz.

Ruzicka, S. (2012), *Trouble in the West: Egypt and the Persian Empire, 525–332 BCE*, Oxford: Oxford University Press.

Ryholt, K. S .B. (1997), *The Political Situation in Egypt during the Second Intermediate Period c. 1800–1550 BC*, Copenhagen: University of Copenhagen, Museum Tusculanum Press.

Sabbahy, L. K. (2021), *Kingship, Power, and Legitimacy in Ancient Egypt: From the Old Kingdom to the Middle Kingdom*, Cambridge: Cambridge University Press.

Sancisi-Weerdenburg, H., A. Kuhrt, and M. Cool Root, eds. (1994), *Achaemenid History, Vol. VIII: Continuity and Change*. Leiden: Brill.

Sapir, E. (1921), *Language*, London: Oxford University Press.

Sartre. J.-P. (1964), *Situations V: Colonialisme et néo-colonialisme*, Paris: Gallimard.

Saussure, F. de (1997), *Cours de linguistique générale*, ed. T. de Mauro, Paris: Payot & Rivages.

Saussure, F. de (2013), *Anagrammes homériques*, ed. P.-Y. Testenoire, Limoges: Lambert-Lucas.

Savan, D. (1988), *An Introduction to C. S. Peirce's Full System of Semiotic*, Toronto: Toronto Semiotic Circle.

Schäfer, D. (2007), "Alexander der Große: Pharao und Priester," in S. Pfeiffer (ed.), *Ägypten unter fremden Herrschern zwischen persischer Satrapie und römischer Provinz*, 54–74, Frankfurt a. M.: Verlag Antike.

Schenke, H.-M. (1960), *Die Orakel im Alten Ägypten*, Berlin: Humboldt-Universität.

Scherer, J. (1947), *L'Expression littéraire dans l'ouvre de Mallarmé*, Paris: Droz.

Schmitt, R. (1990), "The Name of Darius," *Acta Iranica*, 30: 194–9. See further, *Encyclopaedia Iranica* (2012), "DARIUS v. Darius III," VI/1, 51–4.

Schmitt, R. (2014), *Wörterbuch der altpersischen Königsinschriften*, Wiesbaden: Reichert.

Schmitt, R. and P. O. Skjærvø, eds. (1986), *Studia Grammatica Iranica*, Munich: Kitzinger.

Schneider, T. (1998), *Ausländer in Ägypten während des Mittleren Reiches und der Hyksoszeit. Teil 1: Die ausländischen Könige*, Wiesbaden: Harrassowitz.

Searle, J. (1970), *Speech Acts: An Essay in the Philosophy of Language*, Cambridge: Cambridge University Press.

Searle, J. (1985), *Expression and Meaning: Studies in the Theory of Speech Acts*, Cambridge: Cambridge University Press.

Searle, J. R. and D. Vanderveken (1985), *Foundations of Illocutionary Logic*, Cambridge: Cambridge University Press.

Sehshan, R., ed. (2020), *Indo-Hellenic Cultural Transactions*, Mumbai: K. R. Cama Oriental Institute.

Seidl, E. (1968), *Ägyptische Rechtsgeschichte der Saiten- und Perserzeit*, 2nd ed., Glückstadt: Augustin.

Selden, D. (1994), "Genre of Genre," in J. Tatum (ed.), *The Search for the Ancient Novel*, 39–64, Baltimore, MD: Johns Hopkins University Press.

Selden, D. (1998), "Alibis," *Classical Antiquity*, 17: 289–412.

Selden, D. (1999), "Cambyses' Madness, or the Reason of History," *Materiali e discussioni per l'analisi dei testi classici*, 33: 33–63.

Selden, D. (2006), "Vergil and the Satanic Cogito," *Literary Imagination*, 8: 1–45.

Selden, D. (2010), "Text Networks," *Ancient Narrative*, 8: 1–23.

Selden, D. (2011), "Guardians of Chaos," *Journal of Coptic Studies*, 13: 117–55.

Selden, D. (2012), "Mapping the Alexander Romance," in R. Stoneman, K. Erickson, and I. Netter (eds.), *The Alexander Romance in Persia and the East*, 19–60, Groningen: Barkuis.

Selden, D. (2018a), "Alexander in the Indies," in R. Stoneman, K. Erickson, and I. Netter (eds.), *The Alexander Romance: History and Literature*, 69–107, Groningen: Barkuis.

Selden, D. (2018b), "Inundation and Allegory," in A. Maravelia and N. Guilhou (eds.), *Environment and Religion in Ancient and Coptic Egypt: Sensing the Cosmos through the Eyes of the Divine*, 415–28, Oxford: Archaeopress.

Selden, D. (2020), "The Face of Poros," in R. Sehshan (ed.), *Indo-Hellenic Cultural Transactions*, 67–90, Mumbai: K. R. Cama Oriental Institute.

Servajean, F. (2008), "Duality," in J. Dieleman and W. Wendrich (eds.), *UCLA Encyclopedia of Egyptology*, Los Angeles, CA. Available online: http://digital2.library. ucla.edu/viewItem.do?ark=21198/zz0013x9jp (accessed May 7, 2023).

Sethe, K. (1904), *Hieroglyphische Urkunden der Griechisch-Römischen Zeit*, Leipzig: Hinrichs.

Shaw, G. J. (2012), *The Pharaoh: Life at Court and On Campaign*, London: Thames & Hudson.

Shklovskiĭ, V. (1919), "Iskusstvo kak priëm," in V. Shklovskiĭ (ed.), *Poetika: Sborniki po teorii poeticheskogo iazyka*, Petrograd: Gosudarstvennaĭa tipografiĭa.

Shklovskiĭ, V. (1929), *O teorii prozy*, 2nd ed., Moscow: Federatsiia.

Short, T. L. (2007), *Peirce's Theory of Signs*, Cambridge: Cambridge University Press.

Silverman, J. and C. Waerzeggers, eds. (2015), *Political Memory in and after the Persian Period in Egypt*, Atlanta, GA: SBL Press.

Smelik, K. A. D. and E. A. Hemelrijk (1984), "'Who Knows not What Monsters Demented Egypt Worships?': Opinions on Egyptian Animal Worship in Antiquity as Part of the Ancient Conception of Egypt," *Aufstieg und Niedergang der Römischen Welt*, II, 17 (4): 1853–2000.

Sojcher, J. (1969), "La métaphore généralisée," *Revue Internationale de Philosophie*, 23: 58–68.

Spencer, D. (2011), "Roman Alexanders: Epistemology and Identity," W. Heckel and L. A. Trittle (eds.), *Alexander the Great: A New History*, 251–74, London: J. Wiley & Sons.

Spieser, C. (2000), *Les noms du pharaon comme êtres autonomes au Nouvel Empire*, Göttingen: Vandenhoeck & Ruprecht.

Spieser, C. (2010), "Cartouche," in E. Frood and W. Wendrich (eds.), *UCLA Encyclopedia of Egyptology*, Los Angeles. Available online: https://escholarship.org/uc/ item/3g726122 (accessed May 9, 2023).

Stadnikow, S. (1995), "Gottkönig und außerägyptische Bereiche: universalistische Ausdrücke der Könige des Alten Reiches in Ägypten nach den Pyramidentexten," *Mitteilungen für Anthropologie und Religionsgeschichte*, 10: 143–62.

Stanley, J.-D., M. P. Bernasconi, and T. F. Jorstad (2008), "Pelusium, an Ancient Port Fortress on Egypt's Nile Delta Coast: Its Evolving Environmental Setting from Foundation to Demise," *Journal of Coastal Research*, 24 (2): 451–62.

Stanley, J.-D., R. W. Carlson, G. Va Beek, T. F. Jorstad, and E. A. Landau (2007), "Alexandria, Egypt, before Alexander the Great: A Multidisciplinary Approach Yelds Rich Discoveries," *GSA Today*, 17, (8): 4–10.

Stephens, S. (2003), *Seeing Double: Intercultural Poetics in Ptolemaic Alexandria*, Berkeley, CA: University of California Press.

Stephens, S. (2010), "Ptolemaic Alexandria," in J. J. Clauss and M. Cuypers, *A Companion to Hellenistic Literature*, Oxford: Wiley-Blackwell.

Stoneman, R. (2007), *Alexander the Great: A Life in Legend*, New Haven, CT: Yale University Press.

Stoneman, R. (2007–), *Il Romanzo di Alessandro*, 3 vols, ed. R. Stoneman, Milan: Mondadori.

Stoneman, R. (2011), *The Ancient Oracles: Making Gods Speak*, New Haven, CT: Yale University Press.

Stoneman, R. (2022), *A History of Alexander the Great in World Culture*, Cambridge: Cambridge University Press.

Stoneman, R., K. Erickson, and I. Netter, eds. (2012), *The Alexander Romance in Persia and the East*, Groningen: Barkuis.

Stoneman, R., K. Erickson, and I. Netter, eds. (2018), *The Alexander Romance: History and Literature*, Groningen: Barkuis.

Taietti, G. D. M. (2016), "Alexander the Great as a *Herodotean* King," in K. Nawotka and A. Wojciechowska (eds.), *Alexander the Great in the East: History, Art Tradition*, Wiesbaden: Harrassowitz.

Tatum, J., ed. (1994), *The Search for the Ancient Novel*, Baltimore, MD: Johns Hopkins University Press.

Teeter, E. (2002), "Animals in Egyptian Religion," in B. J. Collins (ed.), *A History of the Animal World in the Ancient Near East*, 335–60, Leiden: Brill.

Theodorides, A. (1974), *Le droit égyptien ancien*, Bruxelles: Institut des Hautes Études de Belgique.

Thompson, D. (2021), *Memphis Under the Ptolemies*, 2nd ed., Princeton, NJ: Princeton University Press.

Toby, A. H. (2000), *Royal Annals of Ancient Egypt: The Palermo Stone, and Its Associated Fragments*, New York: Kegan Paul International.

Todorov, T. (1971), *Poétique de la prose*, Paris: Seuil.

Touny, A. D. and S. Wenig (1969), *Der Sport im alten Ägypten*, Lausanne: International Olympic Editions.

Troche, J. (2021), *Death, Power, and Apotheosis in Ancient Egypt: The Old and Middle Kingdoms*, Ithaca, NY: Cornell University Press.

Uphill, E. (1965), "The Egyptian Sed-Festival Rites," *Journal of Near Eastern Studies*, 24: 365–83.

Uphill, E. (1965–6), "The Nine Bows," *Ex Oriente Lux*, 19: 393–420.

Valbelle, D. (1990), *Les neuf arcs: L'égyptien et les étrangers de la préhistoire à la conquête d'Alexandre*, Paris: Armand Colin.

van de Mieroop, M. (2021), *A History of Ancient Egypt*, 2nd ed., Chichester: Wiley Blackwell.

Vandorpe, K. ed. (2019), *A Companion to Greco-Roman and Late Antique Egypt*, Hoboken, NJ: Wiley Blackwell.

Vasunia, P. (2001), *The Gift of the Nile: Hellenizing Egypt from Aeschylus to Alexander*, Berkeley, CA: University of California Press.

Venit, M. S. (2015), *Visualizing the Afterlife in the Tombs of Graeco-Roman Egypt*, Cambridge: Cambridge University Press.

Vercoutter, J. (1975), "Apis," *LÄ*, 1: 338–50.

Véron, A., J. P. Goiran, C. Morhange, N. Marriner, and J. Y. Empereur (2006), "Pollutant lead reveals the pre-Hellenistic occupation and ancient growth of Alexandria, Egypt," *Geophysical Research Letters*, 33 (6): 2–5.

Villany, A. and U. Schlotzhauer, eds. (2006), *Naukratis: Greek Diversity in Egypt: Studies on East Greek Pottery and Exchange in the Eastern Mediterranean*, London: British Museum Press.

Vittmann, G. (2003), *Ägypten und die Fremden im ersten vorchristlichen Jahrtausend*, Mainz: Phillip von Zabern.

von Beckerath, J. (1999), *Handbuch der altägyptischen Königsnamen*, Mainz: Verlag Phillip von Zabern.

von Bomhard, A.-S. (2012), *The Decree of Sais*, Oxford: Oxford Centre for Maritime Archaeology.

von Hofmann, I. and A. Vorbichler (1980), "Das Kambysesbild bei Herodot," *Archiv für Orientforschung*, 27: 86–105.

von Lieven, A. (1999), "Divination in Ägypten," *Orientalische Forschungen*, 26: 77–106.

von Lieven, A. (2016), "Das Orakelwesen im Alten Ägypten," *Mythos*, 10: 17–30.

Wachowski, W. (2019), *Towards a Better Understanding of Metonym*, Bern: Peter Lang.

Wallerstein, I. (2011), *The Modern World-System*, 4 vols, Berkeley, CA: University of California Press.

Wasmuth, M. (2017), *Ägypto-persische Herrscher und Herrschaftspräsentation in der Achämenidenzeit*, Wiesbaden: Steiner.

Weber, M. (1921–2), *Wirtschaft und Gesellschaft*, Tübingen: Mohr.

Weber, M. (1968), *On Charisma and Institution Building: Selected Papers*, ed. S. N. Eisenstadt, Chicago, IL: University of Chicago Press.

Weninger, S., ed. (2011), *The Semitic Languages: An International Handbook*, Berlin: De Gruyter.

Westbroo, R., ed. (2003), *A History of Ancient Near Eastern Law*, vol. 2, Leiden: Brill.

White, H. (1973), *Metahistory: The Historical Imagination in Nineteenth-Century Europe*, Baltimore, MD: Johns Hopkins University Press.

White, H. (1978), *Tropics of Discourse: Essays in Cultural Criticism*, Baltimore, MD: Johns Hopkins University Press.

White, H. (1990), *The Content of the Form: Narrative Discourse and Historical Representation*, Baltimore, MD: Johns Hopkins University Press.

White, H. (1999), *Figural Realism: Studies in the Mimesis Effect*, Baltimore, MD: Johns Hopkins University Press.

White, H. (2010), *The Fiction of Narrative: Essays on History, Literature, and Theory, 1957–2007*, Baltimore, MD: Johns Hopkins University Press.

White, H. (2014), *The Practical Past*, Evanston, IL: Northwestern University Press.

Whorf, B. (2012), *Language, Thought, and Reality: Selected Writings of Benjamin Lee Whorf*, 2nd ed., ed. J. B. Carroll, S. C. Levinson, and P. Lee, Boston, MA: MIT Press.

Wilkinson, T. A. H. (1999), *Early Dynastic Egypt*, London: Routledge.

Wilkinson, T. A. H. (2010), *The Rise and Fall of Ancient Egypt*, New York: Random House.

Wimsatt, W. K. (1954), *The Verbal Icon: Studies in the Meaning of Poetry*, Lexington, KY: University of Kentucky Press.

Wodtko, D. S., B. Irslinger, and C. Schneider (2008), *Nomina im Indogermanischen Lexikon*, Heidelberg: Universitätsverlag Winter.

Wojciechowska, A., V. Grieb, and Krzysztof Nawotka, eds. (2014), *Alexander the Great in Egypt: History, Art, Tradition*, Wiesbaden: Harrassowitz.

Wolohojian, A. (1969), *The Romance of Alexander the Great by Pseudo-Callisthenes*, New York: Columbia University Press.

Woodward, R. D., ed. (2007), *The Cambridge Companion to Greek Mythology*, Cambridge: Cambridge University Press.

Yiftach, U. (2015), "Law in Ptolemaic and Roman Egypt," in E. M. Harris and M. Canevaro (eds.), *The Oxford Handbook of Ancient Greek Law*, 1–64, Oxford: Oxford University Press.

Zinna, A., ed. (1997), *Hjelmslev aujourd'hui*, Turnhout: Brepols.

Part Three

Callimachus

Neglected Splendors

Alcman's Louvre *Partheneion* and Callimachus' Tale of Phrygius and Pieria

Giulio Massimilla
University of Naples Federico II

Archaic lyric poetry, as is well known, had a great influence on Callimachus.[1] He could not fail to be inspired by the kaleidoscopic multiplicity of the lyric tradition, that he not only reinvented in lyric poems of his own composition, but also reworked in his hexameter and elegiac poems.[2] Given his fondness for the adoption of different voices and viewpoints, Callimachus was obviously fascinated by the generic variety of archaic lyric, with its wide range of poetic personae and performative occasions.

Callimachus' engagement with archaic lyric is especially conspicuous in his *Aetia*. In that extremely heterogeneous collection of elegies, with its ever-changing subject matters and different narrative voices, he felt free to appropriate and remold a large number of lyric antecedents. As a matter of fact, the works of all the major archaic lyric poets resonate throughout the *Aetia*. To begin with the most prominent example, the great elegy consisting of the proem and first *aition* of Book 3, now known as *The Victory of Berenice* (frr. 143–156 Massimilla = 54–60j Harder), is modeled after Pindar's and Bacchylides' epinicians.[3] In the same book, just to mention a couple of particularly telling cases, a short poem is set in the mouth of the dead poet Simonides (fr. 163 M. = 64 H.), and the extensive elegy *Acontius and Cydippe* (frr. 166–174 M. = 67–75e H.) more than once echoes the poetry of Sappho, Alcaeus, Ibycus, Simonides, and Pindar.[4] It is also worth remarking that Sappho's songs are a crucial model for *The Lock of Berenice*, the famous last *aition* of Book 4 (fr. 213 M. = frr. 110–110f H.).[5]

My focus here will be on Alcman, whose presence in the *Aetia* seems sometimes to have a special significance.[6] For example, when in the *Aetia* prologue Callimachus expresses his wish to escape old age by changing into a winged cicada (fr. 1.29–35 M. = H.), it is easy to guess that he has in mind, among other poetic forerunners, a passage of Alcman where the aged speaker wishes to become a male halcyon that flies together with the females (*PMGF* 26 = fr. 90 Calame).[7] Also noteworthy is a fragment of uncertain location within the *Aetia* (fr. 69 M. = 119 H., possibly from Book 2), dealing with the division by lot of the honors among the gods, which may well be reminiscent of both Alcman (*PMGF* 65 = fr. 107 Calame) and Pindar (*Ol.* 7.55–61). On a more general note, overtones of Alcman's *Partheneia* have been detected in *Acontius and Cydippe*, where Callimachus' description of Cydippe's unsurpassed beauty (fr. 166.11–14 M. = 67.11–14 H.) recalls the praises of the exceptionally charming girls Agido and Astymeloisa sung by Alcman's maiden choruses (*PMGF* 1.40–41, 3.64–67 = frr. 3.40–41, 26.64–67 Calame).[8]

In what follows, I will expand on a suggestion I have made elsewhere[9] about a possible intertextual link between some lines of Alcman's Louvre *Partheneion* (*PMGF* 1 = fr. 3 Calame) and a specific passage from Callimachus' elegy *Phrygius and Pieria*, belonging to Book 3 of the *Aetia* (frr. 183–185 M.).[10]

It will be useful first to summarize Callimachus' tale of Phrygius and Pieria:

> Phrygius, a young king of Miletus, upon seeing the girl Pieria of Myus during a festival in honor of Artemis, fell in love with her and promised to grant her all she desired. Pieria took the opportunity to ask him whether the long hostility between Miletus and Myus might end, and she achieved her aim. The elegy probably ends with the aetiological outcome of the myth: from then on, Ionian women traditionally express the wish that their husbands may respect them as Phrygius respected Pieria.
>
> Massimilla 2011: 52

The extant papyrus text of this portion of the *Aetia* is incomplete and quite damaged but, by good fortune, we can rely on a late prose paraphrase of Callimachus' *Phrygius and Pieria* included in the collection of love letters ascribed to Aristaenetus (*Letter* 1.15). Aristaenetus' paraphrase is very helpful in reconstructing the outline of Callimachus' story and in interpreting and supplementing its broken text.[11]

Here I will be concerned with the part of Callimachus' poem (fr. 184.5–11 M.) where the narrator addresses Pieria and describes her reaction to Phrygius' generous speech: she was not led astray by all sorts of expensive gifts she might have desired for herself, but modestly set to ask Phrygius to reconcile their respective cities. Given the incomplete state of Callimachus' text, I first offer the text of the corresponding part of Aristaenetus' paraphrase (1.15.35–44 Mazal):

τοιαῦτα μὲν ὁ δίκαιος ἐραστής· σὲ δέ, ὦ πασῶν ὑπερφέρουσα γυναικῶν κςὶ
κάλλει καὶ γνώμῃ, τῆς ἔμφρονος οὐ παρήγαγεν εὐβουλίας οὐχ ὅρμος, οὐχ
ἑλικτῆρες, οὐ πυλεὼν ὁ πολύτιμος, οὐ περιδέραιον, οὐ Λύδιός τε καὶ ποδήρης
χιτών, οὐ πορφυρίδες, οὐ θεράπαιναι τῆς Καρίας οὐδὲ Λυδῶν ὑπερφυῶς
ἱστουργοῦσαι γυναῖκες, οἷς ἅπασιν ἀτεχνῶς ἀγάλλεσθαι τὸ θῆλυ πέφυκε γένος,
ἀλλ᾿ εἰς γῆν ἑώρας τὸ πρόσωπον, ὥσπερ τι συννοουμένη. εἶτα ἔφης ἐπιχαρίτως
πεφοινιγμένη τὰς παρειὰς καὶ τὸ πρόσωπον ἐξ αἰδοῦς ἀποκλίνασα . . .

Thus the just lover. But you, excelling all women in beauty and judgment, were
not led astray from prudent counsel, neither by a necklace, nor earrings, nor a
precious crown, nor a chain, nor a sweeping Lydian robe, nor purple fabrics, nor
by Carian handmaids or marvelous weaving women from Lydia, all those things
that the female sex is utterly crazy about—no, you cast your glance down to the
earth, as though deliberating something. Then you said, your cheeks charmingly
ablush, tilting your head in modesty . . .
Translation by Bing and Höschele 2014: 37

Here is Callimachus' text, as supplemented by Edgar Lobel, Rudolf Pfeiffer,
and Paul Maas (fr. 184.5–11 M.):[12]

ἦ] ῥα· σὲ δ᾿ οὐ πυλ̣εών   οὐ κά]λυκες,   5
Λ]ύδιον οὐ κα[ίρωμα   ]ι Κάειρ[α]ι
  λάτριες, οὐκαγ[.].ικ.[   ]ς,
τ]οῖς ἔπι θηλύτ[ερ]αι .[   ] ἰαίνεσθε
ἔξαιτον, πυκι[νοῦ γ]νώματος ἐξ[έ]βαλο]ν·
ᾳἰδοῖ δ᾿ ὡς φοί[νικι] ţεὰς ἐρύθουσα παρειάς   10
ἤν]επες ὀφ[θαλμο]ῖ̈ς ἔμπαλι .[. . .]ομεν[.].[

He spoke, but neither a headband . . . nor earrings (?)[13] nor a Lydian garment . . .
Carian slaves nor . . ., in which you women especially find pleasure . . .,[14] deterred
you from your sensible judgment. While your cheeks turned red with shame as
if dyed with purple you spoke with your eyes averted . . .[15]
Translation by Harder 2012: vol. 1, 256–7, slightly adapted

As I have briefly remarked elsewhere,[16] the series of luxurious items preceded
by negations in vv. 5–7 seems to have been inspired by vv. 64–73 of Alcman's
Louvre *Partheneion* (*PMGF* 1 = fr. 3 Calame). Here I will focus on this parallel
and further suggest that Alcman's stanza (vv. 64–77) resonates more broadly in
the *Aetia* passage.

Although many aspects of Alcman's vv. 64–77 are much debated,[17] their
general meaning is clear enough. The chorus of girls say that several costly
articles of clothing and pieces of jewelry and a number of beautiful girls

mentioned by name (possibly to be identified with chorus-members)[18] are no match for the extraordinarily charming chorus-leader Hagesichora. Here is Alcman's text:

οὔτε γάρ τι πορφύρας
τόσσος κόρος ὥστ' ἀμύναι,   65
οὔτε ποικίλος δράκων
παγχρύσιος, οὐδὲ μίτρα
Λυδία, νεανίδων
ἰανογ[λ]εφάρων ἄγαλμα,
οὐδὲ ταὶ Ναννῶς κόμαι,   70
ἀλλ᾽ οὐδ᾽ Ἀρέτα σιειδής,
οὐδὲ Συλακίς τε καὶ Κλεησισήρα.
οὐδ᾽ ἐς Αἰνησιμβρ[ό]τας ἐνθοῖσα φασεῖς
"Ἀσταφίς τέ μοι γένοιτο,
    καὶ ποτιγλέποι Φίλυλλα   75
Δαμαρέτα τ᾽ ἐρατά [τ]ε Ϝιανθεμίς"·
    ἀλλ᾽ Ἀγησιχόρα με τείρει.

For abundance of purple is not sufficient for protection, nor intricate snake of solid gold, no, nor Lydian headband, pride of dark-eyed girls, nor the hair of Nanno, nor again godlike Areta nor Thylacis and Cleësithera; nor will you go to Aenesimbrota's[19] and say, "If only Astaphis were mine, if only Philylla were to look my way and Damareta and lovely Ianthemis"; no, Hagesichora wears me out.[20]

Translation by Campbell 1988: 367, adapted

Callimachus may have had in mind this stanza of the Louvre *Partheneion* because he was aware of the relations between archaic Sparta as depicted by Alcman and Ionia,[21] where the story of Phrygius and Pieria is set. The enumeration of splendid items preceded by negations is the most conspicuous shared feature of Alcman's and Callimachus' passages. Besides that, Callimachus' phrase Λ]ύδιον οὐ κα[ίρωμα ("nor a Lydian garment," v. 6) seems to evoke Alcman's οὐδὲ μίτρα / Λυδία ("nor Lydian headband," vv. 67–68),[22] and the term πυλεών that Callimachus uses in v. 5 for his own version of a "headband" is in fact an extremely rare word attested in two other fragments of Alcman (*PMGF* 3.65 and 60.2 = frr. 26.65 and 126.2 Calame).[23]

But a comparative reading of Alcman's stanza on the one hand, and of Callimachus' damaged vv. 5–7 and the corresponding part of Aristaenetus' paraphrase on the other, suggests that Alcman was a source of inspiration for Callimachus in another respect too. As Gregory Hutchinson observes, Alcman's enumeration "begins from material objects, and moves gradually to people (note the incidental description in 68–9)."[24] Now, the same pattern seems to emerge from the remains of Callimachus' text: "neither a headband ... nor earrings (?) nor a Lydian garment ... Carian slaves nor ..." What is more, a reconstruction of the *Aetia* passage along these lines finds support in Aristaenetus' ornate rendering of Callimachus' words: "neither a necklace, nor earrings, nor a precious crown, nor a chain, nor a sweeping Lydian robe, nor purple fabrics, nor Carian handmaids or marvelous weaving women from Lydia."[25]

Given the high quality of Aristaenetus' paraphrase and its overall fidelity to Callimachus' original text, I do not share Pfeiffer's view that Aristaenetus mistakenly included the Carian handmaids and the Lydian weaving women in the list of gifts (οὐ θεράπαιναι τῆς Καρίας οὐδὲ Λυδῶν ὑπερφυῶς ἱστουργοῦσαι γυναῖκες), whereas Callimachus must in fact have mentioned the precious fabrics woven by them. Accordingly, in Callimachus' vv. 6–7 (after Λ]ύδιον οὐ̣ κα[ίρωμα], "nor a Lydian garment") I would not support—as Pfeiffer does—Lobel's supplement [τά θ' ἱστουργοῦσ]ι̣ Κάειρ[α]ι̣ / λάτριες, "and those [garments] which Carian slaves produce at the loom."[26]

By contrast, in light of Aristaenetus' rendering οὐ Λύδιός τε καὶ ποδήρης χιτών ... οὐ θεράπαιναι τῆς Καρίας ("nor a sweeping Lydian robe ... nor Carian handmaids"), after Callimachus' Λ]ύδιον οὐ κα[ίρωμα] I prefer Adelmo Barigazzi's supplement [ποδηνεκές, οὐχ]ὶ Κάειρ[α]ι̣ / λάτριες, so as to have "nor a Lydian garment reaching to the feet, nor Carian slaves."[27] Directly after this, I am also inclined to accept Barigazzi's articulation and supplement οὐκ ἀγ[αϵ]αὶ̣ ("nor skilled ..."), which he attractively refers to the "marvelous weaving women from Lydia" mentioned by Aristaenetus immediately after the Carian handmaids (οὐδὲ Λυδῶν ὑπερφυῶς ἱστουργοῦσαι γυναῖκες). As Barigazzi points out, here Callimachus has in mind a Homeric simile (referring to the wounded Menelaos' blood dripping down his legs), which describes some Maeonian—i.e. Lydian— or Carian woman dyeing ivory with purple to make a cheek-piece for horses, ὡς δ' ὅτε τίς τ' ἐλέφαντα γυνὴ φοίνικι μιήνῃ / Μῃονὶς ἠὲ Κάειρα παρήϊον ἔμμεναι ἵππων (*Il.* 4.141–142).[28]

It seems to me that the influence of this same simile on Callimachus may also be detected in the wording of his v. 10, whose literal meaning is that Pieria "reddens her cheeks with shame as with purple" (αἰδοῖ δ' ὡς φοί[νικι] τεὰς ἐρύθουσα παρειάς). Callimachus is certainly aware of the established metaphorical connection between purple and the cheeks of blushing women,[29] but here he chooses to give prominence to the concrete sense of the word φοῖνιξ through the comparison ὡς φοί[νικι] followed by παρειάς, a combination which echoes the phrasing of the Iliadic simile (ὡς δ' ὅτε ... φοίνικι ... παρήϊον).[30]

At the same time, Callimachus' use of the word φοῖνιξ to describe Pieria's blush may evoke the first luxurious item of Alcman's negative list: οὔτε γάρ τι πορφύρας / τόσσος κόρος ὥστ' ἀμύναι, "for abundance of purple is not sufficient for protection" (vv. 64–65).[31] If this is so, we see that Callimachus reverses the sequence of ideas: while the girls of Alcman's *Partheneion* begin by acknowledging the inadequacy of their glamorous purple robes, Pieria's purple blush (so charming in the eyes of Phrygius) triumphs over all the costly gifts she has chosen to disregard and sets in motion the reconciliation between Miletus and her home city of Myus.[32]

Notes

1 The bibliography on this subject is large: see the references given by Massimilla (2020), 215 n. 1, and add now Kampakoglou (2019), 19–72, 212–350.

2 For a recent discussion of Callimachus' intertextual dialogue with the lyric genres, see Acosta-Hughes and Stephens (2017), who highlight the vitality of lyric compositions and performances in Hellenistic Alexandria.

3 Fuhrer (1992), 55–138, provides the most thorough study of these connections. For the Egyptian overtones in Callimachus' reworking of the epinician genre, see Stephens (2002), 240–52, (2003), 8–9.

4 See Massimilla (2020).

5 See Acosta-Hughes (2010), 63–81; Massimilla (2018).

6 For an assessment of Alcman's influence on Callimachus, see Kousoulini (2019), 102–4.

7 See, e.g., Crane (1986), 273–4.

8 See Curtis (2017), 57; Massimilla (2020), 218 n. 14.

9 Massimilla (2010), 402.

10 I will refer to the fragments of *Phrygius and Pieria* in accordance with the numbering I have used in my edition (Massimilla 2010). Here are the correspondences with the numbering used by Annette Harder in her edition (2012): fr. 183 M. = 81 H.; fr. 184 M. = 80 H.; fr. 185 M. = 83 H.

11 On Aristaenetus' *Letter* 1.15, see Consonni (2000); Zanetto (2005), 298–305; Drago (2007), 270–82; Bing and Höschele (2014), 34–9; Bing (2019). Summaries of Callimachus' tale are also found in Plutarch's *On the Bravery of Women* (16, *Mor.* 253f) and Polyaenus' *Stratagems in War* (8.35).

12 For textual details on Callimachus' passage and its paraphrase by Aristaenetus, see Massimilla (2010), 123–5.

13 The word κάλυκες (v. 5) is already used of bud-like ornaments in the *Iliad* (18.401) and in the major Homeric hymn to Aphrodite (5.87, 163). The scholia to the *Iliad*

passage offer three alternative explanations: "rings," "earrings," or "spiral hairpins." Aristaenetus' rendering suggests that he interpreted Callimachus' κάλυκες as earrings (ἑλικτῆρες). The lacuna between οὐ πυλ.εών and οὐ κά]λυκες may have contained an adjective qualifying πυλ.εών (as could be inferred from Aristaenetus' οὐ πυλεὼν ὁ πολύτιμος, where ὁ πολύτιμος is Lesky's emendation of the transmitted τὸ πολύτιμον), or the negation οὐ followed by a noun referring to another piece of jewelry (maybe a necklace, on account of Aristaenetus' οὐχ ὅρμος . . . οὐ περιδέραιον), or an adjective qualifying κά]λυκες (in that case the anaphoric οὐ could have stood immediately after πυλ.εών).

14 In v. 8 the trace after θηλύτ[ερ]αι resembles *theta*. Pfeiffer's tentative suggestion θ[αλερὰς φρένας] would give the required sense: "to which you women especia_y warm in your blooming hearts."

15 At the end of v. 11, the supplement ἔμπαλι κ[λιν]ομέν[ο]ι[ς (proposed by Herter 1954: 79; and Barigazzi 1976: 17) is particularly attractive both on its own account and because of Aristaenetus' rendering τὸ πρόσωπον ἐξ αἰδοῦς ἀποκλίνασα (see D'Alessio 2007: 494 n. 92; Massimilla 2010: 405; Harder 2012: vol. 2, 684). On lowered or averted eyes as a sign of modesty in ancient Greek poetry, see Massimilla (2010-11).

16 See n. 9 above.

17 The problems of interpretation posed by these lines are further complicated by their close connection (signaled by the initial γάρ) with the immediately preceding vv. 60–63, a very controversial passage where the chorus of girls say that the "Pleiades" fight against them through the night (ταὶ Πεληάδες . . . ἅμιν . . . νύκτα δι' ἀμβροσίαν . . . μάχονται). For discussions of vv. 60–77, see at least: Garzya (1954), 52–62; Calame (1983), 331–40; Campbell (1988), 365–7 nn. 16–21; Davies (1991), 30; Pavese (1992), 71–87; Hutchinson (2001), 90–6; Krummen (2009), 192–3; Tsantsanoglou (2012), 63–77; Budelmann (2018), 75–9. If the word Πεληάδες (whose primary meaning is "Doves") here refers to the star-cluster, we may wonder whether the Pleiades are envisaged as a chorus in the sky, as some scholars have suggested (see Budelmann 2018: 76). In that case, there might be an interesting parallel in a Callimachean fragment of uncertain location (fr. 693 Pfeiffer), corresponding to the first and last parts of a scholion to Theocritus (13.25–28a Wendel). After reporting that according to Callimachus the Πλειάδες (also called Πελειάδες) were the daughters of the queen of the Amazons, the scholiast says that the Pleiades were the first to set up a choral dance and a night-festival of maidens (πρῶτον δ' αὗται χορείαν καὶ παννυχίδα συνεστήσαντο παρθενεύουσαι). If this detail too goes back to Callimachus, he might have had Alcman's passage in mind (see Pfeiffer 1949: 451). Besides that, it is worth noting that fr. 693 Pfeiffer may well belong to the dream scene at the opening of the *Aetia* (fr. 3 M. = frr. 2a–2b H.), since there are reasons to suppose that Callimachus mentioned the Pleiades/Peleiades there (see Massimilla 1996: 240–1).

18 This seems to be the prevailing view: see, e.g., Garzya (1954), 59–60; Calame (1977), 16, 51; and (more cautiously) Hutchinson (2001), 93–4; Budelmann (2018), 77–8. Differently, e.g., Pavese (1992), 86–7.

19 As Budelmann (2018), 78 observes, "we do not know who Aenesimbrota is, except that she evidently is not one of the chorus-members. Since she is named here she is presumably of significance to the performance or festival more widely, e.g. the chorus-trainer" (with further bibliography).

20 Apparently, the final verb τείρει has an erotic meaning: "Hagesichora wears me out with love." The reading τείρει of the Louvre papyrus is supported by a fragmentary scholion to vv. 77–79 preserved on another papyrus (POxy. 2389 fr. 7b, see Römer 2013: 29–30) but some scholars favor the easy correction τηρεῖ ("Hagesichora guards me," which is in fact Campbell's translation here). As a whole, Alcman's stanza has sometimes been identified as a priamel (see, e.g., Calame 1977: 51, 87–8; Race 1982: 54–5; Calame 1983: 335, 339; Davies 1991: 30) but it is best interpreted as a sustained *praeteritio* (see lately Budelmann 2018: 77). In the words of Hutchinson (2001), 94, "the actual flaunting is elegantly conveyed through the narrator's confession of inadequacy" (similarly, e.g., Garzya 1954: 60; Neri 2011: 270; Budelmann 2018: 78). The rhetoric of the passage, I suggest, was not lost on Callimachus.

21 See Krummen (2013), 33–8.

22 Pfeiffer's supplement Λ]ύδιον οὐ κα[ίρωμα is supported by Aristaenetus' paraphrase οὐ Λύδιος . . . χιτών and is very attractive because the word καίρωμα has a distinctly Callimachean flavor (see Massimilla 2010: 234). Alcman's μίτρα Λυδία is paralleled in Sapph. fr. 98a.10–11 Voigt μ]ιτράναν . . . ἀπὸ Σαρδίω[ν and Pind. *Nem.* 8.15 Λυδίαν μίτραν (see Garzya 1954: 59; Calame 1983: 335; Pavese 1992: 85; Hutchinson 2001: 95; Budelmann 2018: 78; Cannatà Fera 2020: 489).

23 Lobel's supplement πυλ.εών is guaranteed by Pollux 5.96. At the same time, Lobel astutely restored the word in Aristaenetus' paraphrase instead of †πόλεων (see Massimilla 2006: 36). In his commentary on Alcman *PMGF* 3.65, Hutchinson (2001), 109, rightly remarks that the occurrence of πυλεών in Callimachus is striking. It is open to doubt whether Alcman's use of the word πυλεών pertains to the Laconian cult of Hera, as might be inferred from Athenaeus 15.678a who relies on the lexicon of Pamphilus (for different views on this point see, e.g., Calame 1983: 407, 526–7; and Hutchinson 2001: 109).

24 Hutchinson (2001), 94; see also 95, on v. 70: "the phrasing forms a transition between things and people." For a similar view, see Race (1982), 55 n. 56: "The ἀλλά (71) . . . indicates a new movement, a heightening with a shift from external adornment to individuals."

25 Harder (2012), vol. 2, 677, adduces other passages "where jewellery, clothes, and servants are also mentioned as part of a dowry or a lover's gift." None of those texts, however, is structured as a negative list and offers such a detailed progression from objects to people.

26 Pfeiffer (1949), 88 (the supplement [ἰστουργοῦσ]ι is based on Aristaenetus' ἰστουργοῦσαι). According to Pfeiffer, in v. 7 the negation after λάτριες was probably followed by the names of articles of clothing.

27 Barigazzi (1976), 16–17. This supplement has also the merit of not interrupting the anaphoric series of negations. Barigazzi's view that Callimachus inserted the Carian slaves in the list of gifts is accepted by D'Alessio (2007), 494 n. 91; Bing (2019), 42 n. 34; and (hesitantly) Harder (2012), vol. 2, 681. Against Barigazzi's supplement ποδηνεκές (which would be mirrored in Aristaenetus' ποδήρης) Harder (2012), vol. 2, 680, argues that "the use of ποδηνεκής and ποδήρης elsewhere suggests that it was not a feature deserving special mention where *women's* dress was concerned," but some of the passages she cites in support of her view refer in fact to women's ceremonial clothes (Eur. *Bacch.* 833, Call. *Iamb.* fr. 193.36 Pfeiffer; on a more general level, one may add, e.g., Dion. Hal. *Ant. Rom.* 7.9.4, Paus. 1.19.1, Lucian. *Ver. hist.* 2.46, Poll. 4.120, Christod. *Anth. Pal.* 2.151). The supplement ποδηνεκές is accepted by Bing (2019), 42 n. 34.

28 Taking his lead from this Homeric simile, after οὐκ ἀγ[αθ]αὶ Barigazzi (1976), 16–17, proposes κε[ρκίδα Μ̣ηονίδε]ς, so as to have "nor Maeonian women skilled with the weaver's shuttle." This latter supplement probably captures the sense of the passage (as observed by D'Alessio 2007: 494 n. 91), but Callimachus' choice of words in the second half of v. 7 must have been different since the trace after *kappa* on the papyrus resembles *omicron* or *omega* rather than *epsilon*. Harder (2012), vol. 2, 682, suggests that, after λάτριες, v. 7 "may contain a summarizing description leading up to the relative clause in 8 f., e.g. 'nor <another of the beautiful or precious gifts>, which you women … especially delight in," but in that case it would be hard to account for the absence of a corresponding phrase in Aristaenetus' paraphrase.

29 Before Callimachus, this metaphor occurs in Euripides (*Phoen.* 1485–1490, *Iph. Aul.* 187–188) and maybe Erinna (fr. 4, 34–35 Neri). For the association of purple with blushing cheeks in Greek poetry, see Massimilla (2010–11), 240–3, 250 (with further bibliography).

30 The Homeric flavor of Callimachus' sequence ὡς φοί[νικι] … παρειάς may be further enhanced by a reminiscence of the *Odyssey* formula νέας φοινικοπαρῄους, "purple-cheeked ships" (11.124, 23.271): see Massimilla (2010–11), 240 n. 40; Harder (2012), vol. 2, 684.

31 On purple as a status symbol, see Budelmann (2018), 78.

32 It is worth noting that a little further on, near the end of the *aition* (fr. 184, 18–23 M.), the narrator remarks that Pieria managed to achieve a long-lasting peace treaty because Aphrodite made her simple words sound more persuasive than any elaborate speech, and the girl actually proved to be more proficient than all the delegations that had traveled in vain between the two cities.

Bibliography

Acosta-Hughes, B. (2010), *Arion's Lyre: Archaic Lyric into Hellenistic Poetry*, Princeton, NJ, and Oxford: Princeton University Press.

Acosta-Hughes, B., L. Lehnus, and S. Stephens, eds. (2011), *Brill's Companion to Callimachus*, Leiden and Boston, MA: Brill.

Acosta-Hughes, B. and S. A. Stephens (2017), "Callimachean 'Lyric,'" *Trends in Classics*, 9 (2): 226–47.

Barigazzi, A. (1976), "L'*aition* di Frigio e Pieria in Callimaco," *Prometheus*, 2 (1): 11–17.

Bastianini, G. and A. Casanova, eds. (2006), *Callimaco: Cent'anni di papiri*, Firenze: Istituto Papirologico G. Vitelli.

Bing, P. (2019), "Thanks Again to Aristaenetus: The Tale of Phrygius and Pieria in Callimachus' *Aetia* (frs. 80–83b Harder) through the Eyes of a Late-Antique Epistolographer," in J. J. H. Klooster, M. A. Harder, R. F. Regtuit, and G. C. Wakker (eds.), *Callimachus Revisited: New Perspectives in Callimachean Scholarship*, 27–49, Leuven, Paris, and Bristol, CT: Peeters.

Bing, P. and R. Höschele (2014), *Aristaenetus: Erotic Letters*, Atlanta, GA: Society of Biblical Literature.

Budelmann, F., ed. (2009), *The Cambridge Companion to Greek Lyric*, Cambridge: Cambridge University Press.

Budelmann, F. (2018), *Greek Lyric: A Selection*, Cambridge: Cambridge University Press.

Calame, C. (1977), *Les chœurs de jeunes filles en Grèce archaïque*, vol. 2, *Alcman*, Roma: Edizioni dell'Ateneo & Bizzarri.

Calame, C. (1983), *Alcman*, Roma: Edizioni dell'Ateneo.

Campbell, D. A. (1988), *Greek Lyric*, vol. 2, *Anacreon, Anacreontea, Choral Lyric from Olympus to Alcman*, Cambridge, MA, and London: Harvard University Press and William Heinemann Ltd.

Cannatà Fera, M. (2020), *Pindaro: Le Nemee*, Milano: Mondadori.

Consonni, C. (2000), "17. Pieria e Frigio. Aristeneto (1, 15)," in A. Stramaglia (ed.), Ἔρως: *Antiche trame greche d'amore*, 243–52, Bari: Levante Editore.

Crane, G. (1986), "Tithonus and the Prologue to Callimachus' *Aetia*," *Zeitschrift für Papyrologie und Epigraphik*, 66: 269–78.

Curtis, L. (2017), *Imagining the Chorus in Augustan Poetry*, Cambridge: Cambridge University Press.

D'Alessio, G. B. (2007), *Callimaco: Inni, epigrammi e frammenti*, 4th ed., Milano: Rizzoli Editore.

D'Alessio, G. B., L. Lomiento, C. Meliadò, and G. Ucciardello, eds. (2020), *Il potere della parola: Studi di letteratura greca per Maria Cannatà Fera*, Alessandria: Edizioni dell'Orso.

Davies, M. (1991), *Poetarum Melicorum Graecorum Fragmenta*, vol. 1, *Alcman, Stesichorus, Ibycus*, Oxford: Clarendon Press.

Drago, A. T. (2007), *Aristeneto: Lettere d'amore*, Lecce: Pensa Multimedia.

Fuhrer, T. (1992), *Die Auseinandersetzung mit den Chorlyrikern in den Epinikien des Kallimachos*: Basel and Kassel: Friedrich Reinhardt Verlag.

Garzya, A. (1954), *Alcmane: I frammenti*, Napoli: Libreria Scientifica Editrice.

Harder, A. (2012), *Callimachus: Aetia*, 2 vols, Oxford: Oxford University Press.

Herter, H. (1954), Review of R. Pfeiffer, *Callimachus*, 2 vols (Oxford 1949–53), *Gnomon*, 26 (2): 74–80.

Hutchinson, G. O. (2001), *Greek Lyric Poetry: A Commentary on Selected Larger Pieces*, Oxford: Oxford University Press.

Kampakoglou, A. (2019), *Studies in the Reception of Pindar in Ptolemaic Poetry*, Berlin and Boston, MA: De Gruyter.

Klooster, J. J. H., M. A. Harder, R. F. Regtuit, and G. C. Wakker, eds. (2019), *Callimachus Revisited: New Perspectives in Callimachean Scholarship*, Leuven, Paris, and Bristol, CT: Peeters.

Kousoulini, V. (2019), *A History of Alcman's Early Reception: Female-Voiced Nightingales*, Newcastle upon Tyne: Cambridge Scholars Publishing.

Krummen, E. (2009), "Alcman, Stesichorus and Ibycus," in F. Budelmann (ed.), *The Cambridge Companion to Greek Lyric*, 189–203, Cambridge: Cambridge University Press.

Krummen, E. (2013), "*Kolymbôsai, klinai* und eine lydische Mitra: Alkman als Dichter der orientalisierenden Epoche Spartas," in P. Mauritsch and C. Ulf (eds.), *Kultur(en): Formen des Alltäglichen in der Antike. Festschrift für Ingomar Weiler zum 75. Geburtstag*, vol. 1, 19–44, Graz: Leykam Verlag.

Massimilla, G. (1996), *Callimaco: Aitia, libri primo e secondo*, Pisa: Giardini Editori.

Massimilla, G. (2006), "I papiri e la tradizione indiretta medievale negli *Aitia*," in G. Bastianini and A. Casanova (eds.), *Callimaco: Cent'anni di papiri*, 31–45, Firenze: Istituto Papirologico G. Vitelli.

Massimilla, G. (2010), *Callimaco: Aitia, libro terzo e quarto*, Pisa and Roma: Fabrizio Serra Editore.

Massimilla, G. (2010–11), "Αἰδώς negli occhi e sul volto: riflessioni su due temi ricorrenti nella poesia greca," *Incontri di filologia classica*, 10: 233–54.

Massimilla, G. (2011), "The *Aetia* through Papyri," in B. Acosta-Hughes, L. Lehnus, and S. Stephens (eds.), *Brill's Companion to Callimachus*, 39–62, Leiden and Boston, MA: Brill.

Massimilla, G. (2018), "Il dolore delle chiome sorelle da Callimaco a Catullo," *Paideia*, 73 (3): 1727–32.

Massimilla, G. (2020), "Riflessi della lirica greca arcaica in Callimaco," in G. B. D'Alessio, L. Lomiento, C. Meliadò, and G. Ucciardello (eds.), *Il potere della parola: Studi di letteratura greca per Maria Cannatà Fera*, 215–27, Alessandria: Edizioni dell'Orso.

Mauritsch, P. and C. Ulf, eds. (2013), *Kultur(en): Formen des Alltäglichen in der Antike. Festschrift für Ingomar Weiler zum 75. Geburtstag*, Graz: Leykam Verlag.

Montanari, F. and L. Lehnus, eds. (2002), *Callimaque: Sept exposés suivis de discussions*, Vandœuvres and Genève: Fondation Hardt.

Neri, C. (2011), *Lirici greci: Età arcaica e classica*, Roma: Carocci Editore.

Pavese, C. O. (1992), *Il grande* Partenio *di Alcmane*, Amsterdam: Hakkert Editore.

Pfeiffer, R. (1949), *Callimachus*, vol. 1, *Fragmenta*, Oxford: Clarendon Press.

Poetarum Melicorum Graecorum Fragmenta (*PMGF*), see Davies (1991).

Race, W. H. (1982), *The Classical Priamel from Homer to Boethius*, Leiden: Brill.

Römer, C. (2013), *Commentaria et lexica Graeca in papyris reperta*, pars 1, *Commentaria et lexica in auctores*, vol. 1, *Aeschines–Bacchylides*, fasc. 2, *Alcman–Antipho*, 1. *Alcman*, Berlin and Boston, MA: De Gruyter.

Stephens, S. A. (2002), "Egyptian Callimachus," in F. Montanari and L. Lehnus (eds.), *Callimaque: Sept exposés suivis de discussions*, 235–70, Vandœuvres and Genève: Fondation Hardt.

Stephens, S. A. (2003), *Seeing Double: Intercultural Poetics in Ptolemaic Alexandria*, Berkeley and Los Angeles, CA, and London: University of California Press.

Stramaglia, A., ed. (2000), Ἔρως: *Antiche trame greche d'amore*, Bari: Levante Editore.

Tsantsanoglou, K. (2012), *Of Golden Manes and Silvery Faces: The* Partheneion *1 of Alcman*, Berlin and Boston, MA: De Gruyter.

Zanetto, G. (2005), "Aristeneto. Lettere d'amore," in F. Conca and G. Zanetto, *Alcifrone, Filostrato, Aristeneto. Lettere d'amore*, 233–417, Milano: Rizzoli Editore.

5

Callimachus' Duplicitous *Iambos*

Don Lavigne

Texas Tech University

In her magisterial study, *Seeing Double*, Professor Stephens has made clear the distinct place Alexandrian poets carved out for themselves and their work, characterizing the socio-poetic goals that guided these authors as a means of finding "ways of redeploying [their Greek literary predecessors] to express the values and cultural experience of the present" (2003: 251). Of course, as Stephens notes, this artistic guideline is not fundamentally different for other Greeks in other times and places; however, among the Alexandrian poets, the regime change that forged their work made connecting to the Greek past particularly fraught. The Alexandrian poets developed various strategies for creating poetry within this new world, strategies that reflect their place within two cultures. According to Stephens, Callimachus clearly situates "himself as a self-conscious ego writing against the past," a poet who regularly creates plausible fictions that reveal his role in fashioning these optical illusions of duplicity (2003: 254–5). One of Callimachus' strategies for creating his position "in between" lies in the poet's choice and deployment of models, as Stephens makes clear in her discussion of the poet's use of Hesiod.

Stephens also mentions Callimachus' use of Hipponax as a model for his self-fashioning as a purveyor of a duplicitous poetics (2003: 254). Hipponax is an excellent choice for a poet who wants to showcase his simultaneous adherence to and difference from his Greek literary predecessors in and through his composition of poetry for his Alexandrian world.[1] One reason lies in the fact that Hipponax himself, from the point of view of Greek literary history before Alexandria, has a profoundly secondary status vis à vis the most famous and celebrated of the Greek iambic poets, Archilochus. Callimachus is no doubt exploiting the duplicity inherent in the literary history of the genre in his choice of Hipponax, but, in addition, the choice of a resurrected Hipponax (a Hipponax who is not one) in *Ia*. 1 prefigures the duplicitous poetics Callimachus creates through his iambic collection. The focus upon the distance between then and now, here and there, this peculiarly Alexandrian identity, is evident in and developed through Callimachus' iambic persona. Moreover, the iambic genre itself offered an attractive site of experimentation for Callimachus and other Hellenistic poets precisely because the genre was multivocal; that is, *Iambos* offered a variety of shifting voices and perspectives, marshaled by the *persona loquens* whose voice itself would, at times, meld with others he presented.[2] For archaic *Iambos*, the opening up of the difference between the speaking voice of the poet and that of the historical poet was a feature of the genre, one further emphasized by the performance context of the poems—within an iambic performance, audience members would be required to make distinctions between these figures.[3] This multivocality and the differences it opened up would have been attractive to Alexandrian poets as they sought to situate themselves in their multiple social and poetic contexts. The divisive potential of the iambic poet-persona is perhaps nowhere clearer than in Callimachus' first *Iamb*, where the poet ventriloquizes the resurrected Hipponax, placing the archaic poet squarely in both the past and present and leaving his readers wondering exactly where "Callimachus" stands.[4] From the first line, Callimachus announces his appropriation and reimagination of the dynamics of iambic speech in the context of the Hellenistic poetry book.[5]

In a recent article on narrative strategy in Greek blame poetry, Chris Carey has emphasized the audience's role in assessing iambic speech and described a successful iambic poem as one that succeeds in convincing the audience that the negative behavior of the blame poet was justified, especially as calling someone out for their faults is always liable to be characterized as *hubris* in a shame culture (2018: 10). Further, Carey argues that the variety of devices marshaled by the controlling poet-persona is a key ingredient for realizing the goals of a poem of blame (ibid., 16–26). While I agree that the successful papering over of the cracks in the morality of the iambic poet contributes to their success, it does not erase them. There remains an element of what scholars have seen as iambic danger, that is, the threat that the poet's own abuse will infect him with the very blame he seeks to inflict on his target.[6] In order to elucidate Callimachus' duplicitous iambic poetics, I will examine this aspect of the iambic poet-persona from the perspective of the performance of masculinity and argue that the iambic poet-persona's revelation of faults in his masculinity is a central feature of the narrative voice of *Iambos*. Iambic narrative style regularly involves stories that reveal the poet's failure of masculinity, even as he seeks to rehabilitate those failures; however, while the archaic iambographers attempt to resuscitate their reputations in the presence of performance, Callimachus draws the process out over the course of the collection, a fact that highlights the contested nature of the poet's represented masculinity and one suited to the uncertain socio-political context of Hellenistic Alexandria.

One feature that all the major iambic poets hold in common is the revelation, implicit or explicit, of a challenge to their masculine privilege. This slight to or fault in their masculinity generates the vituperation that so often characterizes the genre and functions as a poetic attempt at rehabilitating their failed manhood. Nonetheless, the fact remains that these poets advertise their masculine failings and that such advertisement is a key feature of the genre. Often, the vituperation of the iambic poets invokes a gendered rhetoric, bringing enemies on stage so as to tear down their masculine personae by imitating their voices and presenting them as failed men.[7] To put it starkly, the iambic poet starts beaten and then, beating his aggressor, reasserts his masculinity by showcasing the loss of masculine privilege suffered by his enemy.[8] In Callimachus' iambic poetry, which has been removed from the archaic performance context and embedded in the context of the poetry collection, these features play out over the course of the book and can vary from poem to poem, lending an even greater emphasis to the poet's various stages of masculine loss or gain.[9]

Iambic Performativity

The importance of gender for the genre is emphasized by the fact that one of its most common themes is sex, and, in particular, how the *persona loquens* relates to and succeeds or fails with his paramours. Because an iambic poem often involves the narrative self-representation of the *persona loquens* engaged in various acts of masculine prowess, *Iambos*, more than other genres, lingers upon the poet-persona's practice of masculinity. This generic process of gender formation can be seen as akin to the process of real-life gender performance. Drawing on Foucault, Butler argues, "it seems that genders can be neither true nor false, but are only produced as the truth effects of a discourse of primary and stable identity" (1990: 136).[10] According to Butler then, even in the real world, these truth effects show some necessary instability thereby revealing their inherently performative character. The concept of performativity, according to Butler, not only describes the necessary exposure of the arbitrariness of all gender, but can itself be highlighted, and thus provide a means of subverting the stable system. She offers as an example of the latter type of performativity the practice of dressing in drag. When "in drag" individuals emphasize the constructedness of gender precisely by confounding the poles of masculinity and femininity. In other words, the often exacting reproductions of the female ideal on the bodies of men present viewers with a contradiction that reveals the gender system as a practice (a practice that is operative in normative gender performances, although these performances are less readily visible as such).

This formulation has some important implications for the dynamics of masculinity written onto the faces of the iambic poets. The kind of instability that has been revealed in the masculinity of the iambographic poet-persona cannot be said to produce a "primary and stable identity," but rather consistently highlights his multivalent nature.[11] In fact, the virulent masculinity so often adduced in the case of Archilochus and Hipponax as well as the corresponding inversion, the lack of masculinity, so often adduced in the case of Callimachus and Horace, is, for all these poet-personae, not as stable as commentators would lead one to believe. If Butler's notion of performativity is adapted to a theory of the iambic genre and thereby coupled with the multivocal poet-persona, a compelling explanatory model of a key aspect of iambic poetics comes into view. The extremes of masculinity in Archilochus and Hipponax, as well as the emasculated stance of Callimachus and Horace are two sides of the same coin. That is, the extreme positions are always motivated by the threat or promise of their opposite. In the archaic, performed iambic poetry, rather than a complex intratextual hermeneutic, there is a truly intertextual one, one that relies on knowledge of the poet's biography, a biography that often reveals the less than ideal characteristics of the poet's life.[12] For the later iambic poets, Callimachus and Horace, who are reading the now collected works of Archilochus and Hipponax, the dynamic is both intratextual and intertextual, creating a mirage of wholeness within the collection. On the one hand, their intertextuality is governed by their relationship to their generic forebears—a fact encoded and highlighted by the titles of their collections and their self-fashioning as reborn, archaic Greek iambicists. On the other, these iambic collections are intratextual by virtue of the fact that the poems are contained in a papyrus roll; thus, the interrelationship of the poems therein becomes a primary hermeneutic factor.[13] The inherent performativity of *Iambos* provides a way of bridging the hermeneutic gulf between these two fundamentally different modes of composition and the respective strategies of interpretation they engender.

For Archilochus and Hipponax, the poet-persona tends to extremes of masculinity. Indeed, one might say that not masculinity, but rather "hyper-masculinity" is evident in their poems. However, as generic exemplars, each of these "hyper-masculinities" is akin to the Homeric ideal of masculinity, which is also intimately connected to its own genre, epic.[14] In this sense, both Homeric masculinity and iambic hyper-masculinity are generic ideals, fully implicated in the poetry that creates them. Significantly, the poetics of *Iambos* requires such a masculine stance, but, unlike the Homeric ideal of masculinity, the iambic version is always linked to threats to the poet-persona's status as a male.[15] Therefore, the circle of representation, by including not only the hyper-masculine behavior, usually in the form of violent and/or sexual language, but also the "fault" in the persona's male mask, is contradictory, i.e., the poet-persona is simultaneously hyper-male and emasculated. Within this framework, an analogous situation is observed in Callimachus' linking of poetry and sex (or the lack thereof) in *Ia.* 3 and in Horace's *Epodes*, where the poet-persona dramatizes the situation of the archaic poets, but ends up impotent, rather than hyper-male.[16] A primary feature, then, of an iambic poetics is to be seen in the poet-persona's (whether implicit or explicit) self-representation of the faults in his male mask. Simply put, in mocking others, the iambic poet necessarily mocks himself. Masculinity is thus a feature of the multivocality of the iambic genre, one with intimate ties to the self-fashioning of the poet's persona. In writing iambic poetry, Callimachus exploits his masculine stance as an iambic poet in order to both align himself with his archaic predecessors, especially Hipponax, and to showcase his difference from them, thereby creating a duplicitous self perfectly at home in Alexandria.

Platonic Duplicity and *Iambos*

The persona, or mask, of the iambic poet has always fit somewhat poorly, then. In fact, the poor fit between the iambic representation of a person and the actual historical person is addressed in the following passages of Athenaeus. In the 11th book of his *Deipnosophistai*, Athenaeus presents a discussion of the malice of Plato. One of Athenaeus' dinner guests, Pontianus, says:

Λέγεται δὲ ὡς καὶ ὁ Γοργίας αὐτὸς ἀναγνοὺς τὸν ὁμώνυμον αὐτῷ διάλογον πρὸς τοὺς συνήθεις ἔφη "ὡς καλῶς οἶδε Πλάτων ἰαμβίζειν."

The story goes that when Gorgias himself read the dialogue named after him, he said to his friends: "Plato's quite talented at writing abuse-poetry!"

11.505d, trans. Olson 2009

Immediately following his quotation of Gorgias, Pontianus bolsters his case by citing another story about the fifth-century rhetorician, this time citing the Hellenistic scholar, Hermippus, as his source:[17]

Ἕρμιππος δὲ ἐν τῷ περὶ Γοργίου "ὡς ἐπεδήμησε," φησί, "ταῖς Ἀθήναις Γοργίας μετὰ τὸ ποιήσασθαι τὴν ἀνάθεσιν τῆς ἐν Δελφοῖς ἑαυτοῦ χρυσῆς εἰκόνος, εἰπόντος τοῦ Πλάτωνος, ὅτε εἶδεν αὐτόν, 'ἥκει ἡμῖν ὁ καλός τε καὶ χρυσοῦς ὁ Γοργίας· ἔφη ὁ Γοργίας: 'ἦ καλόν γε αἱ Ἀθῆναι καὶ νέον τοῦτον Ἀρχίλοχον ἐνηνόχασιν.'" ἄλλοι δέ φασιν ὡς ἀναγνοὺς ὁ Γοργίας τὸν Πλάτωνος διάλογον πρὸς τοὺς παρόντας εἶπεν ὅτι οὐδὲν τούτων οὔτ᾽ εἶπεν οὔτ᾽ ἤκουσε παρὰ Πλάτωνος."

Hermippus says in his *On Gorgias* (fr. 63 Wehrli): When Gorgias visited Athens after dedicating the gold statue of himself in Delphi, and Plato saw him and said: "Our fine, gold Gorgias has arrived!", Gorgias responded: "And this is a fine new Archilochus that Athens has produced!" Other authorities claim that after Gorgias read Plato's dialogue, he told the people present that he had not spoken or heard a word of this from Plato.

                              11.505d-e, trans. Olson 2009, with slight modification

Athenaeus has here cobbled together a useful group of texts for our understanding of the ancient genre of *Iambos*.[18] The verb Gorgias uses to characterize Plato's technique is *iambizein*, loosely translated above as "to write abuse poetry," perhaps better translated as "to write in the iambic mode."[19] The second quotation, from Hermippus' *On Gorgias*, offers a clarification of Gorgias' word choice by alluding to the *prôtos heurêtês*, "first founder," of the genre *Iambos*, namely, Archilochus. The argument of this passage as a whole seems to be that Plato, like Archilochus, composes in the iambic mode.

The question arises then, what does "Gorgias" mean by *iambizein*, or, put in a slightly different way, to what degree does "Gorgias" reactivate the sense of the verb, "to write in the iambic mode?" The characteristics of the poetic genre, *Iambos*, can be said to be possessed of four main features: an iambic metrical form, a first-person narrator, a critical stance and much ado about sex.[20] In a typical archaic Greek iambic poem, a first-person narrator vehemently criticizes a third party, often in terms that highlight the two parties' genders. Leaving formal metrical concerns aside, certain similarities between Gorgias' treatment by Plato and the iambic genre are evident. In general, the contest, or *agôn*, for wisdom that is a framing device for many of the dialogues often involves a critical stance. Like any Greek *agôn*, these competitions are "zero sum games," where the winner takes all; therefore, they always have implications for the masculinity of the participants.[21] The figure of Socrates in the so-called early dialogues, like the *Gorgias*, regularly deploys his *eironeia* in besting his interlocutors, which, in terms of the public competition for wisdom, amounts to mute shame.[22]

Gorgias' reading of the dialogue named after him suggests that he recognizes his status as inferior to Socrates within the dialogue; he is represented *in propria persona* as bringing about, or at least as being partially responsible for, his own "loss" in this competition with Socrates.[23] In the logic of the dialogue, he is personally complicit in his own downfall at the hands of a better man. From what we can tell from the extant scraps of archaic iambic poetry, these first-person narratives also regularly use the dialogue form.[24] Given this fact, we can see how the Platonic dialogue could be read as a kind of dramatic enactment of a typically iambic narrative situation.[25] What is significant, in generic terms, about Gorgias' comments is the implication that this dramatic enactment does *not* represent reality. At the end of the passage, we see that Gorgias denies outright the existence of the conversation related by Plato. According to Athenaeus (and probably Hermippus), Plato represents real people in his dialogues, but there is a disjunction between the reality of the person and the reality of the situation.[26] Indeed, the relationship of Plato "the author" to Socrates "the voice of Platonic philosophy" emphasizes this disjunction in the dialogues.[27] As has been recognized since antiquity, the real world of the Platonic dialogue is not always as real as it is designed to seem.

Callimachus in the Iambic Mode

While this passage of Athenaeus probably reflects an Alexandrian mode of reading the *Gorgias*, it also presents a useful critical mode for reading Hellenistic *Iambos*. In *Ia.* 1, Callimachus dramatizes the relationship between himself and the tradition of poetry within which he is composing by making a move similar to Plato's staging of Socrates. By beginning his collection in the voice of the archaic poet, Callimachus creates a double space for his poet-persona, which functions both as an active, contemporary critic and as the mere medium of the tradition by wearing the mask of one of the genre's most prominent figures. This is an act of generic appropriation *par excellence*, precisely because the problematic representation of the self as poet-persona is a characteristic mode of archaic *Iambos*. Significantly, the sense of *iambizein* which involves criticism and misrepresentation, is also found in the Diegesis to *Ia.* 5, a poem that has been characterized by Acosta-Hughes as indicative of the polychromatic and variegated *persona loquens* of Callimachus, especially in his iambic poetry (2002: 259–60). The diagete summarizes *Ia*. 5 as follows:

Γραμματο[δ]ιδάσκαλ[ο]ν, ὄνομα Ἀπολλώνιον, οἱ δὲ Κλέωνά τινα, ἰαμβίζει ὡς τοὺς ἰδίους μαθητὰς καταισχύνοντα, ἐν ἤθει εὐνοίας ἀπαγ[ο]ρεύων τοῦτο δρᾶν, μὴ ἁλῷ.

He attacks a schoolteacher, by name Apollonius, but some say a certain Cleon, in iambic fashion because he does vile things to his own students, in the guise of good intention, urging him not to do this, lest he be caught.

Text and trans., Acosta-Hughes 2002

This summary reveals a sense of the poet's use of a mask in this poem (Acosta-Hughes 2002: 256–60), in which, according to the diagete, the poet feigns a friendly attitude, or, perhaps, plays a role in order to accomplish his poetic goal of blame.[28] The use of *iambizein* here parallels that of the passages of Athenaeus and shows that one ancient reader of Callimachus saw the use of masks, by both the poet-persona (Callimachus Friend/Callimachus Enemy) and his target (Schoolteacher/Apollonius or Cleon). Even in the case of Callimachus' presumably unnamed schoolteacher, audiences read real targets into the poem, targets that were perhaps hinted at in the poem itself. Just as Hermippus' account of Gorgias' reading of Plato's dialogue led Gorgias to align Plato with Archilochus, and thus, to reveal a double misrepresentation (Plato: Archilochus::the real Gorgias: represented Gorgias), a double misrepresentation that Athenaeus relates, via the other Gorgianic anecdote, to the idea of the iambic genre, so too does the diagete's reading of *Ia*. 5 lead us to see two faces in the poem's narrator and an open mask under which real-world targets can be seen.

These uses of the verb *iambizein*, then, imply a misrepresentation of reality and suggest that misrepresentation of reality is a characteristic mode of ancient *Iambos*. As is implied in *Ia*. 5, the misrepresentation of people in *Iambos* often occurs along gendered lines, especially concerning the proper performance of masculinity. Improper sexual activity is corrected by the morally superior poet-persona as a way of attacking, in a covert way, the improper masculine sexuality of our anonymous, but knowable, schoolteacher. In general, within the genre of *Iambos*, from Archilochus to his Roman imitator, Horace, and from Hipponax to his Hellenistic imitator, Callimachus, the configurations of gender and criticism contribute to a poetics that constantly calls to the fore its status as a fiction. In other words, a constant feature of ancient *Iambos* is its representation of a seemingly real situation that is somehow always called into question. In contrast to the Platonic dialogues, though, the first-person narrator of ancient iambic poetry is always overtly implicated in this misrepresentation, and therefore becomes emblematic of it, as we can see in the case of Callimachus, *Ia.* 5. The iambic poets themselves all reveal in their own poetry just how bad they are at being men. Each poet-persona's actions in the face of his faulty masculinity vary, but in each, those actions represent a situation that could not exist, other than in the poetry itself. Archilochus, Hipponax, Callimachus and Horace *all* exist as iambic poets only within their iambic poetry and the genre highlights the divide between poet and poet-persona, especially through the portrayal of each poet-persona's problematic masculinity. When a poet makes someone the object of his *iambizein*, then, he represents them as someone they are not, but, he also represents himself as other than he is.

Callimachus' Iambic Masculinity

This multivalent presentation of the self is continued in Callimachus' third *Iamb*, where his problematic masculinity is revealed. The poem focuses on the relationship between poetry and love, through a comparison of the present and past and is summed up by the diagete:

Καταμέμφεται τὸν καιρὸν ὡς πλούτου μᾶλλον ἢ ἀρετῆς ὄντα, τὸν δὲ πρὸ αὐτοῦ ἀποδέχεται ὃς τῆς ἐναντίας ἦν τούτων γνώμης· παρεπικόπτει δὲ καὶ Εὐθύδημόν τινα, ὡς κεχρημένον τῇ ὥρᾳ πορισμῷ, ὑπὸ τῆς μητρὸς πλουσίῳ συσταθέντα.

He (Callimachus) censures the present because it is more concerned with wealth than virtue, and he takes the time before this (to be superior), which was of the opposite opinion to these (times). He also criticizes a certain Euthydemus because he used his beauty for gain when introduced by his mother to a wealthy man.

Text and trans., Acosta-Hughes 2002

From this account, the poem seems to fall into two distinct sections; the first a general critique of the present, and the second a specific rebuke of Euthydemus, the sexy, if greedy, object of Callimachus' affection. The division presented in the diegesis seems to be supported in the surviving text as Euthydemus is mentioned at line 24 with the word ὥς[π]ερ, which indicates a specific comparison to a general situation (Kerkecker 1999: 72).

The poem itself begins with the *persona loquens* expressing, in prayer form, his wish that he lived in another time:

Εἴθ᾽ ἦν, ἄναξ ὤπολλον, ἡνίκ᾽ οὐκ ἦα

If only, Oh Lord Apollo, I was when I was not.

Text and trans., Acosta-Hughes 2002

Callimachus thus strikingly states his anxiety with the present and conjures up a kind of alternate reality in which he simultaneously does and does not exist, a situation the poet actually achieved in *Ia.* 1. Further on in the poem (l. 9), he states that the world is inverted (ζόη μετέστραπται, l. 9).[29] Things are not right. But, is this simply a recasting of the old trope of the myth of the ages as related in Hesiod's story of the decline from the age of gold to his distorted present, the age of iron? The shoddy text suggests that the answer is yes, but with a caveat. Certainly, the remarks in the Diegesis seem to be born out by the remains of the poem, and, therefore, suggest a reading which includes wealth as the evil of the present (l. 17) (με · φεῦ · ἄκληρο[ν, l. 17). The caveat involves the specific complaint that the poet has hinted at in the same line, where φεῦ signals a personal lament, and readies the reader for the ensuing account of Callimachus' failing love life.[30] The Hesiodic model of decline is tempered with a concern not so much for the erosion of egalitarian ideals as for the effects of wealth on a poet's (read poor poet's) ability to get some action.[31]

The second half of the poem casts Callimachus' gripe with the present, topsy-turvy world in specific terms. Here we find out that Euthydemus swore some kind of oath to Callimachus and then broke it. The pederastic connotations secure that this was a homoerotic relationship, but the typical Greek homosexual situation is perverted, in that this would-be *erastes* (adult, pursuer) is reduced to a state of complete erotic inertia. Through some action of Euthydemus' mother, the oath is broken and the poet flounders. By the end of the poem, Callimachus is forced to consider an alternate lifestyle:[32]

     ] . ν μοι τοῦτ᾽ ἂν ἦν ὀνήϊσ[το]ν
.]ϋ[.].[.]Κ[υβή]βῃ τὴν κόμην ἀναρρίπτειν   35
Φρύγ[α] πρ[ὸς] αὐλὸν ἢ ποδῆρες ἕλκοντα
Ἄδω[ν]ιν αἰαῖ, τῆς θεοῦ τὸν ἄνθρωπον,
ἰηλεμίζειν· νῦν δ᾽ ὁ μάργος ἐς Μούσας
ἔνευσα· τοίγα[ρ] ἦν ἔμαξα δει[πν]ήσω.

    This would have been best for me
    [. . .] to cast back my hair for Kybebe
    to Phrygian flute or dragging my ankle-length robe
    to cry, alas Adonis, follower of the goddess.

But now, a desiring fool, I have cast my lot with the Muses.
Therefore I shall dine upon the loaf I have kneaded.

Text and trans., Acosta-Hughes 2002

The images Callimachus chooses to present as alternatives are suggestive. The worshippers of Cybebe are, famously, eunuch priests and the worshippers of Adonis are almost exclusively women.[33] The contrast between these kinds of performers and the kind Callimachus sees himself as is stressed in the word he uses to describe himself, μάργος. This word, which simultaneously connotes "desiring" and "foolish," aptly describes Callimachus' double bind.[34] He cannot satisfy his desire for Euthydemus precisely because of another of his desires, namely, for the Muses, as signaled by the erotic sense of ἔνευσα.[35]

The logic of the poem suggests that poetry causes poverty and poverty in these deteriorated times, leaves one's desires unfulfilled. This schema, however, is problematized by its involvement in the overall implications of the diegete's summary of the first half of the poem, which must be about the poet's anxiety with the present and his relationship with the past. Indeed, a strong argument can be made that the collection as a whole is a constant negotiation of present and past. In generic terms, Callimachus represents his book of *Iambi* in the first and last poems as a derivative form of archaic iambic poetry.[36] Callimachus' exposure of the disjunction between his generic model and his own poetry is constantly highlighted in the remains of the book, perhaps even embraced as a new model of *Iambos* in *Ia.* 13. Paradoxically, the poet's claim to authority as a writer of iambic poetry is called into question within the poetry itself. This self-exposure is paralleled in *Iambi* 3, in which, as we saw, the poet-persona reveals the fissures in his own masculinity. This problematic masculinity, which casts Callimachus' poet-persona as a failed *erastes* in this poem, must provoke a strong contrast with his poet-persona in *Ia.* 5, where the poet-persona, feigning good intent, takes the *erastes* of *Ia.* 5 to task precisely because he was successful in his seductions. Of course, there is a moral dimension grafted onto the criticism, but, nonetheless, the poet-persona's movement from masculine failure to moral authority on masculine sexual performance highlights both the failures and successes of Callimachus' masculine performances in the context of the collection.

As I have argued, this problematic self-representation seems to be characteristic of the archaic iambic poets as well. A double move can thus be discerned, by which Callimachus simultaneously signals his affinity to and difference from his predecessors; this is neatly verbalized in the opening line of *Iambi* 3, Callimachus' present wish for past existence. Such a claim not to "fit" in society seems to be a constant feature of the iambic *persona loquens*.[37] This liminal stance calls into question the possibility of the poet-persona's existence in actual society and suggests the importance of treating the narrating ego as a representation. In *Iambi* 3, Callimachus represents himself as effeminate, precisely because he is poor and unable to perform as a man should. His abuse of the "present" and Euthydemus amounts to a lament for the loss of his own masculinity by virtue of the fact that he is a poet.

Hipponax' Faulty Masculinity

Besides the overt mentions of Hipponax by Callimachus in *Ia*. 1, there are some striking parallels in the extant text of Hipponax to Callimachus *Ia*. 3. Perhaps most striking is Hipponax' prayer to Hermes (32W), preserved in the secondary tradition. In this poem, Hipponax prays to Hermes, the god of thieves, to help him steal some items of clothing:

Ἑρμῆ, φίλ᾽ Ἑρμῆ, Μαιαδεῦ, Κυλλήνιε,
ἐπεύχομαί τοι, κάρτα γὰρ κακῶς ῥιγῶ
καὶ βαμβαλύζω ...
δὸς χλαῖναν Ἱππώνακτι καὶ κυπασσίσκον
καὶ σαμβαλίσκα κἀσκερίσκα καὶ χρυσοῦ
στατῆρας ἑξήκοντα τοὐτέρου τοίχου.

Hermes, dear Hermes, son of Maia, Cyllenian, I pray to you, for I am shivering violently and terribly and my teeth are chattering ... Give Hipponax a cloak, tunic, sandals, felt shoes and 60 gold staters on the other side.

Trans. Gerber 1999

The situation parallels that of Callimachus in an important way, both call on a god (and in many ways very similar gods)[38] in an effort to address their respective states of poverty.[39] While Callimachus prays for a return to a putative past where wealth did not matter, Hipponax' prayer focuses on action in the present.

Hipponax, however, seems to be luckier in love than his imitator. Hipponax, too, is slighted, but not by a lover. The testimonia detail Hipponax' fight with a certain Boupalus, apparently a sculptor who made an obscene statue of Hipponax.[40] According to the biographical tradition, these two artists duke it out on the plains of representation, until, finally, Hipponax is so abusive that

Boupalus and his partner in crime, Athenis, kill themselves.[41] The first fragment of Hipponax hints at the animosity between the two (fr. 1 W):

ὦ Κλαζομένιοι, Βούπαλος κατέκτεινεν

People of Clazomenae, Boupalos has killed ...

In this fragment, the audience is called on to witness the destructive actions of Boupalus. If we imagine the situation of performance, the very utterance of this statement must have struck the listener as odd; does this fragment refer to Hipponax and therefore suggest that his poet-persona is also resurrected? But Hipponax' retaliation is slightly more virulent than that of Callimachus. In fr. 12 W Boupalus has the curious distinction of being the first person in Western literature to be called a "motherfucker":

τούτοισι θηπέων τοὺς Ἐρυθραίων παῖδας
ὁ μητροκοίτης Βούπαλος σὺν Ἀρήτῃ
†καὶ ὑφέλξων τὸν δυσώνυμον ἄρτον.†

deceiving (?) the "Redmen" by means of these things (?), Boupalos, the motherfucker with Arete, about to pull back the ill-named fore-skin[42]

Presumably, Hipponax here describes a sexual encounter between Boupalus and his mother, Arêtê. But that's not the end of the abuse; in fr. 17 W Hipponax describes what may be his own triste with Arêtê:

κύψασα γάρ μοι πρὸς τὸ λύχνον Ἀρήτη.

for Arete, having stooped over for me towards the lamp.

                                                      Trans. Gerber 1999: 367

If we follow the logic of the poetic situation presented in these related fragments, Boupalus has offended Hipponax, who, in turn, accuses Boupalus of sleeping with his own mother. Hipponax then puts the icing on the cake by describing his own sexual escapades with Arêtê.[43] No wonder Boupalus killed himself. When we consider Callimachus' situation in light of these poems, an interesting common figure emerges, namely, the mother. If we believe the summary of *Ia.* 3, then Euthydemus' mother must be acting as a kind of pimp, putting her boy on the market to the highest bidder.[44] In Hipponax, the situation is a bit different; Boupalus' mother is figured as the desired object and the son as the rival for her affections (cf. fr. 15W). Hipponax in these poems simultaneously repairs the cracks in his masculinity and calls into question the masculinity of the very person responsible for those cracks. The fact remains, however, that the cracks have to exist before they can be repaired, exposure must precede retaliation.[45]

There is a major difference, however, between the two poets' representation of their gender and its faults. Callimachus never really strikes a blow against Euthydemus, but focuses his remedy on escape to the past, where this kind of thing would have never happened, whereas Hipponax' frame of reference is decidedly present tense. The focus is on the current state of affairs; and as a result, Hipponax gets the last laugh in the moment of performance. What is striking about the commonality between the two poets is the impossibility of their existence in their respective societies. That is not to say poetry like this was impossible, for, *de facto*, it was. But rather that the poet-personae so represented had no place in society. This is the force of the shiftiness of the poet-persona of Callimachus' collection and the implication of Hipponax fr.1 W. The difference between poetry that is primarily performed and poetry that is primarily textual, that is the difference of the medium, is significant in this regard. In Hipponax, the performer had to play the role of "Hipponax," a fact that would have been readily apparent to the audience, and would have obviated the fiction of the poet. The poet-persona of Callimachus, on the other hand, located solely in the text of the *Iambi*, constantly shifts, starting with the reincarnated Hipponax and ending with a clear attempt at the "real" voice of Callimachus.

The shiftiness of the iambic poet-persona is emblematized by his gendered self-representation, both active and fully masculine, but necessarily simultaneously exposed as a fraud. The iambic poet-persona, whether he focuses on his wounded manhood or showcases his hyper-masculine reactions to such a wound, always represents himself as, in some sense, an impossibility. An iambic poetics virtually demands an awareness of the division between text (or performance) and reality. These poets, like Gorgias, simultaneously do and do not exist in the texts that carry their names, and that is an important part of their narrative strategy, a strategy ideally suited to Callimachus' engagement with the multivalent Alexandrian world.

Notes

1 See Edmunds (2001), 77–9, with scholarship cited there.
2 On the multivocality of the iambic poet-persona, see Lavigne (2008). For a similar view, see Rosen (2007), 203, where, in his reading of *Ia.* 4 as programmatic, he argues that the multiplicity of voices is characteristic of *Iambos*.

3   On this aspect of the iambic performance context, see Lavigne (2008, 2017).

4   See White (2021), who argues that the contrast between oral and literate culture is highlighted through the story of the Seven Sages and thus causes the reader to reflect on the relationship between Callimachus and Hipponax. I would extend that reflection to the relationship between Callimachus the historical person and Callimachus' poet-persona.

5   In reading *Ia.* 1, the likely title of the poetry book would have necessitated a given reader's appraisal of the relationship between poet-persona and poet, a relationship that is bridged through the voice of Hipponax; see Acosta-Hughes (2002), 3–5; and White (2021), although he does not address the likely title of the book roll. On the *Iambi* as a Gedichtebuch, see Kerkhecker (1999), 271–90.

6   Barchiesi (2001), 154, for example, argues that blame can stain poets who would take up invective. While I agree substantially with Rosen's (2007) analysis of ancient satire (especially the comments on p. 244 on the threat to the iambic poet's reputation, although without an explicit focus on masculinity), I would argue that the iambic poet-persona's alignment with the audience is never assumed within the genre, it must be achieved in and through the performance or text; on iambic danger, with a reply to Rosen, see Lavigne (2017), 137–8 (with n. 26).

7   Dialogue was a not unusual narrative mode for archaic iambic. It may even have been the case that Archilochus composed a dialogue featuring his primary target, Lycambes; see Hawkins (2008). See above, p. 129, on iambic dialogue.

8   This pattern is reflected in the *bioi* traditions of Archilochus and Hipponax; e.g., on Archilochus and Lycambes, see the *testimonia* collected by West at frr. 172–81 and, on Hipponax and Boupalos, see *Suda* ii.665.16 Adler and Pliny, *HN* 36.11.

9   See Rosen (2007), 195, who argues that the poet's negative self-portrayal and eventual rehabilitation, as an iambic feature, is deployed programmatically in Callimachus' *Iambi*.

10 Cf. Maud Gleason's succinct statement: "Masculinity in the ancient world was an achieved state, radically underdetermined by anatomical sex" (1995: 59). The remainder of this paragraph summarizes Butler's main argument in *Gender Trouble* (1990).

11 The multivalence of the iambic poet-persona is mirrored in his multivocality, on which, see my discussion above.

12 For Archilochus, this *vita* tradition exists alongside, but not necessarily within the poetry; see Lavigne (2008), 97 and Graziosi (2002) for a parallel argument concerning Homer. In fact, in as much as a given poem relies on knowledge of others in an orally performed context, it could be argued that a inter- rather than intratextual model is appropriate. As far as the performance context of Hipponax is concerned, certainty is impossible, but we see similarities in his *vita* tradition to those of Archilochus, which might suggest a similar performance situation. The

most salient of these examples is the dual citizenship of Archilochus and Hipponax. In every way, though, Hipponax' situation is an exaggeration of what we see in Archilochus. Whereas Archilochus is connected with two *poleis*, Hipponax, we are told is exiled from one and addresses his poetry to his new fellow citizens (see the testimonia for each poet assembled by Gerber 1999). Perhaps we could extend what Demetrius says about Hipponax' adaptation of the trimeter from Archilochus to his overall program; i.e., he has made it more iambic; cf. test. 12 Gerber.

13 Especially given the title of the rolls, which influence their cohesion; cf. Lavigne and Romano (2004) on the use of titles in the Milan Poseidippus roll.

14 On Homeric masculinity, see Graziosi and Haubold (2003), who argue that Homeric masculinity at least attempts to mitigate the destructive potential of masculinity without bounds, especially in the face of an attack on one's masculinity.

15 While Homeric characters certainly negotiate assaults on their masculinity, in general, a measured response is shown to be the ideal; moreover, it is of the utmost significance that we are dealing with the poet-persona's masculine performance in the iambic genre, not simply that of a character featured in a third-person narrative.

16 See Fitzgerald (1988) and Oliensis (1991); Barchiesi rightly stresses that the fluctuations of masculine power throughout Horace's collection are grounded in oscillations and ambiguities found in Archilochus (2001: 161 with n. 50).

17 The pioneering work of Acosta-Hughes and Stephens has made clear the importance of Plato for Callimachus in general and his *Iambi* in particular (2012: 23–83). On Hermippus, see fr. 63 Wehrli and Pfeiffer (1968), 150–1. Rotstein (2010), 298–9, notes that Hermippus wrote on Hipponax as well and that these stories could have been circulating as early as the second half of the fourth century. Hermippus, who was called "Callimachean," and had a reputation as something of a sensationalist, nonetheless reveals that in the Hellenistic period, there was a recognition of the relationship between *Iambos* and Platonic dialogue; cf. Riginos (1976), 93–4.

18 This passage is part of a larger section on the malice of Plato (11.504e–509e) that others have seen in connection to *Iambos*; see Worman (2008), 161–6, and Kurke (2011), 258–9 (via the shared interest in "low" themes between Socratic dialogues and iambic poetry). Although I do not agree with the emendation of *kai neon* later in this passage, Lorenzoni shows that the use of "golden" in this passage draws an iambic charge from parallels in the Platonic corpus (1995); cf. Wehrli (1974), 83.

19 On the use of *iambizein* and its cognates, see Rotstein (2010), 119–28. As will become clear, my sense of the term invovles the fictionality inherent to both the Platonic dialogues and the genre of *Iambos*. Kurke (2011: 258–9) reads this passage as generic criticism masking as biography and sees a strong Aesopic influence via the low tone and themes of the dialogues, which links them with *Iambos*. I would add a shared concern among the three genres with masks and masking and the concomitant ambiguity produced in the various speaking voices represented. As

Blondell (2002: 32) argues (quoting Momigliano 1993: 46): "As a genre, the Socratic discourses occupied a 'zone between truth and fiction . . . Between fact and imagination'. This liminal literary status is perfectly fitted to the Platonic enterprise of appropriating and reinterpreting tradition." She goes on to use this passage to illustrate her point. Incidentally, she also adduces a passage from the Second Letter (314c) in which Plato claims that his writings are not in fact his own, but "of a Socrates become *kalos kai neon*." Though Blondell does not explicitly link the text of the Second Letter with the quotation of Hermippus, it is suggestive to me that the same admittedly common adjectives are applied to such similar ends, i.e., to characterize Plato-as-author as someone who wears a mask in his representations, a mask which is *neos*, new, but also strange. Perhaps the passage of Hermippus and the Second Letter arise from a shared intellectual milieu.

20 See West (1974), 22–39.

21 An instructive anthropological account of the relationship between competition and masculinity is Herzfeld (1985), who argues: "To the extent that a man's performance successfully announces his personal excellence, it fits the poetic canon of Glendiot social life. Glendiot men engage in a constant struggle to gain a precarious and transitory advantage over each other. Each performance is an incident in that struggle, and the success or failure of each performance marks its progress" (11).

22 See Martin (1998) on the competition among sages; he sees Socrates as part of this tradition, but also breaking with it (124). While I agree with Martin that Socrates' performances of wisdom broke the performative frame of earlier wisemen, I would see that frame replaced by the literary context of the dialogue, which itself frames Socrates' elenchic performances as agonistic. The scholarship on Socratic irony is vast; most important to my argument is Vlastos (1991), who characterizes it as "complex irony," i.e., saying something that both is and isn't true at the same time (31). This irony puts Socrates' interlocutors who don't know the true side of his irony at a disadvantage; cf. Nathan (2020): "It is well founded that Socratic Irony has two audiences—an 'in crowd' who get it and an exoteric audience who don't—and this, as mentioned, is why the Greek word for deception could become our word for irony. For the time being we will look to the effect Socrates has on the exoteric audience who are deceived or even shamed by his irony" (77). The strangeness that Socratic irony entails creates a danger akin to that I mentioned above as a property of *Iambos*; cf. Worman (2008), who argues that the iambic abuse Socrates suffers when misunderstood, casts him as an outsider within the dialogues, and he plays the fool in order to ultimately reveal the actual foolishness of those interlocutors (165–6). Socrates' failure modulates with success in and through his ironic persona.

23 On the character of Gorgias in the dialogue, cf. Dodds (1959), 6–12, and his comment: "Plato depicts him as a well-meaning but somewhat muddle-headed old gentleman . . . But, unlike Polus and Callicles, he is a good loser: when his

compromises are exposed for what they are, he accepts his dialectical defeat in a
dignified silence ..." (9–10).

24 Our most famous example is the so-called "Cologne Epode," fr. 196a W; see also
Archilochus fr. 23 W and *Ad. ia.* 55a1 W; Hipponax fr. 36 W offers an imagined
dialogue. The abundance of direct address evident in the poems of both Archilochus
and Hipponax creates a pervasive expectation of dialogue, which may have been
fulfilled. Frr. 19 and 122 W, which begin in the voice of a characters, might involve
dialogue, or, at least editorializing in response by Archilochus' poet-persona.

25 See Worman (2008), 161–6; Edmunds (2001), 92–3, sees similarities between the
Platonic dialogue and the practice of Callimachean *Iambos*. However, as I hope will
be clear, Edmunds' argument for Callimachus' invention of the fictional *persona
loquens* should be pushed back further to the archaic iambicists. On the generic
appropriation that characterizes the Platonic dialogue form, cf. Nightingale (1995).

26 One might compare Old Comedy, a much more conventionally iambic genre; see
Rosen (1988b). Particularly suggestive with regard to this discussion is the portrayal
of Socrates in Aristophanes' *Clouds*. The relationship of Old Comedy to *Iambos* is
significant in this regard, especially in the device of the *parabasis* which strikes me as
a much elaborated version of the iambic poet-persona; see Lavigne (2008), 91,
discussing Hubbard (1991).

27 The confusion of Socrates and Plato is evident in the passage of Athenaeus discussed
above; cf. the story from Diogenes Laertius (3.35) that describes a surprising
reaction by Socrates to his portrayal in Plato's work: "They say that, on hearing Plato
read the *Lysis*, Socrates exclaimed, 'By Heracles, what a number of lies this young
man is telling about me!' For he has included in the dialogue much that Socrates
never said" (trans. Hicks 1925). It strikes me that Plato's ventriloquism of Socrates
might be seen as a self-conscious literary effect meant to mirror the elder
philosopher's characteristic irony. In any event, we, no less than the ancients, wonder
who is behind the mask of Socrates, which is akin to knowing the correct
interpretation of his ironic stances, and, thus, learning to do philosophy.

28 See Acosta-Hughes' discussion of the Diegesis as well as the diegete's comments on
Ia. 1, which suggests that the poet is playing the role of Hipponax in the first *Iamb*
(2002: 257–8).

29 This may be something of a trope in Hellenistic choliambic poetry (Acosta-Hughes
2002: 223–4); cf. Pfeiffer (1949) *ad loc.* l.9.

30 φεῦ is often used to express grief and astonishment, especially in tragedy; see LSJ,
s.v. and Nordgren (2015), 123–6, who quotes (123) Fraenkel (1950) on Aesch. *Ag.*
1143: "There is no example of φεῦ in Aeschylus which is not provoked by an
occurrence affecting the speaker himself." The idea here is unpacked at the end of
the poem, where, at l. 37, the poet-persona claims that he would have been better
offer crying for Adonis; instead he is μάργος, l. 38, and, as we saw, lamenting
himself. φεῦ and its semantics of personal affront may have something of an iambic

ring for Callimachus, as it only appears in Callimachus in his *Iambi* (here, 1.35 f. 4.81, and 5.58).

31 See Pfeiffer (1949), *ad loc.*

32 See Kerkhecker (1999) on the parallel to Hor. *Ep.* 15. Here, Callimachus' appeals to presumably more appropriate and manly gods (l. 32) apparently fail.

33 It is interesting to note that Hipponax mentions Kybebe along with another goddess with particular associations to women in fr. 127 W. The feminine associations of the goddess are clear in Rhianus 7 *HE*. On the cult of Kybebe, see Vermaseren (1977), esp. 13–37; and Martin (1987), 33–4. On the cult of Adonis, see Atallah (1966). In general, see Burkert (1985), 176–9 and 258 with n. 52.

34 See Acosta-Hughes (2002), 247–8, on the sexual meaning. To my mind, the semantics of μάργος have much in common with the poetics of *Iambos*. Both involve bodily deprivation that must be addressed and the loss of status that attends such admissions of lack. The iambic qualities of the Homeric *Margites* are telling in this regard.

35 See Pfeiffer (1949), *ad loc.* and Acosta-Hughes (2002), 247–8, on the sexual meaning.

36 The opening lines of the book suggest as much; see Hunter (1998) on the first and last (if, indeed, it is the last, as Hunter himself acknowledges) poems of the *Iambi*.

37 See Lavigne (2008, 2015). In the archaic context, where the primary mode of dissemination was performance, the liminal quality of the poet-persona would have been immediately recognizable in the distinction between poet and performer. Given the necessary multiplicity of performance venues or occasions (from ritual to symposium), the very nature of a performed poetic tradition elides the problem of derivation. The poet remains a unitary existential being, whence the authority is imputed to performers (cf. Pl. *Ion*). When the primary mode of poetic transmission becomes text-based, poet and performer meld into one figure. No longer is it possible to differentiate poet and performer. This has two implications for the argument presented above; first, that the poet/performer distinction is erased, and, second, that the poet/performer can now see his model as essentially the same as he is, i.e., a text that unifies poetry and performance. The textualization of a performative poetic tradition effectively halts its expansion in traditional terms (no more organic expansion), but it also enables another kind of expansion that has been seen as derivation, usually with negative overtones. I hope to show that besides simply evoking the performative context of the "original" Hipponax, Callimachus, through the highlighting of his derivativeness is dramatizing the marginal status of the iambic poet that would have been readily apparent in performance.

38 In a sense, Callimachus' invocation of Apollo can be seen as a modernizing response to (i.e, an update of) Hipponax' invocation of Hermes. Both gods are seen as in competition for many of the same duties, esp. music and poetry. On the competition

between the two gods, see *H.h.Herm.*; on Callimachus and Apolline poetics, see his *Hymn to Apollo*, with Stephens (2015), 73.

39 On the relationship between this poem and *Ia.* 3, see Acosta-Hughes (2002), 27–8. That Hipponax is here not simply planning a gratuitous raid, cf. fr. 34 W, where he has not as yet gotten his cloak, and fr. 36 W, where Hipponax laments Wealth's blindness, especially to Hipponax.

40 On aesthetic criticism in Hipponax, see Hughes (1996); on Bupalus and Hipponax, Rosen (1988a).

41 See the testimonia collected at fr. 1 W.

42 Text and translation after Rosen (1988a), who follows Masson.

43 For the details, see Hawkins (2015), 234; and Rosen (1988a), 35–9. It is interesting to note in the context of this paper, with Rosen (1988a), 31 n. 10, that it is difficult to question the historicity of Boupalos; could it be that part of Callimachus' choice of Hipponax lies in the fact that he is closer to the representational strategies of Plato than Archilochus is in his depiction of historical figures, especially given the Platonic connections to *Iambos* we have seen?

44 On the mother's role as a panderer, see Acosta-Hughes (2002), 237–8.

45 Compare the slightly different, but complementary argument in Rosen and Keane (2014), 392–4.

Bibliography

Acosta-Hughes, B. (2002), *Polyeideia: The Iambi of Callimachus and the Archaic Iambic Tradition*, Berkeley, Los Angeles, CA, and London: University of California Press.

Acosta-Hughes, B. and S. A. Stephens (2012), *Callimachus in Context: From Plato to the Augustan Poets*, Cambridge: Cambridge University Press.

Atallah, W. (1966), *Adonis dans la littérature et l'art grecs*, Paris: C. Klincksieck.

Barchiesi, A. (2001), "Horace and Iambos: The Poet as Literary Historian," in A. Carvarzere, A. Aloni, and A. Barchiesi (eds.), *Iambic Ideas: Essays on a Poetic Tradition from Archaic Greece to the Late Roman Empire*, 141–64, Lanham, MD: Rowman & Littlefield.

Bassino, P., L. G. Canavero, and B. Graziosi, eds. (2017), *Conflict and Consensus in Early Hexameter Poetry*, Cambridge: Cambridge University Press.

Blondell, R. (2002), *The Play of Character in Plato's Dialogues*, Cambridge: Cambridge University Press.

Burkert, W. (1985), *Greek Religion*, trans. J. Raffan, Cambridge, MA: Harvard University Press.

Butler, J. (1990), *Gender Trouble: Feminism and the Subversion of Identity*, New York and London: Routledge.

Carey, C. (2018), "Narrative, Authority, and Blame," *Mouseion*, 15: 7–27.

Cavarzere, A., A. Aloni, and A. Barchiesi, eds. (2001), *Iambic Ideas: Essays on a Poetic Tradition from Archaic Greece to the Late Roman Empire*, Lanham, MD: Rowman & Littlefield.

Dodds, E. R. (1959), *Plato: Gorgias*, Oxford: Oxford University Press.

Dougherty, C. and L. Kurke, eds. (1998), *Cultural Poetics in Archaic Greece: Cult, Performance, Politics*, Cambridge: Cambridge University Press.

Edmunds, L. (2001), "Callimachus *Iamb* 4: From Performance to Writing," in A. Carvarzere, A. Aloni and A. Barchiesi (eds.), *Iambic Ideas: Essays on a Poetic Tradition from Archaic Greece to the Late Roman Empire*, 77–98, Lanham, MD: Rowman & Littlefield.

Fitzgerald, W. (1988), "Power and Impotence in Horace's 'Epodes,'" *Ramus*, 17: 176–91.

Fraenkel, E. (1950), *Aeschylus: Agamemnon*, Oxford: Oxford University Press.

Gerber, D., ed. and trans. (1999), *Greek Iambic Poetry*, Cambridge, MA: Harvard University Press.

Gleason, M. (1995), *Making Men: Sophists and Self-Presentation in Ancient Rome*, Princeton, NJ: Princeton University Press.

Graziosi, B. (2002), *Inventing Homer: The Early Reception of Epic*, Cambridge: Cambridge University Press.

Graziosi, B. and J. Haubold (2003), "Homeric Masculinity: HNOPEH and AΓHNOPIH," *Journal of Hellenic Studies*, 123: 60–76.

Hawkins, T. (2008), "Out-Foxing the Wolf-Walker: Lycambes as Performative Rival to Archilochus," *Classical Antiquity*, 27: 93–114.

Hawkins, T. (2015), "Bupalus in Scheria: Hipponax's Odyssean Transcontextualizations," in L. Swift and C. Carey, (eds.), *Iambus and Elegy: New Approaches*, 229–52, Oxford: Oxford University Press.

Herzfeld, M. (1985), *The Poetics of Manhood: Contest and Identity in a Cretan Mountain Village*, Princeton, NJ: Princeton University Press.

Hicks, R. D., trans. (1925), *Diogenes Laertius: Lives of Eminent Philosophers, Volume I: Books 1–5*, Cambridge, MA: Harvard University Press.

Hubbard, T. K. (1991), *The Mask of Comedy: Aristophanes and the Intertextual Parabasis*, New York: Cornell University Press.

Hubbard, T. ed. (2014), *A Companion to Greek and Roman Sexualities*, Malden, MA, and Oxford: Wiley Blackwell.

Hughes, B. (1996), "Callimachus, Hipponax, and the Persona of the Iambographer," *Materiali e discussioni per l'analisi dei testi classici*, 37: 205–16.

Hunter, R. (1998), "(B)ionic Man: Callimachus' Iambic Programme," *Proceedings of the Cambridge Philological Society*, 43: 41–52.

Katsonopoulou, D., I. Petropoulos, and S. Katsarou, eds. (2008), *The Proceedings of "Archilochus and His Age," Paroikia, Paros, October 2005*, Athens: Diktynna.

Kerkhecker, A. (1999), *Callimachus' Book of Iambi*, Oxford: Clarendon Press.

Kurke, L. (2011), *Aesopic Conversations: Popular Tradition, Cultural Dialogue, and the Invention of Greek Prose*. Princeton, NJ: Princeton University Press.

Lavigne, D. (2005), "Iambic Configurations: *Iambos* from Archilochus to Horace," PhD diss., Stanford University, CA.

Lavigne, D. (2008), "The Persona of Archilochus and Rhapsodic Performance," in D. Katsonopoulou, I. Petropoulos, and S. Katsarou (eds.), *The Proceedings of "Archilochus and His Age," Paroikia, Paros, October 2005*, 91–113, Athens: Diktynna.

Lavigne, D. (2015), "Archilochus and Homer in the Rhapsodic Context," in L. Swift and C. Carey (eds.), *Iambus and Elegy: New Approaches*, 74–98, Oxford: Oxford University Press.

Lavigne, D. (2017), "ΙΡΟΣ ΙΑΜΒΙΚΟΣ: Archilochean *Iambos* and the Homeric Poetics of Conflict," in P. Bassino, L. G. Canavero, and B. Graziosi (eds.), *Conflict and Consensus in Early Hexameter Poetry*, 132–53, Cambridge: Cambridge University Press.

Lavigne, D. and A. Romano (2004), "Reading the Signs: The Arrangement of the New Posidippus Roll (P. Mil Vogl. VIII 309, IV.7–VI.8)," *Zeitschrift für Papyrologie und Epigraphik*, 146: 13–24.

Lorenzoni, A. (1995), "Platone 'novello Archiloco' e l'aureo' Gorgia (Athen. XI 505de; Plat. Phaedr. 235d–236b)," *Eikasmos*, 6: 109–20.

Martin, L. (1987), *Hellenistic Religions: An Introduction*. Oxford: Oxford University Press.

Martin, R. P. (1998), "The Seven Sages as Performers of Wisdom," in C. Dougherty, and L. Kurke (eds.), *Cultural Poetics in Archaic Greece: Cult, Performance, Politics*, 108–28, Cambridge: Cambridge University Press.

Momigliano, A. (1993), *The Development of Greek Biography*, expanded ed., Cambridge, MA: Harvard University Press.

Nathan, A. R. (2020), "Plato's Use of Irony," PhD diss., University of Sydney.

Nightingale, A. (1995), *Genres in Dialogue: Plato and the Construct of Philosophy*, Cambridge: Cambridge University Press.

Nordgren, L. (2015), *Greek Interjections: Syntax, Semantics and Pragmatics*, Berlin and Boston, MA: De Gruyter.

Oliensis, E. (1991), "Canidia, Canicula, and the Decorum of Horace's 'Epodes,'" *Arethusa*, 24: 107–38.

Olson, S. D., ed. and trans. (2009), *Athenaeus. The Learned Banqueters, Volume V: Books 10.420e–11*, Cambridge, MA: Harvard University Press.

Pfeiffer, R. (1949), *Callimachus, Volume 1: Fragments*, Oxford: Clarendon Press.

Pfeiffer, R. (1968), *History of Classical Scholarship from the Beginnings to the End of the Hellenistic Age*, Oxford: Clarendon Press.

Riginos, A. S. (1976), *Platonica: The Anecdotes Concerning the Life and Writings of Plato*, Leiden: Brill.

Rosen, R. (1988a), "Hipponax, Boupalos, and the Conventions of the Psogos," *Transactions of the American Philological Association*, 118: 29–41.

Rosen, R. (1988b), *Old Comedy and the Iambographic Tradition*, Chico, CA: Scholars Press.

Rosen, R. (2007), *Making Mockery: The Poetics of Ancient Satire*, Oxford: Oxford University Press.

Rosen, R. and C. Keane (2014), 'Greek and Roman Satirical Poetry,' in T. Hubbard (ed.), *A Companion to Greek and Roman Sexualities*, 388–404, Malden, MA, and Oxford: Wiley Blackwell.

Rotstein, A. (2010), *The Idea of Iambos*, Oxford: Oxford University Press.

Stephens, S. A. (2003), *Seeing Double: Intercultural Poetics in Ptolemaic Alexandria*, Berkeley, Los Angeles, CA, and London: University of California Press.

Stephens, S. A. (2015), *Callimachus: The Hymns*, Oxford: Oxford University Press.

Swift, L. and C. Carey, eds. (2015), *Iambus and Elegy: New Approaches*, Oxford: Oxford University Press.

Vermaseren, M. (1977), *Cybele and Attis: The Myth and the Cult*, London: Thames and Hudson.

Vlastos, G. (1991), *Socrates: Ironist and Moral Philosopher*, Cambridge University Press.

Wehrli, F. (1974), *Hermippos der Kallimacheer*, Basel: Schwabe.

West, M. L. (1974), *Studies in Greek Elegy and Iambus*, Berlin and New York: De Gruyter.

White, S. (2021), "Callimachus and the Seven Sages (*Iambus* 1: fr. 191 Pf.)," *American Journal of Philology*, 142: 41–66.

Worman, N. (2008), *Abusive Mouths in Classical Athens*, Cambridge: Cambridge University Press.

6

From a Small Beginning

Of Sibling and Poetic Order in Callimachus

Benjamin Acosta-Hughes

Ohio State University

For my sister
in Alexandrian Studies

The final line of Callimachus' *Hymn to Delos* is one that has long challenged interpreters: χαίροι δ' Ἀπόλλων τε καὶ ἣν ἐλοχεύσατο Λητώ, "hail Apollo, and hail she whom Leto bore." As Artemis is largely absent from the *Hymn to Delos*, her presence here has troubled some editors: Pfeiffer, following Wilamowitz, retained the manuscript reading ἐλοχεύσαο, with the goddess-island Asteria (invoked at line 316) as the subject "hail Apollo, and she for whom you [i.e., Asteria] acted as midwife." In a provocative treatment of the passage M. Fantuzzi (2011: 451–2) proffered the suggestion that Callimachus may have rather thus meant, by evoking Artemis here, in a subtle way to link the two long hymns, those to Artemis and Delos, in a final gesture that binds the two poems together. There is further a tradition that Artemis, born earlier, helped in the delivery of her brother;[1] the order of the two hymns, first that of the child Artemis and then the birth of Apollo, thus recreates the order of their births. The *Hymn to Artemis* opens with a famous scene of Artemis as a small child (line 5 παῖς ἔτι κουρίζουσα, "a child still prattling"), and in the course of the hymn the goddess evolves into a maiden of marriageable age (line 264 μηδέ τινα μνᾶσθαι τὴν παρθένον, "and let no-one woo the maiden").[2] At the conclusion of *The Hymn to Delos* Apollo is born (lines 255–9): our final vision of the infant Apollo is of a babe suckling at his mother's breast (line 274). The two hymns, to Artemis and to Delos, thus highlight a particular birth narrative: of the twins, Artemis is born before Apollo.

In his play on the order of the twins' births Callimachus recreates, in his own way, the play on the chiastic order of the Homeric *Hymn to Apollo* lines 14–16:

χαῖρε μάκαιρ' ὦ Λητοῖ, ἐπεὶ τέκες ἀγλαὰ τέκνα
Ἀπόλλωνά τ' ἄνακτα καὶ Ἄρτεμιν ἰοχέαιραν
τὴν μὲν ἐν Ὀρτυγίῃ, τὸν δὲ κραναῇ ἐνὶ Δήλῳ,

Hail, Leto, blessed one, since you bore glorious children, lord Apollo and arrow-shedding Artemis, her on Ortygia, him on rugged Delos

Given Callimachus' acute ear for sound, one might even posit that the accusative feminine relative ἣν in the final line of his *Hymn to Delos* may be meant to recall the accusative feminine in the article τὴν μὲν ἐν Ὀρτυγίῃ in the Homeric poem. And in his recreation of line 16 of the Homeric hymn in the final line of the *Hymn to Delos* Callimachus playfully reverses the ordering of the siblings ... because of course he does.

One of the arguments that led Wilamowitz (and subsequently Pfeiffer) to prefer the reading ἐλοχεύσαο is that Artemis does not otherwise appear in the 326 line *Hymn to Delos*. It is worth noting though that Apollo only appears twice in the 268 line *Hymn to Artemis*: once as a *comparandus* in the mouth of the infant Artemis herself as she demands boons from her father (line 7 ἵνα μή μοι Φοῖβος ἐρίζῃ, "that Apollo not contend with me"), and once in the narrator's promise of future song to Artemis at lines 137–9, lines which, very strikingly, capture the future pairing of the two long hymns (Artemis and Delos), and the birth narratives again in order (Artemis, Apollo), almost a poetic *mis-en-abyme*:

εἴην δ' αὐτός, ἄνασσα, μέλοι δε μοι αἰὲν ἀοιδή·
τῃ ἔνι μὲν Λητοῦς γάμος ἔσσεται, ἐν δὲ σὺ πολλή,
ἐν δὲ καὶ Ἀπόλλων, ἐν δ' οἵ σεο πάντες ἄεθλοι,

If only I, queen, if only song ever be my concern, in which there will be Leto's wedding, and there will be much about you, and also Apollo, and in it will be all of your feats.

In other words, the presence of Apollo in the *Hymn to Artemis* is very slight indeed: the conceit of the paired hymns is in large part that each of the twin gods is resplendently solo in her/his own hymn, Artemis before Apollo.

The *Hymn to Zeus* and the *Hymn to Demeter*, the first and last hymns of the collection, are again hymns to a sibling pair of gods; Demeter is, also again, an elder sister of Zeus. The *Hymn to Zeus* is now generally believed to be associated with the festival of Zeus Basileus (*Basileia*) in Alexandria.[3] There may be also a similar Alexandrian connection for the *Hymn to Demeter*: a scholion to the hymn records that "Ptolemy Philadelphus, in imitation of the Athenians, established certain customs in Alexandria, among which was also the procession of the basket. For there was the custom at Athens on an established day for the basket to be borne around on a carriage in honor of Demeter."[4] It is worth noting too that Callimachus' *Hymn to Demeter* does not name other cult sites of the goddess than that of the one in Alexandria: the well of Callichorus at line 15, the site at Eleusis where Demeter sat down in her search to rest, is part of the narrative that the poet of *Hymn 6* is deliberately *not* telling. Unlike *Hymns 2–5*, the *Hymn to Demeter* does not name other cult sites, and this is another feature that it shares with the *Hymn to Zeus*.

So, if we consider the hymns as a collection, the first and sixth are dedicated to an older generation of gods, the second through the fifth to a younger generation; Zeus (*Hymn 1*) and Demeter (*Hymn 6*) are siblings, as are Apollo (*Hymns 2 and 4*), Artemis and Athena; Artemis and Apollo are twins, Artemis the first-born. Athena is born without a mother—interestingly whereas Zeus' mother Rhea figures in *Hymn 1*, Kronos only does so in the same hymn as Zeus' patronymic (Κρονίδη, "son of Kronus," at line 91). In other words, each of the two hymns (Zeus, Athena) showcases a single parent. *Hymn 6*, like *Hymn 5*, is mimetic; the hymn evokes an actual progress of women in a ritual procession of Demeter. I wonder whether we might not consider *Hymn 1* to also be mimetic, and the opening lines of the poem to be literal rather than metaphorical:

Ζηνὸς ἔοι τί κεν ἄλλο παρὰ σπονδῇσιν, ἀείδειν
λώιον

At symposia what other thing is better to sing than of Zeus himself?

In other words, are we to read the poem as a hymn appropriate to sing at a symposium, or are we to imagine it, both from the opening occasional statement, and the closing salutation (lines 91–6), as a hymn that *is* in fact sung at a symposium, thus a mimetic hymn in the same sense as the ritual hymns 2, 5, and 6? As Stephens in her 2015 discussion of the passage notes, Athenaeus (*Deipnosophistai* 15.692F–93C) relates that the first libation at a symposium was poured to *Zeus Soter*, whereas a scholion to Aratus attests that the first libation was poured to *Zeus Olympios*; in either case the question of the possible mimetic nature of the hymn remains.

Hymns 5 and 6, as has long been noted, in many ways mirror one another: both celebrate female deities, both are largely in the Doric dialect, both narrate the story of a mortal's punishment, one tragic (Teiresias), one comic (Erysichthon), the two hymns are of very similar length, both are mimetic. Demeter's Egyptian equivalent is Isis: viewed from an Egyptian cultural perspective, Zeus/Demeter, the gods of *Hymns* 1 and 6, are Sarapis/Isis, both brother/sister and husband/ wife.[5] As it happens, one of the earliest literary references to Sarapis, a god who was in some ways a Ptolemaic creation,[6] is in Callimachus *Ep.* 37.5.[7] Athena's Egyptian equivalent is Neith, a goddess worshipped at Sais in the western Nile delta of lower Egypt. Like Athena, Neith is a warrior goddess whose attributes include among other things wisdom and weaving; also, like Athena, most strikingly, Neith is born without a mother. Athena is born adult and fully armed from Zeus' head (*Hy.* 5.134–6):

λωτροχόοι, μάτηρ δ᾽ οὔτις ἔτικτε θεάν,
ἀλλὰ Διὸς κορυφά. κορυφὰ Διὲς οὐκ ἐπινεύει   135
    ψεύδεα   αι θυγάτηρ.

Bath-pourers, no mother bore the goddess, but the head of Zeus. The head of Zeus does not assent to falsehoods ... daughter.[8]

Neith is "born the first, in the time when as yet there was no birth."[9] In other words both goddesses are not part of the usual gendered birth process.

In terms of the dramatic effect of the ordering of *Hymns* 5 and 6 the result is again a tragic or sympathetic one followed by a comic or unsympathetic one. In *Hymn* 5 the young Teiresias is blinded for something he does "unwillingly" (line 78 οὐκ ἐθέλων); at this moment the poet terms him σχέτλιος, "miserable, wretched," a term that, while negative, can also evoke sympathy.[10] His mother, the nymph Chariclo, she who is dearest to Athena,[11] cries out in reproach to the goddess she honors (lines 85–6 'τί μοι τὸν κῶρον ἔρεξας | πότνια; τοιαῦται, δαίμονες, ἐστὲ φίλαι; | ὄμματά μοι τῶ παιδὸς ἀφείλεο. "What have you done to my boy, lady? Are you, the gods, friends like this? You have taken away my son's eyes.") At the end Chariclo is to take consolation in that her now blind son will remain a seer even in death.

Juxtaposed to this tragic narrative of unwitting error is the "comic" one of intentional crime. In *Hymn* 6 Erysichthon is seized by an evil resolve (line 32 ἁ χείρων Ἐρυσίχθονος ἅψατο βωλά, "an evil plan took hold of Erysichthon") to chop down the trees sacred to Demeter; the goddess (in disguise as her own aged priestess Nicippe) tries to dissuade Erysichthon from his violent act, only to be met with his arrogant and harsh threat that he will bury his axe in her own body (line 43). Her following curse upon him results in his unquenchable hunger, which causes his aged father Triopas to throw his hands upon his gray head and cry out to his claimed father Poseidon (line 98): ψευδοπάτωρ, ἴδε τόνδε τεοῦ τρίτον, εἴπερ ἐγὼ μέν | σεῦ τε καὶ Αἰολίδος Κανάκας γένος, αὐτὰρ ἐμεῖο | τοῦτο τὸ δείλαιον γένετο βρέφος, "false father, look upon this your grandson, if indeed I am by birth of you and Canace, daughter of Aeolus, and this wretched offspring is mine." There are a number of motifs at play here, both in individual features and the contrast of the two lamentations, which play upon the ancient myth of the rivalry of Athena and her uncle Poseidon. Chariclo *knows* that she is the mother of Teiresias; Triopas both recalls the ambiguity of paternity that Telemachus first expresses in *Odyssey* 1.215–16, as well as evoking the more self-serving family claim to be descended from Poseidon. In the end, Teiresias, albeit blind, is given second sight and a kind of spiritual immortality; Erysichthon on the other hand ends his life as a beggar seeking refuse from the table-scraps (lines 115–16).

The *Hymn to Delos* also, famously, features the god Apollo speaking *in utero* of the future birth of a different god, Ptolemy Philadelphus (lines 162–70):

ἀλλά ἑ παιδὸς ἔρυκεν ἔπος τόδε· 'μὴ σύ γε, μῆτερ,
τῇ με τέκοις. οὔτ' οὖν ἐπιμέμφομαι οὐδὲ μεγαίρω
νῆσον, ἐπεὶ λιπαρή τε καὶ εὔβοτος, εἴ νύ τις ἄλλη·
ἀλλά οἱ ἐκ Μοιρέων τις ὀφειλόμενος θεὸς ἄλλος   165
ἐστί, Σαωτήρων ὕπατον γένος· ᾧ ὑπὸ μίτρην
ἵξεται οὐκ ἀέκουσα Μακηδόνι κοιρανέεσθαι
ἀμφοτέρη μεσόγεια καὶ αἳ πελάγεσσι κάθηνται,
μέχρις ὅπου περάτη τε καὶ ὁππόθεν ὠκέες ἵπποι
Ἡέλιον φορέουσιν· ὁ δ' εἴσεται ἤθεα πατρός.   170

But this word of her child restrained her. "No, mother, do not bear me there. I do not blame or fault the island, since she is rich and has good flocks, if any other is. But some other god is owed to her from the Fates, the highest race of the Saviors. Under his crown will come, not unwilling to be ruled by a Macedonian, both lands and the lands that dwell in the sea, as far as the ends of the earth and whereunto swift horses carry the Sun. And he will know the ways of his father."

This is another moment in Callimachus' *Hymns* of complex equivalencies. The chiastic ordering of figures is worth noting: child/mother (line 162), child/father (line 170). The divine birth is the equivalent of the royal one, with a series of divine references now emmeshed in the birth of the θεὸς ἄλλος, "another god": the *Moirai*, the race of the *Saviors* and Helios. And as in the same passage just cited of the *Odyssey* on paternity, the child Apollo recognizes she who bears him as his mother (line 162), but the young Ptolemy "will know" the ways of his father (i.e. will show himself to be his father's son by his conduct). In this world paternity is demonstrable rather than simply known.

One of the great papyrus finds of the last century was *P. Lille* 82, which restored to us the opening of Book 3 of Callimachus' *Aetia*, the so-called *Victory of Berenice*. The closing *aition* of Book 4, the *Lock of Berenice*, was known earlier from several sources, among them also several papyri, and in addition from Catullus' Latin adaptation (c. 66). More recent papyrus publications (e.g., *P. Oxy.* 2258 and *PSI* 1092) have filled out our knowledge of the Greek original, and, importantly, shown that Catullus' poem is in many ways his own later adaptation rather than a word-for-word translation from Greek into Latin, as was once thought.[2] Callimachus himself draws attention to Berenice's association with the closing poem of the *Aetia* in one of his extant epigrams (51 Pf.=15 G.-P.):

Τέσσαρες αἱ Χάριτες· ποτὶ γὰρ μία ταῖς τρισὶ τήναις
  ἄρτι ποτεπλάσθη κῆτι μύροισι νοτεῖ.
εὐαίων ἐν πᾶσιν ἀρίζηλος Βερενίκα,
  ἇς ἄτερ οὐδ' αὐταὶ ταὶ Χάριτες Χάριτες.

Four are the Graces, for one in addition to those three has just been fashioned and is still wet with perfume. Berenice, blessed one, envied among all, without whom the very Graces are not Graces.

The grace newly fashioned, still wet with perfume here in the epigram evokes the lock's journey from the queen's head to its settling on the lap of the goddess Arsinoe-Aphrodite in the closing episode of the *Aetia*; there in the *Lock of Berenice* the severing of the lock is imagined as a pained departure from its sister-locks, with the final setting of the new constellation in the sky:

ἄρτι [ν]εότμητόν με κόμαι ποθέεσκον ἀδε[λφεαί,
  καὶ πρόκατε γνωτὸς Μέμνονος Αἰθίοπος
ἵετο κυκλώσας βαλιὰ πτερὰ θῆλυς ἀήτης,
  ἵππο[ς] ἰοζώνου Λοκρίδος Ἀρσινόης,
.[.]ασε δὲ πνοιῇ με, δι' ἠέρα δ' ὑγρὸν ἐνείκας   55
  Κύπρ]ιδος εἰς κόλ[πους   ἔθηκε   ·
αὐτή[μιν Ζεφυρῖτις ἐπὶ χρέο[ς
  ....Κ]ανωπίτου ναιέτις α[ἰγιαλοῦ.
ὄφρα δὲ] μὴ νύμφης Μινωίδος ο[
  .....]ος ἀνθρώποις μοῦνον ἐπι.[,   60
φάεσ]ιν ἐν πολέεσσιν ἀρίθμιος ἀλλ[ὰ γένωμαι
  καὶ Βερ]ενίκειος καλὸς ἐγὼ πλόκαμ[ος,

ὕδασι] λουόμενόν με παρ' ἀθα[νάτους ἀνιόντα
Κύπρι]ς ἐν ἀρχαίοις ἄστρον [ἔθηκε νέον.

My sister-hairs were lamenting me, just now newly severed, and all of a sudden the brother of Ethiopian Memnon appeared, circling his dappled wings, a gentle breeze, the horse of violet-girdled Locrian Arsinoe, ... and with a breath me, bearing me through the wet air, he set me upon the lap of Cypris, Zephyritis herself sent him for that purpose ... the inhabitant of the shore of Canopus, so that of the Minoan girl ... for men only ... but I be numbered among the many lights, I the fair lock of Berenice, me washed in the waters rising up by the immortals Cypris placed me, a new star, among the ancient ones.

I have discussed this passage in terms of its resonances of Sappho elsewhere;[13] here I would like to focus for a moment on the sibling (and other) relationships. The gendered language of the fragment is especially striking.[14] The lock (πλόκαμος line 62, βόστρυχος *Dieg.* V 43), gendered as masculine, is severed from its sister hairs (κόμαι ἀδε[λφεαί line 51) which are feminine; the brother of Ethiopian Memnon (masculine) is Zephyr, a gentle breeze: θῆλυς, however translated, still retains its core sense of "female."[15] Κύπρ]ιδος εἰς κόλ[πους "upon the lap of Cypris" refers here to the cult image of Arsinoe-Aphrodite at Zephyrium, particularly marked, as I have observed before, by the term ἰοζώνου, Callimachus' variation of Sappho's ἰόκολπος.

The figure of Berenice II Euergetes enfolds *Aetia* III–IV; if we follow the play of χάριτες = papyrus rolls that we know from the 16th *Idyll* of Callimachus' contemporary poet Theocritus, the χάριτες of Callimachus' *Aetia* are now complete, as the poet himself proclaims in *Ep.* 15 G.-P. (=51 Pf, cited above). There *may be* a similar play in the opening of *Aetia* I, and this is to come back to an old issue, one now still debated. A scholion to *Aetia* fr. 2 (*Somnium*) responds to the lemma δεκάς as follows (fr. 2a,1 Harder):

δεκας· ρξ.ελυς
παλον . . .τηρ
παιδ( )πα . οκ. τ. ( )
η 'Αρσιγ(όη) δρω
ἦν ἄνω(θεν?) ἦ ὅτι δ(ε)κάτη(ν)
Μοῦσαν ἐκδ(ε) .... ()

.... δεκας· ἤ[τ]οι [.] . του()
...]αριθμ[.]. ταῖς [Μ]ού
σαι]ς τὸν Ἀ[π]όλλωνα
ση]μαίνει· Μουσηγέ-

της] γὰρ ὁ θε[ό]ς· ἢ Ἀρςι-
νόη]ν προςαριθμεῖ[]
ὅτι] τετίμηται ταῖς
τῶν] Μουςῶν τιμαῖ]ς
καὶ] ςυνίδρυται αὐ-
ταῖ]ς ἐν τῶι Μουςείωι.

....ten. Either ... is numbered with the Muses or marks Apollo among the Muses. For the god is leader of the Muses. Or it adds Arsinoe because she is celebrated with the honors of the Muses and she is set up together with them in the Museum.

In her commentary on this passage, Harder, following in part on earlier scholarly discussion, observes first that the text cannot have been very specific, or we would not have the various options proffered by the scholion (pp. 106–7), and that a reference here to Arsinoe as a tenth muse would be especially attractive as she is frequently celebrated as a patroness of the arts as in the new Posidippus epigram 37 AB, where Arion's lyre is dedicated to Arsinoe:

Ἀρςινόη, coì τῆ[ν]δε λύρην ὑπὸ χειρ[......]ῦ
    φθεγξαμ[ένην] δελφὶς ἤγαγ᾽ Ἀριόνιο[ς
ου..ελου[....]ας ἐκ κύματος αλλοτ[
    κεῖνος ἀν[....]ς λευκὰ περᾶι πελά[γη
πολλαπο[....].τητι καὶ αἰόλα τῆι .[
    φωνῆι π[....]ακον κανον ἀηδου[
ἄνθεμα δ᾽, [ὦ Φιλ]άδελφε, τὸν ἤλαςεν [......]ίων,
    τόνδε δέ[χου, .]υςου μ‹ε›ίλια ναοπόλο[υ.

To you, Arsinoe, this lyre from the hand? (...) made to resound, Arion's dolphin brought. (...) from the wave (...), that one crossed the white sea-and many things (...)-with voice (...). As an offering, Brother(-loving one), receive this (which brought? ...) gift from the temple guard.

The figure frequently enrolled as a tenth muse in Greek epigram is the poet Sappho;[16] as I showed in my 2010 study, Sappho's poetry is particularly important for Alexandrian poetical treatments of Arsinoe.[17] The "slippage" of Arsinoe/Sappho as tenth muse thus makes clear aesthetic sense. We might be able to carry this a little further. In the *Lock of Berenice* the sacrificed lock of hair is first borne by Zephyr to rest on the lap of Aphrodite (Cat. 66. 56 *et Veneris casto collocat in gremio*), as Zephyritis (Arsinoe-Aphrodite) instructed, whence the lock will shine as a constellation in the heavens. Might we read this passage also as a metaphor for the concluding episode of the *Aetia*, the *Lock of Berenice* which, first set in the lap of Arsinoe, metaphor here for Arsinoe as Muse from *Aetia* 1–2, will now shine as a constellation *meaning* first the *Lock of Berenice* is first included in the collection of *aitia* associated with her royal mother to then be resplendent in the night sky as a group of stars? In other words, the passage is at once theological and metapoetic: Aphrodite = Arsinoe as Aphrodite-Arsinoe/Zephyritis and Arsinoe as tenth muse = *Aetia* 1–2. We may even be able to bring one of Callimachus' own epigrams into play here, namely epigram 51 Pf.= 15 G.-P. (cited above), where the *Lock of Berenice*, the last episode of *Aetia* 4 and synecdochally representative of the whole book, is now added to *Aetia* 1–3.

In other words, the placement of the lock by Berenike at fr. 110.56-58 on the lap of Aphrodite-Arsinoe is also a metaphor for the completion of the *Aetia*.

We can say very little about the conclusion of *Aetia* 2: some scholars believe that fr. 112 (*Epilogue*) originally concluded *Aetia* 1–2 and was then moved, whether by Callimachus himself or by a later editor, to conclude the final four-book poem.[18] If fr. 112 *were* originally the concluding poem of an earlier two book collection, it is worth noting that line 1 ἐμὴ μοῦσα would further also implicate Arsinoe as one of the muses, and that this might have been given confirmation by line 2 ἀνᾴϲϲηϲ. In other words, *Aetia* 1–2 *may* have been bracketed by poems/passages evoking Arsinoe, here as tenth muse, in a manner similar to the way in which the *Victory of Berenice* (frr. 54–60j Harder) and the *Lock of Berenice* (fr. 110 Harder) bracket *Aetia* 3–4.

The metaphor of Arsinoe/Muse=*Aetia* 1–2 may find some resonances elsewhere in the poem. One example would be the final line of *Aetia* 3.76–7: ἔνθεν ὁ παιδὸϲ | μῦθοϲ ἐϲ ἡμετέρην ἔδραμε Καλλιόπην, which could both be understood as "inspired/came to my poetry" and "joined the *Aetia*." The opening fragment of *Aetia* 4, fr. 86 Pf., Μοῦ]ϲαι μοι βαϲιλη[ἀεί]δειν, "Muses for me royal(?) ......to sing," cited by the *Diegesis*, again associates the Muses and royalty.[19] Whether this line belongs to the *aition* of the Delphic Daphnephoria or another *aition*, the combination of song and royal imagery is still striking: and D'Alessio[20] is surely correct in marking the echo of *Aetia* fr. 1.3 εἴνεκε]ν οὐχ ἓν ἄειϲμα διηνεκὲϲ ἢ βαϲιλ[η.

In the case of the Lyric fragments, we find another striking, if not immediately obvious sibling pair in frr. 228–9. The former, the so-called *Deification of Arsinoe*, features the goddess' translation to Heaven on her death by the Dioscuri: the witness of this apotheosis is the spirit of her sister Philotera, who pre-deceased her. Fr. 229, *Branchus*, tells of the love of Apollo for the shepherd Branchus, whom he entrusts with the care of his oracle at Miletus. Both poems celebrate cult foundations dear to the Ptolemies, one the new cult of Arsinoe-Aphrodite, one the "re-founded" cult of Apollo at Miletus; and they contrast with one another in terms of their erotic imagery. I have written more extensively on these poems elsewhere and would just like to add a note on their arrangement here.[21] Fr. 227 (*Pannychis*) reads as follows:

Ἔνεστ' Ἀπόλλων τῷ χορῷ· τῆς λύρης ἀκούω·
καὶ τῶν Ἐρώτων ἠσθόμην· ἔστι κἀφροδίτη.

.   .   .   .   .   .

.   .   .   .   ]την[...]λ[
θυμηδίην τ[   ]δεῦτε παννυχ[
ὁ δ' ἀγρυπνήσας [συνεχὲς] μέχρι τῆς κο[ρώνης   5
τὸν πυραμοῦ[ντα λήψεται] καὶ κοττάβεια
καὶ τῶγ παρ[ουσῶν ἣν θέλει] χῶν θέλει [φιλήσει.
ὦ Κάστορ [   ] καὶ σὺ Πωλύδ[ευκες
καὶ τῶν ἀ. [   ] καὶ ξενω.[

Apollo is in the chorus; I hear the lyre, and I perceived the Erotes. And there is Aphrodite ... joy ... hither all-night? ... and he who stays awake until the culmination will take the sweets?, and the cottabos-prizes, and of those present will kiss her whom he wishes and him whom he wishes. Oh Castor ... and you Polydeuces ... and of the ... and strangers?

In the fragmentary lines appear the (half-)siblings Apollo and Aphrodite and Kastor and Polydeuces: the latter two will then bear Arsinoe to Heaven in fr. 228, where she is deified as Arsinoe-Aphrodite, and then Apollo is the divine figure of fr. 229. The *Diegesis* to this poem terms the piece a wine-song (*paroinion*) to the Dioscuri and adds that the poem also hymns Helen; in fr. 228 the Dioscuri bear Arsinoe (or Arsinoe/Helen?) to Heaven, then Apollo recurs in fr. 229 where he comes from Delos to the "sacred wood" where he encounters Branchus. The three fragmentary poems (frr. 227–9) are closely entwined, and their ordering plays out something of Ptolemaic religious narrative, one in which sibling imagery is especially marked.

One of the most moving of Callimachus' sepulchral epigrams is one for a dead brother and sister, *Ep.* 20 Pf. = 32 G.-P.:

Ἠῷοι Μελάνιππον ἐθάπτομεν, ἠελίῳ δέ
    δυομένου Βασιλὼ κάτθανε παρθενική
αὐτοχερί· ζώειν γὰρ ἀδελφεὸν ἐν πυρὶ θεῖσα
    οὐκ ἔτλη. δίδυμον δ' οἶκος ἐσεῖδε κακόν
πατρὸς Ἀριστίπποιο, κατήφησεν δὲ Κυρήνη   5
    πᾶσα τὸν εὔτεκνον χῆρον ἰδοῦσα δόμον.

At dawn we were burying Melanippus, and as the sun set the virgin Basilo died by her own hand. For she did not endure to live, after placing her brother on the pyre. And the house of their father Aristippus knew a double misfortune, and all Cyrene grieved on seeing the house of many children now bereft.

In our commentary on this epigram, we suggested that the name *Basilo* with its royal associations might be meant to evoke the Ptolemaic ideology of sibling love present in the epithet φιλάδελφος.[22] In the context of a king and his sister celebrated as *Theoi Adelphoi*, the poem would have an evocative reception.[23]

I would like to close not with a literary text but with one of the more widely known images of the brother-and-sister pair, the so-called Vienna cameo (Plate 12).[24] Using comparison with contemporary coinage portraits, some scholars have identified the figures on the cameo as Ptolemy II and Arsinoe II: on his helmet are the various figures of the Oasis of Siwah legend (serpent, Greek version of the Egyptian uraeus image, thunderbolt, ram of Zeus Amon); her crown is surmounted by a veil that then encircles his image. The effect in the red-brown and blue-white images is almost a realization in stone of the poet Theocritus' lines on the brother–sister pair:

(*Idyll* 17.128–34):
αὐτός τ' ἰφθίμα τ' ἄλοχος, τᾶς οὔτις ἀρείων
νυμφίον ἐν μεγάροισι γυνὰ περιβάλλετ' ἀγοστῷ,
ἐκ θυμοῦ στέργοισα κασίγνητόν τε πόσιν τε.
ὧδε καὶ ἀθανάτων ἱερὸς γάμος ἐξετελέσθη
οὓς τέκετο κρείουσα Ῥέα βασιλῆας Ὀλύμπου·
ἐν δὲ λέχος στόρνυσιν ἰαύειν Ζηνὶ καὶ Ἥρῃ
χεῖρας φοιβήσασα μύροις ἔτι παρθένος Ἶρις.

He and his noble wife, than whom no better woman casts her embrace around a husband in his halls, loving him from her heart as both a brother and a husband. And so was also the holy marriage of the immortals accomplished, whom ruling Rhea bore as kings of Olympos. One bed does Iris, yet a virgin, her hands cleansed with perfumes, strew for Zeus and Hera to sleep upon.

This early image of the *Theoi Adelphoi* clasped in embrace of the first quatrain is a very effective verbal recreation of the physical act (note especially the alternation, even entwinement, of male and female figures) and begins an alignment of the royal brother-sister marriage with that of Zeus and Hera.[25] The final lines are both of sensuality and purity, a last note of delicacy in a comparison that requires a certain tasteful erotic tone.

Another early reference to the *Theoi Adelphoi*, the cult of the brother-sister gods Ptolemy II and his siter-wife Arsinoe II, from this period occurs in Herodas *Mimiamb* I in the old bawd Gylis' numeration of the charms of Alexandria (lines 27–33):

ὅσσ' ἔστι κου καὶ γίνετ', ἔστ' ἐν Αἰγύπτωι·
πλοῦτος, παλαίστρη, δύναμι[ς], εὐδίη, δόξα,
θέαι, φιλόσοφοι, χρυσίον, νεηνίσκοι,
θεῶν ἀδελφῶν τέμενος, ὁ βασιλεὺς χρηστός,   30
Μουσῆιον, οἶνος, ἀγαθὰ πάντ' ὅσ' ἂν χρήιζηι,
γυναῖκες, ὀκόσους οὐ μὰ τὴν Ἅιδεω Κούρην
ἀστέρας ἐνεγκεῖν οὐραν[ὸ]ς κεκαύχηται

For all that exists and occurs anywhere, this is in Egypt. wealth, wrestling schools, power, peace, reputation, goddesses, philosophers, gold, young men, the sanctuary of the *Theoi Adelphoi*, the king is a good one, the *Mouseion*, wine, all good things one might desire, women, so many stars my Kore wife of Hades heaven does not boast to contain . . .

At one time the sense of this reference was one that was compared with the language of inscriptions (e.g., *C.I.G.* 4694 and *C.I.G.* 5127), but more recent images from the Goddio underwater archaeological expeditions off the coast of Alexandria have rendered a possible different sense of this cult, one rather of visual images. Among the colossal statues uncovered by Goddio and his team from the site of Thonis-Heracleion are of a king and queen in pink granite, the king 5 meters, the queen 4.9 meters in height. The figures may be from the reign of Ptolemy II, although they were re-carved at a later date.[26]

From a small beginning, a re-evaluation of the final line of Callimachus' *Hymn to Delos*, to colossal images of the brother and sister monarchs, I have tried to cast a short overview of how artistic culture of this period was influenced by the presence of a royal sibling marriage, a union of older sister and younger brother that for at least a decade in the first half of the third century BCE witnessed an extraordinary flowering of creative talent of many kinds in a new city in Egypt. Through a matrix of cultural analogies, Isis and Osiris, Hera and Zeus, Helen and the Dioscuri, the royal couple propagandized a figure of dual power, dual euergetism, and dual eros that imbued the art and literature of a new period with an extraordinary dynamism that effectively created a new Greek culture, one that we are finally coming to appreciate on its own terms. Susan's remarkable career of revealing inter-cultural discourse has been integral in this process and this essay is meant as a small acknowledgement for a great contribution.

Notes

1 Ps.-Apollodorus *Biblio.* 1.21v. τῶν δὲ Κοίου θυγατέρων Ἀστερία μὲν ὁμοιωθεῖσα ὄρτυγι ἑαυτὴν εἰς θάλασσαν ἔρριψε, φεύγουσα τὴν πρὸς Δία συνουσίαν· καὶ πόλις ἀπ᾽ ἐκείνης Ἀστερία πρότερον κληθεῖσα, ὕστερον δὲ Δῆλος. Λητὼ δὲ συνελθοῦσα Διὶ κατὰ τὴν γῆν ἄπασαν ὑφ᾽ Ἥρας ἠλαύνετο, μέχρις εἰς Δῆλον ἐλθοῦσα γεννᾷ πρώτην Ἄρτεμιν, ὑφ᾽ ἧς μαιωθεῖσα ὕστερον Ἀπόλλωνα ἐγέννησεν. "Of the daughters of Coios, Asteria, after making herself like a partridge, cast herself into the sea to avoid union with Zeus. And from her came a city first called Asteria after her, and later Delos. And Leto, after union with Zeus, was driven over all the land by Hera, until coming to Delos she bore first Artemis, and later, with Artemis as her nursemaid, she gave birth to Apollo."

2 Artemis' request to her father Zeus here replays an Archaic lyric fragment (*P. Fouad* 239) sometimes assigned to Alcaeus, sometimes to Sappho. See Acosta-Hughes (2010), 127–30.

3 Stephens (2015), 48–9.

4 Ὁ Φιλάδελφος Πτολεμαῖος κατὰ μίμησιν τῶν Ἀθηνῶν ἔθη τινὰ ἵδρυσεν ἐν Ἀλεξανδρείᾳ, ἐν οἷς καὶ τὴν τοῦ καλάθου πρόοδον. ἔθος γὰρ ἦν ἐν Ἀθήναις ἐν ὡρισμένῃ ἡμέρᾳ ἐπὶ ὀχήματος φέρεσθαι κάλαθον εἰς τιμὴν τῆς Δήμητρος in Pfeiffer (1953), 77 ("Ptolemy Philadelphus, established, by way of imitation of the Athenians, established some customs in Alexandria, among which was also the progression of the basket. For it was the custom of the Athenians on the appointed day to bear the basket in honor of Demeter on a carriage.").

5 In the *Homeric Hymn to Demeter* the role of Zeus in his daughter's rape arises repeatedly (see Richardson's note to line 3); his relationship to Demeter is less heightened (again see Richardson to 312).

6 Fraser (1972), vol. 1, 268–71; Tkaczow (1963), 68–70.

7 ὁ Λύκτιος Μενίτας | τὰ τόξα ταῦτ᾽ ἐπειπών | ἔθηκε "τῇ, κέρας τοι | δίδωμι καὶ φαρέτρην | Σάραπι· τοὺς δ᾽ ὀιστούς | ἔχουσιν Ἑσπερῖται.", "Menoites from Lyctos dedicated these bows saying 'here, my bow I give to you and my quiver, Sarapis, but the arrows the Hesperitans hold.'"

8 All the mss. have a lacuna in this line. See Stephens (2015), 262.

9 St. Clair (1898), 176.

10 E.g., Callim. *Ep.* 30.1–2: Θεσσαλικὲ Κλεόνικε τάλαν, τάλαν, οὐ μὰ τὸν ὀξύν | Ἥλιον, οὐκ ἔγνων· σχέτλιε ποῦ γέγονας; "Thessalian Cleonicus, wretch, wretch, no, by the harsh Sun, I would not have recognized you. Miserable one, where have you been?" Ap. Rh. III. 445–47: Σχέτλι᾽ Ἔρως, μέγα πῆμα, μέγα στύγος ἀνθρώποισιν, | ἐκ σέθεν οὐλόμεναί τ᾽ ἔριδες στοναχαί τε γόοι τε, ἄλγεά τ᾽ ἄλλ᾽ ἐπὶ τοῖσιν ἀπείρονα τετρήχασιν· "Wretched Eros, great bane, great object of hatred for mortals, from you are fashioned destructive strife, moans and groans, and other endless sufferings for them."

11 Lines 57–9: παῖδες, Ἀθαναία νύμφαν μίαν ἔν ποκα Θήβαις | πουλύ τι καὶ πέρι δὴ φίλατο τᾶν ἑταρᾶν, | ματέρα Τειρεσίαο, καὶ οὔποκα χωρὶς ἔγεντο· "Children, Athena once in Thebes loved one nymph, far, far the most of her companions, the mother of Teiresias, and never were they apart."

12 See further Harder (2012), vol. 2, 793–5; Massimilla 464; and especially the excellent, careful 1997 study of N. Marinone.

13 Acosta-Hughes (2010), 75–8.

14 See esp. Gutzwiller's excellent 1992 study.

15 For further discussion see Harder *ad loc.*

16 Acosta-Hughes (2010), 84–7.

17 Ibid., 16, 63–81 *passim.*

18 Knox (1985, 1993); Cameron (1995), 158 ff.

19 Whether or not fr. 86 is understood to belong to the *Daphnephoria Delphica*: see further Harder (2012), 713; Massimilla (2010), 420.

20 D'Alessio (1996), vol. 2, 500 n. 1.

21 Acosta-Hughes (2003); and Acosta-Hughes and Stephens (2017).

22 Acosta-Hughes and Stephens (2024).

23 On the cult of the *Theoi Adelphoi.*

24 On the cameo see Pollitt (1986), 23–4. On the identification of the figures as Ptolemy II and Arsinoe II, see Eichler and Kris (1927), 47–8.

25 See Hunter (2003), 192, and on the Egyptian parallel of the pharaoh's wife "who loves her brother" see Koenen (1983), 159–60.

26 Yoyotte (2006).

Bibliography

Acosta-Hughes, B. (2003), "Aesthetics and Recall: Callimachus frr. 226–229 Reconsidered," *Classical Quarterly*, 53 (2): 478–89.

Acosta-Hughes, B. (2010), *Arion's Lyre: Archaic Lyric into Hellenistic Poetry*, Princeton, NJ: Princeton University Press.

Acosta-Hughes, B. with S. A. Stephens (2017), "Callimachean 'Lyric,'" in *Trends in Classics*, 9 (2): 226–47.

Acosta-Hughes, B. and S. A. Stephens (2024), *Callimachus: The Epigrams*, Berlin and New York: De Gruyter.

Acosta-Hughes, B., L. Lehnus, and S. Stephens, eds. (2011), *Brill's Companion to Callimachus*, Leiden: Brill.

Adorjáni, Z. (2017), "Arion und Arsinoe Bemerkungen zu Poseidippos P.Mil.Vogl. VIII 309, col. VI 18–25 (= fr. 37 Austin–Bastianini)," *Zeitschrift für Papyrologie und Epigraphik*, 203: 69–75.

Cameron, A. (1995), *Callimachus and His Critics*, Princeton, NJ: Princeton University Press.

Eichler, F. and E. Kris (1927), *Die Kameen in Kunsthisorischen Museum*, Wien: Schroll.

Fantuzzi, M. (2011), "Speaking with Authority: Polyphony in Callimachus' *Hymn*," in B. Acosta-Hughes, L. Lehnus, and S. Stephens (eds.), *Brill's Companion to Callimachus*, 429–5, Leiden: Brill.

Fraser, P. M. (1972), *Ptolemaic Alexandria*, 3 vols, Oxford: Oxford University Press.

Goddio, F. and D. Fabbre, eds. (2006), *Trésors Engloutis D'Égypte*, Paris: Seuil.

Gutzwiller, K. (1992), "Callimachus' *Lock of Berenice*: Fantasy, Romance and Propaganda," *American Journal of Philology*, 113: 359–85.

Harder, A. (2012), *Callimachus: Aetia*, 2 vols, Oxford: Oxford University Press.

Hunter, R. (2003), *Theocritus: Encomium of Ptolemy Philadelphus*, Hellenistic Culture and Society, 39, Berkeley, Los Angeles, CA, and London: University of California Press.

Knox, P. E. (1985), "The Epilogue to the *Aetia*," *Greek, Roman and Byzantine Studies*, 26 (1): 59–65.

Knox, P. E. (1993), "The Epilogue to the *Aetia*: An Epilogue," *Zeitschrift für Papyrologie und Epigraphik*, 96: 175–8.

Koenen, L. (1983), "Die Adaptation ägyptischer Königsidealogie am Ptolemäerhof," in E. van't Dack, P. van Dessel, and W. van Gucht (eds.), *Egypt and the Hellenistic World*, 143–90, Lovanii: Orientaliste.

Massimilla, G. (2010), *Aitia: Libro terzo e quarto*, Rome: Fabrizio Serra Editore.

Pollitt, J. J. (1986), *Art in the Hellenistic Age*, Cambridge: Cambridge University Press.

Pfeiffer, R. (1953), *Callimachus: Hymni et Epigrammata*, vol. 2, Oxford: Clarendon Press.

Richter, G. (1965), *The Portraits of the Greeks*, London: Phaidon.

St. Clair, G. (1898), *Creation Records Discovered in Egypt*, London: D. Nutt.

Stephens, S. A. (2015), *Callimachus: The Hymns*, Oxford: Oxford University Press.

Tkaczow, B. (1993), *Topography of Ancient Alexandria (An Archaeological Map)*, Travaux du Centre d'Archéologie Méditerranéene de lAcadémie Polonaise des Sciences, Tome 32, Warszawa: Zakład Archeologii Śródziemnomorskiej, Polskiej Akadmii Nauk.

van't Dack, E., P. van Dessel, and W. van Gucht, eds. (1982), *Egypt and the Hellenistic World*, Lovanii: Orientaliste.

West, S. (1985), "Venus Observed? A Note on Callimachus, fr. 110," *Classical Quarterly*, 89 NS (35): 61–6.

Yoyotte, J. (2006), "Colosse d'une reine ptolémaïque," in F. Goddio and D. Fabbre (eds.), *Trésors Engloutis D'Égypte*, 102, Paris: Seuil.

7

"Them He Cannot Take"

Callimachus' Epigram for Heraclitus

Phiroze Vasunia
University College London

Susan Stephens taught me Hellenistic poetry during my studies at Stanford. She is an expert reader of Apollonius, Callimachus, and Theocritus, among others, and she opened my eyes to the sophistication of their verses. I offer this chapter to her in gratitude, and for her friendship, inspiration, and scholarly example:

Εἶπέ τις, Ἡράκλειτε, τεὸν μόρον, ἐς δέ με δάκρυ
  ἤγαγεν· ἐμνήσθην δ' ὁσσάκις ἀμφότεροι
ἠέλιον λέσχῃ κατεδύσαμεν. ἀλλὰ σὺ μέν που,
  ξεῖν' Ἁλικαρνησεῦ, τετράπαλαι σποδιή,
αἱ δὲ τεαὶ ζώουσιν ἀηδόνες, ᾗσιν ὁ πάντων
  ἁρπακτὴς Ἀΐδης οὐκ ἐπὶ χεῖρα βαλεῖ.[1]

AP 7.80, 34 GP, 2 Pf.

They told me, Heraclitus, they told me you were dead;
They brought me bitter news to hear and bitter tears to shed.
I wept, as I remembered, how often you and I
Had tired the sun with talking and sent him down the sky.

And now that thou art lying, my dear old Carian guest,
A handful of grey ashes, long long ago at rest,
Still are thy pleasant voices, thy nightingales, awake;
For Death, he taketh all away, but them he cannot take.[2]

William Johnson Cory's version is widely anthologized and disseminated, as it should be, since it is an accomplished and evocative poem. The eight lines of English hexameter and heptameter are no less effective in communicating the tenor of the poet's thought than the six lines of Greek elegiac verse. The emotional notes go deeper and resonate more feelingly in Cory's poem than in Callimachus' epigram. Cory's rendering has a Victorian sensibility to it, but the poem's popularity endures into our own time, perhaps because that sensibility still retains some of its charm.[3] Gildersleeve wrote, grudgingly, of "the tender grace of Cory's version, as a poem a classic, as a translation a failure," and Lloyd-Jones said he found the translation "so far removed from the spareness and tautness of the original."[4] These remarks should not blind us to the English poem's many qualities. A. E. Stallings, herself a distinguished poet, says that while Callimachus' epigram is "a perfect poem in Greek, in jewel-like elegiac couplets," Cory's poem is "a faithful, accurate and instantly memorable translation."[5] Her treatment of the English version analyses the form and structure of the poem and offers an appreciation of its virtues.

I

Many readers have liked and admired Cory's version for its beauty and directness and for saying something profound about death and friendship. The poem, precisely because it is so polished and affecting, raises what is arguably an old question, how to mourn for the dead, how to pay tribute to the dead and be true to them. In particular, the poem, by its poetic virtues, raises the question of mourning in verse. Many cultures, ancient and modern, have traditions in which they commemorate the death of family or friends in song and verse. But inside or without such traditions, questions of versification, sincerity, and rhetoric can be posed. We can't help asking if Cory's poem is a little too perfected, if the last line, for example, is almost too accomplished in the manner in which it offers a note of hope in a situation of loss. Does the poet's virtuosity in this instance draw attention to itself and take away from the tribute being offered to the dead? Does the poem's rhetorical flourish detract from the act of mourning? Funerary verse, of course, need not only be read in antithetical terms: poetry that is accomplished, by its grace and elegance, can enhance or deepen the tribute being paid to the dead. Those who have lost a friend or loved one will draw a great deal of solace and comfort from words that are attractively arranged, chosen carefully, and harmonious. Perhaps all mourning is rhetorical, governed by genre and tradition? But poetic versatility and stylistic brilliance can get in the way of mourning. Elegiac skill may take readers away from grief to self-satisfaction or to a place where admiration of poetry takes precedence over condolence.

These are precisely the issues taken up in the finest English treatise on epitaphs, namely, Wordsworth's sequence, *Essays upon Epitaphs*, which he wrote in the early years of the nineteenth century. The essays quote from many epitaphs, some which the poet saw first-hand, some which he read in books, in order to explore the language and themes found in them. Wordsworth is concerned with propriety and decorum, the kind of arrangements and metres that are appropriate to these compositions, the types of sentiments that they evoke in readers, and the language and rhetoric of the verses. He is not against metaphor or ornament but insists that these be used in a way that is suitable to the genre. The poetic imagery in an epitaph must "elevate, deeper, or refine the human passion, which it ought always to do or not to act at all."[6] Epitaphs should express feelings and views that are so widely held as to be regarded as banal, because they are "grounded upon the universal intellectual property of man." But when the writer of epitaphs conveys, as he must, truths about the human condition, he should do so "with such accompaniment as shall imply that he has mounted to the sources of things— penetrated the dark cavern from which the River that murmurs in every one's ear has flowed from generation to generation."[7] Needless to say, this is a standard that many writers fail to meet, and Wordsworth is severe in his condemnation of them.

Wordsworth appears to be even more concerned with the destructive power of language than with the poet manqué who turns out sepulchral inscriptions in country church-yards. Never shy at reproaching others for their misuse of images or figures, he has recourse to them himself in one of his most memorable passages:

> Words are too awful an instrument for good and evil to be trifled with: they hold above all other external powers a dominion over thoughts. If words be not (recurring to a metaphor before used) an incarnation of the thought but only a clothing for it, then surely will they prove an ill gift; such a one as those poisoned vestments, read of in the stories of superstitious times, which had power to consume and to alienate from his right mind the victim who put them on. Language, if it do not uphold, and feed, and leave in quiet, like the power of gravitation or the air we breathe, is a counter-spirit, unremittingly and noiselessly at work to derange, to subvert, to lay waste, to vitiate, and to dissolve.[8]

Wordsworth had said a little earlier that the language of epitaphs should be "not what the garb is to the body but what the body is to the soul," and he returns now to that image with the help of allusions to the story of Heracles, Deianeira, and the coat of Nessus, or to the poisoned garment sent by Medea to Jason's new bride.[9] Language can be dangerous, poisonous and violent; and Wordsworth's own language here is notably hard and aggressive, as if to drive home the point. The distinction Wordsworth draws is between "incarnation" and "clothing," and his striking turns of phrase have caught the eye of readers, from De Quincey to Geoffrey Hartman to Paul de Man and many others.[10] We are reminded by this body of commentary that Wordsworth's concern is with metaphor and with the appropriate use of figural language in general (and indirectly, perhaps, with literature as a whole). He scarcely denounces "the language of metaphor," but it is clear, from the essays on epitaphs at least, that he worries figural language can be misused or handled recklessly when a writer is commemorating the dead. It may seem like an act of love, as with Deianeira's shirt, but end up inflicting pain and suffering on the beloved. He is anxious about prosopopoeia (προσωποποιΐα) on the grounds that it is, when deployed by a lesser writer, overly sentimental and insufficiently pensive, solemn, or reflective. The gravestone that speaks about the corpse that lies beneath the marble needs to address its readers in a voice that is natural, sincere, and free of extravagance.[11] Metaphors and prosopopoeia have their place in epitaphs, but they need to be crafted with care, discernment, and sensitivity.

Wordsworth in his essays explores the words that people use to share their sadness and commemorate the dead. His writings weigh the language of the sepulchre and mark out the bounds of acceptance. He is not afraid to cast judgement on self-pity, to censure a maudlin thought, or approve this or that piece of epitaphic verse. In the process, he considers the language in which people mourn, and he asks, explicitly, what are good and bad ways to grieve, show bereavement, and express sorrow. Some of us, at a distance of more than two hundred years from Wordsworth's *Essays*, are inclined to say that grief and mourning should be left to an individual's sense of propriety, that people should be allowed to mourn in whatever ways they wish to mourn, and that they should surely not be made to feel the fear of literary reproach when they set about composing an inscription for a grave.

The poet's themes are close to questions which contemporary critics and philosophers have analysed, such as the nature of mourning, the relationship between mourning and language, and whether "true" mourning is possible. For many thinkers, as we suggested earlier, language and rhetoric make it difficult to arrive at an understanding of mourning. The prosopopoeia of the stone is "the fiction of the voice-from-beyond-grave," and as such it participates in modes of rhetoric and literariness that complicate mourning.[12] Metaphor and allegory, in epitaphs and eulogies for the dead, run the risk of saying something else, of transferring meaning to another place, or of making mourning do something in addition to mourning. Of "true 'mourning'" (he places "mourning" in inverted commas), de Man writes that, "The most *it* can do is to allow for non-comprehension . . .," and he is suspicious of its ability to be expressed in a language that is poetic, lyrical, elegiac, or celebratory, or even anthropomorphic. [3] To describe mourning in this way gives the impression that no one can truly mourn and comes close to insinuating that many, if not most, people are not mourning even when they are in a deep state of grief and think they are doing so. Perhaps for this reason, Jacques Derrida, in what might serve as his epitaph for de Man, speaks of "the impossible affirmation of mourning" and adds that "this impossible affirmation must be possible."[14] We mourn the dead in and through language despite the limitations of the human tongue; we mourn them out of love and out of a need to affirm and recall our love. Implicit in Derrida's insistence is the acknowledgement that even "true mourning" has a place for rhetoric.

In the poem for Heraclitus, Callimachus avoids prosopopoeia. This is not a poem in which the tombstone or the deceased address the reader or the passer-by, which is what one regularly finds in funerary epigram. A Greek example taken at random can be found in the elegiac distich recorded in an inscription of uncertain date and found near Thespiae: "I am the monument set up by Osthilos to his son Oligeidas, who brought him grief by his loss" (μνᾶμ᾽ ἐπ᾽ Ὀλιγε[ί]δαι μ᾽ ὁ πατὴρ ἐπέθηκε θανόγτι | Ὀσθίλος, ὃς πένθος θῆκεν ἀποφθίμενος).[15] Examples from Callimachus include: "Here sleeps his holy sleep, Saon of Acanthus, son of Dicon" (*AP* 7.451), or, famously, "Whoever you are who walk past my tomb, know that I am son and father of Callimachus . . ." (*AP* 7.525). Callimachus wrote many sepulchral epigrams—about twenty-five or twenty-six epitaphic epigrams (*epitumbia*) are ascribed to the poet in the standard collections—in which he deployed prosopopoeia or prosopopoeia combined with apostrophe.[16] But Callimachus also liked to work variations on the sepulchral epigram, and here he is playing and experimenting with the tradition. What the epigram presents in this case is apostrophe without prosopopoeia. The biographical or "autobiographical" details are presented to the reader through an address to the deceased poet, and the apostrophe takes the form of a shared memory or reminiscence of time spent together in the past. The address is not directed to the living by one who is dead—which is the presumption of many funerary epigrams—but directed to the dead by one who is living.

The apostrophe to Heraclitus is part of a poem that is extraordinarily alert to figurative language. Callimachus' composition takes de Man's claim that "language, as trope, is always privative" and virtually turns it on its head.[17] Figures may be privative in the sense that they take us away from "the thing itself," but if so, the epigram uses figurative language to complicate the idea that we live in "a world accessible only in the privative way of understanding."[18] The thrust of the epigram's ending is to say that the poems of Heraclitus are not subject to privation and that his verses shall remain among his friends and readers forever. The rejection of Hades—i.e. the rejection of the logic that joins figure to privation— offers a basis for consolation; it stakes a claim for poetic immortality and for restoration. If Heraclitus' verses or "nightingales" will thwart the rapacious violence of Hades, then the friend's death, announced so dramatically in the first line, is countered by the bold declaration made in the last. Callimachus is blunt about the finality of death, but in this epigram he holds out the promise of literary immortality. Negation is transformed into affirmation, and this is accomplished by a versatile language, by metaphor, lexical choice, and literary style. Of these, metaphor seems to me the most powerful of the devices through which Callimachus resolves the string of antinomies—"past and present, presence and absence, light and darkness, loss and preservation"—which form the scaffolding of the poem.[19]

II

Consider Callimachus' handling of the Homeric expression ἠέλιον λέσχῃ κατεδύσαμεν. Where the verb is intransitive in Homer, Callimachus uses the transitive form in his poem and makes the expression metaphorical: "we brought the sun down in conversation." In Homer, the expression ἠέλιον . . . κατεδύσαμεν has a literal or semi-literal connotation and refers to people participating in an activity (conversing, mourning, weeping) together for a long period, until the sun goes down, that is, until sunset.[20] The familiar Homeric words καὶ νύ κ' ὀδυρομένοισιν ἔδυ φάος ἠελίοιο, "and now the light of the sun would have gone down on their weeping," occur in both epics and, as Hunter says, "evoke memory, friendship and loss."[21] The causal, transitive form of the verb καταδύω is attested, but not very frequently: Herodotus, Thucydides, Aristophanes, and Pherecrates use it, in history and comedy, when people or things are making ships sink or disabling sea-faring vessels.[22] In order to find examples of a metaphorical use of the verb *kataduomai* with the noun for the "sun," one has to go to authors who come well after Callimachus. Dio Chrysostom, Aelian, and Aristaenetus "make the sun go down," with the verb in its causal sense.[23]

MacQueen emphasizes the allusions to Homer and points out that the verb *kataduomai* is also used in connection with "going down to the house of Hades" in the *Odyssey*. The "transitive turnaround" of the verb evokes death and indicates that the two friends dispatched the sun to the underworld of Hades.[24] The narrator evidently intends a contrast between the light of the sun and the supposed darkness of the death-world below. In the past, the poet and his friend enjoyed long hours of conversation and companionship, into the darkness, after the setting of the sun. Now the sun has set, and the light of life has been extinguished, but Heraclitus' words and poems endure.

In referring to Heraclitus' poems as "nightingales", Callimachus allusively complicates the sense of loss and desolation that come with the darkness. As Sens writes, "Nightingales were thought not to need sleep (Hes. fr. 312, *Suda* α 651), and the word thus has a special significance for poems that live on after their writer's death."[25] A verse inscription on a tomb from the Roman period also brings together the immortality of the nightingale's song in the face of death (εἴης χῶρον ἐς Ἠλύσιον· ζωούσας ἔλιπες γὰρ ἀηδόνας, ἃς Ἀιδωνεὺς οὐδέποθ' αἱρήσει τῇ φθονερῇ παλάμῃ).[26] But the evocation of the nightingale's song is complicated by the possibility that Callimachus uses the figure of the nightingale to explore his own innovative aesthetics and poetic programme. He appears to be the first person writing in Greek to use the word "nightingale" (ἀηδών) to refer to a poem (the sense "poet" is attested much earlier); later uses of the word in this sense seem to find their inspiration in his work.[27] He arguably uses a form of the word ἀηδών in the *Aitia* and could well be referring to "poems" in that text as well.[28] In the epigram that we have been discussing, the word ἀηδόνες "nightingales" may be a pun and allude to supposed etymological connections to song (ᾠδή), on the one hand, and to knowing (οἶδα), on the other.[29] By speaking of Heraclitus' poems as nightingales, Callimachus expresses his sense of sadness at the death of the poet and affirms that his verses will live on after him; recalls a long literary tradition in which both he and Heraclitus were lately participants; and refers to the distinctive poetics which he is exploring and in which Heraclitus is loosely perceived as a kind of ally.

Callimachus' assertion that the poems of Heraclitus will endure after his death is expressed through a sequence of figures that involves the sun, the nightingales, and, lastly, Hades the robber. The final verse of the epigram contains a new metaphor, or perhaps extends, through enjambment, the metaphor of the nightingales that has begun already in the preceding line since it is these very nightingales that Hades will not steal away. Even if the sentiment ("Hades the thief") is not new, the metaphor is striking, for "ἁρπάζω and its cognates and compounds are often used of sudden death."[30] The poet further draws attention to the metaphor by a novel lexical form (ἁρπακτής), which is a variation on the

Homeric ἁρπακτήρ and which seems to occur for the first time in Greek literature in this poem. With that word, the last line of the poem interestingly begins with a spondee rather than a dactyl: the spondees are regularly in the second metron in the epigram.[31] The vividness of the metaphor is underscored by the way in which the poet prises open, through tmesis, the closing verb/word (ἐπὶ χεῖρα βαλεῖ).[32] Diction, syntax, and figuration work together beautifully to give the poem a stirring and uplifting ending.

Susan Stephens has reminded us that Callimachus' poetic flair and craft should be appreciated in the light of Ptolemaic and Hellenistic socio-political frameworks. The reference to Halicarnassus in Callimachus' poem is interesting: the phrase ξεῖν' Ἁλικαρνησεῦ is not "a line-filler," as MacQueen noted, and conveys something important, namely, that Heraclitus was a friend of the narrator (the one received hospitality from the other) and that he was from Halicarnassus.[33] The point is impressed upon the reader with the help of the vocative form of Halicarnassus, a form which seems to occur only here in all of extant Greek literature. The other vocative expression in the poem is part of the address to Callimachus' friend in the first line, and so the poet presents us with Heraclitus, the guest-friend from Halicarnassus, or, as it were, Heraclitus of Halicarnassus. In his translation, Cory writes "Carian" rather than "Halicarnassian" and obscures the specificity of Callimachus' Greek. The substitution vexed Gildersleeve, but Stallings thinks that the shorter word is "metrically useful" and that there may be "some vague hint to the ear here of 'carrion'"—which is entirely plausible in this context.[34]

Our first literary impulse would be to associate Halicarnassus with Herodotus, who was, already in antiquity, the native most famously associated with the place. An Hellenistic inscription from Salmakis begins by asking the question, "What is it that brings honour to Halicarnassus?" The inscription goes on to say that among those who assuredly bring honour to Halicarnassus is "Herodotus, the prose Homer in the realm of history"; and it is Herodotus who leads the list of mortals mentioned in the inscribed poem.[35] Heraclitus' name appears not to be mentioned at all in the inscribed elegiacs. In his *Geography*, Strabo refers to Herodotus, first, and then Heraclitus and Dionysius as famous natives of Halicarnassus. Again, Herodotus comes first in the triad; and the reference to Heraclitus, in Strabo, may well be based on Callimachus' poem.[36] There is a good precedent for finding echoes of Herodotus of Halicarnassus in Callimachus' work. Susan Stephens is among those scholars who have shown how Callimachus draws on Herodotus' account of Egypt and deftly explores Herodotean themes and motifs in his poetic compositions. Behind the reference to Heraclitus of Halicarnassus, one sees an allusion to a more famous and accomplished writer.

The place name assumes additional connotations in the context of the third century BCE since it was an area over which the Ptolemies were exercising their influence and perhaps their sovereignty.[37] Halicarnassus began to come under the sway of the Ptolemies from about the 280s BCE and it even housed a Ptolemaic garrison under the control of Callias of Sphettos.[38] An inscription from Halicarnassus may "contain a list of mercenaries and members of the Ptolemaic garrison."[39] Scholars have discussed the place of Halicarnassus in Ptolemaic networks from 280 to 260 BCE, an important period in Callimachus' literary career. The historical record shows that citizens of Halicarnassus were involved in transactions with the League of Islanders (*Nesiotai*), which was supported by Ptolemy II Philadelphus. The city also granted honours to Sostratos of Cnidus, who helped with the construction of the Lighthouse in Alexandria and served as a diplomat for Ptolemy I. Jan-Mathieu Carbon and Signe Isager make a robust case for thinking of Halicarnassus as "a key strategic asset of the Ptolemies" and as "closely connected with the high affairs of the Ptolemaic empire."[40] Was Heraclitus, the addressee and poet, a notable resident of Halicarnassus? Wilfried Swinnen suggests that the addressee is the same as one Heraclitus of Halicarnassus, the son of Asclepiades, who is named in three *proxenos* inscriptions.[41] Perhaps this is the very man who composed the one epigram ascribed to Heraclitus in the Anthology. Perhaps so: the perils of biographical criticism are many. The archaeological and epigraphic evidence indicates, at any rate, that Halicarnassus was strategically important to Ptolemaic diplomatic, military, and naval activities in the Mediterranean in the years from about 280 to 260 BCE.

III

"They told me, Heraclitus, they told me you were dead." Cory emphasizes the apostrophe at the beginning of Callimachus' epigram: the latter's expression ("Someone told me," Εἶπέ τις) is doubled and pluralized, as if to draw attention to the figure with which the poem begins.[42] Liddell and Scott define *apostrophe* (ἀποστροφή) as "when one turns away from all others to one, and addresses him specially." That recalls the Latin of Quintilian, who says that speech can be "remarkably effective" (*mire movet*) in a forensic context when it is turned away (*aversus*) from the judge and addresses some other person or law or the natural world in an apostrophe.[43] With Callimachus' epigram, as in older lyric poetry, the text begins with an apostrophe in which the narrator does not explicitly turn away from anything, unless there is an implied audience when the poem commences—but the direct address is remarkably effective. The mention of Heraclitus' name in the initial vocative at the beginning (Ἡράκλειτε) sparks the emotional charge which enlivens the rest of the verses, through the second vocative (ξεῖν' Ἁλικαρνησεῦ), to the sentiment at the very end. The apostrophe enhances the poem's affective and psychological depth, its pathos, and thus conforms to the prescriptions laid down by ancient writers, from Quintilian and Longinus to the scholia on Homer.[44]

The apostrophe gives voice to the relationship that joins together the narrator and Heraclitus. Wordsworth, according to de Man, writes of a similar structure in his essays, but in terms that seem portentous, sinister, and morbid.[45] In the circuit that connects the narrator and the addressee, the apostrophe in Callimachus' epigram gives a specificity and vividness to the ties that bind the two poets together. The epigram works through *energeia* and *enargeia* (Quintilian discusses the latter in proximity to apostrophe), but also through what some modern critics have termed "animation."[46] It is as if the narrator summons up the shade of Heraclitus and animates him with his direct address, so that, in the time of the epigram, he might hear or receive the tribute to his friendship and his poetry. The narrator assures the dead poet that his poetic "nightingales" survive and will continue to be read in the world of the living and delivers this assurance in verse, as one poet to another, to heighten the homage, and, in so doing, the narrator, not incidentally, also inscribes himself into the tribute.[47] The delivery of the tribute, the remembrance of Heraclitus' poetic achievement, the narrator's role in celebrating the other's excellence in verse, and the narrator's own poetic craft are marked, recalled, and animated in every reading of the epigram.

What is striking about Callimachus' epigram is how it denies or defers the potential of loss contained in apostrophe. If apostrophe holds out the promise of animation with every reading, it implies nonetheless that the addressee returns to the dead and to oblivion after the epigram has concluded. There can be no animation without the reading of the apostrophe, no chance for Heraclitus to hear what his friend thinks of his compositions or what he remembers of their camaraderie outside of the time of the poem. But this epigram says that the poems of the guest friend from Halicarnassus shall outlive the structural logic of its master figure. The nightingales of Heraclitus are such that not even the end of the apostrophe can silence them.[48]

Notes

1 Pfeiffer (1949–53), vol. 2, 80–99.

2 In *Ionica* (1858), 7.

3 Goldhill (2017), 429–31, offers a brilliant exposition of Cory's poem and the "exemplary" place it occupies in the classical tradition. Acosta-Hughes (2019) is a stimulating analysis.

4 Gildersleeve (1912), 112 ("Brief Mention"); and Lloyd-Jones (1999), 13.

5 Stallings (2010).

6 In Owen and Smyser (1974), vol. 2, 76.

7 Ibid., 78–9.

8 Ibid., 84–5.

9 Ibid., 84.

10 The idea is vaguely reminiscent of comments made in Porphyry's rhetorical writings: see fragments F4a, 4b, and 4c in Heath (2002).

11 See Owen and Smyser (1974), vol. 2, 73.

12 De Man (1984), 77.

13 Ibid., 262.

14 Derrrida (1986), 32.

15 Text and translation from Friedländer (1948), no. 61, which departs slightly from the Greek in *IG* VII 1880.

16 See Fantuzzi and Hunter (2004), 306–28, for a discussion of the range of styles in Callimachus' epigrams; cf. Gutzwiller (1998).

17 De Man (1984), 80.

18 Ibid., 80, 81.

19 Sens (2020), 131.

20 The interest of Roman poets in the image is explored in the commentary on this epigram in Acosta-Hughes and Stephens (forthcoming).

21 *Iliad* 23.154, *Odyssey* 16.220 and 21.226. Hunter (1992), 122.

22 LSJ, s.v. καταδύω, II.

23 Dio Chrysostom 10.21: "'I grant that, Diogenes,' he said, 'but you are letting the sun go down with all your questions.' 'And is it not better,' he said, 'to let the sun go down if one is listening to useful words than to go on a futile journey?'" (Συγχωρῶ, ἔφη, ὦ Διόγενες· ἀλλὰ καταδύεις τὸν ἥλιον περὶ πάντων ἐπερωτῶν. Καὶ πότερον ἄμεινον, εἶπεν, ἀκούοντα ὧν χρὴ καταδῦσαι τὸν ἥλιον ἢ βαδίζοντα μάτην;). Aelian, *NA* 6.58: "And the priests are obliged to give way and confess that they devote their time 'to putting the sun to rest with their talk'; but they do not know as much as birds" (οἱ δέ, θύειν ἀνάγκη αὐτοὺς καὶ ὁμολογεῖν ὅτι τὸν μὲν ἥλιον ἐν ταῖς λέσχαις καταδύειν ἄγουσι σχολήν, οὐκ ἴσασι δὲ ὅσα ὄρνιθες); text & translation, LCL. The erotic letters of Aristaenetus are dated to the fifth or sixth century CE: "That was the song they

sang almost till cockcrow, and if I wanted to recount each detail, I think I would bring the sun down and still not be finished talking" (... καταδύσειν μοι δοκῶ τὸν ἥλιον ἐπὶ τῷ μήκει τοῦ λόγου, 1.24); text and translation adapted from Bing and Höschele (2014).

24 MacQueen (1982), 50.

25 Sens (2020), 132.

26 Peek (1924), 52 (also in *IGUR* III 1336), cited in part by Gow and Page (1965), 192; and cf. *IK* Kios 79, *IGUR* III 1305 and 1342.

27 See, e.g., *AP* 9.184. The symbolic use of the nightingale in Greek literature is discussed in A. Steier, *RE* 13, 2 (1927), s.v. "Luscinia," at cols. 1864–5; and see Thompson (1936), 22, for the meanings "poet" and "poetry."

28 Harder (2012), vol. 2, 48, on *Aetia* 1.16.

29 See Hesychius α 1498, s.v. ἀηδόνα, and cf. α 1500, with Steiner (2015), 111–12.

30 Sens (2020), 132–3.

31 Snell (1958).

32 Ibid. Sens (2020), 131, reminds us further that Hades "was interpreted to mean 'he who makes invisible'" and refers to Callimachus, *Epigram* 41.1–2 (Pf.). On Hades and invisibility, see e.g. *Iliad* 5.845.

33 MacQueen (1982), 51.

34 Gildersleeve (1912), 486.

35 Isager (1998); Lloyd-Jones (1999); and Gagné (2006).

36 Strabo 14.656; cf. Diogenes Laertius 9.17.

37 Selden (1998), 319.

38 *IG* II³ 911, lines 70–2.

39 Carbon and Isager (2021), 112, referring to a forthcoming publication by Isager.

40 Carbon and Isager (2021), 117.

41 The addressee Heraclitus himself can be glossed only somewhat hesitantly, though he may well be the person whom Swinnen (1970) has identified. Strabo refers to a person of that name as a native of Halicarnassus, as we saw, but Strabo is probably taking his cue from Callimachus. Heraclitus is said to be the author of an epigram which was collected by Meleager in his *Garland* and which survives in the Anthology, and so "only one of Herakleitos' nightingales was actually able to reach safety in the foliage of Melagros' garland" (Swinnen 1970: 41). On the basis of this poem, Wilamowitz (1924), vol. 2, 122, thought that Callimachus' high estimate of Heraclitus' poetry was understandable because the verses indeed were "something very special." That poem may or may not be by Heraclitus: the manuscripts ascribe it to Ἡράκλητος or Ἡρακλείδης, and it was Hecker who emended the name to "Herakleitos" (Ἡράκλειτος).

42 The best recent discussions of apostrophe are Johnson (1986); Culler (2001), chapter 7; and Alpers (2013).

43 Quintilian, *Institutio Oratoria* 9.2.38–9. As noted in LSJ, other relevant sources
   include Longinus, *On the sublime* 16.2; Phoebammon, *On Figures* (*De figuris*, Περὶ
   σχημάτων ῥητορικῶν) 1.1 (Spengel, *Rhetores Graeci*, vol. 3, 45); Alexander, *On
   Figures* (*De figuris*, Περὶ σχημάτων) 1.20 = Περὶ ἀποστροφῆς (Spengel, *Rhetores
   Graeci*, vol. 3, 23–4); and Hermogenes, *On Invention* (*De inventione*, Περὶ εὑρέσεως)
   4.4 (Rabe, p. 187). The reference in LSJ under this heading to Philodemus, *On Frank
   Criticism* (*De libertate dicendi*, Περὶ παρρησίας) fr. 21 (Olivieri, p. 11) is enigmatic.
44 Quintilian, *Institutio Oratoria* 4.1.63–70, 9.2.38–9, 9.3.24–6; Longinus, *On the
   sublime* 16.2 (with D. A. Russell's commentary *ad loc.*); bT scholia at *Iliad* 16.787
   (with Klooster 2013: 153–4; and Budelmann 2020: 64–5); *Rhetorica ad Herennium*
   4.15.22; Lausberg (1998), nos 762–5.
45 De Man (1984), 78.
46 Quintilian and *enargeia*: Steiner (2021), 643–4; animation: Johnson (1986).
47 For a slightly different reading, see Walsh (1990).
48 I am deeply grateful to Dan Selden and to members of a seminar at the Institute of
   Advanced Studies at University College London for their valuable comments on a
   draft of this chapter.

Bibliography

Acosta-Hughes, B. (2019), "Callimachus on the Death of a Friend: A Short Study of
   Callimachean Epigram," in C. Henriksén (ed.), *A Companion to Ancient Epigram*,
   319–35, Hoboken, NJ: Wiley Blackwell.
Acosta-Hughes, B. and S. A. Stephens (2012), *Callimachus in Context: From Plato to the
   Augustan Poets*, Cambridge: Cambridge University Press.
Acosta-Hughes, B. and S. A. Stephens, eds. (forthcoming), *Callimachus: The Epigrams*,
   Berlin: De Gruyter.
Alpers, P. (2013), "Apostrophe and the Rhetoric of Renaissance Lyric," *Representations*,
   122 (1): 1–22.
Bing, P. and R. Höschele, eds. (2014), *Aristaenetus, Erotic Letters*, Writings from the
   Greco-Roman World, vol. 32, Atlanta, GA: Society of Biblical Literature.
Budelmann, F. (2020), "Metalepsis and Readerly Investment in Fictional Characters," in
   S. Matzner and G. Trimble (eds.), *Metalepsis: Ancient Texts, New Perspectives*, 59–78,
   Oxford: Oxford University Press.
Carbon, J.-M. and S. Isager (2021), "Early Ptolemaic Halikarnassos (*ca*. 280–260 BC) and
   Its Network of Interactions," in B. Poulsen, P. Pedersen, and J. Lund (eds.), *Karia and
   the Dodekanese: Cultural Interrelations in the Southeast Aegean II Early Hellenistic to
   Early Byzantine*, 109–24, Oxford: Oxbow Books.
Culler, J. (2001), *The Pursuit of Signs: Semiotics, Literature, Deconstruction*, new ed.,
   London and New York: Routledge.

de Man, P. (1984), *The Rhetoric of Romanticism*, New York: Columbia University Press.

Derrida, J. (1986), *Mémoires: For Paul de Man*, trans. C. Lindsay, J. Culler, and E. Cadava, New York: Columbia University Press.

Eisen, U. E., and P. von Möllendorff, eds. (2013), *Über die Grenze: Metalepse in Text- und Bildmedien des Altertums*, Berlin and Boston, MA: De Gruyter.

Fantuzzi, M. and R. Hunter (2004), *Tradition and Innovation in Hellenistic Poetry*, Cambridge: Cambridge University Press. Originally published in Italian as *Muse e modelli: la poesia ellenistica da Alessandro Magno ad Augusto*, Roma-Bari: GLF editori Laterza, 2002.

Friedländer, P. with H. B. Hoffleit (1948), *Epigrammata: Greek Inscriptions in Verse from the Beginnings to the Persian Wars*, Berkeley, CA: University of California Press.

Gagné, R. (2006), "What is the Pride of Halicarnassus?" *Classical Antiquity*, 25 (1): 1–33.

Gildersleeve, B. L. (1912), "Brief Mention," *American Journal of Philology*, 33 (1): 105–16.

Goldhill, S. (2017), "The Limits of the Case Study: Exemplarity and the Reception of Classical Literature," *New Literary History*, 48 (3): 415–35.

Gow, A. S. F. and D. L. Page (1965), *The Greek Anthology: Hellenistic Epigrams*, 2 vols, Cambridge: Cambridge University Press.

Gutzwiller, K. J. (1998), *Poetic Garlands: Hellenistic Epigrams in Context*. Berkeley, CA: University of California Press.

Harder, A., ed. (2012), *Callimachus: Aetia. Introduction, Text, Translation, and Commentary*, 2 vols, Oxford: Oxford University Press.

Heath, M. (2002), "Porphyry's Rhetoric: Text and Translation," *Leeds International Classical Studies*, 1 (5): 1–38.

Henriksén, C., ed. (2019), *A Companion to Ancient Epigram*, Hoboken, NJ: Wiley Blackwell.

Hunter, R. L. (1992), "Callimachus and Heraclitus," *Materiali e discussioni per l'analisi dei testi classici*, 28: 113–23.

Ionica (1858), London: Smith, Elder and Co.

Isager, S. (1998), "The Pride of Halikarnassos. Editio Princeps of an Inscription from Salmakis," *Zeitschrift für Papyrologie und Epigraphik*, 123: 1–23.

Johnson, B. (1986), "Apostrophe, Animation, and Abortion," *Diacritics*, 16 (1): 29–47.

Klooster, J. (2013), "Apostrophe in Homer, Apollonius and Callimachus," in U. E. Eisen and P. von Möllendorff (eds.), *Über die Grenze: Metalepse in Text- und Bildmedien des Altertums*, 151–73, Berlin and Boston, MA: De Gruyter.

Lausberg, H. (1998), *Handbook of Literary Rhetoric: A Foundation for Literary Study*, foreword by G. A. Kennedy, trans. M. T. Bliss, A. Jansen, and D. E. Orton, ed. D. E. Orton and R. Dean Anderson, Leiden: E. J. Brill.

Lloyd-Jones, H. (1999), "The Pride of Halicarnassus," *Zeitschrift für Papyrologie und Epigraphik*, 124: 1–14.

MacQueen, J. G. (1982), "Death and Immortality: A Study of the Heraclitus Epigram of Callimachus," *Ramus*, 11: 48–56.

Matzner, S. and G. Trimble, eds. (2020), *Metalepsis: Ancient Texts, New Perspectives*, Oxford: Oxford University Press.

Owen, W. J. B., and J. W. Smyser, eds. (1974), *The Prose Works of William Wordsworth*, 3 vols, Oxford: Clarendon Press.

Peek, W. (1955), *Griechische Vers*-Inschriften, *Volume 1: Grab-Epigramme*, Berlin: Akademie-Verlag.

Pfeiffer, R., ed. (1949–53), *Callimachus*, 2 vols, Oxford: Clarendon Press.

Poulsen, B., P. Pedersen, and J. Lund, eds. (2021), *Karia and the Dodekanese: Cultural Interrelations in the Southeast Aegean II Early Hellenistic to Early Byzantine*, Oxford: Oxbow Books.

Selden, D. L. (1998), "Alibis," *Classical Antiquity*, 17 (2): 289–412.

Sens, A. (2020), *Hellenistic Epigrams: A Selection*, Cambridge: Cambridge University Press.

Snell, B. (1958), "Die Klangfiguren im 2. Epigramm des Kallimachos," *Glotta*, 37 (1/2): 1–4.

Stallings, A. E. (2010), "Literary Friendships, Part II," Poetry Foundation. Available online: https://www.poetryfoundation.org/harriet-books/2010/04/literary-friendships-part-ii (accessed 25 October 2022).

Steiner, D. (2015), "The Poetics of Sound: Callimachus' Rereading of Pindar Fragment 70B S.-M.," *Classical Philology*, 110 (2): 99–123.

Steiner, D. (2021), *Choral Constructions in Greek Culture: The Idea of the Chorus in the Poetry, Art and Social Practices of the Archaic and Early Classical Period*, Cambridge: Cambridge University Press.

Stephens, S. A. (2003), *Seeing Double: Intercultural Poetics in Ptolemaic Alexandria*, Berkeley, CA: University of California Press.

Swinnen, W. (1970), "Herakleitos of Halikarnassos, An Alexandrian Poet and Diplomat?" *Ancient Society*, 1: 39–52.

Thompson, D. W. (1936), *A Glossary of Greek Birds*, new ed., London: Humphrey Wilford, Oxford University Press.

Walsh, G. B. (1990), "Surprised by Self: Audible Thought in Hellenistic Poetry," *Classical Philology*, 85 (1): 1–21.

Wilamowitz-Moellendorf, U. von (1924), *Hellenistische Dichtung in der Zeit des Kallimachos*, 2 vols, Berlin: Weidmannsche Buchhandlung.

8

Advisory Tops

Callimachus Ep. 54 Gow and Page (1 Pf.)

Markus Asper
Humboldt University Berlin

for Susan, ὀλίγην λιβάδα

Since the days of Reinhold Merkelbach and Ludwig Koenen, a steadily growing circle of scholars has taught us to look out for Egyptian backgrounds in Ptolemaic court poetry, most notably Susan in her stunning book *Seeing Double*. While there may still be debate as to the actual pervasiveness of intercultural poetics, we should be on our guard even when reading Hellenistic poetry that seems, at first glance, indisputably Greek. In what follows, I present just one little case:

> Ξεῖνος Ἀταρνείτης τις ἀνείρετο Πιττακὸν οὕτω
>   τὸν Μυτιληναῖον, παῖδα τὸν Ὑρράδιον·
> 'ἄττα γέρον, δοιός με καλεῖ γάμος· ἡ μία μὲν δή
>   νύμφη καὶ πλούτῳ καὶ γενεῇ κατ' ἐμέ,
> 5   ἡ δ' ἑτέρη προβέβηκε. τί λώϊον; εἰ δ' ἄγε σύμ μοι
>   βούλευσον, ποτέρην εἰς ὑμέναιον ἄγω.'
> εἶπεν· ὁ δὲ σκίπωνα γεροντικὸν ὅπλον ἀείρας·
>   'ἠνίδε κεῖνοί σοι πᾶν ἐρέουσιν ἔπος.'
> οἱ δ' ἄρ' ὑπὸ πληγῆσι θοὰς βέμβικας ἔχοντες
> 10   ἔστρεφον εὐρείῃ παῖδες ἐνὶ τριόδῳ.
> 'κείνων ἔρχεο', φησί, 'μετ' ἴχνια.' χὠ μὲν ἐπέστη
>   πλησίον· οἱ δ' ἔλεγον· 'τὴν κατὰ σαυτὸν ἔλα.'
> ταῦτ' ἀΐων ὁ ξεῖνος ἐφείσατο μείζονος οἴκου
>   δράξασθαι, παίδων κληδόνα συνθέμενος.
> 15   τὴν δ' ὀλίγην ὡς κεῖνος ἐς οἰκίον ἤγετο νύμφην,
>   οὕτω καὶ σύ, Δίων, τὴν κατὰ σαυτὸν ἔλα.

A visitor from Atarneus asked Pittacus of Mytilene, the son of Hyrras, the following: "My dear old man, two marriages interest me: One girl is, according to wealth and family, like me, but the other one is far ahead. What is better? Please, could you advise me, which of the two I should lead to marriage?" Thus he spoke. But Pittacus, pointing with his stick, the weapon of old men: "Look, *they* will tell you everything." And they, children who had swift whipping tops, let them whirl on a wide cross-road. "Follow their lead!" he said. And he stepped closer. They said: "Keep to your own (place)!" When he heard that, the visitor avoided engagement with the bigger estate; he had understood the children's prophetic utterance. And as this man led the modest bride into his house, so please, Dion, do you: keep to your own.

This epigram (54 Gow and Page 1965: vol. 1, 70–1, 1277 ff. = *Anthologia Palatina* 7.89) is obviously at odds with established epigrammatic sub-genres; rather, it seems close to iambic poetry. Callimachus tells here a little emblematic story about an anecdotal incident, set at early sixth-century Mytilene of Lesbos and within the traditions about the Seven Sages one of which is Pittacus. As Callimachus demonstrates in his first iamb (fr. 191 Pf.), he knows these traditions very well, which is why Diogenes Laertius quotes him often and amply (Thales 1.23 ff., our epigram in Pittacus 1.80).[2] Conventional as Pittacus' advice is,[3] Callimachus tells the story in a way that leaves room for questions, which has perhaps led to the little appreciation modern scholars seem to have had for this epigram ("flat and straightforward," in Gow and Page's words 1965: vol. 2, 205). It is obvious, that we cannot know Dion and thus have to miss the closural point,[4] which is probably somehow derogatory. It might entail a colloquial double entendre on ἐλᾶν, which can also mean "have sex with someone" (Montanari s.v. 1).[5]

Apart from that, the reader will ask herself why Callimachus does not let Pittacus respond himself but lets him refer his visitor to some children. Perhaps for reasons of (imagined) self-presentation of an old and acclaimed sage? One must admit that it makes a great and sage-like scene when an old man, instead of replying with precious advice, slowly raises his stick and points towards an unexpected medium, namely children who are the least probable authorities when marriage is concerned. Ironically, the famous sage refers to playing children as media of his advice. Thus, Pittacus' anecdotal sageness would manifest itself in anticipating the children's words, in a way that is almost prophetic. However, when this advice is associated with any of the Seven Sages outside of this text, of course the sage pronounces it with explicit personal authority as his very own words and original insight.[6]

At this point, I would like to draw attention to the fact that it was Egyptian oracular practice to credit children with prophetic words, inadvertently uttered in play situations. Though remaining skeptical, Gow and Page follow Sinko (1914) in quoting Plutarch's *De Iside et Osiride* 14 (356 E):

ἐκ τούτου τὰ παιδάρια μαντικὴν δύναμιν ἔχειν οἴεσθαι τοὺς Αἰγυπτίους καὶ μάλιστα ταῖς τούτων ὀττεύεσθαι κληδόσι παιζόντων ἐν ἱεροῖς καὶ φθεγγομένων ὅ τι ἂν τύχωσιν.

That is why the Egyptians believe children to have oracular powers, most of all those who foretell with prophetic utterances when playing in sanctuaries and utter whatever fits the situation (in play).

In his rather well-informed treatise on Egyptian religion Plutarch presents this belief as specifically Egyptian and thus certainly as non-Greek.[7] His brief description of the situation (children playing, chance utterances situated in play become significant as actual prophecies) fits the Pittacus epigram beautifully, with one exception: We are to imagine Pittacus, the visitor and the children of Mytilene as standing at a public crossroad (v. 10 εὐρείη . . . ἐνὶ τριόδῳ), not in a sanctuary.

In his chapter on Apis (*De natura animalium* 11.10) Aelian touches upon Apis' oracular strengths and gives more precise information about oracular children than Plutarch, but restricted to the cult of Apis:

μάντις τε ἦν ἄρα ἀγαθὸς ὁ Ἆπις, οὐ καθίζων μὰ Δία κόρας ἢ πρεσβυτέρας γυναῖκας ἐπί τινων τριπόδων, οὐδὲ μὴν πόματος ἱεροῦ ἐμπιπλάς, ἀλλ᾽ ὃ μέν τις εὔχεται τῷ θεῷ τῷδε καί μαθεῖν ἐθέλει αὐτοῦ, παῖδες δὲ ἀθύροντες ἔξω καὶ πρὸς ἀλλήλους σκιρτῶντες, ἐπίπνοοι γενόμενοι σὺν τῷ ῥυθμῷ αὐτὰ ἕκαστα προλέγουσιν, ὥς εἶναι Σάγραν τὰ λεχθέντα.

A good oracle was Apis, indeed—and not by sitting down, by Zeus, young girls or elderly women on some kind of tripod nor by filling them with sacred beverages. Instead, one prays to this god and wishes for instruction by him, and children who are playing outside and hop around (or: dance) with each other, become inspired and rhythmically foretell each single thing, so that their words become a Sagra (i.e., absolutely true).

While Egyptologists acknowledge both Plutarch and Aelian as being well-informed about Egyptian religion,[8] it is not for me to decide whether the cult of Apis provides a specialized instance of a wide-spread belief in oracular powers of playing children (note that in Aelian, the chance- or play-character of the sayings is less distinct) or whether general practice has emerged from this cult.

Perhaps it points to the former that children play a certain role in magical procedure; in addition, there is the prophetic "child of Elephantine" (Papyrus Dodgson).[9] Both the accounts of Plutarch and Aelian seem to find nothing remarkable in the role that children play in Egyptian sanctuaries, by the way.

It seems, thus, that the sage Pittacus refers his guest to Egyptian children, as it were. The scene is Greco-Egyptian in the sense that in order for it to work in the reader's imagination, elements from both cultures have to interlock, to work together in that fictional space. What was a question of only subordinate significance in the days of Gow and Page,[10] however, becomes more meaningful for readers today who look out for Greco-Egyptian "doubleness" in Alexandrian poetry. In the light of Susan's work, especially of *Seeing Double*, even in this modest epigram, quite remote from court literature, a poetical technique of blending becomes visible, with which Callimachus creates a sage past that is firmly set in archaic Greece, yet contains elements of contemporary Egyptian culture. As for the construction of imaginary space, we observe that Callimachus generalizes the situation: The encounter, which by Egyptian standards would probably have to take place in a sanctuary, is set at a non-descript crossroads somewhere in Mytilene.

Acknowledgment: Thanks to my colleague Alexandra von Lieven for her Egyptological expertise.

Notes

1 See, however, Cairns (2008) for the genre of the "epigramma longum."

2 Diogenes motivates the advice by Pittacus' own situation (I 81: εὐγενεστέρα γὰρ αὐτῷ οὖσα ἡ γυνή, ἐπειδήπερ ἦν Δράκοντος ἀδελφὴ τοῦ Πενθίλου, σφόδρα κατεσοβαρεύετο αὐτοῦ— (on Pittacus' wife: "Being of more noble descent than he, because she was the sister of Draco, son of Penthilus, she treated him (i.e. Pittacus) with great arrogance.") It might seem that this fiction means to secure priority to Pittacus' coinage of what was common, even proverbial, wisdom (cf. Aeschylus, *Prometheus vinctus* 887–94).

3 See the material adduced by Gow and Page (1965), vol. 2, p. 206 at l. 1288.

4 The Planudea's last line which reads γ' ἰών, avoids the problem and makes the poem more generally applicable; I thus take it to be the *lectio facilior*.

5 See Sinko (1914), 12, for surface meaning (Callimachus' friend Dion wanted to marry, but did not have a clue, thus Callimachus sent him this epigram). Less probably, the meaning of τὴν κατὰ σαυτὸν ἔλα in v. 16 is "Keep to your own literary strenghts," as Pretagostini (2007) suggests.

6   Chilon in Photius' lexicon s.v. τὴν κατὰ σαυτὸν ἔλα. When ascribed to a certain sage, the advice, transmitted without anecdotal context, claims to preserve the sage's *ipsissima verba* (Cleobulus' in Stobaeus, *Anth.* 3.1.172 (1 Cleobulus), Chilon's ibid. 3.22.105). See Sinko (1914), 5 f. who adduces, among other sources, Plutarch, *De pueris educandis* 19 (13 F).

7   It is true that κληδόνες had mantic meaning in the Greek world, too (cf. Lawson 1910)—but the notion of playing children, so important for our epigram, is absent in the Greek tradition (see Wagenvoort 1974: 189 n. 5).

8   Lieven (1999), 91 f. and *passim*. Sinko (2014), 9 ff. adduces a few more instances, culled from imperial Greek writers.

9   See Lieven (1999), 92.

10 As I see now, Sinko (1914), 12, already suggested a similar blending of Greek and Egyptian elements. In Sinko, however, Callimachus' intention remains a little unclear.

Bibliography

Cairns, F. (2008), "The Hellenistic 'epigramma longum,'" in A. M. Morelli (ed.), *Epigramma longum: da Marziale alla tarda antichità*, 2 vols, vol. 1, 55–80, Cassino: Università degli studi di Cassino.

Erler, M. and S. Schorn, eds. (2007), *Die Griechische Biographie in hellenistischer Zeit*, Berlin and New York: Walter de Gruyter.

Gow, A. S. F. and D. L. Page (1965), *The Greek Anthology: Hellenistic Epigrams*, 2 vols, Cambridge: Cambridge University Press.

Lawson, J. C. (1910), *Modern Greek Folklore and Ancient Greek Religion*, Cambridge: Cambridge University Press.

Lefkowitz, M. R. (2007), "Visits to Egypt in the Biographical Tradition," in M. Erler and S. Schorn (eds.), *Die Griechische Biographie in hellenistischer Zeit*, 101–13, Berlin and New York: Walter de Gruyter.

Lieven, A. v. (1999), "Divination in Ägypten," *Altorientalische Forschungen*, 26: 77–126.

Lozza, G. and S. Martinelli Tempesta, eds. (2007), *L'epigramma greco: Problemi e prospettive*, Milano: Cisalpino. Istituto Editoriale Universitario.

Morelli, A. M., ed. (2008), *Epigramma longum: da Marziale alla tarda antichità*, 2 vols, vol. 1, Cassino: Università degli studi di Cassino.

Pretagostini, R. (2007), "Vita e poetica negli epigrammi 1 e 28 Pf. di Callimaco," in G. Lozza and S. Martinelli Tempesta (eds.), *L'epigramma greco: Problemi e prospettive*, 137–47, Milano: Cisalpino. Istituto Editoriale Universitario.

Sinko, Th. (1914), "Ad Callimachi epigramma I (de uxore eligenda)," *Eos*, 20 (1): 5–12.

Stephens, S. A. (2003), *Seeing Double: Intercultural Poetics in Ptolemaic Alexandria*, Berkeley, CA: University of California Press.

Wagenvoort, H. (1974), "Volkskunde bei Augustin?" *Vigiliae Christianae*, 28: 186–9.

9

On a New Papyrus Fragment of Callimachus' *Hecale* (*P.Ant.* III 179 add.)˘

Giovan Battista D'Alessio
University of Naples Federico II

In a recent publication W.B. Henry has identified a small fragment of a fourth-/ fifth-century papyrus codex as belonging to Callimachus' *Hecale*. In this note I explore some further consequences we can possibly draw from this minute scrap.

As argued by Henry, the new fragment appears to be written in the same hand and format as two previously known fragments of a codex from Antinoopolis with lines of Callimachus' *Hymns* III and VI, *P.Ant.* III 179.[1] Since the new piece, now published as an *addendum* to this papyrus, was found among the still unidentified papyri of the Egypt Exploration Society in the Sackler Library, Oxford, where also the Antinoopolis papyri are housed, it is certainly plausible that the papyri might have belonged to the same codex. In the two previously published fragments *recto* and *verso* are 27 verses apart. It seems reasonable therefore to assume, with Henry, that the two sides of the new fragment too are separated by roughly the same amount of text.

This is Henry's text of the two sides of the fragment, with (a) = → printed before (b) = ↓.

(a)

. . . .

```
        ].[                           ].[
     ]μηνδυρ[                      ]μην δυρ[
     ]ομόδελφ[          – ∞ –    ] ὁμόδελφ[υ
       ....οιϲ[                       ....οιϲ[
   ]ϝενεγω . . λέε[       τὼ μ|ὲ ν ἐγὼ θαλέειϲϲιν ἀνέτρεφον οὐδέ τιϲ οὕτωϲ
```

. . . .

(b)

. . . . .

].[
]υϋδατος[
  ε   εν.[
].υϊ⟦ο⟧c⟦υϊ⟧[
]γικοις[
].κ..[..]..ε.[

. . . . .

. . . . .

].[
]ν ϋδατοc[
      εν.[
].υῖεc ⟦υϊ⟧[
]γικοις[
].κ..[..]..ε.[

. . . . .

The identification is based on the overlap between → l. 4 and fr. 48.1 H(ollis), a line supplemented on the basis of the indirect tradition (fr. 337 Pf., *Sud.* s.v. Θαλέεccι) within the first line of *P.Oxy.* XXIII 2376. Fr. 48 H consists of 10 lines preserved at the foot of column i of a papyrus roll.[2] The foot of the next column of the same papyrus preserves the initial letters of fr. 49.7-16 H. The whole of fr. 49 H is preserved on the → side of another fragmentary papyrus codex, *P.Oxy.* XXIII 2377, whose ↓ side corresponds to fr. 47 H. While the sequence of fragments 48 H and 49 H is, therefore, certain on material grounds, it is not clear whether fr. 47 H precedes or follows fr. 49 H. We have three possibilities: 47-48-49 (Bartoletti, Hollis and others), 48-49-47 (Hutchinson and Henry), and 48-47-49 (Medaglia, who, however, tried to accommodate even 40 H and 42 H in the sequence).[3] My aim in this note is to examine some possible readings of the new fragment and to explore its bearing for the reconstruction of the order.

As for the sequence of the two sides of the new fragment, Henry argues that "as fr. 48.1 Ho(llis) is the first preserved line of *P.Oxy.* XXIII 2376 col. i, and the ↓ side of the new fragment does not appear to contain parts of any of the 20 lines of fr. 49 Ho(llis), to which *P.Oxy.* 2376 col. ii contributes, it seems on the whole likelier that the ↓ side of the new fragment preceded the → side." In fact, however, a look at the format of *P.Oxy.* 2376 shows that this is not necessarily the case. We only have the feet of two columns of this second-century papyrus. The preserved sections, each 10-line long, correspond to a height of approximately 4.3 cm, with a lower margin of slightly more than 3 cm. No line is entirely preserved: the 7 final syllables of the longest preserved portion of any line, fr. 48.7, occupy roughly 3.7 cm. The entire line counted 17 syllables, and its original width would have been around 9 cm. The next column starts around 2.8 cm to the right of the last letter of the line. This allows to work out an original column-to-column width of circa 11.8 cm. If the → side of the new Antinoopolis fragment preceded the ↓ side, the latter part would have fallen within approximately 7.5 cm (corresponding to 17 lines) from the top of column ii in *P.Oxy.* 2376. We should therefore expect to find an overlap with fr. 49 H only if the columns of *P.Oxy.* 2376 were shorter than approximately 15 cm (corresponding to 34 lines). A comparison with the data drawn from papyri of known literary texts from Oxyrhynchus collected by Johnson (2004) shows that a roll with such features is very unlikely to have had a column shorter than 15 cm. Among the fifty-four examples of papyrus rolls from Oxyrhynchus with known verse texts examined by Johnson only thirteen are shorter than 15 cm. In Johnson's Table 3.3, out of 160 papyri whose column height can be ascertained with some degree of probability, only twenty-six have columns tall ≤ 14.9 cm. It follows that, unless *P.Oxy.* 2376 was a roll with columns shorter than usual, we would have no papyrological reason to expect an overlap of the ↓ side of the new fragment with the content of fr. 49 H. We should expect, though, if the roll was not particularly tall, that the new text would belong to a section separated from fr. 49 by not too many lines. Anyway, if this was the case, at least 17 lines must have been lost between fr. 48 H and fr. 49 H, two of which would be represented by the ↓ side of the new fragment. This would have the following consequences for the reconstruction of the sequence:

(1) If fr. 47 H did precede fr. 49 H (Bartoletti, *SH*, Hollis), the codex *P.Oxy.* 2377 would have been at least 47 lines tall, and probably taller if we take into account that its content does not suggest that it was immediately connected to fr. 48 H (now incremented by the new fragment). A codex with such number of lines per page, however, would be by no means a rarity. Turner (1977: 96–7, table 14) lists thirty-three "codices having fifty or more lines per page," fifteen of which contain hexameter texts, and twenty-five are dated between the third and the fourth century, including several with 60 or more lines per page.

(2) It would be more difficult to accommodate fr. 47 H in the intermediate section between 48 H and 49 H: the whole sequence of fr. 47 H (20 lines) and the 4 lines of the ↓ side of the new fragment (unless we imagine that they did fit in the second half of some of the last lines of fr. 47 H) would all need to be accommodated at the top of *P.Oxy.* 2376 col. ii, along with fr. 49.1–6 H and any further missing lines, implying that 2376 was a tall roll, while 2377 was a codex of small format. This is not impossible, but requires squeezing quite a lot of the preserved material in the same gap; one element, though, would make such combination possibly attractive, i.e.

the mention of ὕδατος in the first line of the ↓ side of the new fragment, which would fit neatly in a sequence describing a tragic voyage by sea, and, arguably, a death by water, leading to the loss of one or both of the boys.[4]

(3) There would be no papyrological obstacles in placing fr. 47 H after fr. 49 H (Hutchinson, Henry); but since fr. 49 H has moved from the narrative section of Hecale's speech to her impassionate invective against Kerkyon, including a pathetic address (l.3), and presupposing that another death of a dear one was already mentioned, to have this followed by a section possibly describing a third death (this time by water, and thus by accident: fr. 47 H) might sound as an anticlimax.

Summing up, the new fragment does not settle the question whether fr. 47 H preceded or followed fr. 49 H, while making its collocation between fr. 48 H and fr. 49 H somewhat more difficult. There are, anyway, no papyrological reasons to conclude that in the new fragment the ↓ side (b) preceded the → side (a), as argued by Henry.

The context of the → side, fr. (a), secured by the overlap of l. 3 with fr. 48.1 H, is a speech in which Hecale describes the two young boys whom she raised among delicacies. Line 2 provides a new occurrence of the adjective ὁμόδελφυς ("born from of the same womb"), attested so far only in Callimachus himself, two other times, and in lexicographical sources. Its use in the other Callimachean occurrences (fr. 228.73 and fr. 524 Pf.) may suggest that the focalization here was that of one of the two boys. In fr. 49 H Hecale seems to be lamenting the death of a dear person, possibly one or both of the two boys mentioned in fr. 48 H.

The content of fr. (b), ↓, meagre as it is, does suggest a compatibility with a position between fr. 48 H and fr. 49 H, rather than before fr. 48 H. In my next section I will focus on the text of its third line. The scribe had originally written two consecutive forms of the word υἱός ("son"). As for the first occurrence, Henry argues that the scribe originally wrote υἷος, and then crossed out the omicron with the intention of substituting it with an epsilon written above the line, thus producing a form of the nominative plural υἷες. The second occurrence was then entirely crossed out, and substituted with a word above the line (provided by a different hand and/or with different ink, or a blunter pen), which Henry reads as ευ.[. There are some problems with this interpretation:

a) The letter that Henry interprets as omicron (υἷος) is tall and narrow and has no parallels in other omicrons in other fragments of *P.Ant.* 179;[5] its shape, on the other hand, is similar to the way in which epsilon is drawn by this hand; the stroke supposedly used to cross out the letter starts exactly *within* the interior part of the left arc of the letter, not in its exterior part, as one would expect in case of deletion, thus rather suggesting that it was the cross-bar of epsilon. Henry objects to this that he would expect the cross-bar "to join the first stroke of the <following> sigma at or near the top, where it begins." Within the three tiny fragments of *P.Ant.* 179 (including the new one) there are no further cases of epsilon-sigma sequences. We do have, however, other cases of epsilon with a downward slanting cross-bar in this same fragment, including one before a further epsilon, λέε[, at (a).4, with the same inclination as the stroke Henry identifies as a deleting stroke here, and one, with a lesser inclination, before a gamma, in the same line; furthermore, as a look at other Antinoopolis papyri of similar date and hands—such as those published along with *P.Ant.* 179, and reproduced on Plates I and II of the volume—shows, epsilon's cross-bar does not need to be joined to the following letter "where it begins," as we are not dealing with proper ligatures.

b)   Whatever reading we accept for the correction *supra lineam* of the following word (see below), it is clear that its first syllable opens with a diphthong. This cannot be preceded by a word of the metrical shape of υἱός, as in Henry's reconstruction.

It seems to me that the best way to make sense of all of this would be to understand the correction of the first word as implying: (1) the change of an original epsilon into an omicron (within the line: as shown above, the shape of the letter suggests that the opposite, i.e. the correction of an omicron into an epsilon is less likely) and (2) the addition of another epsilon above the line: this would produce υἱέος (or, less probably, υἱέες), which would also fit the required meter. As for the correction of the second word above the line, the first letter is clearly epsilon, the second can hardly be anything else than hypsilon, as seen by Henry, perhaps corrected from iota (in order to make sense of the "surplus ink in the middle at the top" noted by Henry), and the last trace is most probably "the left-hand side of ν" (Henry).

In the *editio princeps* I have suggested supplementing "forms of εὖνις, 'lacking,' or εὐνή, 'bed,' if ευν- began the sixth foot, or e.g. a form of εὐνάζω, 'put to bed.'" I would now argue that, in consideration of the context, we can be more precise. In fact, among the various options available for the two preserved words, one combination appears to be particularly fruitful in the context of Hecale's speech, and can be corroborated by various arguments. This has potential consequences for the reconstruction of this part of the speech, and for the appreciation of its intertextual background.

The sequence υἱέος εὖνιc (or εὖνιν) would fit naturally well within the account of Hecale's loss.[6] The word εὖνιc, exclusively poetic, has two different meanings (unless, that is, we are dealing with a single word with two different meanings). One is a noun, derived from εὐνή ("bed"), and means "wife, bedfellow." It is first attested in tragedy and has a certain currency in later hexameter and elegiac poetry, with an occurrence Callimachus himself, *Aitia* III fr. 55 Pf.= 267 *SH*= 146 Massimilla. The other is a rare adjective, meaning "bereft," attested twice in Homer (*Iliad* 22.44, *Odyssey* 9.524), thrice in tragedy (only in Aeschylus), once in Empedocles (57.2 D.K.), and once in Apollonius of Rhodes (4.500).[7] In the context of our fragment, it would make much sense if Hecale used the word to indicate herself as "bereft of a son" (which, by the way, would also settle the debate whether the two boys she mentions were actually her sons or her nurslings).

There is, actually, an important piece of lexicographical evidence that seems to corroborate this reading. Apart from the literary occurrences listed above, the adjective εὖνιc has its own life in ancient lexicographical sources, most of which were clearly prompted by its appearance in Homer. To the best of my knowledge, in all these sources the adjective is explained with a *masculine* paraphrase, ὁ ἐcτερημένοc τινόc "the one who has been deprived of somebody/something." The single exception in this textual chain is the entry in the tenth-century lexicon *Suda* (ε 3593) where it is explained using the *feminine*, as ἐcτερημένη τῶν ἐπιτηδείων "a woman deprived of the people/things useful to her."[8] In the apparatuses of her edition of *Suda*, Adler usefully collected a list of similar formulations, tracing the entry and these sources to Δ, a siglum indicating their provenance from the still unpublished *Lexicon Ambrosianum*, a work close to the second-century *Lexicon* of Diogenianus.[9] Adler did not draw attention, however, to the fact that only in *Suda* the adjective is explained as a feminine form. The two Homeric cases, the ones in Empedocles and Apollonius, as well as the one in Antimachus (if this was indeed not a form of the noun) are all masculine. The three occurrences in Aeschylus are feminine, but two of them applies to (metaphoric) animals (*Choephoroe* 247, 794), while *Persians* 289 features the plural εὖνιδαc (cf. the entry εὖνιδεc in the *Lexicon* of Hesychius, where the word is explained as χῆραι, "widows").[10] None of these passages would easily elicit the explanation we find in *Suda* (nor would any of the later passages be a plausible source). As it is well known, however, *Suda* includes many entries ultimately derived from Callimachus' *Hecale*, very often without providing any indication of the title of the poetic work, nor of its author, a fact that has led to the attribution to this poem of several unattributed hexameter entries in the lexicon. This is known as "Hecker's Law," from the name of the brilliant nineteenth-century scholar who first formulated this theory, later confirmed by papyrus finds. The ultimate source of these entries was the ancient commentary on the *Hecale* of the grammarian Salustius.[11] The entry ε 3593 might well be yet another such case: it must certainly deal with a poetic (potentially hexametric) text, but, as we have seen, none of the other extant occurrences of the word can be identified as its source. A neat and economical solution would be to identify here too Salustius as its origin, and our papyrus passage as the actual Callimachean text which prompted Salustius' commentary. This would explain the unique use of the feminine in *Suda*'s entry, which would be compatible with the reconstruction of the papyrus fragment proposed here (feminine singular), corroborating the interpretation of the correction *supra lineam* in the new papyrus as part of the adjective εὖνις, and the reading of the whole sequence as υἱέος εὖνις (or εὖνιν).

This interpretation, in its turn, suggests that the ↓ side (b), mentioning the death of a son, followed the → side (a), mentioning Hecale raising two young boys, and that (b) preceded, probably by not too many lines, fr. 49 H, where Hecale laments the loss of one or more relatives. The new collocation, υἱέος εὖνις, moreover, is important in order to reconstruct the intertextual rhetoric of the passage. If correctly reconstructed it would be a conspicuous echo of the section of Priam's pathetic address to Hector at *Iliad* 22.37–76, where the old father foresees the imminent death of his son at the hands of Achilles, ὅς μ' ὐῶν πολλῶν τε καὶ ἐσθλῶν εὖνιν ἔθηκε ("who rendered me bereft of many and valiant sons" 44). In both passages an old parent reviews his/her previous losses, foresees the great pain he/she will suffer due to a further bereavement, and curses in crude terms the person responsible for the death (or deaths), Achilles in the case of Priam, Kerkyon in that of Hecale. Priam hopes that Achilles may die, providing relief for him (41–43): σχέτλιος· αἴθε θεοῖσι φίλος τοσσόνδε γένοιτο/ ὅσσον ἐμοί· τάχα κέν ἑ κύνες καὶ γῦπες ἔδοιεν κείμενον ("wretched, may the gods love him as much as I do: soon would dogs and vultures pasture over his dead body"). Hecale's declaration against Kerkyon (fr. 49.14–15 H) is even stronger: ζώοντος ἀναι]δέcι|ν| ἐμπήξαι|μι/ cκώλου|c ὀφθαλμοῖcι καί], εἰ θέμ̣ιc, ὠμὰ π|αcαίμην ("I would in person drive stakes into his shameless eyes while he was still alive, and—if it is permitted—devour him raw," trans. Hollis), drawing on other Homeric passages, and, more particularly, on the speech of a mother, Hecabe, lamenting the murder of her son, Hector (24.212–13). If my argument is correct, therefore, this new little fragment would allow us to add a new, small but not insignificant *tessera* to the mosaic of the complex interplay Callimachus creates between the Homeric models and his new innovative characters,[12] while contributing to a slightly better understanding of the structure of this important section of the poem.

Notes

*   Thanks to G. Massimilla and L. Lehnus for comments on a previous draft.
1   See Henry (2022), 37 (for the location of the fragment), 46–9 (for the edition), and 53 fig. 12. For the fragments of the *Hymns*, see Barns (1967).
2   Unless otherwise noted, henceforth all fragments indicated by number alone are those of the edition of Hollis.
3   Cf. Bartoletti (1963); Medaglia (1984); Hollis (2009), 187–9; Hutchinson (2006), 2006: n. 19 = 2008: 76 n. 19 (a solution considered as a theoretical alternative already by Hollis 2009: 198).
4   Medaglia (1984) tried to accommodate also fragments 40 H and 42 H, producing the sequence 40-48-42-47-49, H but the attempt at squeezing so much of the evidence within so little space compounds the margins of unlikelihood. A close proximity between 48 H and 42 H (with no more than 2 lines in the gap between them) is not supported by the content. If we insert the ↓ side of the new fragment in the sequence of Tables II and III in Medaglia 1984, it would fall squarely within fr. 40 H (if it preceded the → side) or fr. 47 H (if it followed the → side). For arguments suggesting that 47 H might deal with earlier events, see Bartoletti 1963: 267–8.
5   Henry (2022), 47, compares the omicron "at the end of P.Ant. 179 fr. 1(a).165, of which only the left-hand side survives on the edge," but too little of that letter survives to make the comparison very useful.
6   As for the metrical position, the sequence might have closed the hexameter after the "bucolic diaeresis" (as suggested also by a comparison with the relative position of the remains of the verses in the → and ↓ sides of *P.Ant.* 179 fragments 1 and 2), but a location in the fourth and the fifth elements cannot be ruled out (e.g. κα]ὶ υἱέος εὖνι[ν ἔθηκε on the model of *Il.* 22.44). The fact that the lemma in *Suda* is at the nominative does not necessarily imply that this must have been the case in the poetic text too: cf. e.g. *Suda* entries ss.vv. σελαγίζω, λαῖφη, or κοκκύαι and Pfeiffer and Hollis on fr. 285 Pf.= 100 H.
7   It is not clear if in Antimachus, 69.3 *SH* (= 121.3 Matthews) the word is to be understood as the noun or the adjective. The adjective is also used in the Imperial period, once in Lollius Bassus, *Palatine Anthology* 7.372.6, once in an inscriptional funerary epigram (*IGUR* III 1354, *GVI* 224), in Quintus of Smyrne 1.113, 7.245 and

279, and once in the Manethonian *Apotelesmatica* (6.275). Of all these occurrences, the only ones where the term is used as a feminine form are those in Quintus of Smyrne, an author very well familiar with Callimachus'*Hecale*: cf. Hollis (2009), 34, and the passages listed in his index p. 390. The adjective, used as a masculine form, occurs also in a remarkable late Hellenistic acrostich inscriptional epigram from Alexandria Arachosia (Kandahar, *SEG* 54.1568, v.5), in a context rich in rare words borrowed from high poetry, and, more particularly, from Callimachus' *Hecale*: cf. Hollis (2011), Garulli (2012), 279–87.

8 The genitive ἐπιτηδείων can be understood as a form of the neuter or of the masculine.

9 Cf. Adler (1928–38), vol. 1, 17 and vol. 3, 459; Hollis (2009), 358.

10 Cunningham (2020) refers to Euripides, *Orestes* 928, but in that passage the word is to be interpreted as a form of the noun meaning "wife." The scholia on Aeschylus, *Persians* 289, waver between understanding the adjective as referring to women who have lost their sons, or to widows (the latter as in Hesychius). This is the only other exegetical or lexicographical passage with an interpretation of the term as a feminine, but the fact that both lemma and interpretation are at the plural makes this case different from that in *Suda*.

11 Cf. Hollis (2009), 41–4, concluding that *Suda* "contains nearly 200 entries (ascribed and anonymous) which certainly, probably, or possibly refer to our poem." In his "Appendix V" (358–61) Hollis draws attention to "several more entries of a Hellenistic or even specifically Callimachean colour which, as far as [he] could see, had as good claim a claim to the *Hecale* as some of the fragments accepted by Pfeiffer," adding that "there is still room for a further painstaking investigation" (358).

12 On this see Hutchinson (2006 = 2008).

Bibliography

Adler, A. (1928–38), *Suidae Lexicon*, ed. A. Adler, I–V, Suttgart: Teubner.

Alexandrou, M., C. Carey, and G. B. D'Alessio, eds. (2022), *Song Regained—Working with Greek Poetic Fragments*, Berlin and Boston, MA: De Gruyter.

Barns, J. W. B. (1967), "179 Callimachus, *Hymns* III and VI," in J. W. Barns and H. Zilliacus (eds.), *The Antinoopolis Papyri*, Part III, 119–20 (and Plates I and II), London: Egypt Exploration Society.

Barns and, J. W., H. Zilliacus, eds. (1967), *The Antinoopolis Papyri*, Part III, London: Egypt Exploration Society.

Bartoletti, V. (1963), "Sui frammenti dell'Ecale di Callimaco nei P.Oxy. 2376 e 2377," in *Miscellanea di studi alessandrini in memoria di A. Rostagni*, 263–72, Turin: Bottega d'Erasmo.

Clarke, M. J., B. Currie, and R. O. A. M. Lyne, eds. (2006), *Epic Interactions: Perspectives on Homer, Virgil, and the Epic Tradition Presented to Jasper Griffin*, Oxford and New York: Oxford University Press.

Cunningham, I. C. (2020), *Hesychii Alexandrini Lexicon. Volumen IIa: E-I*, recensuit et emendavit Kurt Latte, editionem alteram curavit I. C. Cunningham, Berlin: De Gruyter.

Henry, W. B. (2022), "A Papyrological Miscellany," in M. Alexandrou, C. Carey, and G. B. D'Alessio (eds.), *Song Regained—Working with Greek Poetic Fragments*, 33–53, Berlin and Boston, MA: De Gruyter.

Garulli, V. (2012), Byblos Lainee: *Epigrafia, letteratura, epitafio*, Bologna: Patron.

Hollis, A. S. (2009), *Callimachus:* Hecale, 2nd ed., with introduction, text, translation, and enlarged commentary, Oxford: Oxford University Press.

Hollis, A. S. (2011), "Greek Letters from Hellenistic Bactria," in D. Obbink and R. Rutherford (eds.), *Culture in Pieces: Essays on Ancient Texts in Honour of Peter Parsons*, 104–18, Oxford: Oxford University Press.

Hutchinson, G. O. (2006), "Hellenistic Epic and Homeric Form," in M. J. Clarke, B. Currie, and R. O. A. M. Lyne (eds.), *Epic Interactions: Perspectives on Homer, Virgil, and the Epic Tradition Presented to Jasper Griffin*, 105–29, Oxford and New York: Oxford University Press.

Hutchinson, G. O. (2008), *Talking Books: Readings in Hellenistic and Roman Books of Poetry*, 66–89, Oxford: Oxford University Press.

Johnson, W. A. (2004), *Bookrolls and Scribes in Oxyrhynchus*, Toronto, Buffalo, New York, and London: University of Toronto Press.

Medaglia S. (1984), "Su alcuni papiri dell'*Ecale*," in *Atti del XVII Congresso Internazionale di Papirologia*, 2.297–304, Naples: Centro Internazionale per lo Studio dei Papiri Ercolanesi.

Turner, E. G. (1977), *The Typology of the Early Codex*, Philadelphia, PA: University of Pennsylvania Press.

10

No Lyre for Heracles[*]

Peter Parsons
University of Oxford

Callimachus has been central to Susan's work, both in the global significance of his poems and in the nuanced unpacking of his miniatures. This paper, which celebrates her long achievement and our long friendship, represents a miniature within a miniature: the history of a single letter.

The *Victoria Berenices* has been thoroughly explored since the major fragments were first published by Claude Meillier in 1976. It will be agreed that it formed the opening, proclamatory or even programmatic, of *Aetia* Book III: so it stands, with full commentary, in the editions of Annette Harder (frr. 54–60j) and Giulio Massimilla (frr. 143–56). It will be agreed that it offers a Pindaric victory ode by other means, for Berenice's victory in the Nemean games, and that the story of Heracles and the Nemean lion forms the myth at the centre, and perhaps at the end, of the ode. Within this myth Heracles was entertained, as Theseus was by Hecale, by the old peasant Molorcus, engaged in his own battle against invasive mice.

This structuring of the poem depends essentially on the structure of the Lille papyrus.

The craftsman who incorporated it in his mummy-case cut it into rectangular strips. One partly-preserved strip contains the beginning of the poem, as we know from other sources; two further strips, to full height, follow in an order which is reasonably assured from the content. The fourth strip consists of an upper part, with top margin, and a larger part with lower margin; they fit neatly in the space of a typical column, and (more to the point) share on their backs a prominent brown fibre with a stripe of blue-black paint. If the juxtaposition is correct, there may be only two or three lines lost between them.

Quite recently, the original papyrus has been conserved under the supervision of Professor Daniel Delattre. He has kindly let me see a good scan of the newly restored text, which promises to illuminate many obscurities. For the moment, it encourages a second look at fr. 54d Harder = 150 Massimilla. In Harder's edition we read:

```
                  ]. ονεϲτιφ . . [
                  ]πιχορη . . [
                  ]διον καὶ απληϲ . [
                  ]ε χρήϲομαι τη . . [
                  ]ζευϲϲηνδιψαρ[                    5
                  ]πενίαν
                  ]. ειϲιναθωιοϲ . . [
   - - - - - -    ο]ὖτιϲι δῶκαλυρ . [
                  ]. ιν . μοιγεϱον . [
                  ]. κμα [] . . . . [               10
                      ] [
```

Interpreters face a primary difficulty in the unique format of this copy: the scribe inserts glosses and paraphrases which are set off from the poetic text only by indentation. When, as here, the left-hand margin is lost, only style and metre distinguish the poem from the scholia.

Line 1 may or may not be verse. Lines 2–4 clearly contain prose, that is paraphrase, where the first person future χρήϲομαι stands out. Line 5, if the damaged traces are rightly read, remains a mystery. Line 6 ends short: either the end of a scholion, or the end of a pentameter. Line 8 provides a fixed point, universally taken to be verse and in fact a pentameter. A regular sequence of couplets would then make lines 7 and 9 hexameters. In 7 αθωιοϲ spells ἀθῷοϲ, which could indeed be prose, and seemed so, when the traces following were read as μ[. Now οϲ[looks much more likely, but a metrical difficulty remains: the word would not fit in the second part of a Callimachean hexameter, except right at the end. It was Professor Claude Meillier who suggested a way out: we should assume here a prosody αθωϊοϲ in four syllables. That seems highly likely: we have no parallel for the adjective, but of course θωϊη three syllables is well attested in Ionic. In 9 clearly ἐμοί, γέρον would fit the middle part of a hexameter, and γέρον would fit Molorcus, cf. 54h3, 54i10.

For a wider context we must look to fr. 54e, the lower part of the same column. Skirting many obscurities, we find 1–2 clearly "killing the monster, whether I should call it [. . .] or the bain of the Argives." 4 something happens by the well of Danaos, i.e. near Argos; 5 perhaps Bias and Melampus, perhaps as Argive figures, perhaps because in myth Bias acquired a large herd of cattle; 7 "if only I get close . . . you will quickly become rich in cattle," perhaps, that is, the killing of the lion will stop it destroying the livestock of the area; 10 "I shall prove that Zeus has children," then "[If . . .] I fall beneath the tooth . . ." Of course this is full of ifs and buts. The central feature is clearly the repeated first person singular, from which it seems likely that we have a speech; and from 10–11 the "‑" is Herakles: killing the lion will prove that he is Zeus' son; if on the other hand, the lion kills him . . . (and plan B is lost in the much damaged lines following).

This makes it tempting to see the "I" of the smaller fragment as Herakles, and γέρον as addressed to Molorcus. Tempting, because coherent and economical; not proven, given the damage to the text and Callimachus' concern to surprise.

Line 8 provides another first person. The version printed by Harder allows different articulations: δῶκα λύρη[v or δωκ' ἄλυρο[v. But the final trace, clearer on the new scan, looks like an upright, which suits eta better than omicron. That leaves ο]ὔτιϲι δῶκα λύρη[v, metrical and grammatical but hard to interpret.

On the face of it, Herakles says "to no one did I give a lyre." That rings odd, since of course Herakles and a lyre had history. Linos gave lyre-lessons to the young Herakles; Herakles lost patience and killed Linos with the leg of a stool— or in one version with the lyre itself.[1] Callimachus himself alludes to the story in two words at *Aetia* fr. 23.5 Harder. Of course he may not have this in mind, or he may have it well in mind while constructing a paradox. The point might lie in (say) an epithet attached to λύρη[v, now lost. Perhaps οἰκτρόν, "I shall escape unharmed (ἀθῷος): never yet have I given occasion for a song of mourning." Or in a contrast, on the lines of εἰ ϳόπαλον πολλοῖϲ, οὔτιϲι δῶκα λύρη[v, "I shall escape unharmed, since I have put a club at the service of many, a lyre at the service of none": the familiar contrast between the warrior and the artist.

These strain δῶκα and stretch the context. We might avoid it by assuming that Herakles is not after all the subject. Then who? Someone more at home with the lyre? One such person might be the poet himself; another might be the Muse.

So what about the poet? Certainly Callimachus could intrude his poetic persona within his poetry. Later in *Victoria Berenices* he performs a Pindaric manoeuvre, cutting short the narrative and emphasizing the next scene with an emphatic τάδ' ἐξερέω (fr. 54h.1–2 H.). Much more doubtfully, he may sign off from one aition with "I stayed my hand from the lyre" (fr. 137a.4 H.) Could he here say, for example, "I have devoted my lyre to nobody more heroic than this"?

What about the Muse? The sisterhood intervene several times in the first two books of the *Aetia*, which are constructed as question and answer between them and the poet; they are invoked at the beginning of Book 4 (fr. 86 H.). The Muses figure in the traditional Dichterweihe derived from Hesiod, but without the lyre;

in a later form, roughly contemporary with Callimachus, the gift of a lyre from the Muses first inspires Archilochus to poetry (SEG 15.517.34–8). Could the Muse say, for example, "To no one have I given a more melodious lyre"—a comment on the skill of the narrating poet?

Well, with Callimachus one never knows. The hard reality is simply space. If ἀθῴϊος in the line before refers to Herakles escaping scot-free, and if the line after presents Herakles addressing Molorcus, a digressive δῶκα would effectively be limited to a one-line context, with no more than seven syllables at the beginning to mediate the transition.

So, probability forces us back to the assumption that it is Herakles who says δῶκα and to the fact that we do not understand it. No doubt the reader will think of other approaches; or perhaps we have to be content with a scholarly *non liquet*. However, there is one last resource, which indeed ought to have been the first. My teacher H. C. Youtie formulated, among other papyrological laws, the principle: if your papyrus offers something extraordinary, you have probably misread it; and the longer the notes you write about it, the more probable is an error. The basic sequence of letters, as scanned, is shown in Plate 13a–b.

ΔΩKA looks unavoidable, and then ΛΥ. Then apparently the loop and vertical of rho. But together they do not explain extra traces at the foot of the vertical and then further to the right. These might be accidental, but on the enlargement they remain quite solid. The conclusion is clear: not one loop but two, not *rho* but *beta*. And so the lyre gets lost for ever.

Now we work back from the end, and a new word emerges: καλυβη[. This is not elsewhere in Callimachus, but a word of respectable pedigree. Herodotus presents the Paeonians as living each in a shelter above the lake (ἐπὶ τῶν ἰκρίων καλύβης, 5.16). Thucydides describes the refugees in Athens as falling easy victims to the plague, since they lived not in houses but in ill-ventilated shelters (ἐν καλύβαις πνιγηραῖς, 2.52.2). These are the refuges of poor people. So later we find the City of Rome beginning as a collection of herdsmen's huts (βοτηρικαὶ καλύβαι, Plutarch, *Moralia* 321A), Cincinnatus leaving his humble hut (ταπεινὴ καλύβη) to save his country (Dionysius of Halicarnassus, *Antiquitates Romanae* 10.8.4, 10.19.4). The word and the thing cling to real life. Texts of the early Church use the word for the cells of monks, the hovels of saints and the sketes of anchorites.[2] In the *Dictionary of Standard Modern Greek* (1998) καλύβα appears with the definition "rustic dwelling, with only one room, constructed flimsily from very simple materials, commonly with branches, reeds or straw held together with mud and with an earth floor."[3] You can find modern examples built for the benefit of tourists.

In parallel, such structures have a life in poetry. [Theocritus] 21 features two old fishermen who live in shelters woven (from reeds), ὑπὸ πλεκταῖς καλύβαισι (21.1–7, 18). Six centuries later, in the elephants' graveyard of Hellenistic poetry, Nonnus houses his goatherds and shepherds in καλύβαι (*Dionysiaca* 1.456, 48.687). Thus we have no reason to doubt that Callimachus could use the word, and imagine the thing. Molorcus owns a goatskin and a knapsack (fr. 54c.31) and a single ram, which make him rustic and poor. His thematic sister, Hecale, at least had olives and chickens on the rafters in what was clearly another one-room dwelling. Her cottage is described by a different word, καλιή (fr. 263.3 Pf.), perhaps indeed a grander word, since it goes back to Hesiod.[4] The two together have a joint influence on later scenes of theoxeny, like Ovid's *Philemor and Baucis* (*Metamorphoses* 8.616–724), from which further details of the source texts might be inferred. In the novel *Babyloniaka* the fugitive Rhodanes meets an old woman who lives in a hut: the old woman descends from Hecale, but her hut is called καλύβη.[5]

Let us assume, then, that καλυβη[refers to the hut, shack, cabin, hovel, shanty or cottage in which Molorchus lives. Now we work to the left. δῶ is one possibility, but Herakles giving a hut rings odd, so let us try ἰδω instead, "I see the hut." That choice kills off ουτιci, and ο]ῠτιc will hardly suit the new context: so we should try α]ῠτιc. That gives a new half-line: α]ῠτιc ἴδω καλύβη[ν.

Now we need to see if this new construct will fit the context, in subject but also in grammar, since we must explain the subjunctive. If the line before is verse, and if ἀθῶϊος applies to Herakles, we might guess a general sense of "I shall remain unscathed, until I set eyes again on your cottage," a prediction of a safe return. ἔστ' ἂν ceῖο φίλην α]ῠτιc ἴδω καλύβη[ν might give the sense, or more elegantly (a suggestion of Lucia Prauscello) εἰc ὅ κεν ἂψ ἐλθὼν α]ῠτιc ἴδω καλύβη[ν.

One new letter generates one new line, but one still surrounded by uncertainties. I hope at least that the removal of one error will empower others to clear up the whole context. In the meantime, it may be worth considering some wider consequences. Of course, "intertextuality" is a two-way street; a major figure may borrow from a minor figure, as well as the reverse. But in the two cases following we can reasonably assume that Callimachus was the lender.

Leonidas of Tarentum, *Anthologia Palatina* 6. 302 (*HE* xxxvii), an epigram of eight lines, presents himself as an old man whose καλύβη is infested with mice: φεύγεθ' ὑπὲκ καλύβηc, cκότιοι μύεc· οὔτι πενιχρὴ / μῦc cιπύη βόcκειν οἶδε Λεωνίδεω, "Flee from this hut, you darkling mice! Leonidas' flour-bin can never feed mice." Since his larder contains only salt and barley bread, he tells them to try elsewhere. The mice had already suggested a connection with Molorcus; now καλύβης confirms it. That in turn suggests that Leonidas wrote this poem after the *Victoria Berenices,* that is after *c.* 245 BCE. Most handbooks agree that Leonidas worked in the first half of the third century; Gow 1958 put him half a century later, on grounds of stylistic degeneracy. Of course, the earlier Leonidas might still have been writing, in the actual person of an old man, soon after 245; but the glance at Callimachus might make the later Leonidas more plausible.[6]

Not much later, if we accept an early date for the poem, we find more mice rampaging in the *Batrachomyomachia.*[7] Here (30–1), the mouse prince proclaims his parenthood: γείνατο δ' ἐν καλύβῃ με καὶ ἐξεθρέψατο βρωτοῖς / cύκοιc καὶ καρύοιc καὶ ἐδέcμαcι παντοδαποῖcιν, "She bore me in a hut and raised me on edibles, figs and nuts and foods of all kinds." Scholars have discussed whether καλύβη here should have a capital letter, like the homonymous towns in Macedonia and Libya; or whether, since the towns are entirely obscure, the mouse prince regards a hut as a palace to be boasted of. In any case, mice and καλύβη come together. The author may of course be remembering Molorcus' hut as famous in literature for its mice: his boastful prince elevates hut into the city of Hut, and turns Molorcus' meager provisions into a varied feast.

For the most part, then, καλύβαι provide cheap and insubstantial refuges for the poor: farmers, shepherds, swineherds, fishermen and even slaves.[8] Those who live in them lead a life of pain.[9] But we find also scattered references to huts from a different milieu, catering for spiritual or corporeal pleasure. Huts appear in religious contexts, perhaps then temporary structures for outdoor festivals like those of Adonis and Cybele.[10] The philosopher Polemon, head of the Academy in the early third century, liked to spend time in the garden, and so his pupils made themselves small huts and lived close by.[11] An epigram of Philip dwells on the luxurious καλύβη in a vineyard;[12] in the *Copa,* composed perhaps in the early principate, the Greek word is used to entice Latin drinkers to a paradise of taverns: 7–8 *sunt topia et calybae,*[13] *cyathi, rosa, tibia, chordae, / et triclia umbrosis frigida harundinibus,* "There are gardens and shelters, cups, roses, flutes, harps, and dining places cool with shady reeds." Pollux, writing in the second century AD, sums up this aspect (1.74): τὰ μέντοι ἐνδιαιτήματα, καὶ αἱ καλύβαι, ὥсπερ καὶ τὰ ἐνηβητήρια, οὐκ ἐπὶ τῶν ἀναγκαίων οἰκήсεων ἀλλ' ἐπὶ τῶν τερπνῶν τάττεται, "the 'living places' and the 'huts', like the 'party places', are used not for necessary habitations but for pleasurable ones."[14]

An extreme divergence can be illustrated, with all the caution that iconography requires, from the Nile Mosaic of Palestrina.[15] There the Nile is in flood. At one point, herdsmen and their cattle have taken refuge on an island, next to a rounded shelter: the shelter is clearly a καλύβη, just as in Heliodorus' description of the same emergency (Plate 14) (*Aethiopica* 1.5.3). At another, under an arched pergola, a party is in progress, no doubt celebrating the flood that guarantees another prosperous year (Plate 15). The shelter and the pergola are both constructed from reeds, the typical material of καλύβαι in the general tradition, though the pattern of construction is different: the pergola is a hut with open sides.[16] The refuge and the party appear elsewhere in similar Nilotic scenes.[17]

The Palestrina mosaic is normally judged to be Hellenistic, perhaps created and installed in the late second century BC.[18] It can be disputed how far it relies on descriptions of Egypt, how far on earlier and perhaps Egyptian models; it is generally agreed that it has some relation to reality (one which Pollux, who came from Naucratis, might have experienced).[19] That encourages the speculation that Callimachus could have known both the καλύβη of necessity and the καλύβη of pleasure. Did he choose the word deliberately to suit the ambiguous appeal of his rustic chic? The new urban reader takes pleasure in the poverty-stricken peasant of archaic myth: the peasant's shack is the plutocrat's arbor, and the contrast adds relish to the text.

Notes

* Peter Parsons passed away in November 2022, when this book was about to go to press. He was unable to make any revisions to his draft chapter. We have done our best to honour his memory and his wish to offer this tribute to Susan Stephens. The editors are responsible for any errors that remain. — The editors

1 Apollodorus, *Bibliotheca* 2.4.9, Diodorus 3.67.

2 One example among many: St Horus of the Thebaid withdrew to the desert, καλύβιον μικρόν τι ἑαυτῷ κατασκευάσας, λαχάνοις συνθέτοις μόνον ἀρκούμενος, πολλάκις καὶ δι' ἑβδομάδος ἅπαξ μεταλαμβάνων, "making himself a small hutlet meeting his needs with salads and often partaking only once a week." (*Historia Monachorum in Aegypto* 2).

3 χωριάτικο σπιτάκι, με ένα μόνο χώρο, κατασκευασμένο πρόχειρα και με πολύ ατλά υλικά, συνήθ. με κλαδιά, καλάμια ή χόρτα δεμένα με λάσπη, και με χωμάτινο δάπεδο.

4 See West on *Works and Days* 501. The sense "hut" survives in the poetic tradition up to Nonnus, and in the bye-forms καλιός and καλίδιον in Comedy (Epicharmus fr. 36, Cratinus fr. 74, Eupolis fr. 48 KA); more commonly the word refers to a bird's nest. It seems to have died out in the modern language.

5   Photius, *Bibliotheca* cod. 94, 74a 27, see Stephens and Winkler (1995: 191 n. 18).

6   For a balanced discussion of Leonidas', date see de Stefani (2005: 179–84). Campbell (2019) notes how often Callimachus and Leonidas are linked by later imitators.

7   See the detailed discussion in Hosty (2020: 2–11), who concludes that "it is by no means implausible to regard the poem as a product of the late third century or very early second century BCE—only a little later than, if not contemporary with, Callimachus."

8   Farmers, Alciphron 2.27.1. Shepherds, Plutarch *Moralia* 321A. Swineherds, Lucian, *Pro Imaginibus* 20. Peasants, Antipater, *AP* 9.150.6. Fishermen, [Theoc.] 21, Leonidas, *AP* 7.295.7, Plutarch *Marius* 37.10. Slaves, Antipater, *AP* 9.407.2. Elsewhere of a garden shed (Antistius, *AP* 16.243.2, Hesychius s.v. ὀπωροφυλάκιον), a bird-catcher's hide ("Dionysius," *Ixeuticon* (paraphrase) 3.12 etc Garzya), a convalescent's shelter (Galen XII 312), a sentry-box in the suburbs (Pollux 9.150).

9   Strabo 7.5.12 καλυβῖταί τινες καὶ λυπρόβιοι.

10 At the Adoneia, Dioscorides *AP* 5.53.2 (*HE* iii, 1475), τῇ ςῇ . . . πὰρ καλύβη: an al fresco shelter for the celebrant? or a bower for Adonis himself (cf. καλιή as a small shrine, Gow and Page (1968) on Crinagoras *AP* 6.253.3 = *GP* 2024). In the worship of Cybele, Philodemus *AP* 7.222.3 (*GP* xxvi, 3320; Sider no. 33). Two intriguing inscriptions from the Hauran, dated CE 282, record a ἱερὰ καλύβη founded by a village community (*Syria. Publications of the Princeton University Archaeological Expeditions to Syria in 1904–1905 and 1909, Division* IIIA.5.765 = IGRR III 1186): a shrine or aedicula? A problem case: Apollonius Rhodius, *Arg.* 1.775, where the brides in Apollonius' simile appear νηγατέῃσιν ἐεργόμεναι καλύβῃσιν. LSJ translates "bridal bowers," and editors seem to follow this, without finding parallels to such an institution; the scholia comment ταῖς διὰ τῶν ἱματίων, taking καλύβη as equivalent to καλύπτρα. Three epitaphs from Cyrene (second century CE), now republished as *Inscriptions of Greek Cyrenaica* (online) nos 005 and 008–9, mention καλυβοί in the context of wedding celebrations. In 008–9 the latest editor translates "house"; but certainly in 005 it could be argued that καλυβοί and θάλαμοι are equivalent.

11 Diogenes Laertius 4.19 (from Antigonus of Carystus) οὐ μὴν ἀλλὰ καὶ ἐκπεπατηκὼς ἦν διατρίβων ἐν τῷ κήπῳ, παρ' ὃν οἱ μαθηταὶ μικρὰ καλύβια ποιησάμενοι κατῴκουν πλησίον τοῦ μουσείου καὶ τῆς ἐξέδρας. Philodemus, *Index Academicorum* (PHerc 1021) xxiii 39–42, ed. Dorandi (1991), τὸ δὲ πόλ[εω]ς δ[ιαμέ]νειν ἔξω [διε]νο[εῖτ]ο μόγ[ον], [ὥς]τε καὶ τῶγ [γ]ωρίμ[ων τοὺς] πολλοὺς οἰ[κοδο]μησαμέ[ους] ἐν τῶι κήπ[ωι] καλύβια μένειν αὐτοῦ [κ]ατὰ τὸ πλεῖστον, "He thought only of remaining outside the city, so that many also of his acquaintances built themselves hutlets in the garden and stayed there for the most part."

12 *AP* 9.232.4 (*GP* Philip xlii, 2913).

13 *calybae* restored by Scaliger: the MSS have *calybes* and similar variants. This, and 25 *calybita*, are the only uses in Latin, except for the glossators, who record καλύβη and

-βιον with glosses *casa, mapale, pergula, teges, tugurium* (CGL VI: 549). On the general landscape see Westendorp Buerma (1976).

14 Manuscripts A and V omit αἱ καλύβαι; M omits the whole sentence.

15 See Meyboom (1995) for the mosaic and its date. Other Nilotic scenes catalogued on Versluys (2002), some discussed by Barrett (2019). Of the two scenes illustrated here, the former survives at Palestrina, the latter in Berlin.

16 Reeds (κάλαμοι): Herennius Philo FGrH 790 F 2, EtMagn 799 s.v. φορμηδόν, Heliodorus, *Aethiopica* 2.3.2, Nonnus, *Dionysiaca* 1.370: rushes (cχοῖνοι) Leonidas, *AP* 7.295.7. The verb πλέκειν [Theoc.] 21.7, EtGen, Heliodorus, Nonnus, ll.cc. Reeds again in *Copa* 8 *triclia umbrosis frigida harundinibus*: Westendorp Buerma (1976) suggests that *triclia* here refers to just such pergolas as in the Nile Mosaic, for which he finds also a parallel in an erotic painting from Pompeii (Ins. VII 11, Versluys [2002: 103, item 035 L]). Latin elsewhere *trichila*: what was it called in Greek?

17 Nowicka (1969), 129–32 (hut). Meyboom (1995), 33–4 with 250 nn. 94 and 97 and 257 n. 122 (hut and pergola).

18 Meyboom (1995), 16–19, suggests a date roughly contemporary with that of the building that houses it, i.e. the last quarter of the second century.

19 Later, at least from the third century CE, Egyptian houses may boast a καλύβη, apparently an open structure on the roof to catch the cool of the evening (Husson 1983: 122).

Bibliography

Barrett, C. E. (2019), *Domesticating Empire: Egyptian Landscapes in Ponpeian Gardens*, Oxford: Oxford University Press.

Boersma, J. S., W. A. van Es, C. E. s'Jacob-Visser, W. C. Mank, W. T. T. Peters, and A. M. Witteveen, eds. (1976), *Festoen: opgedragen aan A. N. Zadoks-Josephus Jitta bij haar zeventigste verjaardag*, Groningen: H. D. Tjeenk Willink.

Campbell, C. S. (2019), "Variation on Simplicity: Callimachus and Leonidas of Tarentum in Philips' Garland," in M. Kanellou, I. Petrovic and C. Carey (eds.), *Greek Epigram from the Hellenistic to the Early Byzantine Era*, 102–18, Oxford: Oxford University Press.

De Stefani, C. (2005), "Posidippo e Leonida di Taranto: Spunti per un confronto," in M. Di Marco, B. M. Palumbo Stracca, and E. Lelli (eds.), *Posidippo e gli altri: Il poeta, il genere, il contesto culturale e letterario—Atti dell'incontro di studio, Roma, 14–15 maggio 2004*, 147–90, Pisa: Istituti editoriali e poligrafici internazionali.

Di Marco, M., B. M. Palumbo Stracca, and E. Lelli, eds. (2005), *Posidippo e gli altri: Il poeta, il genere, il contesto culturale e letterario—Atti dell'incontro di studio, Roma, 14–15 maggio 2004*, Pisa: Istituti editoriali e poligrafici internazionali.

Gow, A. S. F. (1958), "Leonidas of Tarentum," *Classical Quarterly*, 8 (3–4): 113–23.

Gow, A. S. F. and D. L. Page (1968), *The Greek Anthology: the Garland of Philip*, Cambridge: Cambridge University Press.

Gow, A. S. F. and D. L. Page (1965), *The Greek Anthology: Hellenistic Epigrams*, Cambridge: Cambridge University Press.

Hosty, M. (2020), *Batrachomyomachia (Battle of the Frogs and Mice)*, Oxford: Oxford University Press.

Husson, G. (1983), *Οἰκία: Le vocabulaire de la maison privée en Egypte d'après les papyrus grecs*, Paris: Publications de la Sorbonne.

Kanellou, M., I. Petrovic and C. Carey, eds. (2019), *Greek Epigram from the Hellenistic to the Early Byzantine Era*, Oxford: Oxford University Press.

Meyboom, P. P. G. (1996), *The Nile Mosaic of Palestrina: Early Evidence of Egyptian Religion in Italy*, Leiden: Brill.

Nowicka, M. (1969), *La maison privée dans l'Égypte ptolémaique*, Wroclaw: Zakład Narodowy im. Ossolińskich.

Stephens, S. A. and J. J. Winkler (1995), *Ancient Greek Novels: The Fragments: Introduction Text Translation and Commentary*, Princeton NJ: Princeton University Press.

Versluys, M. J. (2002), *Aegyptiaca Romana: Nilotic Scenes and the Roman View of Egypt*, Leiden: Brill.

West, M. L., ed. (1978), *Hesiod: Works & Days*, Oxford: Clarendon Press.

Westendorp Boerma, R. E. H. (1976), "The Copa Illustrated by Archaeology," in J. S. Boersma, W. A. van Es, C. E. s'Jacob-Visser, W. C. Mank, W. T. T. Peters, and A. M. Witteveen (eds.), *Festoen: opgedragen aan A. N. Zadoks-Josephus Jitta bij haar zeventigste verjaardag*, 653–61, Groningen: H. D. Tjeenk Willink.

11

Strabo's Callimachus

Richard Hunter
University of Cambridge

Strabo's *Geography* is a major source for our knowledge of Hellenistic scholarship and literary activity, and we might well have hoped to learn much from this extraordinary work about Callimachus and the reception of his writings. For Strabo, writing (probably) in the time of Augustus for an audience of educated men involved in public life,[1] Callimachus was clearly a resonant and important name. In the geographer's list of distinguished natives of Cyrene, the city with which Strabo chooses to conclude his work,[2] Callimachus is ὁ . . . ποιητὴς ἅμα καὶ περὶ γραμματικὴν ἐσπουδακώς, "both a poet and a serious grammarian" (17.3.22 = T 16 Pf.), and elsewhere the poet Heraclitus, one of three natives of Halicarnassus whom Strabo chooses to single out (14.2.16 = T 20 Pf.), is simply described as "the friend of Callimachus," as though that were enough. Strabo and many of his intended audience may have known of Heraclitus only from Callimachus' famous funerary epigram in his honour (*AP* 7.80 = 2 Pf. = *HE* 1203–8);[3] Callimachus himself needed no further introduction.

In one sense, Callimacheans cannot really complain about Strabo.[4] Although it seems clear that, despite the geographical and historical subjects of many of Callimachus' prose works, the Cyrenean was not a major source for Strabo, he is mentioned or cited in the *Geography* more often than any other poet except (of course) Homer, Hesiod, Pindar and the three classical tragedians.[5] By contrast, Callimachus is cited only once in what survives to us of Diodorus Siculus' *Universal History*,[6] and Apollonius of Rhodes' only explicit appearance in Strabo, despite the geographer's persistent interest in the travels of Jason, is as "the poet of the *Argonauts*," alongside Dionysius Thrax as two men who were called "Rhodians" but were in fact from Alexandria (14.2.13).[7] On a number of occasions Strabo cites Callimachus as an authority to confirm his own account (1.2.39, 5.1.9, 8.3.19, 10.5.1, 17.1.28, 17.3.21); Strabo's Callimachus is in fact a man after Strabo's own heart. In referring to *Iambus* 10, Strabo (9.5.17) calls Callimachus πολυΐστωρ, "a man of great learning, if anyone was," and apparently cites (the text is uncertain) fr. 178.30 as the poet's own declaration of Strabonian principles:[8]

οὔατα μυθεῖσθαι βουλομέν[οις ἀνέχων

offering ears to those willing to tell a story

Callimachus fr. 178.30 Pf./Harder

Alan Cameron suggested that this passage was in fact the "perhaps indirect" inspiration for Strabo's own declaration (2.5.11) ₁that, despite his own very extensive travels, both he and his predecessors took most of their material from ἀκοή, "what they had heard."[9]

One of the best known facts about Strabo is that the *Geography* brings with it very thorny problems of source criticism;[10] "Strabo says" or "Strabo cites" very often (at one level) means "Strabo, following X, says/cites," and without the *Geography* our corpus of the fragments of lost geographers and historians would be seriously impoverished. Callimachus, however, does not seem to pose too much of a problem. There seems, for example, no good reason to doubt that Strabo knew some at least of the epigrams of Callimachus which have reached us.[11] We have already noted his apparent familiarity with the poem for Heraclitus of Halicarnassus; so too, when Strabo reports (17.3.21) that Callimachus "says that Battos was his ancestor," he is very likely referring to *AP* 7.415 (= *Epigram* 35 Pf. = *HE* 1185–6):[12]

Βαττιάδεω παρὰ σῆμα φέρεις πόδας εὖ μὲν ἀοιδήν
  εἰδότος, εὖ δ᾽ οἴνωι καίρια συγγελάσαι.

You walk past the tomb of the son of Battos, a master of song and one who knew how to make laughter appropriate to wine.

Callimachus, *Epigram* 35 Pf.

At 14.1.18 Strabo cites in full, and offers a sensible interpretation of, Callimachus' epigram on Creophylus of Samos' *Capture of Oechalia* (*Epigram* 6 Pf. = *HE* 1293–6); the epigram involves Homer, and that was always one of Strabo's favourite subjects. Elsewhere, with other poems, we simply do not have enough to go on. At 8.3.30 Strabo reports "some have recorded the measurements of [Pheidias' Olympian Zeus], and Callimachus set them out (ἐξεῖπε) in an iambic poem"; whether or not Strabo had actually read *Iambus* 6 we can hardly say, though it is likely enough, given the subject of the poem. As often, however, *non liquet* might be the safer option.[13]

Beyond the apparent general familiarity of (at least) the *Epigrams* at the time at which Strabo was writing, the other reason why citations of Callimachus in the *Geography* do not seem to pose a major problem of source criticism is that their origin has in fact always seemed plain enough. One of Strabo's principal sources, especially for the descriptions of the Greek mainland and the islands, were the works of Apollodorus of Athens, notably (though by no means exclusively) his extensive commentary on the Homeric "Catalogue of Ships" (*FGrHist* 244 F154–207).[14] Apollodorus was a pupil of Aristarchus and, as such, very firmly rooted in the Alexandrian grammatical tradition, in the history of which Callimachus loomed very large; both Apollodorus' history and his geography, however, followed very much in the wake of Eratosthenes, and this too will have made him both an important, and a problematic, figure for Strabo. Apollodorus "passim Callimachum laudavit" observed Rudolf Pfeiffer,[15] and we know that he made extensive reference to Callimachus both in the commentary on the "'Catalogue" and in his great theological compilation "On the Gods." It would, in turn, not be misleading to suggest that at one time or another virtually every reference to Callimachus in Strabo, including the complimentary ones, has been traced back to Apollodorus. It is indeed, for example, not improbable that Strabo's three citations of verses from Callimachus' Argonautic narrative (1.2.39 = frr. 7.23–6, 11 Pf. = 7c.5–9, 11 Harder; 5.1.9 = fr. 11 Pf./Harder; 10.5.1 = fr. 7.23 Pf. = 7c.5 Harder) derive ultimately from Apollodorus,[16] though it cannot, in the nature of things, be demonstrated. The same may be true for Strabo's three citations (8.3.19, 10.5.1, 17.3.21) of a couplet on Thera as the mother-city of Callimachus' own Cyrene (... μήτηρ εὐίππου πατρίδος ἡμετέρης, "mother of my horse-bearing fatherland," fr. 716 Pf.), which may or may not belong to the same section of the *Aitia*;[17] in 10.5.1 the citation immediately follows that of the opening verse of the Argonautic narrative.[18] The third citation at 17.3.21 is the last verse of poetry we hear in the *Geography*, but whatever homage to Callimachus that might imply, what is equally striking is that these citations are the sum total of Strabo's verbatim engagement with the *Aitia*, and the Argonautic narrative occupied, of course, a very prominent initial position in the *Aitia*; it would not need much familiarity with Callimachus' greatest poem to know these verses. If fr. 716 Pf. also belonged to the Argonautic narrative, the bias towards the early part of Book 1 would be even more impressive, though such an autobiographical couplet is in any case likely to have attracted Strabo's interest, wherever he first came across it; that he cites it three times tells its own story. Citations of the same verses do not necessarily come from the same place; Strabo might well have found a poetic quotation in a source such as Apollodorus and then himself reused it, with or without having made himself more familiar with the poem in the meantime.

In his citation of Callimachus' Argonautic narrative at 1.2.39, Strabo adduces nameless other witnesses to the wanderings:

> Some (τινές) say that Jason and his companions even sailed up the Ister a considerable distance, while others (οἱ δέ) say that he ascended as far as the Adriatic Sea; in part this derives from ignorance of these regions—they assert that a river Ister branches off from the great Ister and empties into the Adriatic Sea, but otherwise what they say is neither improbable nor incredible.
>
> Strabo 1.2.39, trans. H. L. Jones, adapted[19]

For a modern reader, the name "Apollonius of Rhodes" (though not that name alone) is here hard to suppress,[20] and we may wonder (again) how well Strabo knew the Alexandrian epic; the fact that he does not here name names in no way demonstrates, of course, that he did not have specific names in mind. There are plenty of other sources to whom Strabo might here be referring,[21] but whether Strabo's general silence (cf. above) about Apollonius is his silence or Apollodorus' is a question not without interest for the *Nachleben* of Apollonius' poem. If the latter, then we would certainly have another marker of the relative standing of Callimachus and Apollonius within the Alexandrian tradition.[22]

We have seen Strabo's respect for Callimachean authority throughout his citations. In two places he can be seen in fact to defend Callimachus against Apollodorus' criticisms; polemic was another of the Alexandrian traditions which apparently featured notably in Apollodorus' work. In 1.2.37 and 7.3.6, Strabo cites Apollodorus' criticisms (fr. 157 Jacoby) of Callimachus' placing of the wanderings of Odysseus around recognizable Mediterranean locations (fr. 470 Pf.). Apollodorus apparently was at least sarcastic here about Callimachus' scholarly credentials: in 1.2.37 he is said to have erred "though he was a grammarian," and in 7.3.6 Apollodorus is claimed to have said that, unlike others who had fallen into error, Callimachus deserves "no pardon at all, as he claims to practise *grammatikē* (μεταποιουμένωι γε γραμματικῆς)." The quotations here are very obviously derived from Apollodorus, but Strabo's attitude to them is noteworthy. In 1.2.37 Callimachus "might be absolved from blame," because Homer's account of Odysseus' wanderings was not wholly fictitious and Callimachus' identification of places is as probable as any, and 7.3.6 is a long account of Apollodoran errors (some derived from Eratosthenes), and so the criticism of Callimachus is implicitly refuted. Here again we see Strabo making a little go a long way (the same passage of Callimachus is involved in both instances), but what matters is that Callimachus here emerges unscathed. So too, in 10.4.12 Strabo cites unnamed critics of Callimachus' narrative of Britomartis in the *Hymn to Artemis* because he got his Cretan geography wrong;[23] Strabo, however, finds a geographical fact which absolves Callimachus of some at least of the criticism. Callimachus mattered; he was not someone lightly to accuse of error or ignorance.

The search for traces of Callimachus in the centuries after he wrote must inevitably also be concerned with silences. What, for example, is the significance, if any, of the fact that Strabo's account of the cities on the eastern coast of Sicily (6.2.1–4) does not make any obvious use, let alone citation, of fr. 43 Pf./Harder of the *Aitia* on the foundation legends of the cities of Sicily. The indirect tradition of that fragment shows that, as we would have expected, it was excerpted in the grammatical tradition for various purposes, and there is certainly sufficient overlap between Callimachus' verses and the subject-matter of Strabo's account to suggest that citation of the poet would have been unsurprising. As we have seen, however, Strabo's engagement with the *Aitia* seems to have been very circumscribed in its focus. Is this silence, then, just a matter of Strabo's sources, again? One subject of some interest here is the foundation and etymology of Zancle (later Messene), which seems to have been the principal *aition* of fr. 43.[24] Thucydides 6.4.4–5 had bequeathed to the subsequent tradition the history of the foundation and the fact that the town derived its original name from the Sicel word ζάγκλον meaning "sickle" (δρέπανον), because the bay on which the town was located is "sickle-shaped" (δρεπανοειδές). Callimachus clearly used and echoed Thucydides in fr. 43 and adopted the explanation ζάγκλον = δρέπανον, but gave a different explanation; the sickle in question was not the shape of the land, but rather that with which Cronus castrated his father and which was now hidden within the city (fr. 43.68–71). These verses were very well known in the grammatical tradition; it is very likely that Callimachus lies behind the appearance of this version of the etymology in Stephanus of Byzantium's later collection of the various reasons given for the name Zancle (Stephanus ζ 3 s.v. Ζάγκλη).[25]

Strabo's account of Zancle is idiosyncratic:

> Messene is situated in a gulf of Pelorias, which bends considerably towards the east and forms an armpit (μασχάλη), so to speak ... Messene was founded by the Messenians of the Peloponnese, who named it after themselves, changing its name; for formerly it was called Zancle, on account of the crookedness (σκολιότης) of the coast (*zanklion* means "crooked"), having been founded formerly by the Naxians who lived near Catana.
>
> Strabo 6.2.3, trans. H. L. Jones, adapted

Whatever his sources here, Strabo seems to be going out of his way to avoid an explanation involving a sickle;[26] the comparison of the bay to an "armpit" is, as far as I am aware, unique, and the claim that the town's name derives from an adjective meaning "crooked," rather than the noun meaning "sickle," is also unique to Strabo. Strabo and/or his sources may have been consciously (and perhaps polemically) avoiding too close a reproduction of Thucydides, and there was certainly no reason to cite Callimachus, given that the poet offered a different explanation of the name, but we may nevertheless wonder whether the fact that Apollodorus, *On the Catalogue of Ships* naturally did not deal with Sicily has something to do with the fact that Strabo does not seem to have made any use of *Aitia* fr. 43.

One Strabonian citation of Callimachus stands out from all the others. In Book 9 Strabo reaches Athens and immediately confronts the fact that he cannot even attempt to be exhaustive about the city and its history because there is just so much to say on every historical and geographical subject connected with the city and its constituent demes (9.1.16–18). The account has led to a long debate about how well Strabo actually knew the city,[27] but what matters here is what follows Strabo's emphasis on the embarrassment of riches which Athens offers:

> The greater the devotion to learning (τὸ φιλείδημον)[28] about things that are famous and the greater the number of men who have talked about them, the greater the censure (ἔλεγχος), if one is not master of the historical facts (ἐὰν μὴ κρατῆι τις τῆς ἱστορίας). For example, in his *Collection of Rivers* (Συναγωγὴ τῶν ποταμῶν), Callimachus (fr. 458 Pf.) says that it makes him laugh if anyone makes bold to write that the Athenian virgins "draw pure liquid from the Eridanus" (τὰς τῶν Ἀθηναίων παρθένους ἀφύσσεσθαι καθαρὸν γάνος Ἡριδανοῖο) from which even cattle would hold aloof. Its sources are indeed existent now, with pure and potable water, as they say, outside the Gates of Diochares, as they are called, near the Lyceum, and in earlier times there was also a fountain built nearby which provided abundant and excellent water. If that is not the case now, why should it be a thing to wonder at, if in early times the water was abundant and pure, and therefore also potable, but in later times underwent a change? However, it is not possible for me to linger (διατρίβειν) over details, since they are so numerous, nor yet, on the other hand, to pass by them all in silence without even mentioning one or another of them in a summary way (ἐν κεφαλαίωι).
>
> Strabo 9.1.19, trans. H. L. Jones, adapted

The purpose of this chapter is apologetic and explanatory.[29] Athens offers so much to say and so many people have already written on the subject that those who wish to venture into this field can expect greater censure if they are not fully on top of everything, and in particular how Athens has changed over centuries. The Callimachean example illustrates both the ἔλεγχος which awaits, and how real ἱστορία is needed to account for change in every detail.

This is the only explicit citation in Strabo of one of Callimachus' scholarly prose works. It is normally assumed that the verse (*SH* 1180) quoted by Callimachus, perhaps from a roughly contemporary poem, was

<- u> ἀφύσσεσθαι καθαρὸν γάνος Ἠριδανοῖο,

. . . to draw pure liquid from the Eridanus

but the infinitive may be a syntactical adaptation of, for example,

<- u> ἀφύσσονται καθαρὸν γάνος Ἠριδανοῖο
παρθένοι Ἀκταίων.[30]

. . . the virgin daughters of the Athenians draw pure liquid from the Eridanus

Be that as it may, Callimachus' point seems to have been that the idea of young girls drawing "pure water of delight" from the Eridanus was absurd, as the water of that stream as it passed through the city was absolutely filthy; the Eridanus flowed west from the base of Lykabettos to pass through the city north of the Acropolis and then out by the Dipylon Gate, later to join the Ilissos.[31] Callimachus' observation, which, as Adrian Hollis noted, suggests (though does not, of course, prove) personal familiarity with Athens,[32] opens up the whole field of the relationship between poetry and "reality," but let us here remain with Strabo.

Why is this Callimachean example chosen and given such prominence in what amounts to a "programmatic" account of Strabonian method? As we have already seen, τὸ φιλείδημον, "devotion to learning," characterized, in Strabo's view, both Callimachus and Strabo,[33] and so Callimachus is a good choice to stand in for the geographer in this cautionary exemplum. Callimachus is here, I think (*pace* Pfeiffer), not subjected to harsh criticism:[34] he made a mistake, because he was not fully on top of the ἱστορία, but it is precisely the kind of mistake which it is all too easy to make, even for a Strabo. The geographer will, therefore, sidestep the danger by not dwelling (διατρίβειν) on all the details. Callimachus clearly has been subjected to ἔλεγχος in the sense of "censure," though not by Strabo who has limited himself to pointing out the error. Where would a likely source of censure lie? Benedictus Niese long ago suggested that Apollodorus was (again) the culprit, though the only reason he adduced is that this passage is of a piece with the other attacks on Callimachus which we find in

Strabo and which can be securely traced to Apollodorus.[35] As I have argued, Strabo is not here "attacking" Callimachus, although of course the same example could also have been adduced by someone else and embroidered with a good dose of philological polemic. Are there other reasons for thinking that Strabo here may indeed have drawn on the riches of the Apollodoran texts?

Apollodorus may, in fact, have contributed to the chapters (9.1.17–18) immediately preceding the citation of Callimachus,[36] and who more likely, we might think, to seize on a Callimachean error in Athenian matters than Apollodorus of Athens? There is, moreover, another, and strikingly similar, passage of Greek literature which may play with the allegedly "pure" water quality of the Eridanus. In a fragment of his *Nannion* (the name of a courtesan), the fourth-century comic poet Eubulus made a character praise the ready accessibility of cheap female prostitutes as a way of avoiding the shameful dangers of adulterous liaisons:

ὅστις λέχη γὰρ σκότια νυμφεύει λάθραι,
πῶς οὐχὶ πάντων ἐστὶν ἀθλιώτατος;
ἐξὸν θεωρήσαντι πρὸς τὸν ἥλιον
γυμνὰς ἐφεξῆς ἐπὶ κέρως τεταγμένας,
ἐν λεπτοπήνοις ὑμέσιν ἑστώσας, οἵας   5
Ἠριδανὸς ἁγνοῖς ὕδασι κηπεύει κόρας
μικροῦ πρίασθαι κέρματος τὴν ἡδονήν ...

The man who seeks secret liaisons, shrouded in darkness, is not he the most wretched of all men? One can review in broad sunlight (girls), virtually naked, drawn up one after another in a column, standing in very fine transparent fabrics, such as the maidens which the Eridanus waters with its holy streams, and purchase one's pleasure for a small coin ...

Eubulus fr. 67.1–7 K-A/Hunter

Very similar verses were also used in another play, the *Pannychis* (fr. 82 K-A = 84 Hunter), and are cited by Athenaeus in Book 13 immediately before fr. 67. The paratragic v. 6 of fr. 67 suggests a comparison of the prostitutes to the Heliades, Phaethon's mourning sisters, who were metamorphosed into poplars and lined the banks of the (other) Eridanus, commonly identified with the Po, though both Herodotus (3.115) and Strabo (5.1.9) denied that any such river existed;[37] the analogy, which focuses (*inter alia*) on the idea of the girls drawn up "in a column,"[38] is prepared by the reference to the sun in v.3.

James Davidson, however, took the reference in Eubulus to be to the Athenian Eridanus and saw a joke on the filthiness of the stream as it passed through the

Kerameikos and other parts of the Athenian "red-light" district.[39] The idea of some play with the homonymous rivers is very attractive, and helps with the otherwise somewhat surprising, though amusingly paratragic, evocation of the "mythical" Eridanus in Eubulus. As it happens, we know that Apollodorus, alongside a broader interest in Athenian comedy, wrote a work *On the Courtesans at Athens* (frr. 208–12 Jacoby), and one of the ladies whom he discussed in that work was indeed Nannion, the title-figure of Eubulus' play (fr. 211 Jacoby). There was a rich prose literature on Athenian courtesans (cf. Athenaeus 13. 567a, 583d), but it is perhaps not too wild a speculation that one of the sources for the quotation from Eubulus' *Nannion* which finally reached the Ἀθηναίου ποταμοῖο μέγας ῥόος was indeed Apollodorus' work.[40] It is probably going too far to suggest that, either in this work or in another or in more than one place, Apollodorus found cause to discuss the Athenian Eridanus, and it was from there that the example of Callimachus came so opportunely to Strabo, but it is hard to resist the temptation. If there is anything in the suggestion, it may be that there is more originally Callimachean material about the history of the Eridanus, though filtered through Apollodorus, in 9.1.19 than is normally assumed.[41] It is, however, also important to note that, although Strabo may have taken the example from Apollodorus, he did not, at the same time, take over the rather self-satisfied sense of critical superiority which may have accompanied it in the earlier text. Strabo was too well aware, as any scholar should be, that there is a crucial difference between πολυμάθεια and knowing everything.[42]

Notes

1   The time of composition of the *Geography* is a notorious problem: cf. Dueck (2000), 146–51.

2   Roller (2018), 941, implies that this is a nod to Eratosthenes "the inventor of the discipline of geography."

3   Diogenes Laertius 9.17 knows that Heraclitus was "a poet of elegy," but it is Callimachus' poem in his honour which is cited.

4   Pontani (2011), 100, calls Strabo an "admirer" of Callimachus.

5   See the table in Dueck (2005), 88–9.

6   10.6.4 (= 10. fr. 11 Cohen-Skalli) is a corrupt citation of vv. 59–63 of *Iambus* 1, a passage known also to Diogenes Laertius (1.25) or his source. The passage of Diodorus is preserved only in a Byzantine compilation.

7   Cf. further below on Argonautic material in Strabo. Many of the arguments in Nerz (2020) bear on apparent differences in the reception patterns of Callimachus and

Apollonius; for the present context cf. the alleged distinction (Netz 2020: 117) between Callimachus as a "brand name" (the last such, in fact) and Apollonius' place in the canon as due to "the power of a single work."

8　To the standard commentaries add Kerkhecker (1999), 207–9, Hunter (2011), 112; ἀνέχων is Pfeiffer's suggested supplement.

9　Cameron (1995), 38.

10　On Strabo's sources cf. E. Honigmann, *RE* 4A.97–147; Dueck (2000), 180–6.

11　On the *Nachleben* of the epigrams cf. Hunter (2019), citing earlier bibliography.

12　Cf. Radt *ad loc.* (on 837.15f.), Cameron (1995), 8. The only rivals in our corpus of Callimachus would be *AP* 7.525 (= *Epigram* 21 Pf. = *HE* 1179–84) and *Hymn to Apollo* 65, but neither seem very probable.

13　That Strabo did indeed know *Iambus* 6, not just know of it, is assumed, e.g., by Kerkhecker (1999), 165–7, and Pothecary (2005).

14　Cf., e.g., Niese (1877), Schwartz (1894), 2867–70, Jacoby (1930), 775–9.

15　Pfeiffer (1949/53), vol. 2, xxxi. Pfeiffer (1968), 253–66, is a helpful survey of Apollodorus' work.

16　So, e.g., Pontani (2011), 100.

17　Cf. Harder (2012), vol. 2, 147, citing earlier literature.

18　The manner of the quotations, τοτὲ μὲν . . . τοτὲ δέ, leaves unclarified the relation between them.

19　Like Radt, I have adopted the text and interpretation of Wilamowitz (1924), vol. 2, 168 n. 1.

20　Cf. Wilamowitz (1924), vol. 2, 168–9.

21　For a brief account, cf. Hunter (2015), 9–10.

22　Apollodorus makes a number of appearances in the scholia to the *Argonautica* and his scholarly work will no doubt have been much used by Theon and other commentators on Apollonius, but there is very little surviving sign of any major Apollodoran engagement with the Alexandrian epic.

23　I have discussed this passage in Hunter (2011), 108–9. Schwartz (1894), 2864, 2870, identifies the critic in question as (again) Apollodorus.

24　To the standard commentaries add Hunter (2017), 198–212.

25　Pfeiffer regards it as certain, whereas Harder offers a cautious *fortasse*.

26　Elsewhere, however, Strabo is happy to explain the name Δρέπανον as referring to a cape which is δρεπανοειδής (8.2.3).

27　Cf. Waddy (1963), Roller (2018), 505–6.

28　φιλείδημον Meineke: φιλόδημον.

29　I do not understand Roller's statement that the chapter "is a digression on the superior critical sense of Athenian scholarship" (2018: 509).

30　The lost opening of the first verse may, for example, have been οὔ νυν or, taking a clue from the citation itself, οὔ καί.

31 Cf. Dörpfeld (1888; summarized by Frazer 1898: 199–201).

32 Hollis (1992), 2 n. 6. For Callimachus and Athens see esp. Oliver (2002).

33 The adjective φιλειδήμων is virtually unique to Strabo, who uses it six times in the *Geography*.

34 Roller (2018), 509, notes that Strabo's attitude to Callimachus in this passage is unclear.

35 Niese (1877), 275.

36 Cf. Steph. Byz. α 176 = Apollodorus fr. 185 Jacoby.

37 In 5.1.9 the outlandish Ἡλιάδας τὰς ἀπαιγειρουμένας, "the enpoplarised Heliades," mocks the outlandishness of the fiction.

38 Cf. perhaps Ap. Rhod. *Arg.* 1.30 of Orpheus' trees, ἐξείης στιχόωσιν ἐπήτριμοι.

39 Davidson (1997), 85. Davidson does not mention the other Eridanus, and his translation, "the ones the Eridanus refreshes," misrepresents the problematic οἵας (or Meineke's ὅσας) in the Greek text.

40 I have deliberately refrained from pursuing the possibility that fr. 458 has anything to do with the poetic Callimachus' "programmatic" water-imagery.

41 The subject-matter is not far from some of the Callimachean material preserved in later paradoxography, cf. esp. fr. 407 Pf.

42 I am very grateful to Jessica Lightfoot for instructive suggestions on an earlier version of this essay.

Bibliography

Cameron, A. (1995), *Callimachus and His Critics*, Princeton, NJ: Princeton University Press.

Davidson, J. (1997), *Courtesans and Fishcakes*, London: HarperCollins.

Dörpfeld, W. (1888), "Der Eridanos," *Mitteilungen des Deutschen Archäologischen Instituts, Athenische Abteilung*, 13: 211–20.

Dueck, D. (2000), *Strabo of Amasia: A Greek Man of Letters in Augustan Rome*, London and New York: Routledge.

Dueck, D. (2005), "Strabo's Use of Poetry," in D. Dueck, H. Lindsay, and S. Pothecary (eds), *Strabo's Cultural Geography: The Makings of a Kolossourgia*, 86–107, Cambridge: Cambridge University Press.

Frazer, J. G. (1898), *Pausanias's Description of Greece*, vol. 2, London: Macmillan.

Harder, A. (2012), *Callimachus: Aetia*, 2 vols, Oxford: Oxford University Press.

Hollis, A. (1992), "Attica in Hellenistic Poetry," *Zeitschrift für Papyrologie und Epigraphik*, 93: 1–15.

Hunter, R. (2011) "Festivals, Cults, and the Construction of Consensus in Hellenistic Poetry," in G. Urso (ed.), *Dicere Laudes: Elogio, comunicazione, creazione del consenso*, 101–18, Cividale del Friuli: Edizioni ETS.

Hunter, R. (2015), *Apollonius of Rhodes, Argonautica Book IV*, Cambridge: Cambridge University Press.

Hunter, R. (2017), "Callimachus, *Aitia*," in D. Sider (ed.), *Hellenistic Poetry: A Selection*, 186–212, Ann Arbor, MI: University of Michigan Press.

Hunter, R. (2019), "Reading and Citing the *Epigrams* of Callimachus," in J. Klooster, M. A. Harder, R. F. Regtuit, and G.C. Wakker (eds.), *Callimachus Revisited*, 171–91, Leuven: Peeters.

Jacoby, F. (1930), *Die Fragmente der griechischen Historiker*, Vol. IID, Berlin: Weidmannsche Buchhandlung.

Kerkhecker, A. (1999), *Callimachus' Book of Iambi*, Oxford: Oxford University Press.

Netz, R. (2020), *Scale, Space and Canon in Ancient Literary Culture*, Cambridge: Cambridge University Press.

Niese, B. (1877), "Apollodors Commentar zum Schiffskataloge als Quelle Strabo's," *Rheinisches Museum*, 32: 267–307.

Oliver, G. J. (2002), "Callimachus the poet and benefactor of the Athenians," *Zeitschrift für Papyrologie und Epigraphik*, 140: 6–8.

Pfeiffer, R. (1949/53), *Callimachus*, 2 vols, Oxford: Oxford University Press.

Pfeiffer, R. (1968), *History of Classical Scholarship*, Oxford: Oxford University Press.

Pontani, F. (2011), "Callimachus cited," in B. Acosta-Hughes, L. Lehnus, and S. Stephens (eds.), *Brill's Companion to Callimachus*, 93–117, Leiden: Brill.

Pothecary, S. (2005), "Kolossourgia: 'A Colossal Statue of a Work,'" in D. Dueck, S. Lindsay, and S. Pothecary (eds.), *Strabo's Cultural Geography: The Makings of a Kolossourgia*, 5–26, Cambridge: Cambridge University Press.

Roller, D. W. (2018), *A Historiographical and Topographical Guide to the Geography of Strabo*, Cambridge: Cambridge University Press.

Schwartz, E. (1894), "Apollodoros. Schriftstellerei," *Paulys Real-Encyclopädie der classischen Altertumswissenschaft* 1, 2856–86, Stuttgart: J. B. Metzlerscher Verlag.

Waddy, L. (1963), "Did Strabo visit Athens?" *American Journal of Archaeology*, 67: 296–300.

Wilamowitz, U. von. (1924), *Hellenistische Dichtung in der Zeit des Kallimachos*, Berlin: Weidmannsche Buchhandlung.

Part Four

Hellenistic and Roman Culture

Seeing Double

Apollonius' Two Phaethons

Ivana Petrovic

University of Virginian

In her pathbreaking book, *Seeing Double*, Susan Stephens charts the way Alexandrian poets incorporated Egyptian ideas and narrative motifs into their work. In her own words, "the cumulative effect of this poetry would have been to allow the reader to discern Egyptian cultural formations, but contained within or domesticated by its framework of Greekness. The effect is one of an optical illusion—looked at from one angle discrete elements in the narrative are Greek, from another Egyptian; both are complete and distinct without the other, yet interdependent in their final patterning."[1] In her incisive analysis of the fourth book of Apollonius' *Argonautica*, Stephens demonstrates that the homeward voyage of the Argo resembles the path of the Sun through the Egyptian underworld landscape.[2] The journey of the Sun during the night was "much more terrifying than the daily journey, because it traversed a space where time had collapsed, and past met future, where regeneration and rebirth coexisted with putrefaction and death."[3] One of the points of convergence between Apollonius' story and Egyptian myth is the encounter with a fiery lake or a sulfurous pit. According to Stephens, the lake of Phaethon corresponds to the Egyptian underworld fiery lake.[4] My paper discusses this episode with an aim to demonstrate that Phaethon's lake is a rich nodal point of the epic, connecting not only the Egyptian and the Greek points of view, but also myth, paradoxography, and contemporary science. Looking from one, Egyptian, angle, the Argonauts enact the nocturnal voyage of the Sun and encounter putrefaction and death. Looking from the Greek angle, they face death and miasma and enact the wandering and purification typical for those who committed murder which must be expiated.

The reason why the Argonauts end up at the shores of Eridanos in the first place is the pollution of Jason and Medea due to the murder of Apsyrtos. Pollution plays a major role in Apollonius' epic. The reason for the whole quest was the anger of Zeus because of the attempted sacrifice of Phrixos.[5] This anger resulted in the pollution of the whole family of Aiolidai and the only way to remove the pollution was to bring the golden fleece back to Greece.[6] However, in order to bring the fleece back, Jason needs the help of the Colchian princess Medea, who falls in love with Jason, betrays her family and leaves her home. In order to deflect the Colchian pursuit, Medea and Jason treacherously murder her half-brother Apsyrtos, incurring the anger of Zeus, which also manifests itself as pollution.

Zeus is angry, but he still envisages means of purification for Jason and Medea (4.557–61) and the holy plank of Argo communicates Zeus' instructions to the crew (4.585–91):

> Οὐ γὰρ ἀλύξειν
> ἔννεπεν οὔτε πόνους δολιχῆς ἁλὸς οὔτε θυέλλας
> ἀργαλέας, ὅτε μὴ Κίρκη φόνον Ἀψύρτοιο
> νηλέα νίψειεν· Πολυδεύκεα δ᾽ εὐχετάασθαι
> Κάστορά τ᾽ ἀθανάτοισι θεοῖς ἤνωγε κελεύθους
> Αὐσονίης ἔντοσθε πορεῖν ἁλός, ᾗ ἔνι Κίρκην
> δήουσιν, Πέρσης τε καὶ Ἠελίοιο θύγατρα.

It (sc. the plank) said that they could not escape from their suffering on the vast ocean and the terrible storms until Kirke had cleansed them for the pitiless murder of Apsyrtos. It ordered Polydeukes and Kastor to pray to the immortal gods to grant them passage into the Ausonian sea, where they could find Kirke, the daughter of Perse and Helios.

The first stop in their journey is the shore of the river Eridanos, where the Argonauts experience a grim marvel (4.596–603):

> ἐς δ᾽ ἔβαλον μύχατον ῥόον Ἠριδανοῖο,
> ἔνθα ποτ᾽ αἰθαλόεντι τυπεὶς πρὸς στέρνα κεραυνῷ
> ἡμιδαὴς Φαέθων πέσεν ἅρματος Ἠελίοιο
> λίμνης ἐς προχοὰς πολυβενθέος· ἡ δ᾽ ἔτι νῦν περ
> τραύματος αἰθομένοιο βαρὺν ἀνακηκίει ἀτμόν,   600
> οὐδέ τις ὕδωρ κεῖνο διὰ πτερὰ κοῦφα τανύσσας
> οἰωνὸς δύναται βαλέειν ὕπερ, ἀλλὰ μεσηγὺς
> φλογμῷ ἐνιθρῴσκει πεποτημένος.

They entered the remotest part of the stream of the Eridanos,[7] where once Phaethon, half-consumed by fire, fell from Helios' chariot into the waters of the deep marsh, after the blazing thunderbolt had struck him in the chest. To this very day the marsh exhales a heavy vapour which rises from his smouldering wound; no bird can stretch out its fragile wings to fly over that water, but in mid-flight it falls dead in the flames.

Apollonius then describes the eternal lamentation of Phaethon's sisters, whose tears are turned to amber and offers an alternative, Celtic, account about the formation of amber from the tears of Apollo.

Like the body of Phaethon, the marshy lake seems to be half fire: it is water (601: ὕδωρ κεῖνο), but the bird falling into it lands in the fire (603: φλογμῷ ἐνιθρῴσκει). The double nature of the lake allows us, I posit, to read the story both as reminiscent of the Egyptian underworld landscape and as a Greek myth. But there is even more to the lake. The reaction of the Argonauts to the fumes of its waters invites us to interpret the episode from the perspective of Greek medical writing as well. Even though they don't seem to be aware of the source of the stench and lamentation,[8] the Argonauts are nevertheless forced to start expiating the murder of Apsyrtos by entering a state similar to the ritual lamentation for the dead (4.619–26):[9]

> Τοὺς δ' οὔτε βρώμης ᾕρει πόθος οὐδὲ ποτοῖο,
> οὔτ' ἐπὶ γηθοσύνας τράπετο νέος. Ἀλλ' ἄρα τοί γε   620
> ἤματα μὲν στρεύγοντο περιβληχρὸν βαρύθοντες
> ὀδμῇ λευγαλέῃ τήν ῥ' ἄσχετον ἐξανίεσκον
> τυφομένου Φαέθοντος ἐπιρροαὶ Ἠριδανοῖο·
> νύκτας δ' αὖ γόον ὀξὺν ὀδυρομένων ἐσάκουον
> Ἡλιάδων λιγέως· τὰ δὲ δάκρυα μυρομένῃσιν   625
> οἷον ἐλαιηραὶ στάγες ὕδασιν ἐμφορέοντο.

The heroes desired neither food nor drink, nor did their minds have any thought of delights. The days they spent worn out and exhausted, weighed down by the foul smell which rose from the small branches of the Eridanos as Phaethon's corpse steamed; at night they heard the piercing sound of the Heliades' shrill lamentation. As they wept, their tears were carried on the waters like drops of oil.

Scholars have long noted the resemblance of this scene to the horrible murder of Apsyrtos: Phaethon is the nickname given to Apsyrtos by the Colchians (3.245–6); he, too, drives his father's chariot (3.1235–6; 4.224–5) and both are descendants of Helios.[10] Byre (1996: 280) points out that the motif of the stench recalls the punishment of the prophet Phineus who was also prevented from eating by the foul smell the Harpies poured on his food[11] and suggests that, like Phineus, the Argonauts are also in the grip of pollution. In both cases, Zeus punishes the polluted with hardship. Ultimately Byre sees the correspondences between the murder of Apsyrtos and the Eridanos scene as too ambiguous for any firm conclusions: "It is unclear from the narrator's cryptic statements whether the Argonauts have come here despite the plans and wrath of Zeus, or because of them" (p. 281).

In my view, the correspondences between the two scenes are very strong, and the strongest link between them is the ancient Greek view of miasma. In the gory depiction of the murder of Apsyrtos, Apollonius clearly indicates that the source of pollution (*agos*) is the victim's blood gushing from his wound, blood which Apsyrtos smears on the veil of Medea in order to indicate that, as the planner of the deed, she, too, is responsible for his death, and which Jason spits out in his attempt to free himself of pollution.[12] Apollonius uses the word ἄγος three times in the poem, always referring to grave pollution as a result of transgressions against religious norms.[13] Pollution of the *agos*-type is more intense than miasma caused by natural biological processes such as birth, sex, and death.[14] Miasma is unavoidable in human life, whereas *agos* is caused by an avoidable, often intentional transgression. The source of *agos* is a sacrilegious act, an offence against ritual norms or divinely sanctioned social norms. Such offences trigger negative divine attention which amounts to pollution. Both *agos* and miasma are words which denote pollution as a religious category and are not used for ordinary physical dirt. Miasma almost always designates religious pollution which is contagious and therefore dangerous. However, there are a few instances in Greek medical literature where miasma is used to designate noxious vapors which cause epidemic disease. In my view, Apollonius uses the Eridanos episode in order to provide a mythic origin for this type of miasma. The passage effectively romanticizes the notion of disease-causing vaporous miasma.

We have seen that the blood from Apsyrtos' wound is the source of pollution for Jason and Medea. In the case of his double, Phaethon, the lake in which he fell radiates a foul vapor (βαρὺν ἀτμόν) which is also emanating from his wound (τραύματος αἰθομένοιο). This vapor is so toxic, it kills the birds which attempt to fly over the lake.[15] The foul stench prevents the Argonauts from eating and drinking and they fall into a state of lethargy. They are, in fact, "sickened to the point of great weakness," στρεύγοντο περιβληχρόν.[16] The Hippocratic treatise *Breaths*, dated to the late fifth century BCE[17] provides the missing link between pollution (miasma), noxious vapors, and epidemic disease:

Ὅτι μὲν οὖν μεγάλη κοινωνίη ἅπασι τοῖσι ζῴοισι τοῦ ἠέρος ἐστὶν, εἴρηται· μετὰ τοῦτο τοίνυν εὐθέως ῥητέον, ὅτι οὐκ ἄλλοθέν ποθεν εἰκός ἐστι γίνεσθαι τὰς

ἀρρωστίας μάλιστα, ἢ ἐντεῦθεν, ὅταν τοῦτο ἢ πλέον, ἢ ἔλασσον, ἢ **καὶ
ἀθροώτερον, ἢ μεμιασμένον νοσεροῖσι μιάσμασιν**, ἐς τὸ σῶμα ἐσέλθῃ
. . .Ὁκόταν μὲν οὖν ὁ ἀὴρ **τοιουτέοισι χρωσθῇ μιάσμασιν**, ἃ τῇ ἀνθρωπίνῃ
φύσει πολέμιά ἐστιν, ἄνθρωποι τότε νοσέουσιν· ὅταν δὲ ἑτέρῳ τινὶ ἔθνει ζῷον
ἀνάρμοστος ὁ ἠὴρ γένηται, κεῖνα τότε νοσέουσιν.

I have said that all animals partake largely in the air. After this one must simply
state that the source of all diseases is, in all probability, nothing other than this
principle (i.e. air) when there is too much or too little of it, or it has become too
massive, or when it enters the body **stained by morbific miasmata** ... Thus
when the air is **infected with miasmata** whose properties are hostile to human
nature, this is when men are ill; but when the air is not suitable for another type
of living beings, these beings are then ill.[18]

The link between miasma as a religious category and the Hippocratic
rationalizing approach to miasma is the old belief that divinities punish polluted
individuals and even whole cities with disease. We witness this idea already in
the first book of the *Iliad*, where Apollo causes pestilence in the Greek camp.[19]
Pestilence (λοιμός) as a collective divine punishment for grave pollutions looms
large in Greek literature,[20] but individual maladies such as epilepsy or skin
disease were thought to have divine origins, too.[21] The author of the Hippocratic
treatise *On the sacred disease* famously protests against the view that ritual
purification could heal epilepsy—and so proves that this was in fact common
practice.[22] The scarce mentions of miasma in medical texts, in Rufus of Ephesus
(preserved in Oribasius), and in Galen attest to a concentrated effort to rationalize
miasma and provide non-religious explanations for its working and origins.[23]
Miasma as a concept is effectively adopted from the religious sphere and becomes
a rational, medical phenomenon. According to the medical theory, epidemics are
not a consequence of communal pollution and divine anger, but of polluted air.
In his treaties *On Differences Between Fevers*, Galen writes the following:

κατὰ δὲ τὰς λοιμώδεις καταστάσεις ἡ εἰσπνοὴ μάλιστα αἰτία. γίνεται μὲν γὰρ
ποτε καὶ διὰ τοὺς ἐν τῷ σώματι χυμοὺς ἐπιτηδείους πρὸς σῆψιν ὑπάρχοντας,
ὅταν ἀφορμήν τινα βραχεῖαν ἐκ τοῦ περιέχοντος εἰς ἀρχὴν πυρετοῦ λάβῃ τὸ
ζῷον· ὡς τὰ πολλὰ δὲ ἐκ τῆς ἀναπνοῆς ἄρχεται **τοῦ πέριξ ἀέρος ὑπὸ**
σηπεδονώδους ἀναθυμιάσεως **μιανθέντος**. ἡ δὲ ἀρχὴ τῆς σηπεδόνος ἤτοι
πλῆθός τι νεκρῶν ἐστι μὴ καυθέντων, ὡς ἐν πολέμοις εἴωθε συμπίπτειν· **ἢ ἐκ
τελμάτων τινῶν, ἢ λιμνῶν ἀναθυμιάσεις** ὥρᾳ θέρους . . .

In pestilential constitutions, the inhalation (of air) is the most important cause
(sc. of fever). For if the fever is sometimes caused by the humours in the body

that are susceptible to causing putrefaction, when the living being receives a slight impetus from the ambient air for the beginning of the fever most often it is following inhalation that the fever starts, inhalation **of the surrounding air** which is **polluted** by putrefied odors. The origin of putrefaction is either a **mass of cadavers that have not been cremated**, as normally happens during combat, or **fumes from swamps or lakes** during the summer.

He then provides three possible explanations of the famous Athenian pestilence described by Thucydides. One of them is based on Thucydides' mention of a report about the disease originating in Ethiopia:

τάχα δὲ καὶ κατὰ τὸ συνεχὲς ἐξ Αἰθιοπίας ἐρρύη τινὰ σηπεδονώδη **μιάσματα** τοῖς ἐπιτηδείως ἔχουσι σώματα βλαβῆναι πρὸς αὐτῶν, αἴτια πυρετοῦ γενησόμενα.

It could also be, immediately after, a flux of putrefying **miasmata** coming from Ethiopia known to cause fever in those whose body is susceptible to being damaged by them.[24]

Similarly, Diodorus of Sicily explains the plague of Athens as originating from the fumes rising from heated and putrefied stagnant waters which pollute the air. Even though Diodorus does not use the word miasma, Jouanna (2012: 129) rightly notes that his explanation relies on the Hippocratic, rationalizing miasmatic theory:

Προγεγενημένων ἐν τῷ χειμῶνι μεγάλων ὄμβρων συνέβη τὴν γῆν ἔνυδρον γενέσθαι, πολλοὺς δὲ καὶ τῶν κοίλων τόπων δεξαμένους πλῆθος ὕδατος λιμνάσαι καὶ σχεῖν στατὸν ὕδωρ παραπλησίως τοῖς ἑλώδεσι τῶν τόπων, **θερμαινομένων** δ' ἐν τῷ θέρει τούτων καὶ **σηπομένων** συνίστασθαι παχείας καὶ δυσώδεις **ἀτμίδας**, ταύτας δ' ἀναθυμιωμένας διαφθείρειν τὸν πλησίον ἀέρα· ὅπερ δὴ καὶ ἐπὶ τῶν ἑλῶν τῶν νοσώδη διάθεσιν ἐχόντων ὁρᾶται γινόμενον.

As a result of heavy rains in the previous winter the ground had become soaked with water, and many low-lying regions, having received a vast amount of water, turned into shallow pools and held stagnant water, very much as marshy regions do; and when these waters **became warm** in the summer and **grew putrid**, thick foul **vapours** were formed, which, rising up in fumes, corrupted the surrounding air, the very thing which may be seen taking place in marshy grounds which are by nature pestilential.[25]

Finally, Palladius in his sixth-century CE commentary of Hippocrates' *Epidemics* 6 uses the word miasma in the passage which explains that epidemic disease can be caused by the air that receives miasmata either from cadavers or stagnant waters.[26]

In its gradual transformation from a religious category to a rationalizing cause of epidemics in the ancient medical literature, miasma paradoxically goes full circle: whereas in Greek religious belief every corpse exudes miasma which pollutes the house and its inhabitants for a set number of days and prevents them from entering sacred ground,[27] miasma as a medical concept is the air polluted by decomposing corpses, or by stagnant, putrid waters. Death and decay are the source of both types of miasma. The thread of medical explanation of pestilence we can follow for more than 1,000 years, from *Breaths* to Palladius starts with the idea of morbific miasma in the air (*Breaths*). At some point medical writers identify decaying cadavers and marshy fumes as the cause of infectious airy miasma. Apollonius is clearly aware of this explanation because he connects the marshy lake, the decaying corpse, and the noxious, epidemic-causing air, exactly like Galen and Palladius do many centuries later.[28] By using the word ἡμιδαής "half-burnt" (4.598), Apollonius clears the way for a scientific explanation of miasma. As Plutarch notes, the bodies of those killed by lightning do not putrefy,[29] while Galen points out that uncremated cadavers produce miasma in the air. Since Phaethon is only half-burnt, his corpse is capable of polluting the air.

Apollonius' Phaethon episodes bring together the medical and the religious concept of miasma: Phaethon, the son of Helios produces "medical" miasma, whereas the grandson of Helios Phaethon/Apsyrtos produces religious miasma. As the Argonauts travel seeking purification from the murder of Helios' grandson Apsyrtos, their first stop is the lake of one child of Helios, Phaethon, and their final stop is the island of another child of Helios, Circe.[30] In Greek myth, polluted individuals take special care to avoid the sun[31] and the irony of pollution emanating from Helios' grandson and son, as well as the impending doom of Medea's killing of her children intensifies the magnitude of past and future crimes in Apollonius' epic.

The legend about Phaethon's catastrophic driving of the chariot and his fall into Eridanos is very old and seems to have been associated with the origin of amber early on.[32] The lake of Phaethon is described in the Hellenistic paradoxographic text attributed to Aristotle, *On Marvelous Things Heard* 81:

ἔστι δὲ καὶ λίμνη, ὡς ἔοικε, πλησίον τοῦ ποταμοῦ, ὕδωρ ἔχουσα θερμόν· ὀσμὴ δ᾽ ἀπ᾽ αὐτῆς βαρεῖα καὶ χαλεπὴ ἀποπνεῖ, καὶ οὔτε ζῷον οὐδὲν πίνει ἐξ αὐτῆς οὔτε ὄρνεον ὑπερίπταται, ἀλλὰ πίπτει καὶ ἀποθνήσκει. ἔχει δὲ τὸν μὲν κύκλον σταδίων διακοσίων, τὸ δὲ εὖρος ὡς δέκα. μυθεύουσι δὲ οἱ ἐγχώριοι Φαέθοντα κεραυνωθέντα πεσεῖν εἰς ταύτην τὴν λίμνην. εἶναι δ᾽ ἐν αὐτῇ αἰγείρους πολλάς, ἐξ ὧν ἐκπίπτειν τὸ καλούμενον ἤλεκτρον.

There is a lake apparently near the river, containing hot water. A heavy and unpleasant smell comes from it, and no animal ever drinks from it nor does bird fly over it without falling and dying. It has a circumference of two hundred furlongs, and a breadth of ten. The local inhabitants say that Phaethon fell into this lake when he was struck by a thunderbolt. There are many poplars in it, from which oozes the so-called electron.[33]

According to Hunter (2015: 163), *comm. ad vv.* 599–603, Apollonius and Ps-Aristotle most likely shared a common source.[34] By incorporating the story about the hot lake with its heavy fumes into his epic, Apollonius joins myth, paradoxography, and medical theory about epidemics into a unified whole. The episode re-mythologizes the Hippocratic rationalizing explanation of epidemics by presenting Phaethon's decaying corpse as the root cause of pestilential air.

But Apollonius also creates a connection between the religious and scientific origins of disease, as both kinds of miasma ultimately emanate from a corpse. When the Argonauts arrive to Phaethon's lake, they are already engulfed in miasma as a religious category because of the sacrilegious murder of Apsyrtos. At the lake, they experience the symptoms of an epidemic caused by the scientifically construed miasma. Both miasmata are caused by a descendent of the sun called Phaethon. Apollonius' story is underpinned by the contemporary scientific theory about the origins of epidemics and more marvelous than paradoxography.

Notes

1   Stephens (2003), 9.
2   Ibid., 218–37.
3   Ibid., 219.
4   Ibid., 229.
5   *Arg.* 2.1192–5 (Jason's speech to the sons of Phrixos):

> Ἀλλ' ἄγεθ', ὧδε καὶ αὐτοὶ ἐς Ἑλλάδα μαιομένοισι / κῶας ἄγειν χρύσειον ἐπίρροθοι ἄμμι πέλεσθε / καὶ πλόου ἡγεμονῆες, ἐπεὶ Φρίξοιο θυηλὰς / στέλλομαι ἀμπλήσων, Ζηνὸς χόλον Αἰολίδῃσιν.

> But come—we wish to bring the golden fleece to Hellas: help us and guide our voyage, since my expedition is to atone for the attempted sacrifice of Phrixos, which has brought Zeus' anger on the descendants of Aiolos.

Argos elaborates further in his speech to Aietes (3.332–9):

Χρειὼ δ᾽ ἢν ἐθέλῃς ἐξίδμεναι, οὔ σ᾽ ἐπικεύσω. / Τόνδε τις ἱέμενος πάτρης
ἀπάνευθεν ἐλάσσαι / καὶ κτεάνων βασιλεύς, περιώσιον οὕνεκεν ἀλκῇ /
σφωιτέρῃ πάντεσσι μετέπρεπεν Αἰολίδῃσι, / πέμπει δεῦρο νέεσθαι ἀμήχανον·
οὐδ᾽ ὑπαλύξειν /στεῦται ἀμειλίκτοιο Διὸς θυμαλγέα μῆνιν / καὶ χόλον, οὐδ᾽
ἄτλητον ἄγος Φρίξοιό τε ποινὰς / Αἰολιδέων γενεήν, πρὶν ἐς Ἑλλάδα κῶας
ἱκέσθαι.

If you wish to know the reason for the expedition, I shall not conceal it from
you. This man (sc. Jason) has been sent here on a hopeless quest by someone, a
king, who wishes to thrust him out of his homeland and possessions, because
his courage far surpasses that of all the other descendants of Aiolos. He claims
that the family of the Aiolidai will not escape the bitter wrath of implacable
Zeus, from his anger and from the appalling pollution and punishment arising
from Phrixos until the fleece comes to Hellas.

All quotations of *Argonautica* are from Vian's 1974–81 Budé text and the translations
are from Hunter (1993).

6 On the role of the fleece as purifier from pollution, see Petrovic (forthcoming).
7 Apparently, this is either a lake adjacent to the river Eridanos (Po) or its remote
course. We are, however, in the realm of fictional geography and the precise location
of Phaethon's lake is impossible to determine. See Thalmann (2011), 162, with
bibliography.
8 Byre (1996), 279–80, points out that only the narrator knows the backstory in this
passage.
9 According to Beye (1982), 165, the scene is "at one level, a description of the insistent
pressure of choking guilt." Phillips (2020), 98–120, provides a detailed discussion of
the lament of the Heliades and notes that the Argonauts' lack of desire for food and
drink "replicates behavior characteristic of mourning" (p. 102 n. 80).
10 See Livrea (1973), 185. Vian (1981), 35–8; Fusillo (1985), 42–3; Byre (1996), 279–82;
Hunter (2015), 162–3. Phillips (2020), 102, intriguingly attempts to reconstruct the
content of Heliades' lament and suggests repetitive sounds such as αἰαῖ or ὤμοι and
the name of the deceased, concluding at 102 n. 82: "If Phaethon's name was
employed, the Argonauts, not knowing the person whom the name identified, would
have heard a word meaning 'shining' (φαέθων being the active present participle
masculine of φαέθω)." Since Phaethon was Apsyrtos' nickname, Medea would surely
recognize it, so her own behavior would be even more starkly contrasted to that of
the (perhaps all too dutiful) sisters of the other Phaethon, the Heliades.
11 *Arg.* 2.191–3; 228–31.
12 *Arg.* 4.471–9:

λοίσθια δ᾽ ἥρως / θυμὸν ἀποπνείων χερσὶν μέλαν ἀμφοτέρῃσιν / αἷμα κατ᾽
ὠτειλὴν ὑπόσχετο· τῆς δὲ καλύπτρην / ἀργυφέην καὶ πέπλον ἀλευομένης
ἐρύθηνεν. / Ὀξὺ δὲ πανδαμάτωρ λοξῷ ἴδεν οἷον ἔρεξαν / ὄμματι νηλειὴς

ὀλοφώιον ἔργον Ἐρινύς. / Ἥρως δ' Αἰσονίδης ἐξάργματα τάμνε θανόντος, / τρὶς δ' ἀπέλειξε φόνου, τρὶς δ' ἐξ ἄγος ἔπτυσ' ὀδόντων, / ἦ θέμις αὐθέντῃσι δολοκτασίας ἱλάεσθαι.

As his life ebbed away, the hero (sc. Apsyrtos) caught up in both hands the dark blood from the wound; with it he stained red Medea's silver veil and robe though she turned away. With disapproving eye the pitiless Fury, subduer of all, saw clearly the deadly deed they had done. The hero, son of Aison, cut off the dead man's extremities; three times he licked the blood, and three times he spat the pollution out from his teeth, as is the proper way for slayers to expiate treacherous murders.

13 The other two instances are 3.338, 3.203.

14 On miasma and *agos,* see Parker (1983), 3–11, 191–200. For a concise typology of ritual purity and pollution in Greek religion, Petrovic and Petrovic (2016), 25–37.

15 On the motif of "birdless" (Ἄορνος / Avernus) lakes, see Vian (1981), 170.

16 See Hunter (2015), *comm. ad v.* 621.

17 On dating, see Jouanna (1988), 39–50.

18 *De Flatibus* 5–6. Text: Littré, translation is based on Jouanna (2012). Similar ideas about bad air as the cause of epidemic disease (though without the use of the word miasma) can be found in other texts from the Hippocratic corpus from about 400 BCE, see Hoessly (2001), 276–8.

19 On the concept of *agos* in Homer, Parker (1983), 9. On divine vengeance and disease, Parker (1983), 235–56; and Hoessly (2001), 26–7, 90–6. On the concept of miasma in Greek medical literature, Jouanna (2012).

20 Sophocles' *King Oedipus* is a particularly prominent example.

21 Parker (1983), 207–34.

22 *The Sacred Disease* 1.

23 The process is charted in Hoessly (2001), 274–8; and Jouanna (2012).

24 Galen, *On Differences Between Fevers* 1.6, 7. (289–90), ed. Kühn (1965). Translation is based on Jouanna (2012). Thucydides 2.48 does not mention miasma at all. According to Jouanna (2012), 132, "Galen reinterprets Thucydides' text in the light of the Hippocratic theory of miasmas formulated in *Breaths.*"

25 Diodorus 12.58.3. Text and translation, Oldfather (1989).

26 Palladius, *Commentary on Hippocrates' Epidemics* 6 (Preamble, Dietz 2.2.18–23).

27 On pollution caused by death, Parker (1983), 32–48.

28 Apollonius' interest in contemporary medicine is evident from his famous description of Medea's pain at 3.761–5 which is indebted to Erasistratus' and Herophilus' discovery of the nervous system. See Solmsen (1981), 185–97.

29 *Mor.* 665c, where he also notes that this is the reason why some criticized Euripides' tragedy *Phaethon*, where his body is described as rotting. See Hunter (2015), 163, *comm. ad vv.* 599–603.

30 I am grateful to Benjamin Acosta-Hughes for this observation.

31 Although Helios did not play a major role in civic cults, there are several references to the need for polluted individuals to avoid the sun in tragedy: Heracles veils himself after the murder of his children specifically in order to avoid the sun (E. *HF* 1231–2); Kreon orders the attendants to take Oedipus away from the sun and not expose his *agos* uncovered (S. *OT,* 1425–7); Jason asks Medea how she can look at the sun after killing her children (E. *Med.* 1327); the chorus protests at Orestes' displaying of the bloody sword to the sun (E. *Or.* 822). According to Parker (1983), 316–17, "when heroes or their attendants say that they pollute the sun, or that earth itself will not receive them, it is tempting to see this rejection by the very elements as an extreme extension of their exclusion from the society of men." Hesiod's *Works and Days* 727 and Pythagorean *acusmata* (D.L. 8.17, Iambl. *Protr.* 107.16; 115.19) prohibit urination while facing the sun in order to shield it from pollution.

32 See Barrett (1964), 300–1; Diggle (1970), 4–32; Leigh (1998), 88–90.

33 Text and translation, Hett (1936).

34 See also Vian (1981), 36–7.

Bibliography

Barrett, W. S. (1964), *Euripides, Hippolytos*, Oxford: Oxford University Press.

Beye, C. R. (1982), *Epic and Romance in the* Argonautica *of Apollonius*, Carbondale and Edwardsville, IL: Southern Illinois University Press.

Byre, C. S. (1996), "Distant Encounters: The Prometheus and Phaethon Episode in the Argonautica of Apollonius Rhodius," *American Journal of Philology,* 117: 275–83.

Diggle, J. (1970), *Euripides, Phaethon*, Cambridge: Cambridge University Press.

Fusillo, M. (1985), *Il tempo delle Argonautiche*, Rome: Edizioni dell' Ateneo.

Hett, W. S. (1936), Aristotle. *Minor Works: On Colours. On Things Heard. Physiognomics. On Plants. On Marvellous Things Heard. Mechanical Problems. On Indivisible Lines. The Situations and Names of Winds. On Melissus, Xenophanes, Gorgias*, Loeb Classical Library 307, Cambridge, MA: Harvard University Press.

Hoessly, F. (2001), *Katharsis: Reinigung als Heilverfahren. Studien zum Ritual der archaischen und klassischen Zeit sowie zum* Corpus Hippocraticum, Göttingen: Vandenhoeck & Ruprecht.

Hunter, R. (1993), *Apollonius of Rhodes, Jason and the Golden Fleece*, Oxford: Oxford University Press.

Hunter, R. (2015), *Apollonius of Rhodes, Argonautica Book IV*, Cambridge: Cambridge University Press.

Jouanna, J. (1988), *Hippocrate, Tome V, 1re partie. Des vents. De l'art. Texte établi et traduit*, Paris: Les Belles Lettres.

Jouanna, J. (2012), "Air, Miasma and Contagion in the Time of Hippocrates and the Survival of Miasmas in Post-Hippocratic Medicine (Rufus of Ephesus, Galen and Palladius)," in J. Jouanna (ed.), *Greek Medicine from Hippocrates to Galen, Selected Papers*, trans. N. Allies, 121–36, Leiden and Boston, MA: Brill.

Jouanna, J., ed. (2012), *Greek Medicine from Hippocrates to Galen, Selected Papers*, trans. N. Allies, Leiden and Boston, MA: Brill.

Kühn, C. G. (1965), *Claudii Galeni opera omnia*, vol. 7, Leipzig: Knobloch, 1824, repr. Hildesheim: Olms.

Leigh, M. (1998), "Sophocles at Patavium (fr. 137 Radt)," *Journal of Hellenic Studies*, 118: 82–100.

Littré, É. (1962), *Oeuvres complètes d'Hippocrate*, vol. 6, Paris: Baillière, 1849, repr. Amsterdam: Hakkert.

Livrea, E. (1973), *Apollonii Rhodii Argonauticon Liber Quartus*, Florence: "La Nuova Italia" Editrice.

Oldfather, C. H. (1989), *Diodorus Siculus. Diodorus of Sicily in Twelve Volumes with an English Translation*, vols 4–8, Cambridge, MA: Harvard University Press, and London: William Heinemann, Ltd.

Parker, R. (1983), *Miasma: Pollution and Purification in Early Greek Religion*, Oxford: Oxford University Press.

Petrovic, I. (forthcoming), *Crisis, Pollution, and Purification or Why did Jason Bring the Golden Fleece back to Greece? Crisis and Resilience in Hellenistic Poetry*, Hellenistica Groningana, Leuven: Peeters.

Petrovic, A. and I. Petrovic (2016), *Inner Purity and Pollution in Greek Religion, Volume I: Early Greek Religion*, Oxford: Oxford University Press.

Phillips, T. (2020), *Untimely Epic: Apollonius Rhodius'* Argonautica, Oxford: Oxford University Press.

Solmsen, F. (1961), "Greek Philosophy and the Discovery of the Nerves," *Museum Helveticum*, 18 (4): 169–97.

Stephens, S. (2003), *Seeing Double: Intercultural Poetics in Ptolemaic Alexandria*, Berkeley, CA: University of California Press.

Thalmann, W. G. (2011), *Apollonius of Rhodes and the Spaces of Hellenism*, Oxford: Oxford University Press.

Vian, F. and É. Delage (1981), *Apollonios de Rhodes Argonautiques chant IV*, Paris: Les Belles Lettres.

13

"Apollonius Speaks Greek, Petiharenpi Speaks Egyptian"

Cross-Cultural Self-Fashioning in the Serapeum Archive

Edward Kelting
University of California, San Diego

In no small part thanks to Susan's work, it is now clear that Greek literary and intellectual production located in Egypt was influenced *by* Egypt. This is true of the canonical three authors—Callimachus, Theocritus, Apollonius—who immigrated to Egypt. Their texts were shaped by the new social and political realities that hung over Alexandria under the early Ptolemies. Even as Greek ethnic identities were socioeconomically advantaged within Ptolemaic administration, Susan has shown that Greek culture in Egypt was permeable.[1] This is no less true for everyday ethnic Greeks living in Egypt, who offer a valuable view onto how that permeability operated on the ground, outside of Alexandria. Even as ethnic Egyptians took on indices of a Greek identity—like a Greek name—for social advancement in Ptolemaic administration, there was still an intellectual prestige of Egyptian traditions that loomed large for Greeks.[2]

I would like to explore that prestige by drilling down on Greek-language demonstrations of Egyptian intellectual authority. The evidence on which I focus occurred on the "small stage," in texts written out by a Greek named Ptolemaeus, who lived for twenty years in the temple of Serapis in Memphis.[3] Ptolemaeus was occasionally joined by his younger brother Apollonius, who also wrote his own mixed Greco-Egyptian identity into the papyri that he collected. The horizons of Ptolemaeus' life were narrow, contained entirely within a wing of a temple. But his extant papyri shine a light on the rich intellectual life of a down-and-out Greek eking out a living in an Egyptian temple. A portrait emerges of a keen translator of traditional Egyptian culture into a new Greco-Egyptian mixture. In important ways, Ptolemaeus' translations are marked out for their incompleteness. There are moments when Egyptian terminology and concepts are only partially brought into Greek. They remain identifiable as Egyptian even as their new Greek-language environment changes their literal and cultural semantics.

Ptolemaeus and his brother thus show how attention to the social context of papyrological archives can enrich our readings of the literary texts that said archives contain. I will take this as a point of departure for my own discussion of three texts in the Serapeum archive: Ptolemaeus' dream journal, Apollonius' translation of the Egyptian Dream of Nectanebo, and the so-called Art of Eudoxus. In all three cases, moments of deliberately partial translation create a new Greco-Egyptian idiom that mirrors larger processes of identity-formation. The archive's examples of Greek and Egyptian demand a new approach to translation. To borrow from the translation-studies scholar Michaela Wolf, my goal is to show how the Serapeum archive "destabilizes the view of translation as a 'bridge between cultures' or makes it obsolete, since—if we draw on postcolonial theories of culture—translational transfer takes place between cultures that are already contaminated in themselves."[4] The texts, like their authors, speak to a creative mixture of cultural forms that emerged from these ethnic Greeks' residency in a prototypically Egyptian cultural domain, a temple in Memphis. As I argue, the very incompleteness of these translations reflects Ptolemaeus' and Apollonius' inhabitance of a "third space" of Greco-Egyptian self-fashioning that refuses to be collapsed into a Greek-Egyptian dichotomy.[5] Where in their social and economic lives Apollonius and Ptolemaeus were quick to tout their Macedonian ethnic background, in their dreams they inhabited a doggedly in-between identity.

Katochoi: Greeks in an Egyptian World

I can be brief with the biographies of Ptolemaeus and his brother Apollonius, given the thorough overviews offered elsewhere.[6] The broad strokes of their situation, as ethnic Greeks in an Egyptian space, set their interest in Egyptian literary traditions against a backdrop of economic precarity. The reasons why Ptolemaeus was forced to take residence in the Serapeum are unclear. Formally, he was a *katochos*, a term for a temple recluse whose juridical status and motivations are still debated. No matter the reasons which led Ptolemaeus to request asylum in the Serapeum—is it a form of incarceration, a hope for healing, a mechanism to avoid debtors or criminal prosecution?—his status as *enkatochos* required Ptolemaeus to stay within the temple. Thus when the small room that he shared with an Egyptian named Harmais was ransacked by higher-ups among the Serapeum priests, they both had to lodge their complaints *in absentia.* Ptolemaeus' letter, addressed to Ptolemy VI Philometor and Cleopatra II, speaks to a time of turmoil.[7] Egypt had recently been invaded by the Seleucid Antiochus IV, who won a victory near Pelusium in 169 BCE and briefly took control of Egypt. This in turn led to economic collapse and a series of revolts that rocked Egypt and briefly dethroned Ptolemy VI.

The ransacking was, at least initially, a search for cached weapons that might be used against the recently reenthroned Ptolemy VI during his visit to Memphis. But when the police had left, the upper-level priests returned to confiscate the hard-earned personal income of Ptolemaeus and Harmais. To many, this personal vendetta levelled by the higher priests against Ptolemaeus speaks to the perilous position of an ethnic Greek living in an Egyptian world.[8] When a gang of Egyptians who worked odd jobs in the temple assaulted Ptolemaeus twice in one month, he alleges in a letter (*UPZ* I 7) to the *strategos* Dionysius that his Greek identity explains their assault.

Ptolemaeus' Egyptian Dreams

Despite relying heavily on his status as a Greek—his father was a soldier of Macedonian ethnicity—it is clear that Ptolemaeus and his younger brother were immersed in Egyptian language and culture. To have lived for twenty years in the Serapeum, Ptolemaeus must have spoken Demotic well.[9] One hallmark of Egyptian temple culture is well represented in his archive. Ptolemaeus regularly noted down his dreams (*UPZ* I 77–9), where his anxieties and concerns are filtered through the funhouse-mirror of the subconscious.

Ptolemaeus' desire to learn from his dreams speaks to both Greek and Egyptian traditions of dream-interpretation.[10] The oracular potential of dreams had been a dominant part of Egyptian culture. Visitors to the Serapeum practiced temple incubation, in which the dreams of those spending the night in a god's shrine were particularly prophetic. A shared interest in dreams could explain the motivations that brought the *katochoi* into the temple in the first place.[11] That said, there was certainly evidence of Greek oneirocriticism in Memphis, and the safely attested dreams are all written in Greek.[12]

Given this backdrop of a mixed cultural tradition, one of Ptolemaeus' dreams is especially productive. The dream was among several that were written down by Ptolemaeus, but were experienced by Ptolemaeus' friend Nektembes. Apparently because the dreams in question concerned him, Ptolemaeus thought fit to collect them. At the outset, this presents a tricky linguistic situation. The dreamer, Nektembes, was an ethnic Egyptian who presumably (though not definitively) presented his dreams to Ptolemaeus in Demotic. Ptolemaeus' Greek is assured, his ability to speak Demotic is safe to assume, and his ability to write in Demotic is doubtful.[13] The status of the dream language is thus a central concern with which Ptolemaeus' transcription of the dream wrestles (*UPZ* I 79.2–5):

τὸ πρῶτον ἐν⟨⟨εν⟩⟩ύπνιον, ὃ εἶδεν Νεκθονβῆς πρεὶ τοον διδυμῶν καὶ ἐμ᾽ αὑτοῦ·
Ἀπολλώνιον εἶδον, προσπορεύεταί μοι. λέγι· χαῖρε, Νεκθεμβῆς, καλῶς. τὸ δεύτερ[ον]·
Φαφερε σι ενρεηξ Παῦνι ἐν τῷ Βουβαστ⟨εί⟩ῳ χμεννι ἐν τῷ οἴκῳ τῷ Ἄμμωνος πελ λελ χασον χανι.[14]

The first dream that Nekthonbes saw concerning the twins and myself: "I saw Apollonius; he approaches me. He says: 'hello, Nektembes, be well.'" The second: **Phaphere si enreex** Pauni in the Bubasteion **Chmenni** in the house of Ammon **pel lel chason chani**.

The second dream is not exactly informative. The only intelligible information specifies the Egyptian month Pauni and temple locations—specifically of Bastet and of Amun. Even on its own, this insinuates the dream into the broad cultural domain of Egyptian temple incubation and the oracular promise that came along with it. The most striking feature is the string of unintelligible phrases. It is clear that Ptolemaeus is trying to render Egyptian in the Greek script, though nobody can trace these phrases back to anything meaningful in Demotic. The motivations behind Ptolemaeus' decision to opt for transliterated Egyptian have been divisive. Stephen Kidd has argued that the specific context of dream interpretation points both to the privileged status of Demotic as the language of oracular dreams and to a linguistic-based process of interpretation that depends on the sounds of words in their original language. Bernard Legras has suggested that the transliterated phrases are intended by Ptolemaeus to flag that this was a translation of an originally Egyptian-language dream.[15]

What has been lost in this debate is an appreciation of the precarious authority to which this transliteration speaks. It is correct to fixate, with Kidd, on the importance of Demotic as an authoritative dream language. Even in a text intended for Ptolemaeus' own use, there is a display of cultural authority that speaks to the prestige of Egyptian oneirocriticism even among ethnic Greeks. Similarly, it is worth seeing, with Legras, how Ptolemaeus advertises the original Egyptian language from which he has been working.

But one should not lose sight of the productive inelegance of Ptolemaeus' solution. In a quest for an explanation, it is easy to rush past the kind of in-between-ness to which this transliterated dream speaks. I would argue that Ptolemaeus' claims of authority over a Demotic dream tradition and his self-advertisement as a translator should be secondary to what is actually occurring on the page. Ptolemaeus presents a language that is neither Greek nor Egyptian, but which shares in them both. In other words, this is deliberately *not* translation, even as it is embedded into a broader translation process. It is this mediated position that Ptolemaeus is highlighting. Within the mixed tradition of dream interpretation and his own intercultural negotiation of dream languages, Ptolemaeus' Egyptian transcription into Greek creates a third space, a new site of cultural authority specific to an ethnic Greek implicated into, but not wholly enmeshed in, Egyptian dream traditions.

The Dream of Nectanebo

This arrogation of authority through not-quite-translation extends to two literary papyri that Ptolemaeus and his brother possessed. The first text, the "Dream of Nectanebo" (*UPZ* I 81) syncs up with this domain of dream-interpretation—so much so, that Ptolemaeus directly quotes lines from the "Dream" in his own dream papyri.[16] The Dream was written out in Greek by Ptolemaeus' younger brother Apollonius, who had himself become a *katochos* for one year, in 158 BCE.[17] Like his older brother Ptolemaeus, Apollonius displays a clear interest in dreams and their potential prophetic power. Thus, from the larger Egyptian story of Nectanebo, he excerpts a passage that contains the eponymous dream of Nectanebo. Apollonius' Greek translation of an Egyptian story is significant on its own grounds. Apollonius' copy of the Dream has been an essential piece of evidence for the transmission of Egyptian literary traditions to a Greek audience.[18] The larger story is a tale of divine dream-instruction, subsequent quest, and political prophecy typical of the Egyptian genre of "king's tale."[19] The king in question, Nectanebo II, was the last indigenous ruler of Egypt. As such, he became the site of a prophetic body of literature that bemoaned Persian rule of Egypt and naturalized the transition to the Ptolemies. The Dream was a direct forerunner to the Alexander Romance, a text that operated with the same set of goals—legitimating a lineage from the Egyptian Nectanebo to the Macedonian Alexander.[20]

More narrowly, Apollonius' translation of the Dream develops a similar set of Greek-Egyptian juxtapositions. This occurs early in the text, when Nectanebo travels to Memphis—the site of Apollonius' own asylum—and has a prophetic dream. Within the dream, Apollonius pauses to gloss a specific Egyptian term: "it appeared to Nectanebo in a dream that a papyrus boat, which is called a 'rhomps' in Egyptian, came to anchor at Memphis" (ἔδοξεν κατ' ἐνύπν⟨ι⟩ον πλοῖον παπύρινον, ὃ καλεῖται Αἰγυπτιστὶ Ῥω⟨μ⟩ψ, προσορμῆσαι εἰς Μέμφιν, II.5–7).[21] The boat gloss is kindred with, but differs in form from, the transcribed Egyptian in Ptolemaeus' dream. Rather than directly injecting transcribed Egyptian into the stream of the story, Apollonius signals his own status as translator by loudly juxtaposing Greek and Egyptian terms for the same concept (he was likely referring to the Demotic rms). Beyond this one intra-dream gloss and its ambiguous function, Apollonius's broader use of lingual flags—which also include Greek and Egyptian alternatives for gods' names—recasts the story in a mixed cultural form through which Apollonius' expertise is cemented.[22]

Through this exegetical expertise, Apollonius comes to associate himself with the protagonist of the story, a hieroglyph-carver named Petesis.[23] Petesis is chosen to add the hieroglyphic inscriptions to the incomplete temple about which the gods complain to Nectanebo. In the process, Petesis becomes the medium who prophesies the arrival of Greeks who will right the wrongs done by Persian occupation of Egypt. Apollonius' own authority over the text—as a copyist, he occupies a role of extradiegetic narrator—yokes him to this interior protagonist Petesis, whose role as hieroglyph-carver guarantees his unimpeachable authority over Egyptian culture.[24]

This provides a cross-cultural identification that complements Apollonius' self-fashioning elsewhere. In a Demotic-language dream papyrus (*P. Dem. Bol.* 3173), Apollonius highlights his own cultural ambiguity. In the text, he is bifurcated into the version of himself that speaks Egyptian and the part of himself that speaks Greek: "Apollonius speaks Greek, Petiharenpi speaks Egyptian" (ꜣplns mt Wjnn, Pꜣ-tj-ḥr-Pj mt rmṯ (n) Kmj, 9–11).[25] If one follows John Ray's and Bernard Legras' reading, these are alternate names for the same person.[26] Apollonius (or Petiharenpi, to call him by his Egyptian name) is thus subject to the indeterminacy of identity that arises from moving between languages. The inelegant gloss of "rhomps" and the pairing of Egyptian Onouris and Greek Ares are not just one-off markers of Apollonius' authority over Egyptian. Apollonius weaves into the Dream a juxtaposition of Greek and

Egyptian that, by design, refuses to totally translate Egyptian into Greek. It is a seam that creates space for untranslatability. As this Demotic dream text emphasizes, this untranslatability is also central to Apollonius/Petiharenpi's lingually defined, polyonymous sense of self.

Dating Games

The other key moment of cross-cultural juxtaposition within the Dream is more subtle, but equally effective. As is conventional, the Dream of Nectanebo opens with a regnal date. This date is particularly important to the story because the dream was supposed to occur during a full moon: "year 16, 21–22 Pharmuthi according to the god at full moon" (ἔτους ις Φαρμοῦθι κα εἰ κβ, κατὰ θεὸν δὲ διχομηνίαι . . ., I.1–2). The dating is, at first blush, quite boring. But the inclusion of two days (the 21 and 22 of the month Pharmuthi) to denote the one night in question is revelatory. The dating strategy employed by Apollonius exists between two cultural approaches to time. To simplify a more complicated argument made by Anthony Spalinger, the only reason that Apollonius included two days was to render in Greek a mixed Greco-Egyptian date denoted within the Egyptian calendar.[27] Apollonius could have simply listed either individual day, depending on whether he counted days in an Egyptian or Greek style. Instead, he brings together Greek and Egyptian ways of calculating days, the one Greek and lunar— when a day begins at sunset—and the other Egyptian and civil, when a day begins at dawn. Thus a subtle but overt cultural juxtaposition is a cue that resides at the very opening of the text. There is a gesture toward an Egyptian system of counting days that nevertheless highlights the Greek perspective from which that system was being viewed. One should not lose sight of this act of not-quite-translating the Egyptian into the Greek just because it is technical. What is a minute act of time-setting in a new cross-cultural idiom signals the text's larger goals. In this respect, it is essential to note that the other main occurrence of these hybrid dates is in Greek horoscopes rendered within an Egyptian calendar, a tradition that dovetails Ptolemaeus' and Apollonius' interest in dream-interpretation.[28]

To conclude, there is a related text, this time in Ptolemaeus' possession, that offers up a similar mixed dating. This text, the "Art of Eudoxus," gets its name from the Cnidian pupil of Plato who, as the legend goes, travelled to Egypt to learn astronomy from its priests. Ptolemaeus' papyrus (*P. Par.* 1), a recapitulation of earlier Hellenistic astronomy, is so-called because of an acrostic on its verso, which lays out the subject of the text while spelling out with each line's opening letters "The Art of Eudoxus" (EΥΔΟΞΟΥ ΤΕΧΝΗ).²⁹ There are specific flags of cultural mediation that are shared with the Dream of Nectanebo. As in that text, there is specific authority gained by aligning Egyptian and Greek calendars together to calculate the zodiac and other key celestial events. So, in a passage discussing the difficulty but necessity of syncing up lunar and solar years, the author notes Egyptian practices: "astrologers and sacred scribes use the lunar calendar" (οἱ δὲ ἀσ[τρο]λόγοι καὶ οἱ ἱερογραμμ[ατεῖς] χ[ρῶ]νται ταῖς κατὰ σελή[ν]η[ν] ἡμ[έ]ραις, III.20–3).³⁰ The specific reference to the sacred scribe (*hierogrammateus*) locates Egyptian time-reckoning in the same temple hierarchy that Ptolemaeus was surrounded by. The text then peppers in other elements of the Egyptian calendar, like naming the Egyptian months.³¹

This presentation of astronomical and horoscopic data across Greek and Egyptian practices paves the way for "oracles from Serapis," which become a focus of the text. Even as this text only entered Ptolemaeus' life accidentally (its verso consists of models of administrative letters for Ptolemaeus to copy), it still contained an excursus on prophecy that matched Ptolemaeus' own interests in prophetic dreams.³² The utilitarian role of one side of the papyrus—examples of how to write an official letter—sits in productive tension with the other side's prophetic contents, which align well with Ptolemaeus' intellectual activity. The literal flip side, the verso of the cultural mixture of the Art is the set of letters from which Ptolemaeus learned to articulate his unimpeachable Greek identity to local Ptolemaic officials.

Conclusion

These three texts reveal different scales of translation from Egyptian into Greek that are worth juxtaposing. In the end, the archive is valuable because it challenges the very idea that "translation" is the right word for the cultural combination that these texts contain.³³ To repeat my clunky formulation, these are not-quite-translations. These different not-quite-translations represent a range of different authorial strategies within a new Greco-Egyptian third space. In the dream diary, Ptolemaeus directly transcribes Egyptian into a new script. In the Dream of Nectanebo, Apollonius flags a juxtaposition of Greek and Egyptian vocabulary that builds on his own sense of self as a composite of the Egyptian-speaking Petiharenpi and the Greek-speaking Apollonius. Throughout, time-reckoning hybridizes Greek and Egyptian systems.³⁴ In all three approaches, Ptolemaeus and Apollonius can help us move away from a view of translation that casts such an act as a secondary operation posterior to the fossilization of otherwise pure Greek and Egyptian texts. It is only with these new translational practices in view that we can connect these texts to the social context of their composition, to Apollonius' and Ptolemaeus' remarkable backstory.

This reevaluation of translation is most productive when anchored in the discrete ways that Apollonius and Ptolemaeus wrote their identities into these texts. The transcribed Egyptian that Ptolemaeus incorporated into his translation of Nektembes' dream can speak to many different uses of language. But first, it needs to be seen as a manifestation of its author Ptolemaeus' mixed authority. Similarly, the Dream of Nectanebo, the Art of Eudoxus, and Ptolemaeus' birthday records all demonstrate cross-cultural date-reckoning.[35] In a basic way, the Dream of Nectanebo is located in a time that is neither Egyptian nor Greek, or, rather, is both Egyptian *and* Greek. In other words, the exciting work of locating Greco-Egyptian cultural mixture and creating a theoretical perspective that can embrace that mixture is ongoing. Such work demands attention to the specific social contexts—like temple asylum—that facilitated that mixture and the otherwise technical knowledge traditions—astronomy, dream-interpretation—in which it took root. All of which is to repeat what Susan has herself been emphasizing for quite a while.

Notes

1 Particularly Stephens (2003).

2 For the practice of polyonymy in this period, see Coussement (2016).

3 From 172–152 BCE (*UPZ* I 15 and 71 for dates). The archive is collected in Wilcken (1927), who also (104–16) provides a document-based biographical overview of the *katochoi*.

4 Wolf (2008).

5 I am using the concept of "third space" in the original sense of Bhabha (1994), 35–7 (cf. Bhabha 1990). I see these papyri as an "act of cultural enunciation" (36)—i.e., an act in which the symbols of culture are "appropriated, translated, rehistoricized, and read anew" (37). For "self-fashioning," see Greenblatt (1984).

6 Ptolemaeus and his brother are the subject of Thompson (1988), 212–65; and Legras (2011), 169–89, 231–52.

7 For Ptolemaeus' complaint, *UPZ* I 6; for Harmais', *UPZ* I 6a. Legras (2011), 101–43, surveys the potential explanations of temple asylum.

8 Though note that they also stole from the Egyptian Harmais.

9 See, e.g., his Egyptian-influenced misspellings of Greek, per Legras (2011), 231–2.

10 See, most broadly, Näf (2004).

11 Legras (2011), 86–7.

12 As proven by the Memphite inscription of a Cretan dream interpreter (Thompson 1988: plate vii).

13 This differs from his younger brother, who is more likely (*pace* Wilcken 1927: 16, 351) to have written in Demotic (see below, on *P. Dem. Bol.* 3173).

14 Text is from Wilcken (1927), translations throughout are my own. The text in bold is Ptolemaeus' attempt to transliterate Egyptian phrases into Greek. The actual meaning of these phrases is incomprehensible, so by scholarly convention (cf. Wilcken 1927: 366; Legras 2011: 234; and Kidd 2011: 119) they are left untranslated.

15 Kidd (2011), 118–21; Legras (2011), 234–5.

16 The reference to the Dream of Nectanebo in Ptolemaeus' dream (*UPZ* I 78.23–4) was first noticed by Wilcken (1927), 362, but then shown to be a deliberate quotation by Clarysse (1983), 59–60.

17 Gauger (2002), 193–9, offers an overview of the text's publication.

18 Dieleman and Moyer (2010), 434, 36–7, 41–2 (cf. 443 for Art of Eudoxus), locate the Dream in this broad background of intercultural Greco-Egyptian literature. Ryholt (2002), 225–32, offers a textual analysis that shows how Apollonius' text translates traditional Egyptian formulae.

19 A genre discussed by Loprieno (1996); and Hofmann (2004).

20 On the interconnection of these two texts, Jasnow (1997); and Ryholt (2002), 234–41.

21 *UPZ* I 81, text from Koenen (1985).

22 He offers the pair of Ares/Onouris at II.15–16.

23 Note that this was a school assignment rather than a novel composition. I would argue that its status as a copying exercise amplifies, rather than erodes, the function of the Dream as site of cross-cultural identification between copyist Apollonius and protagonist Petesis.

24 Thompson (1988), 263, has emphasized this identification of Apollonius with Petesis.

25 Text from Bresciani et al. (1978), 95. They (102) see this as a different Apollonius and claim that the occurrence of the same set of names (Apollonius, Ptolemaeus, and the twins are all mentioned) is coincidental. Legras (2011), 232–3, justifiably sees this as improbable. Note that my reading does not demand that Apollonius actually wrote this out himself, rather than have it written out for him.

26 Ray (1976), 5 (picked up by Thompson 1988: 263; and Legras 2011: 232–3, with 233 n. 6 for comparative evidence) suggests that the text code-switches between Apollonius' Greek and Egyptian names.

27 Spalinger (1992) generally, 302 for the possibility of one day in the Egyptian system.

28 As discussed by Neugebauer and Van Hoesen (1959), 167–9.

29 Neugebauer (1975), 687, calls it "a rather careless compilation."

30 Text is from Blass (1887).

31 Legras (2011), 248–9. Note that this refers to the Egyptian lunar, religious calendar rather than its solar calendar, as above.

32 *UPZ* I 110–11, 144–5. Note that on the verso Ptolemaeus (Wilcken 1927: 112, 475, for attribution) jotted down the label "Hermes' stuff inside" (εἴσω Ἑρμῆα), which demonstrates his knowledge of the Art of Eudoxus' contents.

33 See the recapitulation of "cultural translation" in Wolf (2008), and the cautious evaluation of "translation" as a cultural theory in Buden et al. (2009).

34 While in this chapter I use the concept of "third space" developed by Bhabha (1994), note the criticisms of his related term hybridity. Hybridity and "third space" both risk reconfirming the purity of cultures which precede hybridization.

35 *UPZ* I 77 II.32, per Clarysse (1983), 58.

Bibliography

Bhabha, H. (1990), "The Third Space", in J. Rutherford (ed.), *Identity: Community, Culture, Difference*, 207–21, London: Lawrence and Wishart.

Bhabha, H. (1994), *The Location of Culture*, London: Routledge.

Blasius, A. and B. U. Schipper, eds. (2002), *Apokalyptik und Ägypten: eine kritische Analyse der relevanten Texte aus dem griechisch-römischen Ägypten*, Leuven: Peeters.

Blass, F. (1887), *Eudoxi ars astronomica qualis in charta Aegyptiaca superest*, Kiel: Prostat in Libraria Academica ex Officina Schmidtii et Klaunigii.

Bresciani, E., E. Bedini, L. Paolini, and F. Silvan (1978), "Una rilettura dei Pap. Dem. Bologna 3173 e 3171," *Egitto e Vicino Oriente*, 1: 95–104.

Buden, B., S. Nowotny, S. Simon, A. Bery, and M. Croni (2009), "Cultural Translation: An Introduction to the Problem, and Responses," *Translation Studies*, 2 (2): 196–219.

Clarysse, W. (1983), "Literary Papyri in Documentary 'Archives,'" in E. van 'T Dack, P. van Dessel, and W. van Gucht (eds.), *Egypt and the Hellenistic World: Proceedings of the International Colloquium, Leuven, 24–26 May 1982*, 43–61, Leuven: Orientaliste.

Clauss, J. J. and M. Cuypers, eds. (2020), *A Companion to Hellenistic Literature*, Chichester: Wiley-Blackwell.

Coussement, S. (2016), *"Because I am Greek": Polyonymy as an Expression of Ethnicity in Ptolemaic Egypt*, Leuven: Peeters.

Dieleman, J. and I. S. Moyer (2010), "Egyptian Literature," in J. J. Clauss and M. Cuypers (eds.), *A Companion to Hellenistic Literature*, 429–47, Chichester: Wiley-Blackwell.

Gauger, J.-D. (2002), "Der 'Traum des Nektanebos'—die griechische Fassung," in A. Blasius and B. U. Schipper (eds.), *Apokalyptik und Ägypten: eine kritische Analyse der relevanten Texte aus dem griechisch-römischen Ägypten*, 189–219, Leuven: Peeters.

Greenblatt, S. J. (1984), *Renaissance Self-Fashioning: From More to Shakespeare*, Chicago, IL: University of Chicago Press.

Hofmann, B. (2004), *Die Königsnovelle: "Strukturanalyse am Einzelwerk"*, Wiesbaden: Harrassowitz.

Jasnow, R. (1997), "The Greek Alexander Romance and Demotic Egyptian Literature," *Journal of Near Eastern Studies*, 56 (2): 95–103.

Kidd, S. (2011), "Dreams in Bilingual Papyri from the Ptolemaic Period," *Bulletin of the American Society of Papyrologists*, 48: 113–30.

Koenen, L. (1985), "The Dream of Nektanebo," *Bulletin of the American Society of Papyrologists*, 22: 171–94.

Legras, B. (2011), *Les reclus Grecs du Serapeum de Memphis: une enquête sur l'Hellénisme Égytien*, Leuven: Peeters.

Loprieno, A. (1996), "The 'King's Novel,'" in A. Loprieno (ed.), *Ancient Egyptian Literature: History and Forms*, 277–95, Leiden: Brill.

Loprieno, A., ed. (1996), *Ancient Egyptian Literature: History and Forms*, Leiden: Brill.

Näf, B. (2004), *Traum und Traumdeutung im Altertum*, Darmstadt: Wissenschaftliche Buchgesellschaft.

Neugebauer, O. (1975), *A History of Ancient Mathematical Astronomy*, Berlin: Springer.

Neugebauer, O. and H. B. Van Hoesen (1959), *Greek Horoscopes*, Philadelphia, PA: American Philosophical Society.

Ray, J. D. (1976), *The Archive of Ḥor*, London: Egypt Exploration Society.

Rutherford, J., ed. (1990), *Identity: Community, Culture, Difference*, London: Lawrence and Wishart.

Ryholt, K. (2002), "Nectanebo's Dream or The Prophecy of Petesis," in A. Blasius and B. U. Schipper (eds.), *Apokalyptik und Ägypten: eine kritische Analyse der relevanten Texte aus dem griechisch-römischen Ägypten*, 221–41, Leuven: Peeters.

Spalinger, A. (1992), "The Date of the Dream of Nectanebo," *Studien zur Altägyptischen Kultur*, 19: 295–304.

Stephens, S. A. (2003), *Seeing Double: Intercultural Poetics in Ptolemaic Alexandria*, Berkeley, CA: University of California Press.

Thompson, D. J. (1988), *Memphis under the Ptolemies*, Princeton, NJ: Princeton University Press.

van 'T Dack, E., P. van Dessel, and W. van Gucht, eds. (1983), *Egypt and the Hellenistic World: Proceedings of the International Colloquium, Leuven, 24–26 May 1982*, Leuven: Orientaliste.

Wilcken, U. (1927), *Urkunden der Ptolemäerzeit 1: Papyri aus Unterägypte*, Berlin: De Gruyter.

Wolf, M. (2008), "Translation—Transculturation. Measuring the Perspectives of Transcultural Political Action," trans. K. Sturge, *Transversal*, April 2008: https://transversal.at/transversal/0608/wolf/en (accessed 5 April 2023).

14

Young Snakes, Old Models

Hellenistic Poetics and Literary Heritage in Nicander, *Theriaca* 343–58

Alexander Sens
Georgetown University

Nicander's *Theriaca* is intensely self-referential about its place in the literary tradition. Not only do its opening lines engage extensively with the language and themes of the beginning of Hesiod's *Works and Days*,[1] but they also include an explicit (if somewhat puzzling)[2] reference to Hesiod's authority for the claim that poisonous creatures originated from the blood of Titans (8–12).[3] As critics have noted, the claim closely follows the unambiguous evocation of the *Works and Days* in verses 1–4, where Nicander's phrase ῥεῖα . . . ἔμπεδα φωνήσαιμι evokes both the quadruple anaphora of ῥέα/ῥεῖα in the Muse-inspired aretalogy of Zeus that opens the *Works and Days* (1–8) and Hesiod's assertion that he would tell his brother the truth (10 ἐγὼ δὲ κε Πέρσῃ ἐτήτυμα μυθησαίμην). Inasmuch as it explains the cause of the conditions that make the narrator's wisdom necessary, the story attributed to Hesiod serves much the same structural function as the story of Pandora in the *Works and Days*, but unlike that poem, the *Theriaca* takes for granted a world in which Hesiod's advice to Perses is unnecessary, since the beneficiaries of his advice are already working hard (cf. 4 πολύεργος ἀροτρεύς), and it focuses instead on the ill-working creatures (cf. 8 κακοεργά) who occupy the brutal landscape.[4] The poem thus presents itself as a successor to the *Works and Days*, much as Callimachus' *Aetia* is framed as a successor the *Theogony*.[5] But Hesiod is not the only ancestor evoked in the opening lines of the poem, for as Bernd Effe observed, Nicander's explicit reference to Hesiodic authority is followed immediately by a reworking of Aratus' account of the scorpion's punishment of Orion (*Theriaca* 13–20 ~ *Phaenomena* 637–46).[6] A similar juxtaposition of Hesiodic and Aratean elements, indeed, occurs in 11–12, where εἰ ἐτεόν περ probably evokes εἰ ἐτεὸν δή in *Phaenomena* 30 (in the context of the first mythological narrative of that poem),[7] and in 4, where Nicander replaces Hesiod's ἐτήτυμα with a word, ἔμπεδα, drawn from the hymn to Zeus at the opening of the *Phaenomena* (13).[8] By fusing Aratus and Hesiod in these ways, the proem of the *Theriaca* creates a miniature "history" of the didactic tradition tracing back to Hesiod's *Works and Days* and running through the *Phaenomena* and so makes a programmatic assertion about its ancestors and their generic relationship to one another.

In this paper, I would like to explore Nicander's use of the same technique in another programmatically significant passage of the *Theriaca*, Nicander's version of an "ancient" story that explains why humans grow old, why the snake known as the *dipsas* (and by extension all serpents) continually renews itself by shedding its skin (*Theriaca* 343–58), and why it imparts a feeling of thirst to its victims:

> ὠγύγιος δ' ἄρα μῦθος ἐν αἰζηοῖσι φορεῖται,
> ὡς, ὁπότ' οὐρανὸν ἔσχε Κρόνου πρεσβίστατον αἷμα,
> Νειμάμενος κασίεσσιν ἑκὰς περικυδέας ἀρχάς
> Ἰδμοσύνῃ νεότητα γέρας πόρεν ἡμερίοισι
> Κυδαίνων· δὴ γάρ ῥα πυρὸς ληίστορ' ἔνιπτον.
> Ἄφρονες, οὐ γὰρ τῆς γε κακοφραδίης ἀπόνηντο·
> Νωθεῖ γὰρ κάμνοντες ἀμορβεύοντο λεπάργῳ
> Δῶρα· πολύσκαρθμος δὲ κεκαυμένος αὐχένα δίψῃ
> Ῥώετο, γωλειοῖσι δ' ἰδὼν ὁλκήρεα θῆρα
> Οὐλοὸν ἐλλιτάνευε κακῇ ἐπαλαλκέμεν ἄτῃ
> Σαίνων· αὐτὰρ ὁ βρῖθος ὃ δή ῥ' ἀνεδέξατο νώτοις
> ᾔτεεν ἄφρονα δῶρον· ὁ δ' οὐκ ἀπανήνατο χρειώ.
> ἐξότε γηραλέον μὲν ἀεὶ φλόον ἑρπετὰ βάλλει
> ὁλκήρῃ, θνητοὺς δὲ κακὸν περὶ γῆρας ὀπάζει·
> νοῦσον δ' ἀζαλέην βρωμήτορος οὐλομένη θὴρ
> δέξατο, καί τε τυπῇσιν ἀμυδροτέρῃσιν ἰάπτει.

In fact, an ancient story circulates among mortals that when the oldest child of Cronus came to control the heavens, having apportioned glorious reigns to his brothers separately, he wisely gave youth as an honor to mortal men, glorifying them; for they denounced the stealer of fire. Fools, they reaped no benefit from their stupidity. For tired with work, they passed on their gifts to the sluggish, smooth-coated one. He, now very lively, rushed off, burning in his throat with thirst, and seeing the crawling beast in its lair it pleaded with it, fawningly, to save him from dread destruction. But the snake asked the foolish creature for a gift of the burden that had assumed on his back, and he did not refuse the request. From that point on snakes always shed their old skin, dragging their bodies, but troublesome old age attends mortals. But the destructive beast received the disease of thirst from the braying one, and he imparts it with weaker strikes.

Here, the echoes of the story of Pandora in the *Works and Days* are well developed. [9] In that Hesiodic narrative, Zeus and the gods create Pandora to punish humans as retribution for Prometheus' theft of fire, and Epimetheus' foolish acceptance of a gift (δῶρον) from Zeus leads to the toil, disease, and death from which they had previously been free (90–2). Nicander's version inverts these features: rather than punishing humans for Prometheus' theft, Zeus means to reward them with a gift of eternal youth, which they foolishly misplace with an ass, and for that reason they must grow old.[10] In some texts of the *Works and Days*, in fact, the story of Pandora leads specifically to the troubles of old age: line 93 αἶψα γὰρ ἐν κακότητι βροτοὶ καταγηράσκουσι, transmitted in several manuscripts and appearing as a marginal notation in others, seems intrusive in its context and is widely considered an interpolation drawn from *Odyssey* 19.360. Though the reading is first attested late,[11] its antiquity is unknowable, and given the thematic intersections between the passages, it is at least possible that Nicander's θνητοὺς δὲ κακὸν περὶ γῆρας ὀπάζει was meant as a specific rewriting of a verse which the poet believed to be connected to the story of Pandora in some way. Whatever the case, the story of the origin of biting animals from the blood of Titans, like the account of the origin of biting creatures earlier in the poem, offers an explanation of the end of the Golden Age (cf. *Works and Days* 113–15) and of human suffering: not only do snakes exist in the first place, but they have the ability to renew themselves while humans grow old and suffer.

Although the narrator explicitly asserts that his story is of great antiquity,[12] it is also, at the stylistic level, quintessentially Hellenistic, a masterpiece of learning, compression, and artifice. Its diction is elevated and recherché, its narrative technique elliptical, with a number of details omitted or suggested only glancingly.[13] At the lexical level, for instance, the adjective πολύσκαρθμος (lit. "much-gamboling"), which has seemed to exclude νωθεῖ from having the sense "sluggish,"[14] may slyly mark the beast's transformation once he has assumed the "burden" of the gift of Youth: having received the gift, the once-sluggish creature is now full of energy. The gods and animals in it are not named directly, but via kennings: Zeus is "the oldest blood of Cronus,"[15] Prometheus the "stealer of fire," the ass a "sluggish ... smooth-coated ... brayer," and the serpent the "dragging destructive beast." But the interpretive demands imposed on the reader extend further, for as scholars have long recognized, the passage is a *sphragis* that conceals the poet's name as an acrostic in lines 345–53. The suppression of the names of key figures, identified only indirectly and obliquely, thus finds a complement in the hidden name of the poet, named directly but in a way that requires detection by the reader.[16]

In hiding his own name in a narrative associated with Zeus' distribution of powers and privileges to gods and humans, Nicander may have an Aratean model in mind. Peter Bing has observed that the hymn to Zeus with which the *Phaenomena* begins contains a pun on the poet's name (1–2 ἐκ Διὸς ἀρχώμεσθα, τὸν οὐδέποτ᾽ ἄνδρες ἐῶμεν | ἄρρητον), and he argues that this pun was recognized at least some of Aratus' close successors, including Callimachus and Leonidas.[17] That Nicander, too, was a sufficiently acute reader of Aratus to have noticed and similarly embedded his name in a passage having to do with the god is *prima facie* plausible and, I shall suggest below, perhaps supported by other circumstantial evidence. One plausible reading of both passages is that the poets, while highlighting Zeus' divine power, covertly signal their own authorial presence, and so suggest their own quasi-divine role in the construction of their poetic universes. Such a reading would, in the case of the *Theriaca*, accord with the enhanced authority that the proem grants to the poet. Clauss has noted that unlike its didactic predecessors, the opening of the *Theriaca* omits any reference to Zeus or the Muses and instead converts the facility with which the Hesiodic Zeus is said to be able to fashion the world as he wishes into an attribute of the poet, who is thus endowed with a quasi-divine power and serves as the ultimate authority for the knowledge which he conveys to his addressee.[18] Whereas in the earlier didactic tradition, the poet, explicitly or implicitly inspired by the Muses, conveys knowledge that directly benefits his audience, in the *Theriaca*, Nicander promises to provide information that will allow his addressee to become an expert (7 περιφρασθέντος) and so benefit others. This tripartite sequence (poet → Hermesianax → rural workers) thus places Nicander in the role traditionally filled by the inspiring deities, whose knowledge is transmitted through the mediation of the poet (Muse → poet → audience).[19] The acrostic may suggest a similar idea: although in the *Works and Days* it is through Zeus that men's names are or are not expressed (3–4 ὄντε διὰ βροτοὶ ἄνδρες ὁμῶς ἄφατοί τε φατοί τε, | ῥητοί τ᾽ ἄρρητοί τε Διὸς μεγάλοιο ἕκητι), in Nicander (as in Aratus) it is the poet who lurks in the background with the power to name himself—or, as in the kennings that run through the passage, to leave things unnamed—and to order his poetic world in accordance with his will.

There may be more to say about the programmatic significance of the acrostic, however, for the narrative in which it occurs shares thematic and linguistic points of contact with a famous and influential passage of the prologue of Callimachus' *Aetia* in which the poet analogizes his compositions to the song of cicada as opposed to the braying of the ass, and expresses the wish that he, like the insect, might shed his old age (fr. 1.29–36):[20]

ἐνὶ τοῖς γὰρ ἀείδομεν οἳ λιγὺν ἦχον
    τέττιγος, θ]όρυβον δ'οὐκ ἐφίλησαν ὄνων.
θηρὶ μὲν οὐατόεντι πανείκελον ὀγκήσαιτο
    ἄλλος· ἐγ]ὼ δ'εἴην οὑλαχύς, ὁ πτερόεις,
ἆ πάντως, ἵνα γῆρας ἵνα δρόσον ἣν μὲν ἀείδω
    προίκιον ἐκ δίης ἠέρος εἶδαρ ἔδων,
αὖθι τὸ δ' ἐκδύοιμι, τὸ μοι βάρος ὅσσον ἔπεστι
    τριγλώχιν ὀλοῷ νῆσος επ' Ἐγκελάδῳ.

We sing among those those who love the clear sound of the cicada, not the noise of asses. Let someone else bray exactly like the long-eared animal, let me be the small one, the winged one, oh, in all respects, in order that, as to old age and as to dew, I may sing like the second—eating the free food from the divine sky— and shed the first again, which weighs on me like the island with three points on destructive Enceladus.

                                       Trans. Harder, modified

Both passages set up an opposition between an ass and a creature—the *aipsas* in Nicander, the cicada in Callimachus—who sheds its external layer and so becomes rejuvenated. In the *Aetia* prologue Callimachus, representing himself as a figurative cicada, imagines casting off the grievous "burden" (βάρος) of his "old age" (γῆρας), and so plays on the idea that a cicada's molting is a form of rejuvenation.[21] In pointed contrast, Nicander imagines the ass giving up the "burden" (βρῖθος) of youth to the snake,[22] who from that time forward sheds "the bark of old age" (γηραλέον ... φλόον) and so, in pointed contrast with humans, perpetually rejuvenates itself.[23] Notably, Nicander refers to the ass by reference to its sound via the kenning βρωμήτωρ "brayer," just as Callimachus refers to the ass as "the long-eared beast" and the cicada as "the light one, the winged one."

The significance of the cicada in Callimachus is complex.[24] At the most basic level, it suggests the purity of Callimachus' song. Because they seemed to be able rejuvenate themselves, cicadas were sometimes represented as immortal,[25] and in associating himself with the creature, Callimachus not only picks up the opposition of old age and childhood with which the prologue opens, but also evokes the idea that poetry can survive the poet's demise (e.g., Callimachus, *Anthologia Palatina* 7.80). At the same time, critics have seen in Callimachus' wish to shed old age like a skin a programmatic desire to cast off the weight of the literary past and to produce the novel sort of poetry recommended by Apollo earlier in the prologue.[26] That Nicander evokes the Callimachean passage in the very narrative in which he hides his own name suggests the possibility that a similar dynamic might be at issue in the *Theriaca*.[27] Although the narrative focuses on the *dipsas*, it accounts for a phenomenon, skin shedding, which is shared by serpents as a whole (cf. 355–6). It thus explains why the creatures who are the principal focus of the poem are perpetually graced with νεότης. The passage may, then, make a claim about the perpetual freshness and novelty of Nicander's subject matter. Whereas in the *Aetia* it is the poet himself who is associated with an insect allegedly blessed with immortality, Nicander stakes his own claim to novelty (and, perhaps, to his posthumous poetic survival) by implying that his topic does not experience old age.[28] In this context, the emphasis placed on the alleged antiquity of the myth (343 ὠγύγιος δ' ἄρα μῦθος) underscores the larger point: just as the *dipsas* sheds the "bark of old age" and is refreshed, so has an ancient narrative been reformed in a novel way.[29]

Given the highly encrypted context, it may be possible to go further. It is likely that ancient readers anticipated modern scholars in recognizing that Aratus *Phaenomena* 783–7 contains a "gamma" acrostic (i.e. an acrostic in which the same word is spelled horizontally and vertically) of the adjective λεπτή,[30] an adjective which Hellenistic poets associated with an elegant and refined approach to poetry, and which Callimachus, perhaps signaling that he has noticed the acrostic, explicitly associates with the *Phaenomena*.[31] Nicander may also have noticed. Although λεπτός comes to mean "fine, small" and so "refined," its original sense is "peeled, husked" (cf. *Il.* 20.497), from the verb λέπω, and its cognates are regularly used of the skin or scales of animals, including snakes and other reptiles (e.g., *Theriaca* 154). In fact, Nicander uses the compound λεπαργής, "having a white hide" (< λέπος), to denote the ass at *Theriaca* 349. The adjective λεπτός does not, as far as I can tell, seem to have been used of snakes which have shed their skins, but λέπω is regularly used of stripping bark (e.g., *Il.* 1.236), an act with which the snake's skin shedding is metaphorically identified at *Ther.* 355–6. I would thus like to suggest that in embedding his "signature" in a narrative explaining how snakes came to shed their skins, Nicander is obliquely evoking the content of Aratus' acrostic: a *dipsas* which has stripped off its old skin could, in a literal sense, be understood as λεπτή.[32] If so, Nicander not only signals his own stylistic affiliation with the *leptotes* of Aratus and Callimachus, but also marks his generic heritage by incorporating a learned reference to Aratus' *Phaenomena* into a narrative inspired by Hesiod's *Works and Days*, just as he has done at the outset of his poem.[33]

Notes

1 Cf. Fakas (2001), 63 n. 108; Clauss (2006); Magnelli (2010), 218; Overduin (2015), 47–9 and *passim*.

2 The scholia (12a Crugnola) note that Nicander is not telling the truth (ψεύδεται), since the story is nowhere attested in Hesiod. Various explanations have been offered. That Nicander nodded seems implausible. Cazzaniga (1975) suggested that Nicander may have known a text of Hesiod in which a now-lost poem contain the story. It may be more likely, however, that the oddity should be understood against the background of Nicander's intense engagement with Hesiod and that poet's concern with poetic authority; cf. Hunter (2014), 25–6; Overduin (2015), 184; Kidder (2018), 75–81. A possible Hellenistic parallel for such tendentious "citation" might be the odd (mis)representation of the Iliadic treatment of the Dioscuri at Theocritus 22.214–20, on which see Sens (1992).

3 ἀλλ' ἤτοι κακοεργὰ φαλάγγια, σὺν καὶ ἀνιγρούς | ἑρπηστὰς ἔχιάς τε καὶ ἄχθεα μυρία γαίης | Τιτήνων ἐνέπουσιν ἀφ' αἵματος, εἰ ἐτεόν περ | Ἀσκραῖος μυχάτοιο Μελισσήεντος ἐπ' ὄχθαις |Ἡσίοδος κατέλεξε παρ' ὕδασι Περμησσοῖο (Indeed, they say that harmful spiders, and along with them grievous reptiles and vipers and the countless burdens of the Earth, derive from the blood of the Titans, if in fact Ascraean Hesiod told the truth on the banks of the most secluded Melisseis by the waters of the Permessus).

4 For the harsh, "anti-bucolic" landscape of the *Theriaca*, see Overduin (2014).

5 Cf. Fantuzzi and Hunter (2005), 51–60. It is perhaps a mark of its self-consciously belated place in the didactic tradition that in addition to regularly noting the threat that snakes pose to workers (e.g., 113, 831), the poem also emphasizes the dangers to those who have finished their work (58, 472–3).

6 Effe (1974).

7 Hunter (2014), 25; Overduin (2015), 183.

8 Overduin (2015), 175.

9 Overduin (2015), 317, notes that the reference to Prometheus evokes Hesiod in general. Sullivan (2013) persuasively reads the story against the "Aesopic" tradition of animal fable, including both the fable of the hawk and nightingale at *Works and Days* 202–12 and Callimachus, fr. 192 Pf.

10 The detail is found otherwise only at Aelian, *Nature of Animals* 6.51, probably depending on Nicander, whom Aelian does not name.

11 West (1978), 168.

12 According to Aelian (*Nature of Animals* 6.51), who (perhaps deliberately) omits any reference to Nicander, the story appears in Ibycus (fr. 342 Davies), Sophocles (362 Radt), Dinolochus (fr. 8 K–A), Apollophanes (9 K–A), and Aristias (fr. 8 Snell).

13 For the recondite style, see Hopkinson (1988), 143; Magnelli (2010), 216. For structural features of the passage, see Luz (2010), 16–19.

14 Cf Hopkinson (1988), 14; Overduin 319, *Il.* 11.558–9.

15 Though πρεσβίστατον αἷμα is capable of referring to status rather than age (Overduin 2015: 311–12), it seems likely that Nicander is engaging with a Hellenistic *zetema* having to do with whether Zeus was the oldest or youngest child of Kronos.

16 Overduin (2015), 314.

17 Bing (1990, 1993). Overduin (2013), 313 and 536, discusses the Aratean pun in connection with Nicander's acrostic.

18 Clauss (2006), 164; cf. Magnelli (2010), 221–2.

19 Hunter (2008), n. 13, notes the programmatic importance of the contrast between Nicander's three levels of knowledge (poet–addressee–laborers) and the two levels of Aratus and Hesiod; cf. Fakas (2001), 108 n. 80.

20 The possible connection between Nicander and the *Aetia* is observed in passing by Harder (2012), vol. 2, 80; Overduin (2015), 321, 322; and Hopkinson (2020), 152, 155. There is, in fact, at least one other evocation of Callimachus in the passages: *Theriaca* 349 cleverly reworks Call. *Hecale* fr. 76 Hollis = fr. 271 Pfeiffer; cf. Overduin (2015), 319; and Hopkinson (2020), 154.

21 Hayden Pelliccia points out to me the interesting case of Aristophanes, *Wasps* 1308–12, where the rejuvenated Bdelocleon responds to a jibe treating him to an ass by comparing himself to a locust which has shed its skin.

22 Overduin (2015), 321, notes that the metaphorical reference to "weight" has an analogy in Call. *Aetia* fr. 1.35.

23 The implicit analogy between the Callimachean cicada and Nicander's spring-guarding *dipsas* and the contrast between each of them and the ass may also play on cicada's alleged ability to feed only on dew, in pointed contradistinction to the ass. Acosta-Hughes and Stephens (2002), 251, note the relevance to Callimachus of an Aesopic fable (184 Perry) in which an ass fatally tries to imitate a cicada by living on dew. That asses must drink (and eat) copiously is of course a central theme of Nicander's story.

24 For discussion, with some of the substantial bibliography on the question, see Harder (2012), vol. 2, 69–71.

25 Davis and Kathirithimby (1986), 113–33; Tsagalis (2008), 115–29.

26 Cf. Harder (2012), vol. 2, 80; Fantuzzi and Hunter (2004), 74–5.

27 Harder (2012), vol. 2, 80, cites the passage in connection to *Aet.* fr. 1.35 and suggests that Nicander may be "inventing his own background for this passage in the *Aetia,*

intending some kind of programmatic statement couplet with the rather puzzling acrosticon in 345 ff."

28 Clauss (2006), 171; Sullivan (2013), 234.

29 Overduin (2015), 317, has plausibly suggested that part of this renovation consists precisely of overlaying elements designed to evoke the Hesiodic Prometheus on a story already attested elsewhere (cf. above, n. 12). Despite these ancient precedents, the claim that the story is Ogygian is only partially true: rather, the narrative as a whole seems likely to be an amalgamation of elements that reimagines the origins of human suffering as described in Pandora story in the *Works and Days*.

30 First noted by Jacques (1960); for further self-referential wordplay within Aratus' acrostic, cf. Hanses (2014). For Virgil's reworking of the passage to include an abbreviate form of his own name, cf. Somerville (2010).

31 Bing (1990, 1993).

32 Castelletti (2012), 90, suggests that ἰδμοσύνη in *Theriaca* 346 might evoke a previously unnoticed "boustrophedon" acrostic in Aratus.

33 I am grateful to Hayden Pelliccia, Charles McNelis, James Clauss, and Michael Sullivan for critiques, advice, and assistance with this paper.

Bibliography

Acosta-Hughes, B. and S. Stephens (2002), "Rereading Callimachus' '*Aetia*' Fragment 1," *Classical Philology*, 97: 238–55.

Bing, P. (1990), "A Pun on Aratus' Name in Verse 2 of the *Phainomena*?," *Harvard Studies in Classical Philology*, 93: 281–5.

Bing, P. (1993), "Aratus and his Audiences," *Materiali e Discussioni*, 31: 99–109.

Castelletti, C. (2012), "Following Aratus' Plow: Vergil's Signature in the 'Aeneid,'" *Museum Helveticum*, 69: 8–95.

Clauss, J. J. (2006), "*Theriaca*: Nicander's Poem of the Earth," *Studi italiani di filologia classica*, 4 (2006): 160–82.

Clauss, J. J. and M. Cuypers, eds. (2010), *A Companion to Hellenistic Literature*, Malden, MA: Blackwell.

Davis, M. and J. Kathirithimby (1986), *Greek Insects*, London: Duckworth.

Fakas, C. (2001), *Der hellenistische Hesiod: Arats Phainomena und die Tradition der aniken Lehrepik*, Wiesbaden: L. Reichert.

Fantuzzi, M. and R. Hunter (2005), *Tradition and Innovation in Hellenistic Poetry*, Cambridge: Cambridge University Press.

Hanses, M. (2014), "The Pun and the Moon in the Sky: Aratus' ΛΕΠΤΗ Acrostic," *Classical Quarterly*, 64: 609–14

Harder, A., ed. (2012), *Callimachus: Aetia*, 2 vols, Oxford: Oxford University Press.

Hopkinson, N. (2020), *A Hellenistic Anthology*, 2nd ed., Cambridge: Cambridge University Press.

Hunter, R. L. (1995), "Written in the Stars: Poetry and Philosophy in the *Phainomena* of Aratus," *Arachnion*, 2. Available online: http://www.cisi.unito.it/arachne/num2/index2.html; reprinted in R. L. Hunter, *On Coming After: Studies in Post-Classical Greek Literature and Its Reception*, 2 vols, vol. 1, 153–88, Berlin and New York: Walter de Gruyter, 2008.

Hunter, R. L. (2008), *On Coming After: Studies in Post-Classical Greek Literature and Its Reception*, 2 vols, Berlin and New York: Walter de Gruyter.

Hunter, R. (2014), *Hesiodic Voices: Studies in the Reception of Hesiod's Works and Days*, Cambridge: Cambridge University Press.

Jacques, J.–M. (1960), "Sur un acrostiche d'Aratos," *Revue d'études grecques*, 62: 48–61.

Kidder, K. (2018), "Representations of Truth and Falsehood in Hellenistic Poetry," PhD diss., University of Cincinnati, OH.

Kwapisz, J., D. Petrain, and M. Syzmánski, eds. (2013), *The Muse at Play: Riddles and Wordplay in Greek and Latin Poetry*, Berlin and Boston, MA: De Gruyter.

Luz, C. (2010), *Technopaignia. Formspiele in der griechischen Dichtung*, Leiden and Boston, MA: Brill.

Magnelli, E. (2010), "Nicander," in J. J. Clauss and M. Cuypers (eds.), *A Companion to Hellenistic Literature*, 211–23, Malden, MA: Blackwell.

Overduin, F. (2014), "The Anti-Bucolic World of Nicander's *Theriaca*," *Classical Quarterly*, 64: 623–41.

Overduin, F. (2015), *Nicander of Colophon's* Theriaca: *A Literary Commentary*, Leiden and Boston, MA: Brill.

Sens, A. (1992), "Theocritus, Homer, and the Dioscuri: *Idyll* 22.137–223," *Transactions of the American Philological Association*, 122: 335–50.

Somerville, T. (2010), "Note on a Reversed Acrostic in Vergil, *Georgics* 1.429–33," *Classical Philology*, 105: 202–9.

Sullivan, M. B. (2013), "Nicander's Aesopic Acrostic and Its Antidote," in J. Kwapisz, D. Petrain, and M. Syzmánski (eds.), *The Muse at Play: Riddles and Wordplay in Greek and Latin Poetry*, 225–45, Berlin and Boston, MA: De Gruyter.

Tsagalis, C. (2008), *Inscribing Sorrow: Fourth-Century Attic Funerary Epigrams*, Berlin and New York: De Gruyter.

West, M. L. (1978), *Hesiod: Works and Days*, Oxford: Oxford University Press.

15

The Death of the Author

Hesiod's Double Burial in Epigrams of Mnasalkes (*AP* 7.54 = 18 GP) and Alkaios (*AP* 7.55 = 12 GP) and in the Biographical Tradition

Peter Bing
University of Toronto

In a famous essay of 1967, the critic Roland Barthes proclaimed the death of the author. By this he meant the idea that we could point to a person outside of the text, an author, whose life, experiences, and intentions provided indispensable guidance in interpreting the work. For Barthes, the death or elimination of the author signaled the birth of the reader as the crucial agent for constituting a text's meaning. While his essay proved widely influential, almost from the start there were those who modified his proclamation (Foucault 1998) or rejected it altogether. And in the intervening years—notwithstanding the work of Mary Lefkowitz (1981), which fundamentally questioned the reliability of ancient Lives as sources of fact about ancient poets—the figure of the author, his biography, and not least of all that critical moment in his life, stories about the circumstances of his death, have been recognized in Classical studies as important and early evidence for ancient reception and interpretation of an author's work. One such story is my focus here: the death of the author, Hesiod. This well-known tale is part of a biographical discourse that arose in response to the poems of Hesiod, and which forms a paratextual corpus spanning various genres of poetry and prose. Several epigrams about Hesiod's burial belong to this discourse[1]—though in varying ways, explicit or implicit: the poems may appear embedded in prose accounts that provide concrete biographical context even as they reflect their authors' viewpoint; they may on the other hand appear separate from such accounts, e.g. in a poetry book, in which case readers must supply information from their own prior knowledge. Since the discourse is present in either case, one and the same epigram may slip easily between contexts, sometimes incorporated into an explicitly biographical framework, sometimes where the discourse is merely implicit. This illustrates the epigrammatic genre's general inclination toward "intermediality," that is, its tendency to migrate between media—monuments, poetry books (collections and anthologies), extended narratives—in each of which the same poem can function to quite different effect.[2]

In its bare bones the saga of Hesiod's death appears already in Thucydides, who mentions its circumstances in a manner that makes clear the fuller story must have been current in his day. In his account of the events of the year 427/6, he describes how the Athenian commander, Demosthenes, made his base at Oineon in Ozolian Locris. There, "after having camped with his army in the precinct of Nemean Zeus, where the poet Hesiod is said to have been killed by the local inhabitants, having been told by an oracle that he was destined to suffer this fate at Nemea, Demosthenes set out at daybreak to invade Aetolia" (Thuc.3.96.1). Thucydides thus knew a tradition in which Hesiod received an oracle foreseeing his death in the grove of Nemean Zeus, but misinterpreted it as referring to Nemea in the Peloponnese rather than in the precinct at Oineon.[3]

Not long after Thucydides, that story appears in far greater detail in the *Certamen Homeri et Hesiodi*, a compilation of the mid-second century CE, but in a section attributed expressly to Alcidamas' *Museum*, datable to the first half of the fourth century BCE:

> When the games broke up, Hesiod [who had been judged victorious over Homer] sailed across to Delphi to consult the oracle and to dedicate a tithe of his victory to Apollo. As he approached the temple, they say the prophetess became possessed, and declared:
>
> . . . .
> . . . beware Nemean Zeus' fair grove,
> for there the end of death is destined for you.

After hearing this oracle, Hesiod withdrew further away from the Peloponnese, thinking that the god meant the Nemea there, and he went to Oinoe in Locris, where he lodged with Amphiphanes and Ganyctor, the sons of Phegeus, not recognizing the reference of the prophecy, for that whole region was called sacred to Nemean Zeus. When he had stayed for some time among the people of Oinoe, the young men came to suspect that Hesiod was fornicating with their sister, and they killed him by drowning him in the sea between Locris and Euboea.[4] His corpse was brought to land by dolphins two days later while a certain local festival was in progress, the Purification of Rhion. Everyone ran to the shore and, recognizing the body, mourned him and gave him burial, and began to seek his murderers. They, fearing their fellow citizens' wrath, pulled a fishing boat down and sailed off towards Crete. In mid voyage Zeus cast a thunderbolt and drowned them, as Alcidamas says in his Museum.

Trans. M. L. West, Loeb, Homeric Hymns, Apocrypha, Lives, 341–3

According to Tzetzes (Schol. Hes. *Op.*, pp. 87–92 Colonna), this story was cited also by "Aristotle" in his *Constitution of the Orchomenians*. Why did Aristotle connect it with Orchomenos? The answer emerges in that same treatise, since— as Plutarch informs us—Aristotle there apparently also recounted how, following the destruction of Ascra by Thespiae, "Orchomenos gave refuge to the survivors, for which reason the god ordered the Orchomenians to take Hesiod's mortal remains and bury them in their own city."[5] The presence of the tale in the Aristotelian *Constitution* is confirmed also by another source, a collection of proverbs (*App. Prov.* 4.92 Leutsch-Schneidewin, *CPG* I p. 456 = "Aristotle" fr.565 Rose = "Pindar," Page *FGE*, pp. 159–60), which cites a poem inscribed on the poet's tomb to illustrate the proverb, "a Hesiodic old age":

τὸ Ἡσιόδειον γῆρας: <Ἀριστοτέλης> ἐν Ὀρχομενίων πολιτείᾳ δὶς τεθάφθαι φησὶ τὸν Ἡσίοδον καὶ ἐπιγράμματος τοῦδε τυχεῖν·

χαῖρε δὶς ἡβήσας καὶ δὶς τάφου ἀντιβολήσας,
        Ἡσίοδ', ἀνθρώποις μέτρον ἔχων σοφίης.

παρόσον τό τε γῆρας ὑπερέβη (Rose, ἀπέβη vulgo) καὶ δὶς ἐτάφη.

1–2 Pindaro adscribunt Tzetz. vit. Hes. p. 3 Solmsen et Suda s.v. Ἡσιόδειον γῆρας

A Hesiodic old age: Aristotle in his Constitution of the Orchomenians says that Hesiod was buried twice and received this epigram:

Hail, you who twice were young and twice received a tomb,
        Hesiod, you who hold the measure of wisdom for human beings.
inasmuch as he surpassed his old age and was buried twice.

Adapted from G. Most, Loeb

The Aristotelian *Constitution* thus included not only the tale of Hesiod's reburial but the epigram allegedly inscribed on his new tomb.[6] What did a "Hesiodic old age" signify? It seems that by citing this epigram Aristotle linked it directly to the narrative that Hesiod at an advanced age made his Locrian host's daughter pregnant. As Wilamowitz put it (1916: 407 n. 2), "Aristotle glosses the double ἥβη as παρόσον τό τε γῆρας ὑπερέβη. Hesiod no doubt proved that when, in extreme old age, he still begot a son."[7] As cited in the *Constitution*, the epigram thus evokes both parts of the story. True to its formal emphasis on doubling—it is, after all, a *distich*, conspicuously dividing its address of Hesiod across the start of two lines (χαῖρε . . . / Ἡσίοδ᾽) and highlighting his double youth and burial—it comprises the twin segments of the tale: It recalls Hesiod's death because of his alleged affair with the daughter of his Locrian host; it evokes his reburial at Orchomenos pursuant to an oracle. The epigram thus responds to and, in Aristotle's account, is integrated with, biographical tales about Hesiod's life and death.

I believe that the doubling that figures so prominently in this epigram gave rise to the pairing of two further epigrams in the *Greek Anthology* (*AP* 7.54–5), a pair of epitaphs on Hesiod. The first is attributed in the *Anthologia Palatina* to Mnasalkes (*AP* 7.54 = 18 GP), a poet of the mid-third century BCE, included by Meleager in his *Garland*; the second, set right beside it in the *GA*, is by another, somewhat later Meleagran poet, Alkaios of Messene (*AP* 7.55 = 12 GP). Here is the text of the first:

Ἄσκρη μὲν πατρὶς πολυλήιος, ἀλλὰ θανόντος
    ὀστέα πληξίππων γῆ Μινυῶν κατέχει
Ἡσιόδου, τοῦ πλεῖστον ἐν ἀνθρώποις κλέος ἐστὶν
    ἀνδρῶν κρινομένων ἐν βασάνῳ σοφίης.

Ascra rich in cornfields was my fatherland, but now that I am dead
    the land of the horse-goading Minyans holds my bones,
Hesiod's, whose fame is greatest among men
    when people are judged in the trial of wisdom.

As previously mentioned, epigrams tend to migrate between media—monuments, anthologies, narratives—and this poem turns up also in multiple accounts of the poet's burial, where it is said to have even been inscribed directly on his tombstone.[8] That's how it appears in the *Certamen*, but it does so in a section coming *after* the citation quoted previously from Alcidamas' *Museum* and *following* a section recounting an alternate version of the poet's death from the *Hesiod* of Eratosthenes. The citation in the *Certamen* therefore does *not* support attributing the poem already to Alcidamas' *Museum* in the early fourth century.[9] As Gow and Page put it in their introduction to the poem (1965: vol. 2, 413), "it is hard to guess why they [scil. the lines] should be ascribed to M[nasalkes] unless he was really their author."

Was the poem ever inscribed as ancient sources suggest (n.8 above)? And if so, when? If we are right that its citation in the *Certamen* does not go back to Alcidamas, then no account of its being inscribed precedes the second century

CE. Mnasalkes could of course have written it for inscription at Orchomenos; alternatively, he could have conceived it purely as literature, set in a collection of his own poems; perhaps he envisioned it intermedially, i.e. embracing both possibilities from the start. Thereafter, the epigram could have made its way into a subsequent anthology such as Meleager's *Garland*. It is from such a source that it likely jumped medium again, landing in the very different context of prose biography. Indeed, perhaps it was only then that it migrated secondarily from literature to inscription, due to the popularity of the *Certamen*.[10]

The epigram itself shows clear signs of being Hellenistic. Though its speaker is impersonal from a grammatical viewpoint, it can be construed as standing in for, or indeed embodying Hesiod's own voice,[11]—he was, after all, both poet and speaking character in his own narrative (naming himself in third person at *Theogony* v.22, as here in v.2)—and the poem is true to that voice inasmuch as πολυλήιος (v.1) is a Hesiodic hapax (fr.240,1 MW), which refers (as here) to a place "rich in cornfields."[12] Through such pointed use of a hapax to mark his speaker's identity, Mnasalkes appears as a typically learned third century poet, actively engaged with Hesiod's text and digging deep into his lexicon. At the same time (and equally typical for the period), he sets that textual inquiry within the paratextual discourse of biography: text and paratext illuminate one another.

As Graziosi has emphasized, ancient poetic biographies reflect contemporary engagement with, and interpretation of, a given author's work.[13] And indeed, Hesiod's voice here may echo cultural politics of the third century BCE. For this is a revisionist Hesiod, describing an improved, idealized Ascra. By the time of Aristotle in the fourth century, the village itself had been destroyed by Thespiae and, according to Plutarch, was never resettled.[14] One anonymous Hellenistic poet opens an iambic poem with the words, "of Ascra there is no longer so much as a trace" (Ἄσκρης μὲν οὐκέτ᾽ ἐστὶν οὐδ᾽ ἴχνος, *SH* 1131 A);[15] comparably, Pausanias remarks that in his day a single tower and no more was left to remember Ascra by (Ἄσκρης μὲν δὴ πύργος εἷς ἐπ᾽ ἐμοῦ καὶ ἄλλο οὐδὲν ἐλείπετο ἐς μνήμην 9.29.2).[16] Ascra had thus become a blank: people could formulate different conceptions of the place without fear of contradiction, at least from the physical evidence.

The rosier view of Ascra quite possibly arose in response to events of the third century BCE, specifically the rising status of the penteteric games in the nearby Valley of the Muses, the *Mouseia*—with their close association to Hesiod—thanks to Ptolemaic patronage.[17] In any case, Mnasalkes' description of Ascra as "rich in cornfields" seems to follow Zenodotus, first director of the Alexandrian Library and tutor to the Ptolemies. In his edition of Homer, the librarian/scholar changed the placename at *Iliad* 2.507 (οἵ τε πολυστάφυλον Ἄρνην ἔχον) from Ἄρνη to Ἄσκρη. In the generation following Mnasalkes, Zenodotus was taken to task by Aristarchus (*Sch. Il.* 2.507a = Σ A, 1, 294, 34ff. Erbse; cf. *ad Il.*7.9 = Σ A H9, 2, 229, 42ff. Erbse), who acidly remarked that Ascra was not "rich in grapes", since Hesiod himself had more credibly described it as "bad in winter, wretched in summer" (*WD* 640): "[the town] therefore could not be called fertile."[18] Zenodotus had, moreover, left Arne unchanged elsewhere in the *Iliad*, so according to Aristarchus he was also inconsistent (cf. *ad Il.*7.9 = Σ A H9, 2, 229, 42ff. Erbse).[19] Yet when Mnasalkes' Hesiod characterizes Ascra as πολυλήιος, it is consistent with the Zenodotean upgrade. Had absence from his home made Hesiod's heart grow fonder—along with a dash Ptolemaic interest in his devastated town?

More generally this idealized Ascra, taken together with esteem for Hesiod as paradigm of human wisdom, may reflect a rising sense of Boeotian national identity in the final decades of the third century BCE.[20] Mnasalkes would have been attuned to the politics of local pride, since he enjoyed close links to Boeotia—he (or a member of his family?) was granted proxeny at Boeotian Oropus in connection with the Amphiareion (*IG* VII 395.1–8 = V. Ch. Petrakos, *Hoi epigraphes tou Oropou*, no. 17),[21] and even his deme in Sicyon evoked close ties to Boeotia: it was called Plataea.[22] Mnasalkes' Hesiod is thus not the parochial Ἀσκραῖος ποιμήν,[23] but one reflecting broader regional awareness, a Βοιωτὸς ἀνήρ, as he appears already in Bacchylides (5.191), thereafter in Hermesianax (fr.7.21–2 Powell = Athen. 597b).

It is in keeping with such awareness that he speaks of "the land of the horse-goading Minyans" (πληξίππων γῆ Μινυῶν v.2) covering his bones, since the adjective πλήξιππος has (once more) a pointedly Hesiodic complexion, and a specifically Boeotian one at that. Homer uses this epithet of heroes from various parts of Greece,[24] but "Hesiod" assigns it specifically to Boeotians, Βοιωτοὶ πλήξιπποι (*Scut.*24)—strikingly, the only reference to Boeotians as a group surviving in the Hesiodic corpus.[25] As with Mnasalkes' choice of the term πολυλήιος, then, his use of πλήξιππος shows him to be learnedly mining the text of Hesiod. At the same time, he is clearly drawing on the paratextual tradition about Hesiod's life and death. For to this general Boeotian tone Mnasalkes adds a more specific Orchomenian hue reflecting Hesiod's (re)burial-site. In the same verse (v.2), he reproduces verbatim the entire pentameter of a sepulchral couplet from the Aristotelian *Peplos*, honoring Orchomenian brothers who had fought at Troy, Ascalaphus and Ialmenus: Ἀσκαλάφου Τροίῃ φθιμένου καὶ Ἰαλμένου ἥδε / ὀστέα πληξίππων γῆ Μινυῶν κατέχει.[26] Arguably, Mnasalkes knew this couplet through the *Peplos* and appropriated its pentameter to give his Hesiod—a relative new-comer to Orchomenos—some local color (the city's name does not otherwise appear in the poem), even as the adjective, πλήξιππος, also retains its particular Hesiodic valence in the mouth of the poet. Thus, just as Hesiod was doubly buried, "the land of the horse-goading Minyans" twice received heroic bones—using the same words.[27]

Orchomenian influence appears also in the second part of Mnasalkes' epigram. Here, the poet seems deliberately to echo that distich about Hesiod's double burial (χαῖρε δὶς ἡβήσας καὶ δὶς τάφου ἀντιβολήσας, / Ἡσίοδ᾽, ἀνθρώποις μέτρον ἔχων σοφίης). Mnasalkes starts his second couplet with Ἡσιόδου (v.3), just as the distich began its second half with Ἡσίοδ᾽ (v.2). In his quatrain's final verse (ἀνδρῶν κρινομένων ἐν βασάνῳ σοφίης), moreover, he lightly modulates his model's ἀνθρώποις with ἀνδρῶν,[28] while leaving intact its final word, σοφίης and conveying the same essential thought, that Hesiod is the standard of wisdom for humankind. In thus varying his exemplar, Mnasalkes evokes the inscriptional practice of setting multiple thematically related epigrams on the same monument or dedication as *Parallelgedichte*, as they are called. It is likely with such a practice in mind that Tzetzes cites both epitaphs as inscribed on Hesiod's tomb (*Scholia on Hesiod's Works and Days*, p.92 Colonna). In this instance, one might even use the competing scholarly term, *Konkurrenzgedichte*, since we are dealing with poems by different authors, and Mnasalkes strikingly tops his model by precisely doubling the original distich which had itself so accentuated the theme of doubling (he will be outdone, in turn, by Alkaios, who increases the epigram's length a further distich).[29] Such allusive play points again to practices of the Hellenistic era. But more than that, given that he alters his prototype by changing the distich's simple acclaim for Hesiod to the explicitly agonistic "when men are judged in the trial of wisdom" (ἀνδρῶν κρινομένων ἐν βασάνῳ σοφίης), we may wonder whether Mnasalkes meant his final verse to refer to the *agon* between Homer and Hesiod; there, poetic σοφίη is indeed the standard by which the winner is judged.[30] The epigram thus appears to engage not only with the paratextual tradition about Hesiod's reburial, but also with that of the contest. It can, in my opinion, be read as a learnèd response to such biographical narratives.[31]

At the same time, one can see how its reference to a judgement in a trial of wisdom eased its incorporation in the *Certamen*. There, endowed with a narrative context, its effect is quite different from what it would be when inscribed or placed in a poetry book. For set in the framework of the *Certamen*, Mnasalkes' reference to men judged in a test of σοφίη becomes concretized. It harks back to the lengthy account of Hesiod's competition with Homer and sums up his glory as victor (τοῦ πλεῖστον ἐν ἀνθρώποις κλέος ἐστίν v.3). The *Certamen* adds further details absent from the epitaph, e.g. that the Orchomenians removed the poet's remains and reinterred them following an oracle, and that it was they who inscribed the verses on his tomb. The epigram thus functions within the narrative as a capstone both for his triumph in the contest and for the tale of his death and reburial.

It is important to bear in mind that other biographical narratives have different axes to grind, and these color their accounts accordingly. Thus, certain sources reveal a strong Orchomenian inflection, more pronounced even than what shines through in Mnasalkes' poem. Pausanias (9.38.9–10), for instance, clearly draws on local sources in saying that the Orchomenians "have a tradition" (μνημονεύουσιν) that the epigram on Hesiod's tomb was by an ἀνὴρ Ὀρχομένιος, the late seventh- / early-sixth-century BCE poet Chersias, thus giving the poem a patina of great age and stressing—in a way that its attribution in the *GA* does not—its homegrown pedigree.[32] The information, moreover, that the people of Orchomenos placed Hesiod's tomb in their city's *agora* (cf. p. 259 below), and that the four-liner was inscribed there alongside the sepulchral distich we examined before—details stemming from Tzetzes' Life in the Hesiodic scholia— sound as though they too could derive from local tradition. In a similar vein, Aristotle, in the *Constitution of the Orchomenians* (as reported by Tzetzes), channels the perspective of his Orchomenian subject, not only assuming the transfer of Hesiod's remains, but in casting the events surrounding his death in Ozolian Locris in a sensational, somewhat scurrilous light: here, in keeping with the citation of the distich about the poet's vigorous second youth, Hesiod is not so much victim as potent agent: Not only did he deflower his hosts' daughter, he begot his poetic heir in the process—Stesichorus the lyric poet (Στησίχορον τὸν μελοποιὸν εἶναί φησιν υἱὸν Ἡσιόδου ἐκ τῆς Κτιμένης αὐτῷ γεννηθέντα τῆς Ἀμφιφάνους καὶ Γανύκτορος ἀδελφῆς, θυγατρὸς δὲ Φηγέως).

Elsewhere, the question of Hesiod's guilt in the affair with his host's daughter appears quite differently.[33] Thus, according to the *Certamen* (245–6), Eratosthenes impugns Hesiod's companion, Demodes, who is consequently killed along with the poet. And in Plutarch's version in the *Dinner of the Seven Wise Men* (162c–f), the poet-statesman Solon, who tells the tale, totally absolves the poet of responsibility; not only was Hesiod innocent of violating the girl, even the suspicion that he had helped conceal the act was utterly baseless: Hesiod, "though guilty of nothing, unjustly fell victim to an accusation made in a moment of anger" (μηδενὸς ὢν αἴτιος, ὀργῆς δὲ καιρῷ καὶ διαβολῆς περιπεσὼν ἀδίκως, 162d). Interestingly, Plutarch sets his dialogue in the house of Periander, tyrant of Corinth between 627 and 585, at a time *before* the Orchomenians seized Hesiod's remains for their second burial: "most foreigners do not know about his grave," says Solon, "but it remains hidden because the Orchomenians are looking for it, as they say, since in accordance with an oracle they want to seize the remains and bury them in their own land" (τὸν δὲ τάφον οἱ πολλοὶ τῶν ξένων οὐκ ἴσασιν, ἀλλ᾽ ἀποκέκρυπται ζητούμενος ὑπ᾽ Ὀρχομενίων, ὥς φασι, βουλομένων κατὰ χρησμὸν ἀνελέσθαι τὰ λείψανα καὶ θάψαι παρ᾽ αὐτοῖς, 162f).

Strikingly, the same Chersias mentioned by Pausanias as author of the epigram commemorating Hesiod at Orchomenos turns up in Plutarch's dialogue as one of Periander's dinner guests. He is there despite having previously been under a cloud at Corinth ("he was absolved of some charge and only recently reconciled with Periander", 156 f). Since he is said to have known the tyrant's father Cypselus personally [died 627] and been present when the latter dedicated the treasury of the Corinthians at Delphi (164 b), he appears as an already older figure.[34] Plutarch does not mention Chersias' native land, but we may wonder: Did he have in mind the Orchomenian tradition about the poet's link with Hesiod's reburial and epigrammatic commemoration?[35] And if so, should we imagine him (spy-like) carefully parsing the tale for clues as to the corpse's whereabouts? Solon does, after all, let slip that "Hesiod was buried near the shrine of Nemean Zeus" (ἐτάφη δ᾽ ὁ Ἡσίοδος πρὸς τῷ Νεμείῳ, 162e). Or was Plutarch casting doubt on his authorship of the quatrain at the site of reburial through his narrative's emphasis on Chersias' age and Orchomenos' ongoing failure to find the grave of Hesiod? In any case, the slant taken by a given biographical account on Hesiod's death and double burial doubtless influences a reader's understanding of the epigrams contained within its narrative frame. On the other hand, readers encountering Mnasalkes' epigram in the *AP* engage in a different interpretative activity: they must fill out the missing backstory and context, which may only be hinted at, through their own knowledge—a more labor-intensive act of reading, but one less constrained by a particular narrative point of view.

We looked before at the two epigrams which, according to the biographical tradition, were juxtaposed on Hesiod's tomb at Orchomenos. I want to turn now to a different kind of collocation, that of Mnasalkes' poem (*AP* 7.54 = 18 GP) and the one that stands beside it in the *GA*, by another Meleagran poet, Alkaios of Messene (*AP* 7.55 = 12 GP):

Λοκρίδος ἐν νέμεϊ σκιερῷ νέκυν Ἡσιόδοιο
   Νύμφαι κρηνίδων λοῦσαν ἀπὸ σφετέρων

καὶ τάφον ὑψώσαντο· γάλακτι δὲ ποιμένες αἰγῶν
     ἔρραναν ξανθῷ μιξάμενοι μέλιτι·
τοίην γὰρ καὶ γῆρυν ἀπέπνεεν ἐννέα Μουσέων
     ὁ πρέσβυς καθαρῶν γευσάμενος λιβάδων.

In Locris' shadowy glade the nymphs washed the corpse
     of Hesiod in their own spring
and raised up his tomb. Shepherds sprinkled it
     with goat-milk mixed with golden honey.
For such a voice the old man exhaled, who had tasted
     the pure streams of the nine Muses.

Though appearing in Cephalas' sequence of poets' epitaphs at the start of *AP* 7, these poems were, I believe, already linked by Meleager as a meaningful pair, since they reflect competing traditions about the whereabouts of Hesiod's tomb: Orchomenos vs. Locris.[36] Indeed, as Alkaios wrote in the late third / early second century, i.e., somewhat after Mnasalkes, he may himself (like Meleager later) have intended his epigram as an answer to Mnasalkes'.

Unlike Mnasalkes', Alkaios' poem was never incorporated into biographical narratives of Hesiod's death, though it clearly also refers to these.[37] It responds to Mnasalkes' epitaph primarily as one epigram to another. It does so, moreover, not as a *Konkurrenzgedicht* carved on the same monument, but referring to an altogether different place (though juxtaposed on the scroll). Significantly, in going through the poems in their transmitted order a reader is compelled to complicate the straightforward chronological sequence of the *Certamen's* biographical account by reversing it. This underlines what a different experience it may be to read epigrams in an anthology *vis-à-vis* in narrative. In a similar vein, although neither author mentions the alternative burial place, the poems form a pair, supplementing each other by allusively evoking the tradition that Hesiod was buried twice: δὶς τάφου ἀντιβολήσας, as the distich from the *Constitution* described. Indeed, one can see in the emphatic opening word of the second epigram, Λοκρίδος, a reminder of that tradition and corrective to the first: Hesiod perished in Locris, where he had tried to elude his prophesied end in the grove of Nemean Zeus, not realizing that there was a *Nemeion* there as well. That fateful location is, I believe, evoked in Alkaios' choice of the word νέμεϊ in v.1 to describe the site of Hesiod's tomb, likely playing on the ancient etymology of Nemea from νέμος ("the wooded district", LSJ s.v. Νεμέα), which thus points readers obliquely to the tale of the oracle Hesiod received.[38] A comparably oblique reference to the tale of Hesiod, redolent of his amorous powers in old age, may lie in Alkaios' description of him in the final verse as ὁ πρέσβυς, that well-known old man. In proximity to πρέσβυς, his prodigious γῆρυς (τοίην . . . γῆρυν v.5), acquired after tasting the streams of the Muses, may suggest a play on γῆρας, the dynamic Hesiodic old age, even as γῆρυν ἀπέπνεεν subtly varies the Muses' original act of inspiration in Hesiod, ἐνέπνευσαν . . . αὐδήν (*Th.*31).

The epigram's obliqueness and non-specificity about the tomb's location apart from pointing vaguely to a grove in the region of Locris, may suggest to readers a further aspect of the biographical tradition about Hesiod's burial there, that noted by Solon in Plutarch's *Dinner of the Seven Wise Men* (162e), namely that his tomb was hidden. In keeping with the secret of its location, the epigram avoids all *deixis*; it gives, moreover, not the slightest hint that it could have been inscribed, which would anchor it materially in a particular spot. We may wonder whether such indeterminacy of setting suggests why the epigram never found a place in biographical accounts. These typically cite an epitaph and its location as a gesture of authenticity, to make the story more believable.[40] Here, by contrast, the secret grave removes the narrative's need for documentation. It is worth pointing out, however, that the mysterious burial is suggestive of hero cult (cf. Oedipus' at Soph. *OC* 1522-3), as is the miraculous detail added by Pausanias (9.38.3-4) that the oracle helped the Orchomenians find the tomb by telling them that a crow would lead them to it.[41]

For all his vagueness about that location, Alkaios' poem assumes the body's removal for a second burial, and is thus keyed to Mnasalkes' epigram in this way, too. How so? Alkaios pointedly refrains from mentioning Hesiod's present location, instead describing the washing of his corpse, raising of his tomb, shepherds' libation, all with historical aorists (νέκυν . . . λοῦσαν vv.1-2, τά·ον ὑψώσαντο v.3, ἔρραναν v.4). In Mnasalkes' poem, by contrast, the Minyan earth covers the bones *now*: κατέχει (v.2). These remains may point to the larger narrative context as well: Pausanias (9.38.3-4) twice specifically mentions Ἡσιόδου τὰ ὀστᾶ as all that is left. The story thus recalls typical legends about repatriating heroes' bones—e.g., Sparta with Orestes' (Hdt.1.68), Athens with Theseus' (Plut. Thes.36.3, Kim.8.7). In this context, should we take Hesiod's mention of only his ὀστέα in Mnasalkes' epigram (v.2) as referring to the tradition about their removal? According to accounts preserved in the Hesiodic scholia, the Orchomenians buried them in the middle of their *agora* (ὀστᾶ θάπτουσιν ἐν μέσῃ τῇ ἀγορᾷ), a location typical for *heroes ktistai*, responsible for keeping a city intact.[42] Both of Hesiod's tombs, then, are places suggesting hero cult. One needn't believe that Hesiod was actually worshipped in either place, yet the nexus of tales in which these epigrams appear certainly allows audiences (ancient and modern) to read them against the backdrop of the biographical tradition about Hesiod's life and death. They can do so in varying ways, resulting in different readerly experiences. On the one hand they encounter poems embedded in prose narratives. Here, as I have argued, the epitaph by Mnasalkes aptly tops off the tale of the contest along with the author's death and reburial, summing up important aspects of the story. That same story, though in this case "untold", is also evoked—allusively—in the *Anthologia* through the juxtaposition of independent epigrams, such as those of Mnasalkes and Alkaios. That evocation invites readers to engage with the text, to reconstitute a narrative—the biographical discourse on the death of Hesiod—based on indications in the poems, along with their own knowledge. Such activity is certainly more arduous for those willing to meet to its demands. More pleasurable, too? That depends on what readers bring to the text and their willingness to connect with it. And for those of us trying to grasp an ancient audience's horizon of expectations, the allusive evocation of biographical legend compels us to "consider how the poet's biography operates in the reader's consciousness."[43]

Notes

1 Epigrams are especially at home in ancient *bioi*, since these often include accounts of an author's dedications, epitaph, and other epigrammatic forms.

2 On intermediality generally, see Rajewsky (2002); Mahne (2007); and Wolf (2008). For discussion of epigram's intermediality in Latin elegy, see Dinter (2011, 2013).

3 This brief account does not mention the poet's burial or reburial. On its function in Thucydides, see Finglass (2013).

4 The geographical detail makes evident that this source was thinking of eastern, i.e. Opountian, Locris rather than Ozolian Locris as in Thucydides. The confusion is present in many of the sources, which fluctuate between these two regions.

5 Plutarch fr. 82 Sandbach = Schol. Hes. *Op.* 633–40 = Aristotle fr. 565 Rose: Ὀρχομενίων δὲ τοὺς σωθέντας δεξαμένων· ὅθεν καὶ τὸν θεὸν Ὀρχομενίοις προστάξαι τὰ Ἡσιόδου λείψανα λαβεῖν καὶ θάψαι παρ' αὐτοῖς, ὡς καὶ Ἀριστοτέλης φησὶ γράφων τὴν Ὀρχομενίων πολιτείαν.

6 On Aristotle as a source for the tale of Hesiod's reburial and the sepulchral distich, cf. Friedel (1878/9), 263.

7 "Die doppelte ἥβη ... deutet Aristoteles παρόσον τό τε γῆρας ὑπερέβη. Das hat Hesiod wohl bewiesen, indem er im höchsten Alter noch einen Sohn zeugte". Cf. Evelyn-White (1920: 127): "a lively, vigorous age, in which ἥβη reasserts itself." In the same note, Wilamowitz suggests how this tale later developed into the idea of the

rejuvenated Hesiod: "Später ward es zu einer Verjüngung wie bei dem Iolaos des Euripides, Schol. Verg., Ecl. 6, 70, Symmachus Ep.7, 20." Scodel (1980: 316) argues that this was the *original* sense: Hesiod had miraculously "been granted a second life". This, she maintains (312), would also square with the distich's later attribution to "Pindar", as its content fit that poet's views of palingenesis. Perhaps, but as cited in the *Constitution of the Orchomenians* the distich had become attached to the story Hesiod's death in Locris and reburial at Orchomenos, where it could illustrate the proverbially vigorous "Hesiodic old age". See Beaulieu (2004), 114–16. Recently, part of the poem was found on a Late Antique epitaph of Kyrion of Nicomedea (*SGO* *09/06/23 Staab 2018: 335). His sons, the authors of the inscription, style him an imitator of Hesiod (Ἡσιόδου ζηλωτά v.2), stress his ripe age at death, and substitute his name for Hesiod's as the standard of wisdom (ἐν σοφίῃ μέτρον Κυρίων v.2). In short, they view Hesiod's life as a model for Kyrion's.

8 Thus, the *Certamen* (l.248 Allen), Proclus' and Tzetzes' prolegomena to the Hesiodic scholia (respectively p. 8 line 28 and p. 19 line 9 Gaisford), and Pausanias (9.38.4). As opposed to the *GA*, Pausanias (9.38.10) says the Orchomenians attribute the epigram on Hesiod's tomb to the late-seventh- / early-sixth-century BCE poet, Chersias of Orchomenos. Debiasi (2010: 260–6) thinks this correct, and suggests we view the quatrain as the model for the distich (attributed to "Pindar"), which imitated its final verse. At this early date, however, an inscribed sepulchral elegy of four verses would be unprecedented.

9 Following Vogt (1959: 200–1) and West (1967: 434–5, 447), most scholars now think that Alcidamas was responsible both for the contest proper and for shaping the careful symmetry between the poets' deaths—in West's formulation, "oracle, death, epitaph" (447). I think it more likely that the last element, the epitaph commemorating Hesiod, was added subsequently since it is not truly parallel: in *Certamen*, Hesiod gets no epitaph upon his death, only later, after the search for and death of his murderers, and once his bones are reburied at Orchomenos (ὕστερον δὲ Ὀρχομένιοι κατὰ χρησμὸν μετενέγκαντες αὐτὸν παρ᾽ αὑτοῖς ἔθαψαν, καὶ ἐπέγραψαν ἐπὶ τῶι τάφωι· *Certamen* 247–9). How much "later" we can't say. The *Constitution of the Orchomenians* connects the reburial with the arrival of the refugees from Ascra after Thespiae destroyed their town. The date of this sack is, however, quite uncertain. Kimmel-Clauzet (2013: 136–41, 166–9) thinks we can date the sepulchral distich together with the sack to the fifth century, but in truth we can say only that they come before Aristotle. Recently Porter (2021: 21) finds Alcidamas "quite possibly" helped create the symmetry between the poets' deaths, yet notably does not extend that parallelism to Hesiod's reburial and epitaph. Symmetry alone, on my view, does not suffice to justify crediting these elements to Alcidamas; no additional grounds presently exist.

10 Whether the poem was ever actually inscribed, however, remains unsettled given the absence of physical evidence. On literary epigrams secondarily inscribed, see Bing (2009: 208–10 = 1998: 33–4).

11 It is translated as Hesiod's own voice by Paton in his 1917 Loeb of the *Greek Anthology*, by M. L. West in his 2003 Loeb of the *Certamen*, and by G. W. Most in his 2018 Loeb Hesiod (T2). On the indeterminate nature of the impersonal voice, which includes the possibility of representing the deceased in epitaph, see Bing (1995), 121–2, 125–6 = (2009), 93–4, 97–8. A nice inscribed instance is *CEG* 545 from Attica (ὀστέα μὲν σάρκας | ἔ{ι}χει χθὼν παῖδα τὸν ἡ | δύν, / ψυχὴ δὲ εὐσεβέων | οἴχεται εἰς θάλαμον./ | εἰ δὲ ὄνομα ζητεῖς, Θεογείτ|ων Θυμόχου παῖς / Θηβα|ῖος γενεὰν κεῖμα<ι>, κλειν|αῖς ἐν Ἀθήνα|ις), where the impersonal voice switches mid-text to the first person, not to signal a new narrator, but to stress its personal knowledge of the deceased foreigner's name, parentage, and ethnicity, as his tomb is in Athens.

12 It is likewise a hapax in Homer (*Il.*5.613), but used of a man (similarly H. H. Hermes 171). Kenyon (1897) proposed it as a supplement at Bacchylides 10.34 to characterize Euboea, Εὔβοιαν πολ.[υλήϊο]ν, followed also by subsequent editors.

13 Thus, e.g., Graziosi (2002: 168): "discussions about authors were a powerful way of expressing thoughts about the poetry."

14 See fr.82 Sandbach: ἀοίκητον δ' αὐτὴν ὁ <Πλούταρχος> ἱστορεῖ καὶ τότε εἶναι.

15 For the reconstitution of this fragment, see West (1979).

16 The tower is identified with the one "that still stands on top of the rocky peak called Pyrgaki . . ., which dominateshe Sanctuary of the Muses from the S," cf. Stillwell, MacDonald, and McAllister (2017: s.v. Askra).

17 Ptolemaic interest in the festival is dated particularly to the reign of Ptolemy IV Philopator and his queen Arsinoe III by Feyel (1942: 88–117) followed by Fraser (1972: 313 w. n. 55) and Bernand (1998: 128–9), while Cameron (1995: 142) argues on the basis of Pausanias 9.31.1 that Arsinoe II Philadelphus may already have been instrumental in the reorganization of the games, cf. also Fantuzzi and Hunter (2004: 52).

18 *Sch. Il.* 2.507a Ἄρνην ἔχον: ὅτι Ζηνόδοτος γράφει ʽἌσκρην ἔχον'. οὐ δύναται δὲ πολυστάφυλος ἡ Ἄσκρη λέγεσθαι· ἀξιοπιστότερος γάρ ἐστιν Ἡσίοδος λέγων· ʽἌσκρη χεῖμα κακή, θέρει ἀργαλέη'· ὥστε οὐδὲ πολύκαρπος λέγοιτο ἄν. See Schironi (2018), 696.

19 Later, Strabo (IX p.413.9–20 Radt) similarly ridiculed Zenodotus' reading: [the scholar] "could not have read what Hesiod said about his own native land, nor the far worse things that Eudoxus said about Ascra."

20 Rigsby (1987), for instance, describes how "in the course of the third century BCE the cities of Boeotia . . . created an elaborate system of religious events that underscored their national unity" (p. 729); and "the religious festivals of the Boeotians served to mark the solidarity of the nation" (p. 740).

21 ἐ[πει]- | δὴ Μνασάλκης Μνασίππου Σικυών[ιος] | διατελεῖ φίλος καὶ εὔνους ὢν τῆι [πόλ]- | ει καὶ λέγων καὶ πράττων πε[ρὶ τὸ ἱε]- | ρον τοῦ [Ἀμφιαρ]ά[ου κατὰ τὸ δυνατὸν] | τὰ συμ[φ]έροντα τοῖς Ὠρωπίοις· δεδόχθαι | τῶι δήμωι· εἶναι αὐτὸν | πρόξενον [καὶ] | εὐεργέτην τῆς πόλεως τῶν Ὠρωπίων. The inscription is dated to the mid-third century BCE, before 220, by Wilhelm (1915), 4–5.

22 Thus Strabo 9.2.31. The name of the deme most likely commemorated the Sicyonians' important role at the battle of Plataea: the city appears prominently on the Serpent Column celebrating the victory.

23 Thus Dionysius of Halicarnassus, *Ars Rhet.*1.1.8. For Hesiod as Ἀσκραῖος, cf. also Nic. *Th.*11.

24 Pelops (*Il.*2.104), Athenian Menestheus (*Il.*4.327), Orestes (*Il.*5.705).

25 Pindar called Thebes πλάξιππον . . . Θήβαν (*Ol.*6.85).

26 The couplet plays on the appearance of these heroes in the *Iliad* (*Il.*2.511–512, cf. 9.82), where—just as its first verse describes—one of the brothers, Ascalaphus, fell in battle: Ἀσκαλάφου Τροίη φθιμένου (thus *Il.*13.477–479, 518–528, cf. 15.111–142). As Gutzwiller (2010: 238) suggests, "the epitaph reflects exactly this epic story, since only Ascalaphus is said to have died at Troy, but the bones of both have come into possession of their homeland, as if Ialmenus brought back his brother's remains." On this epitaph's relationship to Mnasalkes' poem, see Gutzwiller (2010: 237–9).

27 The *Peplos* involved a double set of bones to boot.

28 Mnasalkes transposes ἀνθρώποις to the previous line, τοῦ πλεῖστον ἐν ἀνθρώποις κλέος ἐστίν.

29 On *Parallelgedicht* vs. *Konkurrenzgedicht*, see Hutchinson (2019), 21 n. 20. I owe to Alison Keith the observation that each successive poem increases the length of the original distich.

30 Thus also Skiadas (1965), 41–3, who points to *Certamen* 65, where poetic σοφίη appears as the quality at stake in the contest, and Aristophanes' *Frogs* 882, which describes the competition between Aeschylus and Euripides as an ἀγὼν σοφίας; cf. also Themistius (Or. 30 p. 348c Dindorf).

31 For Hellenistic poets' interest in biographical traditions about poets, see Gabathuler (1937); Bing (1993 and 2018).

32 Incorporating such background elements illuminating a poem's composition is typical in narrative. Thus, while authorial anonymity remained the norm for verse-inscriptions well-into the Hellenistic age, ancient biographical accounts often specify their authorship: At *Certamen* 210–14, for instance, we hear that Hesiod, upon offering to the Muses the tripod marking his victory over Homer at Calchis, himself composed its dedicatory epigram; at 333–8 Homer, after failing to solve the fisher-boys' riddle, devised his own epitaph on Ios. On the other hand, readers encountering those poems in the *AP* (7.53 and 7.3, respectively) hear nothing about their authorship.

33 Pausanias 9.31.6 comments explicitly on such differences.

34 In the dialogue, Periander defers to Chersias in interpreting the decoration of the treasury, as though he himself had been too young to be present at the building's dedication (164a–b).

35 Of course there can be no certainty about this, since the Orchomenian assertion of Chersias' authorship appears only in Pausanias, i.e. well after Plutarch. Pausanias is the only other author to mention this poet.

36 On these competing traditions, see Nagy (2009: 306) and Bershadsky (2011: 19–22, 32–6).

37 Alkaios also wrote on the death of Homer (*AP* 7.1 = 11 GP), likewise responding to a story in the *Certamen*, i.e. the poet's demise through the riddle of the fisher-boys. Campbell (2013: 78–86) reads Alkaios' two poems as a pair, cf. also Bruss (2002/3: 176–7).

38 Campbell (2013: 80 n.171) and Kimmel-Clauzet (2013: 50) also note the play.

39 With his play on the Muses' inspiration at *Th*.31, Alkaios may also intend γῆρυς to recall their own description of their song 3 verses earlier at *Th*.28, as γηρύσασθαι. Curiously, γῆρυς is a Homeric hapax (*Il*.4.437) and does not appear in Hesiod, while γηρύω occurs twice in Hesiod (cf. also *WD* 260) but is absent from Homer.

40 As Gutzwiller (2010: 239) suggests, "the citing of such epitaphs, with a declaration of their reality as inscriptions, served the purpose of validating the authenticity of the story being told." She treats the three epigrams on the tomb of Hesiod ("Pindar," Mnasalkes, and Alkaios) on 238–41.

41 See Beaulieu (2004: 116–17) and Kimmel-Clauzet (2013: 135–6) on possible references to hero cult in this poem.

42 For heroes buried in the agora of cities they founded, cf. Battus in Cyrene (Pind. *P*.5.95) or Brasidas at Amphipolis (Hdt.6.38, Thuc.5.11). As Burkert (1985: 206) puts it, "the hero cult is a centre of local group identity." Currie (2007: 190) sees the evidence for the poet's cult at Orchomenos as clear-cut. Beaulieu (2004: 106–11) is skeptical.

43 Thus Tomashevsky (2017: 83). As he also says (2017: 87), "biographical legends are the literary conception of the poet's life, and this conception was necessary as a perceptible background for the poet's literary works."

Bibliography

Baumbach, M., A. Petrovic, and I. Petrovic, eds. (2010), *Archaic and Classical Greek Epigram*, Cambridge: Cambridge University Press.

Beaulieu, M.-C. (2004), "L'héroïsation du poète Hésiode en Grèce ancienne," *Kernos*, 17: 103–17.

Bernand, A. (1998), *Alexandrie la Grande*, 2nd ed., Paris: Hachette Littératures.

Bershadsky, N. (2011), "A Picnic, a Tomb, and a Crow: Hesiod's Cult in the Works and Days," *Harvard Studies in Classical Philology*, 106: 1–45.

Bing, P. (1993), "The Bios-Tradition and the Poet's Lives in Hellenistic Poetry," in R. M. Rosen and J. Farrell (eds.), *Nomodeiktes: Greek Studies in Honor of Martin Ostwald*, 619–31, Ann Arbor, MI: University of Michigan Press.

Bing, P. (1998), "Between Literature and the Monuments," in M. Harder, R. F. Regtuit, and G. C. Wakker (eds.), *Genre in Hellenistic Poetry*, Hellenistica Groningana, 3, 21–43, Groningen: E. Forsten.

Bing, P. (2009), "Between Literature and the Monuments," in *The Scroll & The Marble Studies in Reading and Reception in Hellenistic Poetry*, 194–216, Ann Arbor, MI: University of Michigan Press.

Bing, P. (2018), "Tombs of Poets' Minor Characters," in N. Goldschmidt and B. Graziosi (eds.), *Tombs of the Ancient Poets: Between Literary Reception and Material Culture*, 147–70, Oxford: Oxford University Press.

Bruss, J. S. (2002/3), "A Program Poem of Alcaeus of Messene: Epigram 16 G-P (= A.P. 7.429)," *Classical Journal*, 98 (2): 161–80.

Bulloch, A., E. S. Gruen, A. A. Long, and A. Stewart, eds. (1993), *Images and Ideologies Self-Definition in the Hellenistic World*, Berkeley, CA: University of California Press.

Burkert, W. (1985), *Greek Religion: Archaic and Classical*, Cambridge, MA: Harvard University Press.

Cameron, A. (1995), *Callimachus and His Critics*, Princeton, NJ: Princeton University Press.

Campbell, C. S. (2013), "Poets and Poetics in Greek Literary Epigram," PhD diss., University of Cincinnati, OH.

Cingano, E., ed. (2010), *Tra panellenismo e tradizioni locali: generi poetici e storiographia*, Alessandria: Edizioni dell'Orso.

Coppola, A., ed. (2007), *Eroi, eroismi, eroizzazzioni*, Padua: Sargon.

Currie, B. (2007), "Heroes and Holy Men in Early Greece: Hesiod's *theios aner*," in A. Coppola (ed.), *Eroi, eroismi, eroizzazzioni*, 163–203, Padua: Sargon.

Debiasi, A. (2010), "Orcomeno, Ascra e l'epopea regionale 'minore,'" in E. Cingano (ed.), *Tra panellenismo e tradizioni locali: generi poetici e storiographia*, 255–98, Alessandria: Edizioni dell'Orso.

Dinter, M. (2011), "Inscriptional Intermediality in Latin Elegy", in A. Keith (ed.), *Latin Elegy and Hellenistic Epigram*, 7–18, Newcastle upon Tyne: Cambridge Scholars Publishing.

Dinter, M. (2013), "Inscriptional Intermediality in Latin Literature," in P. Liddel and P. Low (eds.), *Inscriptions and Their Uses in Greek and Latin Literature*, 303–16, Oxford: Oxford University Press.

Evelyn-White, H. G. (1920), "Miscellanea Hesiodea," *Classical Quarterly*, 14: 126–31.

Fantuzzi, M. and R. L. Hunter (2004), *Tradition and Innovation in Hellenistic Poetry*, Cambridge: Cambridge University Press.

Faubion, J. D., ed. (1998), *Essential Works of Foucault*, vol. 2, New York: The New Press.

Feyel, M. (1942), *Contribution à l'épigraphie béotienne*, Le Puy: Imprimerie de La Haute-Loire.

Finglass, P. J. (2013), "Thucydides and Hesiod," *Quaderni Urbinati di Cultura Classica*, 105: 161–9.

Foucault, M. (1998), "What is an Author," trans. J. Harari, in J. D. Faubion (ed.), *Essential Works of Foucault*, vol. 2, 205–22, New York: The New Press.

Fraser, P. M. (1972), *Ptolemaic Alexandria*, 3 vols, Oxford: Clarendon Press.

Friedel, O. (1878/9), "Die Sage vom Tode Hesiods. Nach ihren Quellen Untersucht," *Jahrbücher der classischen Philologie*, Supplementband, 10: 235–78.

Gabathuler, M. (1937), "Hellenistische Epigramme auf Dichter," PhD diss., University of St. Gallen, Basel.

Goldschmidt, N. and B. Graziosi, eds. (2018), *Tombs of the Ancient Poets: Between Literary Reception and Material Culture*, Oxford: Oxford University Press.

Gow, A. S. F. and D. L. Page (1965), *The Greek Anthology: Hellenistic Epigrams*, 2 vols, Cambridge: Cambridge University Press.

Graziosi, B. (2002), *Inventing Homer: The Early Reception of Epic*, Cambridge: Cambridge University Press.

Gutzwiller, K. (2010), "Heroic Epitaphs of the Classical Age: The Aristotelian *Peplos* and Beyond," in M. Baumbach, A. Petrovic, and I. Petrovic (eds.), *Archaic and Classical Greek Epigram*, 219–49, Cambridge: Cambridge University Press.

Harder, M., R. F. Regtuit, and G. C. Wakker, eds. (1998), *Genre in Hellenistic Poetry*, Hellenistica Groningana, 3, Groningen: E. Forsten.

Hemecker, W. and E. Saunders, eds. (2017), *Biography in Theory: Key Texts with Commentaries*, Berlin and Boston, MA: De Gruyter.

Hutchinson, G. O. (2019), "Gedichte auf Stein und Papyrus lesen: Zwei Arten der Lektüreerfahrung," in C. Ritter-Schmalz and R. Schwitter (eds.), *Antike Texte und ihre Materialität: Alltägliche Präsenz, mediale Semantik, literarische Reflexion*, 13–26, Berlin: De Gruyter.

Keith, A., ed. (2011), *Latin Elegy and Hellenistic Epigram*, Newcastle upon Tyne: Cambridge Scholars Publishing.

Kenyon, F. G. (1897), *The Poems of Bacchylides*, London: Printed by order of the Trustees of the British Museum.

Kimmel-Clauzet, F. (2013), *Morts, tombeaux et cultes des poètes grecs*, Bordeaux: Ausonius Éditions, Diffusion de Boccard.

Kinzl, K. H., ed. (1977), *Greece and the Ancient Mediterranean in History and Pre-History: Studies Presented to Fritz Schachermeyr on the Occasion of His Eightieth Birthday*, Berlin: De Gruyter.

Lambropoulos, V. and D. N. Miller, eds. (1987), *Twentieth-Century Literary Theory: An Introductory Anthology*, Albany, NY: State University of New York Press.

Lefkowitz, M. R. (1981), *The Lives of the Greek Poets*, Baltimore, MD: Johns Hopkins University Press.

Liddel, P. and P. Low, eds. (2013), *Inscriptions and Their Uses in Greek and Latin Literature*, Oxford: Oxford University Press.

Mahne, N. (2007), *Transmediale Erzähltheorie*, Göttingen: Vandenhoek & Ruprecht.

Montanari, F., A. Rengakos and C. Tsagalis, eds. (2009), *Brill's Companion to Hesiod*, Leiden: Brill.

Nagy, G. (2009), "Hesiod and the Ancient Biographical Traditions," in F. Montanari, A. Rengakos and C. Tsagalis (eds.), *Brill's Companion to Hesiod*, 271–311, Leiden: Brill.

Nünning, A., ed. (2008), *Metzler Lexikon Literatur- und Kulturtheorie*, 4th ed., Stuttgart: J. B. Metzler.

Porter, J. (2021), "*P. Mich. Inv.* 2754: New Readings of Alcidamas, 'On Homer,'" *Classical Philology*, 116: 1–25.

Rajewsky, I. O. (2002), *Intermedialität*, Tübingen: A. Francke Verlag.

Rigsby, K. J. (1987), "A Decree of Haliartus on Cult," *American Journal of Philology*, 108: 729–40.

Rimell, V. and M. Asper, eds. (2017), *Imagining Empire: Political Space in Hellenistic and Roman Literature*, Heidelberg: Universitätsverlag Winter.

Ritter-Schmalz, C. and R Schwitter, eds. (2019), *Antike Texte und ihre Materialität: Alltägliche Präsenz, mediale Semantik, literarische Reflexion*, Berlin: De Gruyter.

Rosen, R. M. and J. Farrell, eds. (1993), *Nomodeiktes: Greek Studies in Honor of Martin Ostwald*, Ann Arbor, MI: University of Michigan Press.

Schironi, F. (2018), *The Best of the Grammarians: Aristarchus of Samothrace on the Iliad*, Ann Arbor, MI: University of Michigan Press.

Scodel, R. (1980), "Hesiod Redivivus," *Greek, Roman, and Byzantine Studies*, 21 (4): 301–20.

Skiadas, A. D. (1965), *Homer im griechischen Epigramm*, Athens: Greek Society for Humanistic Studies, Center for Classical Studies.

Staab, G. (2018), *Gebrochener Glanz. Klassische Tradition und Alltagswelt im Spiegel neuer und alter Grabepigramme des griechischen Ostens*, Berlin: De Gruyter.

Stillwell, R., W. L. MacDonald and M. H. McAllister, eds. (2017), *The Princeton Encyclopedia of Classical Sites*, Princeton, NJ: Princeton University Press.

Tomashevsky, B. (1987), "Literature and Biography (1923)," trans. H. Eagle, in V. Lambropoulos and D. N. Miller (eds.), *Twentieth-Century Literary Theory: An Introductory Anthology*, 116–23. Albany, NY: State University of New York Press.

Tomashevsky, B. (2017), "Literature and Biography (1923)," trans. H. Eagle, in W. Hemecker and E. Saunders (eds.), *Biography in Theory: Key Texts with Commentaries*, 83–90, Berlin and Boston, MA: De Gruyter.

Vogt, E. (1959), "Die Schrift vom Wettkampf Homers und Hesiods," *Rheinisches Museum für Philologie*, 102 (3): 193–221.

Walker, S. and P. Higgs, eds. (2001), *Cleopatra of Egypt from History to Myth*, London: British Museum Press.

West, M. L. (1967), "The Contest of Hesiod and Homer," *Classical Quarterly*, 17: 433–50.

West, M. L. (1979), "Four Hellenistic First Lines Restored," *Classical Quarterly*, 29: 324–6.

Wilamowitz-Moellendorff, U. von (1916), *Die Ilias und Homer*, Berlin: Weidmann.

Wilhelm, A. (1915), *Neue Beiträge zur griechischen Inschriftenkunde IV*, "25. Beschluß der Oropier zu Ehren des Mnasalkes aus Sikyon," Sitzungsberichte der Kaiserliche Akademie der Wissenschaften in Wien Philosophisch-historische Klasse 179, 6. Abh., 3–6, Wien: Hölder.

Wolf, W. (2008), "Intermedialität," in A. Nünning (ed.), *Metzler Lexikon Literatur- und Kulturtheorie*, 4th ed., 327–8, Stuttgart: J. B. Metzler.

16

Doomscrolling at Segesta

An Allusion to Lycophron in Virgil, *Aeneid* 5. 552–4

Alessandro Barchiesi
New York University

The work of Susan Stephens, and conversations with her in sunny Stanford, have influenced my understanding of Hellenistic culture and its importance to the Romans: this paper about Lycophron and Virgil is a continuation of our exchanges, written in a spirit of gratitude. My interest here for topics like colonization and intercultural dynamics owes a great deal to Susan's example.

A number of scholars[1] have pointed out possible influences of the *Alexandra* on the *Aeneid*, and some of them are not only inviting but also strategically important

(1) Pride of place belongs to the episode where Anchises explicitly remembers Cassandra's prophetic voice as the first to have revealed the true destination of the Trojans, Italy:

> Tum memorat: "nate, Iliacis exercite fatis,
> Sola mihi talis casus Cassandra canebat.
> Nunc repeto haec generi portendere debita nostro
> Et saepe Hesperiam, saepe Itala regna uocare.
> Sed quis ad Hesperiae uenturos litora Teucros
> Crederet ? aut quem tum uates Cassandra moueret ?"
>
> Virgil, *Aeneid* 3.182–7

He then says: "Son, you who are so tormented by the destiny of the Trojans, only Cassandra was foretelling to me this sort of development. Now I remember how she was predicting this future for our clan, often mentioning the Occident, and a kingdom in Italy. Yet who would have believed that the Teucrians could make it to the shores of the Occident? Who would have been swayed by Cassandra's predictions?"

The passage makes such a strong case for a connection between Cassandra's prophecy and the Western migrations of Trojan survivors that it is hard not to believe in a pointed reference to the *Alexandra*. The force of *sola* and *nunc repeto* is a self-reflexive indication that the poem of Lycophron is perceived as unique and is part of the poetic memory of Virgil, while the emphasis on deaf ears (*aut quem tum uates Cassandra moueret?*) is of course important in Lycophron (cf. *Alexandra* 1472–4), although of course not exclusive to that text. The *Aeneid* answers Cassandra's mysterious voice—her entire raving prophecy is almost a message in a bottle hidden in a complicated Greek poem—by having Apollo's direct voice [2] deliver the simple, sensational revelation that the Trojans have an imperial future in the Occident.

The Roman poet reinforces the point about Cassandra's voice not being heard through a pun that would not be possible in Greek: the jingle *cassus Cassandra canebat* almost reveals that the Latin adjective *cassus* "futile, fruitless, hollow" lurks in *Cassandra*'s name.[3]

The sudden realization by Anchises in *nunc repeto* is recuperated and compensated in 7, 123, where the occasion is the famous foundation omen of "eating the tables": Aeneas, the speaker, utters his "*nunc repeto*" when he suddenly recalls the omen foretold by Anchises—precisely the character who complains about his hindsight in the passage from Book 3. Now things are clear about the destiny of the Trojans—except there is still a dark side to the prophecy, since in our text of the *Aeneid* it is not father Anchises, but the Harpy Celaeno ("the dark one," in Greek) who had made the prophecy to Anchises and Aeneas (3, 250–7). It would be interesting if the *infelix uates* Celaeno (3, 246) turned out to be another avatar of the *Alexandra*: the Virgilian sentence *nunc repeto* harks back to a Lycophronian line from the episode of the *mensae* prodigy

μνήμην παλαιῶν λήψεται θεσπισμάτων

Alexandra 1252

"this will remind Aeneas of old oracles."[4]

(2) The Menelaos section in Lycophron begins with a reference to the Iapygian temple of Athena (cf. 853–5). This is indeed a strategic moment in the text because, while Menelaos is certainly an expected protagonist in a poem of *Nostoi*, his journey into the West and into Southern Italy is a swerve away from the Homeric tradition. Ingrid Edlund has noticed[5] that this moment is echoed in the *Aeneid* when Virgil wants to identify a first landing of Aeneas in Italy, at the so-called *Castrum Minervae*, cf. *Aeneid* 3.530–1: clearly a

significant juncture in the chronotope of Virgil, as pinpointed by the triple shout *"Italia!"* (cf. 3.521–4, with a Hellenistic metrical variation of the first syllable becoming very symbolic of the situation, which is no less than the discovery / "invention" of Italy). Both episodes feature allusions to the struggles of colonization in a warlike land. Anchises interprets the sudden vision of four horses in the new land (3, 537 ff.) as a potential for war. Menelaos comes as a wanderer to the Ἰαπύγων στρατόν (852), and although στρατός can mean "people" (cf. Hornblower ad loc.), if one considers the history of violence between the Iapygians and the Greek settlers (cf. e.g., in a prophetic utterance, Diod. Sic. 8,21; Strab. 6,3,2), the concept of "army" (στρατός) cannot be too far from the surface: I would translate Cassandra's prophetic designation as "the people's army of the Iapygians."

(3) The entire action of the *Aeneid* begins with a Euripidean first scene, Juno stating in a monologue her desire to imitate without constraints the destruction of the Greek fleet by Athena, who was free to strike down the conquerors of Troy because of the individual crime of the Lesser Ajax (*Aeneid* 1.41):

> unius ob noxam et furias Aiacis Oilei

This strategic moment identifies the *Aeneid* as a spin-off of the Greek epic Cycle, since the storm that ensues is in fact a transformation of the storm narrated by the Cycle and by many other illustrious Greek poets. The myth has a rich literary genealogy, but Stephanie West (1984: 132) was right in pointing out that the wording of *unius ob noxam* is a precise allusion to Lycophron 365, where the text has the ghastly quality of being spoken by the future victim of the rape and cause of the divine intervention: ἑνὸς δὲ λώβης ἀντί "in exchange for the sin of one man." A strategically meaningful allusion, since this is the onset of the divine action in Virgil, while in the *Alexandra* the myth of Locrian Ajax and Cassandra functions as a marked articulation of the plot (Hornblower 2015: 195, "In the structure of the poem as a whole, this section is a crucial hinge between the Fall of Troy narrative and the *nostoi* and failed *nostoi* which are the subject of the great central panel").

Stephanie West has also established the useful general guideline that emphasis on prophecy in the *Aeneid*—where there is plenty—frequently facilitates association with Lycophron. (A principle that looks even stronger if we dismiss her argument that the section about Roman power over Greek kingdoms in the *Alexandra* is an Augustan interpolation presumably not read by Virgil.) This is where another example kicks in.

Doomscrolling at Segesta

The *Aeneid* is full of prophecies and haunted by a sense of destiny, but few passages are as mysterious as 5.519–30 where the last arrow of the archery context, shot by Acestes into the sky, becomes a blaze, and the narrator opens up a surprising view into the future (522–4):

> hic oculis subitum obicitur magnoque futurum
> augurio monstrum; docuit post exitus ingens
> seraque terrifici cecinerunt omina vates.

> That's when an omen confronted their eyes: inescapable, sudden
> Symbol of what lay ahead—as events of significance later
> Showed, and as prophets of doom later on sang loudly, but too late.

> Trans. F. Ahl

Countless interpretations of the omen have been proposed, and some of them quite influential.[6] They are however open to objections. A reference to Acestes, who will immediately receive from Aeneas the authorization to found Aigesta / Segesta, is not encouraged by the wording (*magnoque ... augurio monstrum; post ... exitus ingens ... seraque terrifici cecinerunt omina vates*): the event looks at the same time catastrophic and belonging to a distant future. A reference to the future success of Aeneas or of his distant successor Augustus is possible in terms of time distance—actually, Augustus would be a much better temporal context than many—but not a nice fit for the shivering tone of the foreshadowing. An anticipation of the arson of the ships (*Aeneid* 5.604 ff., an episode that seamlessly follows the games for Anchises) seems pointless, given, again, the emphasis on long-distance oracles. It is more likely, considering that this is basically a foundation prodigy, that something about Segesta/Aigesta/Acesta is doomed already in the moment of foundation. A connection with the First Punic War seems to be in the air: Segesta will play a key role in the war precisely for its Trojan associations, and there are reasons to be apprehensive about its future in what will turn out to be the longest war in the whole of ancient history. A promising reference to that war has already been uncovered by David Traill in the parallel episode of the boxing match[7] between the Trojan Dares and the local champ Entellus, a pupil of the mythical athlete Eryx:

> stat grauis Entellus nisuque immotus eodem
> corpore tela modo atque oculis uigilantibus exit.
> ille, velut celsam oppugnat qui molibus urbem

aut montana sedet circum castella sub armis,
nunc hos, nunc illos aditus, omnemque pererrat
arte locum et variis adsultibus inritus urget.

5, 437–42

where the striking, unconventional simile likening the boxers to military skirmishes has an eerie resemblance to a passage in Polybius, where a Roman and a Carthaginian general waging a guerrilla are being compared, with inverse symmetry, to a pair of boxers (Polybius 1.56.1 ff.). The connection is mediated, as in the case of Segesta, via the location: the boxing match is overshadowed by the memory of the hero Eryx and by the view of Mt Eryx, and this landscape[8] is precisely the location of the war of attrition in Polybius. The Polybian text shows how important the connection is between the landscape and its military history: "Here [Hamilcar] he seized on a place called Hercte, lying near the sea between Eryx and Panormus, and thought to possess peculiar advantages for the safe and prolonged stay of an army. It is an abrupt hill rising to a considerable height from the surrounding flat country. The circumference of its brow is not less than a hundred stades and the plateau within affords good pasturage and is suitable for cultivation, being also favorably exposed to the sea-breeze and quite free of animals dangerous to life. On the side looking to the sea and on that which faces the interior of the island, this plateau is surrounded by inaccessible cliffs, while the parts between require only a little slight strengthening. There is also a knoll on it which serves for an acropolis as well as for an excellent post of observation over the country at the foot of the hill. Besides this Hercte commands a harbor very well situated for ships making the voyage from Drepana and Lilybaeum to Italy to put in at, and with an abundant supply of water. The hill has only three approaches, all difficult, two on the land side and one from the sea. Here Hamilcar established his quarters, at great risk indeed, since he had neither the support of any of their towns nor any prospect of support from elsewhere, but had thrown himself into the midst of the enemy. Notwithstanding this, the peril to which he put the Romans, and the combats to which he forced them, were by no means slight or insignificant. For in the first place he would sally out with his fleet from this place, and devastate the coast of Italy as far as Cumae, and next, after the Romans had taken up a position on land in front of the city of Panormus and at a distance of about five stades from his own camp, he harassed them by delivering during almost three years constant and variously contrived attacks by land. These combats I am unable to describe in detail here" (Polybius 1.56). After this emphasis on the identification between landscape and a seven-year war of attrition, and after a *recusatio* of his usual narrative strategies, Polybius goes on to unveil the key simile of the two boxers:

For as in a boxing-match when two champions, both distinguished for pluck and both in perfect training, meet in the decisive contest for the prize, continually delivering blow for blow, neither the combatants themselves nor the spectators can note or anticipate every attack or every blow, but it is possible, from the general action of each, and the determination that each displays, to get a fair idea of their respective skill, strength, and courage, so it was with these two generals. The causes or the modes of their daily ambuscades, counter-ambuscades, attempts, and assaults were so numerous that no writer could properly describe them, while at the same time the narrative would be most tedious as well as unprofitable to the reader. It is rather by a general pronouncement about the two men and the result of their rival efforts that a notion of the facts can be conveyed. Nothing was neglected; neither traditional tactics nor plans suggested by the occasion and by actual pressure of circumstances, nor those strokes which depend on a bold and strong initiative. Yet there were several reasons why no decisive success could be obtained. For the forces on each side were evenly matched; their trenches were so strong as to be equally unapproachable, and the camps were at a quite small distance from each other, this being the chief reason why there were daily conflicts at certain points, but no decisive engagement ...

But Fortune, however, like a good umpire, unexpectedly shifted the scene and changed the nature of the contest, confining both in a narrower field, where the struggle grew even more desperate ...

Polybius 1.57

I had to keep the quotation very long to show how deeply the sport imagery is connected to the military narrative: the description continues at 1.58.1–6 with three years of fighting in the Eryx mountain territory, and Tyche as the referee in a desperate "cockfight."[9]

The Polybius connection is a good example of the alliance between location, prophecy, history, and intertextuality that is so typical of the *Aeneid*. The connection with the First Punic War also affects the meaning of the omen, as Richard Heinze had explained long ago (2012: 165–9 [1 ed. 1903]) in a discussion of unparalleled efficacy. Like Heinze, I believe that the import of the omen is a negative one and that it affects the future of the famous city of Segesta that is in the process of being founded. Yet other texts and events can also contribute to this atmosphere. As we have seen, a reference in the *Aeneid* to *terrifici ... vates* and *sera omina*, to late, scary recollections of prophecy can be seen as a pattern suggesting intertextuality with Lycophron.[10] There is no need to limit the reference to a single occasion, since many locations in the *Aeneid* are historical wormholes, where different associations are kept in play: the Buthrotum area, for example, is fraught with memories/prophecies[11] of Greek menace (Pyrrhus), Roman colonization, and the triumph of Actium. If we are looking for bleak visions of Sicilian history as a history of violence, examples range from Pyrrhus to the Punic wars, to the social and slave wars of the first century BCE. The recent excavations at Selinus by Clemente Marconi have revealed a surprising number of spears and arrowheads in the main sacred precinct, and their setting invites interesting speculations: a militaristic colonial culture, martial rituals, perhaps memories of Greek and Punic recaptures of the city.[12]

Segesta had to suffer for its Trojan affiliation even before the Punic Wars, with the terrific destruction worked by the Greek tyrant Agathocles in 307 BCE, and in fact Aigesta (/Segesta) in Lycophron receives a warning that is dire even by the standards of the *Alexandra*:

Αἰγέστα τλῆμον, σοὶ δὲ δαιμόνων φραδαῖς
πένθος μέγιστον καὶ δι᾽ αἰῶνος πάτρας
ἔσται πυρὸς ῥιπαῖσιν ἠθαλωμένης.
μόνη δὲ πύργων δυστυχεῖς κατασκαφὰς
νήπαυστον αἰάζουσα καὶ γοωμένη
δαρὸν στενάξεις. πᾶς δὲ λυγαίαν λεὼς
ἐσθῆτα προστρόπαιον ἐγχλαινούμενος
αὐχμῷ πινώδης λυπρὸν ἀμπρεύσει βίον.
κρατὸς δ᾽ ἄκουρος νῶτα καλλυνεῖ φόβη,
μνήμην παλαιῶν τημελοῦσ᾽ ὀδυρμάτων.

Unhappy Egesta! For you, by divine ordinance
there shall be great and eternal mourning for my fatherland,
fired by the flicker of flames.
Desolate, you will long mourn for the calamitous destruction
Of its towers, with wailing and groaning
in perpetuity. And all your people, clad
in black suppliant dress,
shall drag out their sad lives in squalor and filth.
Their uncut hair shall beautify their backs,
Nursing the memory of old griefs.

968–77

The passage has a key function in the Greek poem, and well brings out the tragedy inscribed in its poetics (even at the level of metrical choice, tragic iambics not hexameter or elegy). It is the first time in Lycophron that we hear about a "new Ilion,"[13] and the vision of Cassandra is a study in dystopia: Lycophron short-circuits the mourning for the destruction of Troy with the doom that expects Segesta, a city yet to be founded and already haunted by an ill-fated *imitatio Troiae* (remember that both events are as yet existing in the Greek poem only at the level of prophecy). The shattering of the illusion gives even more edge to the unexpected emergence of Rome as a fortunate imitation of Troy at the end of the *Alexandra*. The blur between Troy and the Sicilian city is so complete that the first translation of this passage by Hornblower (2015: 363) has "your towers," later corrected "its towers" in the reprint. This accords well with the dark twist in Virgil's foundation prodigy and suggests a memory/prophecy of catastrophic events in the history of the Elymian city, not only the onset of the Punic wars, but also the tragic story told by Hellenistic historians of what Agathocles did to the city in 307 BCE.[14] The account of Diodorus, whatever its genealogy,[15] is representative of a trend in tragic historiography, and this kind of atmosphere is likely to have been influential on both Lycophron and Virgil, for two reasons: its lurid violence stands out even in the Hellenistic tradition of historiographic pathos, and the historian clearly draws tragic innuendo from the representation of a miniature Troy, a fragile imitation shattered by a repetition of the Ilioupersis (Diodorus Siculus 20. 71 1–4):

> When with all speed Agathocles had crossed from Libya into Sicily, he summoned a part of his army and went to the city of Segesta, which was an ally. Because he was in need of money, he forced the well-to-do to deliver to him the greater part of their property, the city at that time having a population of about ten thousand. Since many were angry at this and were holding meetings, he charged the people of Segesta with conspiring against him and visited the city with terrible disasters. For instance, the poorest of the people *he brought to a place outside the city beside the river Scamander and slaughtered them*; but those who were believed to have more property he examined under torture and compelled each to tell him how much wealth he had; and some of them he broke on the wheel, others he placed bound in the catapults and shot forth, and by applying knucklebones with violence to some, he caused them severe pain. He also invented another torture similar to the bull of Phalaris: that is, he prepared a brazen bed that had the form of a human body and was surrounded on every side by bars; on this he fixed those who were being tortured and roasted them alive, the contrivance being superior to the bull in this respect, that those who perishing in anguish were visible ... While the tyrant in this way was seeking all the wealth, great panic prevailed throughout the city, some burning themselves up along with their houses, and others gaining release from life by hanging. Thus Segesta,

encountering a single day of disaster, suffered the loss of all her men from youth upward. Agathocles then took the maidens and children across to Italy and sold them to the Bruttians, leaving not even the name of the city; but he changed the name to Dicaeopolis and gave it as dwelling to the deserters.[16]

The episode is potentially significant for Virgil, since it predates the devastation of the First Punic War, and anticipates a Trojan connection that makes Segesta a very special place in the Aeneas legend.[17] In the *Alexandra*, if one discounts the famous excursus on the rise of Rome, which in my opinion[18] reflects the first decade of the second century, an allusion to Agathocles would be one of the most recent historical events darkly alluded to by Cassandra.

A small detail in context confirms that the voice of Cassandra is active in *Aeneid* 5. Before the foundation of Acesta (Segesta) authorized by the prodigy, Virgil tells the story of how the Trojan women attempt to burn the ships. The story is highly relevant to the origins of Segesta, since the Trojan women left behind by Aeneas will be a defining part of the new community: we could imagine them among the people in black, suppliant dress who will forever mourn Troy in Lycophron's doomed Aigesta.

The burning of the ships is instigated by Iris, disguised as Trojan Beroe, and she explicitly mentions Cassandra as source and authority for the deed:

> nullane iam Troiae dicentur moenia? nusquam
> Hectoreos amnis, Xanthum et Simoenta, videbo?
> quin agite et mecum infaustas exurite puppis.　　　　　　　　635
> nam mihi **Cassandrae** per somnum **vatis imago**
> ardentis dare visa faces: "hic quaerite Troiam;
> hic domus est" inquit "vobis." iam tempus agi res ...

Time to act: the arson of the ships will be inspired by Cassandra, or more exactly by *Cassandrae uatis imago*, and the dream image emphasizes, like Lycophron, that the new city in Sicily will be the new Troy par excellence.[19] As we have seen, Agathocles will slaughter the Segestans on their own Scamander river.

The situation hangs in the balance, but there is a decisive intervention by another character, Pyrgo, an even older Trojan refugee:

> hic una e multis, quae maxima natu,
> Pyrgo, tot Priami natorum regia nutrix ...
>
> 　　　　　　　　　　　　　　　　5, 644–5

here one of the many, the eldest, Pyrgo, royal nurse of so many children of Priam ...

Pyrgo has been a witness to Iris' transformation into Beroe, and certifies that the speaker is indeed more than human. Her comment certainly contributes to the inflammatory situation,[20] and the Trojan women immediately attack the ships. In the light of the Cassandra connection, I would note that she might have been Cassandra's nurse, cf. 5, 645 *tot Priami natorum regia nutrix*, a Trojan nurse very different from the loyal Caieta who will travel with Aeneas to Italy and give her name to the first Trojan landing in Latium (*Aeneid* 7, 1–4). Perhaps the choice of the name Pyrgo is significant, since her emotional speech will contribute to the foundation of Segesta, where according to Lycophron the "towers," *pyrgoi* of Ilion (above, v. 971) will be mourned and memorialized forever.

This reminiscence of the *Alexandra* in the *Aeneid* complements a model of self-reflexive appropriation that is already familiar to studies of Lycophron's influence in Augustan poetry: the appropriation is accompanied by ideas of prophecy or oracular communication, and of memory; the effect recreates a model that is prophetic, obscure, and comes from the deep past, since the *Alexandra* poet impersonates Cassandra who delivers her prophecy long before the fall of Troy. But there is a second feature which is also important if we want to understand the impact of Lycophron: it is the emphasis on location, and on the location of prophecies in territories. Colonial territories one might say, places of hope and doom. Lycophron's Tower Lady will end up in a city of sorrow, while Virgil's Ashen Lady (Caieta, cf. *Aen.* 7, 1–4) will be a harbinger of Rome reborn.

The *Alexandra* has a special status as a model for Virgil. It is featured as an intertext representing a "study in black" of much the same narrative material, and here lies its special fascination. "The *Aeneid* – writes Emily Gowers–,[21] we know well, is filled with the rustle of alternative dramas." The *Alexandra* is a major provider of this rustle or background effect. It is the *oeuvre au noir* that always offers a worst-case scenario, as an alternative for the Latin poem of Trojan re-foundation and Roman foundation.[22] This darkness visible in the background of the *Aeneid* is the signature style of Lycophron: it is well-known that the *Alexandra* thematises this aspect by using words like *kelainos* and *skotos* and *zophos* in a programmatic, self-conscious way:[23] the messenger, in his programmatic introduction, has in mind fear of the dark as well as inability to grasp the true meanings of the prophecy. Statius, as ever an ace reader of the Greek tradition (cf. *TrGF* 100 T 3 *skoteinon poiema*), picks up those effects in his one-liner about Lycophron: *latebras ... Lycophronis atri* (*silu.* 5.3, 157), where *atri* not only reinforces *latebras* (the riddling, obscure style, a source of toil and pride for Statius' father, the professor of Greek letters who is able to tame the Sphinx) but also connotes "somber, sinister, gloomy, dark" and refers to theme, not only style.

A Study in Black

On the one side, as McNelis and Sens have successfully emphasized, the *Alexandra* prepares a surprising, ameliorative turning point in history: the future glory of the Trojans via Aeneas and the new empire in the West, and paves the way to Virgil.[24] Yet, it is also important to follow the use of the *Alexandra* as a dark foil to the new Latin poem: the imperial poetics of the *Aeneid* requires this background, and draws on the entire tradition of Greek tragedies of Trojan argument, of which Lycophron's poem is an extreme and twisted successor.

If I had to select, perhaps irrationally, a single representative detail, it would be the story of the sow prodigy and the foundation by Aeneas of a city in Latium. This is the version of the story in Lycophron: after the resolution of the oracle of hunger and the eaten tables (on which see above), Aeneas becomes a founder:

κτίσει δὲ χώραν ἐν τόποις Βορειγόνων
ὑπὲρ Λατίνους Δαυνίους τ' ᾠκισμένην,
πύργους τριάκοντ᾽, ἐξαριθμήσας γονὰς
<u>συὸς κελαινῆς</u>, ἣν ἀπ᾽ Ἰδαίων λόφων
καὶ Δαρδανείων ἐκ τόπων ναυσθλώσεται,
ἰσηρίθμων θρέπτειραν ἐν τόκοις κάπρων·
ἧς καὶ πόλει δείκηλον ἀνθήσει μιᾷ
χαλκῷ τυπώσας καὶ τέκνων γλαγοτρόφων

> He will found a place in the regions of the Aborigines . . . thirty towers, numbered after the offspring of *the dark sow*, which he will have brought by ship from the peaks of Ida and the Dardanian regions, the nurse of the same number of piglets, all from one litter. In one of those cities he will dedicate an image of her and her suckling brood, crafting it in bronze.

Kelainos, skotos, Lycophronis atri, dark sow. If we take the passage as typical Hellenistic aetiology, "dark" could be alluding to the *bronze* statue ("bronze" is the first word of line 1260) that finishes the passage: a compression of a typical Hellenistic or Varronian *aition*, with the event + the foundation + the memorial in art. Yet, it remains true that the choice of *kelainos* is intentionally at odds with the tradition about Alba Longa; even more importantly, it hints at a larger truth about the *Alexandra*: the poem is deliberately a "study in black" of many traditional stories, and the "black sow" could be a self-reflexive touch, or a signature by the poet. This is important to Virgil when he appropriates the dark voice of Cassandra in the *Aeneid*. It is in the manner of the Latin poem to turn those clues from black to white:

Ecce autem subitum atque oculis mirabile monstrum,
candida per silvam cum fetu **concolor albo**
procubuit **viridique** in litore conspicitur sus.

Virgil, *Aeneid* 8, 81–3[25]

Acknowledgment

I am grateful to Simon Hornblower for his generous help with this paper. Translations from Lycophron are from his 2015 edition (with reprint 2018; see also his forthcoming (2022) text of Lycophron for Oxford World's Classics.

Notes

1 West (1984) and Horsfall (2005) are influential starters in this discussion.
2 Barchiesi (1994) discusses the revelation on Delos ("The Clear") and its unique character. All Virgilian passages about the search for Italy via oracles, explorations, hints and prophecies are helpfully analyzed in Fletcher (2014).
3 Paschalis (1997), 84, notes the pun. Elaine Fantham has pointed out (see Fantham, 1983, on Seneca, *Troades* 570 and 603) the "obsessive recurrence of *cassus*" in Seneca's *Troades*, a drama where Cassandra is important (cf. also 37 *uana uates ante Cassandram fui*).
4 For the approach in this paragraph cf. West (1984); Klein (2009; with similar situations in Propertius).
5 Edlund (1987).
6 Space forbids a rehearsal of the various positions; for a recent discussion, that includes some really unlikely interpretations, see, e.g., Fratantuono and Smith (2018), *ad loc.*
7 Traill (2001), 405–13.
8 A landscape that is being "made" during the action of the Virgilian text: the narrative of Book 5 of the Aeneid shows how the place acquires the defining hilltop precinct of Venus Erycina, the city of Segesta, and the memorial *lucus* for Anchises: a good instance of what I discuss as "geopoetics" (see Barchiesi 2017, 2021a–b on the landscapes and cityscapes of Buthrotum and Cumae).
9 See also Goldschmidt (2013), 121–2, for the possibility that the similarity between Virgil and Polybius has something to do with the narrative of those

events in the largely lost *Bellum Poenicum* of Naevius, a significant model for the Aeneid.

10 On self-reflexive mentions of prophets, oracles and riddles in connection with echoes of Lycophron in Roman poetry note e.g. the paper by Klein (2009).

11 On the relevance of those associations, see Barchiesi (2017).

12 See the exciting discussion of the discovery in Ward and Marconi (2020), and note in general the papers in Jonasch (2020).

13 Note that many scholars claim that Segesta is a "first" in the history of political invocations of the Aeneas legend and of Trojan ancestry, cf. Erskine (2001), 178–84; Gruen (1993), 44–5; Hornblower (2015), ad 968 and 969.

14 The possible link is not mentioned in the very thorough commentary by Hornblower 2015; one sentence only in Gigante Lanzara (2003), 367. The fact is that the connection with Agathocles had been claimed only once, by Guenther (1889), 13–14, in the context of a clearly untenable attempt to secure a dating of Lycophron's poem between 306 and 285 BCE. Guenther even claims that the passage indicates autopsy of Segesta's recent devastation by the poet of the *Alexandra*. The use of this implied historical reference as an argument for the chronology of the text has been easily dismissed by Geffcken (1892), 26 n. 5 and by others, but once we get rid of Guenther's agenda the similarity of tone with Diodorus remains intriguing.

15 Simon Hornblower kindly points out to me that problems remain about the sources of Diodorus on Agathocles, but I have no contribution to offer in this area. It is enough for me to argue that the episode cannot be entirely an innovation by Diodorus, and must have models in earlier Hellenistic writing about the fall of cities. For the likely derivation of this passage from Timaeus cf. de Lisle (2021), 30–1, 89, 171–3; for hatred of Agathocles as distinctive of Timaeus' history of the West, note e.g. Baron (2012), 19, 61–2.

16 The account is so brutal that I apologize for the full quotation.

17 Cf. note 12.

18 As argued by Hornblower (2015) and (2018).

19 As an analogy, we could think of Buthrotum in Book 3, an imitation of Troy but also a city already under the shadow of Pyrrhus the III century king of Epirus; cf. the hesitations and ominous nuances in Aeneas' speech at 3, 497–505, and on the importance of Pyrrhus in Virgil note the important chapter in Quint (2018), 28–66. On the Beroe passage in Book 5 as a pastiche of Cassandra's voice cf. the comments of Pillinger (2019), 157.

20 Pyrgo's function is sometimes characterized as an attempt to discredit Beroe and stop the sedition, but I fail to see how the testimony that Beroe is more than human could be interpreted as a dissuasion: the situation is quite different from that of Laocoön in Book 2.

21 Gowers (2016), 107.
22 Graziosi (2020), 28–32, has elegant comments on foundations and returns in Homer, Lycophron and Virgil.
23 See Hornblower (2015) on lines 7 and 12, and the index s.vv. *dark, darkness,* and *black*; Sistakou (2012). Note, e.g., 1425 "black thirst."
24 McNelis and Sens (2016). Their view of the poem, like mine, accepts the idea of a composition of the entire text in the early second century by an author conversant with the rise of Rome in the Greek wars of that period.
25 Cf. *Aeneid* 3, 392 *alba . . . albi* in the prophecy of Helenus.

Bibliography

Ahl, F., ed. (2007), *Virgil's Aeneid*, Oxford: Oxford University Press.

Asper, M. and V. Rimell, eds. (2017), *Imagining Empire: Political Space in Hellenistic and Roman Literature*, Heidelberg: Universitätsverlag.

Barchiesi, A. (1994), "Immovable Delos: *Aeneid* 3.73–98 and the *Hymns* of Callimachus," *Classical Quarterly*, 44: 438–43.

Barchiesi, A. (2017), "Colonial Readings in Vergilian Geopoetics: The Trojans at Buthrotum," in M. Asper and V. Rimell (eds.), *Imagining Empire: Political Space in Hellenistic and Roman Literature*, 151–66, Heidelberg: Universitätsverlag.

Barchiesi, A. (2021a), "Aeneas in Campania: Notes on Naevius as a Model for the Aeneid," in S. Oberhelman, P. Baker, and G. Abbamonte (eds.), Habent Sua Fata Libelli: *Studies in Book History and the Classical Tradition in Honor of Craig Kallendorf*, 19–33, Leiden and New York: Brill.

Barchiesi, A. (2021b), "Into the Woods," in B. Gladhill and M. Myers (eds.), *Walking throough Elysium*, 19–33, Toronto: University of Toronto Press.

Baron, C. A. (2012), *Timaeus of Tauromenium and Hellenistic Historiography*, Cambridge: Cambridge University Press.

Belloni, L., L. De Finis, and G. Moretti, eds. (2003), *L'officina ellenistica*, Trento: Università degli studi di Trento, Dipartimento di Scienze Filologiche e Storiche.

Cusset, C. and E. Prioux, eds. (2009), *Lycophron: éclats d'obscurité*, Saint-Étienne: Publications de l'Université de Saint-Étienne.

de Lisle, C. (2021), *Agathokles of Syracuse: Sicilian Tyrant and Hellenistic King*, Oxford: Oxford University Press.

Edlund, I. E. M. (1987), "The Sacred Geography of Southern Italy in Lycophron's Alexandra," *Opuscula Romana*, 16: 43–9.

Erskine, A. (2013), *Troy between Greece and Rome*, Oxford: Oxford University Press.

Fantham, E. (1983), *Seneca's Troades*, Princeton, NJ: Princeton University Press.

Fletcher, K. F. B. (2014), *Finding Italy: Travel, Nation and Colonization in Vergil's Aeneid*, Ann Arbor, MI: University of Michigan Press.

Fratantuono, L. and R. Alden Smith (2018), *Virgil, Aeneid*, Leiden and Boston, MA: Brill.

Geffcken, J. (1892), *Timaios' Geographie des Westens*, Berlin: Weidmann.

Gigante Lanzara, V. (2003), "I difficili approdi. La colonizzazione mitica dell'Occidente nei vaticini di Cassandra," in L. Belloni, L. De Finis, and G. Moretti (eds.), *L'officina ellenistica*, 337–67, Trento: Università degli studi di Trento, Dipartimento di Scienze Filologiche e Storiche.

Gladhill, B. and M. Myers, M., eds. (2021), *Walking through Elysium*, Toronto: University of Toronto Press.

Goldschmidt, N. (2013), *Shaggy Crowns: Ennius' Annales and Virgil's Aeneid*, Oxford and New York: Oxford University Press.

Gowers, E. (2016), "Dido and the Owl," in P. Mitsis and I. Ziogas (eds.), *Wordplay and Powerplay in Latin Poetry*, 107–30, Berlin and New York: Walter de Gruyter.

Graziosi, B. (2020), "Ritorno e fondazione da Omero a Ugo Foscolo," in A. Barchiesi and B. Graziosi, *Ritorni difficili*, 9–25, Roma: Storia e Letteratura.

Gruen, E. (1993), *Culture and National Identity in Republican Rome*, Ithaca, NY, and London: Cornell University Press.

Guenther, P. (1889), "De ea, quae inter Timaeum et Lycophronem intercedit, ratione," PhD diss., Leipzig.

Heinze, R. (2012), *Virgils epische Technik*, Berlin and Boston, MA: B. G. Teubner.

Hornblower, S. (2015), *Lycophron's Alexandra*, Oxford: Oxford University Press.

Hornblower, S. (2018), *Lycophron's Alexandra, Rome, and the Hellenistic World*, Oxford: Oxford University Press.

Hornblower, S. (2022), *The Alexandra of Lykophron*, Oxford: Oxford University Press.

Horsfall, N. (2005), "Lycophron and the *Aeneid*, Again," *Illinois Classical Studies*, 30: 35–40.

Jonasch, M., ed. (2020), *The Fight for Greek Sicily: Society, Politics, and Landscape*, Oxford and Haverton, PA: Oxbow Books.

Klein, F. (2009), "La réception de Lycophron dans la poésia augustéenne: le point de vue de Cassandre et le dispositif poétique de l'*Alexandra*," in C. Cusset and E. Prioux (eds.), *Lycophron: éclats d'obscurité*, 561–92, Saint-Étienne: Publications de l'Université de Saint-Étienne.

McNelis, C. and A. Sens (2016), *The Alexandra of Lycophron: A Literary Study*, Oxford: Oxford University Press.

Mitsis, P. and I. Ziogas, eds. (2016), *Wordplay and Powerplay in Latin Poetry*, Berlin and New York: Walter de Gruyter.

Oberhelman, S., P. Baker, and G. Abbamonte, eds. (2021), Habent Sua Fata Libelli: *Studies in Book History and the Classical Tradition in Honor of Craig Kallendorf*, Leiden and New York: Brill.

Pillinger, E. (2019), *Cassandra and the Poetics of Prophecy in Greek and Latin Literature*, Cambridge: Cambridge University Press.

Quint, D. (2018), *Virgil's Double Cross*, Princeton, NJ: Princeton University Press.

Sistakou, E. (2012), *The Aesthetics of Darkness*, Leuven, Paris and Walpole, MA: Peeters.

Traill, D. A. (2001), "Boxers and Generals at Mount Eryx," *American Journal of Philology*, 122: 405–13.

Ward, A. and C. Marconi (2020), "War and the Life of a Sacred Structure: Weapons from the NYU-UniMi Excavations in the Main Urban Sanctuary of Selinunte," in M. Jonasch (ed.), *The Fight for Greek Sicily: Society, Politics, and Landscape*, 19–45, Oxford and Haverton, PA: Oxbow Books.

West, S. (1984), "Lycophron Italicised," *Journal of Hellenic Studies*, 104: 127–51.

17

Father Ammon and the King

Jay Reed
Brown University

σοφίας καὶ τέχνης χάριν

The *Aeneid* tells that the African king Iarbas, "the son of Jupiter-Ammon by the Garamantian nymph he raped" (4.198 *Hammone satus rapta Garamantide nympha*), "established in his wide realm one hundred vast temples to the god, one hundred altars . . ., and the ground was fat with the blood of livestock and the doorsills abloom with all kinds of garlands" (199–202):

> templa Iovi centum latis immania regnis,
> centum aras posuit . . .,
>   pecudumque cruore
> pingue solum et variis florentia limina sertis.

Hearing rumors of Aeneas' union with Dido, whom he himself had aided and sought to marry, Iarbas makes the rounds of these temples (*dicitur*, "so it is said") and imprecates the god, challenging his inattention and inactivity: "Do you observe all this? Or do we tremble at you for nought, father, when you hurl your thunderbolts?" (208–9 *aspicis haec? an te, genitor, cum fulmina torques, / nequiquam horremus?*). "Yet we bring offerings to your temples," he sardonically concludes, "and cherish an empty story [that I am your son]" (217–18 *nos munera templis / quippe tuis ferimus, famamque fovemus inanem*).

Readers of Rameses II's "Kadesh Poem" (after 1274 BCE) will be reminded of the Egyptian king's desperate (and successful) appeal in battle to the selfsame deity:

> What is this, father Amun?
> Is it right for a father to ignore his son?
> Are my deeds a matter for you to ignore? . . .

What are these Asiatics to you, o Amun,
The wretches ignorant of god?
Have I not made you many great monuments,
Filled your temple with my booty . . .?
I brought you all lands to supply your altars,
I sacrificed to you ten thousands of cattle,
all kinds of sweet-scented herbs . . .[1]

Iarbas' roster of offerings, unlike that of Rameses, is external to his prayer—but Iarbas does indignantly invoke them in lines 217–18. Both kings, moreover, indict the god for favoring the "wretched Asiatic": Iarbas in a Greek-derived gendered othering of Aeneas (215 *ille Paris cum semiviro comitatu*, "that Paris with his crew of half-men"), later to be used against the Trojans by Italian opponents;[2] Rameses in a pharaonic expression of the imperative to maintain the order and integrity (*mꜣꜥt*) of Egypt by repelling foreigners as representatives of chaotic forces (*jsft*), in a chain of conceptual descent and inheritance necessarily claimed by each ruler and each dynasty in turn.[3]

The dense similarities could either be discounted as coincidence or, at the opposite extreme of certainty, ascribed to *in situ* knowledge of the Kadesh inscriptions on Virgil's part (via Egyptian priests, à la Hecataeus or Herodotus?), but Manning points the way toward a more productive explanation: "The behavior of Ptolemy IV in the Raphia decree (217 BC) reads like the much earlier description of Rameses II's battle of Kadesh. In a similar fashion, reading Polybius (V.85.8) one almost has the feeling that he was looking at the Abu Simbel reliefs of Rameses II while he was writing his description of the battle of Raphia." Although such intermediate sources as existed may not be recoverable, elements of Rameses' language could clearly have reached Virgil through Ptolemaic adaptations. "[T]he Ptolemies looked to the New Kingdom pharaohs, the great military conquerors, for inspiration [in legitimating their sovereignty]. Egyptian history was used to justify, and broadcast, Ptolemaic rule."[4] The "Kadesh Poem" represents a recalibration of the reciprocal obligations between god and king, "and Amun's intervention on [the latter's] behalf is an impressive witness to, and confirmation of, Ramesses' divine right to the throne";[5] his victory confirms him as the embodiment of a regal function of preserving *mꜣꜥt* and the proper relations between king, god, and people. The royal significance of Amun-Re's patronage and paternity was consolidated by the New Kingdom and ultimately assimilated by the Ptolemies following Alexander himself, whose rulership in his historical career and in later biographical tradition the god confirmed from both the Egyptian viewpoint (e.g., in Memphis) and the Greek (e.g., in Siwah).[6]

Amun's Hellenization as Ammon and identification with Zeus were already as old as a hymn by Pindar (fr. 36 Maehler) and *Pythian* 4.16, there within the Argonautic myth of Euphemus' clod that guarantees Greek colonialist claims in north Africa.[7]

The *Aeneid*'s image of Iarbas is part of a larger transculturation of imperial symbolism. Hellenists have explicated how the Ptolemies commandeered the native iconography and mythology of rulership to legitimate their own rule in Egypt; Romanists have explored how Augustus and his agents, in remaking the urban landscape, selectively and emulously appropriated this very appropriation—perhaps more precisely, that of his defeated rival Cleopatra—in an advertisement of the passing of supremacy to Rome.[8] Augustus' dedication of obelisks to the sun god in Rome is a replication of the Ptolemies' gestures of overlordship (by which they transported pharaonic monuments to their own capital) and an *interpretatio* of the monuments' function in Egypt. As Kákosy summarizes, "The obelisks, immortalizing the coming of Egypt under Roman dominion, at the same time advertised its glorious past and the greatness of its gods—now champions of Augustus."[9] Egypt functions as the original empire and its icons as the language of empire,[10] even communicating an Alexander-derived dream of world empire that Romans had long entertained and now claimed. Addressing an earlier phase in this program of supersession through imitation, Acosta-Hughes speaks of Julius Caesar's "attempt to transfer Alexandria to Rome … recreating throughout the city the presence of another city, and another imagined imperial space."[11]

Virgil himself had early begun adapting an Egyptian image of the leader. The sacrifices Tityrus promises his "present god" in *Eclogue* 1.40–3 replicate Ptolemaic usage;[12] the "star of Venus' child Caesar" in 9.47, linked to the flourishing of crops, hints at a duly apotheosized ruler's benefits for his country. In *Aeneid* 8.681 that star shines paternally above the new ruler's head at the battle of Actium. In *Georgics* 1.32–5 Augustus himself—by now literally king of Egypt—is expected to become a god in the form of a "new star" between Virgo and Scorpio; the image and phrasing point back to Callimachus' *Lock* and its reimagining of Egyptian royal apotheosis.[13] And in *Georgics* 3.28 the Nile, "flowing big," does not deny Augustus its flood's old symbolic burden of victory, kingship, and the fertility of the land.[14] Virgil, like Alexandrian poets, is "experimenting with a variety of inherited traditions in order to construct a lineation for the king of the Nile, who is neither Greek nor Egyptian, but both"—and now Roman as well.[15] In those passages, however, Virgil projects royal qualities onto Roman leaders; the Iarbas passage rather does so onto the Roman founder's rival. Like Aeneas,

Iarbas descends from Jupiter, but in a combined African and Greco-Egyptian mode. His piety mirrors *pius* Aeneas and models a ruler like Augustus, who on Aeneas' shield is seen consecrating enormous (*maxima*) temples and offering sacrifices (*Aeneid* 8.716, 719). But in answering Iarbas' prayer, Jupiter confirms not his son's claims over Carthage,[16] but Aeneas' Roman destiny; the Jupiter-Mercury-Aeneas relay that ensues will propel Aeneas away from Carthage and ultimately transmit authority to Rome and Augustus.

The image of royal legitimacy in an Egyptianized African king is itself, moreover, enmeshed in the Roman reception and contestation of Hellenistic monarchical discourse. Consider first a late Republican myth of the constellation Aries. A ram, suddenly appearing to Bacchus' army in the African desert, miraculously led it to water. Naming the ram Jupiter Ammon, Bacchus endowed it with a magnificent temple on the spot where water was found (presumably the Siwah oasis); in a further elevation, the ram "achieved the stars of heaven" for its good deed (*aries, dux aquae, caeli sidera consecutus*). This is P. Nigidius Figulus, sidestepping the Argonautic etiology of Aries (the Helle and Phrixus narrative retailed in [Eratosthenes], *Catasterisms* 19) for one ascribed to Hermippus of Smyrna, a follower of Callimachus (*SH* 490 = [Hyginus], *Astronomia* 2.20.3), to which he adds the ram's identification with the ram-horned deity.[17] Evident are further influences close to Ptolemaic ideology, especially Dionysius Scytobrachion's account of the originally "Libyan" Bacchus' conquests, which in turn is indebted to Euhemeristic theology and the biographical literature on Alexander.[18]

Alongside Varro and Cicero, Nigidius (died 45 BCE) was among the most prominent Roman transmitters and reshapers of knowledge in the last generation of the Republic, when waxing autocracy in Rome raised the stakes of the Romanization of discourses of rulership, including Egyptian kingship.[19] Astrology itself, long associated with Egyptian origins and lore, "had emerged in the Roman world as individual generals began to dominate the scene" and ultimately "belonged with the sole ruler, as state diviners belonged with the Republic."[20] In Nigidius' zodiac etiologies—creative, eclectic myths aligned with the intellectual movements of his political class—plays out a contestation between models of governance, one inevitable in the Romans' reception of Greek literature, which was always implicated in its Hellenistic sociopolitical context[21] and pregnant with autocratic challenges to Roman notions of shared aristocratic power. Euhemerus' doctrine, devised in the decades after Alexander's death, that the gods originated as human rulers who achieved divine rewards for their great deeds was part of Roman political thought at least since Ennius[22] and inflected the discursive and pragmatic negotiations in Nigidius' time over divine honors paid to contemporary leaders—negotiations that would lead to the literary and liturgical deifications and catasterisms of Julius Caesar, Augustus, and others.[23]

Nigidius asserts merited immortality for his zodiacal figures for their justice, *pietas*, and euergetism to humanity in general or assistance to particular deities. In his Virgo—a reworking of Aratus' myth[24] as his Aries is of Hermippus—a woman named "Justice" (*Iustitia*), who teaches the people fair dealing, is rewarded for this *pietas* with divinity (*ad immortales merito pervenerit ... immortale praemium pietatis possedit*). His accounts of Libra, Sagittarius, Aquarius, and Pisces likewise involve rewards for culture heroes honored for some combination of *pietas* and *iustitia*—the same qualities that earn statesmen, generals, and civic benefactors a path to heaven in Cicero's *Dream of Scipio* (16). Nigidius' Gemini honors both the Samothracian mystery gods and the Dioscuri, who endured perils "sailing for the golden fleece with Jason and Hercules" and keep the sea safe from pirates and crime (*praedonibus maleficiisque pacatum*).[25] Bacchus, the Samothracian gods, the Dioscuri, and Hercules recall the "Ptolemaic pantheon" of immortalized benefactors—originally cultivated "to bolster [the Ptolemies'] own claims to legitimacy and/or divinity (Dionysus, Heracles), or to articulate Greek claims to North Africa (the legend of the Argonauts, Helen in Egypt)"— that will also emerge in Augustan literature, adjoined to Roman heroes like Quirinus and Julius Caesar.[26]

Negotiating the distance between Republican and monarchical rewards, Nigidius' origin story of Ammon evinces a distinctly Alexandrian discursive nexus of conquest, benefaction, and apotheosis. His Capricorn myth explicitly connects these ideas with Egyptian kingship.[27] To the gods in council, despairing of either sharing the earth with the monstrous Typhon or resisting his brutality (*immanitati*) and unremitting atrocities (*scelera*), Pan gave the advice to disguise themselves as animals until they could secure their vengeance.[28] Typhon, entering Egypt and finding it apparently empty of rulers, made himself the country's master (*dominabatur*), only to be slain by the gods eighteen days later. They thereupon honored Pan with the half-goat constellation and built him the magnificent city of Panopolis. The account transfuses through Greek terms an Egyptian myth of the triumph of order in the primordial vanquishing of Seth, symbolically reenacted by every king,[29] and indeed Nigidius' myth segues— through the location of Typhon's death in the coronation city of Memphis—into a passage of rich detail about the Egyptian coronation ceremony (*solio regio decorari reges*), effecting an implicit etiology of sole rule.[30] Capricorn was to figure prominently in Augustus' iconography after his accession to the Ptolemies' throne, in conjunction with a plethora of symbols expropriated from their rich discourse of rulership.[31]

Now consider a myth composed shortly after the *Aeneid*, one that assimilates Africa to Egypt within a ktistic frame reminiscent of Virgil's plot. King Juba II of Mauretania (a realm contrived by Augustus out of Roman dependencies stretching from west of Carthage to the Atlantic)[32] wrote in Book III of his *Libyca*:[33] "After the sack of Troy Diomedes was cast ashore [ἐξεβράσθη] in Libya, where the king was Lycus, who customarily sacrificed visitors [ξένους] to his father Ares. His daughter Callirhoe, falling in love with Diomedes, betrayed her father and freed Diomedes from his bonds. He, however, sailed away neglectful of his benefactress, and she hanged herself."[34] The myth projects onto "Libya"— basically the southern coast of the Mediterranean and its broad hinterland, minus the Nile delta and valley—a Greek image of Egypt: King Busiris' sacrifice of visitors was a key myth in Athenian constructions of Egypt as other.[35]

In Apollonius' *Argonautica* 4.1393–1457 the parched Argonauts, traversing the Sahara, come upon a spring created by Heracles. Alexander's biographical tradition notes a (possibly miraculous) downpour on his desert journey to Siwah.[36] Hermippus' and Nigidius' myths of the sacred oasis are bound up with etiologies of royal and divine legitimacy and honors. Stephens interprets a sudden access of water amid drought in Ptolemaic myth as a tendentious analogue to the Nile flood, with its import for authorized kingship.[37] In Juba's myth, Princess Callirhoe takes the place of any such "beautiful stream" gushing in the desert in recognition of royal or immortal deserts. As a suicidal African noblewoman she resonates against Sophoniba and Cleopatra (both with personal connections to Juba[38]); as a lovelorn heroine betraying her father she recalls Ariadne and Scylla; as a barbarian princess who rescues the Greek newcomer from her father's cruelty she particularly resembles the Medea of Apollonius and Scytobrachion. Most pertinently, foundational *erōtes* figure in Greek *nostoi* and *ktisis* legends: "The erotic response of a foreign woman to the arrival of an adventuring male is legible as a projection of colonial discourse that functions to legitimate the intruder (and his desires for acquisition) within this alien territory."[39] In Juba's time Dido is the obvious literary parallel.[40] Setting up a Virgilian complex of alterity and destiny in an Africa Egyptianized through distinctly Greco-Macedonian colonialist tropes, Juba rewrites and reconfigures Italian origins to center them on Greek Diomedes, shipwrecked in Libya on his way to found a colony in Italy.

It is tempting to speculate on Juba's engagement with Iullus Antonius' *Diomedeia* in twelve books on Aeneas' old antagonist,[41] whose post-Troy adventures—perhaps including the shipwreck and the princess—could have offered this son of Mark Antony a means to reassess his hero's role as Italian colonist as against *Aeneid* 11.243–95.[42] The Augustan period attests the first multi-book Latin epics on the Trojan War heroes' wanderings, *nostoi*, and colonizations, filling out the stories in and around the *Iliad* and *Odyssey* in a quasi-Cyclic completion of Homer—and now of Virgil. In Largus' epic on Antenor we should certainly see a response to the *problēma* posed by the *Aeneid*'s description of Aeneas as "first" to come from Troy to Italy—where, according to Venus at 1.242–9, Antenor had already settled.[43] The *Diomedeia* of Iullus—the half-brother of Juba's wife Cleopatra Selene (they had all grown up together in Octavia's household)—could have similarly pried open ambiguities in the Virgilian *ktisis*, as could Juba's narrative in prose. But Juba, descendent of Numidian kings and husband of a Ptolemy, was not only imagining but *living* his myth's syllepsis of Egypt and Africa. His *Libyca* was part of a far-reaching scholarly agenda "about the southern reaches of the known world, connecting his wife's ancestral kingdom with his new one."[44] Their realm, "one nation of Egypt and Libya,"[45] was a sort of continuation of Ptolemaic Egypt by other means—contained under Augustan supervision. Their coinage included Capricorn and cornucopias, Augustan golden-age imagery calqued on Ptolemaic; by naming their son Ptolemy they "continue the Ptolemaic dynasty and nullify its deposing."[46] But Ptolemaic monarchy dissipates in the desert; Augustus and his successors inherit the throne of Egypt and its discursive riches.

As Augustus leaves Ptolemaic rulership, in its bodily form, to a Numido-Ptolemaic client kingdom in North Africa, diverting its power and the power of its symbolic language to himself and Rome, so Iarbas—whose name and Garamantian-Gaetulian affinities evoke the historical background to Augustus' disposition of Africa[47]—disappears from the *Aeneid* once he delivers his pharaonic appeal. Bypassing the child of his rape of an indigenous African nymph, Ammon authenticates Aeneas and his lineage as he does Alexander and other rulers of Egypt. Rameses is central to the Kadesh narrative, a complex ratification of his status; Iarbas is one link in a concatenation of rumors, provocations, and responses—a "confluence of stimuli" that "occurs nowhere else in the *Aeneid*"[48]—and his rhetoric, spurred by Fama, is diverted by Jupiter into a different direction. "The Libyan king," Hejduk says, "shrewdly targets Jupiter's two weak spots, questioning both his power and the *fama* that derives from it . . . Jupiter's response, not surprisingly, is couched entirely in terms of *imperium* and *fama*."[49] Inevitably in this poem *imperium* and *fama* collapse into one. *Dicitur* ("so it is said") in 204 defers this story itself—including Iarbas' response to Fama's *rumor* and his meditation on the *fama* of his divine paternity in 217–18—to *fama*, which can include, as well as rumors and oracles, the very words of command and report; the inscriptions (Rameside and Ptolemaic) and intermediary texts through which Egyptian royal protocols passed to Virgil; and the discursive nodes drawn and undone by Scytobrachion, Hermippus, Nigidius, Juba, Iullus, and all others.[50] It is the medium of these claims to power and of the intertexts by which we historicize them. The poem allegorizes its revisions of them and turns us to a more epistemological, as well as a more political, reading. *Fama*, moreover, embraces ambiguity, dialogue, and polycentrism in narrative (or even within an imperial household), the discursive paths not taken, the corrections and supplements to other narratives of authority. As against the "Kadesh Poem," the *Aeneid* divides the content of the king's appeal between the external narrative and Iarbas' words, but it enframes the whole story as something "said," the latest in a series of mythical claims over Africa going back to the Pindaric Pytho's auspicious report of Euphemus' clod.

The reference to Augustus' own "three hundred enormous temples to the gods of Italy" on Aeneas' shield (8.716) occurs during his triumph, a description both historical and deeply embedded in multilayered *fama*, as Vulcan's interpretation of the predictions of "prophetic bards" (627 *vatum*) and as designated by the narrator as the "fame and fate" of Aeneas' descendants (731 *famamque et fata*).[51] The temples and sacrifices here parallel Iarbas' donations; the entryway, however, is abloom not with "all kinds of garlands," but with foreign tribute recalling Rameses' temple-filling spoils (*Aeneid* 8.719–26):

> ante aras terram caesi stravere iuvenci.
> ipse sedens niveo candentis limine Phoebi   720
> dona recognoscit populorum aptatque superbis
> postibus; incedunt victae longo ordine gentes,
> quam variae linguis, habitu tam vestis et armis.
> hic Nomadum genus et discinctos Mulciber Afros,
> hic Lelegas Carasque sagittiferosque Gelonos
> finxerat; Euphrates ibat iam mollior undis . . .

Slaughtered steers have strewn the ground before the altars. Augustus himself, seated at the gleaming threshold of the Bright God, acknowledges the gifts of the nations and fastens them to the proud doorposts. The vanquished populations march in long file, as varied in their garb and weaponry as in their speech. Here Vulcan had imagined the Numidian people and the loose-robed Africans, the Leleges and Carians and Gelonians with their arrows; the Euphrates was flowing more meekly now . . .

The defeat of the motley army and monster-gods of Antony and Cleopatra (685–712) yields to a vision of Augustus' authority that rests precisely on his devotion to, and patronage by, a solar deity and his pacification of "others" to the east, west, and north of Egypt (including Africans). The very message requires accepting Greco-Egyptian convictions as it adds the Roman imperator to a long continuum of global rulership and world order; the pharaonic protocols once adopted by the Greco-Macedonians for use over Egypt—now by Rome over Greco-Macedonian Egypt—are themselves spoils of conquest.

Rome itself is not exactly a "contact zone," in Pratt's terms, of cultural exchange and accommodation between colonizer and colonized. But Roman culture was long a space in which Romans practiced a poetics of *imitatio* and *aemulatio* against earlier world rulers, addressed to both Romans and non-Romans and crafted in terms taken over from the Hellenistic world. Roman "Alexandrianism" was as ideological as aesthetic, and the history of Latin literature—which coincides with the spread of Roman *imperium* beyond Italy—also charts a developing, though ever contested, political identity. Once Rome's *imperium* is headed by a sole ruler (himself king of Egypt), the Ptolemies' appropriation of an Egyptian discourse of legitimate rulership, fused to Greek mythology and thought, gets subsumed into a syncretistic appropriation of the Romans' own—which will then supply symbolic languages for the imperial claims of late antiquity, the Middle Ages, and modernity, with the Roman empire's Byzantine, Arabic, Ottoman, and western European successors casting and recasting their own images of others, selves, and the proper order between them.[52]

Notes

1 Translation by Lichtheim (1976), 65; Egyptian text (*Poem* §§92–102) in Kuentz (1925), 243–5.

2 *Aen.* 9.614–20, 12.99; see Reed (2007), 112–13.

3 Cf. Selden (1998), 293–4, 334 (on the Kadesh inscription); Assmann (2002), 377; Stephens (2003), 42–3, 52–64.

4 Manning (2010), 110 and 78.

5 Ockinga (1987), 48. Cf. Morschauser (1985), 145–53, Pearson (2010), 17.

6 On Alexander and Amun/Ammon see Bosworth (1977); Vasunia (2001), 272–5; Stephens (2003), 64–73; Collins (2014); Pfeiffer (2014), and that volume *passim*.

7 Cf. Vasunia (2001), 27–8. Virgil's form *Hammon* seems to gesture toward the desert location of his oracle (cf. ἄμμος, "sand"). On Apollonius' Ptolemaic refashioning of Pindar's myth (*Arg.* 4.1750–3), see Stephens (2003), 178–82, 195, 202.

8 In addition to Manning (above), see, e.g., Koenen (1993); Selden (1998); Reed (2000); Alfano (2001); Stephens (2003); Vout (2003); Kleiner (2005). For Roman appropriations of (Ptolemaic) strategies of appropriation Trimble (2018), 119 (cf. 134) uses the metaphor of "layering"; Parker (2018), 138, conceiving that "appropriation" offers a *problēma* more than a solution, stresses how any reception fantasizes and redraws identitarian definitions and boundaries. Augustus' legitimation of his rule *in Egypt*, of course, deployed this program more directly: see Hölbl (2000), 9–24; Dundas (2002).

9 Kákosy (1967), 314 ("Az Egyiptom római uralom alá kerülését megörökítő obeliszkek egyúttal ennek dicső múltját és isteneinek—most már Augustus védőinek—nagyságát hirdették"). On obelisks and other Roman architectural appropriations from Egypt, see Swetnam-Burland (2015), 65–104; Trimble (2018), with 132 on the recognizability of such references to Romans; Parker (2018); Reed (2016) and (2021), 711–12.

10 Cf. Trimble (2018), 116, "Ancient Egypt was seen as . . . a touchstone for the sanction of world rule," 119; Parker (2018), 146.

11 Acosta-Hughes (2017), 52.

12 See Clausen (1994), 48–9, citing Wissowa (1902) as well as adaptations of the practice for Octavian.

13 *Aetia* fr. 110.64 Pfeiffer ἄστρον [ἔθηκε νέον; see Selden (1998), 340–4.

14 Cf. the anonymous Greek epigram *SH* 982, a contemporary celebration of Augustus' accession to Egyptian sovereignty in traditional Niliac terms taken immediately from Ptolemaic usage (Koenen and Thompson 1984: 120–31; Barbantani 1998: 292–30).

15 Stephens (2003), 113 (on Callimachus).

16 Note the conflation of imperial and erotic presumptions in *Aen.* 4.211–14 *femina . . . cui litus arandum / cuique loci leges dedimus, conubia nostra / reppulit ac dominum Aenean in regna recepit* ("that woman, to whom I granted shoreland to plow, from whom I exacted conditions of residency, has rejected my offer of marriage and taken Aeneas into her realm as master"); cf. Dido as mere *raptum* in 217.

17 Nigid. fr. 89 Swoboda. His zodiac etiologies, recovered from the so-called scholia on Germanicus' *Phaenomena* and from later sources (Cameron 2004: 18–24), are generally assumed to have formed part of his *Sphaera Graecanica* (on which, see Boll 1903: 349–63).

18 Cf. Nock (1928), 27–9. On Scytobrachion's connection to Alexander mythology and Ptolemaic monarchism, see Rusten (1982), 89, 102–12; Stephens (2003), 39–43, 84.

19 On Nigidius' intellectual milieu and role see Volk (2021), 261–79.

20 Barton (1995), 48, and (1994), 38. Cf. Kelting (2019), 42–3, on a later interpreter of *Aegyptiaca* in Rome: "To Chaeremon, astronomy and astrology are particularly effective planks between Stoicism and Egyptian religion."

21 Feeney (2016).

22 On Ennius' importation of Euhemerism to Rome, see Winiarczyk (2013), 109–22; cf. Stephens (2003), 36–9, 90–1 on its Ptolemaic uses.

23 Cf. Beard, North, and Price (1998), 140–9; Cole (2013), 18–26. Augustan catasterisms: e.g., Virg., *Georg.* 32–5; Ov., *Met.* 15.843–51.

24 *Phaen.* 96–136.

25 This account, like that of Aries, has affinities to Dionysius Scytobrachion and Ptolemaic cult: see Rusten (1982), 88, 95.

26 Stephens (2006), 96. Cf. Reed (2021), 713–19.

27 Nigid. fr. 98 Swoboda; cf. [Eratosth.] *Cat.* 27. For Nigidius' interest in Egyptian monarchism cf. fr. 102 Swoboda = Serv. Auct. *Georg.* 1.19.

28 This adapts an etiology for the part-animal gods cultivated in Egypt, attested as early as Pi. frr. 91–3 Maehler; see Griffiths (1960).

29 See n. 3 above. Typhon's identification with Seth was current in Greek since at least Aesch. *Suppl.* 560 and Hecat. *FGrH* 1 F 300 = Hdt. 2.144.

30 Bergman (1968), 95–9; Stephens (2003), 215.

31 See Barton (1995). Dwyer (1973) argues that Nigidius' etiology was a model for Augustus' Capricorn imagery.

32 Roller (2003), 100–6.

33 Probably completed by 2 BCE: ibid., 183.

34 *FGrH* 275 F 5 = [Plut.] *Par. min.* 311b–c. The source raises suspicions about authenticity (see Cameron 2004: 127–34), but [Plut.] is not always unreliable; e.g., in the two previous paired myths and the following one the Greek citations are verifiable (Parth., *Erot.* 10 and Eur., *Hec.*) or credible (Theodorus *SH* 749). Juba *FGrH* 275 F 60 = Pliny *N.H.* 10.126–7 also concerns Diomedes (and his Apulian connections).

35 Vasunia (2001), 185–93, 207–15; Stephens (2003), 26–30

36 Curtius 4.7.13–14.

37 Stephens (2003), 96–100, esp. on Callim., *H.* 1.

38 Roller (2003), 181 suggests, based on accounts in Dio, that Juba treated the two in parallel ways.

39 Stephens (2003), 191, citing Pratt (1992).

40 The conjunction of the two legendary founders Dido and Aeneas goes back to Naevius on the First Punic War (see Wigodsky 1972: 29–33; Reed 2007: 96–7; Biggs 2020: 64–71).

41 [Acron] on Hor., *Odes* 4.2.33, calling the poem *egeregius*; Hollis (2007), 421. We lack specific information on the contents; the storm scene in Ov., *Met.* 14.470–2 might reflect Iullus' poem (and its engagement with the *Aeneid*).

42 See Fletcher (2006), 219–20.

43 Hollis (2007), 424 = Ov., *Pont.* 4.16.17–18 (cf. the poems on post-Trojan War themes recorded in 4.12.27–8 and 16.20, 25–6); see Leigh (1998), 91–8; Reed (2007), 192–3. Cf. Reed (2021), 715 on Carus' Hercules epic.

44 Roller (2003), 185, 227; cf. 190–6 on Juba's location of the source of the Nile in northwest Africa.
45 Crinagoras *A.P.* 9.235.4 = GP 1914 ἓν γένος Αἰγύπτου καὶ Λιβύης.
46 Roller (2003), 151–2.
47 A Numidian king Hiarbas was defeated by Pompey: Livy, *Epit.* 89; Plut., *Pomp.* 12. Iarbas as Gaetulian: *Aen.* 4.326 (Dido speaking).
48 Estevez (1982), 23–5; cf. Hardie (2012), 88–91.
49 Hejduk (2009), 292–3.
50 Cf. Hardie (2012), 2–3 and *passim*.
51 The scene of the shield's bestowal is itself embedded within (vatic) report and tradition: Apostol (2009), 63–6.
52 Cf. e.g., Tanner (1993).

Bibliography

Acosta-Hughes, B. (2017), "The Shore of Alexandria: A Narrative of a Culture in Motion," in V. Rimell and M. Asper (eds.), *Imagining Empire: Political Space in Hellenistic and Roman Literature*, 23–53, Heidelberg: Universitätsverlag Winter.

Alfano, C. (2001), "Egyptian influences in Italy," in S. Walker and P. Higgs (eds.), *Cleopatra of Egypt from History to Myth*, 276–91, London: British Museum Press.

Apostol, R. A. (2009), "Rome's Bucolic Landscapes: Place, Power, and Prophecy in Aeneid VIII," PhD diss., University of Michigan, Ann Arbor, MI.

Assmann, J. (2002), *The Mind of Egypt*, trans. A. Jenkins, New York: Metropolitan Books.

Barbantani, S. (1998), "Un epigramma encomiastico 'alessandrino' per Augusto (*SH* 982)," *Aevum Antiquum*, 11: 255–344.

Barton, T. (1994), *Ancient Astrology*, London: Routledge.

Barton, T. (1995), "Augustus and Capricorn: Astrological Polyvalency and Imperial Rhetoric," *Journal of Roman Studies*, 85: 33–51.

Beard, M., J. North, and S. Price, eds. (1998), *Religions of Rome*, Cambridge: Cambridge University Press.

Bergman, J. (1968), *Ich Bin Isis*, Uppsala: Berlingska Boktryckeriet.

Biggs, T. (2020), *The Poetics of the First Punic War*, Ann Arbor, MI: University of Michigan Press.

Boll, F. (1903), *Sphaera*, Leipzig: B. G. Teubner.

Bosworth, B. (1977), "Alexander and Ammon," in K. H. Kinzl (ed.), *Greece and the Ancient Mediterranean in History and Pre-History: Studies Presented to Fritz Schachermeyr on the Occasion of His Eightieth Birthday*, 51–75, Berlin: De Gruyter.

Cameron, A. (2004), *Greek Mythography in the Roman World*, Oxford: Oxford University Press.

Clausen, W. (1994), *Virgil: Eclogues*, Oxford: Oxford University Press.

Cole, S. (2013), *Cicero and the Rise of Deification at Rome*, Cambridge: Cambridge University Press.

Collins, A. (2014), "Alexander's Visit to Siwah: A New Analysis," *Phoenix*, 68: 62–77.

Dundas, G. S. (2002), "Augustus and the Kingship of Egypt," *Historia*, 51: 433–48.

Dwyer, E. J. (1973), "Augustus and the Capricorn," *Röm. Mitt.*, 80: 59–67.

Edwards, C. and G. Woolf, eds. (2003), *Rome: The Cosmopolis*, Cambridge: Cambridge University Press.

Estevez, V. A. (1982), "*Oculos ad Moenia Torsit*: On *Aeneid* 4. 220," *Classical Philology*, 77 (1): 22–34.

Fantuzzi, M. and T. Papanghelis, eds. (2006), *Brill's Companion to Greek and Latin Pastoral*, Leiden: Brill.

Feeney, D. (2016), *Beyond Greek: The Beginnings of Latin Literature*, Cambridge, MA: Harvard University Press.

FGrH = F. Jacoby (1923–55), *Die Fragmente der griechischen Historiker*, Berlin: Weidmann and Leiden: Brill.

Fletcher, K. F. F. (2006), "Vergil's Italian Diomedes," *American Journal of Philology*, 127: 219–49.

Goedicke, H., ed. (1985), *Perspectives on the Battle of Kadesh*, Baltimore, MD: Halgo.

GP = A. S. F. Gow and D. L. Page (1968), *The Greek Anthology: The Garland of Philip and Some Contemporary Epigrams*, Cambridge: Cambridge University Press.

Grieb, V., K. Nawotka, and A. Wojciechowska, eds. (2014), *Alexander the Great and Egypt: History, Art, Tradition*, Wiesbaden: Harrassowitz Verlag.

Griffiths, J. G. (1960), "The Flight of the Gods before Typhon: An Unrecognized Myth," *Hermes*, 88: 374–6.

Hardie, P. (2012), *Rumour and Renown: Representations of* Fama *in Western Literature*, Cambridge: Cambridge University Press.

Hejduk, J. (2009), "Jupiter's *Aeneid*: *Fama* and *Imperium*," *Classical Antiquity*, 28: 279–327.

Hölbl, G. (2000), *Altägypten im römischen Reich*, Mainz am Rhein: Verlag Philipp von Zabern.

Hollis, A. S. (2007), *Fragments of Roman Poetry c. 60 BC–AD 20*, Oxford: Oxford University Press.

Kákosy, L. (1967), "Augustus és Egyiptom," *Antik tanulmányok*, 14: 307–15.

Kelting, E. W. (2019), "The Greek Face of Roman Egypt," PhD diss., Stanford University, CA.

Kleiner, D. E. E. (2005), *Cleopatra and Rome*, Cambridge, MA: Harvard University Press.

Koenen, L. (1993), "The Ptolemaic King as a Religious Figure," in A. Bulloch, E. S. Gruen, A. A. Long, and A. Stewart (eds.), *Images and Ideologies: Self-Definition in the Hellenistic World*, 25–115, Berkeley, CA: University of California Press.

Koenen, L. and D. B. Thompson (1984), "Gallus as Triptolemos on the Tazza Farnese," *Bulletin of the American Society of Papyrologists*, 21: 111–56.

Kuentz, C. (1925), *La bataille de Qadech*, Cairo: Institut Français d'Archéologie Orientale.

Kyriakou, P., A. Rengakos, and E. Sistakou, eds. (2021), *Brill's Companion to Theocritus*, Leiden: Brill.

Leigh, M. (1998), "Sophocles at Patavium (*fr.* 137 Radt)," *Journal of Hellenic Studies*, 118: 82–100.

Lichtheim, M. (1976), *Ancient Egyptian Literature*, vol. 2, Berkeley, CA: University of California Press.

Loar, M., C. MacDonald, and D. Padilla Peralta, eds. (2018), *Rome, Empire of Plunder: The Dynamics of Cultural Appropriation*, Cambridge: Cambridge University Press.

Manning, J. G. (2010), *The Last Pharaohs: Egypt Under the Ptolemies, 305–30 BC*, Princeton, NJ: Princeton University Press.

Morschauser, S. (1985), "Observations on the Speeches of Rameses II in the Literary Record of the Battle of Kadesh," in H. Goedicke (ed.), *Perspectives on the Battle of Kadesh*, 123–206, Baltimore, MD: Halgo.

Nock, A. D. (1928), "Notes on Ruler-Cult, I–IV," *Journal of Hellenic Studies*, 48: 21–43.

Ockinga, B. (1987), "On the Interpretation of the Kadesh Record," *Chronique d'Egypte*, 62: 38–48.

Parker, G. (2018), "Monolithic Appropriation? The Lateran Obelisk Compared," in M. Loar, C. MacDonald, and D. Padilla Peralta (eds.), *Rome, Empire of Plunder: The Dynamics of Cultural Appropriation*, 137–59, Cambridge: Cambridge University Press.

Pearson, W. (2010), "Rameses II and the Battle of Kadesh: A Miraculous Victory?," *Ancient History: Resources for Teachers*, 40 (1): 1–20.

Pfeiffer, S. (2014), "Alexander der Große in Ägypten: Überlegungen zur Frage seiner pharaonischer Legitimation," in V. Grieb, K. Nawotka, and A. Wojciechowska (eds.), *Alexander the Great and Egypt: History, Art, Tradition*, 89–106, Wiesbaden: Harrassowitz Verlag.

Pratt, M. L. (1992), *Imperial Eyes: Travel Writing and Transculturation*, London: Routledge.

Reed, J. D. (2000), "Arsinoe's Adonis and the Poetics of Ptolemaic Imperialism," *Transactions of the American Philological Association*, 130: 319–51.

Reed, J. D. (2007), *Virgil's Gaze: Nation and Poetry in the Aeneid*, Princeton, NJ: Princeton University Press.

Reed, J. (2016), "ISIS and Osiris," *Eidolon*, 7 March. Available online: https://eidolon.pub/isis-and-osiris-c506f60f1f05 (accessed 27 April 2023).

Reed, J. D. (2021), "The King's Nectar: Theocritean Encomium and Augustan Poetry," in P. Kyriakou, A. Rengakos, and E. Sistakou (eds.), *Brill's Companion to Theocritus*, 703–22, Leiden: Brill.

Roller, D. W. (2003), *The World of Juba II and Kleopatra Selene*, New York: Routledge

Rusten, J. S. (1982), *Dionysius Scytobrachion*, Opladen: Westdeutscher Verlag.

Selden, D. L. (1998), "Alibis," *Classical Antiquity*, 17: 289–420.

SH = H. Lloyd-Jones and P. Parsons (1983), *Supplementum Hellenisticum*, Berlin: De Gruyter.

Stephens, S. A. (2003), *Seeing Double: Intercultural Poetics in Ptolemaic Alexandria*, Berkeley, CA: University of California Press.

Stephens, S. A. (2006), "Ptolemaic Pastoral," in M. Fantuzzi and T. Papanghelis (eds.), *Brill's Companion to Greek and Latin Pastoral*, 91–117, Leiden: Brill.

Swetnam-Burland, M. (2015), *Egypt in Italy: Visions of Roman Imperial Culture*, Cambridge: Cambridge University Press.

Swoboda, A. (1889), *P. Nigidii Figuli Opera*, Vienna: F. Tempsky.

Tanner, M. (1993), *The Last Descendant of Aeneas*, New Haven, CT: Yale University Press.

Trimble, J. (2018), "Appropriating Egypt for the Ara Pacis Augustae," in M. Loar, C. MacDonald, and D. Padilla Peralta (eds.), *Rome, Empire of Plunder: The Dynamics of Cultural Appropriation*, 109–36, Cambridge: Cambridge University Press.

Vasunia, P. (2001), *The Gift of the Nile*, Berkeley, CA: University of California Press.

Volk, K. (2021), *The Roman Republic of Letters: Scholarship, Philosophy, and Politics in the Age of Cicero and Caesar*, Princeton, NJ: Princeton University Press.

Vout, C. (2003), "Embracing Egypt," in C. Edwards and G. Woolf (eds.), *Rome: The Cosmopolis*, 177–202, Cambridge: Cambridge University Press.

Wigodsky, M. (1972), *Vergil and Early Latin Poetry*, *Hermes* Einzelschriften 24, Wiesbaden: Franz Steiner Verlag.

Winiarczyk, M. (2013), *The* Sacred History *of Euhemerus of Messene*, Beiträge zur Altertumskunde 312, Berlin: De Gruyter.

Wissowa, G. (1902), "Monatliche Geburtstagsfeier," *Hermes*, 37: 157–9.

18

Crinagoras of Mytilene and Octavia

Roland Mayer
King's College London

Maria Ypsilanti's impressive recent edition of the extant epigrams of Crinagoras of Mytilene has rightly been hailed for its accomplished scholarship and, more specifically, for focussing attention on the way a distinguished Greek engineered a place for himself at the highest level of Roman society. One reviewer of her work, Lee Frantantuono (*BMCR* 2019.01.13), felt that Crinagoras had hitherto been a marginalized figure, undeservedly in that he "provides a case study on the question of literary patronage under Augustus." Ypsilanti of course addressed the "nature of Crinagoras' dependence on the family of Augustus" (2018: 7–10, 12–13, 358). Thanks to Crinagoras' high standing within his own community of Mytilene on the island of Lesbos, he represented its interests as an ambassador first to Julius Caesar and in due course to Augustus (Ypsilanti 2018: 2–3, 50, for the inscriptional evidence). He was clearly no starveling Greek in need of financial support, the *Graeculus esuriens* of Juvenal's satire 3.78; his repudiation of the pursuit of wealth in favor of the Muses in *AP* 9.234 = *GP* xlviii is rightly regarded by Ypsilanti (2018: 474) as a literary *topos*. His personal standing and more especially his literary accomplishments enabled him to "enjoy the favour of the Augustan family," a favor he reciprocated by employing his poetic skill in praise of its members in complimentary epigrams. It is on the "Augustan family" that I want to focus in my brief and admittedly speculative contribution to this volume, since I seem to myself at any rate to see a link that draws closely together a number of those persons celebrated in the poems. That link is not as might be supposed the emperor Augustus, but rather his sister Octavia, who now requires a brief introduction.

Born perhaps in 69 BCE, Octavia was the elder sister of Octavius/ Octavianus/ Augustus (himself born in 63). She died round about 11/10 BCE, and was buried in her brother's Mausoleum. Mason Hammond provided a full account of her life in *RE* xvii.1859–68 s.v. Octavius (Octavia) §96 Octavia minor. Historians of the period not unreasonably focus on her considerable political importance, which was founded on her tactical marriages and on her enduring influence with her brother, who clearly loved and respected her. What concerns me now is rather the fruit of those (and of other) marriages, since her children (and the children of others connected with her) were all prominent in the "Augustan family" mentioned above, not least because Augustus himself proved less productive of issue.

The most important of Octavia's children was her son by her first husband, M. Claudius Marcellus. Dynastically valuable were her two daughters, the elder and the younger Antonias, whom she bore to her second husband Marcus Antonius, the Triumvir. He also nimbly sired three children by the Queen of Egypt, Cleopatra. After the deaths of Antony and Cleopatra Octavia heroically took under her wing all three, the twins Alexander Helios and Cleopatra Selene, and Ptolemy Philadelphus. Finally, she took into her household yet another son of Marcus Antonius, Iullus, whose mother was Octavia's predecessor as the Triumvir's third wife, Fulvia. As Sir Ronald Syme put it, "this lady took over the supervision of a whole kindergarten" (1986: 347; see too Plutarch, *Antonius* 87, 35.8, 54.3, 57.4 with Chris Pelling's notes).

Syme's word "kindergarten" may sound lightly dismissive of such a generous act of extended motherhood, but there is a justice to it, since Octavia was a woman of intellectual standing, and so carefully oversaw her brood's education. This leading aspect of her character was overlooked in the articles in the second, third, and even fourth editions of the *Oxford Classical Dictionary*, and so it is high time to make good that deficiency (cf. Hammond in *RE* xvii.1867: 8–23). Literary works were dedicated to her. The Latin grammarian Priscian (x.47 = Keil, *Grammatici Latini* 1855: II 536.6–7) mentioned an unidentifiable work of Maecenas apparently dedicated to Octavia, which he cited for Maecenas' use of a particular (and in his view correct) form, *pexi*, of the perfect tense of the verb *pecto*: "pexisti capillum naturae muneribus gratum" ("you combed your hair, charming with natural gifts"). Granted this is not vastly suggestive of her intellectual qualities (and yet according to Plutarch, *Antonius* 31.2 she was a very beautiful woman, as well as dignified and intelligent), the dedication of a prose work to her has its interest. She appointed an Academic philosopher, Nestor of Tarsus, to be one of the teachers of Marcellus (Strabo, *Geography* 14.5.15 = C675). More significant is Plutarch's reference in *Poplicola* §17 to a work dedicated to her by the Stoic philosopher Athenodorus of Tarsus, son of Sandon (Athenodoros §19 in *RE* ii.2045.23–62); it might have been a consolatory essay upon the death of Marcellus, as suggested by Bowersock (1965: 34).

The most striking piece of evidence for Octavia's intellectual, and more specifically her literary, bent is the building of the Porticus Octaviae, begun probably after 27 and completed after 23 (the cost of its construction was borne by Octavian (A. Viscogliosi in Steinby 1999: vol. 4, 141–5, and see David Wardle's note on Suetonius, *Augustus* 29.4, p. 232)). This seems to be the first public structure in Rome to be named after a woman (the Porticus Liviae is later in date), but that may simply have been a means of distinguishing it from the Porticus Octavia.[1] The significant addition to the elaborate temple complex was a library, which she dedicated to her now dead son, Marcellus (Plutarch, *Marcellus* 30.6). A freedman of Maecenas, C. Maecenas Melissus, was charged with the organization of the collection (Suetonius, *De grammaticis et rhetoribus* §21, with Kaster's commentary, and Paul Wessner in *RE* xv.532–4).

Given her active literary associations, I want to suggest that it was Octavia who commissioned from Crinagoras of Mytilene a number of epigrams dedicated to some of the junior members of the imperial family, her "kindergarten." This possibility was at least hinted at by Conrad Cichorius (to whose work my good friend Ewen Bowie helpfully directed me). Cichorius described Octavia's home as a lively intellectual centre, and he astutely observed that a number of Crinagoras' poems concerned her children, biological and other (1922: 278). He did not however develop this insight, and this seems as good an occasion as any in which to tease out an implication of Cichorius' bare observation. Let us now take a closer look at the poems in question since there are some peculiarities about them which may go some way to encouraging my hunch that Octavia commissioned them or at least encouraged the poet to celebrate the occasions recorded in the poems (texts and translations will be found in the Appendix).

There are two epigrams for M. Claudius Marcellus, Octavia's son by her first husband, C. Claudius Marcellus: *AP* 6.161 = *GP* x, on the first clipping of his beard in 25, and 9.545 = *GP* xi, the gift of a copy of Callimachus' *Hekale*.

There are two, or perhaps even three, poems to Antonia minor, Octavia's daughter by her second husband, Marcus Antonius: *AP* 9.239 = *GP* vii, a (?birthday) gift of an anthology of lyric poems, and 6.244 = *GP* xii, on her pregnancy. The third poem is *AP* 6.345 = *GP* vi, a gift of winter roses to a lady soon to be married; the recipient is unnamed, but she is usually reckoned to be Antonia Minor (Ypsilanti (2018: 96–7) assesses the candidates).

Finally, there is an epigram heralding the marriage of Cleopatra Selene, daughter of Marcus Antonius and Queen Cleopatra, to Juba II king of Mauretania, *c.* 20 (*AP* 9.235 = *GP* xxv).

There are two unusual features of the epigrams accompanying the gift of poetry books to Marcellus and to Antonia that may support the suggestion that someone other than the poet was the giver of the gifts, someone who perhaps was also the instigator of the accompanying poems. When Crinagoras personally gives someone a gift he names himself as the giver, for instance in *AP* 6.227 = *GP* iii (a silver pen for Proclus on his birthday), 6.229 = *GP* iv (an eagle's feather toothpick for Lucius), and 6.261 = *GP* v (a bronze oil-flask for the unnamed son of Simon on his birthday). The practice of naming oneself as donor is natural enough, and found as well in two of Antipater of Thessalonica's gift poems to L. Calpurnius Piso Frugi, *AP* 6.249 = *GP* xlv (a candle), and 9.93 = *GP* xxxi (a poem of his own, written the night before), and in Leonides of Alexandria's poem accompanying the gift of a celestial globe to Poppaea (*AP* 9.355 = *FGE* xxxii). But in just these two poems Crinagoras does not claim that the gifts are his personally. Unsurprisingly, however, his commentators assume that he is the giver, despite his discreet reticence on the point.[2]

The gifts themselves moreover are somewhat unusual. Maria Ypsilanti noted that when an epigrammatist offered poetry as a gift, it was usually his own poems that he offered (2018: 74, 136–7), symbolic of the reciprocity that existed between the giver and the receiver. Is it not therefore strange that when Crinagoras wrote poems to accompany books of poetry given to Marcellus and to Antonia, in neither case were they books of his poems, but rather the work of classical Greek poets, the very poets whose works would be housed in the bilingual library that their mother was building in the complex of the Porticus Octaviae? Even if the gifts were his, we may wonder exactly how he came to know that such works were appropriate to the recipients. The educating hand of Octavia might be detected at work here.

The third gift poem, winter roses to an unnamed lady, shares a peculiarity with the epigrams accompanying the gifts of Greek poetry: the speaker of the poem is also anonymous, and does not claim to be the giver of the flowers.

The poem on Antonia's pregnancy, *AP* 6.244 = *GP* xii, deserves attention next. The date of the poem is unclear (Ypsilanti 2018: 146). In its fifth line there are references to Antonia's husband, her mother (the only such clear reference to Octavia in the group), and to her mother-in-law.[3] A question that arises is the identity of the "speaker" of the poem. The Loeb translator, W. R. Paton, brought out the force of the optative mood of the verb νεύσαιτ᾽ . . . ἵλαοι thus: "I pray," identifying Crinagoras as the "speaker" of the prayer for Antonia's wellbeing. But there is nothing in the actual language of the prayer that compels such an intrusion. The prayer to Hera and Zeus could equally well be made by the trio of family members listed in the fifth line. Once again, Octavia may be behind this, modestly unnamed but clearly party to the prayer.

Finally there is the poem on the marriage of Cleopatra Selene. Though she was no relation at all of Octavia's, she was reared by her in Rome, and according to Plutarch, *Antonius* 87.2, it was Octavia who arranged her dynastic marriage to king Juba; she might thus also have commissioned a poem to celebrate the match. Juba may have had a personal attraction for Octavia, in that he was a scholarly monarch, "the most accomplished of kings," said Plutarch.[4]

We have then five, or possibly six, poems by Crinagoras to members of the imperial family, who all happen to comprise Octavia's "kindergarten." On the other hand, he dedicated only a few poems to other imperial personages. Four centre upon Caesar Augustus (*AP* 9.224 = *GP* xxiii, *AP* 9.562 = *GP* xxiv, *AP* 9.291 = *GP* xxvii, *AP* 9.419 = *GP* xxix), one on Tiberius (*APl* 61 = *GP* xxviii), and there is one to a hard-to-identify Germanicus (*AP* 9.283 = *GP* xxvi) (Ypsilanti 2018: 270–4). The lion's share of the occasional poems written for members of the imperial family clearly goes to the young members of Octavia's household. This may be pure chance, or the accident of opportunity, but given her cultured and literary interests it seems worth suggesting that it was Octavia herself who prompted or encouraged Crinagoras to celebrate the special events in the lives of the children she had borne or fostered. Typically, she herself kept to the background, and promoted others.

Having taken the bit between my teeth, I would like to add a sort of rider to the foregoing discussion, and focus now briefly on Octavia's daughter, Antonia Minor, who seems to have inherited her mother's intellectual bent. Her two sons by Drusus, Germanicus and Claudius, both exhibited literary skills. Germanicus is still generally reckoned to be the author of a now incomplete Latin version of Aratus' astronomical poem. Though Antonia regarded Claudius as a dullard he nonetheless had varied scholarly interests; his literary activity is recorded by Suetonius, *Claudius* 3.1 and 41–2. Now, since Crinagoras had composed poems celebrating events in Antonia's youth, might she not have turned to him, as perhaps her mother had done before her, to laud the achievements of her son Germanicus in the admittedly mystifying *AP* 9.283 = *GP* xxvi? (Ypsilanti 2018: 274 thinks the Germanicus addressed in the poem is the son of Antonia Minor and Drusus.)[5]

Finally, something ought to be said about the nature of the literary bond that I am here suggesting existed between Octavia and Crinagoras. As Ewen Bowie has urged (2008: 235 and 2011: 194), "patronage" does not seem to be the right word, which he put within "frightener" quotation marks, because none of Crinagoras' poetry, even the epigrams about the goat whose milk so pleased Augustus or the parrot which taught a forest of birds to say "Hail, Caesar," can be seen as the products of time-serving flattery. The epigram praising the generosity of C. Sallustius Crispus, *APl* 40 = *GP* xxxvi, is rightly taken by Ypsilanti (2018: 358) to be no exception, since it seems to express gratitude for a particular favor, rather than to appeal for sustained patronage. The same can be said of the poems written for Octavia's brood, all of which are dignified in tone. Crinagoras did not need financial support from Rome's grandees; what he sought on his embassies was favor for his home community of Mytilene, what might be called civic patronage. His poetic gifts made him particularly welcome within the *domus Caesarea*, and naturally he was ready to oblige with poems celebrating events in the lives of the household's members. Since so many of the events celebrated are of a domestic character—birthdays, weddings, the first shaving of the beard— the poet privileged to celebrate them also advertised his intimacy with the powers that be, surely recompense enough for his efforts.

Appendix: Texts and Translations (Adapted) from W. R. Paton's Loeb Library Edition

On Marcellus' first clipping of his beard (*AP* 6.161 = 10)

Ἑσπερίου Μάρκελλος ἀνερχόμενος πολέμοιο
    σκυλοφόρος κραναῆς τέλσα πάρ᾽ Ἰταλίης
ξανθὴν πρῶτον ἔκειρε γενειάδα· βούλετο πατρὶς
    οὕτως, καὶ πέμψαι παῖδα καὶ ἄνδρα λαβεῖν.

Marcellus, returning from the western war, laden with spoil, to the boundaries of rocky Italy, shaved his yellow beard for the first time. Such was his country's wish, to send him forth a boy and receive him back a man.

A gift for Marcellus (*AP* 9.545 = 11)

Καλλιμάχου τὸ τορευτὸν ἔπος τόδε· δὴ γὰρ ἐπ᾽ αὐτῷ
    ὡνὴρ τοὺς Μουσέων πάντας ἔσεισε κάλους.
ἀείδει δ᾽ Ἑκάλης τε φιλοξείνοιο καλιὴν
    καὶ Θησεῖ Μαραθὼν οὓς ἐπέθηκε πόνους,
τοῦ σοὶ καὶ νεαρὸν χειρῶν σθένος εἴη ἀρέσθαι,
    Μάρκελλε, κλεινοῦ τ᾽ αἶνον ἴσον βιότου.

This chiselled poem is Callimachus', for over it he let out every reef of the Muses. He sings of the hut of hospitable Hecale, and the labours that Marathon imposed on Theseus. May the youthful strength of Theseus' hands be yours to secure, Marcellus, and a life of equal renown.

A gift of spring roses (?to Antonia) (*AP* 6.345 = 6)

Εἴαρος ἤνθει μὲν τὸ πρὶν ῥόδα, νῦν δ᾽ ἐνὶ μέσσῳ
    χείματι πορφυρέας ἐσχάσαμεν κάλυκας,
σῇ ἐπιμειδήσαντα γενεθλίῃ ἄσμενα τῇδε
    ἠοῖ, νυμφιδίων ἀσσοτάτῃ λεχέων.
καλλίστης ὀφθῆναι ἐπὶ κροτάφοισι γυναικὸς
    λώϊον ἢ μίμνειν ἠρινὸν ἠέλιον.

Roses used to flower in spring, but we now in mid-winter burst scarlet from our buds, smiling gaily on this thy natal morn that falls so nigh to thy wedding. To be seen on the brow of the loveliest of women is better than to await the sun of spring.

A birthday gift for Antonia (*AP* 9.239 = 7)[6]

Βίβλων ἡ γλυκερὴ λυρικῶν ἐν τεύχεϊ τῷδε
    πεντὰς ἀμιμήτων ἔργα φέρει Χαρίτων.
. . .
δῶρον δ᾽ εἰς ἱερὴν Ἀντωνίῃ ἥκομεν ἠῶ,
    κάλλευς καὶ πραπίδων ἔξοχ᾽ ἐνεγκαμένη.

The sweet quintet of lyric book-rolls in this box brings the works of the inimitable Graces. We come as a gift on a morning sacred for Antonia,[7] supreme in beauty and intellect.

On Antonia's pregnancy (*AP* 6.244 = 12)

Ἥρη, Ἐλειθυιῶν μήτηρ, Ἥρη τε τελείη,
    καὶ Ζεῦ, γινομένοις ξυνὸς ἅπασι πατήρ,
ὠδῖνας νεύσαιτ᾽ Ἀντωνίῃ ἵλαοι ἐλθεῖν
    πρηείας, μαλακαῖς χερσὶ σὺν Ἠπιόνης,
ὄφρα κε γηθήσειε πόσις, μήτηρ θ᾽, ἑκυρά τε.
    ἡ νηδὺς οἴκων αἷμα φέρει μεγάλων.

Hera, mother of the Ilithyiae, and Hera the Fulfiller, and Zeus, the common father of all who are born, graciously grant that gentle pangs may come to Antonia in the tender hands of Epione, so that her husband may rejoice and her mother and her mother-in-law. Her womb bears the blood of great houses.

On Cleopatra Selene's marriage to Juba (*A P* 6.235 = 25)

Ἄγχουροι μεγάλαι κόσμου χθόνες, ἃς διὰ Νεῖλος
    πιμπλάμενος μελάνων τέμνει ἀπ' Αἰθιόπων,
ἀμφότεραι βασιλῆας ἐκοινώσασθε γάμοισιν,
    ἓν γένος Αἰγύπτου καὶ Λιβύης θέμεναι.
ἐκ πατέρων εἴη παισὶν πάλι τοῖσιν ἀνάκτων
    ἔμπεδον ἠπείροις σκῆπτρον ἐπ' ἀμφοτέραις.

Great bordering regions of the world which the brimming Nile separates from the black Ethiopians, you have by marriage made your sovereigns common to both, turning Egypt and Libya into one people. May the children of these princes ever again rule with unshaken dominion over both lands.

Notes

1   Another first for Octavia: she was the first Roman woman to have her portrait on a coin (Doer 1968: 26–7). A silver tetradrachm from Ephesus, dated to 39 BCE, depicted her with her then husband Mark Antony (a portrait of his third wife, Fulvia does appear on earlier provincial coinage, but allegorically, as Nike).

2   Ypsilanti (2018: 21) illustrates Crinagoras' frequent omission of topical information that would have been known to the original audience. Since he does name himself however as the giver of gifts in other poems, I still find suggestive the omission of his name in these poems: he does not claim the gifts as his.

3   There is an odd confusion on the identity of the final person in the list in Gow—Page's account: in their introduction to the poem on p. 221 they say rightly that the three people referred to in the fifth line are Nero Claudius Drusus, Octavia, and Livia, but in their translation they mistranslate ἑκυρά as "wife's mother," not "mother-in-law."

4   Crinagoras also lamented Cleopatra's death, sometime after 11 CE (*A P* 7.633 = *GP* xviii), so that poem cannot be considered as a commission by Octavia.

5   Ypsilanti (2018: 274) is also prepared to countenance the identity of the Germanicus in this poem as Drusus, Antonia's husband; in that case, she might still have had something to do with encouraging the composition of the epigram.

6   Simply for the sake of tidiness, my text follows some editors in omitting a puzzling central couplet, which if it contains reliable information identifies the gift as a five-book edition of the poetry of Anacreon only. Maria Ypsilanti's discussion of the problem is of course thorough, and endorsed recently by Bernsdorff (2020), 49–50.

7 In this translation, I am accepting the argument of Ypsilanti (2018), 110, that
Ἀντωνίη is a "dative of standpoint" to be taken with ἱερὴν rather than with ἥκομεν,
an interpretation endorsed in her note on *AP* 6.242.4 = 9.4 ἠϊθέοισιν on p. 126.
Unfortunately in her own translation (2018: 102) she adopted the interpretation she
rejected. The use of the dative she favored might have been supported by an appeal
to an apparently similar dative in *AP* 6.100.1 = 8.1 τὴν κούροις ἱερὴν ἔριν.

Bibliography

Bernsdorff, H. (2020), *Anacreon: Testimonia and Fragments*, Oxford: Oxford University
Press.

Bowersock, G. W. (1965), *Augustus and the Greek World*, Oxford: Clarendon Press.

Bowie, E. (2008), "Luxury Cruisers: Philip's epigrammatists between Greece and Rome,"
Aevum Antiquum, 8: 223–58.

Bowie, E. (2011), "Men from Mytilene," in T. A. Schmitz and N. Wiater (eds.), *The
Struggle for Identity: Greeks and Their Past in the First Century BCE*, 181–95,
Stuttgart: Franz Steiner Verlag.

Cichorius, C. (1922), *Römische Studien*, Leipzig: Teubner.

Doer, B. (1968), "Octavia: eine außergewöhnliche Frau des alten Rom," *Das Altertum*, 14:
20–31.

FGE = Page, D. L. (1981), *Further Greek Epigrams*, Cambridge: Cambridge University
Press. Poems referred to are numbered according to this edition.

GP = Gow, A. S. F. and D. L. Page, eds. (1968), *The Greek Anthology: The Garland of
Philip*, Cambridge: Cambridge University Press. Poems referred to are numbered
according to this edition.

Schmitz, T. A. and N. Wiater, eds. (2011), *The Struggle for Identity: Greeks and Their Past
in the First Century BCE*, Stuttgart: Franz Steiner Verlag.

Steinby, M., ed. (1999), *Lexicon Topographicum Urbis Romae*, vol. 4, Rome: Edizioni
Quasar.

Syme, R. (1986), *The Augustan Aristocracy*, Oxford: Clarendon Press.

Ypsilanti, M. (2018), *The Epigrams of Crinagoras of Mytilene*, Oxford: Oxford University
Press.

19

Poets, Plants, and Riddles

Kathryn Gutzwiller
University of Cincinnati

In the proem to his *Garland* (*AP* 4.1 = *HE* 1) Meleager names forty-seven poets whose epigrams were included in his anthology.[1] Each is identified with a flower, plant, or tree, which twined together stand for Meleager's grand garland of epigrams. The type of vegetation applied to each epigrammatist has symbolic value, but the link between poet and plant can be difficult to surmise, especially for minor poets. Many if not most of the plants were used in garlands of one type or another, and most have cultural connections that may be relevant to the poet or his epigrams. The plant often stands for the epigrammatist's subject matter, style, or place of origin. For instance, Sappho's poems are "few but roses" (βαιὰ ... ἀλλὰ ῥόδα, *AP* 4.1.6), since the rose, one of the most prized garland flowers, is both an erotic and a poetic symbol in her verse (2.6, 55.2–3, 94.13, 96.13 Voigt). Less certainly, the figuring of Simonides' poetry as a "new branch of a grape vine" (νέον οἰνάνθης κλῆμα, *AP* 4.1.8) may refer to his innovative sympotic elegies (21, 22 W²).[2] It is more difficult to guess why Phaennus, an otherwise unknown poet who contributed two epigrams to the *Garland*, should be associated with a terebinth tree, which produces useful resin (*AP* 4.1.29–30).[3] Meleager perhaps intended the discovery of the connection between poet and vegetative symbol to be a riddle-like game with easier and harder solutions.[4]

I discuss here two instances in which a riddle serves to identify the unmetrical name of a poet.

In *AP* 4.1.43–4 an unnamed epigrammatist is symbolized by Syrian spikenard:

καὶ μὴν καὶ Συρίαν σταχυότριχα θήκατο νάρδον
    ὑμνοθέταν Ἑρμοῦ δῶρον ἀειδόμενον.

And [Meleager] also put in Syrian nard with spikes like ears of wheat,
    a bard who is celebrated as Hermes' gift.

The reader must recognize that the poet celebrated here as Ἑρμοῦ δῶρον is Hermodorus, whose name will not fit in elegiac meter. Since Hermodorus is a minor epigrammatist, known only tenuously as author of two ecphrastic epigrams,[5] ancient readers might not have immediately surmised his name. Nor do these two epigrams provide clues to the presentation of the poet as spikenard. This plant, identified by a spike resembling an ear of wheat,[6] was famed for the perfume made from its root;[7] as a garland flower, it was cherished for its scent.[8] Meleager's choice of spikenard as a symbol for Hermodorus possibly compliments the poet's epigrams, synaesthetically, for their stylistic sweetness. There is likely another point as well. The couplet praising Hermodorus as spikenard directly follows Meleager's pentameter about the more famous and prolific epigrammatist Antipater of Sidon (*AP* 4.1.42):

Φοίνισσάν τε νέην κύπρον ἀπ᾽ Ἀντιπάτρου,

and recent Phoenician henna from Antipater.

The phrase "recent Phoenician henna" represents Antipater as the epigrammatist who was identified as a native of Phoenician Sidon in the *lemmata* of the Palatine Anthology and associated with Phoenician Tyre by Meleager (*AP* 7.428.13–14 = *HE* 122.13–14). Likewise, the specification of Syrian spikenard (Συρίαν σταχυότριχα ... νάρδον, *AP* 4.1.43)—with the parallel structure of adjectives followed by a named plant in the line above (Φοίνισσάν ... νέην κύπρον, *AP* 4.1.42)—may suggest that Hermodorus was a Syrian, and so perhaps even an acquaintance of the Gadaran Meleager, who spent his youth in Tyre. As shown by bilingual inscriptions, theophoric names like Hermodorus, Heliodorus, and Artemidorus served as translations of Phoenician names.[9] Clues then suggest underlying puzzles that extend beyond the play on Hermodorus' unmetrical name to his ethnicity.

A second example of an unmetrical name is that of Diosco(u)rides (*AP* 4.1.23–4):

... ἰδ᾽ ἐν Μούσῃσιν †ἄμεινον†,
ὃς Διὸς ἐκ κούρων ἔσχεν ἐπωνυμίην.

... and one †better† among the Muses,
who has his name from the sons of Zeus.

Here the reader is to understand that the phrase Διὸς ἐκ κούρων, so written, demands the epic-Ionic version of the poet's name, Διοσκουρίδης, which cannot be fit into elegiac meter, rather than the variant Διοσκορίδης which can so fit.

The forty surviving epigrams of Dioscorides (as he is called in the manuscript *lemmata*) place him among the most important of Meleager's anthologized poets, rivaling Asclepiades, Callimachus, and Antipater, and the phrase ἐν Μούσῃσιν may signify Diosco(u)rides' high status as a poet. In the *Garland*'s proem the Muses, who stand for poetry, are connected with Bacchylides in *AP* 4.1.33 (λείψανά . . . εὐκαρπεῦντα μελιστάκτων ἀπὸ Μουσῶν, "fruitful remnants of honey-dripping Muses") and with Meleager in *AP* 4.1.55-56 (Μούσης | . . . σφετέρης . . . λευκόϊα, "white violets of his own Muse") and *AP* 4.1.58 (ὁ τῶν Μουσέων . . . στέφανος, "the Muses' garland").

The corrupt reading ἄμεινον has, however, obscured the name of the plant that is to be identified with Diosco(u)rides. We should note that the surrounding couplets all display a plant name ending in the accusative singular -- σίσυμβρον, "bergamot mint," for Nicias (*AP* 4.1.19); μύρτον, "myrtle," for Callimachus (*AP* 4.1.21); and βότρυν, "grape cluster," for Hegesippus (*AP* 4.1.25). In all likelihood, the plant that represents Diosco(u)rides appeared in the same grammatical form in the same line position (*AP* 4.1.23). Several emendations have been suggested. Heyne proposed ἄμωνον,[10] identified as Nepaul cardamom found in Media or India (Theophr. *Hist. Pl.* 9.7.2, Dsc. 1.15). Hecker preferred ἀνωνίν,[11] a variant of ὀνωνίς, "rest harrow," a flowering plant that grows as a weed in cultivated fields (Theophr. *Hist. Pl.* 6.5.3). Neither suggestion has been generally accepted by editors. Other scholars have been more creative, seeking a corrupt phrase that encompassed ἐν Μούσῃσιν. Boissonade tried ἐν Μούσαις κυκλάμινον, "cyclamen among the Muses,"[12] while Waltz preferred to conjecture εὔμουσον κινάμωμον, "melodious cinnamon."[13] Yet there is no reason to correct ἐν Μούσῃσιν, and we should accept the moveable nu as evidence that the corruption involves a three-syllable word beginning with a vowel. Cataudella observed that the correct reading is "riddling" (γριφῶδες), like Ἑρμοῦ δῶρον in *AP* 4.1.44 and Σικελίδεω . . . ἀνέμοις ἄνθεα φυόμενα in *AP* 4.1.46,[14] where Asclepiades' name is hidden in the puzzling patronymic "Sicelidas" (as in Theoc. *Id.* 7.40)[15] and his symbolic "flowers thriving in the winds" are to be decoded as anemones.

I propose reading ἄμετρον with ἐν Μούσῃσιν: Diosco(u)rides is then a poet "unmetrical among the Muses [i.e., in poetry], who has his name from the sons of Zeus [i.e., the Dioscourides]." While the adjective ἄμετρος commonly designates prose as opposed to poetry, a parallel for the use here appears in an elegiac poem by Critias, who replaces a pentameter with an iambic trimeter in order to fit the otherwise unmetrical name Alcibiades into an innovative couplet form (4 W²; cf. Soph. 1 W²):

καὶ νῦν Κλεινίου υἱὸν Ἀθηναῖον στεφανώσω

Ἀλκιβιάδην νέοισιν ὑμνήσας τρόποις·

οὐ γάρ πως ἦν τοὔνομ᾽ ἐφαρμόζειν ἐλεγείῳ,

νῦν δ᾽ ἐν ἰαμβείῳ κείσεται **οὐκ ἀμέτρως**.

And now I will garland Cleinias' son, the Athenian
　Alcidiades, by praising him with new forms.
For not was there any way to fit his name into elegy,
　but now it will lie in iambics not unmetrically.

Critias' motif of garlanding Alcibiades with song encourages us to think that Meleager had these lines in mind when he addressed the problem of how to convey Diosco(u)rides' "unmetrical" name.

The reading ἄμετρον, however, leaves the epigrammatist without a plant as symbol. Or does it? I propose that Meleager here puns on ἄμετρος, which is offered as an alternative name for βάτος, *bramble*, in some manuscripts of the botanist Dioscorides (4.37). In this way Diosco(u)rides is both unmetrical in name and simultaneously like a bramble, a shrub with thorny stems and spinous leaves.[16] The term ἄμετρος most likely served as an alternative name for βατος because as an adjective it basically means "without moderation" or "unrestrained," often with regard to speech.[17] This is evident from the Homeric hapax ἀμετροεπής (*Il.* 2.212), "immoderate in speech," describing the low-status Thersites who rails against Agamemnon. In later texts βάτος came to symbolize critical invective, often directed by non-elite poets against those of the higher class. For example, in an epitaph anthologized by Meleager, Alcaeus (*AP* 7.536 = *HE* 13) speaks of a bramble (βάτος) that grows, in place of a (sweeter-tasting) grape cluster, on the grave of the invective poet Hipponax. Meleager may have had this epigram in mind when he characterized Diosco(u)ides as ἄμετρος meaning bramble, since in the following line (*AP* 4.1.25) he contrastively presents Hegisippus as a cluster of grapes. Similarly, in a Hellenistic epitaph attributed to Zenodotus (*AP* 7.315 = *HE* 3) or possibly Rhianus, the misanthrope Timon, who typically abuses passersby, asks the dry earth to entwine a "prickly thorn" (τρηχείαν . . . ῥάμνον 1) or the "untamed branches of a twisting bramble" (σκολιῆς ἄγρια κῶλα βάτου 2) all in order to conceal his final resting place. Timon's famed hatred of other humans is here troped by the thorn bush and the bramble that would prevent access to his grave.[18] In the fable narrated in Callimachus' *Iambus* 4, as the *Diegesis* tells us, a laurel and an olive tree engage in a νεῖκος over their status and importance, only to be interrupted by a "prickly bramble" (βάτος τὸ τρηχ., 96 who points out that they play into the hands of their enemies by their criticism of each other. The laurel then vilifies the elderly bramble as an "evil disgrace" (ὦ κακὴ λώβη, *Dieg.* VII 16). The fable is told by one Simos ("Snub-nosed") who happens to pass by as the poet is quarreling with one of his rivals and then offends them by asserting his equal merit. The moral of the fragmentary fable is unclear, but what is important for our purposes is that the low-status bramble plays the role of an invective poet who critiques and corrects other poets of higher status.[19] This dichotomy of high and low plays out also in Meleager's proem where higher-class epigrammatists are associated with symbols of prestige, the laurel for Samius (*AP* 4.1.14), a close associate of Philip V, and the olive for Alexander Aetolus (*AP* 4.1.39), a textual scholar and versatile poet in the courts of Ptolemy II and Antigonus Gonatas.

Why then should Diosco(u)ides be identified with the humble bramble? The solution may lie with two of his epigrams, *AP* 11.195 = *HE* 36 and 11.363 = *HE* 37, now housed in the Palatine Anthology's scoptic book because of their invective nature. In *AP* 11.195, a speaker, perhaps to be identified with the poet, complains that a pantomime artist dancing the role of a Gallus bested him in a contest after his role as a female character from a Euripidean tragedy was harshly condemned by the audience; *AP* 11.363 concerns (rather obscurely) one Moschus who won a torch race in Alexandria despite his apparent low birth. In all probability, Meleager originally anthologized these two epigrams in his diverse, epideictic book since his *Garland* contained no separate book of scoptic epigrams. Both were later apparently removed by Constantine Cephalas to book 11, indicating that this Byzantine anthologizer read them as critical or satiric in nature.[20] Three other epigrams by Diosco(u)rides concern characters who have suffered abuse from invective. In *AP* 7.351 = *HE* 17 the daughters of Lycambes claim from the grave that Archilochus falsely accused them of improper sexual behavior; in *AP* 7.450 = *HE* 26 the Samian Philaenis denies writing pornographic works and proclaims her own chastity; and in *AP* 7.456 = *HE* 29 an old nurse, who was overly fond of wine, was buried by her owner in a field near wine vats. In all three cases the women had apparently been subject to verbal abuse, whether guilty or not. While Meleager mostly avoided scoptic epigrams in his *Garland*, it seems likely that Dioscorides composed a number of such epigrams that have not survived.

On that basis, I propose that Meleager identified Diosco(u)rides with a type of bramble called ἄμετρος, standing for the invective epigrams in his oeuvre.[21]

Notes

1 Meleager also refers to unnamed poets designated ἄλλων τ' ἔρνεα πολλὰ νεόγραοα, "many newly written sprouts of others" (*AP* 4.1.55). There are twelve named poets found in sequences from Meleager's *Garland* that may belong to this group, likely his contemporaries.

2 Fantuzzi and Hunter (2004), 288–9. For the possibility of a poetry book consisting of Simonides' epigrams, see Sider (2007, 2020).

3 Descriptions of the tree are found in Theophrastus (*Hist. Pl.* 3.15.3–4) and Pliny (*HN* 13.54), while Dioscorides (1.71) lists its uses.

4 For other suggested solutions to connections between poets and their plants, see Lai (1995), 129–31, on Nicias imaged as bergamot mint (*AP* 4.1.19–20); Lai (1996/97), 95–6, on Antagoras the Rhodian imaged as oxeye (*AP* 4.1.52); Nicolosi (2015) on Archilochus imaged as the flower of a thistle (*AP* 4.1.37–8); and Nicolosi (2016) on Meleager imaged as white violets (*AP* 4.1.55–6).

5 Gow and Page (1965), vol. 2, 306–7, print only *APl* 170 = *HE* 1, missing from the Palatine but ascribed to Hermodorus by Planudes, and they omit *AP* 9.77, ascribed to Antipater of Thessalonica in the *Palatine Anthology* but to Ariston or Hermodorus in the *Planudean Anthology*.

6 Cf. Nic. *Ther.* 604, νάρδου . . . εὐστάχυος; Plin. *HN* 12.42, *nardi spicas . . . celebrant*.

7 Theophr. *Hist. Pl.* 9.7.2–3, *Od.* 12, 28; Dsc. 1.7.1, 1.62.

8 Luc. 10.164, *sertas nardo florente coronas*. Other references include Lucr. 2.848, *nardi florem, nectar qui naribus halat*; Hor. *Carm.* 2.11.16–17, *Assyriaque nardo potamus uncti*; Tib. 2.2.7, *puro destillent tempora nardo*.

9 E.g., *KAI* 53, *c.* 400 BCE (Bonnet 2015: 452–3) where the Phoenician name of a Sidonian was translated on his tombstone in the Piraeus as "Artemiodorus, son of Heliodorus"; see Parker (2017) 39, 181–3.

10 In *Ephemer. Gotting* (1789), no. 88, according to Jacobs (1794–1814), vol. 6, 8.

11 Hecker (1843), 15.

12 In Dübner (1864–72), vol. 1, 54.

13 Waltz (1928), ad loc.

14 Cataudella (1968), 241–2, though his solution of the riddle in *AP* 4.1.23 is unconvincing.

15 On a possible meaning of the patronymic, see Sens (2011), xxix–xxxi.

16 Theophr. *Hist. Pl.* 1.10.6–7.

17 Poll. *Onom.* 6.146 provides a series of near synonyms.

18 In an epitaph by Hegesippus (*AP* 7.320 = *HE* 8), Timon threatens a passerby with the thorns and stakes that guard his burial site.

19 Cf. Acosta-Hughes' (2002: 204) association of the "the character of the agon" with "poetic style."

20 Interestingly, *AP* 11.195 appears in the Palatine manuscript a second time just preceding Callimachus *AP* 11.362 = *HE* 49, which was directly followed by Dioscorides 11.363. Since Cephalas often moved an epigram from its original Meleagrian sequence to one of his own devising, carelessly leaving it in both sequences (Cameron 1993: 134–5), we may surmise that the trio of *AP* 11.195, 11.362, and 11.363 once appeared in this order in Meleager's *Garland*.

21 In *AP* 4.1.33–8 Meleager's plant imagery refers to the epigrams of Bacchylides, Anacreon, and Archilochus in contrast to the greater body of their other poetry.

Bibliography

Acosta-Hughes, B. (2002), *Polyeideia: The* Iambi *of Callimachus and the Archaic Iambic Tradition*, Berkeley, CA: University of California Press.

Bing, P. and J. S. Bruss, eds. (2007), *Brill's Companion to Hellenistic Epigram*, Leiden and Boston, MA: Brill.

Bonnet, C. (2015), *Les enfants de Cadmos: le paysage religieux de la Phénicie hellénistique*, Paris: De Boccard.

Cameron, A. (1993), *The Greek Anthology from Meleager to Planude*, Oxford: Clarendon Press.

Cataudella, Q. (1968), "Meleagrea," *Rivisita di Cultura Classica e Mediovale*, 10: 241–8.

Dübner, F., ed. (1864–72), *Epigrammatum Anthologia Palatina cum Planudeis et appendice nova epigrammatum veterum e libris et marmoribus ductorum*, 2 vols, Paris: Editore Ambrosio Firmin Didot.

Fantuzzi, M. and R. Hunter (2004), *Tradition and Innovation in Hellenistic Poetry*, Cambridge: Cambridge University Press.

Gow, A. S. F. and D. L. Page, eds. (1965), *The Greek Anthology: Hellenistic Epigrams*, 2 vols, Cambridge: Cambridge University Press.

Hecker, A. (1843), *Commentatio critica de Anthologia Graeca*. Lugduni Batavorum: Apud S. et J. Luchtmans.

Jacobs, F., ed. (1794–1814), *Anthologia Graeca sive poetarum graecorum lusus ex recensione Brunckii*, 13 vols, Leipzig: Insel Verlag.

KAI = Donner, H. and W. Röllig, ed. (2002), *Kanaanäische und aramäische Inschriften.* 5th ed., Wiesbaden: Harrassowitz Verlag.

Lai, A. (1995), "Il χλοερὸν σίσυμβρον di Nicia, medico-poeta milesio," *Quaderni Urbinati di Cultura Classica*, 51: 125–31.

Lai, A. (1996/1997), "Un aneddoto su Antagora di Rodi e l'ΕΥΣΤΡΟΦΟΝ ὌΜΜΑ ΒΟΟΣ nel Proemio della *Corona* di Meleagro," *Lexis* 56: 93–7 = *Quaderni Urbinati di Cultura Classica*, 56: 119–24.

Nicolosi, A. (2015), "Il cardo di Archiloco: Meleag. *AP* IV 1.37s. (= *HE* 1,37s)," *Studi Classici e Orienti*, 61: 47–53.

Nicolosi, A. (2016), "Meleagro e la viola bianca della poesia (*AP* 4, 1, 55 S. = *HE* 3980 S.)," *Quaderni Urbinati di Cultura Classica*, 114: 119–26.

Parker, R. (2017), *Greek Gods Abroad: Names, Natures, and Transformations*, Oakland, CA: University of California Press.

Sens, A. (2011), *Asclepiades of Samos: Epigrams and Fragments*, Oxford and New York: Oxford University Press.

Sider, D. (2007), "*Sylloge Simonidea*," in P. Bing and J. S. Bruss (eds.), *Brill's Companion to Hellenistic Epigram*, 113–30, Leiden and Boston, MA: Brill.

Sider, D., ed. (2020), *Simonides: Epigrams and Elegies*, Oxford: Oxford University Press.

Waltz, P., ed. (1928), *Anthologie grecque, première partie: Anthologie Palatine*, Tome I, Livres I–IV, Paris: Les Belles Lettres.

Part Five

Ancient Prose Fiction

The *Sparagmos* of Parthenope between Ancient Novel and Myth

Jacqueline Arthur-Montagne
University of Virginia

The publication of Stephens and Winkler's *Ancient Greek Novels: The Fragments* opened a new horizon in the study of ancient narrative.[1] While their edition of lesser-known novel fragments like *Sesonchosis* and *Kalligone* was not without precedent—Zimmerman had collated several *Griechische Roman-Papyri* half a century earlier[2]—the volume of accessible texts and translations with essays on the circulation, readership, and statistical representation of ancient novels in the papyri invigorated scholarship on the origin and context of the genre. It also expanded, for newcomers to the field like me, the variety of texts to be considered under the category of "ancient novels." Revising outdated notions of ancient novel readers as juvenile romantics or bourgeois book-buyers, Stephens documented the elevated quality and practiced hands of the novel papyri, "from workmanlike to elegant."[3] Their study encouraged classicists to treat the ancient novels as a part of, and not apart from, the Imperial literary culture to which they certainly belonged.

The second entry in Stephens and Winkler's edition is the Greek novel *Metiochos and Parthenope* which, while fragmentary, achieved a degree of popularity that is difficult to document for other prose fictions of the early Roman Empire.[4] The two (or perhaps three?) columns of the text appear to preserve only the beginning of the narrative, when Metiochos first arrives at the court of Polykrates and converses with Parthenope on the subject of love.[5] But other *testimonia*, namely the satirist Lucian and two floor mosaics from Syrian Antioch, suggest the storyline was known to audiences of the Roman East, perhaps through the medium of pantomime dance.[6] The roots of their tale can be traced to the third book of Herodotus' *Histories*, which records the story of the Samian tyrant Polycrates and his virgin daughter.[7] And the novel had a long afterlife in the literature of the Late Antique and Medieval Near East. A Christian adaptation, *The Martyrdom of St. Parthenope*, reimagines the virgin heroine as the unwilling target of Emperor Constantine's affections; in the Arabic and Coptic versions, she prefers death to marriage. A Persian adaptation entitled *Vāmiq u ʿAdhrā* also survives from an eleventh-century epic poet, who inspired "a rich tradition of stories about *The Lover and the Virgin* in Muslim literature."[8]

Closer to the chronology of the Greek novel's composition, however, the heroine of the *Parthenope* text and pantomime overlapped with a Parthenope of a very different tradition: the Siren of Southern Italy. Homer's *Odyssey* did not offer much in the way of detail on the Sirens' origins or physical appearance, but later poets and mythographers filled in the gaps with local legends and fictions.[9] The most elaborate of these post-Homeric receptions comes from the obscure *Alexandra* of Lycophron, a poet of the third or second century BCE.[10] Displaying a deep familiarity with the geography and cults of Southern Italy, Lycophron revisits the encounter between Odysseus and three Sirens. In this version, Odysseus becomes the "slayer" (κτενεῖ, 712) of the Sirens, who hurl themselves to their deaths in the sea when they fail to seduce the Ithacan hero.[11] The Siren named Parthenope is the first to wash ashore on the Italian coastline near the Glanis, a tributary of the Tiber that runs south towards Naples. There the inhabitants bury her body, erect a tomb, and sacrifice to her annually as a "bird goddess" (οἰωνὸν θεάν, 721). In the centuries that followed, the Siren Parthenope metamorphosed into a patron deity and appellation for the city of Naples.[12] She appears as a sweet nurturer in Vergil's *Georgics* (*dulcis alebat Parthenope*, 4.563–4) and a kindly benefactor in Statius' *Silvae* (*benigna Parthenope*, 3.1.151–2).[13] The two Parthenope stories, of virgin and Siren, originated from and passed through entirely separate literary channels: Herodotean history to prose novel and pantomime versus Homeric epic to Hellenistic and Latin poetry. But it is difficult to know whether audiences in the High Roman Empire would have been able to disambiguate the two.

The confusion of the two Parthenopes is in fact attested in later Greek writing, perhaps as early as the principate. The first Greek *testimonium* of the Parthenope tradition catalogued in Hägg and Utas' *The Virgin and Her Lover* is a passage from Dionysius Periegetes, a geographer of the second or third century CE. In describing Campania, Dionysius marks out the "dwelling of pure Parthenope" (μέλαθρον ἁγνῆς Παρθενόπης, 357–8).[14] Hägg and Utas interpret the adjective *hagnēs*—which can indicate both holiness and virginal purity—as a sign that the two Parthenopes confused Dionysius, "who seems to have contaminated them in his text."[15] This single adjective, on the one hand, seems rather thin evidence that

Dionysius had the novel heroine in mind. Dionysius may instead be responding to the generous adjectives used by Vergil and Statius to describe Parthenope as Naples. It is also reasonable, *pace* Hägg,[16] that Dionysius would have referred to this Parthenope as "holy" given that, by his generation, she was no longer regarded a fearsome Siren so much as a cult goddess. But even if Dionysius was not confused about which Parthenope he meant, his phrasing certainly divided later scholiasts of his *Oikoumenes periegesis*. Two surviving scholia from the Middle Byzantine period suggest that the traditions converged and comingled within classical antiquity.

The first scholiast is known to us by neither name nor exact date. Hägg and Utas posit that the scholiast has no direct knowledge of the *Parthenope* novel or pantomime but instead that "the scholia genre accumulated and transmitted factual knowledge through centuries in a largely closed learned tradition."[17] If that is indeed the case, then the anonymous scholiast preserves a longstanding split in the tradition about precisely which Parthenope Dionysius meant:[18]

Παρθενόπης δὲ μέλαθρον] οὐχ, ὥς τινες ὀρχηστικῇ προσέχοντες ἱστορίᾳ ὑπενόησαν, Παρθενόπης λέγεσθαι τῆς Σαμίας, ἢ τὸν ἄνδρα ζητοῦσα Ἀναξίλαον περιῄει, ἀλλὰ μιᾶς τῶν Σειρήνων, ἥτις λέγεται ἐκεῖσε αὐτὴν δισκεῦσαι. ἡ δὲ ἱστορία κεῖται ἐντελὴς παρὰ τῷ τὴν Ἀλέξανδραν γράψαντι Λυκόφρονι. Παρθενόπη λέγεται διὰ τὸ πολλοῖς ὑποπεσοῦσα ἀνδράσι φυλάξαι τὴν παρθενίαν. ἀπὸ δὲ Φρυγίας ἐρασθεῖσα Μητιόχου καὶ ἀποτεμοῦσα τὰς τρίχας εἰς Καμπανίαν ἦλθε καὶ ἐκεῖ ᾤκησεν. οἱ δὲ μίαν τῶν Σειρήνων φασὶ μετὰ τὸν σπαραγμὸν ἐκβρασθῆναι ἐκεῖ καὶ ὡς θεὸν νομισθῆναι. ἡνίκα γὰρ Ὀδυσσεὺς παρέπλευσεν αὐτὰς καὶ οὐκ ἐθέλχθη ὑπὸ τῆς ᾠδῆς αὐτῶν, οὔτε δέ τις τῶν ἑταίρων αὐτοῦ, τηνικαῦτα ἡ Παρθενόπη, μία δὲ ἦν τῶν Σειρήνων, μανεῖσα, ἐπειδὴ μὴ ἴσχυσε τοὺς περὶ τὸν Ὀδυσσέα καταθέλξαι, ἑαυτὴν κατεπόντισεν. εἰσὶ δὲ τὰ ὀνόματα τῶν Σειρήνων ταῦτα, ὡς καὶ Λυκόφρων, Παρθενόπη, Λευκωσία καὶ Λίγεια.

[*The dwelling of Parthenope*] This does not refer, as some intent on a pantomime narrative conjecture, to Parthenope of Samos, who went around to Anaxilaos[19] looking for her husband, but to one of the Sirens who is said to have thrown herself there. This narrative lies in its entirety in Lycophron, who wrote the *Alexandra*. Parthenope is so named because she protected her virginity, despite falling subject to many men. Having fallen in love with Metiochus and cutting off her hair, she went from Phrygia to Campania and settled there. Others say that she was one of the Sirens who, after the dismemberment, washed ashore there and was revered as a god. For because Odysseus sailed by them and was not bewitched by their singing—nor were any of his companions—then Parthenope, who was one of the Sirens, went mad. When she did not prevail at enchanting Odysseus' men, she threw herself into the sea. According to Lycophron, the names of these Sirens are Parthenope, Leucosia, and Ligea.

This one annotation attests numerous, interwoven strands of Parthenope narratives. First the scholiast distinguishes Parthenope of Samos from Parthenope the Siren, anchoring them to separate literary genres: the former is a pantomime performance (ὀρχηστικῇ ἱστορίᾳ) whereas the latter appears in poetry (τὴν Ἀλέξανδραν). The next two sentences present a confusing background of Parthenope of Samos: she is named for her devotion to virginity but departed for Campania after falling in love with Metiochus, or perhaps in search of a husband. This character straddles the divide between fleeing lover and dutiful wife (τὸν ἄνδρα ζητοῦσα). The following sentences present an equally disjointed description of Parthenope the Siren. Was her death caused by dismemberment (σπαραγμὸν) or Odysseus' escape, and which occurred first? She was revered as a goddess but is here portrayed as a dangerous seductress.

Although this first scholiast is convinced that Dionysius intended Parthenope the Siren, a second scholiast, Eustathius of Thessalonica (twelfth century), favors the opposite reading of Dionysius' adjective.[20] While his commentary recapitulates both interpretations, he tells the story of the novel heroine Parthenope last. Eustathius divulges new details of the novel plot that had not appeared in prior Greek sources: Parthenope cuts her hair (τρίχας ἔτεμεν) to disfigure her beauty and settles in Campania. He also explains that the virgin's characteristic prudence (σωφροσύνην) "is perhaps why Dionysius called Parthenope 'chaste'" (τάχα . . . ἀγὴν ὁ Διονύσιος τὴν Παρθενόπην ὠνόμασεν, 358.26–8). Although Eustathius lends more credence to the theory that Dionysius intends Parthenope the virgin, his synopsis of the novel or pantomime plot shares some puzzling details in common with the first scholiast. To begin, he suggests that Parthenope travels to or perhaps even settles in Southern Italy. Eustathius cites Campania, whereas the first scholiast describes Parthenope's travels to see "Anaxilaos." In a fifth century BCE context, Anaxilaos would be the tyrant of Rhegion who appears in Herodotus' account of Samos after the Ionian revolt.[21] In the Greek novel or pantomime plot, Anaxilaos' realm may have been a waypoint in Parthenope's "wanderings" after she was separated from her lover Metiochus. That these wanderings included Italy is confirmed by the Persian testimonia in Hägg and Utas, which describe Rhegion as a port at which Parthenope arrives and Anaxilaos as a king "full of tricks, fraud and seduction."[22] Of course, Parthenope's travels along the coastline of Southern Italy would also bring her into contact with the territory of the Sirens, where (according to Lycophron) inhabitants worshipped the bird goddess Parthenope.

Another curious commonality between the two *scholia* is the theme of disfigurement, although each scholiast attributes the act to different Parthenopes. In Eustathius, the method of disfigurement is clear: the virgin Parthenope, after being separated from her beloved Metiochus, cuts her hair short and "condemns herself to ugliness" (ἀκοσμίαν ἑαυτῆς καταψηφισζομένη, 358.25). Her short hair would presumably deflect would-be suitors and even allow Parthenope to pass as a young man during her travels.[23] Although the haircutting scene does not survive in any of the Greek novel fragments, the Christian adaptation of the Parthenope story, *The Martyrdom*, may feature a parallel in the first chapter of the Arabic translation. Here the young girl Parthenope enters the convent and has her hair cut by the nuns to make her a model of Christian chastity (1.3). In the anonymous scholiast, on the other hand, the act of disfigurement remains obscure: he reports that the Siren Parthenope committed suicide "after the *sparagmos*" (μετὰ τὸν σπαραγμὸν). The noun *sparagmos*, which means "tearing" or "severing," appears infrequently in Greek literature; its best-known attestation come from Euripides' *Bacchae* when the bacchants "tear apart" cattle and even Pentheus with their bare hands.[24] Other occurrences in Lucian (τὸν Ἀψύρτου σπαραγμὸν, *Salt.* 53) and Herodian (γενείων τε καὶ ὀφρύων σπαραγμοῖς, 8.8.6) confirm that later Greek authors used the word to signify dismemberment or disfigurement of the body by tearing away parts from the whole. In relation to the Siren Parthenope, Hägg and Utas concede that "it is unclear what it [*sparagmos*] may refer to in the story of the Sirens as told by Homer and Lykophron." No scholarship to date has yet identified the scholiast's meaning.

I suspect that the scholiast to Dionysius Periegetes here refers to a myth of the Sirens preserved neither in Homer nor Lykophron, but in later voices of the Greek literary tradition: that the Sirens lost their wings in a contest with the Muses. Pausanias, the geographer and author of *Heliados periegesis* (second century), relates this story in a chapter on Coroneia, where he describes a statue of Hera holding the Sirens in her hand. The sculpture depicts the result of a lyrical contest between the Muses and the Sirens, orchestrated by Hera. According to Pausanias, "When the Muses won, they are said to have plucked the Sirens' feathers (ἀποτίλασαι τῶν Σειρήνων τὰ πτερὰ) and made crowns out of them."[25] Pausanias elaborates on neither the timeline nor the conclusion of this episode: did the removal of the Sirens' wings take place before or after Odysseus? Did it result in their deaths?[26] Another version of the story appears in the epitome of the *Ethnica* by Stephanus of Byzantium (sixth century). Like Pausanias, he records a "quarrel" (ἔριδος) of the Sirens and Muses; in his version, however, the distressed Sirens "took off their [own] wings from their shoulders" (τὰ πτερὰ τῶν ὤμων ἀπέβαλον) before hurling themselves into the sea.[27] Confirming that this myth amounted to more than travelogue trivia is also a sarcophagus from Rome (third century), currently housed in the Metropolitan Museum of Art.[28] One long-side marble panel tells the story of the contest from left to right (Plate 16): the Olympians sitting in judgment (on the far left), the musical performance (center), and the violent rending of the Sirens' wings (far right).[29] Whether the Muses completely severed the Sirens' wings or simply thinned their plumage is not clear from the sarcophagus. But to Eustathius' thinking, at least, it made better sense for the Sirens to be wingless by the arrival of Odysseus in *Od.* 12: "For the Sirens would have pursued Odysseus by flight when he was sailing by, if indeed they were furnished with wings."[30]

The attestation of this myth in Imperial Greek literature and material culture raises some intriguing—if probably unanswerable—questions about the overlap and interaction of the two Parthenope traditions at play in the Roman principate. Scholars of the *Parthenope* novel and pantomime have largely analyzed the plot against its Herodotean backdrop and other Greek romances.[31] But the presence of another and arguably better-known Parthenope in the legends and literature of Magna Grecia prompts me to wonder whether the first-century novelist also drew upon the Siren story in the construction of his plot. If indeed the *Parthenope* novel heroine traveled to Campania or Rhegion, as the scholiasts and Persian *testimonia* indicate, it seems unlikely that the author and audience would fail to recognize that the character wandered in the precise region that shared her name. Another speculation worth entertaining is the possibility that the novelist drew inspiration for the disfigurement of his heroine from the story of the Sirens' own dismemberment. The severing of wings and the cutting of hair both have a disarming effect: the wings of the Sirens afforded them a dangerous advantage over sailors, while the long hair of Parthenope overwhelmed her suitors. In both instances, disfigurement mitigates the threat of danger and allows the two Parthenopes to assimilate into the societies of Southern Italy with new identities. Seductresses are sources of danger in Greek literature, from Homeric epic to the romance novels. While Siren and heroine are Parthenopes of very different orders, they nonetheless embody the same duality of temptation and peril.

The parallels I have identified between Parthenope the novel heroine and Parthenope the Siren are and will likely remain conjectural at best, barring the discovery of new evidence. But they may point the way towards new and contextualized approaches to the romance novels as products of their Imperial landscape. The Greek romances tend to evoke the times and spaces of Archaic and Hellenistic Greece but are deeply embedded in a literary culture that tries to make sense of Greece under Rome. Contemplating one Parthenope in the orbit of the other, as the scholiasts of Dionysius clearly did, may help remind us of how the readers and writers of the ancient novels made sense of romance plots in a contemporary context.

Notes

1 Stephens and Winkler (1995).
2 Zimmerman (1936).
3 Stephens and Winkler (1995), 9.
4 Ibid., 100.
5 Confirmed fragments of the *Parthenope* novel include *O. Bodl.* 2175 and *P. Berol.* 7927, 9588, and 21179. *P. Oxy.* 435 may also belong to the novel and, if so, would depict Parthenope's travels to Corcyra. For the newest edition of *P. Berol.* 7927, see Martínez and Ruiz-Montero (2020), 1–23 (preliminary version).
6 Luc. *Salt.* 2: ἐρωτικὰ γύναια, τῶν πάλαι τὰς μαχλοτάτας, Φαίδρας καὶ Παρθενόπας καὶ Ῥοδόπας τινάς, ed. Harmon (1936). On the two mosaics housed at the Bodmer Library and Zeugma Mosaic Museum, see Hägg and Utas (2003), 57–64. Mignogna (1996), 232–3, remains more skeptical of the association between the novel and pantomime.
7 Hdt. 3.124–6 and 140–2; Metiochos appears in 6.41.
8 Hägg and Utas (2003), 1. On these later adaptations of the *Parthenope* narrative, see pp. 65–187.
9 For an overview of the Sirens in Homer and later Greek literature and material culture, see the chapters of Doherty and Neils in Cohen (1995), 81–92 and 175–84, respectively.
10 For the debates on Lycophron's identity and date, see McNelis and Sens (2016), 10–11.
11 All translations are my own unless otherwise noted.
12 Edlund (1987), 45–7. See also the chapters of Scarrone and Walde in Leopold, Perra, and Scholler (2018), 21–51 and 53–85, respectively.
13 Newlands (2019), 357: "[Statius] represents Parthenope not, however, as a drowned Siren whose body was washed ashore but rather as a traveler by ship seeking refuge and safe harbor."
14 Dionys. Per. 357–8, ed. Brodersen (1994).
15 Hägg and Utas (2003), 48–9, who translate "pure" Parthenope. Stephens and Winkler, *Ancient Greek*, 77 opt for the more neutral translation of "holy" in conjunction with the burial of the Siren.
16 Hägg and Utas (2003), 49: "The epithet 'pure' or 'chaste' can hardly refer to the Siren."
17 Ibid., 49.

18 *Scholia in Dionysii periegetae orbis descriptionem* 358, ed. Müller (1965).
19 The most natural reading here would be "looking for her husband, Anaxilaos." But as Hägg and Utas (2003), 47 note, this more likely refers to Anaxilaos, tyrant of Rhegion in Southern Italy (494–476 BCE). Anaxilaos appears in connection with Samos in Hdt. 6.23, persuading the Samias to capture Zankle for his own political purposes.
20 Eust. *Commentarium in Dionysii periegetae orbis descriptionem* 358.21–9, ed. Müller (1965).
21 Hdt. 6.23.2. Cf. Strabo 6.1.6 and Diod. Sic. 11.48.2.
22 Hägg and Utas (2003), 243.
23 Ibid., on potential motives and parallels in other Greek novels.
24 Eur. *Bacch.* 735 (βακχῶν σπαραγμόν) and 1134–5 (γυμνοῦντο δὲ πλευραὶ σπαραγμοῖς). On the ritual and mythical connotations of the act of *sparagmos*, see Weaver (2009), 1–43.
25 Paus. 9.34.3–4: τὰς γὰρ δὴ Ἀχελῴου θυγατέρας ἀναπεισθείσας φασὶν ὑπὸ Ἥρας καταστῆναι πρὸς τὰς Μούσας ἐς ᾠδῆς ἔργον· αἱ δὲ ὡς ἐνίκησαν, ἀποτίλασαι τῶν Σειρήνων τὰ πτερὰ ποιήσασθαι στεφάνους ἀπ᾽ αὐτῶν λέγονται, ed. Spiro (1903).
26 Weicker (1902), 76–7, regards Pausanias' myth as "naively etiological" and a rationalizing fiction to make sense of the Sirens' suicide. In contrast, Tsiafakis (2001), 20, proposes that this and other myths of the Sirens' destruction "could be symbolic of human victory over death."
27 Steph. Byz. *Ethnica* 1.336: Ἄπτερα, πόλις Κρήτης, ἀπὸ τῆς τῶν Μουσῶν καὶ Σειρήνων ἔριδος, τῆς ἐν τῷ μουσείῳ πλησίον τῆς πόλεως καὶ τῆς θαλάττης τόπῳ τοιῶσδε καλουμένῳ γενομένης, ἐν ᾧ μετὰ τὴν ἐν μουσικῇ νίκην τῶν Μουσῶν αἱ Σειρῆνες δυσφοροῦσαι τὰ πτερὰ τῶν ὤμων ἀπέβαλον καὶ λευκαὶ γενόμεναι εἰς τὴν θάλασσαν ἐνέβαλον ἑαυτάς, ed. Billerbeck (2006).
28 Accession no. 10.104. For images and interpretation, see McCann (1978), 46–50. See Vermeule (1960), 9 and 44 (fig. 13 b) for the lost lid, showing the Sirens seducing Odysseus.
29 Wegner (1966), no. 72, plate 142d reports a similar sarcophagus in the Bibliothèque Nationale of Paris, also dated to the third century CE.
30 Eust. *Od.* 12.167: οὗτοι δὲ καὶ πτερωτὰς αὐτὰς πλάττουσιν, οὐ μὴν οὕτω καὶ ὁ ποιητής. ἢ γὰρ ἂν ἐδίωξαν τὸν Ὀδυσσέα παρελάσαντα προσπετόμεναι, εἴ γε πτεροῖς διῳκοῦντο, ed. Stallbaum (1970).
31 Levi (1944), 420–8; Bowie (2003), 47–63.

Bibliography

Bowie, E. (2003), "The Chronology of the Earlier Greek Novels since B.E. Perry: Revisions and Precisions," *Ancient Narrative*, 2: 47–63.

Coffee, N., C. Forstall, L. Galli Milic and D. Nelis, eds. (2019), *Intertextuality in Flavian Epic Poetry*, Berlin: De Gruyter.

Cohen, B., ed. (1995), *The Distaff Side: Representing the Female in Homer's* Odyssey, Oxford: Oxford University Press.

Edlund, I. (1987), "The Sacred Geography of Southern Italy in Lycophron's *Alexandra*," *Opuscula Romana*, 16: 43–9.

Greenberg, M. ed. (2001), *Studia Varia from the J. Paul Getty Museum*, vol. 2, Los Angeles, CA: Getty.

Hägg, T. and B. Utas (2003), *The Virgin and Her Lover: Fragments of an Ancient Greek Novel and a Persian Epic Poem*, Leiden: Brill.

Harmon, A. M., ed. (1936), *Lucian*. vol. 5, Cambridge, MA: Harvard University Press.

Leopold, S., V. Porra, and D. Scholler, eds. (2018), *Parthenope—Neapolis—Napoli: Bilder einer porösen Stadt*, Mainz: Mainz University Press.

Levi, D. (1944), "The Novel of Ninus and Semiramis," *Proceedings of the American Philosophical Society*, 87: 420–8.

Martínez. M. P. L. and C. Ruiz-Montero (2020), "Parthenope's Novel: *P. Berol.* 7927 – 9588 + 21179, II Column Revisited," *Ancient Narrative*, 17: 1–23.

McCann, A. (1978), *Roman Sarcophagi in the Metropolitan Museum of Art*, New York: Metropolitan Museum.

McNelis, C. and A. Sens (2016), *The Alexandra of Lycophron: A Literary Study*, Oxford: Oxford University Press.

Mignogna, E. (1996), "Narrative greca e mimo: il romanzo di Achille Tazio," *Studi italiani di filologia classica*, 14: 232–43.

Newlands, C. (2019), "Statius' Post-Vesuvian Landscape and Virgil's Parthenope," in N. Coffee, C. Forstall, L. Galli Milic and D. Nelis (eds.), *Intertextuality in Flavian Epic Poetry*, 349–72, Berlin: De Gruyter.

Stephens, S. and J. Winkler (1995), *Ancient Greek Novels: The Fragments*, Princeton NJ: Princeton University Press.

Tsiafakis, D. (2001), "Life and Death at the Hands of a Siren," in M. Greenberg (ed.), *Studia Varia from the J. Paul Getty Museum*, vol. 2, 7–24, Los Angeles, CA: Getty.

Vermeule, C. (1960), "The Dal-Pozzo-Albani Drawings of Classical Antiquities in the British Museum," *Transactions of the American Philosophical Society*, 50: 1–78.

Weaver, B. (2009), "Euripides' *Bacchae* and Classical Typologies of Pentheus' *Sparagmos*. 510–406 BCE," *Bulletin of the Institute of Classical Studies*, 52: 15–43.

Wegner, M. (1966), *Die Musensarkophage*, Berlin: Gebr. Mann Verlag.

Weicker, G. (1902), *Der Seelenvogel in der alten Litteratur und Kunst: ein mythologischarchaeologische Untersuchung*, Leipzig: Teubner.

Zimmerman, F. (1936), *Griechische Roman-Papyri und verwandte Texte*, Heidelberg: F. Bilabel.

21

Alexandria in the Ancient Greek Novels

Stephen A. Nimis
American University in Cairo

Of all the deeds of Alexander the Great, the founding of Alexandria *ad Aegyptum* was perhaps the one of most enduring significance. But as Susan Stephens has recently shown, the real meaning of that famous city with respect to several of the key elements of its history is even today a matter of great dispute, with the same set of facts providing multiple and conflicting evaluations of the city, depending on one's disciplinary perspective (Stephens 2017). Even in antiquity, the city had a remarkably variable set of resonances: the newest and richest city in a very old and wealthy country, a center of Greek culture in an exotic land, the site of intrigue and rebelliousness in a land renowned for continuity and permanence. An onslaught of negative propaganda against the Ptolemies in Augustan literature established many stereotypes that endured for centuries, but the material record of Egyptian references in the Roman Empire tell a much more nuanced view (Maehler 2003; Versluys 2002). Greek imperial literature was often more positive about Egypt, despite the persistence of numerous negative tropes (Monolaraki 2012). The ancient novel fits into this trend, and the following survey of references to Alexandria in them will bear this out.

In the Greek novels that include travel, Egypt is a destination where heroes and heroines travel and have harrowing experiences that hint at the motif of figurative death and renewal, but in only two novels, Xenophon and Achilles Tatius, is the city of Alexandria actually mentioned. Variously set from the Persian period to an indefinite time in the Roman Empire, all the novels are composed when Egyptian Alexandria was still a cultural powerhouse and when Alexandrian literature still an important inspiration. Although the novels are generally Hellenocentric in ideology, their world is a decentered one, ranging from Egypt and Ethiopia, to Sicily and Italy, Anatolia, Babylon and the levant. Indeed none of action in any of the novels (apart from incidents reported in flashbacks) takes place on the Greek mainland. Meanwhile, acknowledgement of the contemporary Roman Empire's material and political existence is studiously avoided, so that characters ranging the Mediterranean neither observe nor acknowledge any aspect of its overwhelming presence at the time the novels were actually written. But this absence does not mean the Roman Empire is completely out of mind. For example, the Persian Empire is sometimes seen as a stand-in for the Roman Empire. So, also, in the two novels set before Alexander the Great (Chariton and Heliodorus), he and his famous Egyptian city still inhabit the story in various ways.

Heliodorus' *Aethiopica* is the latest of the extant novels (fourth century CE) but set in the Persian period of Egyptian history, before the founding of Alexandria. Heliodorus' novel opens at the Heracleotic mouth of the Nile, near the location of the future site of Alexandria. The description and action in this part of the story seems imbued with hints of the future Alexandria in a way that suits the famous cosmopolis that still thrives at the time of the novel's composition. In the novel the area is a site for semi-barbaric "herdsmen," *boukoloi*, who inhabit the nearby marshy areas of the delta region and use the peculiar geography of the place to resist any kind of domination by legitimate authority. These characters figure in several of the novels and also appear in historical sources, such as Dio Cassius (Rutherford 2000). Whatever their historical reality, they are the great boogeymen of the novels who capture heroes and heroines alike, and provide a pretext for testing the chastity and ingenuity of those heroes. In Heliodorus, their home becomes the staging ground for a strange brew of Egyptian, Persian and Greek characters who interact in ways that anticipate the future cosmopolis that Alexandria will become. A detailed ethnography and description of this region, *boukolia*, is given by the author parts of which are based on literary sources like Herodotus. The place itself is a natural fortress, protected not by palisades but by marshes filled with reeds. The natural advantages of the future city of Alexandria seem to be evoked by the natural fortifications of *boukolia*. The ancient sources about the founding of Alexandria all emphasize that Alexander himself recognized and exploited these advantages, especially how it was protected on north and south by two bodies of water and on east and west by narrow land access.

There is also a detailed description of a cave in which the heroes are hidden and where a number of otherworldly incidents occur: it has a long descending channel that leads to a series of chambers, reminiscent of new kingdom tombs or perhaps the catacombs of Kom el Shoqafa, active as a public cemetery until the fourth century CE, or even the underground chambers of the famous

Serapeum in Alexandria. Thus elements of the past and present of Egypt are brought to mind in a way that lends a mystical quality to the novel's setting. Another famous aspect of the real city of Alexandria, commented on by Strabo, Diodorus and others, was its grid of streets that intersect each other at right angles. This famous and powerful rationalizing gesture imposed on this unstable part of Egypt by its Greek-speaking invaders, which transformed Egypt into a country oriented toward the Mediterranean as never before, seems to be negatively evoked in the description of *boukolia's* specially constructed passages:

> By devising many crooked and intricately winding paths through the reeds, and by so constructing passages that are easy enough for themselves, as they know the way through, but quite impossible for anyone else, they have contrived for themselves an impregnable fastness to safeguard them against any attack.[1]

This novel is thus set in the past in a way that brings to mind in an uncanny way the greatness of the city that will bear Alexander's name and be a new center of Hellenic civilization, a new multicultural center, with its Greek-speaking rulers dressed and honored as pharaohs, with its magnificent library of Greek literature, with its double religious consciousness that engages both Greek hero cult and the Egyptian cult of immortality, and with its sylleptic god Sarapis, that engages both Greek and Egyptian ideas of divinity.

So, for example, the beautiful heroine of the novel is immediately compared both to the Greek goddess Artemis and the Egyptian Isis. While Heliodorus emphasizes the savage character of the pre-Alexandrian inhabitants and their resistance to legitimate authority, their leader, who turns out to be a disenfranchised Egyptian priest, conducts himself in some circumstances like a Homeric *basileus*, distributing booty and making heroic speeches. The most important Egyptian secondary character, Calisiris, whose flashback narrative recalls implicitly and explicitly the Homeric tradition—even presenting an elaborate case that Homer himself was an Egyptian—anticipates the complexity of Alexandria as a site of Greco-Egyptian intercultural poetics, what Susan Stephens calls "seeing double," indicating how Alexandrian literature redeploys Greek literature to operate a displacement of the Greek world into the heart of its oriental other.

One of the distinctive features of that literature is its focus on aetiology, accounts of origins that reflect its new Greco-Egyptian focal point, Alexandria, and this move is thematized in another prose text that is closer to the time of the Ptolemies, the *Alexander Romance*, whose first book remakes the origins of Alexander the Great himself as simultaneously the son of the Egyptian god

Amun, the son of Philip of Macedon, and the son of the last Egyptian Pharaoh Nectanebo. But the same kind of displacement and redoubling can be seen in other examples of Ptolemaic literature, such as the epic of Apollonius and the hymns of Callimachus (Stephens 2003, 2012; Selden 1998). The uncanniness produced by these displacements in time and place is intimately linked to the city of Alexandria, itself a site of paradox and somewhat monstrous combinations. The ancient novel finally, as a genre, written so far as we know by Hellenized barbarians from the margins of the Greek world, can be seen as a climax of this Hellenistic aesthetic, since it is a displacement of multiple traditional performed genres into a text that is not meant to be performed at all, is not tied to a specific time and place.

Heliodorus' novel famously begins by casting us into the middle of things, beginning in pre-Alexandrian *boukolia*, and then progressing away from Greece and the Mediterranean through Egypt and finally to Ethiopia. Athens and Delphi are visited retrospectively in flashback narratives, while at the same time Attic drama, Homeric epic and Herodotean narrative are invoked repeatedly (Elmer 2008). Pre-Alexandrian *boukolia* is thus the beginning and also the center from which the novel moves outward geographically, temporally and culturally. The main plot of the novel, meanwhile, is an aetiology, a search for the true origin of Kharikleia, which also happens to follow the Nile river from its mouth in the Delta towards its source, ending in Ethiopia, where even more paradoxical accounts of origins are recounted and affirmed.

Chariton's *Callirhoe* is also set during the Achaemenid Persian period, well before the founding of Alexandria. The hero Chaereas is repeatedly identified as the son of that Syracusan Hermocrates who defeated the Athenians in the course of the Peloponnesian War, and his martial exploits in book seven explicitly recall earlier Greek exploits against the Persians, such as the famous stand at Thermopylae. This section is studded with Homeric quotations that recall the heroic exploits of that generation of heroes as well. But the most important event is the dramatic capture of Tyre, which is clearly meant to invoke the (future) deeds of Alexander the Great in the capture of Tyre in 332 BCE. In several accounts of the siege of that city, Alexander himself exhibits exceptional daring and leadership by leaping up on the city's wall. Although other aspects of the attack are different, the hero Chaereas does display heroism worthy of Alexander by leaping onto the wall of the city and securing victory for the invaders.[2]

Chaereas is at this point in the story acting on behalf of an Egyptian revolt against the Persians, in which he explains to the Egyptian king that "the Persian king has also tyrannized (*tetyrannêke*) us" (Chariton, *Callirhoe* 7.2.4). Not only did the real Alexander represent his attack on the Persian Empire as retribution for Persian aggression, but Ptolemaic propaganda portrayed Alexander as a liberator of Egypt from the oppressive Persians by exaggerating how much the latter despised Egyptian religious and cultural traditions. Indeed, Chariton's *Callirhoe* is one of the novels in which the Persians represent a kind of imperial arrogance that subtly points to the role of the Romans in the east at the time of the novel's writing (Schwartz 2003). Although not overtly political, this novel has been read as a piece of cultural resistance to Roman domination of public life in the imperial period (Alvarez 2001, 2001–2). That said, the representation of the Egyptians in the novel as rebellious, but ineffectual fighters (their king commits suicide rather than being captured) plays into Roman era stereotypes about the Ptolemies, the last of whom also died at her own hands. In this way shifting spatial and temporal coordinates allow Alexandria to be present by implication and to have multiple resonances.

Xenophon's *Ephesian Tale* begins and ends in Ephesus at some unspecified time, but both the hero and heroine independently visit Egypt, along with the chief secondary character, the brigand Hippothoos. The geography of this novel is a good example of the "abstract space" that according to Bakhtin defines adventure-time novels in general, meaning that the specific character of a place does not impact the story (Bakhtin 1981). So, these characters go to Alexandria several times, among other Egyptian cities, but these places are all more or less exchangeable with each other from the standpoint of the novel's plot. Even so, the novel's plot dynamics cannot completely erase the potent symbolism that Egypt had for the ancient world, and the author takes full advantage of the symbolic power of Egypt, as a place of exile, death, and resurrection, in fashioning his characters' adventures. For example, the heroine Anthia is buried alive in upper Egypt, visits the temple of Isis in Memphis twice, and receives an oracle at the temple of Apis. At another point the hero Habrocomes encounters in Sicily a poor fisherman, who had fled Sparta with his beloved, and when she died, embalmed her in the Egyptian style. The story and the storyteller make Habrocomes realize that love has no age limits, impelling him to continue his search for Anthia. Specific visits to Alexandria itself occur in the following manner: In the middle of the novel, the heroine Anthia is buried in a rich tomb in Tarsus, despite being only asleep and not dead. Tomb robbers arrive to steal the riches and kidnap the heroine alive, taking her to Alexandria and selling her into slavery there. Upon hearing this news, Habrocomes decides to go in search of the robbers and Anthia's corpse by boarding a ship to Alexandria, where unbeknownst to him she happens to be living. But he is driven off course and falls afoul of the bandits native to the delta region, here called "shepherds' (*poimenes*) rather than *boukoloi*. These bandits sell Habrocomes into slavery, who is then falsely accused and sentenced to execution twice in Alexandria, once by crucifixion and once by being burnt at the stake. In each case, he is miraculously saved by the gods of Egypt. But the fact that they both have these adventures while in Alexandria at the same time does not actually contribute to any kind of resolution; indeed the two remain ignorant of each other's fate. Even so, Alexandria is a key crossing point between the Greek world and the world of Egypt, where dangerous adventures, savage bandits and near-death experiences await our heroes prior to their restoration in Ephesus.

Whereas Chariton and Xenophon refer to Alexandria obliquely and symbolically, with standard tropes and stereotypes, Achilles Tatius as Koen de Temmerman notes, "was the first of the novelists to draw emphatic attention to the elaborate representation of space" (De Temmerman 2012: 517). Chief among examples of this is his description of Alexandria at the beginning of Book 5, the exact center of the novel and a place that marks a new beginning for the story with clear parallels to the opening of the novel and its equally elaborate description of Sidon there. Before arriving in Alexandria, the main characters pass through *boukolia* in the delta and have harrowing adventures there, including a sacrificial disemboweling of the heroine which turned out to be an elaborate trick using the equipment of a Homeric rhapsode who happened to be on hand. Accompanying the hero and heroine is an Egyptian named Menelaus, whose name cannot but recall his Homeric namesake and that weird episode narrated in *Odyssey* 4, which took place off the island of Pharos, the site of the famous lighthouse of Alexandria. The city itself is described as the hero traverses it:

> As I was coming up to the city entrance whose gates are dedicated to Helios, suddenly the beauty of the city struck me like a flash of lightning, and my eyes were filled to the brim with pleasure. A double row of columns led straight across from the entrance of Helios to the opposite entrance of Selene, Sun and Moon being the guardians of the city gates. Between the columns in the middle there lay the city's open area. Crossing it is such a long journey that you would think you were going abroad, though you were staying at home (*endêmos apodêmia*). Proceeding a little distance into the city, I came to the quarter (*topos*) named for Alexander himself, where I saw a whole other city, whose beauty was split up in separate sections: for a row of columns went in one direction, and another just as long crossed it at right angles. Dividing my gaze to travel along every street, I was left an unsatisfied spectator (*theatês akorestos*). I could not

grasp all the beauty of the spot at once; some parts I saw, some I was on the point of seeing, some I eagerly desired to see, some I was reluctant to pass by. The things to see outstripped my sight; the prospects drew me on. Turning round and round to face all the streets, I grew faint at the sight and at last exclaimed, like a luckless lover (*duserôtiôn*), "Eyes we have been conquered." But then I saw two new and unexpected contests: one between the magnitude of the city and its beauty, and another between the population and the space of the city itself; and both won. The space of the city was larger than a continent (*êpeiros*); the population more numerous than a nation (*ethnous*). If I considered the city, I well might doubt that any swarm of men might fill it; but if I looked at the populace, I was amazed that any urban space could contain them.

5.1

There are many things that could be said about this remarkable passage and it has attracted much attention (Nimis 1998; Zeitlin 2014). First is the detailed evocation of the physical space itself, some of whose details are corroborated by historians and travelers. Most prominent is the grid of streets that intersect each other at right angles. Also striking is the eroticizing of the space as well as the act of seeing and experiencing the space, but there is clearly a rhetorical dimension here as well, with striking antitheses and paradoxes. What I want to focus on briefly is the emphasis on order and control (*taxis*—which is also a rhetorical term), and relate that to the position of Alexandria in the Greek imagination as reflected in this passage.

There is a well-attested link in ancient rhetoric between descriptions of spaces, especially architectural spaces, and memory. According to the rhetorical handbooks, the art of memory consists in setting up in the mind a series of places (*loci*, τόποι) and inhabiting them with "lively images" (*imagines agentes*, εἴδολα). Once this is done, the *loci* can be revisited in the mind and the associations will act as reminders. The rhetorical tradition thus had a specific practice that linked architectural images and places to discourse so that the former generated the latter. Indeed, the very terms τόπος and *communis locus* for "subject matter" and "common idea" indicate the degree to which ancients conceived of the universe of thought as a map of regions able to be traversed along metonymic paths of association. As Bettina Bergmann says, the orator is the "topographer of the imagination" (Bergmann 1994: 226). The description of Alexandria, with its intersecting streets and colonnades, recalls a series of *loci* that, if committed to memory, "can be used again and again for remembering different material."[3]

Commenting on Quintillian's discussion of the use of places and images for mental organization, Bryson states that here "architecture not only stands for the control of self; it is the actual material means by which the self exercises control over its words and its world" (Bryson 1994).

If the architectural elements in the description, with their highly rationalized layout imposing order on the space, suggest the memory systems of the orators on a large scale, the population can be identified with the *imagines agentes*, the lively or acting images with which the orator populates that ordered space, the dynamic narrative elements that occupy that intellectual structure.

But in Achilles Tatius we have a space too large to grasp with the mind and a flood of images too numerous to be disposed of in that space, for it is larger than a "continent" (*êpeiros*, an unbounded region) its inhabitants more numerous than a nation (*ethnos*). Moreover the vision unfolds in a series of more and more striking impressions that gives the sense of a deeper and deeper penetration of the unknown: in the landscape of memory and cognition, the unconscious perhaps, that mysterious and unknown continent that is beyond mastering. Traversing this vast memory space gives Clitophon the strange feeling of making a journey abroad in one's native land (*endêmos apodêmia*: literally, being at home, while being abroad). This expression recalls that peculiar sensation that Freud calls the "uncanny" (*unheimlich*): the sensation that one feels when encountering something familiar (*heimlich*) that has been estranged by the process of repression. What better figure for this than Alexandria, whose origins combine savagery and mysterious ancient wisdom, with its dangerous erotic attractions that famous Romans found so irresistible and frightening, where the logic of the Macedonian phalanx was imposed on this ancient and ever-shifting soil, that recapitulates the whole cosmos, with gates of the sun and moon. The ancient novel itself as a genre is also rooted in Alexandrian aesthetics, with its hybridity and self-consciousness, redeploying elements of the past in uncanny ways, aimed not at particular communities but an international community for whom Greek was a literary *lingua franca*, the kind of multicultural community that Alexandria epitomized. For the Greek-speaking people of the eastern Mediterranean, the exploits of Alexander the great, himself arguably from the periphery of the Greek world, and the most famous and enduring city he founded, whether implicitly or explicitly invoked, represent an alternative Mediterranean center, with various and conflicting meanings and cultural traditions, alternative to Athens, Byzantium and Rome, an erotically charged space of memory and imagination.

Notes

1   Heliodorus, *Aethiopica* 1.6.2. The last clause is a quotation of a passage of Demosthenes (21.138).

2   Compare, e.g., Diodorus Siculus, *Bibliotheca Libraria* 17.46 and Chariton *Callirhoe* 7.4.

3   Yates (1966), 7, discussing *Ad Herrenium* 3, 16–24.

Bibliography

Alvares, J. (2001), "Egyptian Unrest of the Roman Era and the Reception of Chariton's *Chaireas and Callirhoe*," *Maia*, 53: 11–20.

Alvares, J. (2001–2), "Some Political and Ideological Dimensions of Chariton's *Chaireas and Callirhoe*," *Classical Journal*, 97 (2): 113–44.

Bakhtin, M. M. (1981), *The Dialogic Imagination*, Austin, TX: University of Texas Press.

Bergmann, B. (1994), "The Roman House as Memory Theater: The House of the Tragic Poet in Pompeii," *Art Bulletin*, 76 (2): 225–56.

Bryson, N. (1994), "Philostratus and the Imaginary Museum," in S. Goldhill and R. Osborne (eds.), *Art and Text in Ancient Greek Culture*, 255–83, Cambridge: Cambridge University Press.

Cusset, C., N. Le Meur-Weissman, and F. Levin, eds. (2012), *Mythe et pouvoir à l'epoque hellenistique*, Leuven: Peeters.

de Jong, I. J. F., ed. (2012), *Space in Ancient Greek Literature: Studies in Ancient Greek Narrative*, vol. 3, Mnemosyne Supplements 339, Leiden: Brill.

De Temmerman, K. (2012), "Achilles Tatius," in I. J. F. de Jong (ed.), *Space in Ancient Greek Literature: Studies in Ancient Greek Narrative*, vol. 3, Mnemosyne Supplements 339, 517–36, Leiden: Brill.

Elmer, D. (2008), "Heliodoros's 'Sources': Intertextuality, Paternity, and the Nile River in the *Aithiopika*," *Transactions of the American Philological Association*, 138 (2): 411–50.

Goldhill, S. and R. Osborne, eds. (1994), *Art and Text in Ancient Greek Culture*, Cambridge: Cambridge University Press.

Maehler, H. (2016), "Roman Poets on Egypt," in R. Matthews and C. Römer (eds.), *Ancient Perspectives on Egypt*, 203–15, London: Routledge.

Matthews, R. and C. Römer, eds. (2016), *Ancient Perspectives on Egypt*, London: Routledge.

Monolaraki, E. (2012), *Noscendi Nilum Cupido: Imagining the Nile, from Lucan to Philostratus*, Trends in Classics Supplemental Volumes, vol. 18, Berlin: De Gruyter.

Niehoff, M., ed. (2014), *Journeys in the Roman East*, Tuebingen: Mohr-Siebeck.

Nimis, S. (1998), "Memory and Description," *Arethusa*, 31: 99–122.

Rimmel, V. and M. Asper, eds. (2017), *Imagining Empire*, Heidelberg: Klaus Brecht.

Rutherford, I. (2000) "The Genealogy of the Boukoloi: How Greek Literature Appropriated an Egyptian Narrative Motif," *Journal of Hellenic Studies*, 120: 106–21.

Schwartz, S. (2003), "Rome in the Greek Novel? Images and Ideas of Empire in Chariton's Persia," *Arethusa*, 36: 375–94.

Selden, D. (1998), "Alibis," *Classical Antiquity*, 17 (2): 289–412.

Stephens, S. (2003), *Seeing Double: Intercultural Poetics in Ptolemaic Alexandria*, Berkeley, CA: University of California Press.

Stephens, S. (2012), "Writing Alexandria as the (Common)place," in C. Cusset, N. Le Meur-Weissman, and F. Levin (eds.), *Mythe et pouvoir à l'epoque hellenistique*, 137–51, Leuven: Peeters.

Stephens, S. (2017), "The Geopolitics of Imagining Ancient Alexandria," in V. Rimmel and M. Asper (eds.), *Imagining Empire*, 1–22, Heidelberg: Klaus Brecht.

Versluys, M. J. (2002), *Aegyptiaca Romana: Nilotic Scenes and the Roman Views of Egypt*, Leiden: Brill.

Yates, F. (1966), *The Art of Memory*, Chicago, IL: Chicago University Press.

Zeitlin, F. (2014), "*Apodêmia*: The Adventure of Travel in the Greek Novel," in M. Niehoff (ed.), *Journeys in the Roman East*, 157–82, Tuebingen: Mohr-Siebeck.

Aftermath

22

Practicing Orthodoxy

Body Language in Sophronius' *Thaumata*[1]

Maud Gleason
Stanford University

Sophronius, a former sophist and future Patriarch, composed his collection of incubation miracles around the years 610–15. He presents himself as motivated by personal gratitude. Saints Cyrus and John had healed his painful eyes, which were apparently still blinded by paideia's "Homeric fog," despite a long ascetic apprenticeship in the deserts of Palestine.[2] Considerations of theology and politics also contributed to his motivation. Sophronius was an ardent Chalcedonian.[3] But Egypt, outside of Alexandria, tilted heavily to the anti-Chalcedonian side. In Alexandria, Sophronius attached himself to John, the new Patriarch. Though he was Orthodox, John's credentials were not of the strongest. He was a layman and a political appointee of a usurping emperor.[4] Perhaps John was unnerved by the fact that in the fracas of usurpation, his predecessor had been murdered. The new Emperor would doubtless be pleased if John would do something to shore up Chalcedonian orthodoxy in Egypt. And Sophronius the ex-sophist, who was a skilled debater, happened to be on hand. John was only too happy to deputize Sophronius to dispute with anti-Chalcedonians. It was as part of this mission, therefore, that Sophronius decided to write up a collection of the saints' miracles. He intended to claim the shrine of SS. Cyrus and John as a site of Chalcedonian orthodoxy.

He was pushing uphill. Even the priest in charge of the shrine, to whom Sophronius was indebted for some of his material, had a skeptical wife and a monophysite secretary.[5] As in the case with other healing saints in this period whose miracles were written up by rival Christian groups, Cyrus and John were not universally considered Chalcedonians.[6] In fact, there still reposes on Mt Athos an unpublished collection of Cyrus and John's miracles composed by a rival cleric who took the anti-Chalcedonian, anti-Sophronian line of "one activity in Christ."[7] Sophronius' collection of incubation miracles should be seen, therefore, as a polemical move in contemporary doctrinal disputes, part of a general phenomenon observed by Chadwick: Christological controversies having produced a theological stalemate, both sides appealed to the miraculous.[8]

The shrine of Cyrus and John lay 20 kilometers from Alexandria at Menouthis, which had long hosted a shrine of Isis.[9] There had also been a healing temple of Serapis nearby at Canopus. Here, Strabo tells us, cures were sought in the first century by distinguished persons, either incubating themselves, or incubating by proxy. Strabo further notes that these cures were recorded in writing.[10] Sophronius' miracle collection was thus the fruit of an evolving local tradition.[11]

How Cyrus and John took over from Isis and Serapis belongs to the long history of syncretism in Egyptian religious practice; for the purposes of this paper, it begins with late fourth-century efforts to suppress paganism.[12] After Theophilus, bishop of Alexandria, organized the destruction of Alexandria's Serapeum in 391 CE, he destroyed the temple of Serapis at Canopus and built a church dedicated to the Evangelist nearby at Menouthis.[13] It is possible that some of the stone for that church came from a nearby Egyptian temple, presumably of Isis, that appears to have been deliberately destroyed and quarried.[14] By the early seventh century, a shrine in or near the Menouthis church was doing a brisk incubation trade in the name of SS Cyrus and John. These saints were entirely unknown until someone, perhaps Cyril, the Chalcedonian patriarch, or even a Monophysite (there were competing traditions), discovered or invented them and transferred their supposed remains to the Church at Menouthis. Because Cyril was an orthodox Chalcedonian, Sophronius was keen to represent him as the founder, alleging that Cyril received divine instructions to introduce the cult of Cyrus and John to Menouthis.[15] Since the cult of Cyrus and John had a number of foundation-stories, Sophronius' claims about the establishment of their shrine at Menouthis are not, in the words of Phil Booth, "innocent statements of an uncontested tradition, but . . . polemical claims designed both to promote Menouthis as the pre-eminent cultic center and to situate that center within a doctrinally clean history associated with the Chalcedonian Cyril."[16] Sophronius also asserted that the foundation was necessitated by the continuing presence of an eponymous local demon, "dark as an Egyptian in coloring, feminine in mind and form," before whose blood-soaked altar feeble-minded Christians sought healing.[17] This presence of this female "demon" suggests that Lady Isis (*Kyra*) was still active enough, at least in Sophronius' imagination, to require supersession by *Kyros*.

By indeterminate stages, the shrine housing Isis' successors developed an infrastructure of walls enclosing a courtyard, with bathhouse, fountain and latrines (site of spectacular evacuations), with a church or baptistry housing the tomb and relics of the saints. At night the sick fanned out from this central point on little cots, moaning, murmuring, and dreaming. This array, we shall see, reflected the larger social order, with great ladies appropriating the coveted spots closest to the tomb, and lesser mortals sleeping farther and lower, sometimes on the floor, out the door, or in the latrines.[18]

Through the ranks glided the saintly apparitions, pausing and prescribing at will. Keyed up by psalm-singing, fortified by the Eucharist, primed by recitations of previous cures, everyone went to bed in a state of expectation: a sleep-over in a haunted house. This night could be it: a definitive transformation, or a recipe to achieve one. The stakes were high: to dream they passed your bedside by in silence might presage death.[19] Dawn broke to the hum of voices, as the community awoke and the weaving of stories began. "Did you see them?" "That demoniac was yelling all night; I didn't sleep a wink." "They gave me a fig to eat, and now I can't find it!"

Sophronius' collection is a highly stylized reweaving of this material, in which he presents himself both as a grateful devotee of the saints and as an omniscient exegete of their marvels. Like a tour guide, he organizes geographically, beginning with patients from Alexandria, moving to those who came from elsewhere in Egypt and North Africa, and finally to those from farther afield. This organizing principle permits him to culminate with himself, a citizen from Damascus, healed of an eye disease in Miracle No. 70.[20]

Normally, healing miracles were read aloud in the church where they had been originally performed, as preparation for incubation.[21] Experienced on site, these narratives would condition the laity to dream of the saints, and prepare the clergy to interpret their visions.[22] Sophronius, however, intended his collection to circulate beyond the sanctuary. He aspired to an educated audience, as we can surmise from his style, which he admits is more "intense" (σύντονον) and elaborate than the "relaxed" style usually employed to recount miracles. His own explanation for this choice is intriguing: "I have chosen an intense style to indicate the intensity of the Saints' ardent and agile zeal to heal the sick."[23] His saints are no mere simulacra, manipulated by angels, but active agents.[24] Their beatings in a dream produce real bruises upon waking.[25] Sophronius' rhetorical task is to make his readers experience the saints' agency and bodily presence with their own bodies.

In his introduction Sophronius uses the language of physical sensation to describe his own transition, from one who had been only an *auditor* of the saints' grace, to one who has *seen* the truth of what he has heard.[26] This by-play about hearing versus seeing, presence versus absence, points up the ambiguous corporality of the saints, whose presence the hagiographer must somehow evoke by turning dreams into words. He sends these words forth to posterity and "to those far distant *in their bodies*," words that invite us to "come and *see* the works of the Lord" (Psalm 65.5).[27] "Let us wake up the faithful and gather them to *hear* the marvels from God (θεόθεν) brought about *through the agency of* (διά) Cyrus and John."[28] Thus issues of agency and corporality raised by the incarnation, the Word made flesh, are woven through his miracle narratives.

This essay explores how Sophronius' narratives deploy bodies, arguing that this deployment involves a distinctively somatic rhetoric of agency. I will focus on miracles that involve punishment and submission, counter-habitual movement, and changes of posture. My underlying question is, what effect on his audience does Sophronius achieve by using bodies in this way? After touring you through some examples, I will explain how Sophronius' bodies produce a mode of audience engagement that we might call "visceral seeing," and how that mode of engagement is harnessed for the formation of orthodox subjectivities.

Miracle No. 1: Ammonius of Alexandria was a man of considerable wealth who served as collector of the 12 percent tax. Thanks to his good looks, he had been the ornament of the city's youth organization (3) until he developed a hideous array of scrofulous lesions about his neck. The doctors called them *choirades* (piglets) because these lesions resemble pigs. They multiply like piglets in a sow's womb, and make a pigsty of the sufferer's neck.[29] Ammonius' father, a respected financial officer of the orthodox church, sought the doctors' help in vain, then turned to Cyrus and John. The saints perceived that the young man was stiff-necked in more ways than one: as his neck was swollen with scrofula, so his pride was swollen in the conceit of his wealth (7). The saints' response to this spiritual swelling was to prescribe banausic work: they instructed the young aristocrat to sweep the ground in front of their tomb.

Sophronius emphasizes the bodily impact of this intervention: they ordered him to sweep "*so that by means of bending downwards towards the ground* he might learn whence he came and whither he would soon return" (7). We can visualize clearly how the young man is forced to change posture, exchanging the body-language of aristocratic pride for the body-language of humility: "After thus withering the swelling of the young man's soul, and compelling him to recognize who he was, the saints sent [in a dream, presumably] the remedy for the scrofulous malady on the neck of his body"(8).

The saints prescribe lamp oil from their shrine mixed with bread. No sooner is this greasy mix applied than the scrofulous "piglets " burst through the skin and take flight "as if someone were chasing them with a whip" (9). We visualize the saints in a posture of physical coercion, and we visualize the disease itself as *bodies*: the swollen "piglets" race off --sixty seven of them "as those who were counting observed" (9). In the imagination of a Christian audience, the saints repeat Jesus' exorcism at Gerasa, with added specificity as to the number of swine. Sophronius concludes by anchoring these imaginary bodies in the architectural setting of the shrine itself: "Those in charge of the shrine at that time hung them up for many days in front of the saints' tomb to demonstrate the martyrs' power" (9).

You might expect the story to end here. But the young man relapsed. He forgot the lesson he had learned, and his pride recrudesced (10). The martyrs punished him with a stomach ailment. None of the medical men could help— even the *iatrosophists* strutting about in their togas (11). Eventually the patient returned to the saints, who cured his stomach with a purgative (lamp oil mixed in wine this time) and cured his pride with an elaborate staging of self-abasement:

> Coming to him by night, the saints bade him take off his soft flowing garments and put on hempen clothes of courser weave—the sort of thing really impoverished people wear... After telling him to put on these instead of expensive, soft clothing, they ordered him to carry drinking water on his shoulders to the ailing brethren, decreeing that he should heft not one jar only, but two, one upon each shoulder, and they asserted that they would not heal him until he had accomplished this task (13).

He did as they ordered, was healed, and sang their praises, praises *which we are to repeat*. This invitation is the first of many in which the audience is encouraged to perform bodily mimesis of "correct" ritual procedure.

In Sophronius' story, the young man's disfigurement appears to reflect his role as a good-looking member of the *ephebeia*; perhaps the multiplying "piglets" in some way represent his financial work as tax-collector piling up the proceeds of the 12 percent tax. Sophronius associates scrofula with wealth and arrogance.[33] So we may suspect that Sophronius' story was the tip of the iceberg of an unseen social drama—a drama somehow precipitated by the young tax collector's arrogance, rendered concrete by the piglets, and resolved, at first unsuccessfully and at last definitively, by rituals of abasement assigned by the saints that reduce the young man's swollen self-importance and dramatize his submission to the moral norms of the Christian community, specifically service to the poor. These rituals of abasement realign the young man's subjectivity by realigning his physical posture.

About a fifth of Sophronius' miracles involve correction of the soul via the body.[31] If the healing of the scrofulous tax collector was achieved by "rituals of abasement," in Miracle No. 30 we find self-abasement ramped up to self-inflicted charivari. Gesios was a pagan doctor of high intellectual pretensions.[32] As a rational medical man, Gesios considered all disease to be of natural origin. As a pagan who mocked his own "baptism of convenience," he claimed that Saints Cyrus and John borrowed their prescriptions from Hippocrates and Galen, for which he cited chapter and verse (30. 3–4). But one day, as punishment, his back, neck and shoulders seized up like a stick of dry wood, and none of his medicines could cure him (5–6). Eventually his pain drove him to the shrine of Cyrus and John, who instructed him thus: "Take the pack-saddle of an ass, and put it on your suffering shoulders, neck and back. Walk around our sanctuary at mid-day shouting loudly, 'I am a fool and utterly stupid'" (8). When he woke up, Gesios dismissed this dream as mere *phantasia*. The saints returned in another dream and upped the ante: along with the saddle he must hang a huge bell around his neck, and *run* round the sanctuary shouting, "I am a fool." Gesius could make no intellectual sense of this prescription either, and dismissed it. The saints appeared a third time, and raised the stakes again. This time he was to wear a donkey's bridle, like a beast without reason, and be dragged along, "glorying in his saddle and bell" by one of his own slaves walking in front of him (10). The saints' purpose, we are told, was to make his folly even more obvious and to "whip his stupidity with a more stinging shame" (10). Gesios eventually implemented these instructions, and led by his own slave with a bridle in his mouth, crossed the sanctuary ten times, "according to witnesses who were counting." By inserting an internal audience of confirming witnesses into the narrative here, Sophronius encourages us, the external audience, to identify with them and thus place ourselves within the frame. This story, almost certainly apocryphal, shows the saints' power over the bodies of the privileged: only they can force a famous pagan intellectual to adopt subhuman posture as he is led like a pack animal by his own slave.

Although it is usually persons of high status whom the saints command to violate postural and behavioral norms, in Miracle No. 18 we meet Paul, a poor man—an absolute beggar—who suffered from a head full of worms. The saints appeared to him as he incubated and said, "Get up from your bed and go out the gate of the sanctuary that faces the sea. Strike the man you will meet there on the jaw. Once you do that, you will soon find the cure for what ails you" (5).

Understandably, poor Paul took this to be an illusion (*phantasia*). The saints, however, returned twice more, each time giving the same instructions. So Paul got up, went out the gate, and finding there a soldier, slugged him. The soldier thumped his truncheon down on the poor Paul's head. Out burst a great flux of blood and worms, and Paul was cured (7).

Sophronius had predicted that his audience would experience from this story a sort of synesthesia that fuses the spiritual with the carnal: "Let us now also relate the sweetness and charm of the cure that suggests the power of the saints, crafting for the miracle (or rather for its future auditors) spiritual delight mixed with carnal sweetness" (4). At the conclusion of this story he tries to create another sort of fusion: as Paul exits singing, we, the audience, are to take up his hymn of praise

> Having garnered a complete cure, Paul sang a hymn to the martyrs; he raised, as was fitting, a song of praise to God, who through the martyrs accomplished his cure. Paul has become for us an opportunity and a valid reason to honor Christ and the martyrs in song (8).

It is not accidental that this hymn, which we are invited to continue singing, enunciates what Sophronius considers the correct model of joint agency between Christ and the saints.

In this story, the saints demonstrate their power by reversing the gradient of social convention. Normally, a poor man cowers before a soldier and would never dare strike him. Ancient behavioral conventions had a powerful spatial dynamic, as deeply engrained in high and low alike as their habits of command and obedience. In Miracle No. 24, Sophronius demonstrates the saints' power to make people change position. He proposes a diptych: two sufferers of the same sex and name (Juliana), who differ in their ailments and social position (ἀξίωμα). One was rich, the other poor. One had a chest complaint, the other was blind. When they entered the saints' shrine seeking a cure, "they took up even there their characteristic social position. One did not put aside her empty dignity, nor the pride her wealth inspired. *She* lay down upon a couch in front of the martyrs' tomb" (4). The other lay outside the door, like the beggar Lazarus Yet the martyrs appeared equally to both Julianas, "Correcting the arrogant conceit of the one, and encouraging the spiritual lowliness of the other; giving healing to both" (4).

Predictably, the saints tell the rich Juliana that if she wants to be healed of her spiritual and her physical ills, she must leave her couch and sleep on the ground (5). However, though the saints do cure the poor Juliana, they do not instruct her to climb up on the rich Juliana's couch. Was such an upwards reversal of socially sanctioned body position unthinkable for the lowly? Although P. Maraval toys with the idea that Sophronius bashes the rich to please the humbler members of his audience, I think he is more concerned to counter the skeptical and occasionally anti-Chalcedonian tendencies that he found among the rich and well-educated.[33] Take for example Athanasia, the wife of a well-known citizen of Alexandria (No. 29). Sophronius suggests she had pagan sympathies. At any rate, she openly expressed skepticism about Cyrus and John because no contemporary written record of their martyrdom could be found. One day, joking with her friends, she scoffed at the saints. A flea jumped up from the ground "as if to defend them," and bit her ankle. She bent down to swat the flea, and found herself stuck fast in that position (σχήματος), "unable to bend back up again or exhibit that upright capability and bodily conformation that has been allotted to man alone" (9). Since she had unreasonably done wrong to Cyrus and John, "they recalled her to reason by the bent-over posture (σχήματι) of unreasoning beasts" (9–10).

Consider also the postural dimensions of the reform of Theodoros, a gouty contemporary of Sophronios with anti-Chalcedonian convictions (No. 36). The saints afflicted him a with judicial nightmare worthy of Brent Shaw.[34] The sleeping Theodoros found himself before a divine tribunal, with the saints seated on judicial thrones, surrounded by troops and civilian officials. At the saints' command, attendants seized him and bound his hands behind his back. They forced him to bend his neck towards the ground, the way public executioners position (σχηματίζουσιν) the bodies of criminals (11). The saints threaten terrible things, and give orders ("Do this; do that") to the torturers who hold the trembling dreamer, head bowed and body bent. The crowd of functionaries threw themselves at the saints' feet, begging them to pardon Theodoros if he consents to orthodox communion. Ultimately—Theodoros is a hard case, and this is the longest story in the collection—the saints agreed. But even while he was incubating at Cyrus' and John's, his mother secretly brought him take-out communion from a heterodox establishment (24). Eventually, Theodoros dreamed of an icon: Christ, Mary, and John the Baptist, surrounded by apostles, saints, and martyrs, including Cyrus and John. In his dream, the image animates: Cyrus and John are both inside the picture and in front of it, where they repeatedly bend their knees and touch their heads to the ground in supplication for Theodoros (26). They invite him to join them, so that he performs a mimesis of their submissive posture (28) and is eventually healed.

The saints take a similar approach with Count Julian, a heretical aristocrat whose rejected girlfriend had put him under a spell (No. 12). Paralyzed and entirely dependent on others to move his hands and limbs, he presented a miserable spectacle (οἴκτιστον θέαμα, 5). (Again, with this remark, Sophronius effectively positions his own audience among the spectators). The saints at first restore some movement to the sufferer at his parents' request, but stop short of a complete cure because, after all, he's still a heretic. Young Julian, it turns out, was a disciple of the notorious "Julian the Elder," the leader of a miaphysite sect (6). In frequent nocturnal visitations the saints offer him orthodox communion. They go through the motions of taking communion themselves (7), inviting him to perform mimetically an orthodox ritual act. Presumably Sophronius intends this invitation to encompass his listeners. Young Julian refuses. To punish his recalcitrance, the saints intensify his torments (8-9). After repeated nocturnal visitations, Julian knuckles under, but is still reluctant to take communion in public. The saints suggest he visit an orthodox church in Alexandria to take communion privately after Christmas mass. But once he's there, stooped over with head bent low (κάτω νεύων καὶ κεκυφώς), who should walk in but a hundred members of his own heretical community, dumbstruck by the spectacle of his conversion (17). Cyrus and John had tricked him into being caught in the act of obeisance to orthodoxy.

I think Sophronius is exploiting an unconscious rhetorical effect in which the viewer's awareness of their own body mingles with their response to the depicted body. This "visceral seeing" can be a response to bodies in visual depictions (Elkins 1999) or in verbal descriptions (Miller 2004).[35] The protagonists in Sophronius' narratives have bodies, as all protagonists do. But the corporeality of these protagonists is salient: they are protagonists only because of their bodies; they enter the story because they are paralyzed or in pain. As the narrative commands our attention, there is in that attention a kind of heightened awareness that is not purely cerebral, but involves a sympathetic, or secondary, or imaginary physical response. Sophronius' narratives encourage a quasi-kinesthetic experience in which the listener's awareness of their own body mingles with their response both to the pain, and to the healing metamorphosis, of the body being described.

Other collections of incubation miracles, pagan and Christian, may function similarly, leading their audience through a comparable experience of heightened physical awareness followed by wonder, as the divine epiphany effects a transformation. What seems to me especially notable in Sophronius is how he uses his listeners' quasi-kinesthetic response to the described bodily changes as a means to inculcate, or solidify, an orthodox subjectivity via mental mimesis of orthopraxy. I hypothesize that as his listeners responded viscerally to the postural changes in Sophronius' narratives, as they imagined themselves bowing in deference to the saints, or receiving orthodox communion, they mentally rehearsed the piety and submissiveness experienced by his protagonists. As I have mentioned, at the end of many miracles Sophronius specifically invites his listeners to join in the pious acclamations of the dreamer who has been healed. With this invitation to engage in performative language, Sophronius extends his audiences' unconscious identification with the protagonists' behavior into actual mimesis of orthodox piety: "Let us rejoice together with him who has been purified" (No. 57. 3). This synesthesia—in which behaviors inside the narrative frame are fused with (supposedly) "real" behaviors from the audience—is harnessed by the hagiographer to inculcate a correct confessional stance, a new attitude, both physical and mental, toward the saints.

The "realness" of the saints is calqued on the realness of the bodies that they heal. We have seen how the saints in Sophronius' narratives achieve a quasi-corporality by vigorously healing, and sometimes punishing, "real" people's bodies. I have paid particular attention to miracles of a type found only in Sophronius, in which healing saints force people to engage in non-habitual behaviors or adopt non-habitual postures, as when they made the rich Juliana descend from her couch to sleep on the floor, or forced the arrogant woman from Alexandria to stay bent over like a beast, thus depriving her of the upright posture that was her social due. Because posture encoded social difference in the ancient world, narratives in which Cyrus and John impose postural change on humans, especially privileged humans, inculcated the lesson that the saints controlled the temporal order.

My goal has been to explore how bodies function rhetorically in Sophronius' narratives. Composed in an era of intense controversy concerning incarnation, these narratives use sick bodies to make substantial, as it were, the power of the shadowy saints, who fuse divine and human energies to heal. Thus they have a Christological rhetoric. The bodies in these narratives move from disease, via tests of faith and shadowy encounters with a supernatural arbiter, into healing in the full light of day. They recapitulate, as Booth has pointed out, the processes of salvation.[36] Thus they have also a soteriological rhetoric. I have suggested furthermore that in these narratives Sophronius exploits our quasi-visceral response to the experience of seeing bodies, even in the mind's eye, in order to encourage the formation of orthodox subjectivities.

Notes

1   In hopes that these late Egyptian tales please Susan, for so many years a friend and colleague nonpareil. With thanks to Peter Brown for giving me Fernandez Marcos' *Thaumata*, to Allen Romano for inviting me to present some of this material at the

Florida State Epiphanies conference in 2010, and to Phil Booth and Ildikó Csepregi for sharing unpublished work with me at that time. Sarah Wilker gave me invaluable help in the preparation of this manuscript.

2   *Thaumata* No. 70, esp. 9–10. I have used the text of Fernandez Marcos (1975), which is available via the online *Thesaurus Linguae Graecae*, the French translation of Gascou (2006), and Bringel's edition of the *Panegyric* (2008).

3   The Council of Chalcedon convened in 451 to define the relationship between the divine and human aspects of Christ. A majority of its assembled bishops endorsed the position that Christ's nature was both divine and human. But the idea that Christ had a dual nature gave grave offense to those (so-called "Monophysites") who conceived of Christ's nature as unitary and divine and would not accept that Christ's divinity can be qualified in any way. The non-Chalcedonian Oriental Orthodox churches of today prefer the term "Miaphysite."

4   Booth (2014), 50–1.

5   On Christodoros, see Nos 8, 9, 10, 31, 39.10; Gascou (2006), 10; Booth (2014), 56 n. 54. On the secretary, see No. 39.10.

6   For sectarian versions of miracle tales tailored by different confessional groups: Csepregi (2005), 113–17.

7   Booth (2014), 58 n. 66. For an overview of Christological controversies after Chalcedon: Allen (2009), 3–15.

8   Chadwick (1974), 71–2.

9   Kayser (1991), 214–16; Stolz (2008). The complex is now under water in Aboukir ("Father Cyrus") Bay.

10 Strabo 17.1.17.

11 The practice of incubation in Egypt goes way back, perhaps to the late pharaonic period (Renberg 2017: 74–100).

12 On Christianization as syncretism, "a locally negotiated process of selection and recombination" (Frankfurter 2018: 138). On the transition see Sansterre (1991); Gascou (2007); Renberg (2017), 359–79; Frankfurter (2018), 134–6.

13 Rufinus *Church History* 11: 26–7 implies that the two structures were practically contiguous.

14 Decommissioned statues of Isis were found in dump area: Goddio (2007), 43, 46 figs 2.32–4. Goddio thinks the destroyed Egyptian temple in Aboukir Bay was the Canopis Serapeion; Stolz (2008) thinks it was the Isis temple at Menouthis.

15 *Panegyric of Saints Cyrus and John* 23–7, ed. Bringel (2008).

16 Booth (2014), 48.

17 *Panegyric of Saints Cyrus and John* 24–5, 29.

18 Rows: No. 62.4; preferential positions No. 24.4, latrines No. 56.

19 No. 62.4.

20 For the geographical and social origins of the incubants, see Montserrat (1998), 273–6.

21 Sophronius, when incubating himself, looked around in vain for written records (*Panegyric* 1).

22 Cf. Krueger (2004), 69.

23 *Panegyric of Saints Cyrus and John* 6.

24 The simulacra theory posed a skeptical challenge to the "realness" of saints seen in dreams and is attested in the late sixth century: Constas (2002), 267–85.

25 No. 39.11.

26 *Panegyric of Saints Cyrus and John* 33.

27 On the ambiguous corporality of the saints, see Miller (2009).

28 The adverbial θεόθεν conveys a weaker sort of agency than διά.

29 On the porcine terminology see Gascou (2006), 27 and 196 with notes.

30 Miracle No. 58 a rich nobleman with scrofula.

31 Fernandez Marcos (1975: 180–92) terms these "miracles of punishment" (Nos 12, 13, 28, 29, 30, 31, 32, 36, 37, 38, 39, 49, 67).

32 Gesios was an historical figure of the late fifth century (Gascou 2006: 101 n. 579), a prototypical pagan intellectual.

33 Maraval (1981), 392.

34 Shaw (2003). There is a similar judicial nightmare in Miracle No. 38: a recalcitrant heretic named Stephanos reneges on his agreement to continue taking orthodox communion after his healing. The saints appear to him again in the form of the governor of his hometown and indict him for breach of contract (No. 38.9). On these healings via communion, offered only to heretics, see Csepregi (2005), 107.

35 "[V]isceral seeing refers to corporeal responses to word-pictures of the body, responses that implicate the reader in such a way that the boundary between text and reader begins to weaken" (Miller 2004: 396). Elkins (1999), esp. vii–ix.

36 Booth (2009), 53, and (2014), 49, 70.

Bibliography

Allen, P. (2009), *Sophronius of Jerusalem and Seventh-Century Heresy: The Synodical Letter and Other Documents*, Oxford Early Christian Texts, Oxford: Oxford University Press.

Booth, P. (2009), "Saints and Soteriology in Sophronius Sophista's Miracles of Cyrus and John," in P. Clarke and T. Claydon (eds.), *The Church, the Afterlife and the Fate of the Soul: Papers Read at the 2007 Summer Meeting and the 2008 Winter Meeting of the Ecclesiastical History Society*, Studies in Church History, 45, 52–63, Ecclesiastical History Society.

Booth, P. (2014), *Crisis of Empire: Doctrine and Dissent at the End of Late Antiquity*, Transformation of the Classical Heritage 52, Berkeley, CA: University of California Press.

Bringel, P. (2008), *Sophrone de Jérusalem: Panégyrique Des Saints Cyr et Jean*, Turnhout: Brepolis.

Chadwick, H. (1974), "John Moschus and His Friend Sophronius the Sophist," *Journal of Theological Studies*, 25: 41–74.

Clarke, P. and T. Claydon, eds. (2009), *The Church, the Afterlife and the Fate of the Soul: Papers Read at the 2007 Summer Meeting and the 2008 Winter Meeting of the Ecclesiastical History Society*, Studies in Church History, 45, Ecclesiastical History Society.

Constas, N. (2002), "An Apology for the Cult of Souls in Late Antiquity," *Journal of Early Christian Studies*, 10: 267–85.

Csepregi, I. (2005), "Mysteries for the Uninitiated: The Role and Symbolism of the Eucharist in Miraculous Dream Healing," in I. Perczel, R. Forrari, and G. Géreby (eds.), *The Eucharist in Theology and Philosophy: Issues of Doctrinal History in East and West from the Patristic Age to the Reformation*, 97–130, Leuven: Leuven University Press.

Dierkens, A., ed. (1991), *Apparitions et miracles*, Brussels: Université de Bruxelles.

Elkins, J. (1999), *Pictures of the Body: Pain and Metamorphosis*, Stanford, CA: Stanford University Press.

Fernandez Marcos, N., ed. (1975), "Miracula SS. Cyri et Ioanni," in *Los Thaumata de Sofronio: Contribucion al Estudio de La Incubatio Cristiana*, 243–400, Madrid: Instituto Antonio de Nebrija.

Frankfurter, D. (2018), *Christianizing Egypt: Syncretism and Local Worlds in Late Antiquity*, Princeton, NJ: Princeton University Press.

Frankfurter, D., ed. (1998), *Pilgrimage and Holy Space in Late Antique Egypt*, Leiden: Brill.

Gascou, J. (2006), *Sophrone de Jérusalem: Miracles des saints Cyr et Jean (BHG I 477–479)*, Études d'archéologie et d'histoire ancienne, Paris: Université de Strasbourg, De Boccard.

Gascou, J. (2007), "Les origines du culte des Saints Cyr et Jean," *Analecta Bollandiana*, 125: 241–81.

Goddio, F. (2007), *The Topography and Excavation of Heracleion-Thonis and East Canopus (1996-2006)*, Oxford: Oxbow.

Hansen, W. (2003), "Strategies of Authentication in Ancient Popular Literature," in S. Panayotakis, M. Zimmerman, and W. H. Keulen (eds.), *The Ancient Novel and Beyond*, 301–14, Leiden: Brill.

Kayser, F. (1991), "Oreilles et couronnes: A propos des cultes de Canope," *Bulletin de l'Institut français d'archéologie orientale*, 91: 207–17.

Krueger, D. (2004), *Writing and Holiness: The Practice of Authorship in the Early Christian East*, Divinations: Rereading Late Ancient Religion, Philadelphia, PA: University of Pennsylvania Press.

Maraval, P. (1981), "La fonction pédagogique de la littérature hagiographique d'un lien de pèlerinage: l'example des Miracles de Cyr et Jean," in E. Patlagean and P. Riché (eds.), *Hagiographie, cultures et sociétés IVe–XIIe siècles: Actes du Colloque organisé à Nanterre et à Paris (2–5 Mai 1979)*, 383–97, Paris: Études Augustiniennes.

Miller, P. C. (2004), "Visceral Seeing: The Holy Body in Late Ancient Christianity," *Journal of Early Christian Studies*, 12 (4): 391–411.

Miller, P. C. (2009), *The Corporeal Imagination: Signifying the Holy in Late Ancient Christianity*, Philadelphia, PA: University of Pennsylvania Press.

Montserrat, D. (1998), "Pilgrimage to the Shrine of SS Cyrus and John at Menouthis in Late Antiquity," in D. Frankfurter (ed.), *Pilgrimage and Holy Space in Late Antiquity Egypt*, 257–79, Leiden: Brill.

Panayotakis, S., M. Zimmerman, and W. H. Keulen, eds. (2003), *The Ancient Novel and Beyond*, Leiden: Brill.

Patlagean, E. and P. Riché, eds. (1981), *Hagiographie, cultures et sociétés IVe–XIIe siècles: Actes du Colloque organisé à Nanterre et à Paris (2–5 Mai 1979)*, Paris: Études Augustiniennes.

Perczel, I., R. Forrari, and G. Géreby, eds. (2005), *The Eucharist in Theology and Philosophy: Issues of Doctrinal History in East and West from the Patristic Age to the Reformation*, Leuven: Leuven University Press.

Renberg, G. H. (2017), *Where Dreams May Come: Incubation Sanctuaries in the Greco-Roman Worl*, 2 vols, Leiden: Brill.

Sansterre, J. M. (1991), "Apparitions et miracles à Menouthis: de l'incubation païenne à l'incubation chrétienne," in A. Dierkens (ed.), *Apparitions et miracles*, 69–83, Brussels: Université de Bruxelles.

Shaw, B. D. (2003), "Judicial Nightmares and Christian Memory," *Journal of Early Christian Studies*, 11 (4): 533–63.

Stolz, Y. (2008), "Kanopos Oder Menouthis? Zur Identifikation Einer Ruinstätte in Der Bucht von Abuqir in Ägypten," *Klio*, 90: 193–207.

23

Reading Stephens

Lee Palmer Wandel
University of Wisconsin-Madison

I first met Susan Stephens while she and Jack Winkler were working on what became *Ancient Greek Novels: The Fragments* (1995). They were so obviously having fun, their metaphoric fingers pruny with Greek fragments and literary theory. It was only later, when I became acquainted with those who were arguing for a sense of the novel as something northern European and essentially modern, that I was able to see just how original that book was. In the intervening years, I heard about the gestation of the volumes on Callimachus, as well as the deep pleasures of working with Ben, and followed with pure delight the most recent book, *Ancient Greek Athletics: Primary Sources in Translation* (2021), from its origin in undergraduate classes at Stanford, through her conversations with Charles H. Stocking, its co-editor, to its appearance.

But the book I return to, again and again—a reflection of my own interests rather than any objective evaluation of the strengths of her books—is *Seeing Double: Intercultural Poetics in Ptolemaic Alexandria* (2003). Susan and I work in fields that we have come to see, in our decades-long conversation, as similarly governed by ideal types, in her case, of "Greeks," in mine, of "Lutheranism," "Catholicism," "Christianity." In that book, Susan articulates not only a way of reading Alexandrian poets, but more critically a way of thinking about "reading," and, in turn, "reception" and "culture." For those of us who work in what have come to be so tellingly called "premodern" fields, this book models the very vibrancy that ideal types deny:

> Fundamentally, this book is about reading—my own, that of other scholars, and that of ancient poets themselves, though not necessarily in that order. As a scholar trained within the western classical tradition I bring to my reading of Alexandrian poetry the same familiarity with the standard works of archaic and classical Greece that critics of this material normally possess. But to my act of

reading in this book I bring a specific type of knowledge that classical critics only rarely have access to—that of the Egyptian literary and cultural environment contemporary with the poets whom I am discussing. To know these things is to read differently—to see double. Inevitably as I read this poetry, I read it through dual lenses—Greek and Egyptian. I cannot do otherwise; my particular construction of the ancient world will not allow it. Initially my way of reading will seem alien to readers familiar with only Greek literature; therefore, I conceive it my task to present my audience with the kind of material that allows them to repeat my experience as a reader, and to come closer to what I believe would have been the experience of the original audiences of these poets. The ultimate goal is to remove Alexandrian poetry from the ivory tower and locate it more centrally in the social and political life of the city.

Stephens 2003: 18

Susan's voice is not simply inclusive. She consistently imagines multiple and differentiated readers. There is, of course, her own act of reading, more evocative of Hans-Georg Gadamer's sense of the reader who grows in reading and changes both in the moment and over time (Gadamer 1990, 1993) than of Wolfgang Iser's Reader (Iser 1978). *Seeing Double* begins with an acknowledgement that she could not have written the book when she first thought of it. Her reading had to take her into new territories, in the plural—hieroglyphics, Egyptian archaeology, reception theory, among them—in order to do what she aimed to do.

There are the readings of others, woven into the thinking on the page, set in type. Here, for example, are B. G. Gunn and J. Gwyn Griffiths reading Diodorus:

The phrase "beaten by Osiris" is the key to understanding the passage, as B.G. Gunn saw. In a verbal communication to J. Gwyn Griffiths, Gunn suggested that Diodorus was referring to "delineations of the King in a form like Osiris smiting a group of enemies…who are so closely packed together as to appear as monstrous *multicorpores*." This has the ring of truth about it.

Stephens 2003: 63

So, too, are there readings not immediately relevant to her line of analysis, acknowledged in the notes (for example, Stephens 2003: 53 n. 102). These are not mere citations, nor substantiations of her own argument. They build a sense of the richness of her sources and the vulnerability of those sources to multiple readings (Gadamer 1990; Greene 1986), readings whose worth is determined solely by how closely they attend to those sources.

"Reading," in other words, is this book's model for modern scholarship. In our conversations, Susan has spoken of how papyrologists work: from fragments, whose content is incomplete and dependent on the current state of knowledge of the field, not that of just one person. All readings are, reading itself is, thus tentative, contingent on what is known about a particular fragment. And those readings, of necessity, change as knowledge of a fragment and its affiliated fragments change, as fragments are discovered, transcribed, published. She and I share a sense that current readings are tentative, open to revision, even abandonment, as collective knowledge grows—reading is dialogic and dynamic. Reading thus becomes an activity both collective and contingent on so many different factors, not least the changing understanding individuals bring to bear on their sources.

Even as she provides close and illuminating readings of Herodotus and the *Alexander Romance*, as well as Callimachus, Theocritus, and Apollonius, she moves beyond "textual communities" (Stock 1983: 90–2). "Reading" is a broader activity, as her analysis of Herodotus outlines:

> Herodotus was able to observe a variety of monuments firsthand, and, significantly for the themes of this book, he saw a number of religious events. He was able to get information from local priests, especially those in Heliopolis, and to find informants among contemporary Greeks and non-Egyptians resident in Egypt and elsewhere. As we shall see, these four broad categories correspond to sources Greeks actually resident in the country could have availed themselves of without necessarily having access to Egyptian writing.
>
> Stephens 2003: 14

Reading situates individuals in dynamic with objects and texts. As her reading of Herodotus suggests, the encounters are shared, by individuals who see the same monument or observe the same event, but the constellation of encounters is unique to each individual—each reading becomes unique to the human being who has lived a particular life, experiences particular to that person. Herodotus neither reads Egyptian religious events nor hears local priests in the same way as another might have done. Reading *The Histories* is an encounter between two complexly conceived human beings.

That sense of "reading" which encompasses monuments and events thus also rejects literacy as the gauge of reading:

> It is possible to ask to what extent Greeks would have been able to read Egyptian, but the question may not be particularly meaningful in the ancient context. Few Egyptians read hieroglyphics, and even fewer hieratic, but that did not mean that Egyptians were ignorant of their own myths or of the ideologies of kingship.
>
> Stephens 2003: 48

Reading emerges in *Seeing Double* as a singularly complex activity. In the example of the *Alexander Romance*, the focus of reading is the material trace itself (Ginsburg 2012: 4):

> For our purposes, it is immaterial whether this Alexandrian story can be attached with any degree of confidence to the work of a particular Alexander historian, like Cleitarchus, or whether it was cobbled together from a variety of Alexandrian sources. What is significant is the curious nature of Alexander's paternity, found in both A and B versions of the story, or perhaps it would be better to say Alexander's competing paternities.
>
> Stephens 2003: 65

But the unknowability of a particular source's origin does not diminish or simplify its cultural work, its potential to speak to different readers complexly, both rhetorically and conceptually:

> Inevitably the question is asked whether stories like this were circulated with the serious intent of convincing the denizens of Hellenistic Egypt about Alexander's ancestry. Recognizing their inherent improbability, scholars have been inclined to regard such tales as serious or as propaganda only for native Egyptians, while relegating them to the realm of fantastical or romantic fiction for Greeks. But to pose the question in terms of believability or seriousness of intent may overlook a more significant point. It is not important whether Greeks would have believed the Nectanebo tale, if by belief we mean that it was accepted as veridically true. What is important is the fact that was told.... The style and tone of the *Alexander Romance* may predispose us to regard it as satire or parody, and therefore of little consequence, but even this feature of the story is legible within the two different cultures.
>
> Stephens 2003: 71

So, too, one brings lenses to each reading, which in turn, enable one to see what is there in the source, but not visible with other lenses. In the chapters on Callimachus, Theocritus, and Apollonius, Susan offers close readings, an established literary practice, including side-by-side. But those readings are through the new lens, broadly Ptolemaic kingship, here with particular attention to space:

> In Callimachus we saw conflation of two distinct geographic locations deliberately employed to collapse at least momentarily two separate landscapes. Apollonius also exploits geographic doublets but in a markedly different way. Apollonius never indulges in narrative deception, as Callimachus appears to; rather, he applies the same set of features in different places in his narrative to two separate places or customs.
>
> Stephens 2003: 207

These new lenses, in turn, enable a new reading:

By constructing the events in book 4 in such a way that they are coherent in both Greek and Egyptian narrative terms, Apollonius has in fact written a poem of and for the new hybrid political state, by retrojecting into the epic past elements of both worlds and by creating an epic template for new beginnings that partakes of both. . . . By ending with two islands, Apollonius focuses the reader's attention on Egypt of a new order. This is not the older order of Egyptian solar cosmogony or of Greek conquest, but potentially at least a new symbolic realm, signified by the appearance of Apollo and the promise of a new Greco-Egyptian reign of Horus-the-Child. The dawn of this new order requires new symbols and new narratives, the uniqueness of which Apollonius and his contemporaries collectively have striven to articulate.

Stephens 2003: 237

For me, the culmination of the book is neither new readings of these poems, nor a richer sense of Ptolemaic kingship, but the Library of Alexandria:

The Greek-speaking poets who were invited by the Ptolemies to participate in some fashion in the court were necessarily aware of the collective (and collected) Greek literary past as other than or separate from themselves. . . . However, the fact of the Library *did* alter the relationship of past to present. Whatever was embedded in collected texts was available for imitation and appropriation, but it now occupied a space that was temporally and physically separate—like epic, distanced from the present and from the literary events in which these poets participated. Whatever the living performance practices of the Ptolemaic world—and these must have been extensive—they must have been experienced as cognitively different from the repository of literary remembrance gathered in the Library. Or to put it somewhat differently, however scholarly and recondite we may perceive the Alexandrian poets to be, from their own perspective their poetry would have been live experience. The poetry of the past was texts, to be collated, disputed, emended; texts, moreover, that were imbued with an image of Greekness—of who or what Greeks were or had been—against which modern Alexandrians might measure themselves.

Stephens 2003: 250

This image of the Library confounds the usual categories of reception theory (Machor and Goldstein 2001: ix–xvii). Susan posits a more complex temporality, of a place containing material texts in the process of becoming canonical, a place that no longer exists, that became ash between the time of the Alexandrian poets and our own. The Library belongs not simply to a remote past, but to a past materially severed from the present. The poets, in the moment she evokes, have access to the Library, as a site in which texts in Greek have been collected, but Callimachus, Theocritus and Apollonius do not belong to it: they are not yet reduced to the material trace of their lives. They are, in that moment, still living; their speech is both audible and dialogic, directed towards others also living. Most reception theory tends to freeze either reader or text or both. Susan, however, articulates not simply a moment, but a calibrated contingency. In *Seeing Double*, "reading" is a human connection which simultaneously traverses time even as it remains firmly anchored in its distances; lives become linked through a piece of papyrus, itself but a fragment of a world equal to our own in indeterminacy. "Culture" is not a thing, or something which binds—one of the residues of those nineteenth-century archetypes—but lived by human beings who read, are read, and will be read.

Bibliography

Gadamer, H.-G. (1990, 1993), *Wahrheit und Methode*, 2 vols, Tübingen: J.C.B. Mohr.

Ginzburg, C. (2012), *Threads and Traces: True False Fictive*, trans. A. C. and J. Tedeschi, Berkeley and Los Angeles, CA, and London: University of California Press.

Greene, T. M. (1986), *The Vulnerable Text: Essays on Renaissance Literature*, New York: Columbia University Press.

Iser, W. (1978), *The Act of Reading: A Theory of Aesthetic Response*, Baltimore, MD, and London: Johns Hopkins University Press.

Machor, J. L. and P. Goldstein, eds. (2001), *Reception Study: From Literary Theory to Cultural Studies*, New York and London: Routledge.

Stephens, S. A. (1995), *Ancient Greek Novels: The Fragments*, Princeton, NJ: Princeton University Press.

Stephens, S. A. (2003), *Seeing Double: Intercultural Poetics in Ptolemaic Alexandria*, Berkeley and Los Angeles, CA: University of California Press.

Stephens, S. A. (2010), "The New Alexandrian Library," in S. A. Stephens and P. Vasunia (eds.), *Classics and National Cultures*, 267–84, Oxford: Oxford University Press.

Stephens, S. A. and P. Vasunia, eds. (2010), *Classics and National Cultures*, Oxford: Oxford University Press.

Stock, B. (1983), *The Implications of Literacy: Written Language and Models of Interpretation in the Eleventh and Twelfth Centuries*, Princeton, NJ: Princeton University Press.

Stocking, C. H. and S. A. Stephens (2021), *Ancient Greek Athletics: Primary Sources in Translation*, Oxford: Oxford University Press.

A Bibliography of Susan A. Stephens

(up to 2021)

This list excludes book reviews, short notices, and pieces of an informal nature.

Edited Volumes

Lionel Pearson: Selected Papers, with D. Lateiner, Chico, CA: Scholars Press, 1983.

Rituals in Ink, with A. Barchiesi and J. Rüpke, Stuttgart: Franz Steiner Verlag, 2004. Reviews: K. Christ, *Anzeiger für Altertumswissenschaft*, 58, nos 3–4 (2005): 200–1; F. Graf, *Museum Helveticum*, 62, no. 4 (2005): 265; G. Freyburger, *Revue des études latines*, 83 (2005): 392–3.

Classics and National Cultures, with P. Vasunia, Oxford: Oxford University Press, 2010. Reviews: *Bryn Mawr Classical Review*, 2010.11.43; *Choice* 48 (2011); *Greece & Rome* 58 (2011): 279; *Scholia Reviews*, n.s. 19 (2010): 32; *Times Literary Supplement*, 5645 (June 10, 2011): 26–7.

Brill's Companion to Callimachus, with B. Acosta-Hughes and L. Lehnus (eds.), i–xviii, 1–707, Leiden: Brill, 2011. Review: J. J. Clauss, *Bryn Mawr Classical Review*, 2012.05.48; P. Green, *London Review of Books*, 34, no. 24 (20 December 2012).

Books

Oxyrhynchus Papyri XLV, with A. Bowman, J. Shelton, and M. West, London: Egypt Exploration Society, 1977, 1–173. Reviews: J. Irigoin, *Revue des études grecques*, 91 (1978): 211–12; S. Votto, *Studia Papyrologica*, 18 (1979): 154–6; J. D. Thomas, *Classical Review*, 29 (1979): 296–7; H. J. Wolff, *Zeitschrift der Savigny-Stiftung für Rechtsgeschichte (ZRG)*, 95 (1978): 353–60; W. Luppe, *Gnomon*, 51 (1979): 1–8; A. Drochmans-Ruelle, *Chronique d'Egypte*, 54, no. 107 (1979): 156–61; R. T. O'Callaghan, *Orientalia*, 68 (1979): 147; G. Foti Talamanca, *Iura*, 29 (1978 [1982]): 214–20.

Didymi in Demosthenem Commenta, with L. Pearson, Stuttgart: Teubner, 1983, i–xx, 1–87. Reviews: H. Wankel, *Gnomon*, 59 (1987): 213–23; J. Rusten, *Classical Philology*, 82 (1987): 265–9.

Yale Papyri in the Beinecke Library II, American Studies in Papyrology, 24, Chico, CA: Scholars Press, 1985, i–xxxvii, 1–167 + plates. Reviews: H. A. Rupprecht, *Zeitschrift der Savigny-Stiftung für Rechtsgeschichte* (*ZRG*), 104 (1987): 889–90; T. Lenaerts, *Chronique d'Egypte*, 61, no. 122 (1986): 335–9; A. M. Devine, *Classical Bulletin*, 65 (1989): 119–20; W. E. H. Cockle, *Enchoria*, 16 (1988): 169–73; B. Kramer, *Journal of Egyptian Archaeology*, 75 (1989): 291–5.

Ancient Greek Novels: The Fragments. Introduction, Text, Translation and Commentary, with John J. Winkler, Princeton, NJ: Princeton University Press, 1995, i–xvi, 3–541. Reviews: D. Donnet, *Acta Classica*, 66 (1997): 420; N. Marini, *Athenaeum*, 85, no. 1 (1997): 305–7; G. N. Sandy, *Bryn Mawr Classical Review*, 7, no. 1 (1996): 81–4; A. Wouters, *Les Études classiques*, 64, no. 3 (1996): 300–1; A. Billault, *Revue des études grecques*, 109, no. 1 (1996): 310–12; H. Maehler, *Scholia*, 6 (1997): 136–8; J. Griffin, *Times Literary Supplement*, (1996): 9–10; J. R. Morgan, *Classical Review*, N.S., 48, no. 1 (1998): 23–5; E. P. Cueva, *Classical Bulletin*, 75, no. 1 (1999): 85–97. Now in electronic reprint.

Greek Prose Composition, 3rd ed., Bryn Mawr Textbooks, 1996; revised ed., 2016.

Seeing Double: Intercultural Poetics in Ptolemaic Alexandria, Berkeley and Los Angeles, CA: University of California Press, 2003, i–xvi, 1–292 + plates. Reviews: S. Barbantani, *Bryn Mawr Classical Review*, 6, no. 43 (2003); D. Donnet, *Acta Classica*, 73 (2004): 343–4; M. Payne, *Classical Philology*, 99, no. 3 (2004): 267–72; P. Ojennus, *Classical Journal*, 100, no. 1 (2004–5): 99–102; S. Goldhill, *Gnomon*, 77, no. 2 (2005): 99–104; A. M. F. W. Verhoogt, *Journal of the American Oriental Society*, 124, no. 2 (2004): 368–9; J. S. Bruss, *New England Classical Journal*, 31, no. 3 (2004): 307–9; J. J. Clauss, *Phoenix*, 59, nos 1–2 (2005): 161–5.

Callimachus in Context: From Plato to the Augustan Poet, with B. Acosta-Hughes, Cambridge: Cambridge University Press, 2012, v–xvi, 1–328. Reviews: P. Green, *London Review of Books*, December 2012; M. Fantuzzi, *Classical Journal*, 2013; S. Heyworth, *Bryn Mawr Classical Review*, 2013; J. Lightfoot, *Journal of Hellenic Studies*, February 2014. Paperback edition 2015.

The Hymns of Callimachus: Edited with Introduction, Translation and Commentary, Oxford: Oxford University Press, 2015, viii–xiv, 1–324.

The Poets of Alexandria, London: I.B. Tauris, 2018, vii–xiii, 1–192.

Ancient Greek Athletics: Primary Sources in Translation, with Charles Stocking, Oxford: Oxford University Press, 2021, i–xxxiii, 1–429.

Callimachus: The Epigrams, with B. Acosta-Hughes, Berlin and New York: De Gruyter, 2024.

Articles

"Lease of Land," *Collectanea Papyrologica: Texts Published in Honor of H.C. Youtie*, vol. 2, 535–41, Bonn: Rudolf Habelt, 1976.

"Nine Orders to Pay from Oxyrhynchus," *Zeitschrift für Papyrologie und Epigraphik*, 31 (1978): 145–60, reprinted in *The Oxyrhynchus Papyri* XLIX, nos 3513–21, pp. 251–7, Oxford: University of Oxford Press, 1983.

"Aristophanes, *Poiesis*," *Papyri Greek & Egyptian: Edited by Various Hands in Honour of Eric Gardner Turner on the Occasion of his Seventieth Birthday* (= Graeco-Roman Memoirs 68) No. 4, London: Egypt Exploration Society, 1981, 23–5.

Two Fragments of New Comedy, *Oxyrhynchus Papyri* XLIX, nos 3431–2, pp. 1–10, London: Egypt Exploration Society, 1983.

"The Arginusae Theme in Greek Rhetorical Theory and Practice," *Bulletin of the American Society of Papyrologists*, 21, 3–4 (1983): 71–81.

"The Ancient Title of the *Ad Demonicum*," *Yale Classical Studies*, 28: 5–9, Cambridge: Cambridge University Press, 1985.

"A Eulogy for Christian Martyrs?," Festschrift for William Willis, = *Bulletin of the American Society of Papyrologists*, 22, 1–4 (1985): 333–45.

"Book Production," in M. Grant and R. Kitzinger (eds.), *Civilization of the Ancient Mediterranean: Greece and Rome,* vol. 1, 421–36, New York: Charles Scribner's Sons, 1988.

"Complaints of Police Brutality," with T. Caulfield and A. Estner, *Zeitschrift für Papyrologie und Epigraphik*, 76 (1989): 241–54.

"Recycled Demosthenes," *Zeitschrift für Papyrologie und Epigraphik*, 77 (1989): 271–2.

"The Rhetorical Papyrus P. Hamb. 134," *Zeitschrift für Papyrologie und Epigraphik*, 77 (1989): 267–70.

"Hellenistic Queens," in H. Tierney (ed.), *Women's Studies Encyclopedia, Vol. III: History, Philosophy and Religion*, 200–2, Westport, CT: Greenwood Press, 1991, reprinted, 1996.

"Six Documents from the Yale Collection," with Naphtali Lewis, *Zeitschrift für Papyrologie und Epigraphik*, 88 (1991): 169–76.

"An Epikrisis Return and Other Documentary Fragments from the Yale Collection," *Zeitschrift für Papyrologie und Epigraphik*, 90 (1993): 221–6.

"Who Read Ancient Novels?," in J. Tatum (ed.), *The Search for the Ancient Novel*, 405–18, Baltimore, MD: Johns Hopkins University Press, 1994.

"Alcibiades in the Rhetorical Tradition," *Zeitschrift für Papyrologie und Epigraphik*, 105 (1995): 215–24.

"Fragments of Lost Novels," in Gareth Schmeling (ed.), *Handbook of the Ancient Novel*, 655–83, Leiden: Brill, 1996. Revised edition, 2003.

"Callimachus at Court," M. A. Harder, R. F. Regtuit, and G. C. Wakker (eds.), *Genre in Hellenisitic Poetry, Hellenistica Groningana*, vol. 3, 167–85, Leuven: Peeters, 1998

"Writing Epic in the Ptolemaic Court," in G. C. Wakker, M. A. Harder, and R. F. Regtuit (eds.), *Apollonius Rhodius, Hellenistica Groningana*, vol. 4, 195–215, Leuven: Peeters, 2000.

"Aetia fr. 1.5: I told my story like a child," with B. Acosta-Hughes, *Zeitschrift für Papyrologie und Epigraphik*, 136 (2001): 214–16.

"Commenting on Fragments," in R. Gibson and C. Kraus (eds.), *The Classical Commentary: History, Practices, Theory*, 67–88, Leiden: Brill, 2002.

"Rereading Callimachus' *Aetia* Fragment 1," with B. Acosta-Hughes, *Classical Philology*, 97 (2002): 238–55.

"Egyptian Callimachus," *Callimaque. Entretiens sur L'Antiquité classique*, 48, 235–70, Geneva: Fondation Hardt, 2002.

"For You, Arsinoe . . .," in B. Acosta-Hughes and E. Kosmetatou (eds.), *Labored in Papyrus Leaves—Perspectives on an Epigram Collection Attributed to Posidippus (P. Mil. Vogl. VIII 309)*, 161–76, Cambridge, MA: Harvard University Press, 2004.

"Linus Song", *Hermathena* (2002–3): 10–24.

"The Manuscript: Posidippus on Papyrus," with Dirk Obbink in B. Acosta-Hughes and E. Kosmetatou (eds.), *Labored in Papyrus Leaves*, 7–15, Cambridge, MA: Harvard University Press, 2004.

"Posidippus' Poetry Book: Where Macedon Meets Egypt," in W. V. Harris and G. Ruffini (eds.), *Ancient Alexandria: between Greece and Egypt*, 63–86, Leiiden: Brill, 2004.

"Whose Rituals in Ink?," in A. Barchiesi, J. Rüpke, and S. Stephens (eds.), *Rituals in Ink*, 155–8, Stuttgart: Franz Steiner Verlag, 2004.

"Battle of the Books," in K. Gutzwiller (ed.), *The New Posidippus: A Hellenistic Poetry Book*, 220–39, Oxford: Oxford University Press, 2005.

"Lessons of the Crocodile," for "Imperial Trauma: The Powerlessness of the Powerful" Symposium on Imperial Trauma, part I, *Common Knowledge*, 11, no. 2 (2005): 215–39. Reprinted in J. M. Perl (ed.), *Peace and Mind: Civilian Scholarship from Common Knowledge*, 311–46, Aurora, CO: Davies Group Publishers, 2011.

"Ptolemaic Pastoral," in M. Fantuzzi and T. Papanghelis (eds.), *Companion to Pastoral*, 91–118, Leiden: Brill, 2006.

"Cultural Identity," in Tim Whitmarsh (ed.), *Cambridge Companion to the Ancient Novel*, 56–71, Cambridge: Cambridge University Press, 2008.

"Ptolemaic Epic," *Brill Companion to Apollonius Rhodius*, 2nd rev. ed., 95–114, Leiden: Brill, 2008.

"Hellenistic Culture," in G. Boys-Stones and B. Graziosi (eds.), *Oxford Handbook of Hellenic Studies*, 86–97, Oxford: Oxford University Press, 2009.

"Ptolemaic Alexandria," in J. Clauss and M. Cuypers (eds.), *A Companion to Hellenistic Literature*, 46–61, Malden, MA, and Oxford: Wiley-Blackwell, 2010.

"The New Alexandrian Library," in S. A. Stephens and P. Vasunia (eds.), *Classics and National Cultures*, 267–84, Oxford: Oxford University Press, 2010.

"Literary Quarrels," in A. Martina and A.-T. Cozzoli (eds.), *Atti della seconda giornata di studi su Callimaco*, 35–50, Rome: Herder, 2011.

"Introduction," in B. Acosta-Hughes and L. Lehnus (eds.), *Brill's Companion to Callimachus*, 1–19, Leiden: Brill, 2011.

"Remapping the Mediterranean: The Argo Adventure in Apollonius and Callimachus," D. Obbink and R. Rutherford (eds.), *Culture in Pieces: Festschrift for Peter Parsons*, 188–207, Oxford: Oxford University Press, 2011.

"Deregulating Poetry," in A. Peponi (ed.), *The City Dancing: Performance and Culture in Plato's Laws*, 371–91, Cambridge: Cambridge University Press, 2013.

"Writing Alexandria as the (Common)place," in C. Cusset, N. Le Meur-Weissman, and F. Levin (eds.), *Mythe et Pouvior à l'époque héllenistique, Hellenistica Groningana*, vol. 18, 137–53, Leuven: Peeters, 2013.

"Fictions of Cultural Authority," in T. Whitmarsh (ed.), *The Romance Between Greece and the East*, 197–218, Cambridge: Cambridge University Press, 2013.

"The Other Greek Novels," in E. Cueva and S. N. Bryne (eds.), *Blackwell's Companion to the Ancient Novel*, 147–58, Malden, MA: Wiley-Blackwell, 2014.

"The Ancient City in Literature," in K. McNamara (ed.), *Cambridge Companion to the City in Literature*, 31–41, Cambridge: Cambridge University Press, 2014.

"Callimachus and his Narrators," in A. Faulkner and O. Hodkinson (eds.), *Hymnic Narrative and the Narratology of Greek Hymns*, 49–68, Leiden: Brill, 2015.

"Plato's Egyptian Republic," in I. Rutherford (ed.), *Greco-Egyptian Interactions*, 41–59, Oxford: Oxford University Press, 2015.

"The (Geo)Politics of Imagining Ancient Alexandria," in M. Asper and V. Rimell (eds.), *Imagining Empire: Political Space in Hellenistic and Roman Literature*, 11–22, Heidelberg: Universitätsverlag Winter, 2017.

"Callimachean 'Lyric,'" in E. Sistakou (ed.), *Trends in Classics–Hellenistic Lyricism*, 9, no. 2 (2017): 226–47, with B. Acosta-Hughes.

"Alexandria: the new Center," *Electryone*, 5, no. 1 (2018): 1–16.

"P. Oxy. 17.2082 and Berenice I's Victory with Foals (Posidippus 87 AB)," *Zeitschrift für Papyrologie und Epigraphik*, 206 (2018): 35–9.

"Celebrating the Games," in J. J. H. Klooster, M. A. Harder, R. F. Regtuit, and G. C. Wakker (eds.), *Callimachus Revisited, Hellenistica Groningana*, vol. 3, 351–67, Leuven: Peeters, 2019.

"Athletics in Apollonius and Callimachus," *Aevum Antiquum*, 19 (2019): 141–6.

"Cheating and Gaming the System in Ancient Athletics," *Journal of the Philosophy of Sport*, 43, no. 3 (2020): 391–402.

"Sappho in Pieces," in M. Fantuzzi, H. Morales, and T. Whitmarsh (eds.), *Reception in the Greco-Roman World*, 319–43, Cambridge: Cambridge University Press, 2021.

"Forms of Survival," in P. Vasunia (ed.), *The Politics of Form in Greek Literature*, 83–100, London: Bloomsbury Academic, 2022.

Digital Media

Callimachus, *Aetia. Dickinson Classical Commentaries*. Available online: https://dcc.dickinson.edu/callimachus-aetia/preface.

Index

Acanthus, 165
Achilles, 31–3, 187
Achilles Tatius, 328, 333, 335
Acosta-Hughes, Benjamin, 286
Acropolis, 207
acrostic, 233, 242–4
Actium, 274, 286
Adler, Ada, 186
Adonis, 132–3, 196
Adriatic Sea, 204
Aegisthus, 19–20, 26, 30–5
Aegyptus, 67
Aelian (Claudius Aelianus), 166, 178–9
   De natura animalium (*On the Nature*
     of Animals), 178–9
Aeneas, 269, 271, 276–8, 284–7, 289–91
Aeolus, 150
Aeschylus, 17, 19, 22, 26, 29–30, 34, 186
   Oresteia, 19, 34
     Choephoroe (*Libation Bearers*), 17,
       26, 186
   Persians, 186
   Prometheus Bound, 22
aetiology, 112, 278, 287–9, 330–1
Aetolia, 250
Africa, Africans, 284, 286–92. *See also*
     Egypt
Afro-Eurasian, 69, 72
Agamemnon, 18, 22, 25, 31, 34, 311
Agathocles, 274–6
Agathon, 21
Ages of Man, 3, 8–9
Agido, 112
agōn, 34, 57, 128, 255
agora, 256, 259
agos, 218. *See also* pollution
Ahl, Frederick, 271
Ajax (Lesser Ajax), 270
Alba Longa, 278
Alcaeus of Lesbos, 111
Alcaeus of Messene, 249, 252, 255,
     257–60, 311

Alcibiades, 310–11
Alcidamas 250–2
Alcman, 111–16
Alexander Aetolus, 312
Alexander III, of Macedonia ("the Great"),
     45–73, 231–2, 285–7, 289–90,
     300, 328–35, 358
Alexander Romance, 64, 231, 330, 357–8
Alexandria, Alexandrians, 46, 58–61, 65,
     123–5, 127, 129, 136, 146–8, 153,
     157, 169, 179, 201, 203, 215, 227,
     253, 286, 288, 292, 302, 312,
     328–35, 341–4, 348–50, 355–6,
     358–9
   Alexandrianism, 292
   Alexandrian Library, 253, 359–60
   Lighthouse of Alexandria, 169, 333
Amenemḥat I, 63
Amenḥotep III, 48
Ammon, Amun, Amun-Rē, 46–64, 72, 230,
     284–92, 331
Ammonius of Alexandria, 344
Amphiareion, 254
Amphiphanes, 250
Āmū Daryā, 68
Amunia, 46
Anatolia, 328
Anaxilaos, 321–2
Anchises, 268–71
Antenor, 290
Anthia, 332
Anthologia Palatina (*AP*), *Palatine*
     Anthology, 161, 165, 177, 195,
     201–2, 244, 249, 252, 257–8, 260,
     299, 301–6, 308–12
Anthologia Planudea (*APl*), *Planudean*
     Anthology, 303–4
Antigonus II Gonatas, 312
Antimachus, 186
Antioch (Syrian), 319
Antipater of Sidon, 309–10
Antipater of Thessalonica, 302

antistrophe, antistrophes, 21, 31
Antonia, 300–3, 305
Aphrodite, Aphrodite-Arsinoe, Arsinoe-
    Aphrodite, 151–5
    Zephyritis, 152–4. *See also* Cypris
Apis, Apis bull, Apis cult, 48–50, 53, 55–7,
    67, 178, 332
Apollo, 132, 146–8, 150, 153–5, 217, 219,
    244, 250, 269, 359
Apollodorus of Athens, 203–9
Apollonius, brother of Ptolemaeus, 227–35
Apollonius of Rhodes, 3, 130, 161, 186,
    201, 204, 215–22, 227, 289, 331,
    357-60
    Argonautica, 201, 215, 289
Apsyrtos, 216–8, 221–2
Aquarius, 288
Aratus, 148, 239–40, 242, 244–5, 288, 303
    Phaenomena, 239–40, 242, 244–5
Archilochus, 123, 126, 128, 130–1, 194,
    312
Ares, 6, 232, 289
Arete, 91, 135
Argo, 215–16
Argonauts, 215–22, 288–9
Argos, Argives, 26, 28–9, 35, 192
Ariadne, 289
Aries, 287–8
Arion, 153
Aristaenetus, 112–15, 166
Aristarchus, 203, 254
Aristippus, 156
Aristophanes, 21, 29–30, 72, 166
    Aeschylus in, 29–30
    Acharnians, 29
    Frogs, 21, 29
    Lysistrata, 16
Aristotle, 21, 46, 49, 68, 73, 221–2,
    251–4, 256
    [*Constitution of the Orchomenians*],
    251–2, 256, 258
    [*On Marvelous Things Heard*], 221
    [*Peplos*], 254–5
Arne, 254
Arrian, 46, 48, 54–60, 62, 64–8, 70–1
    Anabasis Alexandri, 54, 58–9, 67–8, 73
Arsinoe II, 151–7
Artemidorus, 309
Artemis, 112, 146–8, 205, 330

Ascalaphus, 254
Asclepiades, 169, 310
Ascra, 251–4
Asiatic, Asiatics, 51, 53, 285
Asteria, 146
Astymeloisa, 112
Atarneus, 177
Athanasia, 348
Athena Parthenos, 33
Athena, 33, 148–50, 269–70
Athenaeus, 127–30, 148, 208–9
    Deipnosophistai (*Sophists at Dinner*),
    127, 148
Athenis, 135
Athenodorus of Tarsus, 300
Athens, Athenian, Athenians, 16, 18, 21, 26
    29, 32, 128, 148, 194, 203, 206–9,
    220, 259, 331, 335
Atkin, Albert, 69
Atlantic, 289
Atum, 56
Augustus, 201, 271, 286–92, 299–301,
    303–4
Ausonian sea, 216
Avesta, 72

Ba'al, 49
Bābilim, 68
Babylon, 328
Babyloniaka, 195
Bacchus, 287–8
Bacchylides, 111, 254, 310
Baḥrīya, 46, 50, 62, 71
Barigazzi, Adelmo, 115
Baring, Evelyn, 58
Barque Chapel, 50, 53
Barthes, Ronald, 59–60, 68, 249
Bartoletti, Vittorio, 182–3
Basilo, 156
Bastet, 230
Batrachomyomachia, 196
Battos, 202
Baucis, 195
Berber, 61, 68, 70
Berenice II, 151–4, 191
Bergmann, Bettina, 334
Beroe, 276–7
Bias, 192
Bing, Peter, 113, 242

biography, biographies, biographical, 126, 134, 165, 169, 228, 249–50, 252–60, 285, 287, 289
Boeotia, Boeotians, 254
Booth, Phil, 342, 350
Borthwick, Kerr, 21
Bosch-Puche, Francisco, 51
boukolia, 329–31, 333
Boupalus, 134–5
Bowersock, Glen Warren, 300
Bowie, Ewen, 301, 303
Bright God, 291
Bruttians, 276
Bryson, Norman, 335
Burke, Kenneth, 54
Busiris, 289
Buthrotum, 274
Butler, Judith, 125–6
Byre, Calvin S., 217–8
Byzantium, Byzantine, 205, 292, 312, 321, 323, 335

Caesar, Julius, 286, 288, 299, 303–4
California, 45, 72, 227
Calisiris, 330
Callias of Sphettos, 169
Callichorus, 148
Callimachus, 3, 111–16, 123–36, 146–57, 161–70, 176–9, 181–8, 191–7, 201–9, 227, 239, 242–4, 286–7, 301, 305, 310–11, 331, 355, 357–8, 360
    Aetia, 111–16, 151–4, 167, 186, 191, 193, 203–4, 205–6, 239, 243–4; *Lock of Berenice*, 111, 151, 153–4, 286; *Phrygius and Pieria*, 111–16; *Victoria Berenices* (*Victory of Berenice*), 111, 151, 154, 191, 193, 196; scholia on, 147, 152–3, 192
    Epigrams, 149, 151–6, 161–70, 176–9, 195–6, 201–3, 249–60; epigram on Creophylus of Samos' *Capture of Oechalia*, 202; epigram on Heraclitus, 161–70
    Hecale, 181–8, 301. *See also* papyrus, papyri
    Hymns, 146–50, 155, 157, 181, 205, 331
    Iambi, 123–36, 177, 202, 311

Pannychis (lyric poem), 155
    and Strabo, 201–9
Callisthenes, 70
Calvino, Italo, 67
Cameron, Alan, 202
Campania, 320–2, 324
Campbell, David Aitken, 114
Canace, 150
Canopus, 152, 342
Capricorn, 288, 290
Carbon, Jan-Mathieu, 169
Carey, Chris, 124
Carian, Carians, 113, 115, 161, 168, 291
Carthage, Carthaginian, 272, 287, 289
Cartledge, Paul, 70
Cassandra, 268–70, 275–9
Cassius Dio, 329
Castor, 35, 155
Castrum Minervae, 269
Catana, 205
Cataudella, 310
Catholicism, 355
Catullus, Gaius Valerius
    Carmen 66, 151, 153
Celaeno (Harpy), 269
Cephalas, Constantine, 258, 312
Cephisophon, 21
Certamen Homeri et Hesiodi, 250, 252–3, 255–6, 258
Chadwick, Henry, 342
Chaereas, 331
Chalcedonian, Chalcedonians, 341–2
Chariclo, 149–50
Chariton, 329, 331–3,
    Callirhoe, 331–2
Cheiron, 32
Chersias, 256–7
Chief Prophet, 62
Christ, Jesus, 342, 345, 347–8
    exorcism at Gerasa, 345
Christianity, Christian, Christians, 320, 323, 341–2, 345–6, 349
    Christmas mass, 349
    Christological rhetoric, 350
Church, 194, 342–4
Cicero, 287–8
    Dream of Scipio, 288
Cichorius, Conrad, 301
Cincinnatus, Lucius Quinctius, 194

Circe, 216, 221
Claudius Drusus, Nero, 303
Clazomenae, 135
Cleinias, 311
Cleitarchus, 358
Cleon, 130
Cleopatra II, 229
Cleopatra VII, 286, 289–90, 292, 300–1
Cleopatra Selene II, 290, 300–1, 303, 306
Clitophon, 335
Clytemnestra, 19, 22, 26, 30, 33–5
Colchian, 217
communis locus, 334
Constantine I, "the Great", emperor of
     Rome, 320
Corinth, Corinthians, 257
Coroneia, 323
Cory, William Johnson, 161–2, 168–9
Creophylus of Samos, 202
Crete, 251
Crinagoras, 299–306
Critias, 310–11
Cronus, 205, 240–1. *See also* Kronos
Cumae, 272
Curtius Rufus, Quintus, 46, 53, 61, 67,
     68, 71
Cybele (Cybebe), 133, 196
Cypris, 152. *See also* Aphrodite
Cypselus, 257
Cyrene, 64, 73, 156, 201, 203
Cyril of Alexandria, 342

D'Alessio, Giovan Battista, 154
Dällenbach, Lucien, 68
Damascus, 343
Danaos, 192
Darius III, 45, 53, 68
de Man, Paul, 65, 69, 164–5, 170
De Quincey, Thomas, 164
death-world, 167. *See also* underworld,
     Hades
Death, 161
Deianeira, 163–4
deixis, 259
Delattre, Daniel, 191
Delos, 146–7, 155, 157
Delphi, 128, 250, 257
Demeter, 147–9
Demodes, 256

Demosthenes (Athenian commander), 250
Demotic, 229–33
Derrida, Jacques, 72, 165
Description de l'Égypte, 58
Dicaeopolis, 29, 276
Dicon, 165
Dido, 284, 289
Dio Chrysostom, 166
Diodorus of Sicily, 46, 67–8, 71, 201, 220,
     230, 270, 275, 330, 356
Diogenes Laertius, 177
Diomedes, 289
Dion, 177
Dionysius (*strategos*), 229
Dionysius of Halicarnassus, 168, 194
Dionysius Periegetes, 320–3, 325
Dionysius Scytobrachion, 287, 289, 291
Dionysius Thrax, 201
Dionysus, 288
Diosco(u)rides, 309–12
Dioscuri, 154–5, 157, 288
dirt, 27, 218. *See also* pollution
disease, diseases, 218–22, 241, 343,
     345–6, 350
dream-interpretation, 229–31, 233, 235.
     See also oneirocriticism
Drepana, 272

Eber-Nāri, 45–6
Edlund, Ingrid, 269
Effe, Bernd, 239
Egesta. *See* Segesta
Egypt, Egyptians, 45–69, 71, 73, 149,
     156–7, 168, 176, 178–9, 181, 197,
     215, 217, 227–35, 284–92, 300,
     306, 328–33, 341–3, 356–9
Egypt Exploration Society, 181
eironeia, 129
Elephantinē, 46, 48, 71, 179
Eleusis, 148
Eliot, Thomas S., 66
Elkins, James, 349
Elymian city, 275
Empedocles, 186
enargeia, 170
Enceladus, 243
energeia, 170
enjambment, 167
enkatochos, 228. *See also katochos, katochoi*

Ennius, Quintus, 287
Entellus, 271
epidemics. *See* disease, diseases
epigram, 151, 153–6, 161–70, 177–9,
    195–6, 201–3, 249–53,
    255–60, 299, 301–2, 304,
    308–12
Ephesus, 219, 332–3
elegy, elegies, elegiac, 3–5, 8, 10–11,
    111–12, 161–2, 165, 168, 186,
    275, 308–11
epilepsy, 219
epitaph, epitaphs, epitaphic epigrams,
    163–5, 201–2, 252–60, 311
Eratosthenes, 203–4, 252, 256, 287
Eridanus, 206–9
eros, 157
Erotes, 155
erōtes, 289
Erysichthon, 148–50
Eryx, 271–3
Ethiopia, Ethiopians, 152, 220, 306, 328,
    331
Euboea, 250
Eubulus, 208–9
Eucharist, 343
Eudoxus, 228, 233–5.
euergetism, 157, 288
Euhemerus, Euhemeristic, 287
Euphemus, 286, 291
Euphrates, 291
Euripides, 16–35, 73, 270, 312, 323
    Bacchae, 323
    Electra, 16–35
    Iphigenia at Aulis, 22
    Orestes, 22
Eustathius of Thessalonica, 322–4
Euthydemus, 131–6

Fabbrichesi, Rossella, 70
Faiyum Oasis, 63
Fama, 290–1
Fantuzzi, Marco, 146
Fates, 150
femininity, feminine, 22, 24, 126, 147,
    152, 286–7, 342
figura sententiae, 55
Foucault, Michel, 125, 249
Frantantuono, Lee, 299

Freud, Sigmund, 45, 47, 335
Fulvia, 300

Gadamer, Hans-Georg, 356
Galen, 219, 221, 346
Gallus, 312
Ganyctor, 250
Gates of Diochares, 206
Ġazzah, 45
Gelonians, 291
Gemini, 288
gender, gendered, 125–6, 128, 130, 136,
    149, 152, 285
geographer, geographers, 201–2, 207,
    320, 323
Gerasa, 345
Gerber, Douglas E., 134–5
Germanicus, 303
Gesios, 346
Gildersleeve, Basil Lanneau, 162, 168
Glanis, 320
Goddio, Franck, 58, 157
golden fleece, 216, 288
Goldhill, Simon, 59
Gorgias, 127–30, 136. *See also* Hermippus,
    Plato
Gorgon, 32
Gow, Andrew Sydenham Farrar, 176–9,
    196, 252
Gowers, Emily, 277
Graces, 151, 305
Graziosi, Barbara, 253
Great Chain of Being (*scala naturae*), 49
Greece, Greeks, 18, 33, 35, 46–9, 51, 53–9,
    62, 64–8, 70–1, 73, 123–4, 126,
    128, 132, 151, 153, 156–7, 161–2,
    165, 167–8, 176, 178–9, 194, 196,
    203, 208, 215–9, 221, 227–35,
    252, 254, 269–70, 274–5, 277–8,
    285–9, 292, 299, 302, 319–20,
    322–5, 328–35, 355–60, *and*
    passim
    Greco-Egyptian, 179, 227–8, 233–5,
        287, 292, 330, 359
    Greco-Macedonian, Greco-
        Macedonians, 58–9, 289, 292
    Greco-Roman, 46, 54, 60–1, 64, 68
Greene, Thomas McLernon 356
Greimas, A.-J., 60

Gunn, Battiscombe George, 356
Gwyn Griffiths, John, 356
Gylis, 157

Habrocomes, 332–3
Hades, 6–7, 23, 157, 166–7
Hagesichora, 114. *See also* Alcman
Hägg, Tomas, 320–3
Halicarnassus, 168–70, 194, 201–2
Hall, Edith, 22
Hamilcar, 272
Hammond, Mason, 299–300
Harder, M. A. (Annette), 111, 113,
        152–4, 191–3, 243
Harmais, 229
Harpies, 217
Hartman, Geoffrey, 164
Hecabe, 187
Hecale, 184, 186–7, 191, 195, 305
Hecker, Alfons, 187, 310
    Hecker's Law, 187
Hector, 32, 187, 276
Hegel, Georg Wilhelm Friedrich, 73
Hegesippus, 310
Heinze, Richard, 273
Hejduk, Julia, 290
Helen, 29, 155, 157, 288
Heliades, 208, 217
Heliodorus, 197, 309, 329–31
Heliopolis, 55–6, 58, 66–7, 357
Helios, 150, 216–7, 221, 300, 333
Helle, 287
Henry, W. Benjamin, 181–2, 184–5
Hephaestion, 71
Hephaestus, 31
Hera, 19, 26, 156–7, 302, 305, 323
Heracles, 163, 191–7, 288–9
Heraclitus of Halicarnassus, 161–70,
        201–2
Hercte, 272
Hermes, 32, 134, 308
Hermesianax, 242, 254
Hermippus of Smyrna, 128–30, 287–9, 291
Hermocrates, 331
Hermodorus, 309
Hermopolis, 71
hero, heroes, 18, 22, 217, 254–5, 259, 272,
        288, 290, 320, 328–33
Herodas, 157

Herodian, 323
Herodotus, 48–9, 68, 166, 168, 194, 208,
        259, 285, 319, 322, 329, 331, 357
heroine, heroines, 18–19, 289, 320–2, 324,
        328–30, 332–3
Hesiod, 57, 123, 132, 167, 193, 195, 211,
        239–42, 245, 249–60
    and Mnasalkes, 249, 252–60
    [*Scutum* (*Shield*)], 254
    Theogony, 239, 253
    Works and Days, 239–42, 245, 251, 254–5
Hesychius, 186
hexameter, 111, 161, 183, 186–7, 192, 275
Heyne, Christian Gottlob, 310
Hibis, 71
hieroglyphic, hieroglyphics, 58, 71, 232,
        356–7
hieros gamos, 50
High Priest, 48
Hippocrates, 218–22, 346
Hipponax, 123–7, 130–1, 134–6, 311
Hippothoos, 332
Hjelmslev, Louis, 60–1, 65, 70
Hollis, Adrian S., 182–3, 187
Homer, 32–3, 57, 115, 127, 147, 166, 168,
        170, 186–8, 201–4, 250–1, 253–5,
        269, 290, 311, 320, 323–4, 330–1,
        333, 341
    and *On the Catalogue of Ships. See
        under* Apollodorus of Athens
    Iliad, 18, 31–2, 115, 186–7, 219, 244,
        254, 290, 311
    Odyssey, 18, 150, 167, 186, 241, 290
        320, 324, 333
Homeric Hymn to Apollo, 147
Horace, 126–7, 130–1
Hornblower, Simon, 270, 275
Hornung, Erik, 63
Horus, Horus-Rē, 45, 51–2, 359
Höschele, Regina, 113
hubris, hubristic, 20, 62, 124
Hunter, Richard, 166, 208, 222
Hyksos, 53
hymn, hymns, 3–4, 66, 146–50, 155, 157,
        181, 205, 240, 242, 251, 286,
        331, 347
Hyrcania, 67
Hyrras, 177

Ialmenus, 254
iambic genre, poetry, 3, 10–11, 20, 123–36,
        177, 202, 253, 274, 310–11
    iambic masculinity, 123–36
    iambizein, 128–31
    iambographers, 125
Iapygians, 270
Iarbas, 284–7, 290–1
iatrosophists, 345
Ibycus, 111
Ida, 278
Ilion. *See* Troy
Ilioupersis, 275
Ilissos, 207
Ilithyiae, 305
incubation miracles, 341–2, 349
India, 310
infanticide, 35
inscription, inscriptions, 50, 53, 157,
        163–5, 167–9, 232, 253, 255, 285,
        291, 299, 309
intertextuality, 112, 126, 186–7, 195, 273–4
Io, 22
Iphigenia, 22, 34
Iran, 45–6, 49, 60, 68, 72
Iris, 156, 276–7
Isager, Signe, 169
Iser, Wolfgang, 356
Isis, 149, 157, 330, 332, 342–3
    Lady Isis (*Kyra*), 342
Ister, 204
Italy, 268–70, 272, 276–7, 285, 289–92, 304,
        320, 322, 324, 328
Iullus Antonius, 289–91, 300

Jakobson, Roman, 54–5, 66
Jason, 163, 201, 204, 216, 218, 288
Jendza, Craig, 29
Jerusalem, 48
John the Baptist, 348
Johnson, Barbara, 66
Johnson, William A., 183
Jouanna, Jacques, 220
Juba II (king of Mauretania), 289–91, 301,
        303, 306
Juno, 270
Jupiter, 284, 287, 290
    Jupiter-Ammon, 284. *See also* Zeus,
        Ammon, Amun, Amun-Rē

Justin (Marcus Iunianus Iustinus), 46, 67
Juvenal, 299

Kadesh, 284–5, 290–1
Kákosy, László, 286
Kalligone, 319
Kambyses II, 49
Kant, Immanuel, 70
    neo-Kantian, 57
Karnak, 46, 64, 71
Kaster, Robert, 301
Kastor, 155, 216
katochos, katochoi, 228–9, 231
Kerameikos, 209
Kerkecker, Juliane, 131
Kerkyon, 184, 187
Kharikleia, 331
Kidd, Stephen, 230
Kom el Shoqafa, 329
Kore, 157
Kronos, 148. *See also* Cronus
ktisis, 289–90
Kushite, 53

Lacan, Jacques, 45, 69
Lake Maryūt, 62
Lane Fox, Robin, 59, 70
Langacker, Ronald W., 57
Largus, 290
Latium, 277–8
Lazarus, 347
Lefkowitz, Mary, 249
Legras, Bernard, 230–2
Leleges, 291
Leonidas of Tarentum, 195–6, 242
Leonides of Alexandria, 302
Lesbos, 177, 299
Leto, 146–7
Leucosia, 322
Lexicon Ambrosianum, 186
Lexicon of Diogenianus, 186
Libra, 288
Libya, 51, 196, 275, 287, 289–90, 306
Ligea, 322
Lilybaeum, 272
lingua franca, 335
Linos, 193
Lloyd-Jones, Hugh, 162
Lloyd, Michael, 19–20

Lobel, Edgar, 113, 115
Locris, 250–2, 256, 258–9
Longinus, 170
Lucian, 319, 323
Lucius, 302
Lutheranism, 355
Luxor, 46, 50, 52–3, 71
Lycambes, 312
Lyceum, 206
Lycophron, 268–78, 320–3
  Alexandra, 268–78, 320–1
Lycus, 289
Lydia, 113–15
Lykabettos, 207

Maas, Paul 113
Macedonia, 45–6, 48–9, 53, 56, 58–9, 62,
  67–8, 72, 150, 196, 228–9 232,
  331, 335
MacQueen, James Galloway, 166, 168
Maecenas, Gaius, 300–1
Magna Grecia, 324
Mahaffy, John Pentland, 58–9
Maia, 32, 134
Mallarmé, Stéphane, 66
Malqata, 48
Manning, Joseph Gilbert, 285
Marathon, 305
Maraval, Pierre, 348
Marcellus, M. Claudius, 300–5
Marconi, Clemente, 274
Marcus Antonius, the Triumvir, 300–1
Marsā Maṭrūḥ, 46. *See also* Amunia
Martyrdom of Saint Parthenope, 320,
  323
martyrdom, 348
Mary, 348
Massimilla, Giulio, 112, 186, 191
matricide, 31, 34
Mauretania, 289, 301
Mausoleum, 299
McNelis, Charles, 278
Medaglia, 182
Medea, 163, 216, 218, 221, 289
Media, 310
Mediterranean Sea, 62
Meillier, Claude, 191–2
Melampus, 192
Melanippus, 156

Meleager of Gadara, 252–3, 258, 308–12
Melissus, C. Maecenas, 301
Memnon, 152
Memphis, 46–8, 50–1, 53–64, 66–8, 70,
  227–9, 232, 285, 288, 332
Menelaus (the Egyptian), 333
Menelaus, 29, 115, 269–70
Menouthis, 342
Menṭuḥotep III, 52
Merkelbach, Reinhold, 176
Messene, 205, 252, 257
Metiochos and Parthenope, 319
Metiochus, 319, 321–3
miasma, 215–22
Middle Kingdom, 48, 51–2
Miletus, 112, 116, 154–5
Miller, Patricia Cox, 349
Mimnermus, 8
Minyans, 252, 254–5
Mnasalkes, 249, 252–60
Moirai, 150
Molorc(h)us, 191–6
monophysite, 341–2
Montanari, Franco, 177
Moon, 333
Moschus, 312
Most, Glenn W., 251
Mudrāya, 45, 53
Muse, Muses, 3–4, 133, 153–4, 193–4, 239,
  242, 253, 258–9, 299, 305,
  309–10, 323–4
Mutemwiya, 62
Mysians, 29
Mytilene, 177–9, 299, 301, 304
Myus, 112, 116

Naples, 320–1
Narmer Palette, 49
Naucratis, 64, 197
Nauplia, 32
Naxians, 205
Nectanebo II, 231–235, 358
Neith, 149
Nektembes, 230, 235
Nemea, 191, 250, 257–8
Nereids, 31–2
Nessus, 163
Nestor of Tarsus, 300
New Kingdom, 48, 50, 62, 285

New Music, 18–24
Nicander, 239–45
Nicias, 310
Nicippe, 149
Niese, Benedictus, 207
Nigidius Figulus, Publius, 287–9, 291
Nile, 46–8, 55–6, 62–4, 67, 149, 196–7, 286,
    289, 306, 329, 331
Nine Bows, 51
Nonnus, 195
nostoi, 269–70, 289–90
Nubian, 51, 68
Numidian, 290–1

Octavia Minor, 300
Octavia, 290, 299–305
Octavius/Octavianus. *See* Augustus
Odysseus, 204, 320–4
Oedipus, 259
Old Kingdom, 62
Oligeidas, 165
Olivia, 71
Olson, S. Douglas, 127–8
Olympus, 156, 324
oneirocriticism, 229, 231
Onouris, 232. *See also* Ares
Opet Festival, 50
orator, orators, 334–5
Orchomenos, 251–9
Orestes, 19, 21, 26–30, 35, 259
Orion, 239
Oropus, 254
Orthodoxy, Orthodox, 341–50
    Orthodox church, 344, 349
    Orthodox communion, 348–9
Ortygia, 147
Osiris, 157, 356
Osthilos, 165
Ovidius Naso, Publius (Ovid)
    Metamorphoses, 195
Oxyártēs, 68
Oxyrhynchus, 183

Paeonians, 194
Page, Denys Lionel, 176–9, 251–2
Palermo Stone, 50
Palestine, 341
Palestrina, 196–7
Palladius, 6, 220–1

Pan, 288
Pandora, 239, 241
Pannychis (play), 208
Panopolis, 288
Panormus, 272
pantomime, 312, 319–25
papyrus, papyri, 21, 48, 58, 112, 126, 151–2,
    179, 181–5, 187, 191, 194, 227–8,
    231–4, 319, 360
    P.Ant. III 179 add., 181–8
    P. Dem. Bol. 3173, 232
    P. Lille 82, 151
    P. Oxy. 2258, 151
    P.Oxy. 2376, 182–3
    P.Oxy. 2377, 182–3
    P. Par. 1, 233
    Papyrus Dodgson, 179
    PSI 1092, 151
    P.Vindob. G 2315, 21
paradoxography, 215, 222
paratext, 249, 253–5
paratragedy, 29, 208–9
Paris (Alexander), 285
parody, 21, 29
Pãrsa, 68
Parthenope, Parthenopes, 319–25
Parthia, 67, 69
Paton, William Roger, 302, 304
Paul, 346–7
Pauni, 230
Pausanias, 253, 256–7, 259, 323
Peirce, Charles Sanders, 69–70
Peleus, 31
Pelling, Christopher, 300
Peloponnese, 205, 250
Peloponnesian War, 331
Pelorias, 205
Pelousion (Pelusium), 54–6, 59–60, 64,
    66–7, 229
pentameter, 9, 192, 254–5, 309–10
penteteric games, 253
Pentheus, 323
performance, 18, 20, 23–5, 124–6, 130, 133,
    135–6, 322, 324, 359
performativity, 125–6
Periander, 256–7
Perse, 216
Perses, 239
Perseus, 32–3

Persia, Persians, 46, 48–9, 52–68, 231–2,
        320, 322, 324, 328–9, 331–2
Petesis, 232
Petiharenpi, 227, 232–34
Pfeiffer, Rudolf, 113, 115, 146–7, 203, 207
Phaennus, 308
Phaethon, 208, 215–22
        Phaethon/Apsyrtos, 221
Phalaris, 275
phantasia, 346–7
Phaphere, 230
Pharaoh, Pharaohs, 46–7, 50, 53, 59–60,
        63–4, 285, 330–1
Pharmuthi, 233
Pharos, 333
Phegeus, 250
Pheidias, 33, 202
Pherecrates, 166
Philaenis (Samian), 312
Philemon, 295
Philip (the epigrammatist), 196
Philip II, 68, 331
Philip V, 312
Philitas, 17
Philotera, 154
Phineus, 217
Phrixus, 216, 287
Phrygia, 22, 32, 132, 321
Phrygius, 112, 114, 116
Pi-Ramesses, 63
Pieria, 111–16
Pindar, 111–12, 191, 193, 201, 251,
        286, 291
        Olympian 7, 112
        Pythian 4, 286
Pisces, 288
Piso Frugi, Lucius Calpurnius, 302
Pittacus of Mytilene, 177–9
pity, 19, 25–6, 30, 164
plague. *See* disease
Plataea, 254
Plato, 21, 127–30, 233
Pleiades, 32
Plutarch, 46, 62, 67–8, 71, 178–9, 194, 221,
        251, 253, 256–7, 259, 300–1, 303
        Dinner of the Seven Wise Men, 256, 259
        Life of Antonius, 300, 303
        Life of Marcellus, 301
        Life of Poplicola, 300

Life of Theseus, 259
On Isis and Osiris, 178
Po, 208
poetics, 3, 47, 123–4, 126–7, 130, 135, 167,
        176, 239, 274, 278, 292, 330
Polemon, 196
politics, 52, 253–4, 341
pollution, 35, 216–21. *See also* miasma
Pollux, 196–7
Polybius, 272–3, 285
Polycrates, 319
Polydeuces, 155
Pontianus, 127–8
Poppaea, 302
Porticus Liviae, 301
Porticus Octaviae, 301–2
Poseidon, 150
Posidippus, 17, 153
póthos, 45–6
Pratt, Mary Louise, 292
Prauscello, Lucia, 195
Priam, 187, 276–7
Priscian, 300
Proclus, 302
Prometheus, 241
prose, 57, 112, 168, 192, 201, 207, 209,
        249, 253, 260, 290, 300, 310,
        319–20, 330
proskunesis, 67
prosopopoeia, 164–5
Psalms, 343–4
Ptah, 48
Ptolemaeus, brother of Apollonius, 227–35
Ptolemies, 57–9, 149, 154–6, 168–9, 176,
        227, 231, 234, 253–4, 285–92,
        328, 330–2, 358–9
        Ptolemy I, 169
        Ptolemy II Philadelphus, 148, 150,
                156–7, 169, 300, 312
        Ptolemy IV, 285
        Ptolemy VI Philometor, 229
Punic Wars, 271, 273, 274–6
Pylades, 28
Pyrgo, 276–7
Pyrrhus, 274
Pytho, 291

Quintilian, Marcus Fabius, 169–70
Quirinus, 288

Rames(s)es II, 48, 52–3, 284–5, 290, 291
Raphia, 285
Ray, John, 232
recusatio, 273
Rhakōtis, 46–7, 60–5
Rhea, 148, 156
Rhegion, 322, 324
rhesis, 29
Rhianus, 311
Rhodanes, 195
Rhodes, 186, 201, 204
ring-composition, 4, 7–8, 10
Romans, 46, 268, 272, 286–7, 292, 332, 335,
　　　and passim
Rome, 69, 194, 275–7, 286–7, 290, 292, 301,
　　　303–4, 324–5, 335, *and passim*
Roxane, 68
Rufus of Ephesus, 219

Sagittarius, 288
Sagra, 178
Sahara, 46, 289
Sais, 149
Sallustius Crispus, C., 304
Salmakis, 168
Salustius, 187
Samius, 312
Samos, 202, 321–2
Sandon, 300
Saon, 165
Sapir, Edward, 57
Sappho, 111, 152–3, 308
Šar šarrāni, 52
Sarapis, 149, 330
satire, 299, 312, 358
Satrap Stele, 59
Saussure, Ferdinand de, 60, 65, 69
Scamander, 275–6
scholia, scholion, scholiast, 147–8, 152–3,
　　　170, 192, 251, 254–6, 259, 321–5
Scorpio, 286
Scylla, 289
Sed-Festival, 50
Segesta (Aigesta, Acesta, Egesta), 268–79
Selene, 333
Seleucid Seleucid IV, 229
Selinus, 274
Semonides, 3–11
Sens, Alexander, 167, 278

Serapeum Archive, 227–8
Serapeum, 227–9, 330, 342
Serapis, 227, 234, 342
serekh-panel, 52, 63
Sesonchosis, 319
Sesostris II, 52
Seth, 288
Seven Sages, 177
Supplementum Hellenisticum, 183, 186,
　　　287, 207, 253
Shaw, Brent D., 348
Shoshenq I, 53
Sicelidas, 310
Sicily, 205–6, 220, 275–6, 328, 332
sickness, sick, 5, 7, 343, 350. *See also*
　　　disease, diseases
Sicyon, 254
Sidon, 309, 333
signature, 244, 277–8
Simon, 302
Simonides, 111, 308
Simos ("Snub-nosed"), 312
Sinai, 56
Sinko, Th., 178
Siren Parthenope, 320, 323
Siren, Sirens, 320–4
Sīwah, 46–7, 60–5, 72, 156, 285, 287, 289
Smendes I, 63
Smyrna, 287
Socrates, 129
Sogdiana, 68
Solon, 3–9, 11, 256–7, 259
Sophocles, 17, 19, 26, 34, 259, 310
　　　Electra, 17, 19, 26, 34
　　　Oedipus at Colonus, 259
Sophoniba, 289
Sophronius, 341–50
Sostratos of Cnidus, 169
Spalinger, Anthony, 233
sparagmos, 319–25
Sparta, 114, 259, 332
Sphinx, 32–3, 277
sphragis, 242
Stallings, A. E., 162, 168
Stanford University, 161, 268, 355
Statius, 277, 320–1
Stephanus of Byzantium, 205, 323
Stephens, Susan A., 17, 48, 58–9, 64, 123,
　　　148, 157, 161, 168, 176, 179, 191,

215, 227, 235, 268, 239, 319, 328, 330–1, 355–60, *and passim*
Stesichorus, 256
Stobaeus, 3, 8–9
Stock, Brian, 357
Stocking, Charles H., 355
Stoic, Stoics, 65, 300
Stone, Oliver, 70
Strabo, 168, 201–9, 270, 300, 330, 342
  Geography, 168, 201–9, 270, 300
Suda, 167, 186–7, 251
Suetonius Tranquillus, Gaius, 301, 303
  Claudius, 303
  De grammaticis et rhetoribus, 301
Sun, 150, 215, 333
Swinnen, Wilfried, 169
Syme, Ronald, 300
synecdoche, 54, 57, 59

tagmemes, 54, 56
Tanis, 63
Tarn, W. W., 70
Tarsus, 300, 332
Teffeteller, Annette, 66
Teiresias, 148–50
Telemachus, 150
Telephus, 29
termer, 61, 64
Teucrians, 268
Thebes, 47, 48, 58, 63
Theocritus, 3, 17, 152, 156, 161, 195, 227, 310, 357–8, 360
  Idyll 1, 17
  Idyll 7, 310
  Idyll 16, 152
  Idyll 17, 156
  Idyll 21, 195
Theodoros, 348
Theophilus, bishop of Alexandria, 342
Theophrastus, 310
Thermopylae, 331
Thersites, 311
Theseus, 191, 259, 305
Thespiae, 165, 251, 253
Thetis, 32
Thōnis-Heracleion, Thōnis, Heracleion, 64, 157
Thoth, 51

Thucydides, 166, 194, 205–6, 220, 250
Thule, 67
Thyestes, 34
Tiber, 320
Tiberius, 303
Timon, the misanthrope, 311
Titans, 239, 241
titulary, 50–3, 62, 67, 71
Tityrus, 286
tragedy, tragic, 16–35, 186, 201, 274, 278, 312
Traill, David, 271
Triopas, 149–50
tropology, tropological, 54, 56, 64–5
Troy, Trojan, 25, 31–3, 35, 254, 264–7, 274–8, 285, 289–90
  Trojan War, 18, 25, 34, 290
Tukulti-Nunarta I, 52
Turner, Eric G., 183
Tuthmosis II, 62
Tuthmosis III, 51
Twelfth Night, 71
Two Lands, 46–9, 51–2, 60, 63
Tyche, 273
Tyndareus, 22
Typhon, 288
Tyre, 45, 48, 309, 331
Tyrtaeus, 3
Tzetzes, Ioannes, 251, 255–6

underworld, 7, 167, 215, 217. *See also* Hades
Utas, Bo, 320–3

Vāmiq u 'Adhrā, 320
Varro, Marcus Terentius, 278, 287
Venus, 153, 286, 290
Vergilius Maro, Publius (Virgil), 66, 268–79, 285–6, 289–91, 320–1
  Aeneid, 66, 268–79, 284, 286–7, 289–91
  Eclogues, 286
  Georgics, 286, 320
Virgin and Her Lover, 320
Virgo, 286, 288
Viscogliosi, A., 301
von Lieven, Alexandra, 179

von Ranke, Leopold, 70
Vulcan, 291

Waltz, P., 310
Wardle, David, 301
Wessner, Paul, 301
West, Martin Litchfield, 251
West, Stephanie, 270
White, Hayden, 49, 54–5, 67, 70
Whorf, Benjamin, 57
Wilamowitz-Moellendorf, Ulrich von, 146–7, 251
Wiles, David, 24
Wimsatt, William K., 54
Winkler, John J., 319, 355
Wolf, Michaela, 228
Wordsworth, William, 163–4, 170

Xenophon (novelist), 328, 332–3
Xerxes, 22

Yĕhûdîm, 49
Youtie, H. C., 194
Ypsilanti, Maria, 299, 301–4

Zancle, 205
Zeitlin, Froma I., 19
Zenodotus, 253–4, 311
Zephyr, 152–3
Zephyrium, 152
zeugma, 34
Zeus, 4, 32, 46, 49, 61–2, 64, 73, 147–9, 156–7, 178, 193, 202, 216–18, 239–42, 250–1, 257–8, 286, 302, 305, 309–10
    Zeus Basileus, 147
    Zeus Olympios, 148
    Zeus Soter, 148
    Zeus-Ammon, Zeus Amon, 46, 61, 64, 156
Zimmerman, Franz, 319

Plate 1 Alexander's Egypt.

Plate 2 Barque Chapel, Luxor Temple. Alexander attired as Pharaoh, facing the god Amun.

Plate 3 Veneration of the Apis bull. Year 21 of Psamtik I (*c.* 644 BCE).

Plate 4a The Narmer Palette, verso.

Plate 4b The Narmer Palette, detail of the lower register, verso.

Plate 5 Alexander's route from Pēlousion to Memphis.

Plate 6 Unidentified Pharaoh wearing the *neme*s cloth. Recovered from the sunken harbor of Alexandria, formerly the royal quarters.

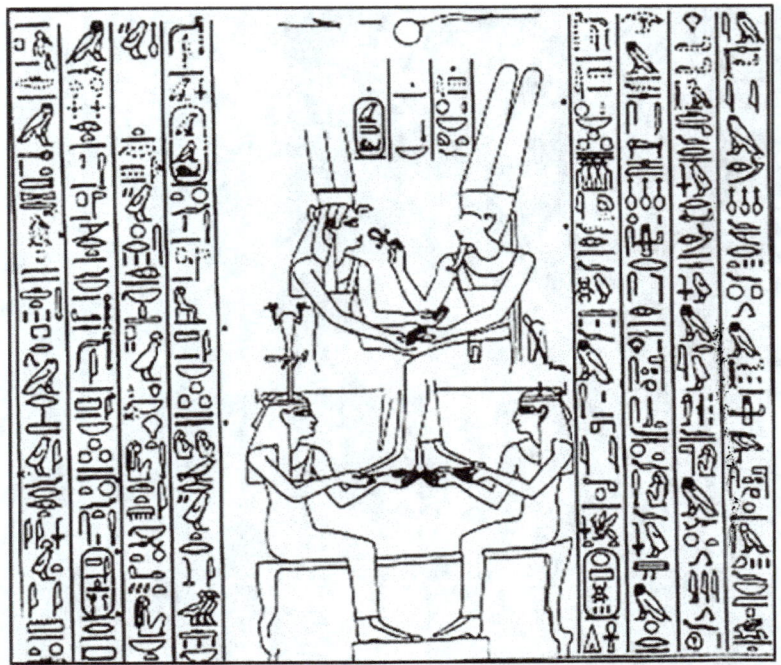

Plate 7 Amun-Rēʿ presents Queen Mutemwiya with the divine breath of life (☥ ʿnḫ). Mortuary Temple of Ḥatšepsut, al-Dayr al-Baḥrī.

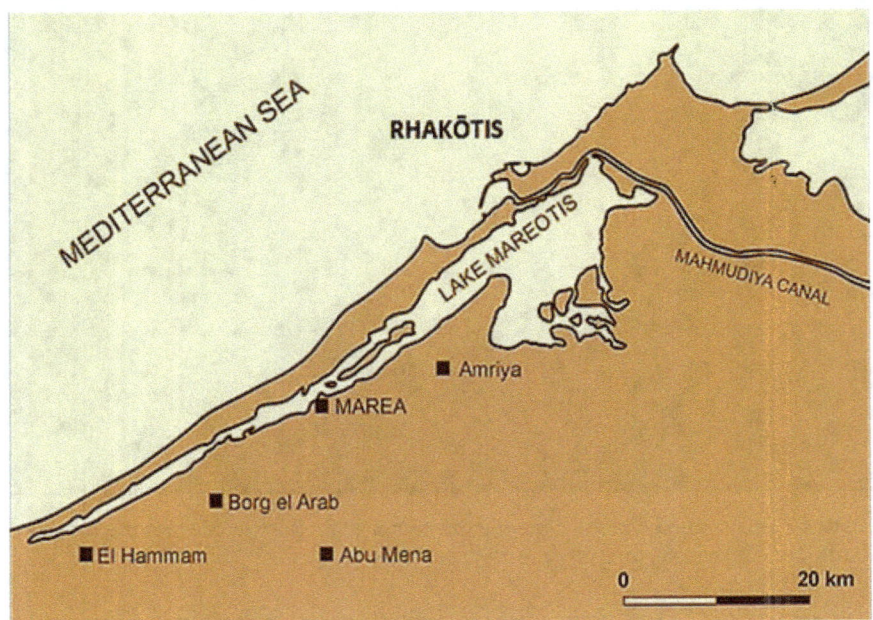

Plate 8 Site of Alexandria / ⲣⲁⲕⲟⲧⲉ.

Plate 9 Flooding of the Nile. Repetition of the First Occasion.

Plate 10 The pyramids at Giza rising out of the flood water of the yearly inundation.

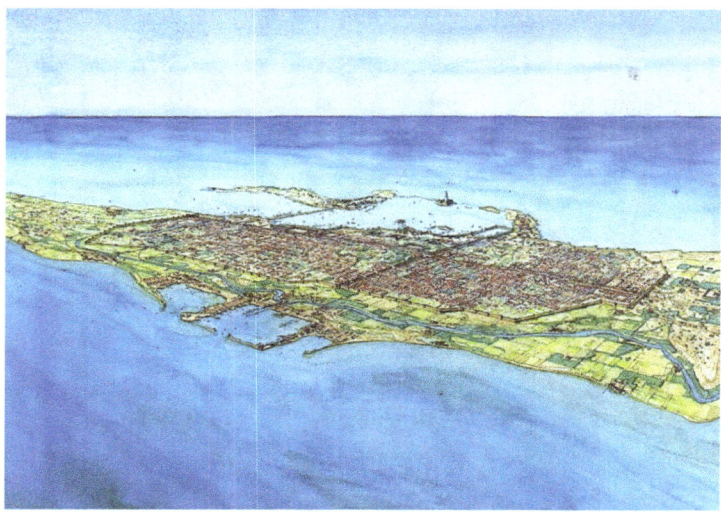

Ἀλεξάνδρεια

Plate 11 Ptolemaic Alexandria seen from Lake Maryūṭ.

Plate 12 Cameo of Ptolemy II and Arsinoe II. Kunsthistorisches Museum, Vienna. Inventory no. Antikensammlung, IXa 81.

Plate 13a Image from the Papyrus, P. Lille 78b. Copyright © IPEL, HALMA UMR 8164 / Th. Nicq.

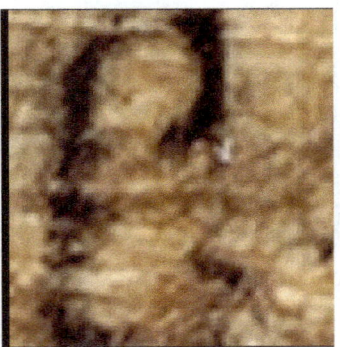

Plate 13b Image from the Papyrus, P. Lille 78b. Copyright © IPEL, HALMA UMR 8164 / Th. Nicq.

Plate 14 Detail of the Nile Mosaic at Palestrina. Image: Wikimedia Commons.

Plate 15 Detail of the Nile Mosaic at Palestrina. Image: Wikimedia Commons.

Plate 16 The Contest between the Muses and the Sirens (long side). 250–275 CE, Rome. The Metropolitan Museum of Art, New York. Rogers Fund, 1910. Accession no.10.104.